EXTERNAL AUDITING AND ASSURANCE AN IRISH TEXTBOOK

2nd Edition

Martin Nolan and Christine Nangle

Chartered
Accountants
Ireland

Published in 2013 by
Chartered Accountants Ireland
Chartered Accountants House
47–49 Pearse Street
Dublin 2
www.charteredaccountants.ie

ISBN: 978-1-908199-46-1

Typeset by Datapage
Printed and bound by GRAFO, S.A.

Contents

Preface

External auditing and assurance is a dynamic area and it continues to evolve in response to the complex changes in business activities and related risks both locally and globally. This text has been written and updated to reflect the myriad changes following on from the International Auditing and Assurance Standards Board (IAASB) 'Clarity Project' and subsequent new developments.

RECENT DEVELOPMENTS IN THE WORLD OF EXTERNAL AUDIT AND ASSURANCE

2012 saw significant reform of the standard-setting environment (UK and Ireland) with the responsibilities previously held by the Auditing Practices Board (APB) being taken on by the Financial Reporting Council (FRC). The FRC is supported in this role by its Codes and Standards Committee while audit and assurance related matters continue to be advised upon by the Audit and Assurance Council. It should be noted, however, that all pronouncements issued by the APB remain effective under the FRC.

The most significant revisions to the International Standards on Auditing (UK and Ireland) (referred to in this textbook with the shorthand form, 'ISAs') during 2012 were those relating to:
- ISA (UK and Ireland) 700 *The Auditor's Report on Financial Statements* ('ISA 700');
- ISA (UK and Ireland) 705 *Modifications to the Opinion in the Independent Auditor's Report* ('ISA 705); and
- ISA (UK and Ireland) 706 *Emphasis of Matter Paragraphs and Other Matter Paragraphs in the Independent Auditor's Report* (ISA 706).

The revision of ISA 700 was made to allow this clarified standard to be used by auditors in the Republic of Ireland as previously it had been adopted in the UK only. Similarly, ISA 705 and ISA 706 have now been adopted by the Republic of Ireland following the revisions. All three of these standards are effective for Irish audits commencing on or after 1 October 2012. The revisions to ISA (UK and Ireland) 700 have been designed to ensure that compliance with it will not preclude the auditor from being able to assert compliance with the International Standards on Auditing issued by the IAASB.

A revised Bulletin Compendium was also issued following these revisions:
- The Republic of Ireland example is based on APB Bulletin 1 (I) *Compendium of Illustrative Auditor's Reports on Irish Financial Statements*.

The UK Bulletin Compendium continues to be effective as follows:

- The UK example is based on APB Bulletin 2010/02 (Revised) *Compendium of Illustrative Auditor's Reports on UK private sector financial statements for periods ended on or after 15 December 2010.*

Other revisions in 2012 included ISA (UK and Ireland) 260 *Communication with Those Charged with Governance*; ISA (UK and Ireland) 265 *Communicating Deficiencies in Internal Control to Those Charged with Governance and Management*; and ISA (UK and Ireland) 720A *The Auditor's Responsibilities Relating to Other Information in Documents Containing Audited Financial Statements.* The objective of these revisions was to enhance corporate reporting and audit. These changes will be complemented by proposed changes to the *UK Corporate Governance Code* on audit committees to enhance board reporting. All of the above are effective for audits of financial statements for periods commencing on or after 1 October 2012.

Two exposure drafts were issued in 2012 relating to:

- ISA (UK and Ireland) 315 *Identifying and Assessing the Risks of Material Misstatement Through Understanding the Entity and its Environment*; and
- ISA (UK and Ireland) 610 *Using the Work of Internal Auditors.*

While both of these ISAs were revised in June 2013, this textbook reflects the pre-revision ISAs. These revisions principally relate to the external auditor's use of internal auditors and remained under debate due to advice issued by the Audit and Assurance Council stating that direct assistance from internal audit staff should be prohibited for external audits conducted in accordance with ISAs (UK and Ireland).

International Standards on Auditing (ISAs) (UK and Ireland) were issued in October 2009 and apply to audits of financial statements for periods ending on or after 15 December 2010. This textbook takes into account the impact of the ISAs (UK and Ireland).

The new ISAs (UK and Ireland) incorporate the clarified ISAs issued by the International Auditing and Assurance Standards Board (IAASB). Where necessary, the FRC has augmented the International Standards with additional requirements to address specific UK and Irish legal and regulatory requirements, and additional guidance appropriate in the UK and Irish national legislative, cultural and business context. Within the publication *Standards and Guidance 2013 – Ireland Edition* (also published by Chartered Accountants Ireland) this additional material is clearly differentiated from the original text of the international standards by the use of grey shading. (A list of the ISAs extant at 1 January 2013 is given in **Appendix A** of this textbook.)

THIS TEXTBOOK

External Audit and Assurance: An Irish Textbook sets out to overcome a perennial difficulty that students of external audit and assurance experience, i.e. putting the audit process into a clear and understandable context. In general, the currently available textbooks on auditing do not seek to relate the audit process specifically to an organisation's financial statements. The audit process in this text is treated as a continuous discussion related directly to the final outcome (end product), i.e. the auditor's report and the financial statements to which it refers.

The textbook includes a full set of financial statements (prepared using IFRS) for illustrative purposes (only) in **Appendix C**. While these financial statements are not intended as the basis for studying financial reporting, they are continually referred to throughout the text in order to simulate the actual activities of the auditor and provide a more practical learning experience. Furthermore, within each chapter (where relevant), extracts are included from the financial statements to help focus on the typical assertions and disclosures that need to be addressed as part of the audit process.

Students in general study financial accounting and reporting under the International Financial Reporting Standards (IFRS) Framework. However, while IFRS is mandatory for Plcs, the FRS (UK and Irish GAAP) framework applies to the vast majority of companies (private) at present. The terms used in the text are as per **IFRS**. As accounting students are aware of the interchangeable terms, there should be no difficulty arising from this approach.

STRUCTURE OF THIS TEXT

This textbook is divided into four **Parts** to group the audit process into its key constituent elements. A set of challenging questions is included at the end of each Part, which are designed to challenge the reader's knowledge using a case study approach. The figure overleaf sets out the overall structure of the textbook:

Part I (Chapters 1 to 3), is structured to provide the reader with an understanding of the external auditing and assurance environment. **Chapter 1** sets the scene by defining the terms 'audit' and 'assurance' and, more specifically, the objectives of the auditor. The chapter outlines the evolution of external auditing and assurance, and discusses the current regulatory and legislative environment. Finally, in **Chapter 1**, the circumstances giving rise to legal liability of auditors is discussed by reference to some of the key legal cases that have shaped auditor liability to date. **Chapter 2** is dedicated to the topics of ethics and corporate governance and shows how the auditing world has responded to both ethical and corporate governance issues. The topic of fraud has been brought forward and covered in **Chapter 3** in order to highlight the part it has played in shaping the world of external auditing and assurance today.

Part II (Chapters 4 to 10), deals with the external audit and assurance issues around the planning and controls considerations undertaken by the auditor. **Chapter 4** provides a brief summary of the audit process, introducing a diagrammatic depiction of the process and providing a basic understanding of two topics highlighted as being those with which students struggle the most (management assertions, and the differentiation between controls testing and substantive procedures). **Chapter 5** introduces the first stage of the audit process: audit acceptance and planning. In **Chapter 6**, the concept of audit evidence is explored with particular attention paid to the concept of sufficient appropriate audit evidence and audit sampling. Risk is the topic of **Chapter 7**, and **Chapter 8** is dedicated to the topic of controls and controls testing. **Chapter 9** covers the topic of computer-assisted audit techniques (CAATs), including a discussion on some key technological advancements of interest to the auditor: cloud computing and the increased relevance of e-commerce. Finally, in Part II, **Chapter 10** deals with the auditor's use of

EXTERNAL AUDIT AND ASSURANCE: TEXT STRUCTURE

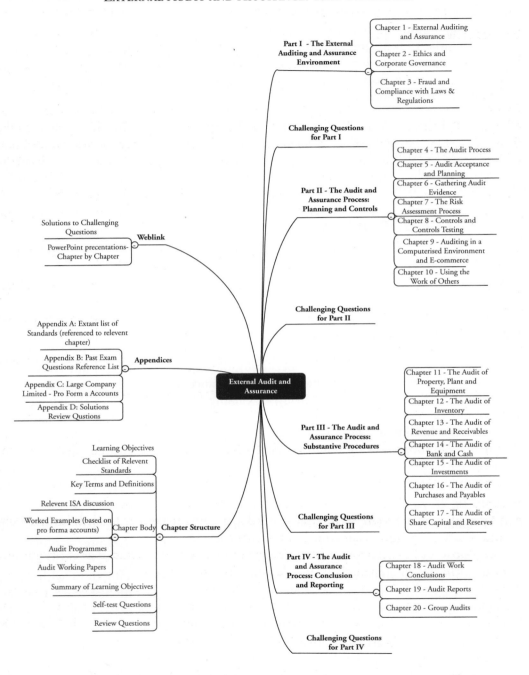

the work of others, being: instances where the client entity uses a service organisation; the use of the work of internal audit by the external auditor; and the use of auditor's experts.

Part III (Chapters 11 to 17) is dedicated to the substantive procedures relating to each financial statement area. These chapters include worked examples of audit procedures and techniques using the Financial Statements included in **Appendix C,** as well as audit programmes and working papers, all of which are intended to aid a better practical understanding.

Part IV (Chapters 18 to 20) deals with the topic of audit conclusion and the auditor's report. **Chapter 18** discusses the final activities of the auditor prior to concluding his opinion on the financial statements and in particular includes a worked example of the auditor's consideration of the errors schedule (summary of unadjusted differences). **Chapter 19** discusses in detail the auditor's report and includes worked examples of the expression of the audit opinion. Finally, **Chapter 20** introduces a new topic to the text, group audits, and takes the reader through the practical considerations of the auditor when auditing the financial statements of a group.

The Appendices include:
- **Appendix A** – Extant List of Ethical and Auditing Standards at 1 January 2013 (including reference to the main chapter where the standard is discussed);
- **Appendix B** – Past Chartered Accountants Ireland Exam Questions Reference List (categorised by topic);
- **Appendix C** – Large Company Limited – Directors' Report and Financial Statements; and
- **Appendix D** – Suggested Solutions to Review Questions.

Other material available to adopting lecturers through the Chartered Accountants Ireland website includes:
- PowerPoint presentations to accompany each chapter of the textbook; and
- Suggested Solutions to the Challenging Questions

THE STRUCTURE OF EACH CHAPTER

Each chapter has a consistent structure which includes:

- **Learning Objectives** – outlining at the outset the objective of the chapter.
- **A Checklist of Relevant Standards** – aimed at guiding the reader towards further technical study of the topics contained in the chapter.
- **Key Terms and Definitions** relevant to the chapter are also included at the beginning of each chapter to prepare the reader for the discussions that follow.
- Each **Chapter Body** includes discussions of relevant ISAs , discussions on the practical application of audit procedures, worked examples (including examples based on the Financial Statements in **Appendix C**), audit programmes (where relevant), audit working papers (where relevant) and reference to relevant current affairs.
- A **Conclusion.**
- A **Summary of Learning Objectives** is included at the end of each chapter to bring the chapter full circle and ensure that the reader understands the main points as set out in the learning objectives at the outset.

- Also at the end of each chapter a series of short **Self-test Questions** is included, providing an opportunity for the reader to focus on the key topics arising in the chapter and to determine whether he or she has fully understood its contents.
- Finally, a set of **Review Questions** is included to allow the student to further test his or her understanding (suggested solutions to which are then provided in **Appendix D**).

For any student of this subject, the volume of knowledge required can be daunting. However, the fundamental challenge in external auditing and assurance is about making sound judgements based on all the available information in a given set of circumstances. Such skill is acquired over time and through practical experience. In exam situations, students are often required to make judgements as if they were experienced auditors. This textbook seeks to narrow the gap between theoretical knowledge and practical experience as much as possible.

RECOMMENDED FURTHER READING

Wide reading is essential to gain the fullest understanding of auditing and assurance. Accordingly, the following sources are recommended:

Journals

- *Accountancy Ireland* (published by Chartered Accountants Ireland, see www.accountancyireland.ie, where as a student you can subscribe to the Accountancy Ireland Extra enewsletter, giving you access to the updated digital edition. You can also download the *Accountancy Ireland* 'App' from your app store.
- *Economia* (published by ICAEW) (http://economia.icaew.com).
- *Accountancy Age*.
- A good daily and Sunday newspaper.

Other textbooks

- FRC (Audit and Assurance), *Standards and Guidance 2013 – Ireland Edition*, Chartered Accountants Ireland, 2013).
- Lyndon MacCann and Thomas B. Courtney, *The Companies Acts 1963–2012* (Student Edition, Bloomsbury Professional, 2013).
- Louise Kelly, *Advanced Auditing and Assurance* (Chartered Accountants Ireland, 2013)
- Brenda Porter, David Hatherly and Jon Simon, *Principles of External Auditing* (4th ed., Wiley, 2013).
- Alan Millichamp and John Taylor, *Auditing* (10th ed,, Cengage, 2012)
- Iain Gray and Stuart Manson, *The Audit Process: Principles, Practice and Cases* (5th ed., Cengage, 2011).
- Emile Woolf, *Avoiding Audit Pitfalls: A Forensic Accountant's Casebook* (August 2010).
- Andrew Brown, *Corporate Fraud* (Chartered Accountants Ireland, 2010).
- David Chitty and John McCarthy, *A Manual on Audit* (2nd ed., Chartered Accountants Ireland, 2012).

Introduction: Current and Future Developments in External Auditing and Assurance

CHALLENGES

The challenges facing independent external auditing and assurance arise principally from the continuously changing global business environment. When buoyant economies grow exponentially they often challenge the slow pace of the various regulators. In particular, the regulators of stock markets, financial markets, and accounting and auditing standards are found wanting. This slow pace of the regulators leads to a time lag in implementing appropriate and effective regulation and hence a vacuum exists that frequently provides fertile ground for sharp/corrupt business practices.

When economies experience downturns, businesses are frequently faced with financial problems evidenced by falling profits or rising losses, declining liquidity and rising levels of debt. The corporate collapses that ensue regularly expose the weaknesses in the regime of the regulators. Frequently, and in this context the answer to such crises is the introduction of new requirements for independent external auditors.

The above scenarios led to an unending discussion of the 'audit expectations gap' which has been a controversial topic since the mid-1970s. It is as if there is some category of stakeholders whose needs can never be satisfied, that this category changes its composition frequently and thus the 'expectations gap' is redefined once more.

The Cadbury Report of 1992, *Financial Aspects of Corporate Governance*, set a baseline for addressing the expectations gap regarding the behaviour and practices of boards of directors. This position was built upon by various subsequent reports such as those of Greenbury, Hampel, Higgs and Smith, which emerged over the next decade. The *UK*

Corporate Governance Code 2012 ('The Code') embodies a broad range of improvements which builds on the *UK Corporate Governance Code* 2010.

Twenty-one years after the publication of the Cadbury Report we are still unhappy with boardroom behaviour and practice. The corporate collapses provide ample evidence of why we should be dissatisfied. It would seem that the 'audit expectations gap' conundrum has been and will continue to drive forward the future agenda of independent external auditing and assurance.

CONFLICTS OF INTEREST

An important difficulty faced in developing the future agenda of independent external auditing and assurance is the mix of players (e.g. the composition of the boards and committees of the various accountancy bodies, the Financial Reporting Council and the International Auditing and Assurance Standards Board (IAASB)), and the public perception of the potential conflicts of interest of those involved. These boards and committees are strongly influenced by the 'Big Four' accounting firms (whose partners and staff make up a sizeable proportion of the membership of the accountancy bodies). As a consequence, the public perception is that the interests of such firms are very likely to have a significant influence on the development of the future agenda.

CURRENT ISSUES IN AUDITING

Recently, renewed focus has been directed to two primary issues of concern for independent external auditing, namely:
1. mandatory joint audits; and
2. audit fees, non-audit fees and auditor independence

Mandatory Joint Audits

Because mid-tier accountancy firms audit only a small fraction of the publicly-quoted companies they have been losing out on audit fees for many years. At the same time there has been growing concern over the concentration of Plc audits by the 'Big Four' firms. The recent proposal to make it mandatory to have joint auditors (Big Four and mid-tier firm) appointed to audit Plcs was lobbied principally by mid-tier firms (in their own self-interest). This is strong evidence of a potential conflict of interest in the area of audit developments. Strong arguments were made for and against the proposal, but finally the proposal was not adopted by the EU.

In 2012, the Institute of Chartered Accountants of Scotland published a research report entitled *What Do We Know About Joint Audit?* in which the authors looked at a wide range of research and empirical evidence on how joint audit has worked in practice and how a requirement to appoint joint auditors might affect audit quality and cost. They found that "there is limited empirical support for the argument that joint audits improve the quality of the work, with different studies of voluntary and mandatory joint audit environments yielding contradictory results. There is also some evidence to suggest that joint audits lead to additional costs."[1]

Audit Fees, Non-Audit Fees and External Auditor Independence

The debate continues about the extent to which independent external auditors may take on the provision of other professional services to their audit clients. It is easily argued that, to ensure full independence, an audit firm should provide only audit assurance services to its audit clients, considering the obvious potential conflict of interest.

Restricting the type of services provided to an audit client is fraught with different arguments for and against. Various jurisdictions have adopted different regulations on the matter.

The proverb, 'he who pays the piper calls the tune', can easily be related to the following question, response and possible solution posed by the **AuditFutures** initiative (see below):

- Question 'How can an audit serve society when a company pays for it?'
- Response: 'In theory, there is no conflict of interest in the audits of public companies; in theory the auditors are picked by the shareholders, and the non-executive directors representing their interests, who will presumably want the most rigorous audit possible. Thus, auditors have a financial incentive to audit rigorously. However, in practice we [i.e. AuditFutures] think the executive could propose the auditor, who is approved "on the nod" by audit committees and shareholders – the fact that the executive holds the de facto power of appointment means the auditor has a financial incentive to do what the executive wants.'
- Possible solution: 'Remake the system much more comprehensively and make audit a public good. The government can either intervene in markets or provide the good itself.'

The debate will continue for some time.

AUDIT ISSUES FOR THE FUTURE

The role of independent external auditing is under serious scrutiny following the recent corporate collapses, particularly in the banking sector. Trust in independent external auditors has been damaged. The gap has widened between what auditors think their role is and what the public more broadly expects of them. It is noticeable that most of the existing discussions and public policy debate about the auditing profession focuses on increased regulation. However, there is a widely held view that overregulation stifles innovation and places a significant burden on small and medium-sized audit practices.

---

[1] Nicole Ratzinger-Sakel, Sophie Audousset-Coulier, Jaana Kettunen and Cédric Lesage, *What Do We Know About Joint Audit?* (Institute of Chartered Accountants of Scotland, 2012).

The International Auditing and Assurance Standards Board (IAASB) is undertaking a major review of the *Audit Quality Framework*. Its objectives are to: raise awareness of the key elements of audit quality; encourage key stakeholders to explore ways to improve audit quality; and to facilitate greater dialogue between key stakeholders on the topic. This review focuses on 'the here and now' and how to make improvements.

However, a more comprehensive and innovative approach to audit issues for the future arises from **AuditFutures**, a partnership between the Institute of Chartered Accountants of England and Wales (ICAEW) and Finance Innovation Lab, which is an initiative that looks at the changes needed so that audit can best serve society.[2] AuditFutures aims to inspire a global discussion about the 21st-Century role of audit in rebuilding public trust and to prototype innovations in audit so that it best serves society.

AuditFutures: KEY AREAS OF INNOVATION

The approach of AuditFutures is worth looking at in detail. The following four areas of innovation have been identified by AuditFutures to drive systemic change within the auditing profession:

Society

Audit should be viewed in the wider social context, considering the higher role of the auditing profession in society for today and tomorrow. The following are examples of emerging issues:
- trust in the profession, the firms, and the expressed audit opinion has suffered;
- the need for an understanding of whom the audit is serving;
- the perceived disconnect with stakeholders and what is important in society.

Information

There is a real challenge to the relevance of audit in a world of growing information complexity where financial data could provide a very limited view of business. The following are examples of emerging issues in the area of information:
- ever increasing complexity of organisations and their disclosed information;
- audit does not capture information beyond financial data;
- lack of simplicity – simplified statements needed to inform the general public.

Institutions

In the search for institutional changes that will enable us to do audit better, we have to re-evaluate the function and governance of the profession: the structure of the firms and markets, the policy process and our regulatory framework. The following are brief examples of emerging issues in the area of institutions:
- the present standards are too prescriptive and this stifles thought and innovation and instead encourages a 'tick-box' mentality;

---

[2] http://auditfutures.org/

- audit can become overly defensive of the risk of getting it wrong, which then creates barriers to having more open and effective relationships with the organisation;
- audit is in danger of losing legitimacy as a crucial element of corporate governance.[3]

People

There is a clear need for a socially-minded professional culture. The following are some examples of emerging issues in the area of people:
- a need for a process for dialogue and/or for challenging thinking;
- cross-disciplinary integration, requiring a mixture of skills that go beyond conventional auditing;
- lack of true leadership in the profession to understand social needs and wants.

OTHER AREAS FOR DEVELOPMENT

Development of Closer Links between External and Internal Auditors

There is a growing view that the roles of management, internal audit and external audit and assurance could be made more congruent and effective and thereby better serve the stakeholders of an organisation. All three parties have a common focus: directors/management, internal auditors and external auditors are concerned with risks to the organisation and internal control systems. By sharing their understanding of and implications of risks a more effective strategy may be devolved to eliminate/reduce risks.

The role of internal audit has grown and is critical to management in carrying out its role regarding risks and controls. It is therefore overdue that the role of internal audit be enhanced and placed in higher regard by external auditors and management. There is a view that the head of internal audit should make a statement for inclusion in the annual report. The contents of this statement should relate principally to the organisation's risks and control processes. Most likely this statement should be included within the directors' report.

Auditing Standards and Guidance

There is also a growing view that current auditing standards are too prescriptive. For instance, the FRC's *Standards and Guidance 2013 (Audit and Assurance) – Ireland Edition* runs to over 2,300 pages. There is a further view (AuditFutures) that there should be less focus on box ticking and increasing paperwork merely to comply with rules and regulations, and concerns about legal liability, and more focus on providing a reliable, professional and useful overall opinion on the financial state of the company. How do we integrate financial, social and environmental audits into one audit?

What form should such an audit report take? Would it be smothered with auditor caveats and thereby rendered meaningless. Therein lies the challenge.

---

[3] http://auditfutures.org/

CONCLUSION

The future of independent external auditing and assurance is not guaranteed. The challenges outlined above must be met head on, treated seriously and with urgency. Another spree of significant corporate collapse could spell the death knell for independent external auditing. Stakeholders will not accept any more excuses. If independent external auditing and assurance is unreliable, then it will have to be replaced.

Acknowledgements

This undertaking was possible through the assistance generously given to the authors by academic and professional colleagues in the preparation and review of the text. This second edition is significantly revised, updated and changed from the first.

In the first edition, the text and the authors received valuable contributions from: Gary Comiskey CISA, Marie Keogh ACA, Bernadette Lea ACA, Patricia Morris FCA, Alan Pitts ACA, Sarah Quirke ACA and Umesh Rana CPA. In this edition we received valuable contributions from Gary Comiskey, CISA in updating the complex area of computer auditing and the new developments in e-commerce and cloud computing affecting auditors.

A special word of thanks to Keith Quigley, BBS (Accounting & Finance), a recent graduate of the Institute of Technology Tallaght and currently a trainee chartered accountant, who dedicated considerable time to providing a student's perspective on the contents of this edition.

We would also like to thank the publishing team at Chartered Accountants Ireland, particularly Becky McIndoe and Liam Boyle, for their work and dedication in preparing this second edition for publication.

Finally, we would like to thank the lecturers from the various universities and institutes of technology for their feedback which has been invaluable in shaping this textbook.

PART I

THE EXTERNAL AUDITING AND ASSURANCE ENVIRONMENT

EXTERNAL AUDITING AND ASSURANCE

LEARNING OBJECTIVES

Having studied this chapter on audit assurance you should be able to:
1. understand what is meant by the term 'assurance engagements';
2. understand the objective of an external audit of financial statements;
3. explain why and how the auditing profession has evolved;
4. demonstrate a detailed understanding of the legal framework and regulatory frameworks that governs external audits in both the Republic of Ireland and Northern Ireland;
5. demonstrate an understanding of the setting and use of International Standards on Auditing (UK and Ireland); and
6. demonstrate an understanding of the case law shaping the legal liability of auditors.

CHECKLIST OF RELEVANT STANDARDS

The relevant standards covered in this chapter are:
- ISA 200 (UK and Ireland) *Overall Objectives of the Independent Auditor and Conduct of an Audit in Accordance with International Standards on Auditing (UK and Ireland)* (ISA 200)
- APB (FRC) Bulletin 2007/2 *The Duty of Auditors in the Republic of Ireland to Report to the Director of Corporate Enforcement*

KEY TERMS AND DEFINITIONS FOR THIS CHAPTER

Assurance   A statement that inspires confidence in the subject matter.

Audit   A formal examination of a company's financial statements, with a formal conclusion on their truth and fairness in the form of an audit opinion expressed in an audit report. For the purpose of this textbook, the term 'audit' will refer to **external audit** unless otherwise explicitly stated.

Audit Opinion   An expression of opinion on the truth and fairness of a company's set of financial statements.

Financial Statements   The financial statements of a client entity represent a compilation of individual reports and statements that show how it has used the funds entrusted by its shareholders and other stakeholders. A set of financial statements normally includes a directors' report, auditor's report, a statement of accounting policies, and primary financial statements, such as the statement of comprehensive income, statement of financial position, statement of cash flows, etc.

Reasonable Assurance   Providing a high degree of assurance but not an absolute assurance.

1.1 INTRODUCTION

Auditing is one of the key accounting disciplines and forms the backbone of many accountancy practices. For the purpose of this text, where we refer to the 'audit firm' this can relate to 'an accountancy practice'. Furthermore, the terms 'auditor' and 'audit firm' are used interchangeably, reflecting the fact that the audit firm may in fact be a sole practitioner.

In very simple terms, an **audit** involves an independent audit firm/auditor examining financial information prepared by a client entity in order to provide assurance on its authenticity and accuracy.

ISA (UK and Ireland) 200 *Overall Objectives of the Independent Auditor and Conduct of an Audit in Accordance with International Standards on Auditing (UK and Ireland)* (ISA 200) defines, at paragraph 3, the objective of a financial statement audit as follows:

"The purpose of an audit is to enhance the degree of confidence of intended users in the financial statements. This is achieved by the expression of an opinion by the auditor on whether the financial statements are prepared, in all material respects, in accordance with an applicable financial reporting framework."

The term 'audit' refers to the process undertaken by the auditor to gather and assess a range of audit evidence that will enable such an opinion to be formed and expressed by the auditor. Evidence is gathered in a number of forms and using a wide variety of methods, which will be discussed in more detail in **Chapters 4–17** of this textbook. The topic of forming an audit opinion will then be covered in **Chapters 18** and **19**, while group audit considerations are covered in **Chapter 20**.

Chapter 2 deals with the ethical requirements imposed on the auditor and outlines how corporate governance impacts on an audit, while **Chapter 3** asks what responsibilities the auditor has with regard to the detection of fraud and non-compliance of the client entity with laws and regulations.

Before one can appreciate what is to come in these chapters, it is important to understand the foundation of the auditing profession and **Chapter 1** is intended to bring the reader through that foundation.

Section 1.2 first considers the role of **assurance engagements** and how that relates specifically to **external audit**. This section introduces two important concepts – '**reasonable assurance**' and '**material misstatement**' – and also discusses the **limitations of an external audit**. Having clarified assurance engagements as they relate to external audits, we then consider the historical development of auditing and assurance in **Section 1.3**. This discussion centers on the '**Agency Theory**'. The agency theory relates to the separation of owners and managers of companies. The term 'management' for the purpose of this text shall incorporate directors and management charged with governance of a client entity. Within the auditing standards the term 'those charged with governance' is also used to describe the directors and management collectively.

In **Sections 1.4** and **1.5** we consider the **Legal and Regulatory environments** that govern external audit, focusing our discussion on the Companies Acts, enforcement authorities and regulatory bodies that issue regulations, guidance and monitoring with respect to auditors and the performance of external audits. Additionally, we introduce the regulatory standards that govern the performance of external audits.

Having set the legal and regulatory scene in which external auditing operates, in **Section 1.6** we further explore the role of the Recognised Accountancy Bodies (RAB) (ROI) or Recognised Supervisory Bodies (RSB), (UK/NI) and the role they play in regulating, monitoring and supervising their members (all auditors must be a member of a RAB). **Section 1.7** reflects on the rights and duties of the auditor with regard to appointment, removal and resignation.

Finally, in **Section 1.8** we discuss the '**legal liability**' of the external auditor by introducing some key legal terms as they apply to external auditing and by considering some of the landmark cases that have shaped the external auditor's legal liability.

Following the introduction of assurance engagements in general, the focus of this textbook is on 'External Audit Engagements' as they relate to the audit of financial statements. Hereafter the word 'Audit' shall mean 'External Audit' unless explicitly stated otherwise.

1.2 THE NEED FOR AUDITING AND ASSURANCE

Introduction

Assurance can be defined as a statement that inspires confidence in the subject matter (i.e. 'he assured me he would be here on time'; 'he assured me that the calculation is correct'). The effect of an **audit** is that stakeholders interested in a set of financial statements are given a level of assurance as to the accuracy and reliability of the accounts.

Auditing is a specific discipline that exists within the wider discipline of assurance reporting. The International Framework for Assurance Engagements, as issued by the International Auditing and Assurance Standards Board (IAASB), provides the following definition for an **assurance engagement**:

> "An engagement in which a practitioner expresses a conclusion designed to enhance the degree of confidence of the intended users other than the responsible party about the outcome of the evaluation or measurement of a subject matter against criteria. The outcome of the evaluation or measurement of a subject matter is the information and results from applying the criteria."[1]

The above definition is broader and less specific than the definition of an audit. The subject matter is not confined to financial statements and, in practice, can involve any number of different things, including both financial and non-financial information. However, common to all assurance engagements, including financial statement audits, is a number of core elements:

- a subject matter, e.g. set of financial statements;
- users of the subject matter, e.g. shareholders;
- a set of criteria, e.g. International Financial Reporting Standards (IFRS);
- an examination and conclusion, e.g. audit procedures leading to an audit report.

Table 1.1 below provides further examples of assurance engagements, demonstrating that assurance can be provided in a wide variety of instances and not just external audit.

When most people think of the provision of 'assurance', they most commonly associate it with the annual statutory audit of a company's financial statements (statutory requirements are discussed in more detail below). In this case, the examiner (the external auditor in the case of external audit) gathers evidence on the items included within the company's financial statements and then expresses an opinion on how these statements were prepared. External audit is the most common form of assurance engagement in practice and, as such, it is the most closely regulated, with guidance and requirements to be found in auditing standards issued by accounting bodies (e.g. International Standards on Auditing (ISA), and within government's (national and EU) legislation. Such regulation adds a degree of uniformity to procedures applied and reports produced in the financial statement audit, and will be discussed in more detail below.

---

[1] International Auditing and Assurance Standards Board, *Handbook of International Quality Control, Auditing Review, Other Assurance and Related Service Pronouncements* (2012 Edition), Volume 1.

TABLE 1.1: ASSURANCE ENGAGEMENTS

Assurance Engagement	Subject Matter	Users of the Subject Matter	Set of Criteria	Examination and Conclusion
External Audit and Assurance	Financial Statements	Shareholders/ Stakeholders	Companies Acts and applicable Financial Reporting Framework	Audit opinion on the financial statements
Audit of pension schemes	Pension plans	Pension-holders	Legislation and pension plan rules	Auditor examines evidence to support pension plan and pension plan movements and issues a report concluding on their accuracy (Actuarial Report)
Forensic audit to uncover fraud	Alleged events of fraud	Company against whom alleged fraud was undertaken/the State	Legislation	Practitioner examines evidence to conclude on alleged fraud – issues a report providing assurance as to whether fraud occured or not
Internal Audit Assurance	Assignments can vary, e.g. assessment of controls within the revenue cycle	Audit committee/ directors /'those charged with governance'	Laid down in client entity's policies and procedures	Internal audit opinion on efficient and effective operation of internal controls within the revenue and receivables cycle of the client entity

Reasonable Assurance

The external auditor provides '**reasonable assurance**' that the financial statements are free from **material misstatements**. The assurance is **not a guarantee**, however; it provides a high degree of assurance but not absolute assurance that the financial statements are correct. For this reason, the term '**true and fair**' is used when concluding on the opinion:

'In our opinion the financial statements: give a true and fair view, in accordance with …'

The auditor's assessment of true and fair is based on his opinion that no **significant errors (misstatements)** exist in the financial statements. Significance is measured by the auditor with reference to **materiality**. As such, the auditor's assessment of true and fair is based on his belief (due to his collection of evidence) that the financial statements are free from **material misstatement**. The terms 'misstatement' and 'materiality' are defined below in **Table 1.2** and are discussed in detail in **Chapter 5**.

TABLE 1.2: 'MISSTATEMENT' AND 'MATERIALITY'

Term	Related Auditing Standard	Definition
'Misstatement'	ISA 450	A difference between the amounts, classification, presentation or disclosure of a reported financial statement item and the amount, classification, presentation or disclosure that is required for the item to be in accordance with applicable financial reporting framework. Misstatements can arise from fraud or error.
'Materiality'	ISA 320	Misstatements are considered to be material if they individually, or in the aggregate, could reasonably be expected to influence the economic decisions of users taken on the basis of the financial statements.

The reason that the concept of 'reasonable assurance' exists is due to the inherent limitations of an audit. The limitations of an external audit are set out in **Table 1.3** below.

1.3 HISTORICAL DEVELOPMENT OF AUDITING AND ASSURANCE

The need for audit has essentially been driven by the increasing separation of the ownership from the management of companies. Although some form of auditing existed in Greece as long ago as 500 BC, it was only with the Industrial Revolution and the growth of publicly owned companies in the 19th Century that the need for auditing really developed. The premise of a publicly owned company is that it is funded by capital raised from the selling of shares to the public. Together, the shareholders own the company but are not responsible for its day-to-day management, which is performed by a team of directors/managers employed by the company (the '**management**'). As such, the directors act as the *agents* of the shareholders and are responsible for the stewardship of the company.

The management should run the company with the aim of maximizing the return of the shareholders. However, there may exist a conflict of interests between the personal interests of the management and the interests of the shareholders (e.g. management may extract resources from the company for personal gain). As a result, shareholders seek to monitor management by requiring them to prepare accounts detailing how they have used the company's resources, and shareholders gain assurance over the accuracy and

TABLE 1.3: LIMITATIONS OF AN EXTERNAL AUDIT

Limitation	Limitation Explained	For further reading see:
Judgement	Auditors must use their judgement throughout the audit in areas such as:	
	• setting materiality;	Chapter 5
	• deciding on the number of items to test;	Chapter 6
	• assessing risk;	Chapter 7
	• extrapolation of errors in a sample.	Chapter 6
Accounting and internal controls	Inherent limitations exist in accounting and internal controls in the:	
	• existence of non-routine transactions;	Chapter 8
	• possibility of human error;	Chapter 8
	• possibility of collusion;	Chapters 7 and 8
	• possibility of management override of controls;	Chapters 3 and 8
	• omission of some controls on grounds that they do not warrant their cost;	Chapter 8
	• need for estimates in accounting.	Chapter 6
The audit report	The audit report itself has inherent limitations, in that:	
	• it has a prescribed standard format, which can be limiting;	Chapter 19
	• it contains auditing jargon which may be difficult for the reader to understand.	Chapter 19
Sampling Risk	For practical reasons, not all items are tested in the set of financial statements. The auditor performs sample testing and extrapolates on the results, which naturally means that some misstatements may go undetected. The results of the sample will indicate what is likely to exist in the rest of the population, but it does not provide a guarantee.	Chapter 6
Timing of the audit report	The audit report is generally issued a long time after the balance sheet date, so even if it does provide a warning (in the way of a modification of opinion), the users may well have made poor decisions in the intervening period which, had the report been available earlier, may have been avoided.	Chapter 19
Audit evidence	While audit evidence is persuasive, it is not always conclusive. The auditor attempts to collect sufficient appropriate audit evidence to support the balances and transactions in the financial statements, but this evidence is often persuasive rather than conclusive.	Chapter 6

legitimacy of these accounts by having them checked by an independent source, i.e. through the annual financial statement audit. The **independent audit report** provides the shareholders with a degree of confidence (**assurance**) that the contents of the financial statements are **true and fair** and can be relied upon to make decisions about their investment.

Figure 1.1 below depicts the above argument, known as the 'agency theory'. It shows that while shareholders appoint directors to run the company, quite often these directors delegate elements of their responsibility to a management team, who are appointed by them. The directors and management should act in the best interest of the shareholder, with an aim to maximising shareholder wealth. Occasionally, however, management can act in a manner that maximises their own wealth to the detriment of the shareholder.

The above scenario causes a concern for the shareholder: how can they be sure that management (those charged with governance) are acting in their best interests? It would be impractical for all shareholders to have a role in the company and they are likely to lack the expertise to do so. Capital markets are designed to give people access to markets and to make profits (through dividends and capital growth) without intervention in the actual running of companies. Over the years, the need for audit services has increased, as the numbers of users of financial statements (and other information produced by companies) has increased. **Users of financial statements** (often referred to as 'stakeholders' due to their common interest in the company) can include the following groups:
- shareholders;
- financial institutions;
- suppliers;
- customers;
- employees;
- governments; and
- the general public.

FIGURE 1.1: THE AGENCY THEORY

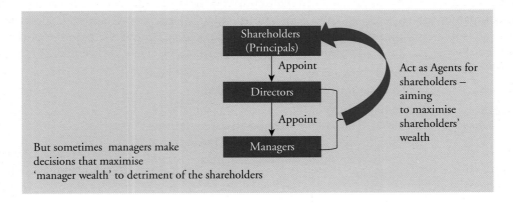

It would not be possible to provide access to books and records to all stakeholders, so the independent audit report offers an unbiased opinion to increase the credibility of the financial statements for all users/stakeholders.

All of the above groups now look for the independent audit report as a means of gaining assurance over financial statements. As the number of users of financial statements has increased, so too has the debate over the issue of whether or not the auditor is liable for negligence to all of these users. Where the audit opinion is found to have been incorrect as a result of negligence on the part of the auditor, to which of these users of the financial statement should he be held accountable? This debate continues to evolve on a case-by-case basis. In essence, auditors are **generally not liable to any parties other than the direct client** (i.e. the shareholders), unless there are very specific circumstances in which the auditor was expressly aware of the intentions of another user to place reliance on the audit report (see **Section 1.8** and **Appendices 1.1.** and **1.2** where landmark legal cases are discussed).

In the last decade or so we have seen a number of high-profile accounting frauds, including, most famously, Enron (2001), along with WorldCom (2001), Xerox (1997/2000) and Parmalat (2002). These cases have resulted in a considerably increased focus on the need for a robust audit of financial statements, and there has been a number of changes in statutory and regulatory guidance over the past number of years to attempt to address these concerns.

Further discussions on the legal liability of auditors are included below at **Section 1.8**. Some of the frauds that have taken place over the last decade or two, leading to the need for increased legal and regulatory framework for the auditor, are discussed in detail in **Chapter 2**, 'Ethics and Corporate Governance' and **Chapter 3**, 'Fraud and Compliance with Laws and Regulations'.

1.4 THE LEGISLATIVE FRAMEWORK

Introduction

Generally, under company law, in both the Republic of Ireland and Northern Ireland (UK), all companies are required to have their annual financial statements audited. However, there are some exemptions afforded under company law that remove the requirements for audit of the annual accounts of small companies meeting certain defined criteria (discussed later in this section).

The Companies Acts in both jurisdictions also set out requirements with respect to directors' and auditors' responsibilities in relation to the preparation of financial statements and the audit of those financial statements.

When producing a set of financial statements, the directors essentially accept responsibility through the inclusion of a '**Directors' Responsibility Statement**'. This statement summarises the directors' responsibilities in relation to the preparation of the financial statements. The directors generally include this statement within the 'Directors' Report' or immediately following it. Directors' responsibilities in the Republic of Ireland and UK/Northern Ireland are as set out below in Examples 1.1 and 1.2, respectively.

With regard to auditors' responsibilities, under both UK/NI (Companies Act 2006 (CA 2006)) and the Republic of Ireland (Companies Acts 1963–2012) company law, there are a number of requirements that set out the scope of audits, which extend beyond that required in the professional standards (professional standards are discussed in Section 1.5 below).

The Office of the Director of Corporate Enforcement (ODCE) was set up in the Republic of Ireland to enforce compliance with the requirements of the Companies Acts. The following, as summarised by the ODCE, are some of the specific responsibilities and duties of the auditor outlined within the Companies Acts 1963–2012.

- **Duty to Provide an Audit Report** The principal duty of the auditors to a company is to report to the members of the company on the financial statements examined by them (section 160 of the Companies Act 1963 (CA 1963), as amended by section 183 of the Companies Act 1990 (CA 1990)).
- **Duty to Report Failure to Maintain Proper Books of Account** Where auditors form the opinion that the company being audited is contravening, or has contravened, its obligations to maintain proper books of account, they are obliged to serve a notice on the company informing it of that opinion (section 194 CA 1990, as amended by section 74 of the Company Law Enforcement Act 2001).
- **Duty to Exercise Professional Integrity** Auditors are under a duty to carry out audits with professional integrity. In preparing their report, auditors must exercise the skill, care and caution of a reasonably competent, careful and cautious auditor (section 193(6) CA 1990).[2]

Legislative Framework within the Republic of Ireland

Requirement for Audit and Audit Exemptions

All private companies in the Republic of Ireland are required to appoint an auditor under section 160 CA 1963. There are, however, some exemptions: the Companies (Amendment) (No. 2) Act 1999 (C(A)(No. 2)A 1999) allows exemption from the audit requirements. These exemptions can only be adopted if a company meets all of the criteria set out in **Table 1.4** below. These thresholds are in line with those set out in the European Union (Accounts) Regulations 2012.[3] In order to be exempt, a company must meet **all three criteria** and the directors must be satisfied that the conditions are met in respect of **current and previous financial years**.

---

[2] See http://www.odce.ie/en/company_responsibilities.aspx
[3] S.I. No. 304 of 2012.

TABLE 1.4: REPUBLIC OF IRELAND AUDIT EXEMPTIONS

Criteria	Reference Item	Threshold
1	Turnover	€8.8 million (or less)
2	Balance Sheet Total	€4.4 million (or less)
3	Average Number of Employees	50 (or less)

The exemptions above do not apply to:
- companies limited by guarantee;
- public companies;
- parent or subsidiary undertakings incorporated in the Republic of Ireland.

Directors' and Auditors' Responsibilities

Earlier in this section we discussed the responsibilities of the auditors as laid down by the Companies Acts. Company directors also have a number of responsibilities under company law (in *both* the UK and the Republic of Ireland), some of which are summarised below:
- to maintain proper books of accounts;
- to prepare annual accounts;
- to have an annual audit performed (subject to exceptions);
- to maintain certain registers and documents.

When producing the financial statements, the directors are required to provide a summary of their responsibilities in relation to their preparation of the entity's financial statements, i.e. a 'Directors' Responsibility Statement'. This summary should either be included in the directors' report or alongside the directors' report, and an example of one for the Republic of Ireland is provided below.

EXAMPLE 1.1: DIRECTORS' RESPONSIBILITIES STATEMENT, REPUBLIC OF IRELAND[4]

The directors are responsible for preparing the Directors' Report and the financial statements in accordance with Irish law and regulations. Irish company law requires the directors to prepare financial statements giving a true and fair view of the state of affairs of the company and the profit or loss of the company for each financial year. Under that law, the directors have elected to prepare the financial statements in accordance with Irish Generally Accepted Accounting Practice (accounting standards issued

---

[4] FRC Bulletin 1(I), *Compendium of Illustrative Auditor's Reports on Irish Financial Statements.*

by the Financial Reporting Council and promulgated by the Institute of Chartered Accountants in Ireland and Irish law).

In preparing these financial statements, the directors are required to:
- select suitable accounting policies and then apply them consistently;
- make judgements and accounting estimates that are reasonable and prudent;
- prepare the financial statements on the going concern basis, unless it is inappropriate to presume that the company will continue in business.

The directors are responsible for keeping proper books of account that disclose with reasonable accuracy at any time the financial position of the company and enable them to ensure that the financial statements comply with the Companies Acts 1963–2012. They are also responsible for safeguarding the assets of the company and hence for taking reasonable steps for the prevention and detection of fraud and other irregularities.

Legislative Framework within the UK/Northern Ireland

Requirement for Audit and Audit Exemptions

All companies are required to appoint an auditor under section 485 of the Companies Act 2006 (CA 2006). Additionally, all companies are required to have their annual accounts audited under section 477 CA 2006. There are some allowances, however; section 75 CA 2006 allows exemption from the audit requirements if a company meets all of the criteria set out in **Table 1.5** below. In order to be exempt, a company must meet **two of three criteria**.

Dormant companies under section 480 CA 2006 are also exempt.

Directors' and Auditors' Responsibilities (UK/NI)

Similar to the requirements in the Republic of Ireland, directors have a diverse range of responsibilities under company law, which they are required to acknowledge in the 'Directors' Responsibility Statement', which is included in either the Directors' Report or alongside the Directors' Report.

TABLE 1.5: UK/NORTHERN IRELAND AUDIT EXEMPTIONS

Criteria	Reference Item	Threshold
1	Turnover	£6.5 million (or less)
2	Balance Sheet Total	£3.26 million (or less)
3	Average Number of Employees	50 (or less)

EXAMPLE 1.2: DIRECTORS' RESPONSIBILITIES STATEMENT, UK/NORTHERN IRELAND[5]

The directors are responsible for preparing the Directors' Report and the financial statements in accordance with applicable law and regulations.

Company law requires the directors to prepare financial statements for each financial year. Under that law the directors have elected to prepare the financial statements in accordance with United Kingdom Generally Accepted Accounting Practice (UK accounting standards and applicable law). Under company law the directors must not approve the financial statements unless they are satisfied that they give a true and fair view of the state of affairs of the company and the profit or loss of the company for that period.

In preparing these financial statements, the directors are required to:
• select suitable accounting policies and then apply them consistently;
• make judgements and accounting estimates that are reasonable and prudent;
• state whether applicable UK accounting standards have been followed, subject to any material departures disclosed and explained in the financial statements;
• prepare the financial statements on the going concern basis, unless it is inappropriate to presume that the company will continue in business.

The directors are responsible for keeping adequate accounting records that are sufficient to show and explain the company's transactions and disclose with reasonable accuracy at any time the financial position of the company and enable them to ensure that the financial statements comply with the Companies Act 2006. They are also responsible for safeguarding the assets of the company and hence for taking reasonable steps for the prevention and detection of fraud and other irregularities.

1.5 THE REGULATORY FRAMEWORK

Introduction

Having established the legislative responsibilities and duties of the auditor, let us now consider the regulatory environment of external auditing.

Louise Kelly, in her book *Advanced Auditing and Assurance,* writes:
  "The regulatory framework includes guidance on how an audit is conducted, who should be allowed to perform an audit, and who should develop auditing standards. It also includes rules and regulations around monitoring of audit firms."[6]

---

[5] Source: FRC, *Compendium of Illustrative Auditor's Reports on United Kingdom Private Sector Financial Statements for periods ended on or after 15 December 2010.*
[6] Louise Kelly, *Advanced Auditing and Assurance* (Chartered Accountants Ireland, 2013).

The regulatory framework relevant to the UK/NI and the Republic of Ireland is summarised below in **Figure 1.2**.

FIGURE 1.2: SUMMARY OF REGULATORY FRAMEWORK IN
THE UK/NI AND THE REPUBLIC OF IRELAND

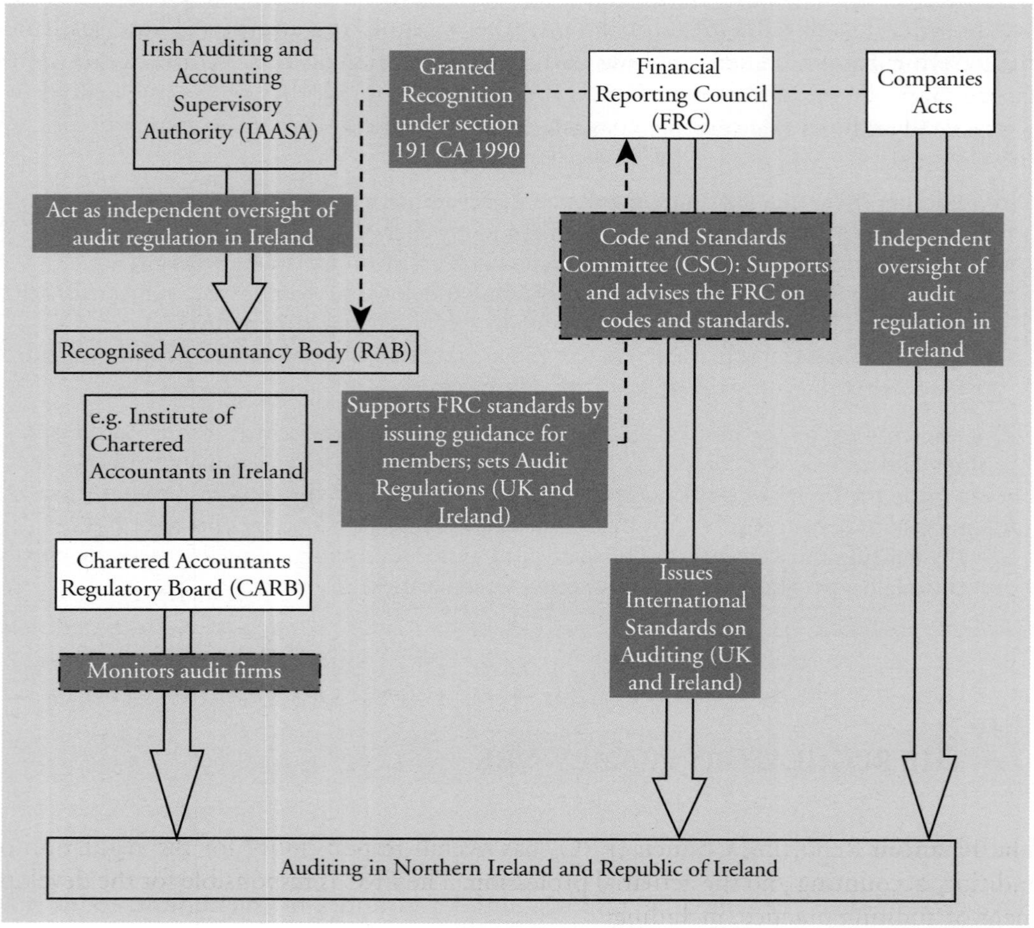

The Role of the Irish Auditing and Accounting Supervisory Authority (IAASA)

The Irish Auditing and Accounting Supervisory Authority (IAASA) aims to support and enhance public confidence in the accountancy profession including acting as an oversight for audit regulation in Ireland. The IAASA also provides information relating to the registration and regulation of audit firms (details of which can be found on its website: www.iaasa.ie).

The Role of a Recognised Accountancy Body (RAB) / Recognised Supervisory Body (RSB)

In order to act as an auditor in either the UK/NI or the Republic of Ireland, the auditor must seek authorisation to do so from a one of the 'Institutes', i.e. all **'recognised supervisory bodies'** (RSB) in the UK/NI and **'recognised accountancy bodies'** (RABs) in the Republic of Ireland, (including the Institute of Chartered Accountants in Ireland(ICAI)) for the purpose of regulating auditors. These Institutes must have rules which set out how auditors are regulated. The Institutes' aim is to ensure that:
- registered auditors maintain high standards of audit work;
- the reputation of registered auditors with the public is maintained;
- the application of the regulations is fair but firm;
- the regulations are clear; and
- the regulations apply to all sizes of firm."[7]

A RAB (Republic of Ireland) is a body that has been granted recognition under section 191 CA 1990. A RSB (UK/NI) is a body that has been granted recognition under the UK Companies Acts 2006.

The Role of the Chartered Accountants Regulatory Board (CARB)

The Institute of Chartered Accountants in Ireland (ICAI) established the Chartered Accountants Regulatory Board (CARB), which carries out the functions of the ICAI as a registering 'Institute'. CARB was established by the ICAI to provide, among other things, the monitoring of the quality of auditing among its members. CARB assists in regulating members, in accordance with the provisions of the Institute's bye-laws, independently, openly and in the public interest. CARB is responsible for developing standards of professional conduct and supervising the compliance of members, member firms and affiliates, which is done by regular reviews of member firms.

The Role of the Financial Reporting Council (FRC)

The Financial Reporting Council (FRC) has overall responsibility for the regulation of auditing, accounting and the actuarial profession. The FRC is responsible for the development of auditing practice, including:
- the setting of standards; and
- issuing guidance on the application of standards in particular circumstances and industries.

---

[7] *Audit Guidance (UK and Ireland) Effective from 1 June 2012* (Institute of Chartered Accountants in England and Wales, Institute of Chartered Accountants of Scotland and Institute of Chartered Accountants in Ireland, 2012) – see www.carb.ie

The role of the Auditing Practices Board (APB), which was responsible for the setting of auditing standards up until July 2012, has been taken over by the FRC, which is supported in this role by the Codes and Standards Committee (CSC). The FRC Board and the CSC are advised on audit and assurance related matters by the Audit and Assurance Council. Pronouncements issued by the APB, however, remain effective under the FRC.

These standards and guidance can be found on the FRC's website: www.frc.co.uk.

The auditing standards issued by the FRC are based on the corresponding international standards issued by the International Auditing and Assurance Standards Board (IAASB). The FRC clarifies its adoption of these International Standards (ISAs) as follows: "The ISAs (UK & Ireland) and ISQC (UK and Ireland) 1 are based on the corresponding international standards issued by the International Auditing and Assurance Standards Board. Where necessary, the international standards have been augmented with additional requirements to address specific UK and Irish legal and regulatory requirements; and additional guidance that is appropriate in the UK and Irish national, legislative, cultural and business context."[8]

The Role of the International Auditing and Assurance Standards Board (IAASB)

The IAASB was set up to serve the public interest by setting high-quality international standards in the areas of auditing and assurance and other related standards. It aims to enhance the quality and consistency of auditing practices throughout the world and in doing so to strengthen public confidence in the global auditing and assurance profession. The IAASB is responsible for setting international standards and guidance for use by all professional accountants.

Figure 1.3 depicts how standards and guidance are set which regulate auditing practices in the UK/NI and the Republic of Ireland, reflecting the above discussion whereby the IAASB produces international auditing and assurance standards, which are then adopted by the FRC having been augmented to ensure their relevance to the UK and Irish legislative, cultural and business environments. Throughout this textbook we will concentrate on and refer to the International Standards on Auditing (UK and Ireland) as set by the FRC (albeit based on the IAASB's standards). **Any reference to 'ISAs' throughout this text refers to ISAs (UK and Ireland), if not otherwise stated**.

You should further note from **Figure 1.3** that the FRC has not adopted the IAASB's standards on assurance engagements or on related services in the same way as it has in relation to those relating to auditing; however, these are applicable for use in the UK and the Republic of Ireland in appropriate circumstances.

---

[8] FRC, *The Financial Reporting Council Scope and Authority of Audit and Assurance Pronouncements*, 2013.

FIGURE 1.3: SUMMARY OF AUDITING AND ASSURANCE STANDARDS
ADOPTED IN UK AND REPUBLIC OF IRELAND[9]

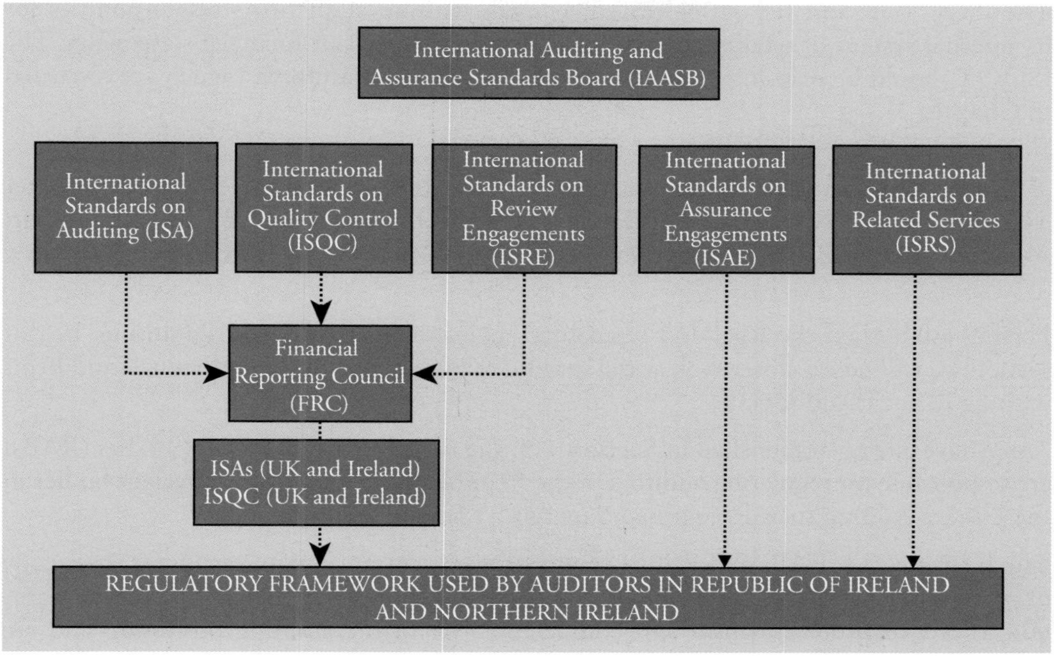

The Role of the International Standards on Auditing ISAs (UK and Ireland) ('ISAs')

The International Standards on Auditing (ISAs) are accepted as best practice by professional accountancy bodies and any auditor who does not apply these standards to an audit engagement leaves himself open to regulatory action. Auditing standards include objectives for and requirements of the auditor, including application and other explanatory material.

Failure to apply these standards in practice could leave the auditor open to accusations of negligence should the **audit opinion** he expresses subsequently prove to be incorrect. Reference to the fact that the audit has been carried out in accordance with ISAs is generally included within the auditor's report (see **Chapter 19**).

The standards issued by the FRC remain largely unchanged from that of the IAASB's and, when altered and published by the FRC, areas of changed text are differentiated from the original text of the international standards by use of grey shading. (See ISA (UK and Ireland) 200, paragraph A14-1 for an example of this.)

---

[9] Based on a Figure in Louise Kelly, *Advanced Auditing and Assurance* (Chartered Accountants Ireland, 2013).

The Role of the International Standard on Quality Control (ISQC (UK and Ireland) 1)

The ISQC (UK and Ireland) 1 (ISQC 1) deals with an audit firm's responsibilities for its internal system of quality control for audits and reviews of financial statements. The ISQC 1 should be read in conjunction with the **Ethical Standards** (which are discussed in **Chapter 2**).

1.6 REGULATION, MONITORING AND SUPERVISION BY THE RECOGNISED ACCOUNTANCY (SUPERVISORY) BODIES

Having established the legal and regulatory environment that governs auditing, in this section we will take a closer look at the specific requirements for the individuals and firms wishing to act as auditors.

As we have already established in **Section 1.5**, the recognised accountancy bodies (RABs) are responsible for regulating auditors in the Republic of Ireland (the equivalent bodies in the UK are referred to as Recognised Supervisory Bodies (RSBs)).

The Institutes, i.e. RABs and RSBs operate stringent entrance requirements, a strict code of ethics and continuing professional development (CPD) for members in order to maintain a level of professionalism and competence within the auditing profession and are responsible for ensuring the following among their members.
- education and work experience;
- eligibility; and
- supervision and monitoring.

Education and Work Experience

In order for the RABs to have confidence in their members' abilities, they insist on strict entry requirements, obliging members to engage in education supported by examination suitable to ensure the member has the necessary technical knowledge to carry out the tasks required of him. Additionally, prior to entry, the member is required to develop a portfolio of experience intended to support the practical application of the technical knowledge gained during the education process. **Table 1.6** below outlines the specific requirements under the 'Three Es': Education; Examination; and Experience.

Eligibility and Ineligibility

In order to practice as an auditor, certain criteria must be met. These criteria are predominantly laid down within company law and enforced by the ODCE in the Republic of Ireland; and by the Department for Business Innovation and Skills (BIS) which does so

TABLE 1.6: THE THREE ES—EDUCATION, EXAMINATION AND (WORK) EXPERIENCE

Education	Examination	Experience
• Compulsory Knowledge (accounting and audit-specific) is required to be held by all members. • Additional knowledge, where relevant. The education provided under RAB/RSB should be sufficient to cover these subjects in a breadth and depth sufficient to enable them to perform their duties to the expected standard.	Each member should demonstrate that they have passed an examination of professional competence: theory and practical application.	Practical application is considered key; therefore each member should complete a minimum period of supervised practical experience, primarily in the area of audit and accountancy (in a suitable professional environment).

through the Insolvency Service for the UK. Eligibility requires membership of an Institute (RAB/RSB). Ineligibility can arise where:
- the auditor fails to meet the eligibility requirements;
- there exists an other independence or ethics issue;
- the auditor is a bankrupt;
- the auditor has been found guilty by court verdict.

Table 1.7 below summarises these requirements.

TABLE 1.7: ELIGIBILITY AND INELIGIBILITY TO ACT AS AN AUDITOR

Eligibility	Ineligibility

✓ Membership of a recognised accounting body (RAB/RSB) is the main prerequisite for eligibility as an auditor (e.g. ICAI). The 'auditor' can be a body corporate, partnership or sole practitioner. Eligibility also requires:
✓ The RAB should have rules to ensure that those eligible for appointment as a company auditor are either:
  • individuals holding an appropriate combination of qualification and experience; or
  • firms controlled by qualified persons.
	× Failure to meet eligibility requirements.
	× Close connection to the client company/client entity – one cannot act as auditor if one is:
	  1. an officer or an employee of the company/client entity;
	  2. a partner or employee of such a person;
	  3. a partnership in which such a person is a partner.
	× The existence of any situation that would be seen to be in breach of the RAB's code of ethics.
	× Bankrupts cannot act as auditors while their debts remain unpaid (or debts are excused by a court).
	× Individuals who have been found guilty on indictment, i.e. under criminal law.

Supervisory and Monitoring Roles

An RAB/RSB is responsible for the adequate monitoring and enforcement of compliance with its rules and should include provisions relating to:

- admittance and expulsion;
- investigation of complaints; and
- compulsory professional indemnity insurance.

In order to supervise and monitor their members, the RABs/RSBs must introduce a 'monitoring body'. This body monitors its members with respect to their continuing professional development (CPD) as well as their competence to carry out audits of financial statements. For the ICAI this takes the form of the Chartered Accountants Regulatory Board (CARB). The following should be evident to CARB on inspection of any audit practitioner:

1. a properly structured audit approach;
2. quality control procedures;
3. commitment to ethical guidelines;
4. technical excellence;
5. adherence to fit and proper criteria;
6. peer reviews;
7. appropriate fees; and
8. strong/complete audit files containing audit evidence to support audit opinions.

1.7 APPOINTMENT, REMOVAL AND RESIGNATION OF AUDITORS

Having established in **Section 1.6** who can act as the auditor of an entity's financial statements, let us now consider how auditors are *appointed* to the role of auditor for a specific company or **client entity**. We will also address the removal and resignation of auditors from their role.

Appointment of Auditors

In the UK/NI and the Republic of Ireland the shareholders of a company appoint an auditor by voting during the first annual general meeting (AGM). A **casual vacancy** (to cover the period prior to the first AGM or prior to the next AGM in instances where the auditor has resigned or been removed) may be filled by the directors while they await approval by the shareholders at the next AGM. However, once appointed, the auditor is in place until the next AGM.

Removal of Auditors

Auditors are generally removed due to:

1. **Tenure** – the length of time for which the auditor has held the **audit engagement** with the client entity, which can be concerning from an **independence** perspective. As will be discussed further in **Chapter 2**, Section 2.5, **long association** between the audit firm and the client entity can develop into a close relationship between the staff of the

respective organisations. When one becomes overly familiar with an individual, it can create a sense of obligation towards that individual. This may be in conflict with one's duty, e.g. in this case to report on one's responsibilities with respect to the financial statements of the client entity.

2. **Incompetence** – where doubts exist over the auditor's continued competency to carry out his duties.

The ultimate removal of the auditor of a company must be subject to a majority vote at an AGM. However, the auditor should be given a notice period. If this removal is during a term of office, the auditor's respective RAB/RSB should be notified by the auditor.

Resignation by Auditors

An auditor can resign from the audit of a client entity for a number of reasons (see **Table 1.8** below). If, however, an auditor acting within the Republic of Ireland does resign, he must comply with certain rights and duties laid down under section 185 CA 1990, which require the auditor: "by a notice in writing … served on the company and stating his intention to do so, resign from the office of auditor to the company; and the resignation shall take effect on the date on which the notice is so served or on such later date as may be specified in the notice." This notice will include:

(a)   a statement to the effect that there are no circumstances connected with the resignation to which it relates that the auditor concerned considers should be brought to the notice of the members or creditors of the company, or

(b)   a statement of any such circumstances (statement of circumstances).[10]

This notice must be sent to the Registrar of Companies within 14 days of serving the notice on the company. Should circumstances be noted (as per (b) above), the company should, within 14 days of receiving the notice, send a copy to everyone entitled to attend an AGM. The auditor has the right to request an extraordinary general meeting (EGM) in which to discuss the circumstances outlined in the statement. The directors should proceed to convene this meeting within 21 days of receipt of request for not more than 28 days from the date of notice convening the meeting.

In respect of the UK/Northern Ireland, sections 522–525 CA 2006 set new requirements for auditors and companies to notify the "appropriate audit authority" when an auditor ceases to hold office. The specific requirements are similar to that laid out above in respect of the Republic of Ireland.

The following **Table 1.8** sets out the reasons why an auditor might resign and the duties and rights of the auditor on resignation.

For the full duties and rights relating to audit resignation, refer to the website of the Office of the Director of Corporate Enforcement at www.odce.ie.

---

[10] Section 185(2) CA 1990.

TABLE 1.8: REASONS, DUTIES AND RIGHTS FOR AN AUDITOR'S RESIGNATION

Reasons	Duties	Rights
Examples include: • inability to work with the management team of the client entity. • identification of ethical issues. • auditor's concerns over association (management integrity as a result of **limitation of scope** (see **Chapter 19**, Section 19.3, breach of laws and regulations, senior management fraud, etc.).	• To notify the share-holders in a '**Statement of Circumstances**', outlining the circumstances giving rise to the resignation. • To notify one's respective RAB/RSB (should the resignation be during a term of office). • To notify the Registrar of Companies (Companies Registration Office (CRO for RoI and Companies House for UK/NI).	• To request the directors to send the written 'Statement of Circumstances' to the members of the company (shareholders) prior to the convening of an EGM. • To request the company to circulate notice of the holding of the EGM and the circumstances relating to the resignation (to be convened by the directors within 21 days of request by the auditor and held not more than 28 days following date of request to convene). • To speak at the EGM.

1.8 AUDITORS' LEGAL LIABILITY

Introduction

The ODCE outlines the main duty of auditors as being:

"… to report to the members on whether in their opinion the company's financial statements give a true and fair view. The auditors' report must be made available to every member and be read at the AGM."[11]

The Companies Acts (UK 2006 and RoI 1963–2012) require, the auditor, within his audit report, to report on failure to maintain proper books of account. Indictable offences (serious enough to be tried before a judge and jury), should be reported directly to the ODCE for RoI or BIS for UK/NI.

In carrying out these duties, the auditor must do so with professional integrity. He has a duty to exercise reasonable care and failure to do so may result in being held liable for damages to the company/client entity or, in particular to its members (i.e. the shareholders).

---

11 http://www.odce.ie/en/company_responsibilities.aspx

Essentially, should the auditor provide an incorrect opinion that causes loss to the client entity or its shareholders and he is found to have not acted with professional integrity and exercised his duties with the expected reasonable care, he may be sued for damages.

Table 1.9 below lists some key legal terms and their explanations, along with some landmark legal cases relating to the legal liability of the auditor.

TABLE 1.9: KEY LEGAL TERMINOLOGY AND THEIR RELEVANCE TO AUDITING

Legal Terminology	Explanation	Case (where applicable)
(Law of) Tort	A 'tort' is a wrongful act or omission, whether intentional or otherwise, whereby a person suffers damages, be they physical or financial, and there is a financial compensation due in return.	
Due professional care	Consideration is given to the relevance of professional standards, i.e. did the auditor apply auditing standards in determining the adequate performance of audit work; and use the relevant financial reporting framework in determining the basis for expressing an opinion as to the truth and fairness of the financial statements?	*Re Kingston Cotton Mill Co* (1896) • A manager exaggerated stock values for years to fraudulently overstate profits. • This eventually came to light when they could not pay debts. • The auditors relied on a certificate from management to confirm the stock value. • The auditors did not attend the stock-take, nor attempt to validate the opening balance of stocks or cross-reference to sales and purchases, which would have highlighted the issue. • The judge held that the auditor must rely on some skilled person (i.e. the manager) for the materials necessary to enable him to enter the stock in trade at its proper value in the statement of financial position. The auditor has to perform with the skill, care and caution of a reasonably competent, careful and cautious professional. **The auditor is a watchdog, but not a bloodhound.**

- This case laid down some fundamental auditing principles, such as the 'watchdog' rule and the concept of the reasonable skill and care of the auditor.

Re London & General Bank (1985), also deals with auditor responsibility. In this case the auditor, while having adequately informed the directors of insufficient security lodged relating to loans and overdrafts guaranteed to customers, **failed to ensure that the financial statements adequately alerted the shareholders to this critical position,** i.e. the financial statements did not adequately disclose the issue and the auditor issued an unqualified opinion. The shareholder was later held liable for the second dividend due to the shareholders (insufficient evidence was believed to exist to hold him liable for the first dividend) and Lindley L.J. described the auditor's duty as follows: "An auditor, however, is not bound to do more than **exercise reasonable care and skill in making inquiries and investigations**."

Negligence

Negligence is conduct that fails to take proper care over something; in law, this entails a breach of any contractual duty or duty of care in tort owed to another person or persons. If auditors have been negligent, the client may sue them for breach of an implicit term of contract to exercise reasonable care and skill in order to recover any consequential loss suffered. A judge will seek to prove not only that the ultimate decision taken by an auditor where damage was suffered was incorrect but also that the method in arriving at the decision was flawed (e.g. that the requirements of the auditing standards and company law were not followed).

Privity of contract

Privity of contract relates to the contractual relationship that exists between two or more contracting parties. Essentially, a contract confers rights and imposes liabilities only on its contracting parties.

The company (client entity) has a contract in the form of an engagement letter with the auditor (see **Chapter 5,** Section 5.3) and hence can sue the auditor for breach of contract if the auditor is negligent in carrying out the terms of the contract. Note that only the company can sue the auditor under the law of contract as other third parties, such as banks, creditors and shareholders, etc., are not in a contractual relationship with the auditor.

A duty may exist to a third party not named in the engagement letter/contract (i.e. who does not have privity of contract) if a relationship was reasonably foreseeable and that third party can prove that a loss suffered was as a result of negligent conduct. Such foreseeable third party might be a bank that requires the company to be audited prior to lending it money. If the auditor was aware of this and failed to give reasonable care, an action may be brought against him by the bank if it suffers a loss as a result of relying on the audited financial statements.

Causal relationship

The question of causal relationship considers the relationship between an event that is said to be negligent, e.g. the auditor is believed not have acted with a duty of care and issued an incorrect opinion on the financial statements that was relied upon, and a second event, e.g. as a result of this negligence somebody suffers a loss. The question a court will seek to answer is 'whether there is a link between the breach and the damages suffered by the innocent party?'

In *Galoo Ltd v. Bright Grahame Murray* (1994), Galoo alleged that had the auditors audited its accounts properly they would have discovered that Galoo was insolvent and this would have caused Galoo to cease trading. Galoo therefore claimed that the auditors' failure to highlight this caused Galoo to continue trading and suffer further trading losses.

It was held that there was no causal relationship between the alleged negligence and the losses incurred. The financial statements may have allowed the company to continue trading, but the company's existence was not the cause of its losses. Event A (the negligent audit) was necessary for Event B (the loss incurred during subsequent trading) to occur but was not in itself the cause of Event B.

Contributory negligence

Contributory negligence is failure of the plaintiff, in this case the client entity, to meet certain required standards of care. Together with the defendant's (auditor's) negligence, it contributes to bringing about the loss in question,

In *AWA Ltd v. Daniels T/A Deloitte Haskins & Sells* (1992):
• the auditors failed to warn management of a control failing which they discovered during their audit – the failing later caused loss to the company;
• the company was held to be partially responsible for not establishing adequate controls in the first place.

Damages   Where auditors fail in their duty to act with reasonable care and skill, whether under contract or in tort, a plaintiff (i.e. a client entity) is entitled to recover any economic loss (i.e. damages) arising out of such breach of duty. Two things need to be considered:

1. Was it the reliance on the financial statements (and in turn the auditor's report) that caused the economic loss and was that reliance reasonably foreseeable by the auditor?
2. To what extent may responsibility for any loss be assigned, on the one hand, to the auditors and, on the other, to other causes/third parties?

Proximity   As introduced above, a duty may exist to a third party not named in the engagement letter/contract if a relationship was reasonably foreseeable and that third party can prove that a loss suffered was as a result of negligent conduct.

Proximity is said to arise where, for example, a company's financial condition is such that it is a likely takeover target, and the auditors in such circumstances should be aware that the accounts may be relied upon by potential investors and a duty of care thus arises.

Considering Auditor Liability

Auditors can face claims under contract law or under the tort of negligence. The auditors must be able to show that they provided the expected duty of care to the plaintiff (client entity) if a legal action is taken. However, if the auditors can show that they carried out the engagement in compliance with generally accepted auditing standards, this may act as their defence. It is up to the courts to decide if the required standard of skill and care has been given.

Caparo Industries plc v. Dickman and Others (1990) is a landmark case that brought the most important ruling with respect to the duty of care of auditors, and is discussed below.

CASE: *CAPARO INDUSTRIES PLC V. DICKMAN AND OTHERS (1990)*

Caparo Industries plc held shares in Fidelity plc. After viewing the audited accounts of March 1984, which showed company profits of £1.3 million, Caparo purchased more shares in Fidelity. Later in the year, Caparo successfully took over Fidelity.

After the takeover, Caparo brought an action against Touche Ross, the auditors, claiming that the accounts were inaccurate and should have shown a loss of £400,000. Caparo claimed that, as auditors, Touche Ross owed a duty of care to the investors and potential investors in respect of the audited accounts.

Caparo claimed that:
(a) the auditors would have known that the company was vulnerable to a takeover as the reported profits had fallen short of those projected of £2.2 million, and the share price had fallen by nearly 50% in the month of March 1984; and

(b) the auditors should have known that any potential investor would be likely to rely on the audited accounts before making his/her investment decision.

The first issue was if a duty of care was owed to Caparo. The High Court held that no duty of care was owed to Caparo.

This decision was appealed to the Court of Appeal, which held that a duty of care was owed to Caparo in respect of them being shareholders, but not as potential investors.

The case upon appeal, due to the significance of the matter (importance to case law), was eventually appealed to the House of Lords, which decided that in making further purchases of shares, existing shareholders were in the same position as any other investors and that they were not owed a duty of care in their capacity as 'potential investors'.

A plaintiff (usually a client entity) wishing to bring a claim of negligence against an auditor must prove three things:
1. that a duty of care existed, which is enforceable at law;
2. that said duty of care was breached; and
3. that the breach caused the injured party to suffer a loss that can be measured, be it a physical or a financial loss.

Because of the interest in the audited financial statements of companies from a broad range of stakeholders, shareholders and potential investors, it is not surprising that auditors can find themselves in court defending various different legal actions.

The costs associated with defending legal actions, or indeed settling such actions, can be very serious. A firm's reputation can be damaged beyond recovery (e.g. Arthur Andersen and Enron). For this reason, it is important to consider the key court rulings arising from various legal actions in this area taken over the years, and therefore the likely thought process of a ruling judge when considering the existence of auditor liability. A 'decision tree' outlines this at **Figure 1.4** below.

FIGURE 1.4: AUDITOR LIABILITY DECISION TREE

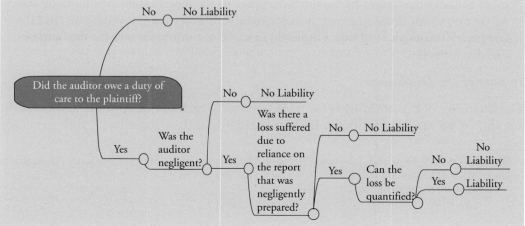

'Deep Pockets', 'No Transaction Claims', etc.

Auditors also need to be mindful of the '**deep pockets phenomenon**' whereby a plaintiff will target the auditors of an entity because losses have been incurred and the auditor firm is the only one deemed to have sufficient financial resources to pay damages.

Similarly, '**no transaction claims**' are common where the auditor is requested to play a small part in a large investment as a type of insurance in case the investment goes wrong. For example, a company wishing to take over another company may request an accounting firm (possibly the auditor of the client entity) to perform the due diligence. An intention of the company (client entity) in the case of a 'no transaction claim' is to use the accounting firm as a sort of insurance policy in case the takeover is not successful. In this instance, the company can bring a case against the accounting firm for negligence causing loss.

For all of the reasons outlined above, it is essential that auditors have (and in fact are required to have) **indemnity insurance** to cover possible liability to their clients and the general public.

A list of landmark cases relating to auditing is included at **Appendix 1.1** at the end of this chapter and expanded upon in **Appendix 1.2**, where they have not been covered in detail in the body of this chapter.

Audit Report Disclaimer

Following the ruling in *Royal Bank of Scotland v. Bannerman, Johnstone, Maclay* (2002) (see below), the ICAI has issued guidance to its members regarding the appropriate additional wording in their audit reports to protect against exposure to third-party claims. Known as the 'Bannerman paragraph' (after the Scottish audit firm that was successfully sued for negligence following the absence of such a paragraph from its audit report), it is suggested that the second paragraph of the audit report should read:

> "This report is made solely to the company's members, as a body, in accordance with Section 193 of the Companies Act 1990. Our audit work has been undertaken so that we might state to the company's members those matters we are required to state to them in an auditor's report and for no other purpose. To the fullest extent permitted by law, we do not accept or assume responsibility to anyone other than the company and the company's members as a body, for our audit work, for this report, or for the opinions we have formed."[12]

Impact of the Disclaimer

The inclusion of this wording is not to be seen to reduce the value of the audit. Audits are still to be carried out to the highest standards and in accordance with generally

---

[12] See also David Chitty and John McCarthy, *A Manual on Audit* (2nd ed. Chartered Accountants Ireland, 2012), Chapter 24.

accepted accounting principles. Its purpose is to inform third parties that, by relying on the financial statements, the auditor does not accept any responsibility to the third party.

CASE: *ROYAL BANK OF SCOTLAND V. BANNERMAN, JOHNSTONE, MACLAY* (2002)

Royal Bank of Scotland (RBS) provided overdraft facilities to APC Limited, which in turn was audited by Bannerman, Johnstone, Maclay. Included in the bank facility letter was the requirement for the company to provide audited accounts each year to the bank. It subsequently transpired that the auditors had failed to detect fraud that had occurred in the company. The bank claimed that they were therefore owed a duty of care by the auditors, as they knew that the bank would be relying on the audited accounts. The auditor, knowing this, should have disclaimed liability to RBS, but they did not do so. The ruling judge held that in absence of the disclaimer, the auditors owed the duty of care to the bank and found in favour of RBS.

1.9 CONCLUSION

The need for audit grew from the increased separation of ownership and stewardship of companies. The owners of organisations (the shareholders/principals) needed confidence that the directors (agents) were acting in their best interests and providing them with accurate financial and other information. The auditor has filled that need by issuing an independent opinion on the financial statements, which increases confidence in the information being produced by those charged with governance.

Increasing numbers of corporate failures have led to increased legislative and regulatory requirements for the auditor. Additionally, the growth of the capital markets, offering more opportunity for investing overseas, has required more uniformity, not just in accounting standards but also in auditing standards. Within the UK and Ireland, international bodies and standards are becoming increasingly recognised and are being adjusted to address key issues within these jurisdictions. While the legal environment has remained quite static, updating existing legislation where required, the regulatory environment is a dynamic landscape that continues to evolve to try to protect the audit profession from negative publicity, by:
- issuing strong standards on auditing;
- ensuring those eligible to audit are members of a RAB/RSB and that those bodies operate stringent entrance requirements, a strict code of ethics and continuing professional development for members in order to maintain a level of professionalism and competence among auditors.

SUMMARY OF LEARNING OBJECTIVES

Learning Objective 1 Understand what is meant by the term 'assurance engagements'.

Assurance engagements deliver statements that inspire confidence in a subject matter. The most common assurance engagement is that of the **external audit**. However, common to all assurance engagements, including financial statement audits, are a number of core elements:

- a subject matter;
- users of the subject matter;
- a set of criteria; and
- an examination leading to an opinion being expressed on the subject matter.

Learning Objective 2 Understand the objective of an external audit of financial statements.

ISA 200 defines the objective of an audit as a process that enhances the "degree of confidence of intended users in the financial statements. This is achieved by the expression of an opinion by the auditor on whether the financial statements are prepared, in all material respects, in accordance with an applicable financial reporting framework."

The auditor issues only a "**reasonable assurance**" as to the "**truth and fairness**" of the financial statements due to the **inherent limitations** of an audit, including the:

- need for **judgement**;
- inherent limitations of **accounting and internal controls**;
- inherent limitations in the **audit report itself**;
- fact that **not all items in the financial statements are tested**;
- **timing of the audit report**; and
- fact that **audit evidence indicates what is probable, not fact**.

Learning Objective 3 Be able to explain why and how the auditing profession has evolved

The need for external audit assurance has increased over the years due to the increase in capital markets and, in turn, the separation of ownership and control of organisations. The auditor offers the shareholder an **unbiased (independent) opinion** that the financial statements are free from **material misstatement.**

Learning Objective 4 Be able to demonstrate a detailed understanding of the legal and regulatory frameworks that govern external audits in both the Republic of Ireland and the UK/Northern Ireland

The Legislative Environment

The Companies Acts in both the Republic of Ireland (CA 1963–2012) and the UK (CA 2006) require companies to **appoint an auditor** and **have their annual**

accounts audited unless they meet all of the following criteria in RoI (two of the three in NI/UK):

	UK/NI	Ireland
Turnover	£6.5 million (or less)	€8.8 million (or less)
Balance Sheet Total	£3.26 million (or less)	€4.4 million (or less)
Average Number of Employees	50 (or less)	50 (or less)

The Companies Acts also require the inclusion of a **statement of directors' and auditors' responsibilities** to be included somewhere with the financial statements.

The Regulatory Environment

The regulatory environment is made up of the following:

- **IAASB** – which develops and promotes ISAs and other assurance standards and improves uniformity of auditing practices and related services throughout the world.
- **IAASA** – which aims to support and enhance public confidence in the accountancy profession by acting as an oversight body for audit regulation in Ireland. IAASA requires anyone wishing to act as an external auditor to be a member of a Recognised Accounting Body (RoI) or Recognised Supervisory Body (UK/NI).
- **FRC** – which holds overall responsibility for the regulation of auditing, accounting and the actuarial profession, and which is responsible for the development of auditing practice in the UK and Ireland. The FRC is responsible for setting auditing standards (ISAs (UK and Ireland)), which are adapted from the International Standards issued by the IAASB, amended to suit the legal, cultural and business environment in the UK and Ireland.
- **ISAs** – standards accepted as best practice by professional accountancy bodies; any auditor who does not apply these standards to an audit engagement leaves himself open to regulatory action.
- **RAB/RSB** – these bodies lay down rules that require adequate: education and experience; eligibility; and supervision and monitoring of their members (i.e. auditor practitioners).

Appointment, Removal and Resignation of Auditors

Auditors are appointed by shareholders at the AGM and may be removed only by shareholders at an EGM. The auditor, should he wish to resign, has a duty to report to the shareholders his reasons for doing so through a "**statement of circumstances**". He has the right to address the shareholders at an EGMs providing them with reasons for his resignation.

Learning Objective 5 Demonstrate an understanding of the setting and use of ISAs (UK and Ireland)

The ISAs (UK and Ireland) are accepted as best practice by professional accountancy bodies and any auditor who does not apply these standards to an audit engagement leaves himself open to regulatory action. Auditing standards include objectives for and requirements of the auditor, including application and other explanatory material. As noted above, the FRC has adopted and adapted the International Standards on Auditing (ISAs) for use in the UK/NI and the Republic of Ireland. The ISAs of the FRC are distinguishable in their title: ISA (UK and Ireland) XXX.

Learning Objective 6 Demonstrate an understanding of the case law that has shaped the legal liability of auditors.

Duties are laid down in company law and breach of these duties due to negligence toward a person for whom the auditor owed a duty of care, and who suffered loss as a result of that negligence, may be subject to liability.

QUESTIONS

Self-test Questions

1.1   What is an audit?

1.2   Why are audits required?

1.3   What is meant by the term 'reasonable assurance'?

1.4   Name and explain four limitations of an audit.

1.5   What is meant by 'agency theory'?

1.6   What conditions must be met for a company to be eligible for audit exemption in both the UK and Ireland?

1.7   Distinguish between the auditor's and directors' responsibilities.

1.8   What is the role of the IAASA?

1.9   What is the role of the FRC?

1.10 What is the role of the CARB?

1.11 What is the role of the IAASB?

1.12 Outline your understanding of the 'Three Es' of education, examination and work experience required by the auditor.

1.13 In what circumstances might an individual be ineligible to act as an auditor?

1.14 Who is responsible for appointing and removing the auditor?

1.15 What duties and rights does the auditor have when he chooses to resign (withdraw from the engagement)?

1.16 What is meant by the term 'duty of care' and to whom does the auditor owe a duty of care?

1.17 What is meant by the term 'negligence'?

1.18 What are the key questions a judge will try to answer when deciding on a legal claim against an auditor?

1.19 What is professional indemnity insurance?

Review Questions

(See Suggested Solutions to Review Questions in **Appendix D**.)

Question 1.1

You have recently joined an auditing firm to complete a training contract. You are telling a friend about your recent appointment as 'audit trainee'.

Your friend has never heard of the term auditor and asks you to explain what auditing is and the role of an auditor. Your friend likes the sound of this type of career. She has an accounting qualification and has been thinking of setting up her own business, she thinks she might set up an auditing firm. Outline to her the eligibility requirements to act as an auditor in the Republic of Ireland.

Having reconsidered her decision to open an audit practice, your friend decides she might instead join her family retail business, which has recently seen significant growth. It now employs 60 people nationwide, has revenue of €9.3 million and balance sheet worth approximately €3 million. She says they are not currently being audited and asks you if they should be.

Requirement

(a) Outline for your friend what is meant by auditing and what is the role of an auditor.

(b) Set out the requirements to be eligible to be a registered auditor in the RoI.

(c) Outline the audit exemption criteria applicable to a company in the RoI.

Question 1.2

The audit and assurance regulatory framework includes guidance on how an audit is conducted, who should be allowed to perform an audit, and who should develop auditing standards. It also includes rules and regulations around monitoring of audit firms.

Requirement

(a) Depict the regulatory framework in diagrammatic form and outline the role of three authorities/bodies therein.

(b) Who is responsible for the appointment and removal of auditors in the UK and the RoI?

(c) What guidance does the Office of the Director of Corporate Enforcement (ODCE) – RoI and the Department of Business Innovation and Skills – UK provide with regard to the resignation of auditors?

Question 1.3

"Because of the interest in the audited financial statements of an entity from a broad range of stakeholders, shareholders and potential investors, it is not surprising that the auditor may find himself in court defending various different legal actions."

Requirement Discuss the above comment with reference to the auditor's duty of care, referring to any relevant legal cases and explaining the decision-making process of a judge ruling on a legal claim against an auditor. Outline how stringent adherence to the International Standards on Auditing might help to avoid liability for the auditor.

Question 1.4

Certain legal cases have been noted as landmark cases with regard to shaping the legal liability of auditors. For each of the landmark cases below, outline the facts of the case, the outcomes and the impact on the audit profession:

- *Royal Bank of Scotland v. Bannerman, Johnstone, Maclay and Others* (2002);
- *Re Kingston Cotton Mill Co.* (1896);
- *Caparo Industries Plc v. Dickman and Others* (1990).

APPENDIX 1.1: SCHEDULE OF LANDMARK LEGAL CASES SHAPING AUDIT LEGAL LIABILITY

Year	Case Name and Key Findings
1896	***Re Kingston Cotton Mill Co.*** (UK) Auditor must use reasonable skill and care. Auditor is a "watchdog, not a bloodhound".
1931	***Ultramares Corporation v. Touche*** (USA) Accountant only has a liability to those in contractual relationship – not to third parties.
1932	***Donoghue v. Stevenson*** (UK) A duty of care is owed to a third party where it is reasonably foreseeable that one's acts or omissions could result in injury to that third party.
1951	***Candler v. Crane*** (UK) If no contractual relationship exists, auditors are not liable for losses suffered by a third party.
1963	***Hedley Byrne & Co v. Heller & Partners*** (UK) A duty of care is owed to third parties where the third party is known to the auditor, or ought to have been known to the auditor, as having the intent to rely on the audited financial statement for a particular reason. (E.g. if the client entity made the auditor aware that the bank were waiting on the signed financial statements in order to make a final decision on a large loan, then the auditor would know of the intent to rely on the financial statements for the purpose of the provision of a loan.)
1977	***Anns v. Merton London Borough Council*** (UK) Special relationship is replaced by the proximity principle and loss must have been reasonably foreseeable. The duty of care for financial loss is significantly extended.
1981	***Jeb Fastner Ltd v. Marks Bloom & Co.*** (UK) Duty of care extended to those who may use accounts for investment decisions.
1983	***Twomax Ltd v. Dickinson McFarlane & Robinson*** (UK) Duty of care extended to virtually anyone who can prove that they relied on negligently prepared financial statements to make an investment decision.
1990	***Caparo Industries plc v. Dickman and Others*** (UK) Auditors usually only owe a duty of care to the client entity and its shareholders. Duty of care owed to third parties only when there is: • forseeability of damage; • proximity of relationship; and • the fairness of imposing a duty of care.

1990	***James McNaughton Paper Group Ltd v. Hicks Anderson & Co.** (UK)* When deciding if a special relationship exists, one needs to consider six steps (see details of this case below).
1991	***Morgan Crucible Co. plc v. Hill Samuel Bank Ltd** (UK)* By making specific representations after a known bidder was identified, a relationship of proximity exists and a duty of care is owed to the bidder.
1994	***Galoo Limited v. Bright Grahame Murray** (UK)* A plaintiff can only claim for loss when breach is the cause of the loss, not where it provides an opportunity for the loss.
1996	***ADT Ltd v. BDO Binder Hamlyn** (UK)* A partner of Binder Hamlyn who made specific negligent representations during a takeover discussion was held to owe a duty of care to third party as he knew they would rely on the information.
2003	***Royal Bank of Scotland v. Bannerman, Johnstone, Maclay** (UK)* A duty of care, in the absence of a disclaimer, may be held to have been owed when information is passed on to a third party for a specific purpose and the third party will rely on the information.

APPENDIX 1.2: OTHER LANDMARK LEGAL CASES

Donoghue v. Stevenson (1932) – 'Duty of Care'

The facts of this case were as follows: a woman was drinking ginger beer. When she went to pour some more out of the bottle, she discovered the remains of a snail in the bottle. She brought an action against Stevenson, the producer of the drink, claiming damages for her injuries. Although there was no contract between the two, the manufacturer was found to have owed a duty of care to Donoghue and was ordered to pay damages. This case established the '**neighbour principle**', whereby a person will owe a duty of care not to injure those whom it can be reasonably foreseen would be affected by their acts or omissions. The importance of this case is that it is now shown that a duty of care may be owed to people who may not be in a contractual relationship with the company.

Candler v. Crane (1951)

In this case, a set of accounts had been negligently prepared for a client. A third-party plaintiff used these accounts for the purpose of making an investment. The investment failed and the third party sued the accountants. The court ruled, by majority, that as there was no contractual relationship between the parties, the action for negligence failed.

The dissenting judge, Lord Justice Denning stated:

"They owe a duty to their client and also, I think, to any third party to whom they themselves show the accounts, or to whom they know their employer is going to show the accounts so as to induce him to take some action on them. I do not think, however, the duty can be extended further so as to include strangers of whom they have heard nothing and to whom their employer without their knowledge may choose to show their accounts. Once the accountants have handed the accounts to their client, they are not, as a rule, responsible for what he does with them without their knowledge or consent."

Hedley Byrne & Co. v. Heller & Partners (1963)

In this case a certificate of creditworthiness was negligently given by a firm of merchant bankers to an advertising agency in relation to a client of Heller's. Heller had said that the company was good for normal business arrangements and for the proposed advertising contract about which they were being approached. The bank claimed that they owed no duty of care to the plaintiff in the absence of any contractual or fiduciary relationship with the advertising agency. The courts held that the duty of care was owed and applied the findings of Lord Justice Denning, the dissenting judgment in the *Candler v. Crane* case (see above).

Heller & Partners, however, did not have to pay any damages as they had a clause in the contract disclaiming any liability if their advice was relied upon.

Lord Denning stated:

"I can see no logical stopping place short of all those relationships where it is plain that the party seeking information or advice was trusting the other to exercise such a degree of care as the circumstances required, where it is reasonable for him to do that, and where the other gave the information or advice when he knew or ought to have known that the inquirer was relying on him. I say 'ought to have known' because in questions of negligence we now apply the objective standard of what the reasonable man would have done."

The decision by the House of Lords in *Hedley Byrne* indicated that actions for professional negligence may arise if financial loss is suffered by third parties through their reliance on the professional skill and judgement of persons with whom they were not in a contractual or fiduciary relationship.

The effect of the *Hedley Byrne* decision is that someone possessed of a special skill, quite irrespective of contract, may be considered to have undertaken to apply that skill for the assistance of another person and thereby to have accepted a duty of care to that person. A negligent though honest misrepresentation which causes financial loss to another may thus, in certain circumstances, give rise to an action for damages at the suit of a person with whom no contract exists.

Legal counsel in the case drew attention to the US case of *Ultramares Corporation v. Touche*, where the court decided that auditors were not liable for negligence to a plaintiff who lent money on the strength of accounts on which the auditor had reported, but which they did not know were required for the purpose of obtaining financial assistance or would be shown to the plaintiff. In so deciding, the court recognised that it would be quite wrong to expose the auditors to a potential liability "in an indeterminate amount for an indefinite time to an indeterminate class".

Conclusion The *Hedley Byrne* decision modified the liability of accountants for professional negligence in an important but limited respect. It did not introduce a new concept of negligence. Negligence must first be shown. Auditors may owe a duty of care to those not having a contractual or fiduciary relationship and may be negligent if, and only if, they know, or ought to have known, that a financial report, account or statement prepared by them has been prepared for a special purpose or transaction, will be shown to a particular person or class of persons and may be relied upon by that person or class of persons in that particular connection.

The *Hedley Byrne* decision underlines the importance of observing best practice, and legal counsel has further advised that, where an accountant specifically restricts the scope of his report or expresses appropriate reservations in a note attached to and referred to in the financial statements he has prepared or the report to which he has made thereon, this can constitute a disclaimer, which will be effective against any action for negligence brought against him by the third parties.

Anns v. Merton London Borough Council (1977)

In this case, a local authority did not adequately inspect a building (block of flats), which was later found to have inadequate foundation, causing the flats to suffer from structural defects. The court held that the local authority owed a duty of care to the residents. This introduced the principle of proximity and the concept of reasonably foreseeability (in that the council would have been expected to reasonably foresee that an inadequate inspection of the building could have led to later structural defects impacting on the residents).

This was recognised in the Irish case of *Siney v. Dublin Corporation* (1980), where the Supreme Court ruled that the local authority providing housing was under a duty of care to a tenant to ensure that the housing was fit for human habitation.

These cases, although not involving auditors, led to a wider definition of third-party liability than that given in the *Candler v. Crane* case (see above). The courts will consider the relationship between the person suffering the injury and the alleged wrongdoer, and whether there is any factor that can reduce or limit the duty of care owed.

Jeb Fastners v. Marks Blooms & Co. (1981)

In this case, the defendant was the auditor of a company which was aware it was in need of refinancing. The company's accounts contained assets that were significantly overvalued and the auditors failed to detect this misstatement. The court said that the auditor owed a duty of care to any person or any class or class of persons whom they do not know but should be able to reasonably foresee might use the audited financial statements of the company for their investment decision.

It was held that the auditor should have foreseen that the audited financial statements would have been used for a purpose of valuing the company in a takeover and that by doing so would suffer a financial loss.

No damages were awarded, however, as the main reason for the takeover was to obtain the services of two of the directors of the company being acquired. It was held that the plaintiff would not have acted any differently had they known that the assets were overvalued and therefore it was not shown that they had suffered economic losses due to the auditor's negligence.

James McNaughton Paper Group v. Hicks Anderson & Co. (1991)

James McNaughton was considering the takeover of a group of companies. Draft accounts were prepared by a firm of accountants, Hicks Anderson & Co., and they held meetings with the claimant where they made representations that the target company was breaking even. Following the takeover, this was found to be inaccurate and the target takeover group was, in fact, insolvent. James McNaughton Paper Group took an action against Hicks Anderson, claiming that they would not have proceeded with the takeover had they known the true financial position and they had relied on the representations in making their decision. The court decided that no duty of care was owed to the plaintiff because:
- the accounts were prepared for the target company and not for McNaughton;
- the accounts were in draft form;
- the accountants were not involved in negotiations;
- the accounts showed a loss, so it was clear that the company was in a poor state;
- it was expected McNaughton would consult with their own financial experts; and
- the representations made were general and did not change the figures in the accounts.

This case would seem to put more obstacles in front of third parties in attempting to take an action following on from the *Caparo* decision (see above).

Morgan Crucible v. Hill Samuel & Co. (1991)

Morgan Crucible made a takeover bid for First Castle Electronics Plc. The chairman of the target company recommended to the shareholders that the bid be rejected in a circularisation sent. More circulars, which were also issued by the merchant bank

Hill Samuel, referring to the audited financial statements and the unaudited interim statements, were sent. They also circularised a profit forecast showing an expected increase in profits of 38%. This forecast contained a letter from the company's auditors stating that the forecast had been prepared in accordance with the company's stated accounting policies and the forecast was made after due and careful inquiry.

Morgan Crucible had an increased offer accepted. They subsequently found that the company they had acquired was worthless and sued the merchant bank, the auditors and the directors as they felt it was foreseeable that they would rely on the circularisations that were issued and the profit forecast. They claimed that the accounting policies were flawed and statements negligently prepared, with the profit being overstated. They argued that all these factors had led them to their bid price.

The court, relying on the *Caparo* decision, initially dismissed the claim. Morgan Crucible appealed. The Court of Appeal found that, as they were an identified bidder, it was reasonable that they would rely on the representations. It was held that there was, in fact, a relationship of proximity between each of the defendants and the plaintiffs, thus giving rise to a duty of care. The case was sent forward for trial.

ADT Ltd v. Binder Hamlyn BDO (1996)

Binder Hamlyn issued an unqualified audit report on the financial statements of Britannia Securities Group, which ADT was considering taking over. A partner of Binder Hamlyn attended a meeting with ADT, where he confirmed that the financial statements showed a true and fair view of the target company's state of affairs. ADT, relying on this representation, completed the takeover, only to find that the company was worth £40 million and not the £105 million purchase price paid.

The judge held that Binder Hamlyn owed a duty of care to ADT based on the representations made at the meeting, as Binder Hamlyn knew the purpose for which the information was to be used. The judge awarded ADT £65 million, the difference between the price paid and subsequent value found to be correct. Binder Hamlyn stated that it intended to appeal and the case was subsequently settled out of court.

2

ETHICS AND CORPORATE GOVERNANCE

LEARNING OBJECTIVES

Having studied this chapter on ethics and corporate governance you should:

1. understand the contents and purpose of the FRC's 'Auditors' Code';
2. understand the importance of Ethical Standard 1 (ES 1) on integrity, objectivity and independence;
3. know the threats to integrity, objectivity and independence as outlined in ES 2 – ES 5;
4. be able to demonstrate your understanding of ES 1–ES 5 by being able to identify examples of threats and their respective safeguards;
5. know what is expected of the firm with regard to the internal system of quality control as laid down by ISQC 1; and
6. understand the relevance of *The UK Corporate Governance Code* and the *Irish Corporate Governance Annex* to the external auditor.

CHECKLIST OF RELEVANT STANDARDS

The relevant standards covered in this chapter are:
- Ethical Standard 1 (Revised) *Integrity, Objectivity and Independence* (ES 1);
- Ethical Standard 2 (Revised) *Financial, Business, Employment and Personal Relationships* (ES 2);
- Ethical Standard 3 (Revised) *Long Association with the Audit Engagement* (ES 3);
- Ethical Standard 4 (Revised) *Fees, Remuneration and Evaluation Policies, Litigation, Gifts and Hospitality* (ES 4);
- Ethical Standard 5 (Revised) *Non-Audit Services Provided to Audit Entities* (ES 5);
- International Standard on Quality Control (UK and Ireland) 1 *Quality Control for Firms that Perform Audits and Reviews of Financial Statements, and other Assurance and Related Services Engagements* (ISQC 1).

KEY TERMS AND DEFINITIONS FOR THIS CHAPTER

Independence   Independence from parties that have an interest in the results of the financial statements of an entity.

Integrity   Adherence to moral and ethical principles or soundness of moral character, essentially the ability to act with honesty.

Objectivity   "Objectivity is a state of mind that excludes bias, prejudice and compromise and that gives fair and impartial consideration to all matters that are relevant to the task in hand, disregarding those that are not" (ES 1, para 10).

Self-interest   Where a situation exists that may result in the auditor's decisions being influenced by his own self-interest in the matter. For example, if the auditor holds shares in an audit client, he may be reluctant to make a decision that will impact the opinion expressed in the auditor's report and therefore the value of his shares.

Self-review   This arises where, during an audit, the auditor is reviewing a non-audit service provided by the audit firm. For example, if the auditor was seconded to the audit client to assist with their payroll function. In the course of the audit the auditor may need to re-evaluate the work performed in the non-audit service.

2.1 INTRODUCTION

The Financial Reporting Council (FRC) is responsible for issuing pronouncements, which include the following:
- quality control standards;
- a framework of fundamental principles;
- ethical and engagement standards for audits of financial statements; and
- guidance for auditors of financial statements.

In this chapter we will be concerned with the first three of these audit and assurance pronouncements. In **Section 2.2** we examine the '**framework of fundamental principles**', which includes the '**Auditors' Code**', issued by the FRC in order to guide the conduct of auditors. In **Sections 2.3–2.7**, we then discuss the '**Ethical Standards**', starting in **Section 2.3** with Ethical Standard 1 (ES 1), introducing the concept of professional **ethics** and the **importance of integrity, objectivity and independence** to the auditor. Also in this section, we introduce the types of **threat** that can exist around objectivity and independence. **Sections 2.4–2.7** deal with specific circumstances that can give rise to the threats discussed in **Section 2.3**, as well as covering the remaining ethical standards, ES 2–ES 5 which provide guidance for auditors on circumstances to which they should be alert that could cause threats to their objectivity and independence. These standards also provide guidance on how to safeguard against such threats. As outlined in the Learning Objectives above, after completing these sections you will be expected to demonstrate your knowledge of the ethical standards by being able to identify situations and circumstances that create threats and also being able to make recommendations on how the auditor should safeguard against these threats.

Section 2.8 then briefly discusses the quality control standard, International Standard on Quality Control (UK and Ireland) 1 *Quality Control for Firms that Perform Audits and Reviews of Financial Statements, and other Assurance and Related Services Engagements* (ISQC 1). This quality control standard includes objectives for the auditor, along with requirements and related application and other explanatory material around the area of the **internal quality control system** of the **audit firm**. In studying this section you should understand the requirements on the audit firm with regard to implementing a sound system of quality control, as well as examples of policies and procedures which audit firms are expected to put in place.

Finally, in **Section 2.9** we introduce the topic of '**corporate governance**'. While corporate governance is apparently unrelated to the role of the external auditor, it has a number of impacts on the audit profession. At the close of this section you should have an appreciation of the similarities between the UK Corporate Governance Code and the Ethical Standards and the importance of the Code on the performance of individual audits and on the auditing profession in general.

2.2 FRAMEWORK OF FUNDAMENTAL PRINCIPLES

In Appendix 2 to its *Scope and Authority of Audit and Assurance Pronouncements*, the FRC sets out the 'The Auditors' Code' which it expects to guide the conduct of auditors. This is summarised in **Table 2.1** below, which outlines the manner in which the FRC expects an auditor to behave with reference to fundamental principles.

TABLE 2.1: THE AUDITORS' CODE

Fundamental Principle	Explanation of the behaviour expected of the auditor
Accountability	Auditors act in the interest of the primary stakeholders whilst having regard for the public interest.
Integrity	Auditors act with integrity (honesty, fairness, candour, courage and confidentiality).
Objectivity and Independence	Auditors are objective and provide impartial opinions unaffected by bias, prejudice, compromise and conflicts of interest. An auditor's independence should be both actual and perceived (i.e. he should not only strive to have independence in fact, he should strive to avoid any situations which would *call into question* his independence).
Competence	Auditors act with professional skill, derived from their qualification, training and practical experience.
Rigour	Auditors approach their work with thoroughness and with an attitude of professional scepticism.
Judgement	Auditors apply professional judgement, taking account of materiality in the context of the matter on which they are reporting.
Clear, complete and effective communication	Auditors' reports contain clear expressions of opinion and set out information necessary for a proper understanding of the opinion.
Association	Auditors allow their reports to be included in documents containing other information only if they consider that the additional information is not in conflict with the matters covered in their report and they have no cause to believe it is misleading.
Providing Value	Auditors add to the reliability and quality of financial reporting; they provide to directors and officers constructive observations arising from the audit process; and thereby contribute to the effective operation of the business capital markets and the public sector.

The FRC supports the Auditors' Code with the use of Ethical Standards, which take the form of requirements along with related guidance intended to promote fairness, trust and an overall system of moral values. There are five Ethical Standards:

- Ethical Standard 1 (Revised) Integrity, Objectivity and Independence (ES 1);
- Ethical Standard 2 (Revised) *Financial, Business, Employment and Personal Relationships* (ES 2);
- Ethical Standard 3 (Revised) *Long Association with the Audit Engagement* (ES 3);
- Ethical Standard 4 (Revised) *Fees, Remuneration and Evaluation Policies, Litigation, Gifts and Hospitality* (ES 4); and
- Ethical Standard 5 (Revised) *Non-Audit Services Provided to Audit Entities* (ES 5).

The nature of ethics is essentially a study of morality and moral choices, as well as ethical decision-making processes. Professional ethics for accountants encompasses standards of behaviour, professionalism, highest levels of performance and serving the public interest.

Each of the five ethical standards is discussed in turn below.

2.3 INTEGRITY, OBJECTIVITY AND INDEPENDENCE

Introduction

The primary objective of the audit of the financial statements of an entity is for the auditor to provide independent assurance to the shareholders/members that the directors have prepared the financial statements correctly. There are a number of ethical issues which are of great importance to the client entity–auditor relationship because of the need for the auditor to be seen to be impartial and independent of the client entity, which in turn creates greater confidence in the opinion the auditor provides.

Ethical Standard 1 (Revised) *Integrity, Objectivity and Independence* (ES 1), paragraph 6, states:

> "Auditors shall conduct the audit of the financial statements of an entity with integrity, objectivity and independence."

'**Integrity**' refers to the application of honesty and fairness when carrying out an audit. '**Objectivity**' refers to the absence of bias and prejudice and asks that auditors avoid any conflicts of interest that may call into question their objectivity.

'**Independence**' is the cornerstone of auditing. Independence is the freedom from situations and relationships which make it probable that a reasonable and informed third party would conclude that objectivity either is impaired or could be impaired. For example, if an **audit engagement partner's** wife were the CFO of the client entity, he may be reluctant to issue a negative opinion on the financial statements and risk damaging her career, or worse. Even if he was of a very high moral standing and acted with complete objectivity and integrity, the general public might be sceptical of whether a clean **audit opinion** was, in fact, the correct opinion. For reasons such as this, it is important that the auditor does not put himself in a position where his ability to act with honesty is questioned, as doing so reduces the credibility and trust associated with the **auditor's report**.

Establishing Policies and Procedures to Protect Integrity, Objectivity and Independence

ES 1, paragraph 16 states that the audit firm shall:

"… establish policies and procedures, appropriately documented and communicated, designed to ensure that, in relation to each audit engagement, the audit firm, and all those who are in a position to influence the conduct and outcome of the audit, act with integrity, objectivity and independence."

The standard also states (para 22) that the audit firm shall designate a partner in the firm (the 'Ethics Partner') as having responsibility for the **adequacy of the policies and procedures** relating to integrity, objectivity and independence, its **compliance with the Ethical Standards** and the **effectiveness of its communication** to partners and staff on these matters within the firm. This individual should also provide guidance to individual partners to ensure a consistent approach to the applicable ethical standard.

Such policies and procedures of the audit firm should review the existence of:
- interests in audited entities (by partner or staff member on the engagement);
- economic dependence on audited entities;
- the performance of non-audit services;
- audit partner rotation;
- family and other personal relationships involving an entity audited by the firm; and
- decisions with respect to joining an audited entity.

These and other examples are discussed in more detail below.

The Ethical Standards require the existence of any threats to the integrity, objectivity and independence of the auditor/audit firm to be documented, as well as action taken to remove the identified threat. **Table 2.2** outlines the categories of threats that can exist along with a description of each. Specific examples of matters giving rise to each type of threat are discussed throughout the rest of the chapter.

ES 1, paragraph 43, further states:

"If the audit engagement partner identifies threats to the auditor's objectivity, including any perceived loss of independence, he or she shall identify and assess the effectiveness of the available safeguards and apply such safeguards as are sufficient to eliminate the threats or reduce them to an acceptable level."

Should the **engagement partner** conclude that the threat cannot be reduced to an acceptable level, then he or she shall not accept or continue the audit engagement.

ES 2, ES 3, ES 4 and ES 5 present situations that may pose threats to integrity, objectivity or independence and outline the possible safeguards audit firms and auditors can implement to mitigate these threats.

TABLE 2.2: THREATS TO OBJECTIVITY AND INDEPENDENCE

Self-interest threat	This threat arises where an audit firm or an auditor in the firm has a financial or other interest in the client which might cause the auditor to be reluctant to take actions that would adversely impact on his own interests (e.g. ownership of shares in the client entity).
Self-review threat	This arises when the results of a non-audit service performed by the auditor, or by others within the audit firm, are reflected in the amounts included or disclosures in the financial statements. The auditor is going to be reluctant to highlight errors if he himself, or his audit firm, performed and got paid for the work.
Management threat	Management threats arise when partners or employees of the audit firm take decisions on behalf of the **management** of the audited entity. Management threats also arise where the results of non-audit services work carried out are used to make judgements and take decisions. In such instances, the auditor is not sufficiently objective when assessing the outcome of those decisions giving rise to the figures and disclosures in the financial statements.
Advocacy threat	This arises when the audit firm or auditor acts as an advocate on behalf of the audited entity (e.g. acting on behalf of the company, *say* as a legal advocate). To do so requires the auditor to adopt a position closely aligned to that of management, which creates an actual and perceived threat.
Familiarity threat	This threat arises when the audit firm or auditor accepts or insufficiently questions the audited entity's point of view due to the close relationship held, usually as a result of long association.
Intimidation threat	This arises when the auditor's conduct is influenced by fear or threats due to aggressive or dominating characters within the audited entity's management team.

2.4 FINANCIAL, BUSINESS, EMPLOYMENT AND PERSONAL RELATIONSHIPS

Ethical Standard 2 (Revised) *Financial, Business, Employment and Personal Relationships* (ES 2) provides requirements and guidance on specific circumstances arising out of financial, business, employment and personal relationships with the audited entity, which may cause threats to the audit firm's or the auditor's objectivity, or result in a perceived loss of independence. It also gives examples of safeguards that can, in some circumstances, eliminate the threat or reduce it to an acceptable level.

Examples of threats and their possible safeguards are included in **Table 2.3** below. For the purpose of this Table, 'influential individual' refers to any individual in a position to influence the conduct and outcome of the audit other than the engagement partner, and 'any connected person' refers to a close family member of the partner or the influential individual. This Table is intended to demonstrate specific instances or matters that may give rise to a threat to auditor independence and, in turn, identify possible safeguards that an audit firm can adopt to avoid actual or perceived independence issues.

TABLE 2.3: FINANCIAL, BUSINESS, EMPLOYMENT AND PERSONAL
RELATIONSHIPS – THREATS AND POSSIBLE SAFEGUARDS

Examples of Specific Threats	Type of Threat	Possible Safeguards

The holding by the auditor of a direct or indirect financial interest in the client entity	Self-interest	• First, it is important to note that the ethics partner should be made aware of any direct or indirect financial interests of partners, staff and of connected persons.
		• The influential individual and his connected persons should:
		  ◆ not be permitted to work on the audit engagement or non-audit services and where possible in any department servicing the client; or
		  ◆ they dispose of the interest; or
		  ◆ there is a policy permitting a minimum shareholding which is not material to either the entity or the individual.
		• If the partner (or person connected to him) holds such a direct or indirect interest he should either dispose of the interest or the firm should decline (or withdraw from) the engagement where disposal of the shares is not an option.

Acceptance or provision of loans or guarantees **or** Existence of a business relationship	Self-interest, Intimidation	• The audit firm, its partners, influential individuals and connected persons to the audit of a client entity are not to be permitted to accept or provide loans or guarantees to clients other than in the normal course of business under normal business terms (arm's-length transactions). • If influential individuals or their connected persons engage in such activities, they should not be permitted to work on the audit engagement or non-audit services and, where possible, in any department servicing the client entity; alternatively, they should cease the activity.

		• If the firm or the partner (or connected person) has engaged in such activities and cannot withdraw from the activity, then the firm should decline (or withdraw from) the engagement.
Secondment of staff of audit firm to client entity	Self-review	• These should be avoided where partners are concerned; for individuals working in the audit firm these should be for a short period only and should not be to perform non-audit services that would not be permitted under ES 5. • Individuals seconded should have no future involvement in the audit.
Individuals from the audit firm taking direct employment with client entity	Familiarity	• The audit firm should take swift action to ensure that no further work is performed by the individual on that audit client and that no significant connections remain between the firm and the individual after his departure.
Family members employed by a client entity	Self-interest, Familiarity	• Individual with connected party shall not be permitted to work on or have any influence on the respective audit. • If connected party is that of a partner, decline or withdraw from the engagement.

2.5 LONG ASSOCIATION WITH THE AUDIT ENGAGEMENT

Naturally, long association between the auditor/audit firm and the client entity can develop into a close relationship between the staff of the respective organisations. When one becomes overly familiar with an individual, it can create a sense of obligation towards that individual, which may be in conflict with one's duty to report on their responsibilities with respect to the financial statements.

Ethical Standard 3 (Revised) *Long Association with the Audit Engagement* (ES 3), paragraph 5, states:

> "The audit firm shall establish policies and procedures to monitor the length of time that audit engagement partners, key partners involved in the audit and partners and staff in senior positions, including those from other disciplines, serve as members of the engagement team for each audit."

Table 2.4 below demonstrates the types of threat that long association with a client entity can give rise to and, in turn, identifies the possible safeguards that an audit firm can adopt to avoid actual or perceived independence issues.

TABLE 2.4: LONG ASSOCIATION WITH THE AUDIT
ENGAGEMENT – THREATS AND POSSIBLE SAFEGUARDS

Examples of Specific Threats	Type of Threat	Possible Safeguards
Long association with the audit engagement	Self-interest, Self-review, Familiarity	• Rotation of partners and senior members of the engagement team after a pre-determined number of years. (Note: with respect to listed entities, there is a more prescriptive ruling that requires, e.g. the audit engagement partner to rotate every five years.) • Introduction of a review partner with no prior involvement. • Applying an independent quality reviewer to the engagement in question.

2.6 FEES, REMUNERATION AND EVALUATION POLICIES, LITIGATION, AND GIFTS AND HOSPITALITY

This Standard (ES 4) addresses some critical issues that have led to concerns and significant frauds over the years. For example, the issue of high proportional fees is said to be a main factor in the failure of Arthur Andersen to report Enron's accounting irregularities. Naturally, a business will strive to maintain its most significant customers. When it comes to audit firms, however, clients who represent a significant percentage of the overall fees of a firm can cause it to behave in a manner that protects the relationship at the cost of the firm's integrity. Put simply, the auditor does not want to jeopardise losing a large-fee client and for this reason may be reluctant to issue a qualified audit opinion.

ES 4 also deals with the issues of remuneration and evaluation policies connected to audit staff; litigation between the audit firm and the client entity; and the receipt of gifts or hospitality from the client entity to the audit engagement team or partners. Each of these topics is dealt with in detail below.

Fees

With respect to fees, Ethical Standard 4 (Revised) *Fees, Remuneration and Evaluation Policies, Litigation, and Gifts and Hospitality* (ES 4) states that:
• the audit engagement should be assigned to sufficient partners and staff with appropriate time and skills to perform the audit in accordance with all applicable auditing and ethical standards, irrespective of the audit fee to be charged;

- audit fees shall not be influenced or determined by the provision of non-audit services;
- an audit shall not be undertaken on a contingent fee basis (fee calculated based on a pre-determined basis relating to the outcome of the audit);
- where outstanding fees from the audit client to the auditor are regarded as more than trivial, then the engagement partner and ethics partner should consider whether the audit firm can continue as auditor (overdue fees, if substantial, may influence decisions);
- where combined audit and non-audit fees of a listed entity exceed 10% of the annual fee income (or, for a non-listed entity, exceed 15% of the annual fee income) of the firm, the auditor shall not act as auditor, resign as auditor or not stand for reappointment, as appropriate, or alternatively relinquish non-audit services. The size of the fee relative to the total fees of the firm may influence the decision-making of the auditor if he feels that his decision will jeopardise the future of the engagement (i.e. the firm will lose a large client that is influential to its profitability).

The auditor should be able to act with objectivity, and freely question and disagree with management where necessary, regardless of the consequences to his own position. Not abiding by the above with reference to fees may call into question the auditor's objectivity.

Remuneration and Evaluation Policies

ES 4 requires an audit firm to ensure that the remuneration packages and performance reviews of audit team members are not based on the selling of non-audit services to the entity that they are auditing. If the **audit engagement team** is focused on winning non-audit services with audit clients in order to boost their remuneration, they may place the importance of this above their responsibility to adequately and fairly audit the financial statements (i.e. there is a risk that when trying to win new business, the auditor may not want to upset the client and so might let a few errors slide to maintain a good relationship).

Threatened and Actual Litigation

Litigation instances can arise where the client entity sues the audit firm for damages. For example, while testing the client's computer system the auditor could cause the client's system to crash and cost the client entity thousands in down-time. The client entity may, in turn, commence a law suit against the audit firm. With respect to threatened and actual litigation against the auditor by the client entity, the guidance from ES 4 is straightforward: where actual or threatened litigation arises with an audit client, which is anything other than insignificant, then the audit firm shall either not continue with or not accept the audit engagement.

Gifts and Hospitality

ES 4 further provides that the audit firm, its partners and 'influential individuals' (including their connected persons – see **Section 2.4**) are not permitted to accept gifts or hospitality from an audit client, unless the gift is insignificant. Cash of *all* values is deemed significant. The auditor should use his judgement in assessing gifts and hospitality offered by the client and when in any doubt he should consult with the **ethics partner**.

Table 2.5 below is intended to demonstrate specific instances or matters, under ES 4, which may give rise to a threat to auditor independence and, in turn, to identify possible safeguards that an audit firm can adopt to avoid actual or perceived independence issues.

TABLE 2.5: GIFTS AND HOSPITALITY – THREATS AND POSSIBLE SAFEGUARDS

Examples of Specific Threats	Type of Threat	Possible Safeguards
Excessive fees	Self-interest, Intimidation	• Reduce or decline non-audit services to audit clients. • Withdraw from or decline the engagement where non-audit services cannot be reduced. • Withdraw/decline audits which will represent >15% (10% PLCs) of overall fee income. • Introduce early warning policy and procedure whereby fees approaching >5% <10% for listed companies and >10% <15% for non-listed companies are flagged for monitoring by the ethics partner.
Threatened/actual Litigation by the client	Self-interest, Advocacy, Intimidation	Decline or withdraw from the engagement.
Gifts and hospitality	Self-interest, Familiarity	Determine policies and procedures outlining what is reasonable in terms of frequency, nature and value of hospitality and gifts.
Remuneration and evaluation of audit personnel	Self-interest	A policy should exist prohibiting any element of remuneration or performance reviews to be connected to the winning of non-audit services of audit clients.

2.7 NON-AUDIT SERVICES PROVIDED TO AUDIT ENTITIES

The provision of non-audit services to an audit client gives rise to a multiple of threats and so for many it is the most significant of the ethical standards. Non-audit services include the provision of services such as tax consultancy, IT consultancy, performance of due diligence for proposed acquisitions, performance of payroll on behalf of the audit client or assistance with investment appraisals.

Ethical Standard 5 (Revised) *Non-Audit Services Provided to Audit Entities* (ES 5) describes non-audit services as comprising any engagement in which an audit firm provides professional services (such as those noted above) to an audited entity, an audited entity's affiliates or another entity in respect of the audited entity.

Table 2.6 below outlines the types of threats that the provision of non-audit services can give rise to and, in turn, identifies possible safeguards that an audit firm can adopt to avoid actual or perceived independence issues.

TABLE 2.6 NON-AUDIT SERVICES – THREATS AND POSSIBLE SAFEGUARDS

Examples of Specific Threats	Type of Threat	Possible Safeguards

Provision of non-audit services	Self-interest, Self-review, Management, Advocacy, Intimidation	• Introduce policies and procedures that require intended non-audit services to be communicated to the audit engagement partner for his or her consideration.
		• If considered to be inconsistent with the objectives of the audit of the financial statements, the audit firm should:
		  ♦ not undertake the non-audit service; or
		  ♦ not accept/withdraw from the audit engagement.

Before accepting an engagement for the provision of non-audit services, the **audit engagement partner** should be notified. He or she should consider the relevance and impact of the subject matter on the financial statements of the entity, how much professional judgement will be required in the service, the size of the engagement and its associated fee, the basis on which fees are to be calculated and, finally, the staff who would work on or be involved in the non-audit service.

As one can see from the above Table, the provision of non-audit services to an audit client gives rise to a larger number of threats than any other matter discussed. A pertinent example is Arthur Andersen whose non-audit services to Enron represented 52% of its fee income from the client.

AN OVERVIEW OF THE ENRON SCANDAL[1]

The Enron Scandal, which occurred at the turn of the century, led to the bankruptcy of the Enron corporation. Arthur Andersen, having audited Enron's accounts for 16 years, was initially found guilty of obstruction of justice connected to the reported shredding of documents relating to Enron. The United States District Court later overturned this ruling, but Arthur Andersen had already closed its doors due to the mass of audit engagements brought to an end by their other clients.

---

[1] To follow the events that led to the collapse of Enron, see the documentary films *Enron: The Smartest Guys in the Room* – a documentary based on a book about the scandal – and *The Crooked E: The Unshredded Truth about Enron* – a film about the rise and fall of Enron.

Their downfall was caused by a series of issues concerning revenue recognition, market-to-market accounting and the use of special-purpose entities to manage risks associated with poorly performing assets. Fuelling the above was a series of corporate governance failures relating to excessive executive remuneration (which ultimately drove a dysfunctional corporate culture), and a lack of financial risk-management (hedging of risk through special-purpose entities owned by Enron itself). Arthur Andersen is alleged to have engaged in the reckless application of auditing standards, which was driven by their conflicts of interest. This cannot be fully determined due to the shredding of thousands of documents that related to its audit of Enron. The Houston firm of Arthur Andersen responsible for the Enron engagement obtained fees representing approximately 27% of its public fee income. It is believed that Andersen's audit was either:

(a) influenced by the size of annual fee; or
(b) was carried out incompetently. The audit committee of Enron claimed its members did not have the technical knowledge to question any of what was presented by the auditors.

While now over a decade old, the Enron collapse continues to be a good example with which to illustrate the importance of safeguarding against threats to auditor independence. The magnitude of the effects felt by the collapse lead to the introduction of the Sarbanes–Oxley Act of 2002 (SOX), the main provisions of which include:

- the restriction of public accounting companies providing non-audit services to audit clients;
- the introduction of the Public Company Accounting Oversight Board;
- the requirement that directors sign-off on the annual reports and, in particular, on their confidence with respect to internal controls;
- the increased disclosure of company relationships with unconsolidated entities;
- the requirement for the audit committee of the entity to be independent; and
- the renunciation of certain director emoluments.

SOX is a US federal law and as such relates only to those companies (and their subsidiaries) listed on the New York Stock Exchange (NYSE). While the Act is not enforced in either the UK or Ireland, local auditors are often exposed to companies who are required to comply with the Act due to their connection with a company listed on the NYSE.

2.8 INTERNATIONAL STANDARD ON QUALITY CONTROL (ISQC 1)

We have established above the need for auditors and audit firms to act within the ethical standards laid down by the FRC. However, in order for any auditor/audit firm to protect him/itself from instances of actual or perceived threats to independence, he/it will need to implement a system of internal control within the audit firm itself. Without detailed policies, procedures and guidance around ethical issues, staff may knowingly or inadvertently engage in activities that could be damaging to the audit firm. When we refer to **quality control**, we must consider it at two levels: at a 'macro' level that considers the ethical quality control of the organisation as a whole; and at an 'engagement' level, which considers the ethical quality control of a specific engagement being carried out.

The FRC's International Standard on Quality Control (UK and Ireland) *Quality Control for Firms that Perform Audits and Reviews of Financial Statements, and other Assurance and Related Services Engagements* (ISQC 1) outlines an audit firm's responsibility with respect to a '**System of Quality Control**' for audits of financial statements and reviews the performance of that audit. ISQC 1 should be read in conjunction with the Ethical Standards.

ISQC 1, paragraph 3, describes the audit firm's system of control as consisting of "policies and procedures designed to achieve the objective set out in paragraph 11 and the procedures necessary to implement and monitor compliance with those policies". Paragraph 11 of ISQC 1 states that "the objective of the firm is to establish and maintain a system of quality control to provide it with reasonable assurance that:
(a) The firm and its personnel comply with professional standards and applicable legal and regulatory requirements; and
(b) Reports issued by the firm or engagement partners are appropriate in the circumstances."

The standard prescribes guidelines on what elements should be included in an audit firm's internal quality control environment by outlining the areas where a set of policies and procedures should exist to support the ethical behaviour of the auditor. ISQC 1 requires the following policies and procedures to exist.
1. **Leadership responsibilities for quality** within the audit firm should be assigned and should clearly set out the responsibilities to promote an internal culture that recognises the importance of quality.
2. Relevant **ethical requirements policies and procedures**, which allow the firm to monitor its compliance with ethical requirements.
3. **Policies and procedures for acceptance and continuance** of client relationships.
4. **Human resources policies and procedures** that help to ensure sufficient, competent and capable personnel are available to carry out audits.
5. **Engagement performance policies and procedures** promoting consistency, supervision and review of responsibilities with respect to the performance of each engagement carried out by the firm.
6. **Monitoring of quality control** procedures and evaluation, communication and remedy of deficiencies.

The above demonstrates the expectations of the FRC with regard to the manner in which an auditor/audit firm should ensure his/its compliance with the Ethical Standards. It is not sufficient for an audit firm to rely on the ethics of its individual staff members; instead it should introduce a system that prevents, detects and safeguards against threats to independence.

The issue of professional ethics is an increasingly important topic for discussion, both globally and locally, following the myriad corporate scandals that have occurred over the last decade. Considering the importance of independence not only to the individual firm but also to the auditing profession as a whole, it is essential that the auditor repairs the negative perception held by the public by ensuring strict adherence to the Ethical and Quality Control Standards laid down by the FRC.

The importance of business and professional ethics is not just one associated with the auditing profession but one that has received dedicated attention following a wave of corporate governance failings in the UK in the early 1990s. Corporate governance encourages directors to carry out business with integrity and fairness and so is essentially an ethical guide for company directors. In **Section 2.9**, we will discuss the concept of corporate governance and how it relates to the external auditor.

2.9 CORPORATE GOVERNANCE

What is Corporate Governance?

"'**Corporate governance**' is the system by which companies are directed and controlled" (*Cadbury Report* 1992). The 2012 *UK Corporate Governance Code* (formerly the *Combined Code*) sets out standards of good practice, or 'principles', in relation to board leadership and effectiveness, remuneration, accountability and relations with shareholders (see **Figure 2.1** below).

Each principle contains provisions intended to support a strong corporate governance environment, and these provisions are summarised in **Table 2.7** below.

FIGURE 2.1: THE PRINCIPLES OF THE *UK Corporate Governance Code*

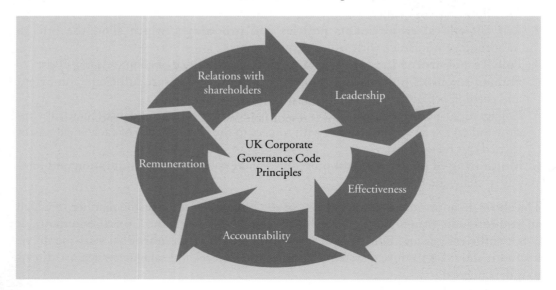

TABLE 2.7: PROVISIONS OF THE *UK Corporate Governance Code*

PRINCIPLE	Examples of provisions contained within each principle:
Leadership	• Every listed company should be headed by an **"Effective board"**. • There should be a **clear division of responsibilities**: "running of board" and "running of company". • The **Chairman runs the board**. • The board should **meet sufficiently regularly** to discharge its duties effectively. • **The board should** be comprised of both **executive and non-executive directors**. • A nomination, a remuneration and an audit committee should exist. • The board is collectively responsible for the long-term success of the company. • The roles of Chairman and Chief Executive Officer (CEO) must be held by separate individuals. • Appointments to the board should be by nomination. • Professional development of the board members should be considered. • The board members should be subject to performance evaluation. • A process of re-election of board members should be in place.
Effectiveness	• The directors should possess the right balance of skills, expertise, independence and knowledge to discharge their duties. • The board should have the right combination of executive and non-executive directors (NEDs). • NEDs should be independent. • Rigorous procedures around board appointment should exist.

Accountability and Audit	• The board should present:
	  ◆ a balanced and understandable assessment of company's financial position and prospects;
	  ◆ both financial and business reporting.
	• The board is responsible for risk-management and internal control.
	• The audit committee holds responsibility for internal audit.
	• The board should be mindful of its responsibilities with respect to external auditors.

Relations with shareholders	• The board should ensure dialogue with shareholders to ensure mutual understanding of objectives. • The board should make constructive use of the AGM.

Irish Stock Exchange Listing Rules – Appendix 4: The Irish Corporate Governance Annex

The Irish Stock Exchange (ISE) recognises that the *UK Corporate Governance Code* (formerly the *Combined Code*) has set the standard for corporate governance internationally. It is regarded as being the pre-eminent corporate governance code and is widely emulated. Since the Irish Stock Exchange Act 1995, the Listing Rules of the Irish Stock Exchange have required every company listed on the Main Securities Market to state in its annual report how the principles of the *UK Corporate Governance Code* have been applied, and to give details of whether the company has complied with all relevant provisions. Where a company has not complied with all relevant provisions of the *UK Corporate Governance Code*, it is required to set out the nature, extent and reasons for non-compliance.

Figure 2.2 below summarises the evolution of corporate governance in the UK and Ireland.

Corporate Governance and the External Auditor

Set out below are some provisions included in the *UK Corporate Governance Code* of 2010, as well as changes made in the 2012 revision that are of relevance and interest to external auditors:

- Provision C1.1: "The directors should explain in the annual report their responsibility for preparing the annual report and accounts, **and state that they consider the report and accounts, taken as a whole, is fair, balanced and understandable and provide the information necessary for shareholders to assess the company's performance, business model and strategy**. There should be a statement (in the financial report) by the auditor about their reporting responsibilities."
- Provision C3.4: "**Where requested by the board, the audit committee should provide advice on whether the annual report and accounts, taken as a whole, is fair, balanced and understandable and provides the information necessary for shareholders to assess the company's performance, business model and strategy.**"

With respect to C1.1 and C3.4, the text in bold was added in 2012 and reiterates the responsibilities of those charged with governance.

- Provision C.3.7: "The audit committee should have primary responsibility for making a recommendation on the appointment, re-appointment and removal of the external auditors. **Companies should put the external audit contract out to tender at least every ten years.** If the board does not accept the audit committee's recommendation, it should include in the annual report, and in any papers recommending appointment or re-appointment, a statement from the audit committee explaining the recommendation and should set out reasons why the board has taken a different position."

Again, the text in bold highlights a change made in 2012, which supports the ethos of the safeguards included in the Ethical Standards.

FIGURE 2.2: THE EVOLUTION OF CORPORATE GOVERNANCE IN THE UK AND IRELAND

Failures in corporate governance in the UK in the early 1990s, such as Maxwell Communications and the Bank of Credit & Commerce International (BCCI), lead to the Financial Reporting Council (FRC), the London Stock Exchange and the accounting profession setting up a committee to investigate the growth in numbers of such failures. This committee, headed by Sir Adrian Cadbury, leads to the introduction of the *Cadbury Report* in 1992.

A number of subsequent reports are issued relating to corporate governance, including the *Greenbury Report* and the *Hampel Report,* which are combined in 1998 with the *Cadbury Report* to produce the *Combined Code.*

In the wake of the Enron Scandal in the US and the collapse of Arthur Andersen, the *Smith Report* on the independence of external auditors is issued to the UK Government in 2003. Additionally, Derek Higgs carries out a review of the role and effectiveness of non-executive directors fuelled again by unrest caused after the Enron, WorldCom and Tyco collapses in the US. In 2002 the US introduces new legislation under the Sarbanes–Oxley Act, which is designed to protect investors by improving accuracy and reliability of corporate disclosures. Instead of introducing new legislation, the UK opts to review the internal control provisions within the *Combined Code.*

Essentially a consolidation and refinement of all reports and codes issued to date relating to good corporate governance, *The UK Corporate Governance Code* is published in 2010. The Code requires listed companies to disclose how they have complied with the code and also to explain where they have not complied with it (known as the 'comply or explain' approach). The crisis in the banking sector in Ireland, causing some banks to be nationalised, leads the Central Bank of Ireland to issue a new corporate governance code dedicated to the reform of the financial services sector – *The Corporate Governance Code for Credit Institutions and Insurance Undertakings.* The *UK Corporate Governance Code* is still in use with respect to non-financial listed companies.

UK Corporate Governance Code 2010 is updated.

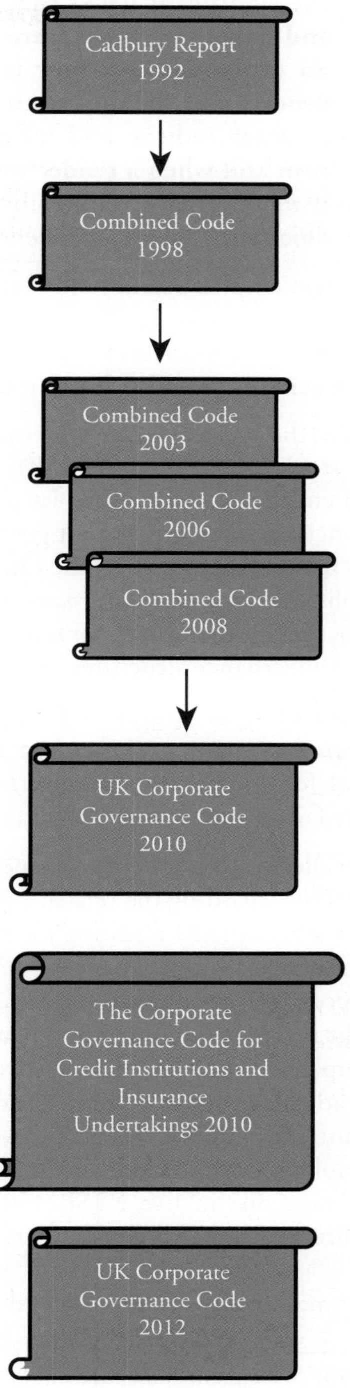

- Provision C.3.8: "A separate section of the annual report should describe the work of the audit committee in discharging its responsibilities. The report should include:
  - **the significant issues that it considered in relation to the financial statements, and how these issues were addressed;**
  - **an explanation of how it has assessed the effectiveness of the external audit process and the approach taken to the appointment or re-appointment of the external auditor, and information on the length of tenure of the current audit firm and when a tender was last conducted; and**
  - if the external auditor provides non-audit services, an explanation of how auditor objectivity and independence is safeguarded."

The text emphasised in bold here was added in 2012 and reiterates the importance of the attention given to significant items that will support the audit engagement. Additionally, this provision emulates ES 3 with respect to long association and ES 5 with respect to non-audit services provided to audit clients.

While the *UK Corporate Governance Code* only relates directly to those entities listed on the stock exchange (LSE, ISE), some larger private companies, i.e. non-listed entities, also endeavour to embrace its principles and provisions, particularly in the wake of the financial crisis and now that good corporate governance is more important than ever. For this reason, in early 2010 the European Confederation of Directors' Associations (EcoDa) published *Corporate Governance Guidance and Principles for Unlisted Companies in Europe*, a document intended to serve as a practical tool for unlisted companies seeking to improve their governance structures and policies.

Additionally, in Ireland the Central Bank of Ireland issued a *Corporate Governance Code for Credit Institutions and Insurance Undertakings* in 2010, recognising the increased require-ment for good corporate governance in financial institutions considering the impact of their failure on the wider economy.

The alleged corporate governance failures with respect to the banking sector have raised concerns regarding the related external auditors, who are now facing the risk of being sued for losses allegedly resulting from their failure to uncover the transactions involved in the governance failings. For this reason, the auditing world will welcome further reform of corporate governance in the UK and Ireland, which can only serve to reduce the level of audit risk to which the external auditing firms are exposed. For now, however, governance compliance continues to improve, albeit at a slow rate, and there is much debate around the adequacy of the 'comply or explain' method of regulation (see below). Highlights from Grant Thornton's *Corporate Governance Review 2012*, demonstrating the current levels of compliance to the Code, include[2]:

- almost one in five FTSE 350 companies had insufficient numbers of non-executive directors throughout the year;
- 49% of companies have not achieved full compliance and of those not achieving full compliance, only 44% intend to do so within the next year;

---

[2] http://www.grant-thornton.co.uk/corporategovernancereview

- while an increasing number of non-financial companies have a risk committee (up 7% on 2011), it still lies at just 40%;
- the average tenure of the external auditor is 33 years and 75% of companies gave little or no information with regard to future intentions on the matter.

Regulation Through 'Comply or Explain'

With respect to its 'comply or explain' approach, the *UK Corporate Governance Code* states: "The 'comply or explain' approach is the trademark of corporate governance in the UK. It has been in operation since the Code's beginnings and is the foundation of the Code's flexibility. It is strongly supported by both companies and shareholders and has been widely admired and imitated internationally."

'Comply or explain' is essentially a self-regulating approach with respect to corporate governance. Directors are required to state their compliance with corporate governance provisions and, where they have not complied, state the reasons for non-compliance. The self-regulating element comes into play by the shareholders choosing not to invest or divesting where they are not satisfied with the corporate governance compliance as outlined by the directors in the annual financial statements.

2.10 CONCLUSION

An auditor relies on his independence, therefore protecting it is central to his success. The Ethical Standards exist not only to protect the stakeholders but also to protect the auditor by giving him the tools to ensure that at all times he maintains a high standard of integrity, objectivity and independence. The Ethical Standards provide practical examples of threats to independence or perceived independence and give examples of how these can be safeguarded. Finally, the Standards outline the policies and procedures which should be in place in all auditing firms to control the quality of work and compliance with ethical requirements.

With respect to corporate governance, the auditor has both a **direct and indirect** link to its provisions. **Directly**, the provisions make reference to the appointment of external auditors and the conduct expected of directors and the audit committee when engaging with external auditors.

Corporate governance is described as:
"a system of law and sound approaches by which corporations are directed and controlled, focusing on the internal and external corporate structures with the intention of monitoring the actions of management and directors and thereby mitigating agency risks stemming from the devious deeds of these corporate officers."[3]

This being so, **indirectly** the auditor will expose himself to fewer risks in an organisation that has strong corporate governance.

---

[3] Anazett Sifuna (2012), "Disclose or Abstain: The Prohibition of Insider Trading on Trial", *Journal of International Banking Law and Regulation*.

SUMMARY OF LEARNING OBJECTIVES

Having studied this chapter on ethics and corporate governance you should:

Learning Objective 1 Understand the contents and purpose of the FRC's 'Auditor's Code'.

The FRC's 'Auditor's Code' outlines the manner in which the FRC expects an auditor to behave by reference to fundamental principle, including: accountability, integrity, objectivity and independence, competence, rigour, judgement, clear complete and effective communication, association and providing value.

Learning Objective 2 Understand the importance of the Ethical Standards on integrity, objectivity and independence (ES 1).

ES 1 requires an auditor to carry out the audit of financial statements with integrity, objectivity and independence and identifies a number of threats to integrity, objectivity and independence as follows: self-interest threat; self-review threat; management threat; advocacy threat; familiarity threat; intimidation threat. Independence is considered the cornerstone of auditing as it provides the freedom from situations and relationships which make it probable that a reasonable and informed third party would conclude that objectivity is either actually impaired or perceived to be impaired. It is the independence of the auditor that supports the credibility of the audit opinion issued by the auditor.

Learning Objective 3 Know the threats to integrity, objectivity and independence as outlined in ES 2–ES 5.

Specific circumstances around the areas of: *Financial, Business, Employment and Personal Relationships* (ES 2); *Long Association with the Audit Engagement* (ES 3); *Fees, Remuneration and Evaluation Policies, Litigation, and Gifts and Hospitality* (ES 4); and *Non-Audit Services Provided to Audit Entities* (ES 5) give rise to the threats noted in ES 1 above.

Learning Objective 4 Be able to demonstrate your understanding of ES 1–ES 5 by being able to identify examples of threats and their respective safeguards.

The audit firm should appoint an ethics partner to deal with the specific threats outlined in ES 2–ES 5 by implementing safeguards that protect against their impact on the independence and objectivity of the auditor. The most significant of these circumstances is that around the provision of Non-audit Services, due to the number of threats that it gives rise to, and as such the firm should have strong policies and procedures to manage the provision of non-audit services.

Learning Objective 5 Know what is expected of the firm with regard to the internal system of quality control as laid down by ISQC 1.

ISQC 1, paragraph 3 describes the audit firm's system of control as consisting of "policies and procedures designed to achieve the objective set out in paragraph 11 and the procedures necessary to implement and monitor compliance with those policies." Paragraph 11 of ISQC 1 states that "the objective of the firm is to establish and maintain a system of quality control to provide it with reasonable assurance that:

(a) The firm and its personnel comply with professional standards and applicable legal and regulatory requirements; and

(b) Reports issued by the firm or engagement partners are appropriate in the circumstances."

Learning Objective 6 Understand the relevance of *The UK Corporate Governance Code* and the *Irish Corporate Governance Annex* to the external auditor.

Corporate governance has evolved over the years and exists in Ireland and the UK in the form of the *UK Corporate Governance Code* which attempts to define standards with respect to: board leadership; effectiveness; remuneration; accountability; and relations with shareholders.

This Code impacts the auditor directly, in that its provisions make specific reference to the auditor's appointment, and also indirectly by way of reducing risk in organisations and hence reducing 'audit risk' for the auditor.

QUESTIONS

Self-test Questions

2.1   What is the purpose of the 'Auditor's Code'?

2.2   What is the primary objective of an audit of financial statements?

2.3   What is meant by the terms 'integrity', 'objectivity' and 'independence' with respect to Ethical Standard 1 (ES 1)?

2.4   Name and explain five threats to integrity, objectivity and independence.

2.5   What type of threat would exist if a director held shares in an audit client?

2.6   What type of threat would exist if an audit manager moved to an audit client?

2.7   What type of threat would exist if an audit firm guaranteed a loan to an audit client?

2.8   What type of safeguard would you expect to be in place to protect against the self-interest threat of a family member of an audit partner working as CFO in an audit client?

2.9   What type of safeguard would you expect to be in place to deal with the numerous threats caused by long association with an audit client?

2.10 Besides the Ethical Standards, what other standards/codes exist to deal with the threat of long association?

2.11 Besides the direct provisions relating to the auditor in the *UK Corporate Governance Code,* why else would the auditor be interested in a company adopting its provisions?

Review Questions

(See Suggested Solutions to Review Questions in **Appendix D**.)

Question 2.1

Your firm has been the auditor of Trafford Ltd since the company's formation 10 years ago. The company's owner and Managing Director, Arnold Ferguson, is an old school friend of an audit partner in your firm, who has also acted as the partner on the audit of Trafford Ltd throughout the client's relationship with your firm. Arnold Ferguson has a reputation for being a very hands-on managing director, and is involved in many aspects of the business. He does not suffer fools gladly; indeed, he has been known on occasion to be vocal in his castigation of underperforming staff. He has also been quite curt in the past in response to questioning from members of the audit team and does not respond well to questioning of his judgements. This approach has, however, served him well over the years, and under his leadership Trafford Limited has grown to be one of the largest manufacturers of fertiliser in Ireland. As a result of this growth, the scope of the Trafford Ltd audit has grown significantly, with the audit fee increasing over the years. The fee for last year's audit was some €65,000. Your firm's total fee income from audits last year was approximately €250,000. As a result of Trafford Ltd's growth, Arnold Ferguson is keen to keep a close watch on internal controls. He has recently contacted your audit partner to enquire about the possibility of your firm providing internal audit services to Trafford Ltd.

Requirement From the above passage regarding an audit client of your firm, identify four threats to your firm's integrity, objectivity and independence and suggest what action your firm should take prior to commencing the next annual financial statement audit for this client, quoting relevant guidance.

Question 2.2

An audit client of your firm, Istanbul Ltd, has informed you that they are considering raising funds through a stock market flotation. You have had a meeting with the Finance Director, Rick Parry, who has explained that he is aware that Istanbul Ltd will have to look closely at improving their corporate governance arrangements prior to listing. Rick has asked you for some advice on the types of structure and arrangement he needs to introduce within Istanbul Ltd.

Requirement Draft a memo to Rick explaining the types of corporate governance arrangement required of a listed company, including relevant guidance.

3

FRAUD AND COMPLIANCE WITH LAWS & REGULATIONS

LEARNING OBJECTIVES

Having studied this chapter on fraud, and compliance with laws and regulations you should:

1. understand fraud in the context of audit;
2. understand the types of fraud that can occur and the forms it can take;
3. be able to demonstrate your understanding of the 'fraud triangle' by identifying conditions which give rise to fraud;
4. be able to explain the respective responsibilities of the management of the entity and the auditor with regard to fraud;

5. be able to identify the necessary audit procedures to detect fraud;
6. know the duty and right of auditors to report to third parties;
7. understand what is meant by the term 'aggressive earnings management';
8. be able to identify ways in which computer-assisted audit techniques (CAATs) can assist the auditor in detecting fraud; and
9. know the auditor's responsibilities with respect to the entity's compliance with laws and regulations.

Checklist of Relevant Standards and Guidance

The relevant standards covered in this chapter are:
*   ISA (UK and Ireland) 200 *Overall Objectives of the Independent Auditor and the Conduct of an Audit in Accordance with International Standards on Auditing (UK and Ireland)* (ISA 200)
*   ISA (UK and Ireland) 210 *Agreeing the Terms of Audit Engagements* (ISA 210)
*   ISA (UK and Ireland) 240 *The Auditor's Responsibilities Relating to Fraud in an Audit of Financial Statements* (ISA 240)
*   ISA (UK and Ireland) 250 – Section A *Consideration of Laws and Regulations in an Audit of Financial Statements* (ISA 250A)
*   ISA (UK and Ireland) 315 *Identifying and Assessing the Risks of Material Misstatement through Understanding the Entity and its Environment* (ISA 315)
*   ISA (UK and Ireland) 330 *The Auditor's Responses to Assessed Risks* (ISA 330)
*   FRC Selected FRC Guidance – Briefing Paper *Professional Scepticism*

Key Terms and Definitions in this Chapter

Analytical Review   Comprises the analysis of movements and relationships between items of data. It involves the comparison of recorded values with expectations developed by the auditor.

Auditor's Expert   If expertise in a field other than accounting or auditing is necessary to obtain sufficient appropriate audit evidence, the auditor shall determine whether to use the work of an auditor's expert.

Auditor Scepticism   Referring to professional scepticism, this is a particular state of mind that an auditor must maintain to help him conduct audit engagements appropriately. The 'scepticism approach' enables the auditor to recognise that circumstances may exist that cause the financial statements to be materially misstated, therefore he should be alert and remain cautious about such information and events that indicate the existence of material misstatement in the financial statements.

Fraud Risk Factors   Events or conditions indicating an incentive or pressure to commit fraud or provide an opportunity to commit fraud.

Going Concern   The going-concern assumption that the business will continue in existence in its present form for a defined period (usually at least 12 months). The directors/management and auditors are expected to be mindful of conditions that may indicate a company is not a 'going concern' (e.g. changing business environment or significant litigation, which could impact on the future of the business).

Management Representations   A written statement by management provided to the auditor to confirm certain matters or to support other audit evidence.

Segregation of Duties   The division of key tasks in a transaction to ensure that no one individual can perform a transaction from beginning to end.

3.1 INTRODUCTION

There is a 'perception gap' between the public and the auditing profession in relation to the auditor's duty in respect of the detection of fraud and error. Auditors place their emphasis on ensuring that, subsequent to their independent examination, the financial statements show a true and fair view of the state of the entity's affairs at the reporting date and of its profit or loss for the period then ended. In order to do this, they must determine, with reasonable certainty, whether or not the financial statements are materially misstated as a result of fraud or non-compliance with laws and regulations. The public believes, however, that it is the duty of the auditor to detect and prevent fraud and error. It is the responsibility of management, not the auditor, to ensure that the operation of the entity is conducted in accordance with relevant laws and regulations and steps are taken to prevent and detect the occurrence of fraud.

In planning and performing the audit to reduce audit risk to an acceptably low level, the auditor should consider the risks of material misstatements in the financial statements due to fraud or error. The auditor is concerned with both fraud and error since either may cause a material misstatement in the financial statements on which the auditor is giving an opinion.

The financial crisis has brought with it a surge in the risk of fraud. As we have learned, the impact of fraud can have extreme effects on many stakeholders. Where there is fraud, the shareholders, without doubt, suffer a loss, but so too do lenders, employees and suppliers.

The existence of the following factors increases the risk of fraud and error occurring:
• lack of segregation of duties amongst the various functions;
• unnecessarily complex corporate structures;
• understaffed accounting departments;

- inadequate working capital;
- significant transactions with related parties; and
- volatile business environments.

Based on his risk assessment, the auditor should design audit procedures so as to have a reasonable expectation of detecting misstatements, arising from fraud or error, which are material to the financial statements. The auditor must gather sufficient appropriate audit evidence to determine whether the financial statements give a true and fair view of the state of the entity's affairs at the reporting date and of its profit or loss for the period then ended. Therefore, the auditor should aim to identify all material fraud and error as these directly affect his opinion on the true and fair presentation of the financial statements. The auditor should, however, be mindful that there are various factors that hamper the detection of fraud.

It is important to note at this point that IAS 8 *Accounting Policies, Changes in Accounting Estimates and Errors*, at paragraph 41 states that the:

"Financial statements do not comply with international standards if they contain either material errors or immaterial errors made intentionally to achieve a particular presentation of an entity's financial position, financial performance or cash flows."

This chapter sets the scene of fraud today and the impact that fraud has had on the auditing profession. **Section 3.2** first outlines the difference between fraud and error, then **Section 3.3** discusses the primary types of fraud surrounding the audit of financial statements. This section also discusses some large-scale frauds, starting with the infamous collapse of Enron.

In **Section 3.4** we explore the conditions that are said to be present that cause people to commit fraud. This is known as the 'Fraud Triangle'. Having set the scene of fraud, these sections lead to a discussion on who is responsible for the prevention and detection of fraud, which we consider in **Section 3.5**.

Section 3.6 discusses ISA (UK and Ireland) 240 *The Auditor's Responsibilities Relating to Fraud in an Audit of Financial Statements*. In this key section of the chapter, we outline the audit procedures that the auditor is required to carry out with respect to detecting fraud impacting on the financial statements of an entity. This section also discusses the auditor's responsibilities with regard to reporting actual or suspected fraud.

In **Section 3.7** we will briefly discuss the concept of 'aggressive earnings management' before moving on to **Section 3.8**, where we consider the limitations that exist around audit procedures with regard to their ability to detect fraud and error. The use of computer-assisted audit techniques (CAATs), although discussed more fully in **Chapter 9**, is also considered in **Section 3.9** relating to how it can assist the auditor specifically in the detection of fraud.

Section 3.10 gives the reader an insight into the world of fraud today, discussing some key statistics on fraud in the UK and Ireland.

Finally, in **Section 3.11** we examine auditors' responsibilities and related audit procedures surrounding compliance by the client entity with laws and regulations.

3.2 ERROR VERSUS FRAUD

An '**error**' is considered a simple, 'unintentional' mathematical or clerical mistake in the financial statements. Examples include:
- the unintentional misapplication of an accounting policy;
- an incorrect accounting estimate arising from oversight;
- a misinterpretation of facts; or
- a mistake in the gathering of the initial data.

The auditor must design and implement procedures to prevent, detect and disclose **material** errors in the financial statements (the methods used are discussed in detail later in this chapter). At the completion stage of the audit, the auditor assesses the total level of errors and misstatements detected by the audit and forms an opinion as to the adequacy of the records kept and their impact on the '**true and fair**' presentation of the financial statements. Depending on conclusions reached, a **modified** report may have to be issued.

ISA 240 at paragraph 11(a) defines fraud as "an intentional act by one or more individuals among management, those charged with governance, employees, or third parties, involving the use of deception to obtain an unjust or illegal advantage". The standard also explains that the auditor is required to be concerned with fraud that causes a material misstatement in the financial statements.

3.3 TYPES OF FRAUD

Material misstatements may arise from **fraudulent financial reporting** or from the **misappropriation of assets**. While, according to the Association of Certified Fraud Examiners, misappropriation of assets represents approximately 91% of fraud schemes, it is not the most expensive type of fraud. The average fraud associated with misappropriation of assets is believed to be in the region of €110,000. In contrast, fraudulent financial reporting (also known as financial statement fraud), although occurring less frequently, is believed to cost companies on average $ 1 million (circa €750,000) per case.[1]

---

[1] See Gerard Zack, *Financial Statement Fraud: Strategies for Detection and Investigation* (John Wiley & Sons, 2012) and the Association of Certified Fraud Examiners (ACFE), *Survey 2012*.

Fraudulent Financial Reporting

Fraudulent financial reporting involves intentional misstatements. The fraudulent acts centre on the creation of financial opportunities for an individual or entity, e.g. through the manipulation of stock price or performance-related bonuses. The intention is to present financial statements that give a misleading impression of the financial affairs of the entity. These may include omissions of amounts or disclosures in financial statements to deceive financial statement users. **Generally, management are the perpetrators of this type of fraud**, motivated by what they consider to be their own best interests in terms of reporting of the financial position and performance of the entity. Methods employed include:

"• Manipulation, falsification (including forgery), or alteration of accounting records or supporting documentation from which the financial statements are prepared.
• Misrepresentation in, or intentional omission from, the financial statements of events, transactions or other significant information.
• Intentional misapplication of accounting principles relating to amounts, classification, manner of presentation, or disclosure." (ISA 240, paras A2–A3)

Management are in a better position to perpetrate this type of fraud due to their ability to override controls. **Table 3.1** below outlines some of the fraudulent financial reporting that can happen as a result of management overriding controls.

TABLE 3.1: EXAMPLES OF FRAUDS INVOLVING MANAGEMENT OVERRIDING CONTROLS

Fraudulent Act	Description	Auditor Response
Fictitious journal entries	The recording of fictitious journal entries generally tends to occur close to the year-end, when final results are becoming clearer and do not represent the results desired by management, causing them to reverse and alter valid journal entries and to create fictitious ones.	Review all journal entries around the year-end and obtain back-up as to their validity. Give particular attention to: 1. high value journal entries; and 2. reversed journal entries.
The deliberate application of inappropriate judgement or assumptions	This involves management altering their point of view with respect to judgements or assumptions to achieve a desired result (e.g. making light of significant uncertainties surrounding the going-concern assumption, or changing position on the collectability of receivables in order to justify a light provision).	Ensure an appropriately qualified and experienced member of the audit team is assigned to the audit of balances requiring the application of judgement and assumptions.

Concealing or not disclosing facts	The concealment or non-disclosure of facts that could impact amounts recorded in the financial statements is quite common and includes such things as omitting to share details of legal claims, or product quality issues.	Review: • board meeting minutes, • interim accounts (issued after the date of the financial statements), and • legal invoices and correspondence to identify any undisclosed matters. Inquire of management and obtain management representations for any oral disclosures.
Omission, advancement or delaying of recognition of financial statement items	This involves the smoothing of profits by knowingly moving transactions from one period to another (inappropriate application of cut-off) to achieve a desired result.	Perform cut-off testing, be mindful of incentives (such as bonus targets) and assign appropriately qualified and experienced audit staff to perform searches for unrecorded liabilities (missing liabilities). Adequately qualified and experienced audit personnel should also be assigned the review of complex revenue recognition transactions due to the high degree of fraud in this area. At all times the auditor should apply professional scepticism.
Complex transactions	Often complex transactions can be structured in a manner to misrepresent the financial position or performance of the entity.	Assign the audit of complex transactions to an appropriately qualified and experienced member of the audit team and obtain the advice of an auditor's expert, where necessary.

Misappropriation of Assets

Misappropriation of assets involves the theft of an entity's assets and is often perpetrated by **employees** in relatively small and immaterial amounts. It may also involve management, who are usually better able to disguise or conceal misappropriations in ways that are difficult to detect. Often, false or misleading records are created in order to conceal the fact that assets are missing or have been pledged without authorisation. Unlike fraudulent financial reporting, **misappropriation of assets** usually occurs **solely** for personal gain. Methods employed include:

- "Embezzling receipts (for example, misappropriating collections on accounts receivable or diverting receipts in respect of written-off accounts to personal bank accounts).
- Stealing physical assets or intellectual property (for example, stealing inventory for personal use or for sale, stealing scrap for resale, colluding with a competitor by disclosing technological data in return for payment).
- Causing the business to pay for goods and services not received (for example, payments to fictitious vendors …).
- Using an entity's assets for personal use (for example, using the entity's assets as collateral for a personal loan or a loan to a related party)" (ISA 240, para A5).

Perpetrators of fraud are generally those who come to auditors for explanations and assurance of information. For example, if an individual has committed fraud, he becomes more interested in how the auditor is going to carry out his tasks, and hence is more inquisitive about the auditor's approach in order to either settle his concerns that the auditor might discover the fraud or to better understand how to hide it. The auditor should maintain **professional scepticism** when conducting his duties in light of his knowledge of the entity and evidence he has obtained. Other general characteristics of behaviour or signs that may be indicative of fraud of which the auditor should be aware are as follows:

- unusual behaviour, e.g. defensiveness or failure to reassign work when overloaded;
- stale items in the bank reconciliation, missing lodgements or missing cheques. With each reconciliation performed, the reconciling items may be on the increase;
- excessive journal entries posted or credit notes issued;
- missing documents and lack of explanations and procedures to locate the documents;
- absence of original invoices, which are substituted by copies;
- common names, addresses, etc. that relate to an employee or family and friends of employee;
- excessive purchases relative to the nature of the entity;
- duplication of payments;
- fictitious employees noted on wages records;
- inventory levels relative to the nature of the entity, e.g. inventory levels held inconsistent with expectations;
- large and often round-sum payments made with little or no back-up documentation;
- post-office boxes used as shipping addresses;
- undue pressure from the client to complete the audit.

We have discussed the two types of fraud that can happen and established that fraudulent financial reporting has the potential to lead to a larger impact. **Table 3.2** below outlines a decade of fraud, starting with the largest impacting fraud in history – the Enron Scandal – and ending with some of the more recent reports of fraudulent corporate activity. The table highlights the types of fraud (fraudulent activities) undertaken by management, their impact (both financial and non-financial) and how they were discovered.

TABLE 3.2: EXAMPLES OF ACCOUNTING FRAUDS PERPETRATED SINCE 2001

Who	When	Type of Fraud/ Alleged Fraud	The Impact of the Fraud/ Alleged Fraud	How the Fraud/Alleged Fraud was Uncovered
Caterpillar and ERA Mining Machinery Limited	2012/ 2013	**Alleged** – improperly recognised revenues and inventories. **Alleged** – engagement by senior management in "deliberate misconduct beginning several years prior to Caterpillar's acquisition".	$580 million write down of $734 million investment.	Discovered by Caterpillar in January 2013 following its investment made in 2012.
Barclays	2012	Libor rate fixing and concealment of toxic assets through 'off balance sheet' accounting.	Immeasurable market impact. £7.47 billion sale of toxic assets. £290 million fine to Barclays. Allegations of other banks' involvement leads to Deutsche Bank advising it has set aside €1 billion to deal with potential litigation around Libor fixing.	At the onset of the financial crisis, liquidity concerns drew public scrutiny towards Libor.
Hewlett-Packard and Autonomy	2012	**Alleged** – autonomy improperly recognised revenue (upfront booking of long-term sales commitments and of sales made on a sale or return basis). **Alleged** – Autonomy's then management made misrepresentations and failed to make required disclosures. HP believe this was done to mislead investors and potential buyers.	$8.8 million write down by HP of its investment in Autonomy ($5 million of which is alleged by HP to be resulting from improprieties).	Actual margins of 20% rather than the expected 40% on acquisition led to investigations by HP, revealing alleged fraud.

Olympus	2012	Concealment of investment losses, which were secretly liquidated.	$1.7 billion	Internal whistle-blower (who was fired for questioning dubious deals).
Saytam	2009	Falsification of revenues, margins and cash balances. Improperly recognised revenue.	INR1.5 billion	Perpetrator, wrote to the board about his involvement.
Lehman Brothers	2008	**Alleged** – removal of 'Toxic Assets' from the balance sheet by selling them to Cayman Island Banks on a promise that they would buy them back.	$50 billion	The company went bankrupt.
American Insurance Group	2005	**Alleged** – told traders to inflate stock prices as well as booked loans as revenue and encouraged their clients to go to insurers from which they obtained a payoff.	$3.9 billion	Believed to be a whistleblower tip-off that led to SEC-regulator investigations.
Healthsouth	2003	**Alleged** – instructed subordinates to falsify transactions to inflate revenue to meet shareholder expectations.	$1.4 billion	Posted a massive trading loss following posting of $75 million in stock market value a day – this lead to SEC suspicions.
Tyco	2002	Set aside cash through unapproved loans and fraudulent stock sales and then extracted this cash from the company disguised as executive remuneration payments.	$500 million inflation of revenue (financial reporting fraud). $150 million misappropriation of funds.	Investigations by SEC and Manhattan D.A. revealed questionable accounting practices.

WorldCom	2002	Capitalised expenses and falsified revenue to inflate profits.	$11 billion inflation of assets. $180 billion losses for investors. Loss of 30,000 jobs. Led to introduction of Sarbanes–Oxley (discussed in **Section 2.7** of **Chapter 2**).	Internal Audit uncovered part of the fraud, leading to further investigations.
Enron	2001	Inappropriate revenue recognition. Inappropriate use of special-purpose entities. Market-to-market accounting (method of valuing assets at their current price). Capitalisation of expense items.	$74 billion in losses for shareholders; loss of thousands of employee and investor pensions. Also a factor in the introduction of Sarbanes–Oxley.	Internal whistle-blower.

3.4 THE 'FRAUD TRIANGLE' – WHY PEOPLE COMMIT FRAUD

Introduction

While **misappropriation of assets** is the most commonly perpetrated fraud, **fraudulent financial reporting** is more destructive and has a more significant impact. In the current recessionary economic climate, there is increased pressure to deliver unattainable targets in order to satisfy shareholders, lenders and the parent companies, which can lead to financial statement misrepresentation.

For example, bonus targets became quite common in the boom period and the receipt of bonus payments became commonplace; they were regularly paid out due to the healthy financial performances and positions of companies. Such bonuses came to be relied upon as regular sources of income by those who received them, typically those in management positions. The sudden financial and economic crash, which brought to an end that period of apparent, ever-improving performance, has left management out of pocket as they can no longer achieve the assigned targets and therefore the connected bonuses. As demonstrated above, the management of an entity can often easily override controls to manipulate financial reporting records and hence they may be tempted to smooth profits in order to assist the achievement of targets, feeling robbed of their right to receive a bonus they have taken for granted. Three conditions, **incentive**, **opportunity** and **rationalisation**, are now present for fraud to take place, as demonstrated in **Figure 3.1**:

FIGURE 3.1 CONDITIONS GIVING RISE TO FRAUD IN THE
CURRENT RECESSIONARY ENVIRONMENT

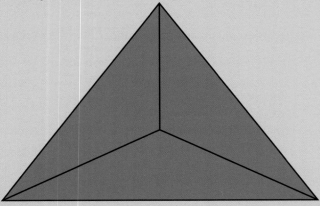

Incentive/Pressure to Commit Fraud Both incentive and pressure exist, in that the fall in financial performance and position is causing increased pressure from parent companies, shareholders, lenders, etc. Additionally, with personal bonuses at stake, management has incentive.

Rationalisation by the Individual or Company Management may be aggrieved by their loss of bonus, which they have become so accustomed to receiving that they do not perceive the harm in 'getting what they are entitled to'. Additionally, they may justify it by concluding that it is the only way to retain employment as otherwise responsibility for waning profits may be unfairly placed on their shoulders.

Opportunity for Fraud to Occur Management are best placed to commit fraud due to their ability to override controls. Additionally, organisations were not diligent enough in implementing controls during the boom period as they were satisfied with the profits they were making and failed to prioritise controlling the business and managing risk.

The Fraud Triangle Explained

As we can see from the above, generally there are three conditions present when fraud occurs. This is known as the 'fraud triangle' and is outlined in more detail in **Table 3.3** below, which shows examples of fraud risk factors relating to misstatements arising from fraudulent financial reporting, within each of the three elements of the fraud triangle explained above at **Figure 3.1**.

TABLE 3.3: THE FRAUD TRIANGLE

Stage 1: Incentive/Pressure to Commit Fraud
Employee   – individual is living beyond his means;   – personal debt and/or unforeseen expenses;   – pressure to meet expectations/targets that may be unrealistic;

– performance-related bonus/pay incentives;
– impossible targets set.

Company Directors/Management
– company has performed badly and is making a loss;
– market is expecting a certain level of profit from the company;
– company does not wish to make shareholders and the market aware of its liquidity problems;
– continual growth expectation puts management under pressure to sustain trends.

Stage 2: Opportunity for Fraud to Occur

Employee
– oppportunity may be perceived or actual and there is a belief that no one will notice the fraud;
– individual is in a position of trust;
– ineffective or absent controls;
– knowledge of specific weakness in an area of internal control;
– the ability of management to override control;
– no internal audit function.

Company Directors/Management
– complex overseas transactions allow opportunities for fraudulent transactions and reporting.

Stage 3: Rationalisation by the Individual or Company

– prevailing rationalisations of action/culture of the entity;
– acceptable competitive behaviour either internal to the entity or external with third parties;
– no visible harm – 'other people are doing it';
– no alternative employment opportunity;
– previous fraudulent activities have occurred in the company.

While this Table provides some examples of fraud risk factors, ISA 240, Appendix 1 gives further examples of fraud risk factors for both misstatements arising from fraudulent financial reporting and from the misappropriation of assets.

We can consider the 'fraud triangle' by applying it to the recent fraud case relating to the interest rate (Libor) rigging and concealment of toxic assets at Barclays Bank – see **Example 3.1**:

EXAMPLE 3.1: THE FRAUD TRIANGLE IN PRACTICE – BARCLAYS AND LIBOR

"A network of traders working on both sides of the Atlantic conspired to influence both the Libor and Euribor interest rates – the rates at which the banks lend to each other. It was, in effect, a worldwide conspiracy against the free functioning of the market."

The Observer, 30 June 2012

The Libor scandal cost Barclays £290 million in fines. 'Libor' is the term used to describe the average interest rate that banks pay to borrow money, and can represent the health of a bank. If the Libor is healthy, then the bank is deemed healthy and therefore gets offered lower interest rates. Derivative traders took bets on which way the Libor would go and subsequently fixed the rate (by colluding with fellow bankers) to support their preference. The reality of the troubled Barclays and its losses from toxic structured products was then concealed through an offshore company, Protium (this questionable accounting practice is the same as that operated by Lehman Brothers). The substance of the transaction was not that of a sale of the assets to Protium but a temporary transfer, funded by Barclays themselves through loans to Protium. Essentially, Barclays sold the toxic assets to themselves but through this 'off balance sheet' approach they remained out of view of the shareholders. Bankers at Barclays were rewarded well for the generation of large profits, creating an aggressive bonus culture. Additionally, ex-employees of Barclays were said to be paid substantial fees for arranging the sale through Protium.

Barlcays' employees told the City Watchdog and various other authorities that all the banks that comprise the Libor panel "were contributing rates that were too low". Misconduct was said to be "widespread, involving staff in New York, London and Tokyo as well as external traders".

With the above in mind, were the three conditions present for this fraud to take place?

Stage 1: Incentive/Pressure to Commit Fraud

Employee **(rigging of the rate)**
– pressure to meet expectations/targets that may have been unrealistic;
– performance-related bonus/pay incentives – "Aggressive bonus culture" and "substantial fees" paid for organising sale to Protium.

Company Directors/Management **(concealment of toxic assets)**
– Barclays was performing badly;
– market was expecting a certain level of profit from the company;
– Barclays did not wish to make shareholders and the market aware of its liquidity problems.

Stage 2: Opportunity for Fraud to Occur

Employee
– opportunity and a belief that no one would notice; the opportunity arose in the willingness of other bankers to participate;

– it is evident that ineffective controls existed or there was an absence of controls;
– knowledge of a specific weakness in the system gave the fraudsters an avenue.

Company Directors/Management
– use of 'off balance sheet accounting' – Special Purpose Entities (now outlawed under financial reporting by warranting inclusion of subsidiaries by reference to the definition of 'control' (*Note*: IFRS 10 *Consolidated Financial Statements* outlines when an entity must consolidate another entity and addresses the issue of special purpose entities).

Stage 3: Rationalisation by the Individual or Company

Employee
– prevailing rationalisations of action/culture of the entity – all the banks that comprise the Libor panel "were contributing rates that were too low";
– acceptable competitive behaviour internal to the entity – driven by an aggressive bonus culture;
– no visible harm – "Misconduct was said to be '*widespread, involving staff in New York, London and Tokyo as well as external traders'.*"

Company Directors/Management
– it is apparent that the justification was 'It's for the good of the shareholder; it will come good in the end'.

To summarise the theory of the fraud triangle: if an individual cannot see a reason to commit fraud (i.e. incentive/pressure), then he will not proceed; if he cannot perceive a way (opportunity), then he cannot proceed; finally, if he cannot justify or rationalise the wrong to himself, if even the first two conditions exist, then he is unlikely to proceed.

3.5 RESPONSIBILITIES FOR PREVENTION AND DETECTION OF FRAUD AND ERROR

The primary responsibility for the prevention and detection of fraud rests with the audited entity's directors (particularly the finance director), management and those charged with governance. This is highlighted in ISA (UK and Ireland) 210 *Agreeing the Terms of Audit Engagements,* paragraph 6, where the standard indicates that it is the responsibility of directors to maintain adequate internal controls and safeguard the assets of the company. The auditor is not required to assist in this function, but he should inform directors and relevant management of their responsibilities through the **engagement letter** issued at the start of the audit and through other relevant communications, which could include the **planning meeting**. The fact that an audit is carried out may, however, act as a deterrent to potential fraudsters.

Responsibilities of Management

The auditor should advise management on how to set the '**tone at the top**' for the running of their business. Management can do this through:

- Developing an accepted **Code of Conduct** for all employees – for example, Barclays issued a code of conduct to be signed by all staff following the scandal surrounding the 'fixing of the Libor rate'. Staff are mandatorily required to sign the document, which centres on five key values: respect, integrity, service, excellence and stewardship.
- Promoting a **culture of honesty and integrity** within a positive working environment – this is often demonstrated in a tone-at-the-top document but more importantly should be embodied in the actions of the senior management of an organisation, encouraging employees to follow their example.
- Implementing an **ethics programme** based on a strong set of core values to be communicated to the entire organisation.
- Establishing penalties and procedures for dealing with prosecutors – usually implemented through HR disciplinary procedures.
- Implementing e-banking for payroll and other recurring outgoings.
- Establishing an **appropriate control environment** and maintaining strong internal controls that provide reasonable assurance with regard to reliability of financial reporting, effectiveness and the efficiency of operations and compliance with applicable laws and regulations.
- Establishing an **internal audit function**, an **audit committee** and an **independent compliance function** to which the auditor can report any incidence of suspected fraud.
- Taking action in response to actual, suspected and alleged fraud; and
- Developing an employee '**whistleblower**' charter – as can be seen from **Table 3.2**, above some of the largest fraudulent financial reporting cases were revealed by whistleblowers so organisations should create a safe environment that encourages whistleblowing.

Responsibilities of the Auditor

The auditor is required to provide reasonable assurance that the financial statements are free from material misstatement, whether caused by fraud or error. There is the unavoidable risk that some material misstatements may, however, go undetected. The auditor's responsibility is to obtain sufficient appropriate audit evidence to support his opinion on the true and fair presentation of the financial statements. More specific requirements of the auditor are dealt with in **Section 3.6**.

3.6 AUDIT PROCEDURES UNDER ISA 240

ISA 240 outlines the following key requirements for the auditor when discharging his responsibility with respect to the detection of fraud:

- application of **professional scepticism**;
- ensuring adequate discussion among the engagement team;

- application of appropriate risk procedures and related activities;
- identification and assessment of the risks of material misstatement due to fraud;
- adequate response to the assessed risks of material misstatement due to fraud;
- evaluation of audit evidence;
- obtaining written representations;
- communicating suspicions of fraud; and
- documentation.

These are considered in turn below.

Professional Scepticism

A briefing paper on professional scepticism was issued by the Financial Reporting Council (FRC), with the aim of establishing a common understanding and reaffirming the central role of professional scepticism in delivering audit quality.[2] Three important points are highlighted in the paper with regard to the origins of the term 'scepticism':
- the essence of scepticism is doubt, and that doubt stimulates informed challenge and inquiry;
- in the face of doubt, the suspension of judgement about the truth; and
- in its extreme forms scepticism is not pragmatic as it may lead to the conclusion that no judgements about the truth can be made.

The **Ethical Standards** reflect a fear that auditors will develop close ties with the management teams of audited entities that will lead them to develop a trust (familiarity), hence leading either to a lack of, or reduced levels of, professional scepticism. According to the FRC's briefing paper on professional scepticism, "the rigorous assessment of when, and the degree to which, professional scepticism is required is fundamental to an effective audit". The importance of the application of this professional scepticism is never more relevant than when recognising the possibility that a material misstatement due to fraud could exist.

Discussion among the Audit Engagement Team

ISA 240, at paragraphs A10–A11, requires the members of the **audit engagement team** to discuss the susceptibility of the entity's financial statements to material misstatements due to fraud and how it might occur. This discussion should occur with a questioning mind and professional scepticism. Items to be discussed include:
- how and where the financial statements may be susceptible to material misstatement due to fraud, how management could perpetrate and conceal fraudulent financial reporting, and how assets of the entity could be misappropriated;
- the circumstances that might indicate earnings management and the practices that might be followed by management to manage earnings that could lead to fraudulent financial reporting;

---

[2] *Professional Scepticism – Establishing a common understanding and reaffirming its central role in delivering audit quality* (FRC Briefing Paper, March 2012) – see http://www.frc.org.uk/getattachment/1aecac64-6309-4539-a6d9-690e67c93519/Briefing-Paper-Professional-Scepticism.aspx

- how external and internal factors affecting the entity could create an incentive or pressure for management or others to commit fraud, provide the opportunity for fraud to be perpetrated, and indicate a culture or environment that enables management or others to rationalise committing fraud;
- management's involvement in overseeing employees with access to cash or other assets susceptible of misappropriation;
- any unusual or unexplained changes in behaviour or lifestyle of management or employees which have come to the attention of the engagement team;
- the importance of maintaining professional scepticism and a proper state of mind throughout the entire audit process regarding the potential for material misstatement due to fraud;
- circumstances that could indicate the possibility of fraud, the risk of management override of controls, how an element of unpredictability must be incorporated into the nature, timing and extent of procedures performed and how the audit procedures are selected relative to the likelihood of material misstatement; and
- allegations of fraud that have already come to light.

Risk Assessment Procedures and Related Activities

There are some specific procedures that the auditor must carry out when trying to establish if any risk of fraud exists within the client entity. Throughout ISA 240 the auditor is guided with regard to the types of procedures he can perform relating to his risk-assessment of the client entity including:
- The auditor must discuss with management and those charged with governance the procedures they follow when fulfilling their responsibilities for detecting fraud. Discussions should include management's assessment of fraud occurring, procedures to minimise fraud occurring and the ethical attitudes communicated to the organisation.
- The auditor should ascertain if management and those charged with governance are aware of any fraud that has occurred or is occurring.
- The auditor should determine the procedures implemented by the internal audit team aimed at detecting fraud and what conclusions they have reached.
- Those charged with governance should be approached to determine what processes and procedures have been used by management to identify the risks of fraud occurring and how management responded to these risks.
- The auditor should consider what fraud risk factors, if any, already exist.
- Analytical review techniques should be used by the auditor to identify any unexpected relationships that might suggest the possibility of material misstatement due to fraud.

Identification and Assessment of the Risks of Material Misstatement Due to Fraud

The auditor must identify situations where there is a higher than usual risk of fraud or error occurring. He should also identify what types of transaction and assertion he believes could be impacted.

"There is no special recipe, checklist or manual for detecting fraud, no such thing exists and no such thing is truly capable of being developed to address all forms of fraud."[3]

While the above statement is true, fraud investigations over the years have revealed that fraudulent behaviour tends to exist where:

- there are no controls or weak/inadequate controls;
- there is inadequate segregation of duties;
- there is inadequate management of staff;
- there are inherent risks of fraud existing in the industry;
- the entity has financial difficulties;
- the entity is suffering a loss of market share;
- there are aggressive bonus structures;
- there is unusual behaviour; or
- there are unusual circumstances/transactions or swings in business.

(See also **Section 3.4**.)

Responses to the Assessed Risks of Material Misstatement Due to Fraud

Once the auditor identifies risks, he must now decide how to address these identified risks. He must plan his audit procedures to ensure that he assigns appropriate levels of staff and audit techniques to minimise the risk of not detecting a **material misstatement**. As will be discussed further in Chapter 4, errors (and therefore risks) can exist at the **financial statement level** (i.e. the entire sets of financial statements are affected by the risk) *or* at the **assertion level** (e.g. when an individual account balance is affected by the risk). The auditor needs to determine the level of the risk and then apply appropriate procedures to address that risk. Risks at the financial statement level are naturally more concerning as their impact is far greater.

Responses at the Financial Statement and Assertion Levels

ISA 240 requires that the auditor responds to risk both at the financial statement level (risk that impacts on the entire set of financial statements) and at the assertion level (risks that impact on *say* the completeness of revenue – a further discussion on assertions is included in **Chapter 4**). ISA 240, paragraph 29, advises that to assess risk at the overall financial statement level, it is essential to assign and supervise audit personnel appropriately. Additionally, it notes the need for unpredictability in the selection of the nature, timing and extent of audit procedures.

Audit Procedures to Address Risks of Management Override of Controls

Section 3.3, 'Fraudulent Financial Reporting', outlines the susceptibility of financial statements to fraud through management override of controls. **Table 3.1** above also identifies various types of fraud resulting from management override of controls and the audit procedures that can address these risks. In particular, ISA 240 states the need for testing the

---

[3] Corné Mouton, "Fraud Prevention", *Accountancy Ireland*, April 2013, Vol.45, No. 2, pp. 37–38.

appropriateness of journal entries and for reviewing accounting estimates for bias. The standard does, however, advise the auditor to perform audit procedures that respond to the identified risks in the particular situation(s) in the entity being audited (i.e. the auditor needs to draw upon his experience and expertise to assess what procedures are required within each unique situation).

Evaluation of Audit Evidence

At the conclusion stage of the audit, the auditor performs a '**final analytical review**' (see **Table 3.4**), which is designed to analyse movements and relationships between figures in the financial statements and consider these against expectations. The auditor, at this conclusion stage of the audit, should have gained sufficient understanding of the financial statements to be able to appreciate the movements and relationships and justify them with **corroborating evidence**. During this review, if he identifies a movement or relationship that is not corroborated by previous audit procedures, it might indicate an unidentified risk and as such the auditor needs to perform further audit procedures that are appropriate to deal with the newly identified risk.

Table 3.4 below demonstrates the process the auditor undergoes when performing a final analytical review. First, the table outlines an example of the auditor's expectation of how bad debts should look in the financial statements, based on conversations with management. Then, during his final analytical review, he realises that this expectation is not consistent with other reported financial information. In turn, this realisation triggers the auditor to perform further investigation and conclude on whether he will need to perform further testing.

TABLE 3.4: FINAL ANALYTICAL PROCEDURE PROCESS

Expectation	Identification	Investigation	Evaluation
During testing the auditor concluded on the bad debt provision and through inquiry of management and review of the adequacy of their calculation determined that it was reasonable. During inquiry with management it was noted that the bad debt provision was reduced this year due to the significant write off of items previously provided for. The expectation is, therefore, that bad debts in the current year will be higher than in prior years.	During final analytical procedures the auditor notices that bad debts written off in the year are significantly less than in the prior year and amount to only €100,000, while the reduction in the bad debt provision is €950,000. This does not tie in with his expectation and may indicate a risk not previously identified.	Further inquiry with management revealed that the bad debt write off, to which management had referred, was actually written off in the prior year and as such the fall in the provision is not justified by this initial explanation.	Further audit procedures will be required around the reduction in the bad debt provision.

Written Representations

Throughout the audit, **management** will make statements to the auditor that are often verbal and therefore cannot be put onto the auditor's audit working file. As such, the auditor, in order to solidify some of those statements, will present management with a list of statements made (implicitly or explicitly) in order to obtain confirmation that their understanding is correct and that the directors stand over any **management representations** that may have been made.

'Written representations' are routinely obtained from management in which management confirms, in writing, significant representations made to the auditor (a detailed discussion on written representations (commonly known as 'management representations') is included in **Chapter 18**, Section 18.5).

ISA 240, paragraph 39, details specific representations required from the management of an entity, that it:
- acknowledges its responsibility for designing, implementing and maintaining internal controls to prevent and detect fraud;
- has disclosed to the auditor:
  - the results of its assessments of the risk that the financial statements may be materially misstated as a result of fraud;
  - its knowledge of fraud or suspected fraud affecting the entity involving management, employees who have significant roles in internal controls and others where the fraud could have a material effect on the financial statements;
  - its knowledge of any allegations of fraud, or suspected fraud, affecting the entity's financial statements communicated by employees, former employees, analysts, regulators or others.

Communicating Suspected or Actual Instances of Fraud

Having identified all risks, responded to those risks and obtained written representations from management, the auditor may be faced with an actual or suspected fraud. The auditor now needs to consider how he communicates this fraud both to management and potentially to third parties.

If the auditor suspects fraud or discovers a material error, having obtained all the necessary evidence, he should report his findings to an appropriate level of management, the directors or those charged with governance. The auditor must make sure he is fully informed of the nature of the fraud and the magnitude of the situation. The situation must be fully documented in the working papers.

Discussion with Directors and/or Those charged with Governance

If a material fraud is discovered that affects the financial statements, directors and/or those charged with governance should be asked to consider amending the financial statements to reflect the impact of the fraud. The impact on other audit work must also be considered. Management can be asked to carry out additional procedures to determine if the auditor has uncovered the full extent of the fraud. If management, other than the directors, are suspected of committing a fraud, the directors should be informed.

Even if fraud or suspected fraud has not been encountered, the auditor should discuss with the directors the concerns they have relating to fraud. For example:
- concerns about the nature, extent and frequency of management's assessments of the controls in place to prevent and detect fraud;
- a failure of management to appropriately address identified material weaknesses in internal control, or to appropriately respond to an identified fraud;
- the auditor's evaluation of the entity's control environment, including questions regarding the competence and integrity of management;
- actions by management that may be indicative of fraudulent financial reporting; and
- concerns about the adequacy and completeness of the authorisation of transactions that appear to be outside the normal course of business.

Indifference of Management to Reported Fraud Suspicions

Once the auditor reports his suspicions, it is expected that those charged with governance take action. If management and directors are indifferent to investigating the fraud, the auditor will need to reassess their integrity and the control environment and will need to consider the impact on the **audit report**.

If the auditor believes that the financial statements are materially affected by a fraud or error, an explanatory paragraph should be added to the audit report to qualify his report, depending on the circumstances (audit reports are discussed in detail in **Chapter 19**). Additionally, the auditor should seek legal advice about reporting to a third-party authority.

Audit Continuance

If the auditor suspects that fraud exists at the management level then this calls into question the integrity of the client entity and, as such, the auditor may feel that he cannot continue the engagement. If a misstatement resulting from fraud or a suspected fraud is discovered and it brings into question the auditor's ability to continue performing the audit, the auditor should:
- consider the professional and legal responsibilities applicable in the circumstances, including whether there is a requirement for the auditor to report to the person or persons who made the audit appointment or, in some cases, to regulatory authorities;
- consider the possibility of withdrawing from the engagement; and
- if the auditor withdraws from the engagement, he must discuss with the appropriate level of management and those charged with governance the reason for the withdrawal. The auditor must also consider whether there is a professional or legal requirement to report to the person or persons who made the audit appointment or, in some cases (e.g. in the case of money laundering, discussed in **Section 3.11**, or any reason in the public interest), to regulatory authorities. As a result of the Company Law Enforcement Act 2001 (CLEA 2001), auditors are now required to make a report to the Director of Corporate

Enforcement (ODCE) where, during the course of, and by virtue of, carrying out an audit, information comes into their possession which leads them to form the opinion that the company, or an officer or agent of it, has committed an indictable offence under the Companies Acts (section 194(5) CA 1990 as inserted by section 74 CLEA 2001).

The following table (**Table 3.5**) outlines the process the auditor must follow when considering who to communicate actual and suspected instances of fraud. The table identifies the various parties to whom the auditor may communicate and the obligations they hold to each of those parties.

TABLE 3.5: AUDITOR'S OBLIGATION TO REPORT FRAUD OR ERROR

Party	Obligation
Shareholders	Shareholders/members must be informed (through the audit report) if the auditor concludes that the financial statements do not give a true and fair view, do not comply with applicable accounting framework, or that proper books and records have not been kept.
	Where professional and legal responsibilities permit, and the auditor encounters exceptional fraudulent circumstances that bring into question the auditor's ability to continue performing the audit, he may consider it appropriate to withdraw. This should be discussed with those charged with governance and reported to the persons who made the audit appointment. The auditor has the right to make known his reason for withdrawal to the shareholders.
Management	If lower level management is suspected of being involved in fraudulent activities, senior management and/or the audit committee must be informed.
	Lower level management should be informed of all errors and irregularities noted by the auditor. This can be done through the management letter.
Third Parties	When reporting to third parties, confidentiality is very important. The auditor should consider obtaining legal advice to determine the appropriate course of action.
	Where breaches of the law have occurred, there is a public duty to disclose the breach and the relevant authority must be notified (e.g. money laundering – see above).
	Also in instances where either: 1. directors (those charged with governance) have failed to report a suspicion of fraud outlined to them by the auditor; or 2. directors (those charged with governance) are suspected to be involved in the suspected of fraud, then the auditor should seek legal advice before informing third-party authorities.

Documentation

Having identified all risks, responded to those risks, obtained representations from management and reported actual and suspected instances of fraud, the auditor now needs to ensure that his audit file reflects the process followed. In order to be able to demonstrate that he carried out his duties in accordance with auditing standards, the auditor must be able to demonstrate all steps taken and evidence gathered, and he does this by documenting the details surrounding each risk identified and concluded upon.

There has been an increase in regulatory requirements relating to the documentation of audit procedures performed to detect fraud and the steps taken to report detected and/or suspected fraud. Matters that must be documented include (ISA 240, paras 44–47):

- discussions with management regarding fraud – see **Appendix 3.1** of this chapter for a sample client fraud questionnaire;
- significant decisions reached during the audit engagement team discussions regarding the susceptibility of the entity's financial statements to material misstatements due to fraud[4];
- identified and assessed risks of material misstatements due to fraud at financial statement and assertion level;
- overall responses to the assessed risks of material misstatements due to fraud at financial statement level and the nature, timing and extent of audit procedures performed in response to assessed risks of material misstatement at the assertion level;
- the results of audit procedures performed, including those designed to address the risk of management override of controls;
- communications about fraud made to management, those charged with governance, regulators or others; and
- if the auditor has concluded that improper revenue recognition does not present a risk of material misstatement due to fraud, the reasons supporting that conclusion.

3.7 AGGRESSIVE EARNINGS MANAGEMENT

A discussion of the topic of fraud cannot be adequately concluded upon without reference to the practice of **aggressive earnings management**. Aggressive earnings management is the use of methods by management to paint an unrealistic, positive picture of company results. It is a form of fraudulent financial reporting and usually takes the form of inappropriate revenue recognition or delaying of expense recognition. These practices are also known as 'profit smoothing'.

In 2001 the APB issued a Consultation Paper entitled *Aggressive Earnings Management*, which defines aggressive earnings management as:

---

[4] See Louise Kelly, *Advanced Auditing and Assurance* (Chartered Accountants Ireland, 2013) Chapter 3, Example 3.3.

"accounting practices including the selection of inappropriate accounting policies and/or unduly stretching judgements as to what is acceptable when forming accounting estimates.

These practices, while presenting the financial performance of the companies in a favourable light, do not necessarily reflect the underlying reality."[5]

Auditors should be alert and responsive to the existence of aggressive earnings management. The auditor should:
- recognise the pressures on directors or management to report a specific level of earnings;
- act with a greater professional scepticism when alerted to circumstances indicative of aggressive earnings management;
- take a strong stance with directors when requesting adjustments for misstatements identified during the audit; and
- communicate openly and frankly with the entity, in particular the directors and the audit committee.

3.8 LIMITATIONS OF AUDIT PROCEDURES IN DETECTING FRAUD AND ERROR

There are unavoidable limitations where, even though the audit will be properly planned and performed, fraud or error may not be detected. ISA (UK and Ireland) 200 *Overall Objectives of the Independent Auditor and the Conduct of an Audit in Accordance with International Standards on Auditing* (ISA 200), at paragraph 3, states that the purpose of an audit is to enhance the degree of confidence of intended users in the financial statements. This is achieved by the expression of an opinion by the auditor on whether the financial statements are prepared, in all material respects, in accordance with an applicable financial reporting framework. Thus, the primary responsibility is not to detect fraud. In addition, the auditor is only required to give an opinion on the financial statements, not a guarantee. Therefore, the evidence gathered in terms of persuasiveness is limited to that required to arrive at their opinion.

Due to the volume of transactions going through an entity's general ledger and bank accounts, including all journal entries and other adjustments, the auditor uses sampling methods when performing audit tests. It is inevitable that every error or misstatement is not going to be detected. Management could also have concealed fraud from the auditors, deliberately manipulated the books and records of the entity, made intentional misrepresentations or deliberately not recorded transactions. Where judgement has been exercised, by management (e.g. when determining whether a receivable needs to be provided against or not, management applies judgement), it may be difficult to ascertain whether misrepresentations were caused by fraud or error. Additionally, unless 100% of transactions are tested, the auditor must accept the possibility that the fraud may simply go undetected

---

[5] Auditing Practices Board, Consultation Paper: *Aggressive Earnings Management* (CCAB Ltd, 2001).

in the financial statements. This is referred to as '**sampling risk**', i.e. the fraudulent item may not have been selected in the sample tested by the auditor and hence go undetected. Sampling risk is discussed in more detail in **Chapter 6**, Section 6.7.

Additionally, fraud usually involves collusion (an act involving two or more people working together to achieve a fraudulent or deceitful purpose). Collusion overrides segregation of duties, which may have been implemented by the client entity and therefore it is more difficult to detect the fraud. By collaborating together, the fraudsters can create an apparent existence of corroborating evidence.

3.9 FRAUD AND CAATs

Computer-assisted audit techniques (CAATs) are discussed in detail in **Chapter 9** and are a very important tool for auditors in their detection of fraud. In order to work effectively, CAATs must be strategically adapted to the situation and the various audit objectives and procedures of the entity under review. There are many benefits to utilising CAATs when searching for indications of fraudulent activity.

CAATs can be used to:
• search for duplicate payments;
• match vendor address to employee address;
• search for matching employee and supplier details;
• search for matching addresses, e.g. payroll, payables and receivables;
• analyse overridden transactions;
• identify large round-sum payments;
• identify scrapped inventory followed by re-orders;
• list missing items, e.g. items on cheque-payments summary to bank reconciliation;
• identify any employee's or director's account with a large volume of transactions for large amounts;
• search for classes of transactions known to have high exposure e.g. loans, health claims; and
• search for patterns, e.g. customers changing their payment methods, sales returns following a disputed account.

According to Andrew Brown in his book, *Corporate Fraud*, CAATs are particularly effective with respect to fraud to avoid 'auditor fatigue':
> "This arises when an individual is looking for anomalies or mistakes in a population but the vast majority of the population does not contain any anomalies. The risk is that the auditor gets so used to seeing acceptable transactions that they fail to identify the anomalies or mistakes when they do come across them."[6]

In order to combat this, the auditor can use 'data analysis tools', which allow mass review of large populations. The process surrounding data analysis using CAATs involves cleaning

---

[6] Andrew Brown, *Corporate Fraud* (Chartered Accountants Ireland, 2010), p. 101.

the data to ensure it is adequate for auditor review, preparing the test, sample testing to ensure it is correctly set up and then reviewing highlighted transactions. Andrew Brown, as noted above, further outlines the specific requirements and application of 'Proactive Fraud Prevention Using Data Analysis'.

3.10 THE CURRENT ECONOMIC ENVIRONMENT AND FRAUD

In times of recession and financial difficulty, the occurrence of fraud becomes more and more prevalent as incentive and opportunity increase. In such times, where individuals and companies suffer financially, behaviour can change and the line of morality (and legality) can be crossed, resulting in activities undertaken in order to maintain the lifestyles, financial performance, etc. to which individuals and business have become accustomed.

In 2011, Alan Shatter, TD, Minister for Justice, Equality and Defence, on publishing the Criminal Justice Bill:
> "… the publication of this Bill … is an important step in delivering on the Government's strong commitment to tackle white-collar crime".

The Minister's words are not surprising given the public frustration over the nationalisation of the banks and the general economic collapse suffered since 2008.

While Ireland does not have *detailed* statistics relating to fraud, in the UK the National Fraud Authority commenced the Annual Fraud Indicator (AFI) in 2010. The AFI 2011 report indicated that the cost of fraud to the UK economy was approximately £38.4 billion. Figures from the Irish Central Statistics Office show that recorded fraud, deception and related offences were up, from 5,370 in 2011, to 5,544 in 2012 (+3.2%). This figure in 2009 was 4,947, and so in just three years has increased by circa 12%. Statistics show that perpetrators of fraud tend to be males aged between 25 and 44. While the statistics give an indication of the upsurge of fraud in the Republic of Ireland, they do not give any indication of their gravity.

The Prevention of Corruption (Amendment) Act 2010 ('the Act') was signed into law on 15 December 2010. This Act attempts to improve the strength of anti-corruption legislation while providing specific **protection to the whistleblower**. Throughout the world people are generally afraid of being penalised by their employer if they blow the whistle. This is truer, however, in countries where little or no protection exists for the whistleblower. The Act, while welcomed, is somewhat piecemeal in its application in that it refers to corruption offences against a public office/department only (not private sector companies). As we can see from **Table 3.2**, whistleblowers play an important role in the detection of fraud and as such can be seen to be truly fighting corruption. However, legislation is needed that stretches to all industries and sectors of the economy. For now, at least, private sector investors and indeed the public will have to hold their breath and hope that directors stand by the spirit of the *UK Code on Corporate Governance* (see **Chapter 2**).

The area of '**forensic audit**' is becoming an increasingly popular area of the profession due to the rise in corporate fraud. The primary objective of a fraud audit (a special investigation a forensic auditor might be asked to perform) is to either prove or disprove the occurrence of fraudulent behaviour for use as evidence in court. More recently, the role or skill set of the forensic accountant is being increasingly called upon to assist entities in their anti-fraud efforts.

3.11 CONSIDERATION OF LAWS AND REGULATIONS IN AN AUDIT OF FINANCIAL STATEMENTS

Introduction

A topic closely connected to that of fraud is the area of client entity compliance with laws and regulations. When a company does not act within the constraints of the law, it is said to be **non-compliant** with laws and regulations. During the course of an audit, the auditor can frequently become aware of instances of non-compliance with laws and regulations and he must consider if he has a duty to report the respective non-compliance areas. The auditor also needs to ensure he is familiar with his responsibilities in detecting non-compliance of the client entity with laws and regulations.

ISA (UK and Ireland) 250 – Section A *Consideration of Laws and Regulations in an Audit of Financial Statements* ('ISA 250A') outlines the auditor's consideration of laws and regulations in an audit of financial statements.

Table 3.6 below outlines the respective responsibilities of directors and auditors with respect to adherence to laws and regulations. The types of law and regulation are considered later in this section.

The responsibilities outlined in **Table 3.6** are not dissimilar to those with respect to fraud. There are essentially two categories of laws and regulations that the auditor must consider:
• those that relate directly to the financial statements (Category 1); and
• those that support the legal framework in which the business of the client entity is conducted (Category 2).

Laws and regulations that relate directly to financial statements include company law disclosure requirements, distribution rules, requirements in relation to accounting records and taxation laws. The legal framework in which the company operates can be more far reaching and the auditor should gain a general understanding of this through inspection of correspondence and inquiry of directors. Adherence to legal and regulatory requirements will always form part of the **written management representations** (as discussed above in **Section 3.6**).

The auditor should remain alert to instances of non-compliance. He must obtain **sufficient appropriate audit evidence** in relation to Category 1 (those laws and regulations impacting directly on the financial statements). However, with respect to Category 2, the auditor is only required to carry out procedures to identify non-compliance with other laws and regulations that may have a material effect on the financial statements.

TABLE 3.6: RESPECTIVE RESPONSIBILITIES OF DIRECTORS AND
AUDITORS WITH RESPECT TO LAWS AND REGULATIONS

Directors:	**Auditors:**
Have an **active role** with respect to adherence to laws and regulations (i.e. they must actively put measures in place to ensure compliance with laws and regulations).	Have **no preventative role** (i.e. they are not responsible for preventing client non-compliance with laws and regulations).
Have a **preventative role** in ensuring no instances of non-compliance with laws and regulations can occur.	Frequently, the auditor plays a **deterrent role**, in that client entity is less likely to knowingly engage in non-compliance if it feels there is a chance the auditor will detect it.
Have a **detective role** in ensuring that instances of non-compliance with laws and regulations are identified and rectified.	Have a **detection role**, which is based on '**reasonable expectation**', similar to their responsibility to detect **material misstatements**.

Audit Procedures when Non-compliance is Identified or Suspected

Where the auditor becomes aware of actual or suspected non-compliance, according to ISA 250A, he shall obtain an understanding of the nature of and circumstances giving rise to the act and obtain further information to evaluate the possible effect on the financial statements.

Similar to the fraud requirements noted above, the auditor should discuss suspected instances of non-compliance with the directors/**those charged with governance** and give them the opportunity to rectify it. Failure by the directors to do so should lead to legal advice being sought by the auditor. This may have an impact on the **auditor's report** and may give indications of risk (e.g. management integrity). **Table 3.7** below considers the steps taken by the auditor in reporting non-compliance.

TABLE 3.7: REPORTING NON-COMPLIANCE BY THE AUDITOR

Step 1	Obtain all information to support suspicions.
Step 2	Where those charged with governance/management are not suspected, then the auditor should disclose suspicions to them and give them time to investigate and report the matter to the necessary authorities (where required). Failure to do so by management should lead the auditor to seek legal advice regarding the next course of action.
Step 3	Where most of the senior management of the organisation is believed to be associated with non-compliance, the auditor should obtain legal advice before proceeding to inform the relevant regulatory authority.
Step 4	Where the auditor concludes that the non-compliance has a material impact on the financial statements, he should consider the implications for his report (see **Chapter 19**, 'Audit Reports').
Step 5	The auditor must determine if he has a responsibility to report the identified or suspected non-compliance to parties outside the entity.

Money Laundering

In recent times greater attention has been given internationally to the issue of **money laundering**, which is described as follows by Vaeni Mac Donnell in *An Introduction to Business Law*:

> "Money laundering is the process by which the proceeds of crime, either money or other property, are converted into assets that appear to have a legitimate rather than an illegal origin. The aim of the process is to disguise the source of the property in order to allow the holder to enjoy it free from suspicion as to its source."[7]

An auditor who knows, suspects or has reasonable grounds to suspect money laundering, on the basis of information obtained in the course of carrying on his business (as an auditor), shall make a report to the relevant authorities as set out in the Acts.

The legal objectives are to deter, detect and disrupt money laundering and terrorist financing. The legislation applicable to the Republic of Ireland is the Criminal Justice (Money Laundering and Terrorist Financing) Act 2010 as amended by the Criminal Justice Act 2013. For the UK/NI, the Money Laundering Regulations 2007 apply. An auditor who knows, suspects or has reasonable grounds to suspect money laundering or terrorist financing, on the basis of information obtained in the course of carrying on business (as an auditor), must make a report to the relevant authorities as set out in the legislation.

Concluding on and Documenting Non-Compliance

All identification and conclusions drawn with regard to client entity non-compliance with laws and regulations should be fully documented in the audit file. The auditor needs to

---

[7] Vaeni Mac Donnell, *An Introduction to Business Law* (Chartered Accountants Ireland, 2009).

demonstrate that he has adequately carried out his responsibilities with respect to the detection of client entity non-compliance. He does so by ensuring adequate documentation is included on the audit file, which shows the process followed by the auditor and the conclusions reached, all of which should be supported by audit evidence. Where having found instances or suspected instances of non-compliance, the auditor must document the reasons for reporting, or for not reporting, these to the necessary regulatory authorities.

3.12 CONCLUSION

Frauds are being committed in all parts of the world and have been committed throughout time. Many or most entities have been victims of fraud to some extent, even though they may not know it. As we can see from **Table 3.2**, the cost of fraud can be immeasurable and far exceeds just a financial cost. All frauds have the following in common: there must be an **incentive** or pressure to commit it; there must be an **opportunity** that reveals itself, giving rise to its occurrence; and the perpetrator must be able to **rationalise** or justify it to himself.

While it is true that fraud is unavoidable, companies must still seek to prevent it insofar as is possible by strengthening their fraud prevention and detection controls and increasing internal reviews to identify control weaknesses. All the while, the auditor must remain vigilant and apply professional scepticism with respect to the existence of fraud while watching out for warning signs that fraud could occur.

ISA 240, paragraphs 17–24, detail specific procedures to be undertaken by the auditor when considering the possibility of fraud and these are summarised in **Table 3.8** below.

TABLE 3.8: SUMMARY OF AUDIT PROCEDURES PERFORMED
BY THE AUDITOR RELATING TO FRAUD

Procedures to be performed by the auditor	Expansion on procedure
Make inquiries of management	The auditor should engage in discussions with those charged with governance and others, as appropriate, to obtain an understanding of how management exercise control of the processes in place for identifying and responding to the risks of fraud. Additionally, the auditor should discuss with management the internal controls that have been established to mitigate these risks.
Perform audit procedures to identify the risk of material misstatements due to fraud	This will include evaluating the integrity of management and the inherent risks relating to the client's business. Evaluate any unusual or unexpected relationships.

Perform walkthrough tests	Walkthrough tests should be performed to confirm the adequacy of the system and related documentation and whether the control objectives are met.
Identify and assess risk at both the individual transaction level and the financial statements as a whole	The auditor should identify and assess the risk of fraud occurring at both levels. This will include evaluating the efficiency of the internal control procedures relevant to the assessed risks.
Use audit software known as computer-assisted audit techniques (CAATs) to test controls	For example, searching for journal entries over a certain limit.
Determine audit responses to the assessed risks	This will include the assignment and supervision of personnel, the accounting policies used and the unpredictability when selecting the audit procedures.
Design and perform audit procedures responsive to management override of controls	See examples included at **Table 3.2** and further examples in **Appendix 3.2** of this chapter.
Consider whether any identified misstatements or errors indicate the possibility of fraud occurring	The auditor must consider for each misstatement or error found whether he believes it to be intentional or unintentional (i.e. caused by fraud or error).

Summary of Learning Objectives

Having studied this chapter on fraud and compliance with laws and regulations, you should:

Learning Objective 1 Understand fraud in the context of audit.

Error is considered a simple, unintentional mathematical or clerical mistake in the financial statements. Fraud, on the other hand, is an intentional act using deception to obtain an unjust or illegal advantage.

Learning Objective 2 Understand the types of fraud that can occur and the forms it can take.

Fraud can be classified into two categories:
- **Fraudulent financial reporting** The intention is to present the financial statements to give a misleading impression of the performance or position of the entity for personal gain. This is usually perpetrated by management due to their ability to override controls.

- **Misappropriation of assets** This involves the theft of an entity's assets and is often perpetrated by employees (as opposed to senior management), generally for immaterial amounts.

(Note: you should be familiar with the cases noted in **Section 3.3**, **Table 3.2.** above, which support an understanding of the different types of fraud.)

Learning Objective 3 Be able to demonstrate your understanding of the 'fraud triangle' by being able to identify conditions which give rise to fraud.

Generally, there are three conditions present when fraud occurs:
- Incentive or pressure to commit fraud;
- Opportunity for fraud to occur; and
- Rationalisation by the individual or company.

To summarise the theory of the fraud triangle: if an individual cannot see a reason to commit fraud (i.e. incentive/pressure), then he will not proceed; if he cannot perceive a way (opportunity), then he cannot proceed; finally, if he cannot justify or rationalise the wrong to himself, even if the first two exist, then he is unlikely to proceed.

Learning Objective 4 Be able to explain the respective responsibilities of the management of the entity, and the auditor with regard to fraud.

Directors have an active role to both prevent and detect fraud. While they may act as a deterrent, auditors have no obligation with respect to prevention. The auditor's detection responsibility is limited to 'reasonable expectation' and is concerned with fraud causing material misstatement in the financial statements.

Learning Objective 5 Be able to identify the necessary audit procedures to detect fraud.

ISA 240 advises the following audit procedures to assist the auditor in the detection of material misstatements in the financial statements resulting from fraud:
- Maintain a state of **professional scepticism** when considering the possibility of fraud.
- Ensure adequate discussion occurs among the engagement team regarding the possibility of fraud.
- Apply appropriate risk procedures and related activities to identify and assess the risk of material misstatement due to fraud and adequately respond to those assessed risks.
- Evaluate and conclude on audit evidence through appropriately designed audit procedures.
- Obtain written representations from management and those charged with governance with regard to fraud.
- **Ensure adequate documentation exists to support risks identified and conclusions thereon**.

Learning Objective 6 Know the duty and rights of auditors to report to third parties.

Reporting to third parties is a delicate matter for the auditor, as he has a duty of confidentiality to the client entity and so must ensure he follows a systematic approach before reporting any suspected frauds (or breaches in laws and regulations) to regulatory authorities. The auditor should always maintain a state of professional scepticism when considering the possibility of fraud. The auditor should always ensure he has sufficient audit evidence before making any accusations and he should consider the suspected involvement of management (at various levels) when deciding to whom in the organisation to report the actual or suspected fraud or breach. Finally, before ever reporting to a third party, the auditor should always seek legal advice.

Learning Objective 7 Understand what is meant by the term 'aggressive earnings management'.

Aggressive earnings management is the use of methods by management to paint an unrealistically positive picture of an entity's results.

Learning Objective 8 Be able to identify ways in which computer-assisted audit techniques (CAATs) can assist the auditor in detecting fraud.

CAATs are a very important tool for the auditor in the detection of fraud. It involves the use of computer techniques in the form of audit software programmes or the interrogation of the client computer systems and reports to help in the detection of fraud. 'Data analytics tools' are the most common form of CAATs adopted by the auditor when detecting fraud.

Learning Objective 9 Know the auditor's responsibilities with respect to the entity's compliance with laws and regulations.

When a company/client entity does not act within the constraints of the law, they are said to be non-compliant with laws and regulations. The auditor's duty with respect to the detection of client entity non-compliance with laws and regulations is limited to two categories:

- Category 1 – Laws and regulations that relate directly to the financial statements; and
- Category 2 – Laws and regulations that support the legal framework in which the business of the client entity is conducted.

The auditor has an active role to play in detecting Category 1 non-compliance, whereas he only has a responsibility with regard to Category 2 if he becomes aware of a non-compliance during the course of other audit procedures. The reporting of non-compliance should be given the same consideration as that discussed above, in **Learning Objective 6**.

QUESTIONS

Self-test Questions

3.1   What is the difference between fraud and error?

3.2   Material misstatements can arise from what two types of fraud?

3.3   What is the difference between these two types of fraud?

3.4   Why are management in a better position to perpetrate fraudulent financial reporting?

3.5   What types of 'fraudulent acts' might a manager engage in when committing fraudulent financial reporting?

3.6   What are the three conditions that are said to be present when fraud occurs?

3.7   What types of incentive/pressure might be in place that could contribute to fraud?

3.8   Who is responsible for preventing and detecting fraud?

3.9   What types of audit procedure might the auditor use to identify fraud?

3.10 What is meant by the term 'professional scepticism'?

3.11 In what type of control environment might fraud be more likely to occur?

3.12 What responsibility has the auditor to report fraudulent activity to third parties?

3.13 What matters relating to fraud must be documented by the auditor?

3.14 What is aggressive earnings management?

3.15 Why is it more difficult for the auditor to detect fraud than error?

Review Questions

(See Suggested Solutions to Review Questions in **Appendix D**.)

Question 3.1

Qualitax Limited, a manufacturer of electrical goods, is a large company with good growth prospects. There is always the possibility that it could become a takeover target. You have been appointed audit senior in respect of the audit for the year ending 31 December 2012. The audit partner is concerned about the risk of fraud at Qualitax Limited and is planning a meeting of the audit team in advance of the interim audit visit to brief them about his concerns.

Requirement As part of the briefing meeting, prepare a memo outlining the key requirements of ISA 240 *The Auditor's Responsibilities Relating to Fraud in an Audit of Financial Statements*.

Question 3.2

The cost of fraud to businesses in Ireland is believed to be significant. However, it is difficult to estimate because not all fraud is discovered, not all uncovered fraud is reported, and civil or criminal action is not always pursued. Frequently, it is the 'trusted and valued' employee (the term employee includes directors) who commits business fraud.

Requirement
(a) Briefly discuss the auditor's responsibility for detecting fraud.
(b) Discuss whether fraud by management or employees not in management positions is more easily perpetrated.

APPENDIX 3.1 EXAMPLE OF A CLIENT FRAUD QUESTIONNAIRE[8]

Large Company Limited

31 December 2012

	Initials	Date
Prepared by:		
Reviewed by:		

Client Fraud Questionnaire

Meet with those charged with corporate governance (Board of Directors or a Director representing the Board) and a member of management/senior staff (separate to the Board) to discuss Fraud. Use the Checklist below as a template to record the discussion. Copy and paste the template for each person you speak to:

Question #	Questions	Yes	No
Attendees:	**Thomas Hogan (Chairperson)** **John Kelly**		
1	Do you have any knowledge of any fraud or suspected fraud that could result in a material misstatement of the financial statements? *If Yes, Please give particulars:*	☐	☐
2	Have there been any allegations of fraud with in or against the Company during the financial period? *If Yes, Please give particulars:*	☐	☐
3	Have any types of fraud ever occurred within the Company? *If Yes, please state what types of fraud have occured:*	☐	☐
4	Do you know of any unusual activity relating to making journal entries and other adjustments in the accounts? *If Yes, Please give particulars:*	☐	☐
5	Where do you believe the greatest risk of fraud is likely to occur in the Company? *Record Response here:*		
6	How do you monitor operations and procedures in order to prevent or detect fraud? *Record Response here:*		
7	What controls has management established to manage fraud risks that have been identified, or that prevent, deter and detect fraud? *Record Response here:*		

---

[8] Source: based on *Procedures for Quality Audit* (© Chartered Accountants Ireland, 2010), Appendix 2.

APPENDIX 3.2: EXAMPLES OF FRAUD

Exploitation of Systems Flaws

When employees become aware of system flaws, they can often use them to their advantage. One such fraud involved an accounts payable clerk discovering that the cancelling of a purchase invoice resulted in the system placing it for payment. The clerk, using dormant supplier accounts, changed the associated bank account details and cancelled invoices resulting in him receiving payment directly to his bank account. This cost the company approximately €260,000.

To identify such a fraud the auditor can use data analysis tools to match employee and supplier bank account details. Additionally, he can review changes to masterdata and agree to supporting documentation that backs up the change. From a management perspective, adequate segregation of duties, separating the roles of masterdata editing and accounts payable functions would have prevented this fraud from occurring.

Pyramid Schemes

A number of frauds involving pyramid schemes have occurred over the years where, for example, an individual posing as an investment advisor convinces unsuspecting investors that they could make above-average returns. He pays a return to these individuals with their own money, and then as he secures new funds from new investors, he uses this new money to pay further returns, encouraging more investment. One such scheme eventually collapsed, and this borrowing 'from Peter to pay Paul' exercise resulted in a loss of €4 million to investors.

The Fictitious Firm

Here, the fraudster sets up a fictitious supplier, which may even be registered with the CRO, or equivalent. Invoices are submitted and payments are made to this company. The key to concealing this type of fraud is keeping the payments small. The auditor should review any new suppliers detected. The company address should be checked to ensure the company is not assigned to a PO box number. The address of the individual authorising the payments to such a company should also be investigated.

Inventory Theft

Inventory is the balance sheet item most susceptible to theft. It may be written off as a loss, scrap stolen to sell as scrap or simply not entered onto the balance sheet. The auditor should investigate inventory shortfalls relative to the nature of the entity, investigate journal entries relating to write offs and stock write downs and perform variance analysis procedures.

Tampering with Employee Records

This is especially prevalent in large companies, where not everyone knows everyone else's names. When an employee leaves the firm, the fraudster, who generally is associated with the payroll department, instead of removing the employee from the records, alters their bank account details to those of the fraudster's own bank account. The auditor should identify employees who have ceased employment with the client entity and ascertain whether payments were made to those individuals or their bank accounts after their leaving dates.

Additionally, it is common for fictitious employees to be added to the payroll with the bank details matching those of the fraudster. The auditor can catch such instances by first reviewing changes to masterdata and matching these to requested back-up and, secondly, using data analysis tools to identify duplicate bank accounts. Once again the company protects itself from this type of fraud by implementing adequate segregation of duties between masterdata editing and payroll functions.

Identity Theft

Identity theft is the misuse of personal information to impersonate someone for financial gain. It can take the form of identity cloning (assuming someone else's identity), financial theft (from existing accounts or the setting up of a new accounts used to misappropriate assets) and benefit theft (impersonating an individual to obtain benefits). The most common method of stealing personal information is by way of a 'phishing attack', where an individual receives an email requesting personal information from a trusted individual or organisation. This information is then used to steal the individual's identity. The auditor and, indeed, management, have a duty to protect their clients and employees. The auditor has a legal duty to protect his client's personal and financial information, and thus his clients must be protected from the risk of identity theft. The auditor must ensure that his client's management are alert to the occurrence of identity theft and that management protect their staff from this crime. Personal records should be safeguarded, passwords changed regularly, memory keys encrypted, anti-virus and anti-spyware programmes installed, only reputable suppliers dealt with and clear policies and procedures implemented and reviewed regularly.

CHALLENGING QUESTIONS FOR PART 1

(Suggested Solutions to Challenging Questions are available through your lecturer.)

This Challenging Question aims to test your knowledge of **Chapters 1–3**. It is intended to test your practical application of what you have learned in these chapters and so you are presented with a case study on which you are asked to deliver on a number of requirements.

Question 1.1

You are an audit manager for Smith & Reilly, a long-established accountancy practice. Generally, Smith & Reilly tends to deal with smaller entities, however or a strategic decision has been made to go after larger company audits. Recently a partner of Smith & Reilly met the directors of Décor Company Limited (Décor) at a conference and gave them his business card. The partner has been a believer in Décor's long-term success for quite some time and bought shares in it two years ago. Recently the partner received a call from the directors of Décor, due to the sudden departure of the previous auditors. The partners advise you that James Collins will actually perform the audit (in the role of audit manager) if Smith & Reilly decide to proceed, but he is currently out on stress leave due to the bankruptcy of a family business that he has been a part of for many years. The partners of Smith & Reilly are really keen to get business like this, as Décor alone would increase their fee income by 21%. This type of business, along with the expected new business won due to the new bonus structure introduced by Smith & Reilly, which weights performance of its employees based on their ability to win new business with existing audit clients, will really help to put the firm on the map.

Requirement
(a) The audit engagement partner for Décor has asked you, in the absence of James Collins:
   (i) to identify any ethical, regulatory or legislative reasons why they should not accept this audit;
   (ii) to advise the partner of Smith & Reilly of any issues you have identified, as well as methods of overcoming any potential acceptance risks.
(b) The directors of Décor have specifically requested that the audit report state that the auditors guarantee the accuracy of the financial statements, as there is a potential for them to be taken over by a potential buyer and they want the buyer to use the audited financial statements as part of their due diligence for purchasing the company. The directors have indicated that they will pay extra for such a guarantee. You have been asked to outline a response to the directors specifically addressing this request.
(c) During your review of Décor you come across a newspaper clipping in relation to one of their non-executive directors (see Appendix 1), alleging his involvement in a fraud in a US company, where he also serves as director. A partner of Smith & Reilly

comments on the increase of fraud and is concerned that the staff members of the firm are not sufficiently knowledgeable about the presence of conditions that can lead to fraud. You are required to draft your opinion on what conditions are present in a business for such large-scale frauds to be occurring in companies of all sizes and in all types of industries (i.e. the Fraud Triangle).

APPENDIX 1: NEWSPAPER CLIPPING

ADG Accounting Scandal

Reports emerging today reveal that the directors (Fred Alter and John Roche) of Handy Store Limited allegedly used improper revenue recognition in order to boost revenue and therefore the profit on which their bonus was based. The company was allegedly suffering due to the economic downturn, resulting in a reduction in salary of many top executives. Additionally, with bonuses being tied to waning profits, the directors had taken a hard knock to the comfortable lifestyles to which they had become accustomed. The internal audit department, which now operates with just two staff following cost-cutting exercises, is alleged to have defended itself from not having found the error sooner due to a lack of resources.

PART II

THE AUDIT AND ASSURANCE PROCESS: PLANNING AND CONTROLS

THE AUDIT AND ASSURANCE PROCESS

The figure below outlines the stages involved in the completion of an audit engagement. This is a detailed overview and the coming chapters will deal with each of these areas in turn. As a new area of this Figure is introduced you will see this diagram repeated, with the respective area to be discussed highlighted.

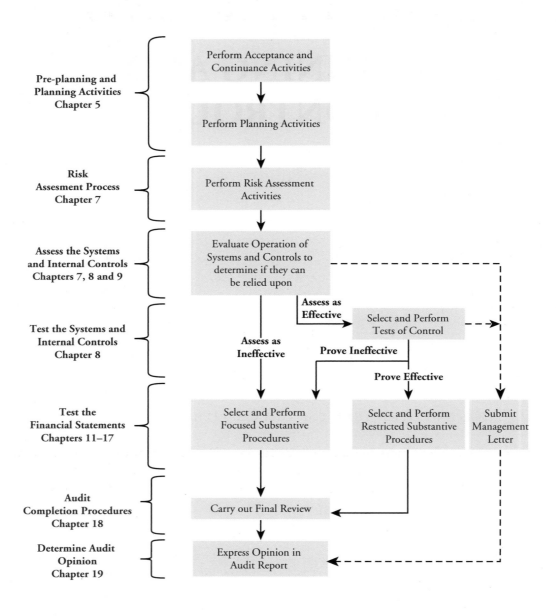

THE AUDIT PROCESS

LEARNING OBJECTIVES

Having studied this chapter on the audit process you should:
1. understand the key terms used in the external auditing environment;
2. understand the main stages of an external audit process;
3. gain an initial understanding of the terms 'management assertions' and 'audit objectives';
4. understand the difference and relationship between controls testing and substantive testing.

KEY TERMS AND DEFINITIONS FOR THIS CHAPTER

Before we move into more specific audit discussions, it is important to understand some key auditing terms used in this chapter, and indeed in this textbook. It is important to familiarise yourself with these terms and their meaning in order to understand the context of further discussions.

Analytical Procedures   These comprise the analysis of movements and relationships between figures in the financial statements. They involve the comparison of recorded values with expectations developed by the auditor.

Assertions   Explicit or implicit representations made by **management** in presenting a set of financial statements to the auditor (i.e. in providing the auditor with financial statements, management are saying, "we believe these financial statements to be valid, complete, accurate, results pertain to the organisation and are fairly classified and disclosed"). The objective of the auditor is to prove or disprove these assertions by obtaining evidence.

Audit Engagement   When a company has to go through the audit process, an auditor may use the term 'audit engagement'.

Auditor Scepticism   Professional scepticism refers to the state of mind which an auditor must maintain to help him in conducting the audit engagement appropriately. The 'scepticism approach' enables the auditor to recognise that circumstances may exist that cause the financial statements to be materially misstated, therefore he should be alert and remain cautious about such information and events that indicate the existence of material misstatement in the financial statements.

Controls Activities   Policies and procedures adopted by management of the entity to assist in ensuring the orderly and efficient conduct of its business, including adherence to internal policies, the safeguarding of assets, the prevention and detection of fraud and error, the accuracy and completeness of the accounting records and the timely preparation of reliable financial information.

Emphasis of a Matter   This is a paragraph in an **unqualified audit report** that draws the reader's attention to a particular matter disclosed in the financial statements which the auditor believes to be of significance.

Financial Statements   A set of financial statements consists of a summary of how the firm has utilised the funds provided by the shareholders. The auditor concentrates his testing on the parts of the financial statements that make up the accounting policies, accounting statements and disclosure notes therein, reviewing the other information with the financial statements for consistency.

Going Concern   A going concern is a business that operates without the threat of liquidation for the near future, usually evaluated for the next 12 months. The directors of a client entity must perform an assessment on going concern to satisfy themselves that it is appropriate to prepare the financial statements on that basis. If a client entity is not a going concern, the financial statements are prepared on a **break-up basis**.

Materiality   The magnitude of an omission or misstatement of accounting information that, in light of surrounding circumstances, makes it probable that the judgement of a reasonable person relying on the information would have been changed or influenced by the omission or misstatement. Essentially, the concept of significance to the readers of financial statements is what auditors refer to as the concept of 'materiality'.

Misstatement   An instance where a financial statement assertion is not in accordance with the criteria against which it is audited (e.g. IFRS). Misstatements may be classified as fraud (intentional), as other illegal acts, such as non-compliance with laws and regulations (intentional or unintentional), or as errors (unintentional).

Modified Opinion   A modified opinion suggests that the information provided to the auditor was limited in scope and/or the company being audited has not maintained IFRS accounting principles (i.e. the financial statements do not give a true and fair view or the truth and fairness of the financial statements cannot be determined.

Policies and Procedures   Policies outline the principles or rules that guide decisions (e.g. it is company policy to only accept return of goods within 28 days of sale). Procedures outline what action is to be taken or what steps are to be followed when performing a particular task (e.g. when a customer presents a return: request a receipt or invoice and check that the date on the receipt of invoice is within 28 days of sale; for returns over €100; contact a supervisor to approve the return).

Unqualified Auditor's Opinion   A 'clean' audit report, indicating the auditor's opinion that a client's financial statements are truly and fairly presented in accordance with agreed-upon criteria (e.g. IFRS). This is the desired auditor's opinion of each company.

4.1 INTRODUCTION

This chapter provides an overview of the external audit process from beginning to end. The individual topics are not dealt with in any depth here; rather they are introduced *in outline* to allow the reader to appreciate the overall complexity of the audit process from the outset. Topics introduced within this chapter include a reference to the chapter in which they are then discussed in more detail.

Two specific topics have been selected for expansion at this point, in order to help the reader with earlier chapters. The first of these topics relates to '**management assertions**' also known as '**audit objectives**'. An early understanding of the concept of assertions/objectives is essential for the reader to be able to understand the discussions throughout the coming chapters. **Section 4.3** in this chapter is intended to provide this.

The second selected topic relates to the distinction between '**controls testing**' and '**substantive testing**'. The area of controls testing is dealt with in detail in **Chapter 8**, and then **Chapters 11–17** fully examine the required audit procedures relating to substantive testing. These terms and concepts, however, are used from the outset of **Chapter 5** and it is important that you come to terms early on with the meaning of these two types of audit procedure. **Section 4.4** of this chapter is intended to help you to understand the difference and the relationship between controls and substantive testing.

4.2 AUDIT PROCESS OVERVIEW

Introduction

The audit process is comprised of a number of stages and it is important to have an appreciation of the broad process involved in an audit engagement. **Figure 4.1** below provides an overview of the stages for which the auditor must gather evidence in order to enable him to form an opinion on the financial statements of the client entity. It may come as a surprise that the auditor does not commence direct testing on the financial statements until quite late in the process, following a number of other key stages, i.e. he does not start to actually test the numbers in the financial statements until he completes an extensive **planning stage**.

Audit Acceptance

As we have seen in **Chapter 2**, the auditor is bound by the 'Auditors' Code',[1] which prescribes the manner in which auditors should behave. For this reason, the auditor cannot simply accept any engagement without first asking, in line with International Standard on Quality Control (UK and Ireland) 1 *Quality Control for Firms that Perform Audits and Reviews of Financial Statements, and other Assurance and Related Services Engagements* (ISQC 1), if he can act:

1. without infringing on any of the **Ethical Standards**;
2. considering the **competency, capabilities and resources** within his firm;
3. considering the **integrity of the client**.

FIGURE 4.1: AUDIT PROCESS OVERVIEW

AUDIT STAGE	RELATED CHAPTERS
Audit Acceptance	Chapter 5
Audit Planning	Chapters 5, 6, 7, and 10
Assessment of Controls	Chapters 7 and 8
Tests of Controls	Chapters 8 and 9
Substantive Tests	Chapters 11 – 17
Audit completion Steps	Chapter 18
Audit Report	Chapter 19

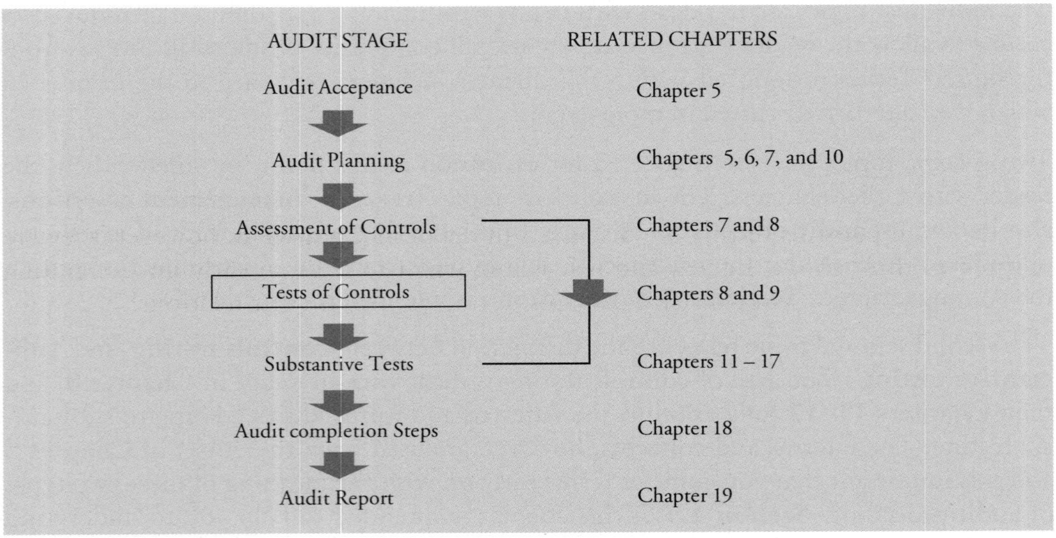

[1] Financial Reporting Council, *Scope and Authority of Audit and Assurance Pronouncements*, Appendix 2, in *Standards and Guidance 2013* (FRC, 2013).

(Each of the above is expanded upon in **Chapter 5,** Section 5.2.)

In **Chapter 2** we learned of the importance of an auditor's reputation – that this is essentially what the auditor relies upon to gain new clients and obtain confidence in his reports. As such, the auditor will not want to get involved with a client that may damage his reputation, either by association or due to the risk of issuing an inappropriate opinion.

Finally, the auditor will always contact the **outgoing auditor**, to ensure there are no circumstances of which the incoming auditor should be aware. (We will discuss this further in **Chapter 5**, Section 5.2.)

Once acceptance is confirmed, an **engagement letter** (see **Chapter 5**, Section 5.3) is prepared by the auditor for the client, outlining the agreed terms of the engagement. Both the auditor and the directors will sign the engagement letter, which effectively is a contract.

Audit acceptance is discussed in full in **Chapter 5**, Sections 5.2 and 5.3 – at this stage you should just need to be aware of the basic considerations the auditor must undertake before accepting or continuing engagement with a client entity.

Audit Planning

ISA (UK and Ireland) 300 *Planning an Audit of Financial Statements,* paragraphs 7–11, states that the auditor shall plan the audit so that the engagement is performed in an effective manner. In order to plan the engagement, the auditor needs to gain an understanding of the client's business and perform a risk assessment that will allow the auditor to develop an audit strategy, defining the nature, timing and extent of testing in response to identified risks. It is at the audit planning stage that the auditor will set the **materiality level** against which audit activities and findings will be measured. (The concept of **materiality** was introduced in **Chapter 1** and a full discussion on the topic is contained within **Chapter 5**, Section 5.4.)

Assessment of Controls

Controls and controls testing are discussed in detail in **Chapter 8**, however, they are referred to throughout the text and is it is important to have an early understanding of the importance of controls and controls testing as well as their relationship to substantive testing. It is the assessment of controls that determines the next stage of the audit and an incorrect assessment can lead to an inefficient and costly audit process. If the auditor concludes that he believes the controls to be operating effectively and consistently throughout the period being audited, he can test these controls to prove his initial assessment and reduce the volume of substantive testing that he performs. If his initial assessment is proved, through testing, to be incorrect, then the auditor will have wasted valuable time testing the controls and will still need to perform a focused level of substantive testing. A more detailed discussion of this is contained in **Chapter 8**.

Tests of Controls

Tests of controls are audit procedures performed to test the operating effectiveness of controls in preventing or detecting material misstatements at the relevant assertion level (a fuller discussion on assertions and controls testing can be found below at **Sections 4.3** and **4.4**). An auditor might use inspection of documents, observation of specific controls, re-performance of the control, or other audit procedures to gather evidence about controls. (As noted above, controls are explained further in **Section 4.4** below and discussed in detail in **Chapter 8**.)

Substantive Procedures

Substantive procedures (also referred to as **substantive testing**) are audit procedures performed to test material misstatements (monetary errors) in an account balance, transaction class or disclosure component (notes to the financial statements) of financial statements. There are two categories of **substantive procedures**:
1. **tests of details**; and
2. **substantive analytical procedures**.

Chapters 11–17 (the substantive procedures stage chapters) deal with the audit of each significant class of transaction and balance in the financial statements and these two categories of substantive procedures are explained in detail in these chapters.

Audit Completion Steps

As an audit draws to a conclusion, the auditor will perform audit procedures to obtain further audit evidence in order to draw a conclusion and finalise the audit process. The auditor will perform the following when concluding on a client entity's financial statements:
- final analytical review procedures;
- evaluation of misstatements identified during the audit;
- a subsequent events review;
- a provisions, contingent liabilities and contingent assets review;
- a going concern review;
- obtaining a letter of representation; and
- issuing a management letter.

Each of these topics is discussed in detail in **Chapter 18**.

Auditor's Report

The **auditor's report** is essentially the final product of the audit. It contains the auditor's opinion on the financial statements and is presented alongside the financial statements of the client entity. As discussed in **Chapter 1**, the audit report is intended to add credibility to the financial statements.

ISA (UK and Ireland) 700 *The Auditor's Report on Financial Statements* (Effective for audits of financial statements for periods commencing on or after 1 October 2012), paragraph 8 states:

"The Auditor's Report shall contain a clear written expression of opinion on the financial statements taken as a whole."

At this stage, the auditor makes a final decision on the truth and fairness of the financial statements after considering all errors found during the audit.

4.3 MANAGEMENT ASSERTIONS/AUDIT OBJECTIVES

Now that we have established an understanding of the stages involved in an audit engagement, we can consider two important concepts or topics that will further aid your understanding of earlier chapters. The first of these topics relates to the concept of '**management assertions**', which is the subject of this section.

Throughout this textbook the phrase 'management assertions' (or just 'assertions') is used regularly. 'Management assertions' are also frequently referred to as 'audit objectives', as explained below. (A further discussion on management assertions is contained within **Chapter 6**, Section 6.2.)

Let us first consider what the auditing standards have to say about **assertions**:

ISA (UK and Ireland) 315 (Revised) *Identifying and Assessing the Risks of Material Misstatement Through Understanding of the Entity and Its Environment*, at paragraph A110 states that:
"In representing that the financial statements are in accordance with the applicable financial reporting framework, management implicitly or explicitly makes assertions regarding the recognition, measurement, presentation and disclosure of the various elements of the financial statements and related disclosures."

Essentially, this means that in providing an auditor with a set of financial statements, the directors or those charged with governance are asserting that:
• the financial statements only include valid transactions (supported by real events);
• all balances included in these financial statements exist at the year end;
• transactions and balances are complete (all events that occurred are represented in these financial statements);
• the transactions and balances that are recorded pertain to the client entity;
• all transactions and balances have been recorded accurately and are properly classified;
• all balances are recorded at their correct value;
• all transactions have been recorded in the correct period; and
• disclosures are complete, accurate and valid.

The audit objective is to validate these assertions with respect to all transaction classes and account balances by considering the types of potential misstatement that may occur. In achieving this objective, the auditor gains comfort over the truth and fairness of the financial statements (and the assertions made by the directors).

Table 4.1 below lists the assertions that are relevant to:
(a) financial statement transactions (e.g. in the area of revenue and receivables, revenue is a transaction, each sale represents an individual transaction); and

(b)   financial statement balances (e.g. in the area of revenue and receivables, receivables is a balance representing the money owed by customers).

The assertions alter slightly, depending on whether the auditor is auditing a transaction class or balance in the financial statements. A brief explanation of the objective of each assertion is also included at **Table 4.1**. You will repeatedly see this Table adapted for each financial cycle as we walk through the audit process throughout this textbook. For now you need to familiarise yourself with the objective of each type of assertion. **Note**: assertions by financial cycle will be discussed throughout **Chapter 8** and again in the substantive **Chapters 11–17**.

Note: the terms 'assertions' and 'objectives' are used interchangeably, as the items above represent both the *assertions* made by management (management assertions) and the *objectives* of the auditor (audit objectives).

TABLE 4.1: ASSERTION CATEGORIES ABOUT TRANSACTION CLASS AND ACCOUNT BALANCE

Financial Statement Transactions		Financial Statement Balances/ Presentation and Disclosure	
Assertion/ Objective	**Transaction Class Audit Objective**	**Assertion/ Objective**	**Account Balance Audit Objectives**
Occurrence	Transactions and events that have been recorded pertain to the entity.	Existence	The asset or liability in the year-end balance sheet actually exists.
Completeness	Transactions that should have been recorded have been recorded.	Completeness	All assets and liabilities that should have been recorded have been recorded.
Rights and Obligations	Risks and rewards pass to the entity resulting from the transactions.	Rights and Obligations	The entity holds the rights to the asset and has obligations.
Accuracy/ Classification	All transactions are recorded correctly and are classified correctly in the financial statements.	Valuation	All assets and liabilities are included in the financial statements at correct valuations and are classified correctly in the financial statements.
Cut-off	Transactions and events have been recorded in the correct accounting period.		
Presentation and Disclosure	Compliance with appropriate legislation and applicable accounting standards.	Presentation and Disclosure	Compliance with appropriate legislation and applicable accounting standards.

4.4 CONTROLS VERSUS SUBSTANTIVE TESTING

In this section we will discuss the second key topic of this chapter: 'Controls versus Substantive Testing'. Controls testing, substantive testing and audit assertions will be discussed and explained extensively in later chapters. However, it is important to understand at this point the differences between controls and substantive testing. The discussion here, including the two examples, is not intended to be a full discussion on the subject of controls and substantive testing; rather it is intended to allow you to appreciate the fundamental difference and relationship between these two audit procedures.

Controls Testing and the Control Environment

Figure 4.2 below demonstrates the control environment that exists in a client entity and shows that the financial statements lie at the heart of this control environment, i.e. a weak control environment will produce a poor quality set of financial statements, whereas

FIGURE 4.2: ORGANISATIONAL ENVIRONMENT IN WHICH
FINANCIAL STATEMENTS ARE PRODUCED

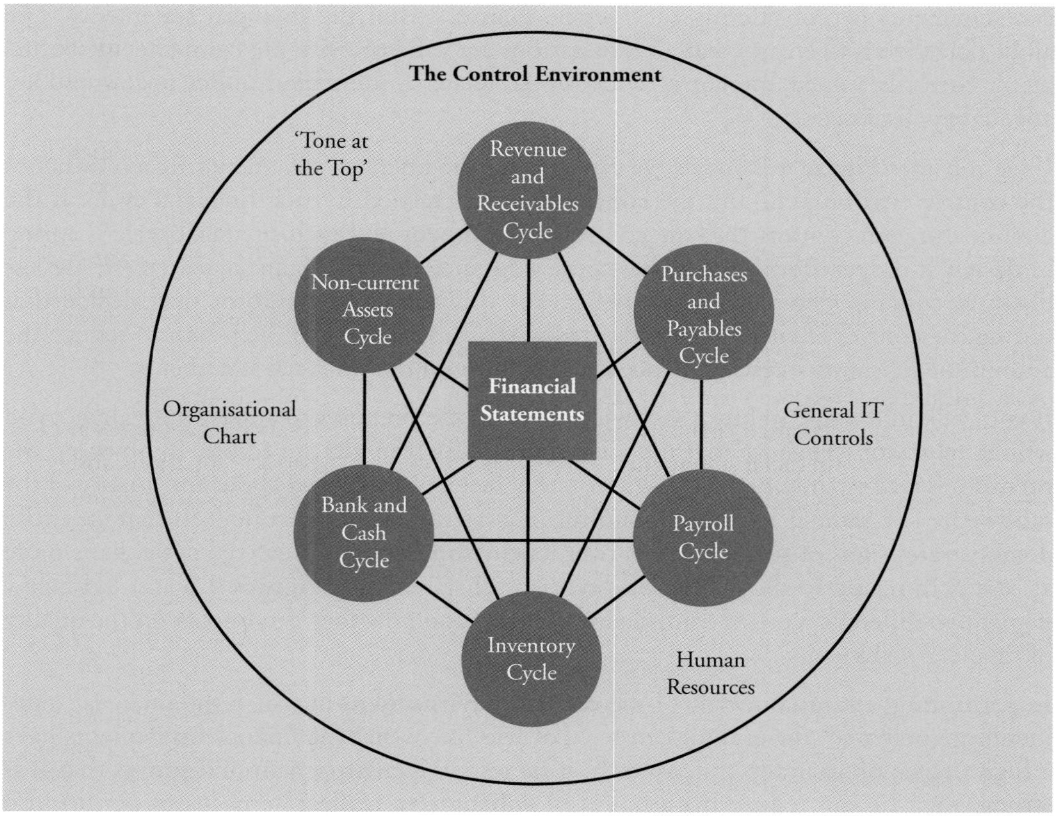

a strong control environment is more likely to produce a set of financial statements that is free from material misstatement. The figure also demonstrates that controls can exist at a 'macro level' (i.e. they serve the client entity as a *whole*) or at a transaction and account balance level (i.e. they are specific to a *particular* financial cycle). The controls noted on the outer ring of the figure are referred to as **organisational controls** (e.g. the existence of a '**tone-at-the-top**' document) whereas those noted within the inner ring are financial, cycle specific (e.g. revenue and receivables cycle).

Controls are concerned with the operating effectiveness of internal controls. The auditor's assessment of controls aims to answer:

- Is the design of the control environment and the specific control activities related to the various financial cycles strong?; and
- Did the controls operate according to the control design?; and
- Did the controls operate for the entire period under review?

Chapter 8 deals with controls and the control environment in great detail; thus, at this point, you need to understand only that the control environment and the control activities within the client entity have the ability to impact on the quality of a set of financial statements and for that reason are of great interest to the auditor.

Substantive testing is concerned with testing the truth and fairness of a set of financial statements by considering the specific figures within the financial statements. The audit objective is to ensure that all transactions are valid or exist, are complete, are accurate or correctly valued, are correctly classified, relate to the period under review and are adequately disclosed.

If we consider **Figure 4.2** above, we can see that the financial statements are a product of the control environment and the control activities related to each financial cycle. If the auditor can gain comfort that the control environment and each financial cycle is strong in design and operation, then he has some assurance that the financial statement are less likely to contain material misstatements. For this reason, the auditor may decide that testing the control environment and proving that it is strong will help him to reduce the amount of substantive testing he needs to perform on the financial statements.

If you walk into a café to buy a sandwich and find the premises to appear unhygienic, you will be reluctant to believe that the sandwich and its contents are edible. If, however, the premises is well-maintained, you will instantly feel less concerned about the quality of the sandwich. The same is true for an auditor in a client entity: when he feels that an entity demonstrates signs of strong control over its environment and financial cycle, he is more at ease with regard to the quality of the financial statements. **Figures 4.3** and **4.4** below depict two different types of control environment and how they can impact on the quality of financial statements.

In performing an initial review of the **control environment** in which the financial statements are prepared, the auditor can see that it is likely that the financial statements have a high degree of accuracy and, as such, if he tests the environment and proves that it is strong, then he can reduce the amount of **substantive testing** he needs to perform on

FIGURE 4.3: IMPACT OF A STRONG CONTROL ENVIRONMENT ON THE
AUDITOR'S CONFIDENCE IN A SET OF FINANCIAL STATEMENTS

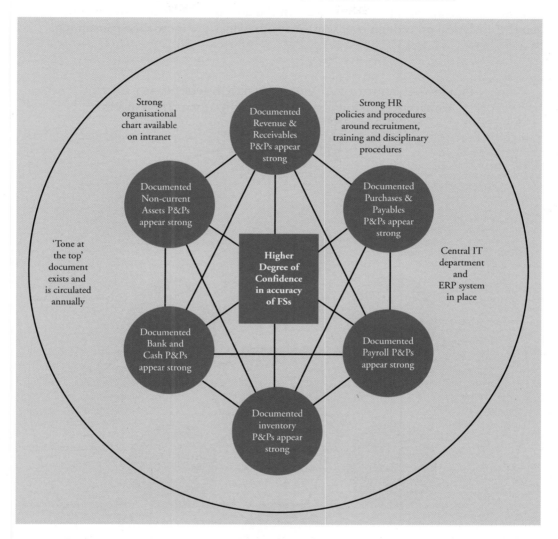

the financial statements, because he receives **assurance** from the strength of the control environment. (For the purposes of **Figures 4.4** and **4.5**, 'P&P' refers to policies and procedures, and 'ERP' refers to a type of computer system, 'enterprise resource planning' (which integrates the processes and procedures of the client entity and is generally a more robust computer system).)

In **Figure 4.3** above, by performing an initial review of the control environment in which the financial statements are prepared, the auditor can see that there is a **low probability** that the financial statements contain errors. As such, he may choose to test the environment and if he can prove that the control environment is strong, he can reduce the level of substantive testing he needs to perform on the actual set of financial statements. This reduced testing comes in the form of: performing an increased level of audit procedures prior to the year end; reducing sample sizes; and the use of substantive analytical procedures over tests of details, which are more time-consuming.

FIGURE 4.4: IMPACT OF A WEAK CONTROL ENVIRONMENT ON THE AUDITOR'S CONFIDENCE IN A SET OF FINANCIAL STATEMENTS

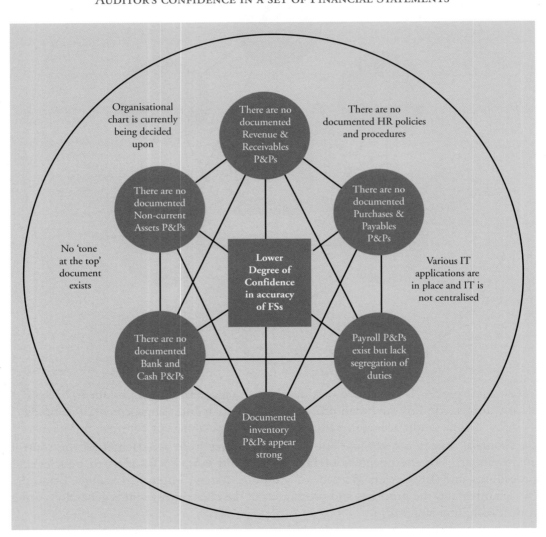

In **Figure 4.4**, by performing an initial review of the control environment in which the financial statements are prepared, the auditor can see that there is a **high probability** that

the financial statements contain errors. As such, he would choose not to test the environment as it would likely prove that the control environment is weak and therefore not allow the auditor to reduce the level of substantive testing he needs to perform on the actual set of financial statements. His testing of the control environment would give him no assurance and, essentially, would have been an inefficient use of his time.

Each of the above topics is discussed in considerable detail in the coming chapters; as mentioned, at this point the objective is to appreciate some key auditing terminology and activities, which will enhance the reading of earlier chapters.

4.5 CONCLUSION

The **audit opinion** is intended to provide reasonable assurance that the financial statements are presented fairly, in all material respects, and give a true and fair view in accordance with the financial reporting framework. The single biggest risk to the auditor is in issuing an incorrect opinion. Similar to many organisations, the auditing firm aims to make a profit and as such the auditor needs to strike a balance between minimising auditing risk and maximising audit efficiency. The auditor must take on clients with acceptable risk, plan the audit to deal with risk areas in the most efficient way and issue an audit opinion, while at the same time make an acceptable profit from the engagement. All of the stages of the audit are designed to address these two priorities.

SUMMARY OF LEARNING OBJECTIVES

Having studied this chapter on the audit process you should:

Learning Objective 1 Understand the key terms used in the external audit environment.

The Key Terms and Definitions provided at the outset of this chapter should be fully read and understood by the student before progressing on to further chapters.

Learning Objective 2 Understand the main stages of the external audit process.

The audit process is comprised of a number of stages and it is important to have an early appreciation of the broad process involved in an audit engagement. The broad stages include: audit acceptance; audit planning; assessment of controls; test of controls; substantive tests; audit completion steps; and the audit report. The actual financial statements are only considered in detail at the **substantive** stage and much of the procedure prior to this is centred on planning. These various planning activities are aimed at ensuring that the nature, timing and extent of audit procedures are adequate to address the risks and assertions that exist in the financial statements so as to ensure that the auditor detects material misstatements.

Learning Objective 3 Gain an initial understanding of the terms 'management assertions' and 'audit objectives'.

In providing the auditor with a set of financial statements, the directors implicitly imply that the financial statements are complete, accurate, relate to transactions and balances that actually occurred or exist, contain only transactions that relate to the period under review, are appropriately classified and include adequate and complete disclosures. These are referred to as 'management assertions' or just the 'assertions'. The audit *objective* is to validate these assertions with respect to all transaction classes and account balances by considering the types of potential misstatement that may occur. In achieving this objective, the auditor gains comfort over the truth and fairness of the financial statements. As such, the terms 'management assertions' and 'audit objectives' are often used interchangeably.

Learning Objective 4 Understand the difference and relationship between controls testing and substantive testing.

'Controls testing' is concerned with the operating effectiveness of the client entity's internal controls. The auditor may choose to test these controls to prove that the financial statements were prepared in a strongly controlled environment. If the auditor can prove (through testing) that the financial statements were prepared within a strong control environment, then he gains 'comfort' over the assertions of the transaction classes and balances in the financial statements. This comfort or assurance gained allows the auditor to perform a reduced level of substantive testing (i.e. testing of actual figures and disclosures in the financial statements) and hence perform a more efficient audit. This reduced testing is reflected by an increased level of audit procedures prior to the year-end; reducing sample sizes; and the use of substantive analytical procedures over tests of details.

QUESTIONS

Self-test Questions

4.1   What are the main stages of an external audit?
4.2   What is the significance of the 'acceptance stage' of an audit?
4.3   What is meant by the term 'audit assertions'?
4.4   List five audit assertions.
4.5   Why would an auditor not test the control environment in every instance?
4.6   What is the difference between controls and substantive testing?

Review Questions

Note: no review questions are included in this chapter as each topic is dealt with and examined in detail in later chapters. At this point you should have a basic appreciation for the broad stages involved in an audit, what is meant by the term audit assertions, what the difference is between controls and substantive testing and the relationship between them and, finally, the limitations of an audit.

THE AUDIT AND ASSURANCE PROCESS

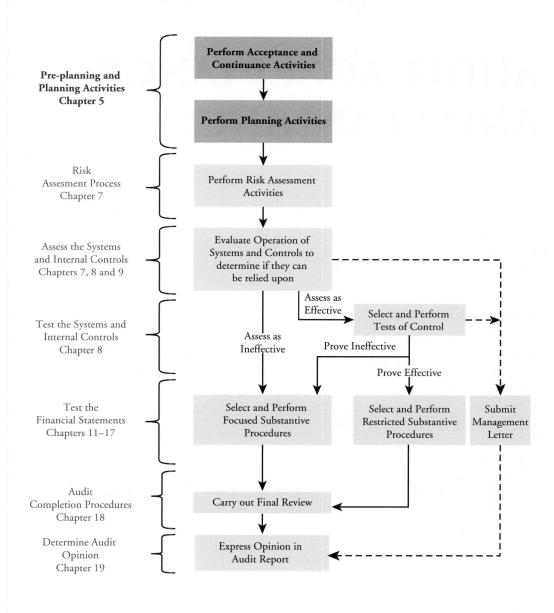

Pre-planning and
Planning Activities
Chapter 5

**Perform Acceptance and
Continuance Activities**

Perform Planning Activities

Risk
Assesment Process
Chapter 7

Perform Risk Assessment
Activities

Assess the Systems
and Internal Controls
Chapters 7, 8 and 9

Evaluate Operation of
Systems and Controls to
determine if they can
be relied upon

Assess as
Effective

Test the Systems and
Internal Controls
Chapter 8

Select and Perform
Tests of Control

Assess as
Ineffective

Prove Ineffective

Prove Effective

Test the
Financial Statements
Chapters 11–17

Select and Perform
Focused Substantive
Procedures

Select and Perform
Restricted Substantive
Procedures

Submit
Management
Letter

Audit
Completion Procedures
Chapter 18

Carry out Final Review

Determine Audit
Opinion
Chapter 19

Express Opinion in
Audit Report

5

AUDIT ACCEPTANCE AND PLANNING

5.1 Introduction
5.2 Audit Acceptance
5.3 Audit Engagement Letters
5.4 Audit Planning
5.5 Conclusion

LEARNING OBJECTIVES

Having studied this chapter on audit acceptance and planning you should:
1. understand and be able to apply the audit acceptance and continuance considerations;
2. know the role and contents of an engagement letter;
3. know the stages of audit planning and be able to distinguish between the overall audit strategy and the audit plan;
4. have developed an understanding of the role of analytical procedures at the planning stage;
5. appreciate the concept of materiality including how and why it is calculated; and
6. able to discuss the options available to the auditor with regard to nature, timing and extent of audit procedures when designing the audit plan.

CHECKLIST OF RELEVANT STANDARDS

The relevant standards covered in this chapter are:

- ISA (UK and Ireland) 210 *Agreeing the Terms of Audit Engagement* (ISA 210)
- ISA (UK and Ireland) 220 *Quality Control for an Audit of Financial Statements* (ISA 220)
- ISA (UK and Ireland) 300 *Planning an Audit of Financial Statements* (ISA 300)
- ISA (UK and Ireland) 320 *Materiality in Planning and Performing an Audit* (ISA 320)
- ISA (UK and Ireland) 330 *The Auditor's Reponses to Assessed Risks* (ISA 330)
- ISA (UK and Ireland) 520 *Analytical Procedures* (ISA 520)
- ISA (UK and Ireland) 570 *Going Concern* (ISA 570)
- ISA (UK and Ireland) 620 *Using the Work of an Auditor's Expert* (ISA 620)
- ISQC 1 (UK and Ireland) *Quality Control for Firms that Perform Audits and Reviews of Financial Statements, and Other Assurance and Related Services Engagements* (ISQC 1)

KEY TERMS AND DEFINITIONS FOR THIS CHAPTER

Analytical Procedures   These comprise the analysis of movements and relationships between figures in the financial statements. They involve the comparison of recorded values with expectations developed by the auditor.

Audit Plan   The audit plan is more detailed than the overall audit strategy. It includes the nature, timing and extent of audit procedures to be performed.

Audit Strategy   The audit strategy includes the more general audit requirements, such as the resources required, the budget, the timing and the management of how the audit is to be carried out.

Auditor's Expert   If expertise in a field other than accounting or auditing is necessary to obtain sufficient appropriate audit evidence, the auditor shall determine whether to use the work of an auditor's expert. For example, if the entity has revalued property in the period, the auditor will require the use of an auditor's expert in the form of a property valuer as the auditor is not an expert in this field.

Engagement Letter   A written document, signed by the client and the audit firm, confirming the auditor's acceptance of the appointment and including a summary of the responsibilities of those charged with governance and of the auditor, the scope of the engagement and the form of any reports to be issued by the auditor.

Going Concern   A going concern is a business that operates without the threat of liquidation for the near future, usually evaluated for the following 12 months.

Recurring Audit   Long-standing audit client.

Random Sampling   The process of applying auditing procedures to less than 100% of a population, such that each unit has an equal chance of being selected.

Sample Population   All of the items that make up the balance or transaction being tested by the auditor, e.g. the receivables balance population is made up of all the customers' individual balances.

5.1 INTRODUCTION

This chapter deals with the issues and activities facing the auditor prior to commencement of the fieldwork of an audit. These are referred to as the audit acceptance and planning stages. Collectively, these stages allow the auditor to identify key areas of risk and concerns, which will help him make decisions such as:

- whether to accept or continue an engagement;
- what level of audit staff is required to carry out the audit;
- whether outside experts will be needed; and
- the nature, timing and extent of the work to be done.

Section 5.2 outlines the considerations that the auditor must take into account when deciding whether or not to accept or continue an audit engagement. Once the engagement is accepted, the auditor issues an audit engagement letter, which is discussed in **Section 5.3**.

In **Section 5.4** we consider the requirements of ISA (UK and Ireland) 300 *Planning an Audit of Financial Statements* (ISA 300). Within this section we discuss the overall '**audit strategy**' and the '**audit plan**'. This section deals with some specific procedures that the auditor needs to carry out at the planning stage. Two topics are of particular importance as they are regularly referred to in later chapters: the concept of '**materiality**' and the use of '**analytical procedures**'. The audit plan is introduced later in this section. The audit plan is more detailed than the overall audit strategy and determines the '**nature**', '**timing**' and '**extent**' of further audit procedures. Finally, within this section we address the importance of documenting the audit plan and audit strategy.

5.2 AUDIT ACCEPTANCE

Introduction

When approached by a new client who wishes to engage an audit firm for performance of an audit of its financial statements, the auditor is required to consider whether he should accept the engagement. Similarly, each year in relation to existing audit clients, the auditor must consider whether he should continue the engagement with the client. This process for new and existing clients is known as **acceptance and continuance**.

Acceptance and Continuance

As stated in ISQC 1 (UK and Ireland) *Quality Control for Firms that Perform Audits and Reviews of Financial Statements, and Other Assurance and Related Services Engagements* (ISQC 1), audit firms should establish policies and procedures for the acceptance and continuance of client relationships and specific engagements. These should be designed to provide the audit firm with reasonable assurance that it will only undertake or continue relationships and engagements where it:

1. has considered the **integrity of the client** and does not have information that would lead it to conclude that the client lacks integrity;
2. is **competent to perform** the engagement and has the capabilities, time and resources to do so; and
3. can comply with **Ethical Standards**.

ISA (UK and Ireland) 220 *Quality Control for an Audit of Financial Statements* (ISA 220), states that:

"The engagement partner shall be satisfied that appropriate procedures regarding the acceptance and continuance of client relationships and audit engagements have been followed, and shall determine that conclusions reached in that regard are appropriate." (ISA 220, para 12)

There may be instances where there is an outgoing auditor (predecessor auditor) that the potential engagement is replacing. Under ISA (UK and Ireland) 300 *Planning an Audit of Financial Statements* (ISA 300), the auditor should communicate with the " ... predecessor auditor, where there has been a change of auditors, in compliance with relevant ethical requirements" (ISA 300, para 13(b)).

The overriding theme is that an audit firm will want to avoid engaging with a client entity that brings with it unacceptable levels of risk and it is therefore essential that a thorough assessment is made of the prospective engagement prior to the audit firm commencing or continuing engagement with the client entity.

Table 5.1 summarises the auditor's considerations when deciding whether to engage with a new client entity.

The final decision as to whether to engage with a new client or continue engaging with an existing client is the responsibility of the audit engagement partner. Where he determines that the audit firm can engage successfully with the client entity, the next stage in the initial phase of the audit process is the issuance of an **engagement letter** (see below, **Section 5.3**).

While the considerations above are essential for new client entities, they are as important when considering whether or not to continue engagement with existing client entities. When it comes to continuing audits, the auditor should reconsider each of the points noted above with respect to continued management integrity, audit firm competence and ethical compliance, to ensure there is no change to the initial assessment of these areas. ISA 220, paragraph 13, states:

"If the engagement partner obtains information that would have caused the firm to decline the audit engagement had that information been available earlier, the engagement partner shall communicate that information promptly to the firm, so that the firm and the engagement partner can take the necessary action."

TABLE 5.1: QUESTIONS AN AUDITOR MUST CONSIDER BEFORE COMMENCING OR CONTINUING AN AUDIT ENGAGEMENT

1. Should I Act? Is it wise to accept this engagement considering:

(a) Client Integrity Are there any questions over the potential client that will create unacceptable risk?	What is the identity and business reputation of the client entity's principal owners, key management, related parties and those charged with its governance? What is the nature of the client entity's operations, including its business practices? What are the attitudes of the client entity's key players towards such matters as aggressive interpretation of accounting standards and the internal control environment? Is the client entity aggressively concerned with maintaining the audit firm's fees as low as possible? Are there indications of an inappropriate limitation on the scope of audit work? Are there indications that the client entity might be involved in money laundering or other criminal activities? What are the reasons for the proposed appointment of the firm and non-reappointment of the previous firm?

2. Can I Act? Is there any reason why I should not or cannot accept this engagement considering:

(b) Competence and Resources Do I have the competency and resources to perform this engagement?	Do the audit firm's personnel have the knowledge of the relevant industry or subject matters? Do the audit firm's personnel have experience with relevant regulatory or reporting requirements, or the ability to gain the necessary skills and knowledge effectively? Does the audit firm have sufficient personnel with the necessary capabilities and competences? Will the firm require the use of outside experts? Does the audit firm have individuals meeting the criteria and eligibility requirements to perform 'engagement quality control review' in place, where applicable? Will the audit firm be able to complete the engagement within the reporting deadline?
(c) Ethics Will this contravene any ethical requirements?	Is my audit firm sufficiently independent of the client? Will acceptance of the audit create an actual or perceived conflict of interest with an existing audit client?
(d) Outgoing Auditors Have I contacted the outgoing auditors?	Do the outgoing auditors indicate any reason why they feel they were unjustly removed from the position of auditor?

EXAMPLE 5.1: THE ACCEPTANCE DECISION

You are an audit manager in an audit firm, called Baxter & Hynes, that has been approached by Minder Ltd. Minder Ltd has decided to change its auditors as the directors are not happy with the efficiency and professionalism of the existing audit firm. Minder Ltd received a qualified opinion from its auditors in the prior year with which it continues to disagree. Minder Ltd is the parent of two subsidiaries, Black Ltd and Red Ltd. You recall something in the newspaper with respect to the alleged fraud of a director within Black Ltd. Red Ltd is the direct competitor of one of your largest clients. From a query with the entity's accounts department, you note that the payroll function for Black and Red Ltd is carried out by your firm. The year-end is 30 June 2012 and the entity is requesting that the audit be completed by the end of August 2012. July and August are the busiest periods for Baxter & Hynes, which struggles to resource Sarbanes–Oxley (SOX) audits during this time period.

Should Baxter & Hynes engage with this client entity?

Baxter & Hynes would be advised not to engage with this client entity after considering the following:

- **Integrity of the Client** A senior member of the client entity is alleged to have committed fraud, which calls into question the integrity of the client entity. There may be reasons, other than those stated, behind their intention to remove the existing auditors. The existing auditors should be contacted to enquire if there are any reasons why they feel Baxter & Hynes should not accept the engagement. This may be driven by the qualification in the prior year rather than the efficiency and professionalism of the existing auditors. The existence of that qualification brings with it a risk that most audit firms would prefer to avoid. Finally, with respect to integrity, the client entity appears to be putting undue pressure on the audit firm to complete the accounts and audit within an eight-week period.
- **Ethical Considerations** Acceptance of this audit would create an actual or perceived conflict of interest with an existing audit client of Baxter & Hynes, due to the fact that Red Ltd is the direct competitor of the existing client. Additionally, a self-review threat exists due to the fact that Baxter & Hynes carry out other services for the client entity in the form of payroll.
- **Competence to perform** Baxter & Hynes may not have the resources to complete this audit in the time period requested due to existing commitments to SOX audits.

5.3 AUDIT ENGAGEMENT LETTERS

Introduction

When an audit is accepted, an **engagement letter** must be issued by the audit firm to the client entity. As stated in ISA (UK and Ireland) 210 *Agreeing the Terms of Audit Engagements* (ISA 210), the auditor and the client entity should agree on the terms of the engagement and the terms should be recorded in writing. Issuance of an engagement letter is in the interest of both the audit firm and the client entity as it helps avoid any misunderstandings with respect to the engagement. The client entity and the auditor should agree on all the terms of the engagement and this agreement should be recognised through the signing of the engagement letter by both parties.

Engagement Letter Contents

As outlined in ISA 210, in the UK and Ireland the auditor should ensure that the engagement letter documents and confirms the scope of the appointment and includes: a summary of the responsibilities of those charged with governance; a summary of the responsibilities of the auditor; the scope of the engagement; and the form of any reports to be issued by the auditor.

The following are the main points to be included in an engagement letter:
- the objective of the audit of the financial statements;
- management's responsibility for the financial statements;
- the scope of the audit, including reference to applicable legislation, regulations, or pronouncements of professional bodies to which the auditor adheres;
- the form of any reports or other communications resulting from the engagement;
- the fact that, because of the test nature and other inherent limitations of an audit, together with the inherent limitations of internal control, there is an unavoidable risk that even some material misstatement may remain undiscovered;
- a request for unrestricted access to whatever records, documentation and other information are required in connection with the audit; and
- the basis of the audit fee calculation.

See **Appendix 5.1** at the end of this chapter for a sample engagement letter sourced from the FRC's website.

Recurring Audits

A new engagement letter may not be required each year of a continuing engagement (**recurring audit**). However, each year the auditor should "… assess whether circumstances require the terms of the audit engagement to be revised and whether there is a need to remind the entity of the existing terms of the audit engagement" (ISA 210, para 13).

Factors that could trigger the need for a new letter may include the following:
- any indication that the client misunderstands the objective and scope of the audit;
- any revised or special terms of the engagement;
- a recent change of senior management or those charged with governance;
- a significant change in ownership;
- a significant change in nature or size of the client entity's business; and
- legal or regulatory requirements.

In some cases, the client entity may request a change to the terms of the engagement. Should this arise, the auditor and the client entity should agree on the new terms, as outlined in ISA 210, paragraphs 14–17, provided that the auditor feels there is reasonable justification for changing the terms. Where the auditor is unable to agree to a change of the engagement and is not permitted to continue the original engagement, the auditor should withdraw and consider whether there is any obligation, either contractual or otherwise, to report to other parties, such as those charged with governance or shareholders, the circumstances necessitating the withdrawal.

Once the auditor has accepted the new engagement, or agreed to continue an existing engagement, he must commence audit planning.

5.4 AUDIT PLANNING

Introduction

ISA 300 states that the auditor should plan an audit so that the engagement will be "performed in an effective manner" (ISA 300, para 4) and reduce audit risk to an acceptably low level. In order to achieve this, planning an audit at two levels is necessary, with ISA 300 requiring the auditor to:
1. establish an overall **audit strategy** (ISA 300, paras 7–8); and
2. develop an **audit plan** (ISA 300, para 9).

It is important at this point to understand what is meant by the terms 'overall audit strategy' and 'audit plan'. An audit strategy essentially describes the general terms of how an audit is to be carried out and an audit plan details the specific procedures to be carried out to implement the strategy and complete the audit.

Audit engagement partners and key audit team members should be involved in the planning phase of the audit in order to share knowledge and experience with junior team members and alert the team to areas where the assessed risk of misstatement could be high. It also helps to ensure that audit work is assigned to team members with the appropriate level of skill and experience. The nature and extent of planning activities will not be the same on all engagements and will depend on the size and complexity of the client, the auditor's previous involvement with the client and changes in circumstances that occur during the audit engagement.

It is important for the audit team to realise that planning is not a discrete activity; while it initially takes place at the commencement of the audit, planning does not cease at this point. Planning is a dynamic process that should continue during the entire audit cycle, being amended and adapted as new information becomes available or issues arise during the course of audit testing.

The Overall Audit Strategy

Before the auditor can develop a detailed **audit plan**, which outlines the testing that the audit team must perform in order to gain sufficient appropriate audit evidence, the auditor must consider a number of key factors at the outset in order to ensure that the detailed plan is the most efficient approach to the completion of the audit. This process leads to the development of the overall **audit strategy**, which guides the detailed audit plan. Outlined below are the key areas the auditor must consider when developing the overall audit strategy:

1. characteristics of the engagement;
2. roles and responsibilities within the audit team;
3. the need for experts;
4. determining **materiality**;
5. understanding the client entity (risk and internal control assessment);
6. preliminary **analytical procedures**; and
7. going concern.

Characteristics of the Engagement

It is important for the auditor to gain an understanding of the broad characteristics of the client he is dealing with. In doing so, the auditor should consider:

- the **characteristics of the engagement that define its scope**, such as the financial reporting framework used, industry-specific reporting requirements or the locations of the divisions within the entity;
- the **reporting obligations** for the entity in order to determine the timing of the audit (i.e. to ensure filing dates are met);
- key dates and format for **communication with management**;
- identification of **material balances within the financial statements**;
- consideration of **prior years' issues and errors**;
- consideration of **experience gained** during other engagements performed for the client entity or during the acceptance and continuance phase;
- consideration of **laws and regulations** which apply to the client entity (including tax laws); and
- identification of **related parties** and transactions with related parties requiring disclosure.

Roles and Responsibilities within the Audit Team

As part of the planning stages of the audit, the resourcing of the engagement must be considered. ISA 300, paragraph 11, states:

"The auditor shall plan the nature, timing and extent of direction and supervision of engagement team members and the review of their work."

An audit team usually consists of a partner, manager, audit senior and junior (see **Table 5.2**). The following are factors to be considered when selecting the audit team.

- Does the proposed audit team have the necessary skills and resources?
- Does the proposed audit team have the correct level of staff for the job?
- Are all staff members independent of the client?
- Is continuity of staff required?
- Has an engagement quality control reviewer been assigned?
- Is each member of the team aware of his role and responsibility within the audit team?

- Have dates for audit team meetings been set?
- Have dates been agreed with the client for the commencement of the audit, attendance of stocktakes, etc.?
- If the work of experts or other auditors is to be relied on, have these parties been contacted and dates agreed by which their fieldwork is to be completed (ISA (UK and Ireland) 620 *Using the Work of an Auditor's Expert* (ISA 620))?
- Has a budget been set for the audit engagement?

Note: continuity of team members from year to year can introduce efficiency into the audit as the team members will have gained knowledge and experience on working with the client and therefore be more prepared than newly introduced staff.

TABLE 5.2: ROLE OF TEAM MEMBERS

	Audit Partner	**Audit Manager**	**Audit Senior**	**Audit Junior**
Roles and Responsibilities	Acceptance and continuance procedures.	Review of audit file.	Liaise with manager with regard to audit planning.	Perform audit work.
	Planning and completion stages.	Responsible for planning.	Review audit junior's work.	Notify audit senior of any issues.
	Reviewing critical areas of the file.	Review of financial statements prior to audit partner's review.	Notify manager of contentious issues.	
	Reviewing the financial statements prior to being issued.	Review of critical matters prior to audit partner's review.	Perform audit work.	
	Signing of audit report on financial statements.	Review of client audit file prepared by audit senior.	Provide on-the-job training for audit junior.	
			Prepare client audit working file and/ or reports to other auditors.	

The Need for Experts

ISA 620 states:

"If expertise in a field other than accounting or auditing is necessary to obtain sufficient appropriate audit evidence, the auditor shall determine whether to use the work of an auditor's expert" (ISA 620, para 7).

Instances where experts may be required include areas such as: valuation of complex financial instruments, property, jewellery, works of art, etc.; actuarial calculation of liabilities associated with insurance contracts or employee benefit plans; and estimation of oil and gas reserves.

ISA 620 does not, however, diminish the fact that the auditor has "sole responsibility for the audit opinion expressed". The auditor must takes steps, as necessary, to determine that "the work of that expert is adequate for the auditor's purposes" and only then may he "accept that expert's findings or conclusions in the expert's field as appropriate audit evidence" (ISA 620, para 3).

Before engaging the work of the expert, the auditor is responsible for evaluating the necessary qualifications, competence, capabilities and objectivity of the expert.

In evaluating the work of the expert, the auditor must evaluate the adequacy, including:
• considering "the relevance and reasonableness of that expert's findings or conclusions, and their consistency with other audit evidence" obtained;
• considering the "relevance and reasonableness" of any assumptions or methods used by the expert;
• considering the "relevance, completeness and accuracy of that source data" used by the expert to draw on his conclusion. (ISA 620, para 12)

Determining Materiality

In **Chapter 1** it was established that the auditor expresses an opinion with reasonable assurance that the financial statements are free from material misstatement. Reasonable assurance is measured by reference to materiality.

What is Materiality? Before we discuss ISA (UK and Ireland) 320 *Materiality in Planning and Performing an Audit* (ISA 320), we must first refer back to ISA (UK and Ireland) 200 *Overall Objectives of the Independent Auditor and the Conduct of an Audit in Accordance with International Standards on Auditing* (ISA 200), which states:
"... the overall objectives of the auditor are:

(a) To obtain reasonable assurance about whether the financial statements as a whole are free from material misstatement, whether due to fraud or error ...". (ISA 200, para 11)

Let us remind ourselves of these key terms, introduced in **Chapter 1**:

Misstatement ISA (UK and Ireland) 450 *Evaluation of Misstatements Identified During the Audit* (ISA 450), paragraph 4: "A difference between the amounts, classification, presentation, or disclosure of a reported financial statement item and the amount, classification, presentation, or disclosure that is required for the item to be in accordance with applicable financial reporting framework. Misstatements can arise from fraud or error."

Materiality Misstatements are considered to be material "if they individually or in the aggregate, could reasonably be expected to influence the economic decisions of users taken on the basis of the financial statements" (ISA 320, para 2).

Basically speaking, when a misstatement (or the aggregate of all misstatements) is significant enough that it could change or influence the decision of an informed person, a material misstatement has occurred.

We now consider the following examples, which address the concept of materiality.

EXAMPLE 5.2: SCENARIOS ASSISTING WITH THE UNDERSTANDING OF MATERIALITY

Scenario 1
The inventory balance included in the financial statements is the highest balance on the balance sheet at €10,000,000. The auditor has discovered during the performance of audit testing that inventory has been **understated** by €2,500,000 (i.e. 25%).
If the error identified is not adjusted, then the financial statements will be materially misstated due to the size of the error in relation to the financial statements taken as a whole.

Scenario 2
The inventory balance included in the financial statements is the highest balance on the balance sheet at €10,000,000. The auditor has discovered during the performance of audit testing that inventory has been **understated** by €2,500 (i.e. 0.025%)
If the error is not adjusted, the financial statements will not be materially misstated due to the size of the error in relation to the financial statements as a whole.

How do I calculate Materiality? There is no prescribed mathematical formula that will generate **materiality** for every client and ISA 320, paragraph 4, advises:
> "The auditor's determination of materiality is a matter of professional judgment, and is affected by the auditor's perception of the financial information needs of users of the financial statements."

The standard does, however, offer guidance on how to approach the calculation of materiality:
1. identification of a benchmark (critical balance); and
2. application of a percentage against that benchmark.

A benchmark, or critical balance, is the key figure in the financial statements. ISA 320, paragraph A3, indicates areas that can assist the auditor in identifying what the benchmark may be for a particular client's accounts and includes:
- **Financial Statement Elements** What makes up the financial statements, e.g. assets, liabilities, equity, revenue, expenses, etc.?
- **Items of User Focus** Is the user focused on financial performance and therefore more interested in revenue and profit?
- **Nature of the Entity** Lifecycle, industry, economic environment, for example, if the client is in property development, then the revenue could be nil in some years and so the benchmark may be assets held for resale.
- **Ownership Structure** If the company is financed primarily by debt rather than equity, then the user may be more interested in assets and the claims on assets than on the equity earnings.

TABLE 5.3: MATERIALITY BENCHMARK PERCENTAGES

Benchmark	%
Earnings before tax	5–10%
Total Revenues	½–1%
Total Assets	½–2%
Equity	1–2%
Net Assets	½–1%

The standard avoids giving quantitative guidelines on what percentages to apply to the benchmark. However, common methods have developed in practice that can be used to quantify materiality, as set out in **Table 5.3**.

What is Performance Materiality? The context of performance materiality is set out in ISA 320. It is defined in the standard as:

> "the amount or amounts set by the auditor at less than materiality for the financial statements as a whole to reduce to an appropriately low level the probability that the aggregate of uncorrected and undetected misstatements exceeds materiality for the financial statements as a whole." (ISA 320, para 9)

Performance materiality can also be set at transaction or account balance level.

EXAMPLE 5.3: DETERMINATION OF MATERIALITY, PLANNING MATERIALITY
AND USING MATERIALITY TO ASSESS MISSTATEMENTS

(Refer to **Appendix C** at the end of this textbook, Large Company Limited (Pro-forma Financial Statements).

Step 1 – Determining the overall materiality level for the financial statements as a whole

From the Directors' Report in the accounts of Large Company Ltd, we note that this company is involved in the manufacture of furniture and revenue has increased by 41% to €280,250,000. We also note that it is believed revenue will continue to grow due to a push into the luxury market. It is fair to say that any shareholder would be interested in revenue growth and how it drives the profitability of the company (i.e. taking into account the effect on margins of the purchasing of higher value products). As such we conclude that the benchmark (critical balance in the financial statements) is profit before tax. Profit before tax in the statement of profit or loss and other comprehensive income is €72,850,000. If we were to apply common methods (**Table 5.3**), we would take 5–10% of this profit before tax as materiality. We will assume that we are prudent auditors and as such we choose materiality at the lower end of this percentage range, and therefore we apply 5% (the application of a percentage within the range is completely judgemental and is based on the auditor's experience and is sometimes based on the internal guidance and practice of the audit firm). Applying the 5% would derive a materiality level for the financial statements as a whole to be €3,642,500.

Step 2 – Setting a performance materiality

The auditor will still need to consider materiality levels for particular classes of transactions, account balances or disclosures, where appropriate. This can be achieved by setting a performance materiality level, which can be set at, *say*, 75% (again a judgement call by the auditor) and acts as a cushion to take account of undetected errors by taking in more balances to be tested than otherwise would have been, if the higher materiality level was applied (i.e. the application of the lower materiality means more items get tested). By creating a performance materiality of €2,731,875 (€3,642,500 × 75%), we create a cushion of €910,675, which reduces the risk of the auditor issuing an unqualified opinion on a set of accounts that contain a material misstatement.

Step 3 – Using materiality in assessing misstatements

If, during testing, the auditor was to find a misstatement with respect to investment revenue resulting in investment revenue being overstated by €50,000. Would the auditor consider this to be a material misstatement? No, the €50,000 is well below materiality and does not pose a concern for the auditor. He will, however, take this €50,000 to an error schedule to ensure that when added to other misstatements, they do not, in aggregate, create a material misstatement.

Now consider that the auditor during his testing finds that Property, Plant and Equipment is overstated by €3,200,000. Is this material? Yes, if we consider performance materiality, then the overstatement is material as it exceeds €2,731,875. If we had assessed it against materiality level for financial statements as a whole it would not have been material but would not have left room for, first, further errors and, secondly, undetected errors and, as such, the application of the performance materiality offers the auditor a margin for error.

Understanding the Client Entity (Risk and Internal Control Assessment)

ISA (UK and Ireland) 315 *Identifying and Assessing the Risks of Material Misstatement Through Understanding of the Entity and Its Environment*, outlines the auditor's responsibilities with respect to:
1. risk assessment procedures and related activities;
2. the required understanding of the entity and its environment, including the entity's internal control;
3. identifying and assessing the risks of material misstatement; and
4. documentation.

A full discussion of the requirements of ISA 315 is contained within **Chapter 7**, "The Risk Assessment Process", and **Chapter 8**, "Controls and Controls Testing".

Preliminary Analytical Procedures

ISA (UK and Ireland) 520 *Analytical Procedures* (ISA 520) defines **analytical procedures** as:
"evaluations of financial information through analysis of plausible relationships among both financial and non-financial data. Analytical procedures also encompass such

investigation as is necessary of identified **fluctuations or relationships that are inconsistent** with other relevant information or that differ from expected values by a significant amount." (ISA 520, para 4)

The following outlines the stages where analytical procedures are used:
- **Planning stage** As part of understanding the client and assisting the risk-identification process.
- **Substantive Stage** As an efficient method of testing.
- **Final Stage** As a method of ensuring (prior to the signing of the audit report) that the auditor now understands all fluctuations or unusual relationships identified at the planning stage and during the audit.

Essentially, preliminary analytical procedures assist the auditor in understanding the entity and allow him to better plan the nature, timing and extent of audit procedures. The main objective of the analytical procedures at this stage in the audit is to understand the client entity's business and transactions and to identify financial statement account balances and transactions that are likely to contain misstatements. It is important to note that preliminary analytical procedures do not aim to prove why there are unusual variances to prior year or why unusual relationships exist but rather highlight the fact that something unusual exists and therefore warrants further investigation for better understanding.

Preliminary analytical procedures are considered in more detail in **Chapter 7**, 'The Risk Assessment Process', where worked examples are discussed.

Going Concern

ISA (UK and Ireland) 570 *Going Concern* (ISA 570) deals with the auditor's responsibilities in the audit of financial statements relating to management's use of the going concern assumption in the preparation of the financial statements. The bulk of the **going concern** review is generally left to the completion stage of the audit. However, some consideration should be given to it at the planning stage where risks identified indicate that the company may not continue as a going concern. If a serious risk with respect to going concern exists, the entire basis of the financial statements would be incorrect as the going concern assumption is one of the fundamental assumptions on which financial statements are prepared. If the auditor proceeds without initial consideration of going concern, the entire audit may prove to be inefficient as the financial statements would look very different if they needed to be prepared on a break-up basis.

It is the responsibility of management to determine whether the going concern assumption is appropriate in the preparation of financial statements. If, however, the going concern assumption is invalid, the financial statements would need to be prepared on a break-up basis.

Indications of going concern problems can include:
- deteriorating liquidity position not backed by sufficient financing arrangements;
- aggressive growth strategy not backed by sufficient finance, which ultimately leads to overtrading;

- bankruptcy of a major customer of the company; or
- continuous losses.

Going concern is considered in more detail in **Chapter 18**, 'Audit Work, Conclusions'.

The Audit Plan

The **audit plan** is more detailed than the overall audit strategy and determines the nature, timing and extent of audit procedures to be performed by the audit team in order to gain sufficient, appropriate audit evidence over account balances and transactions and allow the audit firm to issue an opinion on the financial statements.

The audit plan includes the following elements, which are defined in ISA 330 (paras A5–A7).

- **Nature of audit procedures** "… refers to its purpose (i.e. test of controls or substantive procedure) and its type (that is, inspection, observation, inquiry, confirmation, recalculation, reperformance, or analytical procedure). The nature of audit procedures is very important in responding to the assessed risks." (ISA 330, para 5)
- **Timing of audit procedures** "… refers to when it is performed, or the period or date to which the audit evidence applies." (ISA 330, para 6)
- **Extent of audit procedures** "… refers to the quantity to be performed, for example, a sample size or the number of observations of a control activity". (ISA 330, para 7)

Nature of Audit Procedures

The two types of audit procedure used are **testing of controls** and **substantive testing**. An appropriate approach might include a combination of tests of controls and substantive tests. The auditor should consider which type of testing will address the assessed risk in the most efficient and effective manner and reduce the risk of material misstatements to an acceptably low level. When determining which combination of controls and substantive testing should be used, the auditor should give consideration to a number of factors, including:

1. how the controls were applied at relevant times during the period under audit;
2. the consistency with which they were applied; and
3. by whom, or by what means, they were applied.

Timing of Audit Procedures

When the auditor has decided upon the nature of the audit procedures to be performed, consideration must then be given to the timing of the procedures, i.e. when the audit team will carry out the testing.

Audit procedures can be performed at an interim date or after the period end.

The interim audit occurs a few months before the year-end and generally covers the planning activities, including testing of controls. Some substantive testing may also be performed at this stage, however roll-forward procedures must then be performed to audit the transactions from the interim testing date to the year-end date. The most common substantive procedure carried out is on the receivables balance, whereby the auditor will audit the receivables balance at, *say*, the end of November and then after the year-end, he will only have to audit the transactions that occurred from1 December to 31 December hence reducing the amount of time needed on the audit after the balance sheet date. Other areas normally tested at interim stage include non-current assets and their related additions and disposals. Care should be taken by the auditor to ensure that the interim audit does not take place too short a time before the year-end or he creates unnecessary risk in the period from the interim audit to the balance sheet date. An interim audit can assist in balancing the workload of the audit team, as well as helping to identify issues at an early stage and giving the audit team, time to respond to issues. In deciding whether to perform interim testing the auditor should consider the following:

- How good is the overall control environment? (Performing a roll-forward between interim date and the period end is unlikely to be effective if the general control environment is poor.)
- How good are the specific controls over the account balance or class of transactions being considered?
- Is the required evidence available to perform the test?
- Would a procedure before the period end address the nature and substance of the risk involved?
- Would the interim procedure address the period or date to which the audit evidence relates?
- How much additional evidence will be required for the remaining unaudited period between the date of the interim audit and the period end?

Activities such as attendance at the physical inventory count usually occur at the reporting date (although occasionally can take place before or after that date as discussed in **Chapter 12**, Section 12.8).

Substantive testing is generally left until the **final audit (after the balance sheet date)**, after the books and records have been completed and a draft set of financial statements has been prepared.

Extent of Audit Procedures

Finally, the audit plan requires consideration of the extent of audit procedures. Extent of testing refers to the quantity of transactions (sample size) upon which specific audit testing is to be performed. As a general rule, where the assessed risk is deemed to be high, the extent of testing to be performed will be greater. The objective of the audit team is to obtain audit evidence that is sufficient and appropriate to gain comfort over the assertions surrounding the transactions, balances or disclosures that are being tested.

Sufficient appropriate audit evidence can be obtained by:

- selecting all items (100% of the population), which is appropriate when:
  - the population constitutes a small number of high-value items;

- there is a significant risk and other means do not provide sufficient appropriate audit evidence; or
  - where computer-assisted audit techniques (CAATs) can be used in a larger population to electronically test a repetitive calculation or other process.
- selecting specific items, which is appropriate for:
  - high-value or key items;
  - all items over a certain amount;
  - items to obtain information about matters such as the nature of the entity, the nature of transactions, and internal control; and
  - items to test control activities.
- selecting a representative sample of items from the population. This can be performed using judgemental or statistical sampling methods.

Audit evidence and **sampling** are dealt with in more detail in **Chapter 6**, 'Gathering Audit Evidence'.

Documentation of Audit Plan and Strategy

As discussed further in **Chapter 6**, Section 6.6, audit documentation supports the auditor's audit conclusions and ultimately his audit opinion, therefore the collection of audit documentation is an integral part of any audit procedure.

It is important for the audit team to document each step involved in developing the overall **audit strategy** and the detailed **audit plan**. This is specified in ISA 300:

"The auditor shall include in the audit documentation:
(a) The overall audit strategy;
(b) The audit plan; and
(c) Any significant changes made during the audit engagement to the overall audit strategy or the audit plan, and the reasons for such changes." (ISA 300, para 12)

The auditor should document the details of the strategy and audit plan as evidence that it was completed and to record the key decisions considered necessary to appropriately plan the audit and to communicate significant matters to the audit team.

The usual means of documenting the detailed audit plan is to outline the following:
- the nature of testing to be performed;
- the extent of testing to be performed;
- the assertions which testing addresses (assertions are dealt with in detail in **Chapter 6**); and
- the details of who is to perform the testing.

Communication of the Audit Plan

The audit plan should be made available to all members of the audit team, however it can be helpful for the audit team to communicate elements of the detailed audit plan to management or those charged with governance. This allows management to gain a greater insight into the audit process and to identify the information which the audit team will request from the client entity's personnel.

5.5 CONCLUSION

A considerable amount of audit work is performed well before the client provides the final set of financial statements on which the auditor is required to provide an opinion.

The auditor wishes to make a profit from the performance of the audit, but without taking any unnecessary risks on his reputation and as such:
- he does not take on or continue engagements with client entities that bring with them undue risk;
- he clearly outlines the terms of the engagement in the form of an **engagement letter** to avoid any misunderstandings with respect to the audit; and
- he plans the audit to ensure it is efficient (achieves maximum productivity) without compromising its effectiveness in identifying material misstatements.

It is important for the audit team to realise that audit planning is a continuous process that does not cease when the overall strategy and the detailed plan are developed. Both should be updated and changed as necessary throughout the audit cycle in response to risks identified and results of audit testing performed. Reasons for significant changes should be documented along with the auditor's response to the events, and conditions or results of audit procedures that resulted in such changes.

SUMMARY OF LEARNING OBJECTIVES

After having studied this chapter on audit acceptance and planning you should:

Learning Objective 1 Understand and be able to apply the audit acceptance and continuance considerations.

When considering accepting or continuing an audit, the auditor will assess the client entity's integrity, the audit firm's competence to perform the audit and ethical requirements. He will also contact the outgoing auditor in the case of a new engagement to ensure there is no reason why he should not accept the engagement.

Learning Objective 2 Know the role and contents of an engagement letter.

An engagement letter should be drawn up and signed by both parties to avoid any misunderstandings with respect to the engagement. There may be instances in the case of a recurring audit where the engagement letter will need to be updated due to, for example, changes in scope or legislation. There are many points which may be included within an engagement letter, for example, the objective of a financial statement audit, management's responsibility for the financial statements, etc.

Learning Objective 3 Know the stages of audit planning and be able to distinguish between the overall audit strategy and the audit plan.

The audit strategy essentially describes the general terms of how an audit is to be carried out. The audit plan details the specific procedures to be carried out to implement the strategy and complete the audit.

Overall Audit Strategy Where the auditor considers, for example:
* characteristics of the engagement;
* roles and responsibilities within the audit team;
* the need for experts;
* the determination of materiality;
* understanding the client entity (risk and internal control assessment);
* preliminary analytical procedures; and
* going concern.

Audit Plan Once the audit strategy is determined, the auditor should refine this into a detailed plan that dictates:
* nature;
* timing; and
* extent of audit procedures.

Learning Objective 4 Develop an understanding of the role of analytical procedures at the planning stage.

Preliminary analytical procedures assist the auditor in understanding the client entity and in doing so allow him to better plan the nature, timing and extent of audit procedures. The main objective of the analytical procedure at this stage in the audit is to understand the client entity's business and transactions and to identify financial statement account balances and transactions that are likely to contain misstatements.

Learning Objective 5 Appreciate the concept of materiality, including how and why it is calculated.

When a misstatement (or the aggregate impact of all misstatements) is significant enough that it could change or influence the decision of an informed person, a material misstatement is said to have occurred. In order to assess if an item is material, the auditor sets a monetary amount which represents a benchmark by which to measure the significance of misstatements as well as plan which balances will be tested and to what degree. The auditor must use his judgement when setting materiality by first identifying a benchmark (a key figure in the financial statements) and then applying a percentage to that benchmark (see **Table 5.3**).

Learning Objective 6 Be able to discuss the options available to the auditor with regard to the nature, timing and extent of audit procedures when designing the audit plan.

The nature of the audit procedures refers to the purpose and type. The auditor can adopt more substantive analytical procedures if he has assessed the client entity control environment to be strong. The timing of audit procedures refers to when the auditor carries out his testing. He can carry out more testing prior to the reporting date if he has assessed the client entity control environment to be strong. Finally, extent refers to the quantity of the testing performed by the auditor (for example, smaller sample sizes can be taken if the auditor has assessed the client entity control environment to be strong).

QUESTIONS

Self-test Questions

5.1 What four key areas would you as auditor consider before accepting an audit engagement?
5.2 What factors is the auditor interested in when assessing client integrity?
5.3 What factors is the auditor interested in when assessing his competence to perform an audit?
5.4 Name three ethical considerations the auditor should take into account when assessing whether to accept a new audit client or to continue an existing audit engagement?
5.5 What is an engagement letter and what does it contain?
5.6 Distinguish between the terms 'audit strategy' and 'audit plan'.
5.7 What are the key stages involved in developing the overall audit strategy?
5.8 What is meant by the term 'materiality'?
5.9 What is meant by the term 'analytical procedures'?
5.10 At what stages during the audit does the auditor use analytical procedures?
5.11 Why is it necessary for the auditor to consider going concern early on in the audit?
5.12 What is meant by the terms 'nature', 'timing' and 'extent' with regard to audit procedures?
5.13 Why is it important to document the audit plan and the audit strategy?

Review Questions

(See Suggested Solutions to Review Questions in **Appendix D**.)

Question 5.1

Your audit firm has been asked to accept the position of auditor to CAT Ltd, as the incumbent auditor is retiring. CAT Ltd is a long-established and successful large company, which manufactures medicines. Your audit firm's first audit of the company will be for the year ended 31 December 2012 and you have been asked by the audit partner to draft an engagement letter for the audit and to begin initial planning.

Requirement
(a) Explain the procedures that an auditor should adopt before accepting an appointment.
(b) Identify the matters that should be included in a letter of engagement.

Question 5.2

You are employed by a practising audit firm, one of whose client entities is Leoville Ltd (Leoville), a family-owned company in the textile industry. Leoville has recently reached agreement with a rival company, Poyferre Ltd (Poyferre), to jointly develop and manufacture a new range of children's clothing for sale through multiple retailers. A new company, Las Cases Ltd, will be formed for this purpose, with Leoville and Poyferre each owning 50% of the share capital.

Several days ago, you accompanied the audit partner to a meeting with Leoville's shareholders and management at which they explained that the company would need to raise an amount of €4 million to fund its investment in Las Cases Ltd. They propose that this will be funded entirely from debt and have already held a preliminary meeting with their bankers.

Leoville has agreed with its bankers that it will make a formal presentation to them in four weeks' time in relation to this application for finance. The principal elements of the presentation will be:
• a business plan for the new venture; and
• Leoville's management accounts for the six months ended 30 June 2012.

At your meeting with Leoville's management, they indicated that they require assistance from your firm in relation to both of these matters. This assistance is to include the drafting of the business plan and preparation of trading projections for the new venture for the period from 1 January 2013 to 31 December 2013. It is apparent that management from both Leoville and Poyferre will have significant input into drafting the plan and, in addition, you are aware that they intend to retain specialist textile industry consultants to advise on particular aspects of the venture. In essence, it seems that your firm will be involved in 'project managing' the preparation of the business plan.

As Leoville's bankers have requested that the management accounts for the six months to 30 June 2012 be reviewed by Leoville's auditors, your audit firm has been requested to undertake such a review as soon as possible. You understand that the bank merely wishes your audit firm to confirm that the management accounts have been 'properly prepared'.

Your audit firm's operating procedures require that an engagement letter should be issued for all assignments it is asked to undertake. The audit partner has asked that you prepare a draft of this letter for his review at a meeting to be held in two days' time.

Requirement Prepare a draft engagement letter for the work which Leoville Ltd has asked your audit firm to undertake.

Question 5.3

You are an audit senior working for a firm of Chartered Accountants. The partner responsible for staff training has asked you to prepare some training material on the firm's audit approach for the trainees about to join. In particular, the partner has asked you to prepare the material on your audit firm's approach to planning, controlling and recording of an audit in order to ensure that the trainees are aware of the high standards expected of an auditor in this area.

Requirement Prepare a memorandum to new trainees, highlighting the key points they should be aware of in:
(a) planning an audit;
(b) controlling an audit; and
(c) documenting audit work.

APPENDIX 5.1 EXAMPLE OF AN AUDIT ENGAGEMENT LETTER[1]

The following is an example of an audit engagement letter for an audit of general purpose financial statements prepared in accordance with International Financial Reporting Standards. This letter is not authoritative but is intended only to be a guide that may be used in conjunction with the considerations outlined in ISA 210. It will need to be varied according to individual requirements and circumstances. It is drafted to refer to the audit of financial statements for a single reporting period and would require adaptation if intended or expected to apply to recurring audits (see ISA 210, para 13). It may be appropriate to seek legal advice that any proposed letter is suitable.

To the appropriate representative of management or those charged with governance of ABC Company: (Note 1)

[*The objective and scope of the audit*]

You (Note 2) have requested that we audit the financial statements of ABC Company, which comprise the balance sheet as at December 31, 20X1, and the income statement, statement of changes in equity and cash flow statement for the year then ended, and a summary of significant accounting policies and other explanatory information. We are pleased to confirm our acceptance and our understanding of this audit engagement by means of this letter. Our audit will be conducted with the objective of our expressing an opinion on the financial statements.

---

[1] Source: ISA (UK and Ireland) 210 *Agreeing the Terms of Audit Engagements*, Appendix 1.

[*The responsibilities of the auditor*]

We will conduct our audit in accordance with International Standards on Auditing (ISAs). Those standards require that we comply with ethical requirements and plan and perform the audit to obtain reasonable assurance about whether the financial statements are free from material misstatement. An audit involves performing procedures to obtain audit evidence about the amounts and disclosures in the financial statements. The procedures selected depend on the auditor's judgment, including the assessment of the risks of material misstatement of the financial statements, whether due to fraud or error. An audit also includes evaluating the appropriateness of accounting policies used and the reasonableness of accounting estimates made by management, as well as evaluating the overall presentation of the financial statements.

Because of the inherent limitations of an audit, together with the inherent limitations of internal control, there is an unavoidable risk that some material misstatements may not be detected, even though the audit is properly planned and performed in accordance with ISAs.

In making our risk assessments, we consider internal control relevant to the entity's preparation of the financial statements in order to design audit procedures that are appropriate in the circumstances, but not for the purpose of expressing an opinion on the effectiveness of the entity's internal control. However, we will communicate to you in writing concerning any significant deficiencies in internal control relevant to the audit of the financial statements that we have identified during the audit.

[*The responsibilities of management and identification of the applicable financial reporting framework (for purposes of this example it is assumed that the auditor has not determined that the law or regulation prescribes those responsibilities in appropriate terms; the descriptions in paragraph 6(b) of ISA 210 are therefore used).*]

Our audit will be conducted on the basis that [management and, where appropriate, those charged with governance (Note 3) acknowledge and understand that they have responsibility:

(a) For the preparation and fair presentation of the financial statements in accordance with International Financial Reporting Standards; (Note 4)

(b) For such internal control as [management] determines is necessary to enable the preparation of financial statements that are free from material misstatement, whether due to fraud or error; and

(c) To provide us with:

   (i) Access to all information of which [management] is aware that is relevant to the preparation of the financial statements such as records, documentation and other matters;

   (ii) Additional information that we may request from [management] for the purpose of the audit; and

(iii) Unrestricted access to persons within the entity from whom we determine it necessary to obtain audit evidence.

As part of our audit process, we will request from [management and, where appropriate, those charged with governance], written confirmation concerning representations made to us in connection with the audit.

We look forward to full cooperation from your staff during our audit.

[*Other relevant information*]

[*Insert other information, such as fee arrangements, billings and other specific terms, as appropriate.*]

[*Reporting*]

[*Insert appropriate reference to the expected form and content of the auditor's report.*]

The form and content of our report may need to be amended in the light of our audit findings.

Please sign and return the attached copy of this letter to indicate your acknowledgement of, and agreement with, the arrangements for our audit of the financial statements including our respective responsibilities.

XYZ & Co.

Acknowledged and agreed on behalf of ABC Company by

(signed)

....

Name and Title

Date

Note 1: The addressees and references in the letter would be those that are appropriate in the circumstances of the engagement, including the relevant jurisdiction. It is important to refer to the appropriate persons – see paragraph A21 of ISA 210.

Note 2: Throughout this letter, references to "you," "we," "us," "management," "those charged with governance" and "auditor" would be used or amended as appropriate in the circumstances.

Note 3: Use terminology as appropriate in the circumstances.

Note 4: Or, if appropriate, "For the preparation of financial statements that give a true and fair view in accordance with International Financial Reporting Standards."

6

GATHERING AUDIT EVIDENCE

LEARNING OBJECTIVES

Having studied this chapter on gathering audit evidence you should:
1. understand what is meant by 'sufficient appropriate audit evidence';
2. be able to identify whether audit evidence is sufficient and appropriate with respect to specific assertions;
3. have an understanding of how the methods of obtaining audit evidence are carried out;
4. have an appreciation of the types of testing carried out for controls and substantive testing to support further learning in later chapters;
5. understand the concept of 'substantive analytical procedures' and the essential considerations that must be taken into account when deciding whether or not to use substantive analytical procedures;
6. understand how to carry out external confirmations;

7. understand the importance of audit documentation and audit working papers as well as their form;
8. obtain a strong insight into sampling, its risks, methods and projection techniques;
9. understand the auditors responsibility with regard to opening balances; and
10. understand the auditing procedures applied to accounting estimates.

CHECKLIST OF RELEVANT STANDARDS

The relevant standards covered in this chapter are:
- ISA (UK and Ireland) 230 *Audit Documentation* (ISA 230)
- ISA (UK and Ireland) 500 *Audit Evidence* (ISA 500)
- ISA (UK and Ireland) 505 *External Confirmations* (ISA 505)
- ISA (UK and Ireland) 510 *Initial Audit Engagements – Opening Balances* (ISA 510)
- ISA (UK and Ireland) 520 *Analytical Procedures* (ISA 520)
- ISA (UK and Ireland) 530 *Audit Sampling* (ISA 530)
- ISA (UK and Ireland) 540 *Auditing Accounting Estimates, Including Fair Value Accounting Estimates, and Related Disclosures* (ISA 540)

KEY TERMS AND DEFINITIONS FOR THIS CHAPTER

Appropriate Evidence   In the context of 'sufficient appropriate audit evidence', 'appropriate' refers to the requirement for evidence to be of a high quality and be of relevance to the objective of the audit procedure.

Assertions   Explicit or implicit representations made by management in presenting a set of financial statements to the auditor (i.e. in providing the auditor with financial statements, management are saying, "we believe these financial statements to be valid, complete, accurate results pertaining to the entity and are fairly classified and disclosed"). The objective of the auditor is to prove or disprove these assertions by obtaining audit evidence.

Audit Evidence   All information used by the auditor in arriving at the conclusions on which the audit opinion is based, including the information contained in the accounting records underlying the financial statements and other information.

Control Risk   Control risk is the risk that a material misstatement could occur in an assertion. Controls should be put in place to address risks and these controls should prevent, detect or correct fraud and errors that may occur. Absence of these types of controls increases control risk. For example, where cash reconciliations are not performed daily, this poses a control risk.

Corroborative Evidence   Evidence or information that strengthens or supports other evidence or information received.

Detection Risk   This is the risk that the auditor will not detect a material misstatement that exists in an assertion.

Directional Testing   Directional testing refers to the direction in which the auditor performs a test. For example, to test for completeness, the auditor performs tests from source documents to the general ledger, whereas to test for occurrence, the auditor performs tests in the opposite direction, i.e. from the general ledger to source documents.

Dual Test   A test that can be used to support both controls and substantive testing procedures.

Inherent Risk   Inherent risk is the susceptibility of an assertion to a misstatement that could be material. Inherent risks exist due to the nature of the industry in which the client entity operates, product type or transaction types. For example, an entity that deals predominantly in cash is inherently risky.

Sufficient Evidence   In the context of 'sufficient appropriate audit evidence', 'sufficient' refers to the requirement for evidence to be 'enough in terms of quantity'.

6.1 INTRODUCTION

This chapter is concerned with audit evidence both in general and as it relates to specific auditable classes of transactions and balances in the financial statements.

The most appropriate place to start is with the definition of **sufficient appropriate audit evidence** (SAAE). This is discussed in **Section 6.2**, which outlines the various layers of interpretation surrounding this term. Essentially, the term sufficient appropriate audit evidence defines what is expected of the audit evidence that is gathered by the auditor. In this section you must understand that beneath this term lies the requirement for audit evidence to be sufficient in quantity, reliable in source and relevant to the management assertions (audit objectives) being tested. The concept of relevance is the most difficult to understand and so it is supported by a number of examples included in **Table 6.2** and again in **Table 6.4**.

Once we have established, in **Section 6.2**, what standard of evidence is required, in **Section 6.3** we then explore the various **methods of obtaining evidence** that are open to the auditor, as laid down in ISA (UK and Ireland) 500 *Audit Evidence* (ISA 500) paragraphs A14–A25. A significant discussion is dedicated to one particular method of gathering evidence. This method is **analytical procedures**, which warrants particular attention due to the fact that analytical procedures are used at three key stages throughout the audit process: the planning stage; the substantive testing stage; and the audit completion stage.

Having gained an appreciation of how audit evidence is collected and the standard of audit evidence required, in **Section 6.4** we then discuss how the auditor goes about evaluating the evidence gathered. In **Section 6.5** we discuss the types of testing procedure used by the auditor at the controls testing stage and at the substantive testing stage. While **tests of details** is the testing approach used during controls testing, when performing substantive testing the auditor has two methods open to him: tests of details and **substantive analytical procedures**.

Section 6.6 deals with the specific audit technique of '**external confirmations**', which forms one of the most reliable forms of audit evidence because it is independent, obtained directly by the auditor and exists in documentary form.

Audit documentation and the requirements of ISA (UK and Ireland) 230 *Audit Documentation* (ISA 230) are the subject of **Section 6.7** which outlines the importance of audit documentation and demonstrates the typical contents of an audit working paper by way of **Example 6.10**.

Auditing would not be possible without the use of '**audit sampling**' and **Section 6.8** takes us through the various sampling methods, the sample design considerations, the risks associated with using a sample and the factors that influence sample size. Finally, the chapter concludes with three examples: **Example 6.11**, which demonstrates the projection of an error onto the population; **Example 6.12**, which demonstrates the benefits of stratification; and **Example 6.13**, which demonstrates the extrapolation (projecting of errors) considering the existence of anomalies (or isolated instances).

The final two sections deal with two specific types of balances that exist in the financial statements: **Section 6.9** addresses how the auditor approaches the opening balances (comparatives figures) in the financial statements; and **Section 6.10** outlines the audit procedures used when auditing accounting estimates.

The chapters that follow this chapter require you to have a full understanding of what is denoted by audit evidence and how the auditor collects and evaluates audit evidence.

6.2 SUFFICIENT APPROPRIATE AUDIT EVIDENCE

Introduction

The primary purpose of an audit is for the auditor to issue an audit opinion on the financial statements. In order to do this, he must gain evidence that supports the balances, transactions and disclosures in the financial statements. An **audit opinion** cannot be issued where **sufficient appropriate audit evidence** has not been obtained.

ISA (UK and Ireland) 500 *Audit Evidence* (ISA 500) defines **audit evidence** as all the information used by the auditor in arriving at the conclusions on which the audit opinion is based; it includes the information contained in the accounting records underlying the financial statements and other information. In summary, audit evidence is what the auditor requires in order to support and conclude whether or not the financial statements give a **true and fair view**. Examples of audit evidence include:

- sales/purchase/sundry invoices;
- supplier statements;
- contracts for work to be performed;
- client entity's spreadsheets, e.g. budgets;
- client entity's control manuals;
- valuation reports, e.g. from surveyors or inventory valuation experts;
- minutes from shareholders'/directors' meetings;
- third-party confirmations, e.g. bank confirmations, legal confirmations or debtor confirmations; and
- audit working papers, e.g. audit working papers containing recalculations of depreciation, or workings and results of analytical procedures.

The term 'sufficient appropriate audit evidence' is a complicated term and its meaning has many layers, as depicted in **Figure 6.1**. Sufficiency refers to the quantity of evidence whereas appropriateness refers to quality, and quality in this regard is a twofold term. Quality refers to both the reliability and the relevance of the evidence. These concepts are expanded upon later in this chapter.

Each element of the term 'sufficient appropriate audit evidence' is now considered to explain what is required of the auditor with regard to the collection of sufficient appropriate audit evidence.

What is Sufficient Evidence?

ISA 500 states that the auditor must obtain evidence that is sufficient and appropriate. **Sufficiency** is the measure of the quantity of audit evidence, while **appropriateness** is the measure of the quality of the evidence, i.e. its **relevance** and **reliability**

FIGURE 6.1: SUFFICIENT APPROPRIATE AUDIT EVIDENCE

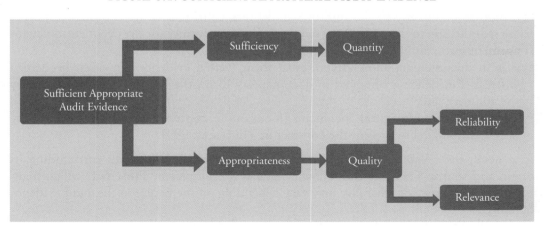

in providing support for or detecting misstatements in account balances, classes of transactions and disclosures.

The quantity of audit evidence is directly linked to the risk of material misstatement identified at the assertion level. For example, if the auditor believes there is a risk that not all expenses are recorded he will perform a greater degree of testing to search for unrecorded expenses. As a general rule, the higher the assessed level of risk, the more audit evidence is required. The quantity of audit evidence is also directly linked to the quality of the evidence. As a general rule, the better the quality of the evidence, the less the quantity of evidence required. Hence the sufficiency and appropriateness of audit evidence are interrelated. However, simply obtaining a greater quantity of audit evidence will not necessarily compensate for poor quality.

Now that the meaning of 'appropriateness' audit evidence has been clarified, consideration will be given to the meaning of 'appropriate' audit evidence.

What is Appropriate Audit Evidence?

As can be seen in **Figure 6.1**, 'appropriateness' refers to both the reliability and relevance of evidence. These terms will now be discussed.

Reliability

Reliability of audit evidence varies and often the auditor needs to use **professional judgement** in deciding whether the audit evidence received is sufficient to be relied upon. ISA 500 states that audit evidence is more reliable when:
- it is obtained from an independent source, e.g. a bank confirmation letter;
- entity controls are effective (if generated internally); however, if the controls operating within the entity are not deemed to be effective, then the quality of the evidence produced by the entity will most likely not be reliable, (for example, reports generated from an accounting system that has been found to be unreliable and susceptible to errors should not be assessed as reliable);
- it is obtained directly by the auditor, e.g. debtors' confirmation letters where responses are sent directly to the audit firm, removing the opportunity for the client entity's management to manipulate responses;
- it is in documentary rather than verbal form (verbal evidence can often be denied whereas if evidence is obtained in documentary form, the facts are held on record by the auditor); and
- it is provided from **original** documents (for example, **copies** of sales contracts may have been manipulated to present the contract in a different light).

In general, the reliability of evidence depends upon the circumstances surrounding its origin and source. Consider the following practical examples in **Table 6.1**, which highlight how the degree of reliability may vary depending on the nature of the audit evidence obtained.

In all instances the auditor should endeavour to gain the most reliable evidence available.

TABLE 6.1: RELIABILITY OF EVIDENCE

Reliable audit evidence	Less reliable audit evidence
Confirmation of receivables balance received directly from the client entity's customer (it is completely independent of the client entity).	Receivable balance per year-end ledger provided by the client entity (not as independent as direct third-party confirmation).
Year-end receivables aged listing (showing all customers' balances by reference to the amount of time they have been outstanding), if tests of controls have concluded that system can be relied upon (strong control environment equates to more confidence over information produced in that environment).	Year-end receivables aged listing, if tests of controls have concluded that the system has material weaknesses and cannot be relied upon (weak control environment equates to less confidence over information produced in that environment).
Observation of the application of a control by the auditor, e.g. the need for two people to authorise an electronic payment through the bank by entry of passwords on the computer system (seeing is believing).	Documentation of the control by the client entity and given to auditor (I would rather witness the event than be told it happens).
Letter from solicitor confirming that there are no claims against the entity at the period end.	Oral representation from client entity stating that there are no claims against it at the period end.
Original bank statement (authenticity).	Fax of period-end bank statement from client.
Attendance by auditor at period-end inventory count.	Inspection of period-end inventory listing supplied by the client entity.

Relevance

'**Relevance**' refers to the logical connection of the evidence or test with the management assertion/audit objective that the auditor is trying to address (management assertions were covered in **Chapter 4**, Section 4.3). For example, if the auditor was testing the valuation assertion with respect to receivables and obtained confirmations from the client entity's customers regarding their account balances this evidence would not be sufficient because it is not **relevant** to the assertion. The circularisation has merely proved that the customer acknowledges that they owe the money, but not that they have the ability to pay it. The following table, **Table 6.2**, gives some further examples of the consideration of the relevance of audit evidence. The table outlines a sample of financial cycles and specific assertions that the auditor would try to address. Within the Table, suggested tests are put forward and the question is asked, "Are these tests relevant to the assertion being tested by the auditor?". In each case a more relevant test is presented which addresses the assertion in question.

TABLE 6.2: ASSESSING THE RELEVANCE OF AUDIT EVIDENCE

Transaction Class / Account Balance	Management Assertion / Audit Objective	Suggested Test	Is the suggested test relevant to address the assertion / objective	Why?
Non-current Assets	Existence	Obtain original invoice	No	Obtaining original invoice only proves that the asset was purchased but not that it exists at year end. A more appropriate test would be to inspect the physical asset and confirm it is in use at the year end.
Receivables	Valuation	Obtain confirmation from the client entity's customer that the balance is correct	No	Obtaining confirmation from the customer that it owes the amount does not provide comfort that the customer has the ability or inclination to pay. A more appropriate test to cover the valuation of a receivable would be to review receipts dated after the reporting date to see whether the balance has been paid.
Inventory	Completeness	Review of sales order book for the new year	No	Reviewing the sales order book for new year helps to prove the valuation assertion (i.e. the inventory is saleable) but is not appropriate to prove completeness of inventory. A more appropriate test would be to observe the client entity's physical inventory count and make comparison to the final inventory listing in the general ledger.
Revenue	Completeness	Select invoice from general ledger and trace it to the invoice, the signed dispatch note and the original sales order	No	When testing for completeness, the auditor should not start with the general ledger; he should start from the books of first entry. Tracing from general ledger to books of first entry tests for occurrence, not completeness.

The last row of **Table 6.2** illustrates the importance of the **direction** of the test (i.e. from books of first entry / source documents to general ledger, or from general ledger, to books of first entry). This is referred to as directional testing. The direction of the test is important when considering the relevance of the test. In order to appreciate the concept of directional testing, consider **Example 6.1** below.

EXAMPLE 6.1: DIRECTIONAL TESTING

As an auditor, you are provided with a computer system listing of customer orders raised during the period under review. You are also provided with the list of all the invoices that support the €3,000,000 revenue balance in the draft financial statements. You are testing the completeness assertion.

From the invoice listing that supports the €3,000,000 revenue figure in the financial statements, you select 20 invoices and trace them back to related signed customer POD (purchase order delivery) notes. You successfully trace all of the invoices back to a valid signed POD note. Have you satisfied your objective to test the completeness assertion?

No, you have not satisfied your objective to test the completeness assertion. You have proved the occurrence assertion (i.e. that the transactions recorded in the general ledger are supported by valid events, in this case, the delivery of the goods). However, you have not yet proved the completeness assertion (i.e. all orders placed by customers and delivered to them are included in the general ledger). In order to prove completeness, you must start with the books of first entry and trace the transactions recorded in them to the general ledger. The correct test would be to select 20 customer orders, trace them to signed customer POD notes **and** ensure that these were recorded in the general ledger.

A single test may well provide evidence with respect to more than one assertion. In our example above we refer to inspecting receipts from customers after the balance sheet date, which provides evidence with respect to not only the valuation assertion but also the existence assertion as customers would not have paid the balance if it did not exist.

The term 'sufficient appropriate audit evidence' should now be fully understood. Remember that the auditor will seek sufficient appropriate audit evidence to satisfy all of the audit objectives (management assertions). Assertions are dealt with in **Chapter 4**, Section 4.3, and below is a summary to remind you of the assertions that the audit seeks to prove for transactions and balances within the financial statements, as well as the adequacy of the presentation and disclosure of the financial statements. **Table 6.3** below provides a summary of the management assertions (audit objectives) as they relate to (a) transactions (for example, revenue transactions); (b) balances (for example, the receivables balance); and (c) presentation and disclosure (for example, the disclosure note required to show the receivables bad debt provision movement).

Different types of testing will be necessary in order to address each assertion at the financial statement level and in some instances a combination of tests will be used. The detailed audit testing plan will be developed during the planning phase of the audit and will be updated as necessary throughout the audit process.

TABLE 6.3: MANAGEMENT ASSERTIONS/AUDIT OBJECTIVES

Transactions	Balances	Presentation and Disclosure
Occurrence	Existence	Occurrence
Completeness	Completeness	Completeness
Accuracy	Valuation and Allocation	Accuracy and Valuation
Cut-off	Rights and Obligations	Rights and Obligations
Classification	Classification	Classification

TABLE 6.4: DEVELOPMENT OF AUDIT TESTS TO COVER ASSERTIONS

Financial Statement Area	Audit Test	Nature of Audit Test	Assertions Addressed
Non-current Fixed Assets	Agreeing fixed asset additions to supporting documentation.	Substantive	Accuracy, existence/occurrence, cut-off
Sales	Invoices are system-generated and are issued in sequential number order, choose an invoice number and confirm that the following 50 invoices have been posted to the receivables ledger.	Controls	Completeness
Accounts Payable	Reconciliation of balance per payables ledger to supplier statements.	Substantive	Completeness, accuracy, existence/occurrence
Inventory	Attendance at period-end physical inventory count.	Substantive	Completeness, accuracy, existence/occurrence, valuation

Consider the practical examples included in **Table 6.4** above which identify how audit tests are developed to cover assertions relating to classes of transactions and balances in the financial statements. The Table gives examples of financial cycle areas and tests and then identifies the nature of the test and the assertions that this test covers.

As we can see from the above Table some tests will provide the auditor with evidence to both substantive test of details and controls test of details. These types of test are referred to as dual tests and are best described by way of example, included at **Example 6.2** below.

EXAMPLE 6.2: DUAL TESTING

When testing controls, the auditor, using statistical sampling methods, selects, for example, 50 purchase orders (POs) and performs the following test:
- ensures each PO was approved;
- traces each PO to a goods received note (GRN);
- compares the details on each PO to the details on the corresponding GRN to ensure they match;
- traces each transaction to its entry on the system to ensure it was accrued;
- traces each GRN to a matching purchase invoice; and
- compares the details per each GRN to the matching purchase invoice.

Remember: the above test, being a control test, is referred to as 'attribute testing' and therefore there are two possible answers to each part of the test itemised in the bulleted list above: "Yes" or "No". If the auditor establishes that in each case the answer is 'Yes', then he concludes that controls with respect to the completeness and accuracy assertion are strong/effective.

The auditor still needs to carry out substantive procedures to validate the purchases figure in the financial statements with respect to all other assertions (i.e. occurrence, cut-off and classification). However, with respect to the completeness and accuracy assertions, the above test will suffice and hence the test has acted as a dual purpose test in providing evidence to support both control testing and substantive testing.

We now know what type of audit evidence is acceptable, in that it must be sufficient appropriate audit evidence and it must support all assertions for all transactions, balances and disclosures in the financial statements. The question we must address next is, "What methods can the auditor adopt to obtain this audit evidence?"

6.3 METHODS OF OBTAINING AUDIT EVIDENCE

There are a number of methods by which an auditor can obtain audit evidence. The method used will depend on the nature of the testing being performed. Some of the key methods are discussed below.

The auditor obtains evidence using one or more of the following procedures (see ISA 500, paras A14–A25):
- inspection,
- observation,
- external confirmation,
- recalculation,
- re-performance,
- analytical procedures, and
- inquiry.

Inspection

Inspection involves examining, reviewing, vouching, tracing or verifying records or other documents, processes, conditions or transactions. Inspection also relates to the inspection of physical assets for existence. However, further documents must be inspected to verify rights and obligations to the asset. Inspection in general means physically checking, for example, physically inspecting an invoice or physically inspecting an asset.

Inspection of documents provides auditors with varying degrees of reliability depending on:
- whether the documents were generated internally or externally. Externally generated documentation is naturally more reliable due to its independence of the client entity;
- whether they were received directly by the auditors. If the auditor receives something directly from a third party, it is more reliable than if it was sent to the client entity and then passed to the auditor through the client entity. The client has had the opportunity to tamper with the document;
- whether its source is reliable. The auditor will have to consider the connection of the source to the client entity to ensure there is no conflict of interest.

EXAMPLE 6.3: USES OF INSPECTION

Examples of the use of inspection when gathering audit evidence are as follows.
- The auditor inspects the bank statement to prove the existence of the bank balance (reliable third-party confirmation).
- The auditor vouches a receivable's confirmation letter to that receivable's balance per the receivables listing (reliable third-party confirmation).
- The auditor vouches the value of an investment to the price on the stock exchange (reliable third-party source).

Observation

Observation consists of looking at a process or procedure being performed by others. It allows the auditor to obtain audit evidence on how adequately the process or procedure is performed. Observation will seldom gain adequate audit evidence on its own, but may identify areas where further audit evidence is required.

EXAMPLE 6.4: USES OF OBSERVATION

Examples of the use of observation when gathering audit evidence include:
- observation of inventory count to confirm the inventory exists at the date of the statement of financial position,
- observation of processes surrounding the sales system – inquiry of management would have indicated that there are processes; observation would then be used to verify that the systems are in place. If the observation concludes that the systems are strong, substantive testing on the **debtors listing** would be reduced. However, if observation indicated weak controls, increased substantive tests would need to be designed around the existence and completeness of the receivables listing.

External Confirmation

Confirmation is the process of receiving direct representation from a third party to verify information included in the financial statements. The auditor usually contacts the third party directly, or through the client entity, and requests the confirmation to be sent directly to him.

Since confirmations are written representations from independent third parties received directly by the auditor, they are highly persuasive evidence. ISA 505 *External Confirmations*, deals with this topic and is discussed in more detail in **Section 6.6**.

EXAMPLE 6.5: USES OF CONFIRMATION

Examples of the use of confirmation when gathering audit evidence include confirmation:
- from banks of period-end balances;
- from customers of period-end receivables balances;
- from public warehouses holding inventory for the client; and
- from suppliers regarding terms of agreement or transactions.

Recalculation

As a method of obtaining audit evidence, recalculation consists of verifying the mathematical accuracy of documents and accounting records and re-computing financial statement amounts or supporting details, including client schedules. Some examples of recalculation are set out below:

EXAMPLE 6.6: USES OF CONFIRMATION OF RECALCULATION

Examples of the use of recalculation when gathering audit evidence include:
- re-checking totals in inventory, payables and receivables listings (as discussed in more detail in **Chapters 11–17**);
- extending inventory values by quantities and checking calculations (as discussed in more detail in **Chapter 12**;
- recalculating balances denominated in a foreign currency to ensure that they are carried in the financial statements at the correct amount. This will be done using a suitable exchange rate obtained from a suitable third party;
- recalculating the depreciation charge for the period under review, comparing this to the charge per the client and assessing for reasonableness (as discussed in more detail in **Chapter 11**).

Re-performance

Re-performance is the auditor's independent execution of procedures or controls, which were originally performed as part of the entity's internal control system, either manually or through the use of computer-assisted audit techniques (CAATs).

EXAMPLE 6.7: USE OF RE-PERFORMANCE

> Re-performing the bank reconciliation by obtaining a copy of the bank statement, general ledger balance and confirming cheques and receipts listed on the reconciliation as outstanding.

Analytical Procedures

As methods of obtaining audit evidence, analytical procedures involve evaluating financial and non-financial information and comparing actual results to expectations. They also involve identifying significant fluctuations and relationships that deviate from expectations. Expectations should be developed based on the auditor's knowledge of the operations of the entity during the period under review and information obtained through performance of other audit tests.

Where deviations from expectations are significant, the auditor will use inquiry to discuss with management the reasons for these movements. Reasons for deviations should be corroborated through inspection of documentation, which will underpin the reasons disclosed by management. This approach is outlined in ISA (UK and Ireland) 520 *Analytical Procedures* (ISA 520):

> "If analytical procedures performed in accordance with this ISA (UK and Ireland) identify fluctuations or relationships that are inconsistent with other relevant information or that differ from expected values by a significant amount, the auditor shall investigate such differences by:
> (a) Inquiring of management and obtaining appropriate audit evidence relevant to management's responses; and
> (b) Performing other audit procedures as necessary in the circumstances." (ISA 520, para 7)

It is important to point out that analytical procedures occur within three stages of the audit process, as outlined below in **Figure 6.2**.

Planning analytical procedures is addressed in **Chapter 7**, 'The Risk Assessment Process', which includes a worked example that illustrates the planning of analytical procedures. Substantive analytical procedures are addressed throughout **Chapters 11–17** and more detail on final analytical procedures can be found in **Chapter 18**, 'Audit Work Conclusions'.

EXAMPLE 6.8: USES OF ANALYTICAL PROCEDURES

> Examples of the use of analytical procedures when gathering audit evidence include:
> * comparing profit and loss expenses year-on-year to identify any unexpected fluctuations (planning analytical procedures are performed at the planning stage to identify possible risks);
> * comparing period-end accruals and prepayments to prior-period balances and investigating any unexpected fluctuations (substantive analytical procedure);
> * comparing income statements year-on-year to see if unexpected fluctuations have been explained and corroborated throughout the audit, i.e. fluctuations make sense (final analytical procedures).

FIGURE 6.2: USES OF ANALYTICAL PROCEDURES IN THE AUDIT PROCESS

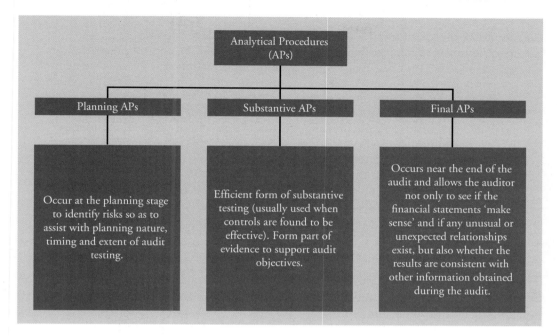

All of the audit procedures discussed above, or combinations thereof, may be used as risk assessment procedures, tests of controls or substantive procedures, depending on the context in which they are applied by the auditor.

Inquiry

Inquiry is the most utilised technique for gathering audit evidence. It consists of seeking information from knowledgeable persons inside or outside the entity. It is seldom used alone to provide sufficient audit evidence, but rather is used in conjunction with other corroborating evidence.

Inquiries may consist of oral or written requests for information from persons inside the entity or from third-party sources. The response to these inquiries will either necessitate the auditor getting **corroborative evidence** to substantiate the inquiry, or the auditor may receive information which differs significantly from other information that he has received and will therefore provide a basis for the auditor to modify or perform additional audit procedures. As included in Key Terms above, corroborative evidence is evidence or information that strengthens or supports other evidence or information received.

In some instances, where no additional evidence exists to corroborate management responses/oral representations, then the auditor may consider it necessary to obtain written representations from management.

Below are some examples of where the auditor might use the method of inquiry.

EXAMPLE 6.9: USES OF INQUIRY

Examples of the use of inquiry when gathering audit evidence include:
- inquiries made to management of the client entity about the control procedures around the sales process. In order to rely on the information that the management of the entity provides, the auditor must back this up with further corroborative evidence, for example, by observing the process;
- the auditor inquires why motor expenses have increased significantly. Management may state that this is because of rising fuel prices throughout the year. In order to rely on this information, the auditor must corroborate this information by reviewing invoices or looking at industry trends;
- the auditor inquires as to the presence of 'other receivables' on the balance sheet. When an explanation is received from management, the auditor must obtain sufficient audit evidence to substantiate the existence of this asset as inquiry in itself is not sufficient.

Thus far, in **Section 6.2** we established what is acceptable audit evidence and, in **Section 6.3**, how to collect audit evidence, which leads us to **Section 6.4**, where how to evaluate the audit evidence is explained.

6.4 EVALUATING AUDIT EVIDENCE

The goals in evaluating audit evidence are to decide, after considering all relevant audit evidence obtained, whether:
- the assessments of the risks of material misstatement at the assertion level are appropriate; and
- sufficient evidence has been obtained to reduce the risks of material misstatement in the financial statements to an acceptably low level.

When misstatements or deviations are found in the course of performing audit testing, consideration should be given to the following.
- The reason for the misstatement or deviation:
  - are there indicators or warning signals of possible fraud?
- Do the misstatements/deviations:
  - indicate a previously unidentified risk or weakness in an internal control that could be material?
  - impact on risk assessments and other planned procedures? or
  - point to the need to modify or perform further audit procedures?

Remember: an audit is a cumulative process of gathering and evaluating audit evidence. All evidence obtained should be evaluated together and the auditor should ensure that evidence is corroborative and not contradictory.

Having established in **Sections 6.2–6.4** what evidence should be collected and how to collect it and evaluate it, the types of audit procedure (audit testing) available to the auditor are now discussed.

6.5 TYPES OF TESTING

Introduction

Three types of audit procedure can be used by the auditor to gain sufficient appropriate audit evidence. These are set out in **Table 6.5**.

TABLE 6.5: TYPES OF AUDIT TESTING

Type of Testing	Type of Procedure	Discussed in detail in:
Risk Assessment	Inherent Risk Control Risk Detection Risk	**Chapter 7**, 'The Risk Assessment Process'
Tests of Controls	Tests of Details	**Chapter 8**, 'Controls and Controls Testing'
Substantive Testing	Tests of details; or Substantive analytical procedures	**Chapters 11–17**, on substantive procedures

Tests of Controls

There are a number of factors to consider when designing tests of controls. As a general rule, it is not worth testing controls that are believed to be unreliable, i.e. controls where there is a strong likelihood that exceptions will be found, because the sample sizes commonly used for testing controls are based on the expectation of no exceptions being found – otherwise the sample sizes required would be much larger.

In considering the controls of an organisation, a two-step approach is usually involved:
- **Step 1** – Assess the control environment and move on to Step 2 (testing of controls) only if the assessment indicates that the control environment is strong. If the assessment indicates that the control environment is weak, do not spend time testing controls; instead, perform focused substantive testing.
- **Step 2** – Test the controls (only where the control environment is assessed as being strong).

The assessment of the control environment and its impact on substantive testing is discussed at length in **Chapter 7**, 'The Risk Assessment Process'. A full discussion on the testing of controls can be found in **Chapter 8**, 'Controls and Controls Testing'.

Substantive Procedures

While, as indicated above, it is possible to reduce the level of substantive testing where the control environment is identified as strong, ISA (UK and Ireland) 330 *The Auditor's Responses to Assessed Risks* (ISA 330) states that the following substantive procedures should be performed at a minimum for each material class of transactions, account balance and disclosure, irrespective of the assessed risk of material misstatement:

> "(a) agreeing or reconciling the financial statements with the underlying accounting records; and
>
> (b) examining material journal entries and other adjustments made during the course of preparing the financial statements." (ISA 330, para 20)

Substantive testing should be performed over:
- areas that have been identified as significant risk areas; and
- material classes of transactions, account balances and disclosures.

Substantive procedures aim to obtain evidence to support the financial statement assertions either using **tests of details** or **substantive analytical procedures**. The nature, timing and extent of substantive procedures will depend on the assessed levels of inherent and control risks.

Tests of Details

Tests of details are procedures that are used to obtain audit evidence that will substantiate a financial statement amount. They are used to obtain audit evidence regarding certain assertions, such as existence, accuracy and valuation. As discussed earlier in this chapter, when designing a procedure, the auditor needs to consider carefully the nature of the assertion for which evidence is required. This will determine the type of evidence to be examined, the nature of the procedure, and the population from which to select the sample. Practical examples of substantive tests of details and the assertions that they address are set out below in **Table 6.6**.

Substantive Analytical Procedures (SAPs)

Substantive analytical procedures (SAPs) involve a comparison of amounts or relationships in the financial statements, with a precise expectation developed from information obtained from understanding the entity and other audit evidence gained during the engagement. **Table 6.7** identifies the stages involved in building an expectation, the considerations required by ISA 520 as well as a worked example by way of explanation.

The degree of reliability of the data (or information) used to develop expectations needs to be consistent with levels of assurance and precision intended to be derived from the analytical procedure. Other substantive procedures may also be required to determine whether the underlying data is sufficiently reliable. Tests of controls may also be considered to address other assertions, such as the data's completeness, existence and accuracy. Internal controls over non-financial information can often be tested in conjunction with other tests of controls.

In considering whether the source data is sufficiently reliable for achieving the audit objective, the following questions can be asked.

- Is the data from an internal source or a source external to the entity?
- If it is internal data, was it obtained by persons not directly responsible for its accuracy?
- Was the data developed under a reliable system with adequate internal controls?
- If broad industry data was used in developing an expectation is it comparable for use within the entity?
- How relevant is the data?
- Was the data subject to audit testing in the current or prior year?

TABLE 6.6: EXAMPLES OF SUBSTANTIVE TESTS OF DETAILS

Financial Statement Area	Test of Detail	Assertion Addressed
Sales and accounts receivable	Testing sales cut-off.	Cut-off.
Accounts receivable	Assessing adequacy of allowance for doubtful debts.	Valuation.
Accounts payable	Reconciling balances per accounts payable listing to supplier statements.	Completeness, accuracy, existence/occurrence and rights and obligations.
Accounts payable	Testing for unrecorded liabilities.	Completeness and cut-off.
Non-current Fixed Assets	Verification of ownership of fixed assets.	Existence/occurrence and rights and obligations.
Non-current Fixed Assets	Re-computation of depreciation expense.	Accuracy.
Bank	Testing bank reconciliations.	Accuracy, existence/occurrence and completeness.
Bank	Confirmation of bank accounts.	Accuracy, existence/occurrence, rights and obligations and cut-off.
Prepayments	Testing prepaid expenses.	Accuracy, existence/occurrence, cut-off and completeness.
Other tax and social security	Testing compliance with tax regulations.	Accuracy.

TABLE 6.7: STEPS, CONSIDERATIONS AND WORKED EXAMPLE OF A SUBSTANTIVE ANALYTICAL PROCEDURE

Step	Considerations	Worked Example
Identify balance/transaction and assertion(s) to be addressed.	The auditor needs to consider the suitability of the substantive analytical procedure given the assertion/s being addressed (i.e. ensure the test is relevant to cover the assertion/s).	Payroll – Completeness, Occurrence, Recording, Rights and Obligations. Payroll figure in the statement of comprehensive income is €1,000,000.
Calculate the tolerable misstatement value.	The tolerable misstatement value is the maximum difference which the auditor is permitted to accept between his calculated expectation and the actual value of the transaction/balance in the financial statements. The size of the tolerable misstatement is influenced by materiality and risk.	The tolerable misstatement value will be influenced by the materiality of the payroll figure and the identified risks associated with the payroll. Tolerable misstatement is set at, e.g. 5% and calculated to be €50,000.
Consider the practicality of calculating a precise expectation within the tolerable misstatement (i.e. is it going to be possible to calculate an expected value or are there too many variables making up the value that the auditor is trying to prove).	Consider how practical it is to be able to build a precise expectation of the payroll value in the statement of comprehensive income to be within the tolerable misstatement. If there are not too many variables influencing the base number (i.e. the environment is stable), then it is more likely to be possible to build a precise expectation.	The audited payroll figure for the prior year was €1,100,000. Three staff were let go at the beginning of the year. Their combined salaries were €110,000. No pay increases were granted during the year. There is no overtime or bonuses. Using the above information it seems that it is practical that the auditor could build a precise expectation to be within the tolerable misstatement calculated.

Consider the reliability of the source information being used to build the expectation.	All source information will need to be subject to audit procedures to validate it is complete, accurate, valid, etc. As a result, it may prove to be inefficient to perform the substantive analytical procedure if the source information needed to build the expectation requires extensive tests of details.	Information needed: Prior-year payroll figure – reliable? – yes, audited last year. Salaries of the three members of staff let go – reliable? – easily validated by checking their employment contracts, P45s/ termination letters. We do not expect that anything else has changed, so the information to be used to build the expectation is reliable/easily auditable (the environment is relatively stable).
Calculate the expectation.	All calculations must be retained as audit evidence and each piece of source information must be cross-referenced to evidence supporting its validity, completeness, etc.	Prior Year Payroll €1,100,000 Less Reduction in salaries (€110,000) Expected Payroll €990,000
Compare the calculated expectation to the actual figure in the financial statements and compare the difference to the tolerable misstatement.	If the calculated difference between the figure in the financial statements and the calculated expectation is less than the tolerable misstatement, then no further testing is required. However, if it is greater than the tolerable misstatement, then the auditor must investigate the difference by inquiring of management and performing appropriate other audit procedures as necessary in the circumstances.	Figure per Financial Statements €1,000,000 Calculated Expectation €990,000 Difference €10,000 Tolerable misstatement €50,000 Margin of safety €40,000

Table 6.8 below provides examples of common substantive analytical procedures the auditor might carry out on various classes of transactions and account balances (indicated in the first column). The second column in the Table briefly outlines the type of substantive analytical procedure that can be applied.

TABLE 6.8: EXAMPLES OF SUBSTANTIVE ANALYTICAL PROCEDURES

Financial Statement Amount	Relationship and Procedure
Revenue	Selling price applied to volume information about shipments (i.e. volume sold multiplied by price should equal revenue). This would have to be applied to an organisation with a simple and stable pricing structure.
Depreciation expense	Depreciation rates applied to fixed asset balances after allowing for the effect of additions and disposals.
Payroll expense	Pay rates applied to number of employees.
Commission expense	Commission rate applied to sales.
Interest charge	Interest rate for loan agreement applied to the reducing balance of the loan.

Other analytical procedures can take the form of:

- detailed comparisons of current financial statements with those of a prior period or with current operating budgets. For example, an increase in accounts receivable where there is no corresponding increase in sales could indicate an issue with the collectability of receivables (i.e. there could be an issue with the valuation assertion related to receivables);
- comparison of sales results year-on-year by product type or by customer – this could help explain month-to-month or year-to-year sales fluctuations.

6.6 EXTERNAL CONFIRMATIONS

Introduction

As outlined earlier in this chapter, **external confirmation** (the receiving of direct representation from a third party to verify information included in the financial statements) is one of the methods of obtaining audit evidence. External confirmation can form a very reliable source of evidence, provided the process is controlled adequately, as it ticks three essential boxes when it comes to reliability;

- its source is an independent third party;
- it is obtained directly by the auditor; and
- it exists in documentary form.

ISA (UK and Ireland) 505 *External Confirmations* (ISA 505) outlines some guidance with regard to the use of external confirmations to ensure their reliability is not compromised, and these are discussed below.

Designing External Confirmation Requests

Due to the fact that the design of the confirmation request can affect the response rate and the reliability of the responses, it is important that the auditor carefully considers:
- the layout and presentation of the request;
- previous experience from similar audit engagements (e.g. if response rates for receivables confirmations in a particular industry tend to be low, it may be inefficient to use this method);
- the method of communication (i.e. hard or soft copy response); and
- the existence of authorisation by the client entity's management within the request (i.e. permission to third party to release requested information to the auditor) can encourage a higher response rate.

The request, overall, should be easy for the third party to understand and easy to respond to.

A **positive external confirmation request** is generally the most efficient and reliable type of response. It requests the confirming party to reply in all cases (i.e. whether they agree or disagree with the balance). Positive external confirmation requests can take two forms, as outlined in **Table 6.9** below; and each form has its advantages and disadvantages.

TABLE 6.9: ADVANTAGES AND DISADVANTAGES OF INCLUDING CONFIRMABLE BALANCES ON THE CONFIRMATION TO THE CONFIRMING PARTIES

	Advantages	Disadvantages
1. Information to be confirmed included on the request. Example: requests sent to a sample of debtors to confirm the balances outstanding at year end. The balance is included on the request and the confirming party need only sign in agreement.	Less work required by the confirming party, which might increase the response rate.	Not very reliable audit evidence as the confirming party may reply to the request without actually verifying that the information is correct.
2. Information to be confirmed not included on the request. Instead the confirming party is required to add the information. Example: requests sent to a sample of debtors to confirm the balances outstanding at year end. The balance is not included on the request and the confirming party needs to complete the request by adding in the balance they believe was outstanding at the stated year end.	More reliable audit evidence, as confirming party cannot sign without checking the balance; he must include the balance on the request.	Due to the extra work involved, the response rate may be reduced.

The auditor can either include the balance per the financial statements on the confirmation request or ask the third party to confirm what they believe the balance to be. **Table 6.9** discusses the advantages and disadvantages of each of these approaches.

ISA 505 also suggests that the auditor perform some testing on the addresses of the third parties to whom the confirmations are being sent, supplied by the client entity, to ensure their validity prior to posting.

A **negative external confirmation request** is a request that the confirming party respond directly to the auditor only if the confirming party disagrees with the information provided on the request. This is not a very reliable form of request as a non-response may simply indicate that the confirming party did not receive the request. This is not considered a reliable form of confirmation request.

Controlling Responses to External Confirmation Requests

It is essential that the auditor instruct the confirming party to respond directly to him rather than to the client entity. If the response goes directly to the client, it may be subject to manipulation and its reliability would be compromised. In order to encourage responses directly to the auditor and to improve the response rate, the auditor usually includes a self-addressed, stamped envelope. If the response is in the form of an e-mail or fax, the auditor should be confident of its source. If there is any doubt about the source, the auditor should modify or add procedures to resolve doubts over the reliability of the information to be used as audit evidence.

The auditor may need to send a reminder or follow-up the confirmation request with a phone call or e-mail to encourage a response. Confirmation by telephone is not sufficient audit evidence under the standard and alternative procedures will be required where such a confirmation is received.

Evaluating Responses to External Confirmation Requests

ISA 505 indicates four possible results from external confirmation requests, as outlined in **Table 6.10** below.

6.7 AUDIT DOCUMENTATION

According to ISA (UK and Ireland) 220 *Quality Control for an Audit of Financial Statements* (ISA 220): "On or before the date of the auditor's report, the engagement partner shall, through a review of the audit documentation and discussion with the engagement team, be satisfied that sufficient appropriate audit evidence has been obtained to support the conclusions reached and for the auditor's report to be issued" (ISA 220, para 17). Thus, the audit firm/auditor cannot establish if sufficient appropriate audit evidence has been obtained unless he has audit documentation which can be reviewed.

TABLE 6.10: EXTERNAL CONFIRMATION RESPONSE TYPES AND AUDITOR ACTIONS

Response Type	Auditor Actions Required
Appropriate: confirming party agrees with information provided or provides information requested without any exception.	No further procedures with respect to this test are required.
Response deemed **unreliable**.	Modify or add procedures to resolve doubts over the reliability of the information to be used as audit evidence.
A **non-response** to a positive confirmation.	Perform alternative procedures.
A response indicating an **exception**.	Identify reason for exception. The exception may indicate an error or not. For example, cash in transit, goods in transit may not render the client balance incorrect. Where the exception does relate to an error on the client's behalf, then they should be recorded on an error schedule (which is a document that summarises all errors found – a fuller discussion on the error schedule is contained in **Chapter 18**).

ISA (UK and Ireland) 230 *Audit Documentation* (ISA 230), paragraph 2, outlines the main purpose of **audit documentation** as providing:
"(a) Evidence of the auditor's basis for a conclusion about the achievement of the overall objectives of the auditor; and
(b) Evidence that the audit was planned and performed in accordance with ISAs (UK and Ireland)and applicable legal and regulatory requirements." (ISA 230, para 2)
The documentation also assists the audit team in planning and performing the audit, reviewing work and conclusions, referring to prior-year work and conclusions, as well as enabling the conduct of quality review. Audit documentation is commonly referred to as audit working papers. Audit working papers should record all of the evidence gathered during the course of the audit and can take the form of copies of source files (e.g. invoices) viewed by the auditor as well as calculations performed by the auditor (e.g. substantive analytical procedures).

ISA 230 outlines the required standard of audit documentation by referring to the documentation's intended purpose. The standard states that an experienced auditor with no previous connection with the audit should be able to pick up the audit file and understand clearly the nature, timing and extent of procedures performed to comply with the ISAs, the results of such procedures and any significant matters that arose during the audit, as well as the conclusions reached on those matters.

A sample audit working paper is provided below at **Example 6.10** and includes such basic items as:
- the preparer, reviewer and partner name and date;
- working paper reference number;
- name and year end of the company;
- nature of test and assertion being addressed;
- test objective; and
- test details and extent (i.e. what is being tested and the size of the sample being tested).

As can be seen in **Example 6.10**, as well as the basic elements, note that each characteristic of the test is recorded (i.e. which week was selected, which PO number was selected, etc.). These details are important to allow a reviewer to validate the conclusions reached. Note also that beside each week selected a 'working paper reference' is given, which means that a copy of the open PO report review can be obtained in the audit file at that reference; the same is true of the explanation obtained. Finally, a conclusion is drawn on the test to determine if the objective was reached. All of the above information helps to address the objective of a working paper audit document (i.e. it supports the decision drawn by the auditor).

EXAMPLE 6.10: SAMPLE AUDIT WORKING PAPER

		Working Paper Reference	PC1
Name of the Client	Woodco	**Working Paper Preparer**	Mary Foley
Year End	31-Dec-12	**Preparation Date**	17-Jan-13
Testing Type	Controls Testing	**Reviewer**	Brian Maher
Cycle Under Testing	Purchases	**Review Date**	22-Jan-13
Assertion	Completeness	**Partner**	Gerry Nolan
		Partner Review Date	21-Mar-13

Objective	To ensure all purchases are recorded timely as the goods or service is received by confirming that "Open Purchase Orders" (POs) are reviewed weekly by the finance reporting manager in accordance with company written policy and POs greater than one month old are followed up for investigation.

Control Activity Identified to Cover Assertion	Open PO report is reviewed weekly by the Finance Reporting Manager and items greater than one month old are followed up.

Test Details	Randomly selected five weeks from 1 January 2012 to 31 December 2012 and requested a copy of the Open PO review. **(See sample size calculation @ Working Paper Reference PC1a)** *Ensured review was signed off as being reviewed by the Finance Reporting Manager. *From each review I selected one item greater than one month old to ensure explanations were obtained for its age.

Week	PO review obtained	Working Paper Reference	PO Number Selected	PO Date	Explanation Available	Working Paper Reference
2	Yes	PC2	PO00012678	12-Dec-11	Yes	PC7
14	Yes	PC3	PO00013787	01-Feb-12	Yes	PC8
30	Yes	PC4	PO00036372	03-Mar-12	Yes	PC9
41	Yes	PC5	PO00046529	19-Jun-12	Yes	PC10
49	Yes	PC6	PO00026383	19-Jul-12	Yes	PC11

Conclusion	Open PO review is performed weekly to ensure goods are receipted timely and accruals recorded timely.
Is the Control Effective?	Yes

Such a working paper can be a 'hard' or 'soft' copy document; the references to the reviews and the explanations contained within the working paper can also be either in print or electronic versions. Working papers can also take the form of audit programmes, analyses carried out in Excel, summaries of significant matters, receivables confirmations, as well as board meeting minutes or correspondence with respect to significant matters.

Once all matters are concluded upon and an opinion reached, the 'Final Audit File' should be reviewed to ensure it supports the audit opinion. This file, once completed, should not be amended without noting the specific reasons why the amendments were made, when and by whom.

6.8 AUDIT SAMPLING

Introduction

ISA 530 *Audit Sampling* (ISA 530) defines audit sampling as: "The application of audit procedures to less than 100% of items within a population of audit relevance such that all sampling units have a chance of selection" (ISA 530, para 5(a)).

The objective of the auditor when using audit sampling is to provide an appropriate basis from which to draw conclusions about the population from which the sample is selected. Audit sampling can use either a statistical or non-statistical approach.

In general terms, sampling is the examination of a few items (or sampling units) drawn from a defined mass of data (or population), with a view to inferring characteristics about the mass of data as a whole.

Sampling has been an accepted auditing technique since the early part of the 20th Century and today is recognised as an essential feature of most audits. Three main reasons for the importance of sampling are as follows.

1. In the modern business environment it is **not economically feasible** to examine the details of **every transaction** and account balance.
2. Testing a sample of transactions is **faster** and **less costly** than testing the whole population.
3. Auditors are required to form an opinion about the truth and fairness of the financial statements. They are **not required to reach a position of certainty** or to be concerned about the statements' absolute accuracy. The task can usually be accomplished by testing samples of evidence; there is no need to test the whole population.

Sampling may not be appropriate in certain circumstances. Such circumstances are primarily:

- when the auditor has already been advised of **a high level of errors or systems failures** or a **possible fraud**;
- where **populations are too small** (e.g. only 10 non-current fixed assets were purchased in the period) it may be more effective to check them all;
- where all the transactions in a population are **material**, e.g. a manufacturer of airplanes – they may only sell a few in a year, but each contract is worth several million Euros;
- where data is **required by law to be fully disclosed** in the financial statements, e.g. directors' emoluments;
- where the **population is not homogeneous**.

Non-statistical Judgemental Sampling versus Statistical Sampling

There are two key types of sampling, judgmental and statistical sampling, and it is important to be able to distinguish between these two approaches. They are discussed in turn below.

Judgemental Sampling

Judgemental sampling refers to the use of sampling techniques in circumstances where the auditor relies on his own judgement to decide:

- how large the sample should be;
- which items from the population should be selected; and
- whether to accept or not accept the population as reliable, based on the results obtained from the sample units examined.

This sampling method has advantages over statistical sampling in that it is generally **faster**, and therefore **less costly** to apply. However, unlike statistical sampling, the method provides **no measure of sampling risk** and, should the auditor's judgement be challenged (particularly in a court of law), the conclusions reached with respect to the sample may be **difficult to defend**. Furthermore, when using judgemental sampling it is **difficult not to introduce sample bias** – whether it be in relation to sample size, the items selected or the conclusions reached with respect to the population.

Statistical Sampling

Statistical sampling refers to the use of sampling techniques which rely on probability theory to help determine:
- how large the sample should be; and
- whether to accept or not accept the population as reliable based on the results obtained from the sample units examined.

ISA 530, paragraph 5, defines statistical sampling as "[a]n approach to sampling that has the following characteristics:
   (i) Random selection of sample items; and
   (ii) The use of probability theory to evaluate sample results, including measurement of sampling risk."

This sampling method has certain important advantages over judgemental sampling:
- it is **unbiased**;
- should aspects of the sampling be challenged, because it is based on probability theory and, therefore, considered to be objective (rather than based on the auditor's subjective judgement), it is **readily defensible**; and
- it **permits quantification of sampling risk**. For example, if a sample is selected on the basis of a 5% sampling risk, there is a 5% chance that the sample is not representative of the population and, as a result, a 5% chance that an inappropriate conclusion may be reached about the population.

However, statistical sampling can be more **complex and costly to apply** than judgemental sampling due to the time associated with setting it up and the associated skill.

Designing the Sample

The design of a sample requires the auditor to give some consideration to the specific purpose to be achieved and the combination of audit procedures that are most likely to assist in the achievement of these objectives.

When designing the sample, auditors need to consider the following.
- **Population** The population (classes of transactions or account balances) is the data set from which the sample will be chosen. In order to draw valid conclusions about the whole population from a sample, the essential feature of the population is that it be homogeneous.
- **Level of confidence (level of desired assurance)** Auditors work to levels of confidence which can be expressed precisely. For example, a 5% confidence level means that there are 19 chances out of 20 that the sample is representative of the population as a whole.

Stated differently, there is one chance in 20 that the sample, on which the auditor draws conclusions, is non-representative of the population as a whole.

- **Precision** From a sample it is not possible to say that the auditors are, *say*, 95% certain that, for example, the error rate in a population of inventory calculations is 5%, but only that the error rate is 5% ± y% where ± y% is the precision interval. The level of confidence and the precision interval are related in that, for a given sample size, higher confidence can be expressed in a wider precision interval and vice versa.

- **Tolerable rate of deviation** "A rate of deviation from prescribed internal control procedures set by the auditor in respect of which the auditor seeks to obtain an appropriate level of assurance that the rate of deviation set by the auditor is not exceeded by the actual rate of deviation in the population." (ISA 530, para 5)

- **Tolerable misstatement** " … the application of performance materiality, as defined in ISA (UK and Ireland) 320, to a particular sampling procedure. Tolerable misstatement may be the same amount or an amount lower than performance materiality" (ISA 530, para A3). The auditor seeks to obtain an appropriate level of assurance that the monetary amount set by the auditor (i.e. the tolerable misstatement) is not exceeded by the actual misstatement contained in the balance.

  The essential procedure is to set a tolerable misstatement, then to project the error rate implied by the sampling results onto the population and to compare the two (e.g. the tolerable misstatement is set at €100, 20% of the population was tested and an error of €4 was found. The total population value is €1,000, 20% of population was tested, which is €200, and a €4 error was found, which is an error rate of 2% (4/200). The sample tested is representative of the entire population, which means there is likely a 2% error rate in the balance of the population not tested. The population not tested is €1000 × 80% = €800 and 2% of this is €16. The total error in the population is deemed to be €20 (€4 + €16). The auditor now compares this error of €20 to the tolerable misstatement set at €100 and because the €20 is within the tolerable misstatement set, no further testing is required. If the projected error is larger than the tolerable misstatement, then further auditing procedures will be necessary in the area.

- **Materiality** This is a subset of risk. Materiality is fundamental to auditing and, with all populations being sampled, materiality should be considered in fixing the sample size because populations that are material to the overall audit opinion (e.g. inventory, receivables, payables) must be sampled with smaller precision intervals and higher confidence levels.

Sample Selection Methods

The methods used to select the sample are as important as the number of items tested. In order for the results of the sample to be used to calculate a projected misstatement, the sample should be:

- Random – a random sample is one where each item of the population has an equal (or specified) chance of being selected. Statistical inferences may not be valid unless the sample is truly random.

- Representative – the sample should be representative of the items in the whole population. For example, it should contain a similar proportion of high- and low-value items as that of the population.

The following are some examples of sample selection methods as outlined in ISA 530, Appendix 4.

Random sampling This is simply choosing items subjectively while trying to avoid bias. Bias might come in by tendency to favour items in a particular location or in an accessible file or, conversely, in picking items because they appear unusual. Simple random sampling means that all items in the population have (or are given) a number. Numbers are selected by a means which give every number an equal chance of being selected. This is done using random number tables or computer- or calculator-generated random numbers.

Systematic selection This method involves making a random start and then taking every nth item thereafter. The sampling interval is decided by dividing the population size by the sample size, e.g. if the population is 1,000 and the number to be sampled is 100, the sampling interval will be every tenth transaction. The starting point is determined randomly within the first ten items.

Block sampling This method involves randomly choosing one block of items, e.g. all March invoices. This sampling method has none of the desired characteristics and is not recommended. Analogous to this is **cluster sampling**, where data is maintained in clusters (groups or bunches), as wage records are kept in weeks and purchase invoices in months. The idea is to select a cluster randomly and then to examine all the items in the cluster chosen. The problem with this method is that the sample may not be representative as the month or cluster chosen may have unique characteristics.

Monetary Unit Sampling (MUS) The application of value-weighted selection is appropriate for those populations within which there are large variances. Large variance populations are those like receivables or inventory, where the individual units of the population are of widely different sizes. The method is suited to populations where errors are not expected. It implicitly takes into account the auditor's concept of materiality.

Two further methods of sampling are explained below:

Attribute sampling This provides results based on two possible attributes, e.g. correct/not-correct, and is used primarily in connection with the testing of internal controls, e.g. non-monetary testing. It is generally used in compliance testing where the extent of application of a control is to be determined, i.e. the test is "complies/does not comply". Each deviation from a control procedure is given an equal weight in the final evaluation of results. (MUS is an attribute sampling technique as it measures monetary deviations.)

Multi-stage sampling This method is appropriate when data is stored in two or more locations. For example, inventory in a chain of shops. The first stage is to randomly select a sample of shops and the second stage is to randomly select inventory items from the chosen shops.

Sampling Risk versus Non-sampling Risk

Having considered the methods open to the auditor in selecting his sample, it is important now to discuss the risks that exist when performing testing using sampling. The methods of sampling discussed above should help to reduce sampling risk but can never eliminate the risk associated with sampling. Let us first consider the question "What is sampling risk?" ISA 530 defines sampling risk as "The risk that the auditor's conclusions based on a sample may be different from the conclusion if the entire population were subjected to the same audit procedure" (ISA 530, para 5(c)). Naturally, if you extrapolate an error rate onto a total population, you will not predict the actual error contained in that population, rather it suggests the likely outcome of testing 100% of the population.

Non-sampling risk is the risk that the auditor reaches an erroneous conclusion for any reason not related to sampling risk. Examples of non-sampling risk can include the use of inappropriate procedures to test noted assertions (e.g. vouching invoices from the general ledger to the signed POD to test for completeness), the audit evidence yielded will be inappropriate whether 100% of the population is tested or just a sample.

Calculation of Sample Size

Now that the term 'sampling' has been explained as well as the methods used by the auditor when carrying out sampling, how the sample size is calculated will now be discussed.

The sample size can be determined by the application of a formula from statistics or through the exercise of professional judgement. ISA 530 does not provide formulas, but it does provide factors that may impact on the auditor's determination of sample size.

Table 6.11 below summarises the factors that influence the size of a sample when the auditor is testing the controls of the client entity.

Table 6.12 summaries the factors that influence the size of a sample when the auditor is testing an item from the financial statements (i.e. performing substantive testing procedures). It is important to understand the difference between the two tables.

TABLE 6.11: FACTORS INFLUENCING SAMPLE SIZE FOR TESTS OF CONTROLS

Factor	Impact on Sample Size
Risk	The greater the reliance on the results of a test of control using audit sampling, the lower the sampling risk the auditors are willing to accept and, consequently, the larger the sample size (i.e. if inherent risks identified are high, then the auditor will have gained no comfort with respect to inherent assurance and as such cannot take too many risks and will avoid sampling risk by testing a larger volume of the population.)
Tolerable rate of deviation	The lower the tolerable misstatement rate, the higher the sample size and vice versa.
Expected Deviation Rate	The higher the expected rate of deviation, the larger the sample size needs to be so that the auditor can more accurately estimate the actual rate of deviation. High expected misstatement values may result in a decision not to perform tests of control at all.

Desired level of assurance	The greater the level of assurance the auditor wishes to achieve, the larger the sample size in order to more accurately predict the actual deviation in the population.
Population Volume	The population volume has virtually no effect on the sample size (unless population is small, in which case the auditor would likely decide that it is more efficient to just test 100%).

TABLE 6.12: FACTORS INFLUENCING SAMPLE SIZE FOR SUBSTANTIVE TESTS OF DETAILS

Factor	Impact on Sample Size
Audit risk components (inherent, control and detection risk)	The higher the assessment of inherent risk, the more audit evidence is required to support the auditor's conclusion and therefore the larger the sample size at the substantive stage (unless the control environment is strong enough to mitigate any inherent risk noted). If there are low inherent risks and low control risks, then detection risk will be high and therefore sample sizes will be small (a full discussion on this can be found in **Chapter 7**, 'The Risk Assessment Process').
Existence of Other Substantive procedures addressing the same assertion	The more the auditor is relying on other substantive procedures (tests of details or substantive analytical procedures) to reduce to acceptable level the detection risk regarding a particular population, the less assurance the auditor will require from sampling and therefore the smaller the sample size can be.
Desired level of assurance	The greater the level of assurance the auditor wishes to achieve, the higher the sample size in order to more accurately predict the actual value of the misstatement in the population.
Tolerable misstatements	The lower the tolerable misstatement, the larger the sample size that is required.
Expected Misstatement	If errors are expected, a larger sample needs to be examined to confirm that the actual value of the misstatement is less than the tolerable misstatement.
Population value	The less material the monetary value of the population to the financial statements, the smaller the sample size that may be required.
Stratification	Should stratification be possible, then the auditor will be able to achieve lower sample sizes (see **Example 6.13**, which demonstrates this).
Population volume	Virtually no effect on the sample size unless population is small (in which case it may be more efficient to test 100%).

Projecting the Error into the Population

Now that we understand what is meant by the term 'sampling', and we know the various approaches used to select a sample and determine its size, we must now consider how to use the results of the sample tested. Let us return to an example we introduced earlier in this section: 20% of a population is tested and an error of €4 is found. The total population value is €1,000; 20% of population was tested, which is €200, and a €4 error was found, which is an error rate of 2% (4 ÷ 200). The sample tested is representative of the entire population and so we expect that errors will arise at the same rate throughout the population. This means there is likely a 2% error rate in the balance of the population not tested. The population not tested is €1,000 × 80% = €800 and 2% of this is €16. The total error in the population is deemed to be €20 (€4 + €16). We have 'projected' the error found in the population tested against the balance of the population not tested.

Before further discussing the projection of errors into the population as a whole, it is important to familiarise ourselves with some key terms included at **Table 6.13**.

TABLE 6.13: KEY TERMS FOR SAMPLING AND ERROR PROJECTION

Anomaly "A misstatement or deviation that is demonstrably not representative of misstatements or deviations in a population" (ISA 530, para 5(e)) (i.e. an isolated incident).

Deviation Refers to the departure from a prescribed internal control (i.e. the control did not work as described by management).

Error Monetary value representing an error found with respect to the financial statements.

Sampling Unit "The individual items constituting a population" (ISA 530, para 5(f)) (e.g. within the receivables balance either the individual invoices outstanding or the individual receivables balances may be considered as the sampling units).

Stratification "The process of dividing a population into sub-populations, each of which is a group of sampling units which have similar characteristics" (ISA 530, para 5(h)) (e.g. within the receivables balance you may divide the receivables into categories of value: greater than €100,000, between €50,000 and €100,000 and less than €50,000).

Tolerable Misstatement Monetary amount set by the auditor which represents the maximum monetary error value he is willing to accept to obtain an appropriate level of assurance.

Tolerable Rate of Deviation Maximum number of deviations the auditor is willing to accept in order to determine that the control being tested is sufficiently strong. Remember, 'deviation' refers to attribute testing, where the items being tested have only two possible outcomes (e.g. a document is either signed or not signed). If the auditor determines that he can accept one document not being signed and still determine that the control being tested is strong, then one is the tolerable rate of deviation, anything above this and the auditor will conclude that the control being tested does not work and cannot be relied upon to reduce substantive testing.

For tests of details, the auditor should project the errors found in the sample to the population as a whole (ISA 530, para 14). Once errors have been identified, they should be projected to the population after considering any anomalies that may impact on the projection (ISA 530, application note 19).

Projection of an error (or extrapolation of an error) is best described by way of example:

EXAMPLE 6.11: PROJECTING ERRORS

An auditor is performing substantive tests of details on the revenue figure in the financial statements, which is €8,560,000 (made up of 2,210 invoices). He has decided that the most appropriate test is to select, using statistical methods, a sample of invoices from the sales (revenue) account in the general ledger and vouch the invoices back to signed customer purchase order delivery (POD) documents. This will test for occurrence, rights and obligations and recording and classification. Using the sample size formula prescribed by your firm, you have calculated a sample size of 200.

You obtain the general ledger listing and select your 200 invoices, which total a value of €774,661. You find three invoices where the signed POD cannot be obtained and inquiry of management has yielded no acceptable answers. The total value of these invoices is €25,231. You are required to project the error to the population.

Materiality is €430,000.

Projecting the Error

	€
Value of Balance Tested	774,661
Value of Total Population	8,560,000
Value of Balance not Tested	7,785,339
Value of Errors found (not noted as anomalies)	25,231
Error Rate *(value of errors found/value tested)*	3.3%
Projected *(error rate × value not tested)*	**253,572**

The €25,231 is a known error (it is confirmed to be wrong). The €253,572 is likely to be wrong (projection based on error rate found). The amounts of the misstatements are not individually material, however both amounts will be recorded on the errors schedule, to be assessed at the end of the audit in aggregate with other errors found. If in aggregate a material error is found, the auditors will return to the projected error to see if they can more accurately quantify the error rate by testing more of the population to see if they get a more favourable error rate, hence reducing the known error value.

Let us now consider stratification and the benefits it may bring. At the beginning of the discussion on sampling, the advantages and disadvantages of judgemental and statistical sampling were discussed. Stratification combines these two methods so as not to reduce the reliability of the judgemental influence, i.e. it takes advantage of the best parts of both methods: judgement, which can help with efficiency, and statistics, which avoids bias. Stratification, as noted above, divides the population into groups based on a characteristic. The use of stratification can help to reduce sample sizes, making the audit more efficient while also increasing the value of the population being tested, but in a way that does not reduce reliability or introduce bias in a negative way. The information supplied in **Example 6.11** is now used in **Example 6.12** to illustrate how stratification can improve on efficiency and effectiveness of sample testing.

EXAMPLE 6.12: STRATIFICATION OF THE POPULATION

The details are the same as in **Example 6.11** above, but on receiving the general ledger listing, the auditor uses CAATs (computer assisted audit techniques) to divide the population (invoices) according to their value. The following is the result of the stratification.

	Stratification of Population			
	Block 1	**Block 2**	**Block 3**	**Total**
Value in €	1,240,000	3,220,000	4,100,000	8,560,000
Number of units in stratum	10	1,000	1,200	2,210
Value of sample taken	1,240,000	750,000	170,833	2,160,833
Number of units in sample taken	10	35	50	95
% value tested	100%	23%	4%	25%
% units tested	100%	3.5%	4%	4%

Now that stratification has been applied, we can see that vouching just 10 of the invoices will cover €1.24 million of the total value of the population, leaving the rest of the population at a lower value, which will result in a lower sample size. By stratifying further we can ensure our sample covers a range of middle-value invoices by applying statistical sampling methods to the middle range of invoices. This leaves the high-volume, low-value invoices, which again we can apply statistical sampling methods to in order to determine an appropriate sample size.

Now let us compare the two approaches taken.

	Stratification Applied	No Stratification Applied
Value of total population	€8,560,000	€8,560,000
Number of units	2,210	2,210
Value of sample taken	€2,160,833	€774,661
Number of units in sample taken	95	200
% value tested	25%	9%
% units tested	4%	9%

We can see from the above that the stratification approach has given us significantly more coverage of the total value, which is more important than the number of items tested. This is acceptable provided that statistical methods are used on the remaining population, and all invoices have an equal chance of being selected.

Finally, let us consider the effect of the existence of an anomaly, again using the details from **Example 6.11**.

EXAMPLE 6.13: CONSIDERING ERRORS RELATING TO ISOLATED EVENTS

The details are the same as in **Example 6.11** above, however you find three invoices where the signed POD cannot be obtained and inquiry of management has yielded no acceptable answers with respect to two of those invoices, valued at €15,340. With regard to the third invoice you were advised that the driver crashed on the way to the delivery and the inventory was destroyed. The settlement clerk (who normally validates the delivery on receipt of the signed purchase order delivery note) misheard what had happened and thought the event had taken place after delivery of the goods. As such she recorded the delivery as successful and issued the invoice. This was the driver's only delivery that day and the invoice, for €9,891, was sent to the customer. You validated this story to the insurance claim and corroborated it with the settlement clerk.

Projecting the Error

The invoice error of €9,891 is considered an anomaly (an isolated incident) and it is not representative of the population. It should be excluded from the error rate calculation.

	€
Value of sample taken	774,661
Value of total population	8,560,000
Value of population not tested	7,785,339
Value of sample tested excluding anomaly (€774,661 – €9,891)	764,770
Value of Errors found (not noted as anomalies)	15,340
Error Rate *(value of errors found ÷ value tested excluding anomaly)*	2.0%
Projected *(error rate × value not tested)*	156,161

A known error of €25,231 still exists, however the projected error (likely total error in the population) is only €156,161.

6.9 OPENING BALANCES

When collecting audit evidence regarding the figures in the financial statements, the auditor cannot forget that comparative figures (which ultimately represent the opening balances) are included in a set of financial statements and so he must obtain audit evidence relating to those comparative figures.

IAS 1 *Presentation of Financial Statements* (IAS 1) requires that comparative information shall be disclosed in respect of the previous period for all amounts reported in the financial statements, both on the face of financial statements and notes, unless another Standard requires otherwise. According to ISA 510 *Initial Audit Engagements – Opening Balances,* paragraph 3, states that it is essential that the auditor obtains sufficient appropriate audit evidence about whether opening balances contain misstatements that materially affect the current period's financial statements and that consistent accounting policies were applied to both opening balances and current year balances.

With respect to continuing audit engagements, the audit of opening balances is not so onerous. The auditor compares the draft financial statements of the current period with the signed financial statements of the prior period (which are supported by his own audit files). He is simply ensuring that the prior period's closing balances have been correctly brought forward to the current period.

An issue arises, however, for initial audit engagements where either:
- the financial statements were not audited in the prior period (perhaps due to exemptions from needing to be audited, as discussed in **Chapter 1**); or
- the financial statements were audited by a predecessor auditor (i.e. you were not the auditor in the prior year).

In these circumstances:
- review predecessor's working papers to obtain evidence in relation to opening balances;
- evaluate whether audit procedures performed in the current period provide evidence relevant to the opening balances of the prior period;
- perform specific audit procedures to obtain evidence regarding the opening balances.

If, through this review, the auditor identifies that misstatements do exist in the opening balances that could materially affect the current period's financial statements, then he must perform additional audit procedures to determine the effect on the current period financial statements. Where that effect is material, the auditor must qualify his opinion if the necessary adjustments are not made.

It is important to note that opening balances encompass matters requiring disclosure that existed at the beginning of the period, such as contingencies and commitments (ISA 510, para 4(b)).

If the auditor cannot obtain sufficient appropriate audit evidence with respect to opening balances, he must issue a qualified opinion or disclaim an opinion, i.e. "I don't know if these financial statements give a true and fair view because I cannot obtain the evidence I need to form an opinion" (audit opinion types are discussed in more detail in **Chapter 19**).

6.10 AUDITING ACCOUNTING ESTIMATES

Where financial statement items are estimated due to the fact that they cannot be measured precisely, the nature and reliability of source information to support the estimate can vary greatly. This is therefore a risky area for auditors as it can be difficult to obtain sufficient appropriate audit evidence to support the estimate.

Coupled with the possible lack of supporting evidence is the fact that accounting estimates can also be influenced due to the different requirements of the various financial reporting frameworks relevant to the financial statement item being audited.

To deal with the above, ISA 540 *Auditing Accounting Estimates, Including Fair Value Accounting Estimates, and Related Disclosures* (ISA 540) gives the auditor some guidance on how to approach the audit of estimates. ISA 540 advises that, before commencing the audit of estimates, it is essential that the auditor:

- familiarise himself with the reporting framework relevant to the accounting estimate (including disclosure requirements);
- understand how management identifies transactions, events and conditions that may give rise to the need for accounting estimates to be recognised;
- understand how management makes the accounting estimate, including an understanding of the data and assumptions and experts (if applicable) used to build that estimate. The auditor will also seek to understand if there is a change in how the estimate was applied in prior periods and how management has assessed estimation uncertainty. ISA 540 defines estimation uncertainty as "The susceptibility of an accounting estimate and related disclosures to an inherent lack of precision in its measurement." (ISA 540, para 7(c));
- review the outcome or re-estimations of accounting estimates included in prior periods to assess the information used in those estimates and management's ability to measure estimates as precisely as is practical with information available at that time.

The degree of review will, of course, be impacted by the risk assessment procedures and in responding to the assessed risks of material misstatement, the auditor shall undertake one or more of the following activities (ISA 540, para 13):

- determine whether **events occurring up to the date** of the auditor's report provide audit evidence regarding the accounting estimates;
- test management's **methods and assumptions** used in deriving the accounting estimate;
- test effectiveness of any **related controls** that support the estimate;
- calculate his own estimate or an estimate range to evaluate management's estimate;
- where **estimation uncertainty** exists, the auditor should, in addition, understand how management has considered **alternative assumptions** and why they were rejected over assumptions used. Where management has not adequately considered alternative assumptions, the auditor shall assess such alternatives and their impact on the estimates compared to that of management's;
- assess management's **decision to recognise, disclose or exclude** accounting estimates;
- evaluate the **adequacy of disclosures with respect to estimation uncertainty**;
- apply professional scepticism with respect to the existence of **management bias**; and

- obtain **written representations** from management regarding whether those charged with governance believe significant assumptions used in making accounting estimates are reasonable.

6.11 CONCLUSION

According to ISA 220, "On or before the date on the auditor's report, the engagement partner shall, through a review of the audit documentation and discussion with the engagement team, be satisfied that sufficient appropriate audit evidence has been obtained to support the conclusions reached and for the auditor's report to be issued" (ISA 220, para 17). The above therefore tells us that we cannot establish if sufficient appropriate audit evidence has been obtained unless we have audit documentation which can be reviewed.

ISQC 1 *Quality Control for Firms that Perform Audits and Reviews of Financial Statements, and Other Assurance and Related Services Engagements* prescribes that "the firm shall establish policies and procedures for engagement teams to complete the assembly of the final engagement files on a timely basis after the engagement reports have been finalised" (ISQC 1, para 45). Again, this reiterates the importance of audit evidence and documentation. An engagement quality control reviewer must be able to pick up a final audit file and appreciate/agree with the audit conclusion reached.

The discussion of audit evidence quantity, reliability and relevance highlights the importance of the risk assessment – as a key factor in deciding on the type of audit testing and quantity and quality of audit evidence required.

It is not practical for the auditor to test 100% of transactions and balances that support the figures in the financial statements and, for this reason, sampling is an acceptable tool used to gather evidence and reach conclusions. This is only so, however, if the sample design is carried out in accordance with ISA 530. The auditor seeks to reduce audit risk to a minimum to avoid drawing the wrong conclusion and expressing an incorrect opinion, but he seeks to do this at the lowest possible cost and so, through planning, risk assessment and the use of sampling techniques, he strives to perform an efficient audit that concentrates on risk and materiality.

SUMMARY OF LEARNING OBJECTIVES

Having studied this chapter on gathering audit evidence you should:

Learning Objective 1 Understand what is meant by 'sufficient appropriate audit evidence'.

Sufficient Appropriate Audit Evidence (SAAE) (ISA 500)

Sufficiency refers to the **quantity** of evidence that must be obtained. Quantity will have a direct link to reliability of the audit evidence available in that the more reliable the evidence, the less of it that is required.

Appropriateness refers to the **reliability** and the **relevance** of audit evidence. The reliability will depend on factors such as source (independent of entity and received direct by the auditor), form (written or oral), effectiveness of controls and whether they are original documents. Relevance relates to the appropriateness of the test in addressing the noted assertions.

Learning Objective 2 Be able to identify whether audit evidence is sufficient and appropriate with respect to specific assertions.

The requirement for audit evidence to be sufficient appropriate audit evidence (SAAE) requires the evidence to be relevant. Relevance specifically refers to the appropriateness of the test in addressing the noted assertions. Throughout the text examples are provided which demonstrate how the auditor considers the relevance of audit procedures with regard to the assertion being tested.

Learning Objective 3 Have an understanding of how the methods of obtaining audit evidence are carried out.

ISA 500 outlines the following methods of obtaining audit evidence: inquiry; inspection; observation; external confirmation; recalculation; re-performance; and analytical procedures.

Learning Objective 4 Have an appreciation of the types of testing carried out for controls and substantive testing to support further learning in later chapters.

Tests of Controls are generally concerned with **tests of details** whereby attribute sampling is used to assess if the control is operating consistently as described by management ("Yes" or "No") and that control is effective is addressing the financial statement assertions. Testing controls and proving their effective operation will assist in reducing the quantity of substantive procedures when testing the financial statements.

Substantive Tests of Details uses samples of the population of transactions and balances to determine an error rate that can be applied to the total population. **Substantive analytical procedures** can also be used as a form of substantive testing.

Learning Objective 5 Understand the concept of 'substantive analytical procedures' and the essential considerations that must be taken into account when deciding whether or not to use substantive analytical procedures.

Substantive Analytical Procedures involve the building of an expectation (an estimate) of what the value of the balance or class of transactions should be and comparing that to the draft financial statements to see if it is within a tolerable misstatement. Substantive analytical procedures also encompass the comparison of comparative figures, ratios and relationships.

All of the above are designed in response to identified risks, ensuring that appropriate audit evidence is obtained to support all balances and classes of transactions at the assertion level.

Learning Objective 6 Understand how to carry out external confirmations.

External Confirmations The auditor must give careful consideration to the **design of the confirmation request** to ensure it provides a reliable source of evidence and to encourage a high response rate. This can be achieved by the use of **positive confirmations or negative confirmations**. Additionally, the auditor must consider carefully the responses to ensure their source is reliable and, where **questions over reliability of source** arise, perform additional audit procedures as necessary. Similarly, where **no response is obtained,** alternative procedures must be carried out to meet the assertions. Where **management refuses to permit the use of external confirmations** and the reasons are not considered valid, then the auditor should consider the implications for his report (**limitation of scope**).

Learning Objective 7 Understand the importance of audit documentation and audit working papers as well as their form.

Audit Documentation Audit documentation forms the backbone of audit evidence: without it, review is impossible. Audit documentation supports the basis of audit opinion and the planning activities carried out. Audit documentation can exist in hard copy documentation or soft copy files within an audit programme or application.

Learning Objective 8 Obtain a strong insight into sampling, its risks, methods and projection techniques.

Audit Sampling All samples should be **random** (no bias) and **representative** of the population (to support projection of sample results).

Sampling risk is introduced when sampling is used, which is the possibility that an alternative outcome would have been achieved if 100% of the population was tested. **Non-sampling risk** is the risk that an erroneous conclusion is reached which is not related to sampling risk (i.e. it relates to auditor competency).

Statistical sampling has significant benefits over **judgemental sampling** when it comes to reliability and defence if questioned, however judgemental sampling takes into account experience and is usually easier to apply. **Stratification of a population** can help to combine the benefits of both statistical and judgemental sampling.

Sample size is influenced by a number of factors, predominantly related to **risk**, **materiality** and **tolerable misstatement**.

On completion of sampling, the errors found need to be projected to the population. When projecting the error to the population, the **error rate** should be adjusted for noted and supported **anomalies**.

Learning Objective 9 Understand the auditor's responsibility with regard to opening balances.

Opening Balances When collecting audit evidence regarding the figures in the financial statements, the auditor cannot forget that comparatives (which ultimately represent the opening balances) are included in a set of financial statements and so he must obtain audit evidence relating to those comparative figures.

Learning Objective 10 Understand the auditing procedures applied to the area of estimates.

Estimates When assessing estimates, the auditor needs to familiarise himself with the **financial reporting framework** and the **estimate type** as well as gain a clear understanding of the **methods and assumptions** used by management to build the estimate. The auditor should also consider **estimation uncertainty** and how management has considered alternative outcomes and that these are adequately disclosed. The auditor should gain comfort that **adequate procedures** are in place for management to **identify the existence of transactions or events giving rise to accounting estimates**.

QUESTIONS

Self-test Questions

6.1   What are the advantages of statistical sampling over judgemental sampling?
6.2   What does sufficient appropriate audit evidence mean?
6.3   What is your understanding of relevant evidence?
6.4   Define your understanding of analytical procedures.
6.5   Name the methods of obtaining audit evidence.
6.6   What are the two types of substantive testing?
6.7   What should the auditor take into consideration when designing substantive analytical procedures?
6.8   What are the benefits of external confirmations?
6.9   What should the auditor take into consideration when designing an external confirmation?
6.10 Why is audit documentation so important?
6.11 Distinguish between sampling and non-sampling risk.
6.12 What is an anomaly with respect to sampling?
6.13 What factors influence the sample size for a substantive test of details?
6.14 What problem is the auditor faced with when auditing the financial statements of an initial engagement?
6.15 What should the auditor consider when auditing accounting estimates?

Review Questions

(See Suggested Solutions to Review Questions in **Appendix D**.)

Question 6.1

(a) Identify and explain three substantive tests of detail and for each one outline the following:
(i) the financial statement area that it addresses;
(ii) the financial statement assertions that it addresses.
(b) Identify and discuss the work an auditor will usually perform to gain sufficient appropriate audit evidence over obsolete and unsaleable inventory.

Question 6.2

Big Match Ltd is an audit client of your firm. The annual audit for the year ended 31 March 2012 has just been completed, however the audit senior has taken unexpected leave and has left the following list of issues to be followed up with the client:
(a) A liability of €350,000 has been included in the results of the company in relation to shareholder dividends.
(b) Company land and buildings were revalued during the year and have been included in the financial statements at the revalued amount.
(c) A significant customer of Big Match Ltd went into liquidation in November 2010. The company manufactured a specialised product for this company, which was exclusively sold to them and manufactured to meet their specific needs. At the year end the company has €500,000 inventory in its books manufactured solely for this company. The company has not sold any of this inventory since the customer went into liquidation. The client is currently attempting to win a contract with a new customer who uses the same product.
(d) On review of invoices for legal fees, a pending case against the company was identified.

Requirement In order to finalise the audit, what further information/audit evidence would you require from management in respect of these items?

Question 6.3

State four audit procedures you would undertake to ensure the completeness of sales and receivables balances.

Question 6.4

Fresh Food Ltd is a supplier of food and drink to supermarkets. You, as audit senior, have been asked to review the work performed by the audit junior on payables and purchases for the year end 31 December 2009 audit. Total purchases were €38 million in the last year and the company has 175 suppliers on its records.

You have received the following summary information on the work performed by the assistant on supplier statement reconciliations.

Supplier Name	Balance Per Aged Payables Listing €000	Balance Per Supplier €000	Assistant's Comments
A	34	80	Appears to be cut-off issue as supplier has recorded €45,200 in invoices in December not recorded by client.
D	89	55	Credit note on statement but not on the client ledger.
R	120	122	Difference is not material for further work.
W	61	70	Difference is due to €3,000 cash payment from October not yet received by the supplier and claim by Fresh Food Ltd for discount of €4,000, which has not been granted on supplier statement

Requirement

(a) Explain the purpose of the audit procedures carried out in respect of supplier statement reconciliations.

(b) What follow-up work would you request of the assistant?

THE AUDIT AND ASSURANCE PROCESS

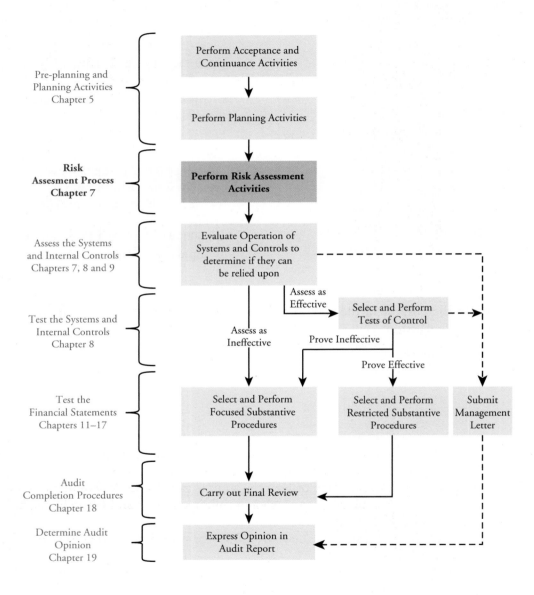

7

THE RISK ASSESSMENT PROCESS

LEARNING OBJECTIVES

Having studied this chapter on the risk assessment process you should:
1. demonstrate detailed knowledge of the risk environment;
2. demonstrate an understanding of how the auditor gains an understanding of the entity, what types of information he should collect and why, and where he might find the required information;
3. understand the principal considerations of the auditor when assessing the risk of material misstatement;
4. demonstrate a detailed understanding of how the auditor responds to risk (and, separately, significant risk) in the design of the nature, timing and extent of further audit procedures;
5. demonstrate an appreciation of the assessment of the sufficiency and adequacy of evidence and the importance of documenting the risk process; and
6. have an appreciation of the relationship between materiality and audit risk.

CHECKLIST OF RELEVANT STANDARDS

The relevant standards covered in this chapter are:
- ISA (UK and Ireland) 200 *Overall Objectives of the Independent Auditor and the Conduct of an Audit in Accordance with International Standards on Auditing (UK and Ireland)* (ISA 200)
- ISA (UK and Ireland) 315 *Identifying and Assessing the Risks of Material Misstatement Through Understanding of the Entity and Its Environment* (ISA 315)
- ISA (UK and Ireland) 320 *Materiality in Planning and Performing an Audit* (ISA 320)
- ISA (UK and Ireland) 330 *The Auditor's Responses to Assessed Risks* (ISA 330)
- ISA (UK and Ireland) 500 *Audit Evidence* (ISA 500)

KEY TERMS AND DEFINITIONS FOR THIS CHAPTER

Assertions   "Representations by management, explicit or otherwise, that are embodied in the financial statements, as used by the auditor to consider the different types of potential misstatement that may occur." (ISA 315, para 4(a))

Audit Risk   The risk that the auditor will fail to reach an appropriate conclusion about the entity and the accounting information on which the auditor is reporting.

Business Risk   "A risk resulting from significant conditions, events, circumstances, actions or inactions that could adversely affect an entity's ability to achieve its objectives and execute its strategies, or from the setting of inappropriate objectives and strategies." (ISA 315, para 4(b))

Control Risk   This risk is directly linked to the design and implementation of the entity's internal control function (e.g. an entity that lacks segregation of duties may pose many control risks).

Inherent Risk   A risk that exists due to the nature of the client entity's industry, products or transactions (e.g. a company governed by management with a poor reputation is inherently risky).

Internal Control   "The process designed, implemented and maintained by those charged with governance, management and other personnel to provide reasonable assurance about the achievement of an entity's objectives with regard to reliability of financial reporting, effectiveness and efficiency of operations, and compliance with applicable laws and regulations. The term 'controls' refers to any aspects of one or more of the components of internal control." (ISA 315, para 4(c))

7.1 INTRODUCTION

As previously discussed, the objective of an audit of financial statements is to enable the auditor to express an opinion as to whether the financial statements give a **true and fair view**, in accordance with an applicable financial reporting framework, of the state of the company's/entity's affairs at the reporting date. The auditor should plan and perform an audit with an attitude of **professional scepticism**, recognising that circumstances could exist that may cause the financial statements to be materially misstated (ISA 315 (UK and Ireland) *Identifying and Assessing the Risks of Material Misstatement Through Understanding of the Entity and Its Environment* (ISA 315)). In order to mitigate **material misstatement**, the auditor must consider the risks of it arising at the **assertion level** and plan the audit in a manner that will reduce such risks to an acceptable level.

This chapter discusses the concepts of **business risk** and **audit risk** and the approach of the auditor with regard to identifying and responding to such risks.

We commence our discussion in **Section 7.2** with an overview of the 'risk environment', distinguishing between business risk and audit risk, and then taking an in-depth look at the question: 'What is audit risk?' The answer to this question leads us into extensive discussions on the **components** of audit risk: **inherent risk**, **control risk** and **detection risk**.

In **Section 7.3** we consider: the risk assessment procedures used by the auditor to gain an understanding of the entity and its environment (and hence answer the question, "**How** does the auditor gain this understanding?"); the types of information of interest to the auditor and why these types of information can assist the auditor in assessing risk (answering the question, "**What** information does he collect and **Why**?"); and the sources to which the auditor can look to obtain the required information (i.e. **Where** does the auditor find the information he is looking for?)

Having established how, what, why and where the information is obtained, in **Section 7.4** we then examine how the auditor goes about assessing the risk of material misstatement based on his findings. This is discussed under three main headings:
- What risk has been identified?
- What is the potential magnitude of the potential misstatement?
- How likely is it to occur?

Once the risks have been assessed, the auditor must then design a **response** to that risk, which is reflected in the **nature, timing and extent of the audit procedures**. We discuss the auditor's approach to this in **Section 7.5**. This is expanded upon in **Section 7.6** when we consider the specific response to significant risks, concentrating on **non-routine transactions and judgemental matters**.

In **Section 7.7** we discuss the auditor's considerations with regard to the collection of **sufficient appropriate audit evidence** and documentation. In **Section 7.8** the importance of communicating deficiencies in internal controls to those charged with governance is emphasised. Finally, in **Section 7.9** we remind ourselves of the relationship between materiality and audit risk.

> Remember: the risk assessment process commences at the planning stage of the audit and impacts on the nature, timing and extent of future audit procedures, which should be designed to ensure audit procedures minimise the risk of material misstatement not being detected by the auditor.

7.2 THE RISK ENVIRONMENT

The risk environment can be a complicated subject to understand. The word 'risk' is generally used to indicate exposure to danger. Within audit, exposure may exist in the **macro environment** or in the **micro environment**. For example, in the **macro environment** the Euro to sterling conversion may be volatile, creating a risk in the macro environment (which is economy driven). However, in the **micro environment** (i.e. the client entity's immediate area of operations), all transactions are in Euro and so they have no exposure to this macro environment risk. If the client entity did engage in Euro to sterling transactions, then it would be exposed to what is referred to as an '**inherent risk**', in that the mere fact that it is involved in foreign exchange transactions creates a risk. If the entity does not attempt to hedge this risk, then it may be exposed to losses that will impact on its profitability, which in turn poses a '**business risk**'.

The auditor, however, is concerned with the correct recording of the foreign exchange transactions and not necessarily the related business risk. The fact that the client entity engages in foreign exchange transactions causes an inherent risk from the auditor's point of view, in that foreign exchange transactions can be difficult to account for and therefore are prone to error. This inherent risk can be reduced if the company has strong **controls** in place to ensure that all foreign exchange transactions are recorded correctly. If the entity does not adequately control foreign exchange transactions, then it has an inherent risk **and** a **control risk**.

The auditor is seeking to avoid '**audit risk**', which is the risk that he could conclude an inappropriate opinion (i.e. issue a clean audit opinion when a material misstatement exists, or vice versa). **Audit risk is made up of three types of risk**:

- inherent risk (discussed above);
- control risk (discussed above); and
- **detection risk**, which is the risk that audit procedures will fail to detect a **material misstatement**.

> To summarise the key points of this discussion:
> - **Business risk** is the existence of a risk that will impact on the client entity's goals and objectives, e.g. transacting in foreign exchange where rates are volatile may create unexpected losses that impact on the profitability objectives of the client entity.

- **Audit risk** is the risk that the auditor will issue an inappropriate audit opinion. Audit risk is made up of: inherent risk, control risk and detection risk.
- **Inherent risk** exists due to the nature of the client entity's industry, products or transactions, e.g. the client entity transacts in foreign exchange transactions, which can be difficult to account for and increases the risk that there might be a material misstatement in the financial statements.
- **Control risk** is directly linked to the design and implementation of the entity's internal control function, e.g. the client entity that engages in foreign exchange transactions has no specific controls to monitor the accuracy of such transactions, further increasing the risk that there is a material misstatement in the financial statements.
- **Detection risk** is the risk that the auditor will fail to detect a material misstatement that exists in the financial statements, e.g. the auditor applies insufficiently rigorous testing procedures in the area of foreign exchange transactions and balances and hence fails to detect a related material misstatement.

At this point, you are not expected to fully understand the world of **risk**, as it will be discussed in much greater detail throughout the rest of this chapter. **Table 7.1** below gives an overview of the risk environment that the auditor must consider. This shows business risk as being separate from audit risk. As explained above, though it bears repeating, business risk relates to the entity failing to meet its objectives (which can include profitability, growth or any number of typical business objectives), whereas audit risk is concerned with the issuing of an incorrect audit opinion. Audit risk is made up of three key components: inherent risk, control risk and detection risk. Two other risks are included below, which cover **engagement risk** (this relates to the acceptance considerations discussed in **Chapter 5**, Section 5.2) and **independence in fact risk** (which relates to the **Ethical Standards** discussed throughout **Chapter 2**).

We can now further consider each of these components of the risk environment in turn.

Table 7.1: The Risk Environment

'Business Risk' Risk that the entity will fail to meet its objectives						
'Audit Risk' Risk that the auditor may give an inappropriate audit opinion on the financial statements						
Engagement Risk	Inherent Risk		Control Risk	Detection Risk		Independence in Fact Risk
	Entity level	Account balance and class of transactions level		Sampling Risk	Quality Control Risk	

Business Risk

All entities are exposed to business risks; the types of business risk involved will depend on the nature of the entity's activities and the industry in which it operates, how it is regulated, its size and the complexity of its operations. It is management's responsibility to consider the business risks facing the entity and respond appropriately.

> **Remember**: not all business risks will translate into risks associated with the preparation of the financial statements. Ultimately, the auditor is concerned only with those risks that could affect the financial statements and lead them to being materiality misstated.

EXAMPLES OF BUSINESS RISKS

The following are examples of risks that may impact on the entity's ability to meet its goals or objectives:
- attaining a certain level of profitability;
- maximising shareholder wealth;
- ensuring efficiency and effectiveness of operations;
- meeting a desired market share;
- giving customer satisfaction (however measured);
- maintaining a desired level of liquidity;
- maintaining reputation;
- effective change management;
- adherence to accepted principles of corporate governance; and
- corporate social responsibility (CSR).

Engagement Risk

The concept of **engagement risk** is discussed in detail in **Chapter 5**, 'Audit Acceptance and Planning'. Engagement risk relates to the risks considered by the auditor prior to commencement of an audit engagement. An example of engagement risk would be where a competitive tendering process has forced the auditor to accept an unreasonably low fee, thus restricting the time available to perform an effective audit (affecting audit quality) and/or increasing pressures on **independence in fact** (see below).

A further example of engagement risk is that the auditor may accept a client whose inherent risk at the entity level is unduly high because of, for instance, management with low integrity.

Independence in Fact

Independence in fact is the risk that, even though the auditor's procedures have detected misstatements that cause the financial statements to not give a **true and fair view**, the auditor may fail to report the misstatement because of lack of independence. (Independence in fact is discussed in detail throughout **Chapter 2**, 'Ethics and Corporate Governance'.)

Audit Risk

With every audit that is conducted, an audit opinion is expressed on the truth and fairness of the financial statements. This opinion is issued only after the auditor has obtained sufficient appropriate audit evidence over the account balances and classes of transactions in the financial statements, which provides **reasonable assurance** about the truth and fairness of the financial statements. The concept of reasonable assurance acknowledges that there is a risk that the audit opinion may not be appropriate. The risk that the auditor will fail to reach a proper conclusion about the company and the accounting information on which the auditor is reporting is known as **audit risk**.

The auditor should plan and perform the audit to reduce audit risk to an acceptably low level that is consistent with the objective of the audit. In order to do so, the auditor must design and carry out a detailed **audit plan** that will provide sufficient appropriate audit evidence to allow him to draw reasonable conclusions on which to base an audit opinion. When audit risk is reduced to a reasonably low level, reasonable assurance has been obtained.

Figure 7.1 below depicts audit risk and its components. We have already established that audit risk is the risk that the auditor will issue an inappropriate audit opinion. If he does, he does so because a material misstatement existed in the financial statements and he failed to detect that material misstatement. As such, the auditor must first assess the risk of the financial statements containing a material misstatement. He does this by assessing

FIGURE 7.1: THE COMPONENTS OF AUDIT RISK

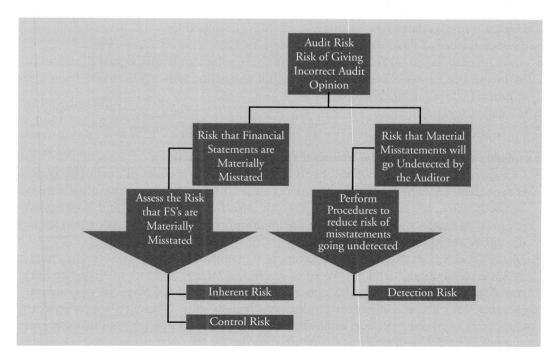

'inherent risk' and 'control risk'. Once he understands the level of inherent and control risk, he can better manage his chances of detecting any errors by applying a detection risk that is appropriate to inherent and control risk. This is considered further as we proceed through this section and the remainder of the chapter.

Before we discuss the components of audit risk, we will first consider the levels of material misstatement that might exist in the financial statements. The auditor is only concerned with risk that could potentially lead to a material misstatement in the financial statements. As such, it is important to first understand the levels of material misstatement that can arise from risk before considering the components of risk.

Levels of Material Misstatement

The auditor's primary concern is detecting material misstatements in the financial statements. In order to assess whether there are misstatements that materially impact on the financial statements taken as a whole, the auditor must consider risk at two levels:
1. the financial statement level; and
2. the classes of transactions, account balances, disclosures and the related assertions level.

1. The Financial Statement Level

At this level, the risk of material misstatement is deemed to be **pervasive**; it can impact the entire set of financial statements and, therefore, can impact on many assertions. Risks of this nature are often related to an entity's control environment, fraud risk or the risk of management override of controls.

The auditor's response to risks at this level includes considering:
- the significance of these types of risk;
- ensuring that personnel assigned to the audit have sufficient knowledge, skill and ability to adequately assess and conclude on the risk and at the same time ensure there is an appropriate level of supervision;
- the need for experts; and
- the existence of indicators that the company is not a **going concern**.

Examples of such risks at the financial statement level include:
- *Controls* Lack of existence of an organisational structure or **chart of authority** (a document detailing who has authority to perform which acts within the organisation). Without these, there is a risk that there is insufficient hierarchy and control over approval of transactions in the entire organisation; thus, this type of risk could impact the **entire set of financial statements**.
- *Fraud* There is a risk that management is engaged in profit-smoothing to secure their bonus, which is based on profitability. The act of 'profit-smoothing' calls into question the integrity of management and also raises concerns over the **entire set of financial statements**.
- *Inherent Risk* A new competitor product was launched on 1 January, which rivals the company's top-selling product and will likely require the company to sell this inventory at a loss. The risk is that the company may not be able to continue as a going concern,

as its top-selling product has been replaced. If the company is not a going concern, the accounts will have to be prepared on a **break-up basis** and therefore the risk impacts the **entire set of financial statements**.

2. The Classes of Transactions, Account Balance, and Disclosure and the Related Assertion Level

The risk of material misstatement at this level is considered in order to assist the auditor in determining the nature, timing and extent of further audit procedures at the assertion level. This type of risk is generally more isolated to a specific class of transactions (e.g. revenue transactions), account balance (e.g. receivables), and disclosures (e.g. adequacy of disclosure relating to **factoring**). Furthermore, this risk may be related only to one assertion within a class of transactions or account balance.

The auditor's response to risks at this level would include appropriately planning the nature, timing and extent of audit procedures to address the identified risks.

Examples of such risks (at the financial statement level) include:
- *Controls* No credit checks are performed on new credit customers and no credit limits are applied. There is a risk that the receivables (account balance) are not collectable and therefore have an impact on the valuation assertion. Note how this risk is more focused than the one referred to with respect to financial statement level above. While this risk will require the auditor to adapt the nature, timing and extent of his audit procedures, it does not pose as significant a risk as the control risk noted above for material misstatement at the financial statement level.
- *Inherent Risk* A new competitor product was launched on the 1 January which will rival one of the company's smaller lines and likely require the company to sell this inventory at a loss. The risk relates to the inventory balance and again impacts the valuation assertion, as the inventory that existed at 31 December will need to be written down to the lower of cost and net realisable value (NRV). Again, the risk is concentrated in one area, does not impact the entire set of financial statements and so is not as concerning as the inherent risk noted above at the financial statement level.

We can now return to the topic of audit risk and more specifically the components of audit risk.

Components of Audit Risk

Having examined the different levels of material misstatements, we need to be able to categorise the types of risk that can lead to material misstatements and these are known as the **components of audit risk**. As depicted in **Figure 7.1** above, audit risk can exist at three different levels. This is further illustrated in **Table 7.2** below, which shows the three components of audit risk – inherent, control and detection risk – along with the subcategories of these risks. Risks relating to **inherent and control risk** can exist on two different levels:
- financial statement (entity) level; or
- account balance and class of transaction level (related specifically to a figure in the financial statements).

TABLE 7.2: COMPONENTS OF AUDIT RISK

Audit Risk					
Risk that the auditor may give an inappropriate audit opinion on the financial statements					
Inherent Risk		Control Risk		Detection Risk	
Entity level	Account balance and class of transactions level	Entity level	Account balance and class of transactions level	Sampling risk	Quality Control Risk

With regard to detection risk, two types of risk can arise:
- **sampling risk** (introduced in **Chapter 6**, Section 6.8); and
- **quality control risk** (also known as '**non-sampling risk**') (introduced in **Chapter 6**, Section 6.8).

Let us now consider each of these components in turn.

Inherent Risk

Inherent risk is "the susceptibility of an assertion … to a misstatement that could be material, either individually or when aggregated with other misstatements, before consideration of any related controls" (ISA 200, para 13(n)(i)). Some factors may pose inherent risks, but be adequately controlled by the entity to mitigate or reduce the risk. Inherent risks tend to exist due to the nature of the client entity's industry, product or transaction types. Examples of inherent risks are included in **Table 7.3** below.

TABLE 7.3: EXAMPLES OF INHERENT RISK AT THE FINANCIAL STATEMENT
LEVEL AND ACCOUNT BALANCE AND CLASS OF TRANSACTIONS LEVEL

Inherent Risk	
Financial Statement (Entity) Level	**Account Balance and Class of Transactions Level**
These types of risk are usually related to the environment in which the client entity operates and therefore have a pervasive impact on the financial statements.	These types of risk are generally confined to a particular class of transactions or account balance, and in some cases to a particular assertion within the account balance or class of transactions.
• Management integrity/reputation. • Profitability relative to the industry. • Management experience and competence. • High turnover of key personnel. • Unusual pressures on management.	• Susceptibility to misappropriation or loss (e.g. cash). • Complex transaction (e.g. pensions). • High degree of judgement (e.g. provisions are often quite subjective).

- Nature of entity's business (e.g. technological advancement often renders inventions quickly obsolete).
- Nature of industry (e.g. building trade).
- Complex computer systems.
- Quality of computer systems.
- Qualified opinion in previous years.

- Quality of specific computer applications (e.g. the payroll package).
- Non-routine transactions (e.g. property revaluation).
- Existence of consignment stock.

Control Risk

Control risk is the second component of audit risk. **Control risk** is the risk that a material misstatement (or series of misstatements that are material) could occur relating to an assertion and will not be prevented, or detected and corrected in a timely manner by the entity's internal controls. This risk is directly linked to the design and implementation of the entity's internal control function. The entity should put controls in place to address risks and these controls should prevent, detect or correct fraud and errors that may occur. Examples of control risks are provided in **Table 7.4**.

TABLE 7.4: EXAMPLES OF CONTROL RISK AT THE FINANCIAL STATEMENT LEVEL AND ACCOUNT BALANCE AND CLASS OF TRANSACTIONS LEVEL

Control Risk

Financial Statement (Entity) Level	**Account Balance and Class of Transactions Level**
These types of risk are normally entity-level control related (i.e. the types of control that impact the entire organisation).	These types of risk are derived from lack of controls related to a particular financial statements cycle, such as the revenue cycle, and so the risk is isolated to a specific balance in the financial statements or class of transactions (and assertion).
<ul><li>Poor management attitude and lack of action regarding financial reporting.</li><li>Culture of management overriding of controls.</li><li>Complex or poor-quality computer systems.</li><li>Lack of existence of a chart of authority (document prescribing authority to perform various acts within the organisation, such as stating who has the authority to purchase fixed assets).</li></ul>	<ul><li>Not directed to non-routine transactions (e.g. the purchase of non-current fixed assets, because they occur ad hoc and in small volumes, generally do not have specific controls related to them).</li><li>Changes in third parties carrying out controls, e.g. moving the outsourcing of payroll from one third party to another.</li><li>Controls changing in line with changes in procedures/business.</li></ul>

continued overleaf

- Lack of written policies and procedures.
- Lack of business planning, budgeting and monitoring of performance.
- Lack of procedures around risk management.
- Lack of internal audit function.

- Lack of segregation of duties within a particular cycle.
- Lack of effective, competent personnel specific to a particular cycle.

Detection Risk

This is the risk that the auditor "will not detect a misstatement that exists" in an assertion "that could be material, either individually or when aggregated with other misstatement." (ISA 200, para 13(e)). Detection risk is a function of an audit procedure and of its application by the auditor. Detection risk cannot be reduced to zero – there will always be a risk that the auditor has not detected a misstatement predominantly due to the fact that the auditor tests on a sample basis. **Table 7.5** below shows how sampling can impact on detection risk.

TABLE 7.5: EXAMPLES OF DETECTION RISK

Detection Risk	
Sampling Risk	**Non-sampling Risk/Quality Control Risk**
The auditor does not examine all of the items within the population of a class of transactions, account balance or disclosure and therefore increases the chances of missing something.	The possibility that the auditor may choose an inappropriate auditing procedure or a sample that is not representative of the population to gain assurance over an assertion; **or** that he may choose an appropriate procedure but use it incorrectly or interpret the results incorrectly. Such mistakes can be avoided through proper audit planning (see **Chapter 5**). The auditor must apply professional scepticism, adequately staff the engagement and plan the nature, timing and extent of procedures in response to identified audit risks.

We will now examine how the auditor assesses each of these components of audit risk in order to determine his audit approach. **Figure 7.2** below shows how the auditor considers each layer of the components of audit risk. First, he assesses the existence of inherent risks that might impact on the client entity's financial statements; then the auditor considers if the entity's control environment mitigates these inherent risks or presents any new risks. This combined assessment of inherent and control risk gives the auditor an indication of the volume and extent of errors that could have flown into the financial statements, and hence gives him an indication of how much testing he needs to perform to provide **reasonable assurance** that the financial statements are free from material misstatement.

FIGURE 7.2: INHERENT, CONTROL AND DETECTION RISK ASSESSMENT

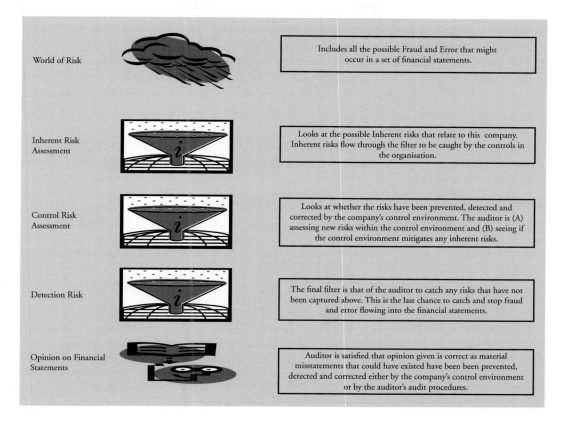

World of Risk	Includes all the possible Fraud and Error that might occur in a set of financial statements.
Inherent Risk Assessment	Looks at the possible Inherent risks that relate to this company. Inherent risks flow through the filter to be caught by the controls in the organisation.
Control Risk Assessment	Looks at whether the risks have been prevented, detected and corrected by the company's control environment. The auditor is (A) assessing new risks within the control environment and (B) seeing if the control environment mitigates any inherent risks.
Detection Risk	The final filter is that of the auditor to catch any risks that have not been captured above. This is the last chance to catch and stop fraud and error flowing into the financial statements.
Opinion on Financial Statements	Auditor is satisfied that opinion given is correct as material misstatements that could have existed have been been prevented, detected and corrected either by the company's control environment or by the auditor's audit procedures.

Using an earlier example where, in the risk environment ('the world of risk') there exists a volatile rate of exchange rate between Euro and sterling: if the client entity only transacts in Euro, then this risk does not flow to the financial statements; if, however, the client entity does engage in Euro to sterling transactions, then an inherent risk exists. If the client entity sufficiently controls foreign exchange transactions, then the risk of error, relating to these transactions, flowing into the financial statements is low and hence the level of testing required by the auditor would be lower than if the entity did not have sufficient controls in place to control the accuracy of foreign exchange transactions.

Relationship between the Three Components of Audit Risk

The relationship between the three components of audit risk can be summarised as follows.

- The greater the risk of material misstatement (i.e. due to high inherent and control risk), the lower the level of detection risk that can be accepted. The auditor has obtained no assurance from the inherent and control risk assessment and so he must carry out focused **substantive procedures** in order to ensure that he captures all possible misstatements that may have flown into the financial statements as a result of the high-risk environment.

The chances of the existence of an error in the financial statements is higher if they have been prepared in a high-risk environment and as such, the auditor, in order to ensure he issues an appropriate opinion, must perform a high level of substantive testing (i.e. by taking a low detection risk approach).

- The lower the risk of material misstatement (i.e. due to low inherent and control risk), the higher the level of detection risk that can be accepted, i.e. not too many risks have been taken and so the auditor can carry out a reduced level of substantive testing, as he is not expecting that too much fraud and error flowed into the financial statements due to the low-risk environment.

If there is low inherent and control risk, not much risk has been taken by the entity, so the auditor can afford to take some risk at the detection stage by performing a reduced level of substantive testing.

Table 7.6 below depicts the above in a summarised format.

TABLE 7.6: RELATIONSHIP BETWEEN INHERENT, CONTROL AND DETECTION RISK

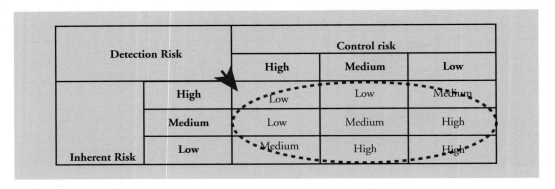

7.3 THE AUDITOR'S APPROACH TO ASSESSING THE RISK OF MATERIAL MISSTATEMENT

Introduction

Only after the risk of material misstatement is assessed can a meaningful audit plan be developed that will provide the auditor with sufficient appropriate audit evidence to express an opinion on the financial statements. In order to do this, the auditor needs to understand the entity and the environment within which it operates. ISA 315 "deals with the auditor's responsibility to identify and assess the risks of material misstatement in the financial statements, through understanding the entity and its environment, including the entity's internal control" (para 1).

This understanding will allow the auditor to assess the risks of material misstatement and develop an audit plan in response to these risks. For example, the findings will be used when considering the following:

- setting an appropriate **materiality** level (the more risks associated with an entity, the lower the level of materiality should be – see discussion in **Chapter 5**, Section 5.4);

- the ability of the entity to continue as a **going concern**;
- significant risk areas that need special audit consideration; and
- the appropriateness of management's oral and written representations.

The auditor should use professional judgement when assessing the level of understanding that is required of the entity and its environment, with the overriding consideration being whether the understanding that has been obtained is sufficient "to assess the risks of material misstatement at the assertion level and design further audit procedures responsive to assessed risks." (ISA 315, para 20)

Note: it is important to note that the understanding that is required by the auditor is less than the understanding held by the entity's management.

Risk Assessment Procedures Used by the Auditor to Obtain an Understanding of the Entity

Obtaining an understanding of the entity is a continuous process during the audit. As introduced in **Chapter 6**, Section 6.3, there are a number of ways the auditor can obtain audit evidence. Below we consider how these methods can be used specifically relating to **gaining an understanding of the entity and its environment sufficient to identify risk**. First, let us remind ourselves of the methods introduced in **Chapter 6**:
- inquiries of management and others within the entity;
- analytical procedures (see **Section 6.3**);
- observation and inspection (also **Section 6.3**);
- cumulative audit knowledge and experience; and
- discussion among the engagement team.

In addition to these, the auditor can decide to perform other auditing procedures to help in the identification of material misstatements, such as contacting external independent parties, e.g. the entity's legal representative or valuation experts used by the entity.

Inquiries of Management and Others within the Entity

The audit team should carry out preliminary information-gathering at meetings with management and other entity employees in order to gain an understanding of, for example, the following:
- the controls processes in place within the entity, such as the revenue and receivables cycle, purchases and payables cycle, and treasury cycle;
- the management structure;
- instances of fraud taking place during the reporting period;
- changes in key personnel taking place during the reporting period;
- application of accounting policies within the entity; and
- related parties and related-party transactions taking place during the reporting period.

Inquiries of personnel other than management are also important to allow corroboration of information obtained from management and to provide the auditor with a different perspective in identifying risks of material misstatements.

Analytical Procedures

The performance of **analytical procedures** at the beginning, during and at the end of the audit may identify unusual transactions, incorrect treatment of transactions/balances and omissions from the financial statements. When using analytical procedures as risk-assessment tools, the auditor develops expectations for classes of transactions and account balances based on factors such as the economic climate, changes in the entity's trading operations during the reporting period or information obtained from management. Where actual results differ significantly from expected results, this may alert the auditor to areas where material misstatement might exist at the early stages of the audit for further investigation during substantive testing.

Now that we understand the types of risk that the auditor is alert to (i.e. inherent and control risks) and we are more familiar with the methods used to identify risk, we can apply this understanding by way of **Example 7.1**.

EXAMPLE 7.1: IDENTIFICATION OF INHERENT AND CONTROL RISKS

You are the auditor of Large Company Limited (a company involved in the manufacture of furniture for sale in Ireland and abroad) and have been asked to carry out a risk assessment. Information available to you is as follows:
- inquiries of the company's directors on performance in the year – they have provided you with a draft copy of the Directors' Report; and
- the draft statement of comprehensive income and statement of financial position.

These documents can be referred to in **Appendix C** of this textbook, which contains the financial statements of Large Company Limited. You should now refer to **Appendix C** and review the Directors' Report, the statement of comprehensive income and the statement of financial position. For this example, assume that these are the only documents available to you.

Using these documents you are required to:
1. identify the possible inherent and control risks that exist in Large Company Limited;
2. identify if these risks are at the entity level (financial statement level), or account balance and class of transactions level.

To work through these requirements, we first compare the results of 2012 with those of 2011 (i.e. perform a **preliminary analytical review**) to identify any risks. The table below shows each line item in the statement of financial position and then in the statement of comprehensive income, and the changes in absolute terms and in percentage terms from 2011 to 2012. The auditor's aim is to identify any large, unexpected variances or relationships between the figures.

Preliminary Analytical Review – Workings Example

STATEMENT OF FINANCIAL POSITION

	2012	2011	Absolute Change	% Change
Non-current Assets	€000	€000	€000	
Intangible assets	1,150	1,140	10	1%
Property, Plant and Equipment	130,050	140,500	–10,450	–7%
Financial assets	112,200	110,200	2,000	2%
Derivative financial instruments	1,900	1,460	440	30%
Pension Assets	1,200	1,000	200	20%
	246,500	**254,300**	**–7,800**	
Current assets				
Inventories	49,774	35,020	14,754	42%
Receivables:				
amounts falling due after one year	8,700	10,250	–1,550	–15%
amounts falling due within one year	6,500	7,250	–750	–10%
	15,200	**17,500**	**–2,300**	**–13%**
Derivative financial instruments	390	170	220	129%
Available-for-sale investments	4,200	5,000	–800	–16%
Cash at bank and in hand	104,200	105,530	–1,330	–1%
	173,764	**163,220**	**10,544**	**6%**
Payables:				
amounts falling due within one year	–135,680	–142,600	6,920	–5%
Net current assets	**38,084**	**20,620**	**17,464**	**85%**
Total assets less current liabilities	**283,384**	**273,920**	**9,464**	**3%**
Payables:				
amounts falling due after more than one year	109,940	116,630	–6,690	–6%
Provision for liabilities	750	500	250	50%
	–110,690	**–117,130**	**6,440**	**–5%**
Net assets excluding pension asset	172,694	156,790	15,904	10%
Pension asset	1,200	1,000	200	20%
Net assets including pension asset	**173,894**	**157,790**	**16,104**	**10%**

continued overleaf

Capital and reserves

Called-up share capital	84,050	78,160	5,890	8%
Share premium account	2,990	570	2,420	425%
Other reserves	1,600	28,700	−27,300	−95%
Retained earnings	85,254	50,360	35,094	70%
Shareholders' funds	**173,894**	**157,790**	**16,104**	**10%**

STATEMENT OF COMPREHENSIVE INCOME

	2012	2011	Absolute Change	% Change
	€000	€000	€000	
Turnover – continuing operations	280,250	198,500	81,750	41%
Cost of sales	−140,250	−120,800	−19,450	16%
Gross profit	140,000	77,700	62,300	80%
Distribution costs	−23,000	−20,000	−3,000	15%
Administration costs	−35,000	−34,000	−1,000	3%
	82,000	23,700	58,300	246%
Other operating income	750	700	50	7%
Operating profit – continuing operations	82,750	24,400	58,350	239%
Exceptional items				
Profit/(Loss) on sale of tangible fixed assets	420	−120	540	−450%
Impairment of investment property	−10,000	–	−10,000	100%
Loss on disposal of available-for-sale investments	−120	–	−120	100%
Profit on ordinary activities before interest	73,050	24,280	48,770	201%
Investment income	350	330	20	6%
Interest payable and similar charges	−550	−550	0	0%
Profit on ordinary activities before taxation	72,850	24,060	48,790	203%
Tax on profit on ordinary activities	−12,456	−8,500	−3,956	47%
Profit on ordinary activities after taxation	60,394	15,560	44,834	288%

Below are some risk observations from the review of the Directors' Report, coupled with the preliminary analytical procedure above.

Inherent Risks:
- A new line of furniture has broken into the luxury market; this is a dramatic change for the company, considering the impact on revenue, and therefore imposes an entity-level risk.
- According to the directors' report, foreign trade has increased by €42 million, which will add to the complexity of transactions and pose a risk at the account balance and class of transaction level.
- A key member of staff is retiring (John Hogan).
- Considerable political donations were made during the year, which will require additional disclosure, posing a risk at the disclosure level.
- Complicated transactions exist in the form of derivatives (which are up 30% for long-term and 129% for short-term on the prior-year balance sheet number), which pose a risk at the class of transactions and account balance level.
- Provisions for liabilities are up 50% – provisions require a high degree of judgement and so pose an inherent risk at the account balance, class of transactions, assertion and disclosure level.

Controls Risks:
- Revenue has increased by 41% in just one year, which may indicate a cut-off risk and, due to the impact this would have on revenue, cost of sales, inventory, receivables and payables, this is considered to be an entity-level risk (financial statement level).
- Revenue has increased by 41%, yet receivables have decreased 13% overall. This may indicate some incorrect classification or netting of receivables and payables balance (account balance level risk).
- Cost of sales has risen by only 16%, compared to a 41% increase in sales. Additionally, inventory balances are up 42% on the prior year, which may indicate that closing inventory has been overvalued (account balance level risk), or that incorrect cut-off/counting procedures have been applied. This may be explained by the fact that some furniture lines have been classified in the luxury market and so are generating higher margins (gross margin is up 11%), but it will be highlighted as a risk until investigated further.
- Payables: amounts falling due within one year are down 5% despite all categories of expenses being up and inventory levels being up, which may indicate that accruals are not complete (account balance, class of transaction and assertion level risk).
- Distribution costs, which are normally a function of sales, are up only 15%, while sales have risen by 41%. This may indicate that accruals are not complete (account balance, class of transactions and assertion level risk).
- Pension assets are up despite the retirement of a long-standing employee during the year, which may indicate a control risk around non-routine transactions (account balance, class of transactions and assertion level risk).
- Interest has not changed; one would expect that interest charged to the income statement would decrease in line with the 6% decrease in long-term payables noted on balance sheet. The calculation of accruals will need to be validated (account balance level risk).

continued overleaf

> While the above are some examples of risks that an auditor may highlight as a result of his review, they do not form an exhaustive list. ***Note***: though the details in the notes may explain some of the concerns around the risks identified, at the time of the risk review you only have access to the three documents provided: a draft of the directors' report, and the draft statement of comprehensive income and statement of financial position. An auditor would now request further information to gain a further understanding of the risks identified.
>
> ***For illustration purposes, note also some consistencies which exist with respect to relationships:***
> - Fixed assets are down, and we note a large profit from the sale of fixed assets, which indicates fixed assets were disposed of during the period.
> - Financial assets are up as is investment income.

Observation and Inspection

As tools of risk assessment, observation and inspection can be used to corroborate information obtained from management and other personnel. Such audit procedures include the following:
- observation of the entity's activities and operations;
- inspection of documents and entity records, e.g. business plans, internal control manuals, etc.;
- reading reports prepared by management and those charged with governance, e.g. quarterly management accounts, monthly/annual budgets, minutes of directors'/management meetings; and
- tracing transactions through the information system relevant to financial reporting – **walkthrough testing** (which is often used for the purpose of controls testing and is discussed in **Chapter 8,** Section 8.4).

Cumulative Audit Knowledge and Experience

For continuing audit engagements, i.e. audits that are performed annually by the auditor, information obtained in prior years in relation to the entity and the environment in which it operates can be used, provided that the auditor determines whether changes have occurred during the reporting period that may affect the relevance of such information in the current period audit.

Discussion among the Audit Engagement Team

Prior to the commencement of the audit, it is worthwhile for the **audit engagement team** to discuss the potential for the entity's financial statements to be materially misstated. This will allow more experienced team members, such as the engagement leader and the team manager, to share their knowledge of the entity, including significant risk areas and past instances of fraud or misstatement, with the rest of the team.

Types of Information Considered when Gaining an Understanding of the Entity and its Environment

As stated in ISA 315, paragraphs 11–12, the auditor's understanding of the entity and its environment consists of familiarity with the following

1. The Entity and its Environment, including;
    (a) industry, regulatory and other external factors, including the applicable financial reporting framework;
    (b) nature of the entity, including its operations, ownership and governance structures, types of investment and its structure;
    (c) the entity's selection and application of accounting policies;
    (d) the entity's objectives and strategies and related business risks; and
    (e) the measurement and review of the entity's financial performance.
2. The Entity's Internal Control Environment (discussed in detail in **Chapter 8**).

Focusing on each of these components will provide the auditor with a detailed knowledge and understanding of the entity before assessing the risk of material misstatements and developing the audit plan.

In order to gain a suitable understanding of areas outlined under 1(a)–(e) and 2 above, there are certain factors that the auditor should consider. The application notes to ISA 315 provides examples of these, some of which are presented below, according to their categories.

1(A) INDUSTRY, REGULATORY AND OTHER EXTERNAL FACTORS

Industry – ISA 315, paragraph A17: "relevant industry factors include industry conditions such as the competitive environment, supplier and customer relationships, and technological developments."

Regulatory – ISA 315, paragraph A19: "the regulatory environment encompasses, among other matters the applicable financial reporting framework and the legal and political environment". For example, the applicable tax laws that govern the client entity form part of the regulatory environment.

Other External Factors – other external factors include such things as interest rates, credit availability or currency revaluation (ISA 315, para A22).

The applicable financial reporting framework (e.g. IFRS) is also considered by the auditor under this heading.

1(B) NATURE OF THE ENTITY

Its Operations – this is normally one of the first things the auditor will consider and includes such things as: client entity revenue sources and markets; involvement in e-commerce; whether the entity is involved in, for example, retail or manufacture; geographical dispersion and industry segmentation; warehouse and office locations; and key customers, (ISA 315, para A24).

continued overleaf

Its Ownership and Governance Structure – ISA 315, paragraph A23: "this understanding assists in determining whether related party transactions have been identified and accounted for appropriately".

Existing and Potential Investment Types – investment information such as: "planned or recently executed acquisitions or divestures; investment and dispositions of securities and loans; capital investment activities; or investments in non-consolidated entities, including partnerships, joint ventures and special purpose entities" (ISA 315, para A24) provides the auditor with an insight into possible complicated accounting transactions and valuations, as well as giving the auditor an insight into the direction of the client entity.

Entity Structure and Financing – ISA 315, paragraph A23 explains: "Whether the entity has a complex structure, for example with subsidiaries or other components in multiple locations. Complex structures often introduce issues that may give rise to risks of material misstatement. Such issues may include whether goodwill, joint ventures, investments or special-purpose entities are accounted for appropriately." The financing structure is also of interest to the auditor. What is the debt to equity ratio? Or is there a use of derivative financial instruments? This type of information again gives the auditor an insight into the existence of complex accounting transactions and going concern (ISA 315, para A24).

Financial Reporting – gaining an understanding of the accounting principles and industry-specific practices will give the auditor an insight into potential issues around areas such as: revenue recognition; valuing of long-term contracts; or accounting for fair values (ISA 315, para A24).

1(C) SELECTION AND APPLICATION OF ACCOUNTING POLICIES

ISA 315, paragraph A28 states that: an understanding of the entity's selection and application of accounting policies may encompass such matters as methods to account for significant or unusual transactions; accounting policies selected surrounding controversial or emerging issues; changes in accounting policy; or new adoption of financial reporting standards and laws and regulations.

1(D) THE ENTITY'S OBJECTIVES AND STRATEGIES

An entity sets objectives and strategies which define the overall plans of the entity. These plans can be subject to business risk, which is broader than the risk of material misstatement of the financial statements. ISA 315, paragraph A31, explains that: "An understanding of the business risks facing the entity increases the likelihood of identifying risks of material misstatement, since most business risks will eventually have financial consequences and, therefore, an effect on the financial statements. However, the auditor does not have a responsibility to identify or assess all business risks because not all business risks give rise to risks of material misstatement."

Examples of business risks provided by ISA 315, paragraph A30, include: "development of new products or services which may fail; or flaws in a product or service that may result in liabilities and reputational risk".

ISA 315, paragraph A32 provides examples of matters which the auditor should be alert to that may indicate business risk and in turn lead to a material misstatement. Some of these examples include: new products or services giving rise to product liability; expansion of the business without accurate estimation of demand; or the introduction of a new IT system where systems and processes are incompatible.

1(E) MEASUREMENT AND REVIEW OF THE ENTITY'S FINANCIAL PERFORMANCE

ISA 315, paragraph A37 explains that "the measurement and review of financial performance is not the same as the monitoring of controls, though their purpose may overlap:
- the measurement and review of performance is directed at whether business performance is meeting the objectives set by management (or third parties).
- Monitoring of controls is specifically concerned with the effective operation of internal control."

The company/entity typically might measure its financial performance using key performance indicators, period-on-period financial performance analysis or comparison of financial results with that of its competitors. (See ISA 315, para A38 for further examples.)

2. INTERNAL CONTROL

The auditor must gain an understanding of internal controls within the entity that is relevant to the audit. This understanding is then used to identify potential areas where misstatements could occur, consider factors that affect the risk of material misstatement and design the nature, timing and extent of further audit procedures (ISA 315, para 12).

As defined in ISA 315, paragraph A44:
"Internal control is designed, implemented and maintained to address identified business risks that threaten the achievement of company objectives that concern:
- the reliability of the entity's financial reporting;
- the effectiveness and efficiency of its operations; and
- its compliance with applicable laws and regulations."

The 'Internal Controls' of an entity have the following components:
- the control environment;
- the entity's risk assessment process;
- the information system, including the related business processes relevant to financial reporting and communication;
- control activities; and
- monitoring of controls.

These are discussed in more detail in **Chapter 8**, Section 8.2.

At this stage of the risk assessment process, the auditor must consider how the design and implementation of the entity's system of internal control prevents material misstatements from occurring and, if they did occur, how the system would detect and correct these material misstatements. It must also be noted that this consideration by the auditor could also identify weaknesses in the internal control function. Where weaknesses are detected, the risks of material misstatement will be increased. (Internal control weaknesses are discussed in **Chapter 8**.)

Internal Control Limitations

No matter how well internal controls are designed and implemented by the entity, they can only provide **reasonable assurance** over the achievement of financial reporting management assertions (audit objectives). Possible limitations to internal control include the following:
- human error/mistake;
- human decision-making – the correct decision is not always made;
- controls can be circumvented as a result of collusion by two or more people;
- controls can be circumvented as a result of management override of control; or
- segregation of duties is often not possible within smaller entities, resulting in internal control functions not operating in an ideal manner.

(Again, a full discussion on the internal control environment is contained in **Chapter 8**.)

Sources of Information

Having discussed the type of information which the auditor should obtain, we will now consider where the auditor can find the information that he requires, i.e. the sources of this information.

The auditor can obtain both financial and non-financial information necessary to gain an understanding of the entity from external and internal sources. **Tables 7.7** and **7.8** below offer examples of where, respectively, such financial and non-financial information can be obtained.

TABLE 7.7: SOURCES OF FINANCIAL INFORMATION

Internal Sources	External Sources
• Budgets.	• Industry information.
• Management accounts.	• Competitive intelligence.
• Financial reports.	• Credit rating agencies.
• Financial statements.	• Creditors/suppliers.
• Minutes of directors' meetings.	• Government agencies.
• Income tax returns.	• Franchisors.
• Decisions made on accounting policies.	• The media and other external parties.
• Judgements and estimates.	

TABLE 7.8: SOURCES OF NON-FINANCIAL INFORMATION

Internal Sources	External Sources
• Vision of the organisation.	• Trade association data.
• Mission of the organisation.	• Industry forecasts.
• Objectives.	• Government agency reports.
• Strategies.	• Newspaper/magazine articles.
• Organisational structure.	• Information on the Internet.
• Minutes.	
• Job descriptions.	
• Operating performance.	
• Business drivers.	
• Capabilities.	
• Policy and procedure manuals.	
• Non-financial performance measures/metrics.	

7.4 ASSESSING THE RISKS OF MATERIAL MISSTATEMENT

When the auditor has obtained an understanding of the entity and its environment, including the internal control function, an assessment must be made as to the risk of material misstatement occurring at the financial statement level, and at the assertion level for classes of transactions, account balances and disclosures. In order to make this assessment the auditor shall, according to ISA 315, paragraph 26:

"(a) Identify risks throughout the process of obtaining an understanding of the entity and its environment, including relevant controls that relate to the risks, and by considering the classes of transactions, account balances, and disclosures in the financial statements;

(b) Assess the identified risks, and evaluate whether they relate more pervasively to the financial statements as a whole and potentially affect many assertions;

(c) Relate the identified risks to what can go wrong at the assertion level, taking account of relevant controls that the auditor intends to test; and

(d) Consider the likelihood of misstatement, including the possibility of multiple misstatements, and whether the potential magnitude is of a magnitude that could result in a material misstatement."

This assessment will dictate the nature, timing and extent of further audit procedures to be performed, which will be designed and performed in response to the assessed risks.

The risk assessment process should be adequately documented by the audit team and include information such as:
• engagement team discussions on the entity's control environment;
• how the understanding has been obtained;

- key points of the understanding obtained;
- the identified and assessed risks of material misstatement;
- identification of significant risks that need to be specifically addressed; and
- risks for which substantive procedures alone will not provide sufficient appropriate audit evidence.

Factors to be Considered when Making a Risk Assessment

Some of the factors that should be considered by the auditor when making a risk assessment are outlined in **Table 7.9** below. These considerations are dealt with under three key areas:
1. What risks have been identified, are they at the entity (financial statement) level or assertion level, and are there related internal control procedures that mitigate the risk?
2. What magnitude of misstatement could possibly occur and is this at the entity (financial statement) level or the assertion level?
3. How likely is the event or risk to occur?

Table 7.9 provides examples of the specific types of risk that the auditor should consider with respect to three key questions:

1. What risks have been identified?
2. What magnitude of misstatement (monetary impact) could possibly occur?
3. How likely is the event (risk) to occur?

7.5 THE AUDITOR'S RESPONSE TO ASSESSED RISKS

When the auditor has assessed the risks of material misstatement at the financial statement (entity) level, further audit procedures should be designed whose nature, timing and extent are in response to the assessed risks (ISA 330, para 6). There should be a clear link between the risks identified and the audit procedures performed to mitigate these risks. The overall aim of the auditor's response to assessed risks is to reduce audit risk to an acceptably low level.

ISA (UK and Ireland) 330 *The Auditor's Responses to Assessed Risks*, paragraph 7, states that the auditor should consider the following when designing further audit procedures:
"(a) Consider the reasons for the assessment given to the risk of material misstatement at the assertion level for each class of transactions, account balance, and disclosure including:
  (i) The likelihood of material misstatement due to the particular characteristics of the relevant class of transactions, account balance, or disclosure (that is, the inherent risk); and
  (ii) Whether the risk assessment takes account of relevant controls that is, the control risk), thereby requiring the auditor to obtain audit evidence to determine whether the controls are operating effectively (that is, the auditor intends to rely on the operating effectiveness of controls in determining the nature, tiraing and extent of substantive procedures); and
 (b) Obtain more persuasive audit evidence the higher the auditor's assessment of risk."

The nature of audit procedures used in response to assessed risks is critical in order to reduce audit risk to an acceptably low level.

TABLE 7.9: RISK ASSESSMENT FACTORS

1. What Risks have been identified?

Financial Statement (Entity) Level	• Risks resulting from poor entity-level internal controls or general IT internal controls. • Risk factors relating to management override and fraud. • Risks that management has chosen to accept, such as a lack of segregation of duties in an entity.

Assertion Level	• Specific risks relating to the completeness, accuracy, existence or valuation of:
	  ♦ revenues, expenditures, and other transactions;
	  ♦ account balances; and
	  ♦ financial statement disclosures.
	• Risks that could give rise to multiple misstatements.

Related Internal Control Procedures	• Significant risks. • The appropriately designed and implemented internal control procedures that help to prevent, detect or mitigate the risks identified. • Risks that can only be addressed by performing tests of controls.

2. What magnitude of misstatement (monetary impact) could possibly occur?

Financial Statement (Entity) Level	• What events, if they occurred, would result in a material misstatement in the financial statements? Consider management override, fraud, unexpected events and past experience.

Assertion Level	• Consider:
	  ♦ the inherent nature of the transactions, account balance or disclosure;
	  ♦ routine and non-routine events and past experience.

3. How likely is the event (risk) to occur?

Financial Statement Level	• Consider:
	  ♦ 'tone at the top';
	  ♦ management's approach to risk management;
	  ♦ policies and procedures in place; and
	  ♦ past experience.

Assertion Level	• Consider:
	  ♦ relevant internal control activities; and
	  ♦ past experience.

Related Internal Control Procedures	• Identify the elements of management's risk response that are crucial in reducing the likelihood of an event from occurring.

Considering the Nature, Timing and Extent of Further Audit Procedures in Response to Assessed Risks

Nature

The 'nature' of audit procedures refers to their **purpose** and their **type**.

Purpose:
- controls testing; and
- substantive testing.

Type:
- inspection;
- observation;
- inquiry;
- confirmation;
- recalculation;
- re-performance; or
- analytical procedures.

It is important to realise that certain forms of testing are more appropriate for some assertions than for others. For example:
- controls testing is not appropriate for gaining comfort over the cut-off assertion, whereas substantive testing is appropriate;
- substantive testing is usually more appropriate than controls testing for gaining comfort over the completeness and accuracy of the assertions for accounting estimates, such as prepayments, accruals or provisions (e.g. provision for bad debt, provision for slow-moving inventory); and
- when it comes to revenue, controls testing is more suitable for addressing risks relating to the completeness assertion, whereas substantive procedures are better for addressing risk relating to the occurrence assertion.

When considering the nature of the testing to be performed, the auditor must remain firmly focused on the risks identified and the related risk assessment, i.e. the higher the assessed risk, the more reliable and relevant must be the audit evidence obtained by the auditor from substantive testing.

Timing

'Timing' simply refers to when the audit procedures are performed. Audit procedures can be performed at an interim date or at the period end, and later. As a general guide, the higher the assessed risk, the more likely it is that the auditor will consider it more effective to perform audit procedures nearer to and after the period end. In some circumstances, in order to introduce an element of unpredictability into audit testing, it is worthwhile to perform some audit procedures at an unpredictable time or unannounced. In other instances, performing audit procedures before the period end can alert the auditor to significant matters at any early stage of the audit. Key points to consider when deciding whether to perform audit procedures at an interim date (i.e. before year end) are summarised as follows.

- How good is the overall control environment? Performing a **roll forward** between an interim date and the period end is unlikely to be effective if the general control environment is poor.
- How good are the specific controls over the account balance or class of transactions being considered?
- Is the required evidence available to perform the test? Electronic files could subsequently be overwritten or procedures to be observed could occur only at certain times.
- Would a procedure before the period end address the nature and substance of the risk involved?
- Would the interim procedure address the period or date to which the audit evidence relates?
- How much additional evidence will be required for the remaining period between the date of procedure and period end?

It is important to remember that certain procedures can only be performed at or after the period end, such as cut-off testing, unrecorded liabilities testing and post balance-sheet events testing.

Extent

'Extent' relates to the quantity of a specific audit procedure to be performed, e.g. the sample size to be used when testing client cut-off procedures, the number and value of receivables balances to be circularised or the number of observations of a control activity to be performed.

The extent of the testing to be performed is determined by the judgement of the auditor after considering the following:
- materiality;
- assessed risk; and
- the degree of assurance necessary.

Where the assessed risk is greater, the extent of testing to be performed will be increased as appropriate. As a general rule:
- where the risk is assessed as high, the greater the extent of testing to be performed; and
- where the risk is assessed as low, the extent of testing to be performed is less.

7.6 SIGNIFICANT RISKS

As discussed in **Section 7.5** above, as part of the risk assessment process within an entity, the auditor must consider each risk individually and how pervasive it could be in the financial statements. However, not all risks will be of equal significance and, therefore, not all risks will have the potential to lead to a material misstatement in the financial statements. Risks that have the potential to impact significantly on the financial statements and which need special audit consideration as a result in order to mitigate the risk are known as 'significant risk' (ISA 315, para 4(e)).

When determining significant risks, which will arise on most audits, the auditor must use professional judgement and assess the following:
- the nature of the risk;
- the likely magnitude of the potential misstatement; and
- the likelihood of the risk occurring.

When considering the above points, the auditor must ignore the controls in place within the entity to mitigate the risk and make an assessment that does not consider the safeguards in place against the risk.

Significant risks often relate to:
- significant transactions that are not usual for the nature of the business; and
- matters that require significant judgement.

Significant transactions that are outside the normal routine transactions of the entity give rise to the risk of incorrect processing, classification and disclosure in the financial statements.

Matters requiring significant judgement are inherently risky, given that they are often very subjective in nature, represent the views of a small number of individuals, e.g. the directors, and cannot be substantiated by third-party evidence.

Significant **non-routine transactions** and judgemental matters are often the basis of significant risks, particularly in smaller entities. This is considered in **Table 7.10** below, which outlines some characteristics of risks for both non-routine transactions and judgmental matters.

The Auditor's Response to Significant Risks

The auditor must gain an understanding, if this has not already been obtained, of the controls designed and implemented around any significant risks identified.

Assessment of the robustness of the controls surrounding significant risks is necessary in order for the auditor to have all the information needed to develop an appropriate audit approach. As a general rule:
- where the controls identified around significant risk areas are weak or where no controls exist, the auditor must perform appropriate substantive testing in order to mitigate the risk of a material misstatement going undetected; or
- where the controls identified around significant risk areas are strong, the level of substantive testing performed can be reduced as is deemed appropriate by the auditor.

Where it is concluded by the auditor that management has not responded appropriately to a significant risk through the design and implementation of appropriate controls, this is noted as an 'internal control weakness' and should be communicated to those charged with governance. (Communicating internal control weaknesses is discussed in **Section 7.8**.) However, at this point it is appropriate to explain that, where the system of internal control is weak or does not exist, and the auditor does not believe that substantive

TABLE 7.10: RISKS RELATING TO NON-ROUTINE
TRANSACTIONS AND JUDGEMENTAL MATTERS

Subject Matter/ Information	Characteristics

Significant Non-routine Transactions	• High inherent risk (likelihood and impact).
	• Occur infrequently.
	• Not subject to systematic processing.
	• Unusual due to their size or nature (such as the acquisition of another entity).
	• Require management intervention:
	  ◆ to specify accounting treatment; or
	  ◆ for data collection and processing.
	• Involve complex calculations or accounting principles.
	• Nature of transactions makes it difficult for the entity to implement effective internal controls over the risks.

Significant Judgemental Matters	• High inherent risk. • Involve significant measurement uncertainty (such as the development of accounting estimates). • Accounting principles involved may be subject to differing interpretation (such as preparation of accounting estimates or application of revenue recognition). • Required judgement may be subjective, complex, or require assumptions about the effects of future events (such as judgements about fair value, valuation of inventory subject to rapid change).

(**Source**: *Guide to using International Standards on Auditing in the Audits of Small- and Medium-Sized Entities* (IFAC).)

procedures alone can reduce the risk of material misstatement to an acceptably low level, then the impact of this on the audit opinion must be considered.

It is important to note also that, where controls exist around significant risks, these controls must be tested during each audit engagement by the audit team. Reliance on evidence attained in previous audits is not permitted without some key considerations, outlined in ISA 330, paragraph 13.

For all significant risks identified, it is essential that the auditor documents the following:
• the nature of the significant risk identified;
• management's response to the significant risk; and
• audit response to the significant risk, i.e. audit testing to be performed to mitigate the audit risk (i.e. the risk that the auditor expresses an inappropriate opinion when the financial statements are materially misstated as a direct result of the significant risk identified).

Examples of Significant Risks

Examples of significant risks that often arise on audit engagements include the following:
- fraud risk;
- management override of controls;
- revenue recognition; and
- personal expenditure of directors being included in the expenses of the company.

7.7 EVALUATING THE SUFFICIENCY AND APPROPRIATENESS OF AUDIT EVIDENCE OBTAINED

Once audit procedures have been performed and audit evidence obtained, the auditor should consider the initial risk assessment at the assertion level and conclude if the risks identified still remain appropriate. Overall, the auditor should then make an assessment as to whether the audit evidence obtained is sufficient and appropriate to reduce the **audit risk** (i.e. the risk that the auditor expresses an inappropriate opinion when the financial statements are materially misstated) to an acceptably low level (ISA 330, para 25). Whether audit evidence is sufficient and appropriate is a matter of professional judgement for the auditor.

Where the auditor concludes that sufficient appropriate audit evidence has not been obtained, attempts should be made to obtain such evidence. Where it is not possible to obtain such evidence, the auditor must consider the impact on the audit opinion to be issued.

As discussed in detail in **Chapter 6**, 'Gathering Audit Evidence', it is essential that the auditor document the nature, timing and extent of audit procedures that have been performed in response to assessed risks of material misstatement at the assertion level. Equally, the auditor must document the results of the testing performed.

7.8 COMMUNICATING WITH THOSE CHARGED WITH GOVERNANCE AND MANAGEMENT

The auditor should communicate in writing significant deficiencies in internal control identified during the audit to **management** on a timely basis (ISA 265, para 9). Such communication should include:
- the weakness identified;
- the level of risk associated with the weakness, i.e. low, moderate or high; and
- suggestions as to how the control environment can be improved in order to remove the weakness.

It should be noted that the risk assessment process does not end after the initial assessment is made and communication of control weaknesses is made to those charged with governance/management. Rather, the auditor must remain alert throughout the audit for additional risk areas that are identified and for evidence of internal controls not operating as intended. When this occurs, the original risk assessment must be updated to reflect the new information. The audit plan should also be amended, if necessary, in response to the new risks identified.

7.9 THE RELATIONSHIP BETWEEN MATERIALITY AND AUDIT RISK

When planning the audit, the auditor considers what would cause the financial statements to be materially misstated. The auditor's understanding of the entity and its environment establishes a frame of reference within which the auditor plans the audit and exercises professional judgement about assessing the risks of the existence of material misstatement in the financial statements and responding to those risks throughout the audit. It also assists the auditor to establish materiality and in evaluating whether the judgement about materiality remains appropriate as the audit progresses.

For instance, where significant risks of material misstatement are identified, audit materiality should be adjusted to reflect the new information obtained. Where this is the case, the auditor must consider the impact on the audit approach and may consider it necessary to alter the nature, timing and extent of the audit plan. An example of this in practice would be as follows:

EXAMPLE 7.2: RELATIONSHIP BETWEEN MATERIALITY AND AUDIT RISK

- The auditor has established preliminary materiality level as €35,000.
- Total trade receivables balance at the period end is €275,000.
- Trade receivables balances equalling €240,000 have been circularised, resulting in the untested balance being immaterial for further testing.
- Factors are identified during the preliminary assessment of materiality which result in the auditor exercising judgement and reducing materiality to €21,000 due to further risk assessment.
- The impact on the audit testing performed on trade receivables balance is that the balance, which has not been tested through circularisation, is no longer immaterial to the financial statements. The result is that further testing, to the extent of €14,000, must now be performed in order to reduce the untested balance to below the amended materiality level.

Remember: the key point is that there is an inverse relationship between audit risk and materiality:
- the greater the audit risk, the lower the level of materiality; and
- the lower the audit risk, the greater the level of materiality.

7.10 CONCLUSION

Assessing the risk of material misstatements occurring in the financial statements is critical for the auditor in order to determine an appropriate audit plan that will reduce the **audit risk** (i.e. the risk that the auditor expresses an inappropriate opinion when the financial statements are materially misstated) to an acceptably low level. This is a complex process and the auditor must develop the skills necessary in order to achieve the following:

- understanding the business and related business risk;
- obtaining an understanding of the system of internal control (to include evaluating the design of the controls and determining whether they have been implemented);
- assessing the risks of material misstatement;
- developing overall responses to risks; and
- developing responses to risks at the assertion level.

A suitable risk assessment process should be carried out by the auditor that should include appropriate audit procedures responding to identified risks. Failure to carry out an adequate assessment of risks exposes the auditor to a high level of 'audit risk', which may resuh in him issuing an incorrect audit opinion.

SUMMARY OF LEARNING OBJECTIVES

Learning Objective 1 Demonstrate detailed knowledge of the risk environment.

The 'risk environment' is made up of:
- Business risk – the auditor is only concerned with business risks that could impact on the financial statements and lead to material misstatements;
- Audit risk – the risk of the auditor issuing an inappropriate audit decision.

'Audit risk' comprises:
- Engagement risk (dealt with in **Chapter 5**);
- Independence risk (dealt with in **Chapter 2**);
- Audit Risk Components
  1. Inherent risk – driven by the environment in which the company operates.
  2. Control risk – driven by the organisational controls introduced by management.
  3. Detection risk – driven by the strength of the auditor's substantive testing

The auditor will assess inherent and controls risks that exist in the client entity and plan substantive testing at an appropriate level to respond to the risks identified. Detection risk is the only risk component within the control of the auditor.

Risk can exist at two levels of material misstatement:
- the financial statement level;
- the class of transaction, account balance and disclosure, and related assertions level.

Risks that occur at the financial statement level (also known as the entity level) are more significant for the auditor, so he will ensure that he assigns an appropriate level of staff with relevant expertise and experience to deal with the risks at hand.

Learning Objective 2 Demonstrate an understanding of how the auditor gains an understanding of the entity, what types of information he should collect, and why and where he might find the required information.

In order to gain an understanding of the entity and its environment, the auditor can use a number of methods, including: inquiries of management; analytical procedures; observation and inspection; cumulative audit knowledge and experience; and discussion among the audit engagement team.

ISA 315, paragraphs 11–12 (A17–A64), offers guidance on **what** type of information the auditor should try to obtain in order to gain an understanding of the entity and its environment. Broadly, these include: the entity and its environment, and the entity's internal controls. Focusing on each of these components will provide the auditor with a detailed knowledge and understanding of the entity before assessing the risk of material misstatements and developing the audit plan.

The auditor should look for both financial and non-financial information to support his understanding and obtain his understanding from both internal and external sources to the entity.

Learning Objective 3 Understand the principal considerations of the auditor when assessing the risk of material misstatement.

When assessing the risk of material misstatement, the auditor will consider:
1. What risk has been identified and whether it is at the entity (financial statement) level or the assertion level?
2. What is the potential magnitude of the risk identified?
3. How likely is the risk to occur?

The above will allow the auditor to better **plan** a response to the risks identified.

Learning Objective 4 Demonstrate a detailed understanding of how the auditor responds to risk (and, separately, significant risk) in the design of the nature, timing and extent of further audit procedures.

The design of the **nature, timing and extent** of audit procedures to respond to risks:

Low detection risk – Nature: perform tests of details (as opposed to substantive analytical procedures).
Timing: perform audit procedures after or very close to year end.
Extent: large sample sizes.

High detection risk – Nature: perform more substantive analytical procedures, less tests of details.
Timing: Perform more audit procedures at **interim** stage.
Extent: sample sizes will be smaller.

Not all risks will be of equal significance and, therefore, not all risks will have the potential to lead to a material misstatement in the financial statements. Risks that have the potential to impact significantly on the financial statements and which need special audit consideration as a result, in order to mitigate the risk, are known as **'significant risk'** (ISA 315, para 4(e)).

Learning Objective 5 Demonstrate an appreciation of the assessment of the sufficiency and adequacy of evidence and the importance of documenting the risk process.

Whether audit evidence is sufficient and appropriate is a matter of professional judgement for the auditor. Where the auditor concludes that sufficient appropriate audit evidence has not been obtained, attempts should be made to obtain such evidence. Where it is not possible to obtain such evidence, the auditor must consider the impact on the audit opinion to be issued.

Learning Objective 6 Have an appreciation of the relationship between materiality and audit risk.

Factors may be identified during the course of the audit that impact on the preliminary assessment of materiality. This may result in the auditor exercising judgement and reducing materiality due to risk assessments performed. Earlier audit procedures may need to be revisited, to see if the change in materiality impacts on the required nature, timing and extent of audit procedures performed.

QUESTIONS

Self-test Questions

7.1 Explain the relationship between materiality, audit risk and audit planning.

7.2 Distinguish between inherent risk, control risk and detection risk.

7.3 What is the overall aim of the auditor's response to assessed risks?

7.4 Distinguish between business risk and audit risk.

7.5 Identify and explain the components of audit risk.

7.6 Identify three key ways the auditor can obtain an understanding of the entity.

7.7 Identify and give details of two sources of external and internal information from which the auditor can gain an understanding of the entity.

7.8 Identify five internal control limitations.

7.9 How should the auditor communicate material weaknesses in the entity's internal control environment to those charged with governance?

7.10 Outline the considerations the auditor should make when designing further audit procedures.

7.11 What are the two types of audit procedure an auditor can use to assist in reducing the assessed risk of misstatement to an acceptably low level?

Review Questions

(See Suggested Solutions to Review Questions in **Appendix D**.)

Question 7.1

You are the audit senior on the audit of Oh So Chic Ltd, which is a retailer of cutting-edge designer fashion clothing. The audit is scheduled to commence in two weeks. The audit partner has drawn the following information to your attention and would like to know your thoughts.

Significant Risk The company financial director explained, during a recent meeting with the audit partner, that sales have slowed down during the year under review. Normally, the company experiences a very quick turnaround time for inventory, given that its retail cutting-edge designer fashion of the moment has been very much in demand in the past. As fashion trends are moving away from designer to high street, the financial director is concerned about the appropriateness of the year-end inventory valuation. The value of inventory held at the year end is €2.75 million, which is material to the financial statements.

Internal Control The financial director also revealed at the meeting that a key member of the accounts team had been absent from work through sickness for the final five months of the accounting period under review. His responsibility included preparation of the following key reconciliations:
- daily till reconciliations; and
- monthly supplier statement reconciliations.

In his absence, the above reconciliations were not prepared.

Other Information The company is considering commencing a contract to supply goods to Gorgeous Shoes Ltd, a company that is owned by a director of Oh So Chic Ltd, in an attempt to improve company sales.

Requirement
(a) Outline the approach you would adopt to address the significant risk identified above in relation to inventory.
(b) Discuss the impact of the absence of the key member of the accounts team noted above on the audit plan and approach, including a discussion of the financial statement areas and assertions which may be affected.
(c) Document briefly the audit considerations if a contract is to be agreed between Gorgeous Shoes Ltd and Oh So Chic Ltd.

Question 7.2

You are currently auditing County Builders Ltd, a long-established building company whose principal activity is building residential housing developments. You are performing the audit for the year to May 2013. As a result of a recent contraction in the housing market, the company's trading results have been significantly affected. See financial information below:

	2013	2012	2011
	€	€	€
Revenue	2.2 million	4.6 million	6.2 million
Net profit/Loss	(750,000)	(300,000)	750,000
Reserves	150,000	900,000	1.2 million
Gearing	75%	60%	50%

The company is coming under increasing pressure to fulfil interest payments on significant loans held by the company.

The company has not secured any significant contracts for the coming year and 35 houses remain unsold out of a total of 50 houses built on the previous significant contract secured by the company. You are required to discuss the risk that the above presents to the current year's audit. Outline how the auditor should respond to any risks identified.

Question 7.3

The following is a description of the payroll function in a company you are auditing.
- Employees record hours worked each day on a manual time sheet.
- Each week, time sheets for each employee are reviewed for accuracy by line managers.
- Reviewed time sheets are passed to the payroll assistant for processing onto the payroll system.
- Hourly wage rates, PAYE rates and PRSI/NIC rates are maintained as standing data on the payroll system.
- Wages are paid via Bankers Automated Clearing System (BACS) each week.
- The payroll manager reviews the BACS payment listing for all employees prior to authoring the BACS payment.
- Authorisation codes are required from the payroll manager and the accounts manager in order to process the BACS payment.

Requirement Describe the testing that the auditor should perform in order to obtain assurance that the total wages figure recorded in the financial statements is accurate.

Question 7.4

As audit senior, you are involved for the first time in the audit of a long-standing client of your auditing firm. The engagement leader has alerted you to the fact that the company has a board consisting of three directors, with two of these directors being perceived to exert dominant influence over the operations of the company.

Requirement Discuss the risks this may create for the audit and how the audit plan should be tailored to respond to these risks.

Question 7.5

Parallel Ltd is a long established FMCG Company owned by an Australian holding company and has been audited by Brett & Co for the past four years. 80% of their sales are to Irish supermarkets. You are audit manager for the year ended 31 December 2012 and through you conversations with management have learned the following.

- The group company was disappointed with the fall in profits in 2011 and warned the management that they needed to take more control of costs considering that up to October of 2011 they were on target to meet profit expectations and then, due to unforeseen expenses, they could not meet this profit for year end.
- A number of staff was on strike during 2012 due to disputes over pay decreases, the striking staff was mainly finance support functions (accounts receivable and accounts payable) related and distribution.
- Due to the striking of distribution staff, some invoices needed to be marked as delivered without signed Purchase Order Delivery dockets.
- Marketing costs have been cut by approx. 60% as part of the cost saving exercise.
- All service contracts (outsourced activities) were sent out for tender during 2012 to ensure the best price was being achieved. As a result payroll is now under a new service provider.
- The Financial Controller has recently been replaced (management did not go into details regarding his departure). There was a one-month gap between the old and new financial controller.

You have prepared an analytical review based on comparison of 2012 Actual versus Budgeted figures as follows.

	2012 Actual Figures	Budget	Variance	Variance
	€000	€000	€000	%
Sales	4,900	4,812.00	–88.00	2%
Production Costs				
Material A	1,180	1,000.00	180.00	18%
Material B	1,150	1,200.00	–50.00	–4%
Material C	500	520.00	–20.00	–4%
Material D	152	150.00	2.00	1%
Factory Electricity	170	160.00	10.00	6%
Labour 133	111.00	22.00	20%	
Factory Rent	8	8.00	0.30	4%
Machinery Depreciation	20	20.00	0.00	0%
Total Production Costs	3,313	3,169	144.30	5%

Gross Profit	**1,587**	**1,643**	**–56.30**	**–3%**
Overheads				
office Rent	40.00	83.00	–43.00	–52%
Sales Salaries	235	240.00	–5.00	–2%
Distribution Salaries	295	300.00	–5.00	–2%
Marketing	180	300.00	–120.00	–40%
Finance Salaries	325	330.00	–5.00	–2%
Deprecation Office Equipment	100	58.00	42.00	72%
Debtors Write off	25	100.00	–75.00	–75%
	1,200	1,411	–211.00	–15%
Net Profit	**2,400**	**2,822**	**–422.00**	**7%**

Requirement

(a) Your audit partner has asked you to wrhe a memo outlming the inherent and control risks you have identified during your discussion with management.

(b) List five questions you would raise with management based on your analytical review (you should take your earlier discussion into account).

THE AUDIT AND ASSURANCE PROCESS

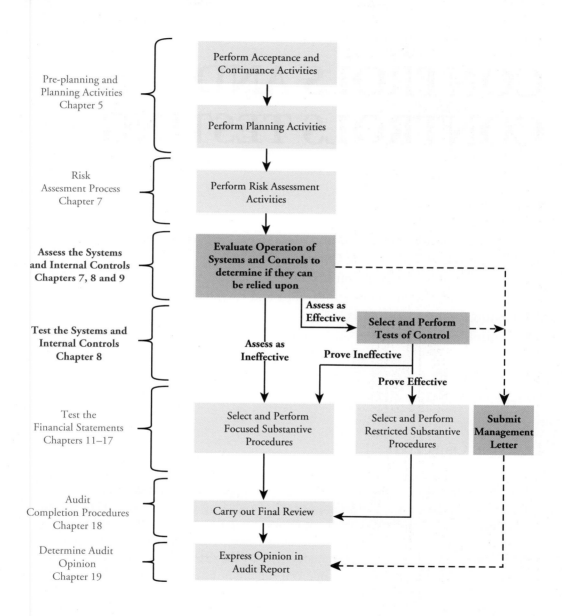

CONTROLS AND CONTROLS TESTING

LEARNING OBJECTIVES

Having studied this chapter on controls and controls testing you should:
1. demonstrate a detailed knowledge of what makes up the internal control system;
2. appreciate the importance of client entity internal controls to the auditor;
3. demonstrate a detailed knowledge of the stages involved in the review of the internal control system of the client entity by the external auditor;
4. gain an understanding of the financial statement assertions (audit objectives) relative to each financial cycle;
5. appreciate the control activities that should exist relative to each financial cycle;
6. gain an appreciation of when it is most efficient to test controls;
7. be able to select and apply appropriate control tests to typical financial cycles, which address the financial statement assertions (audit objectives); and
8. explain how the auditor communicates control deficiencies to the client entity.

CHECKLIST OF RELEVANT STANDARDS

The relevant standards covered in this chapter are:
- ISA (UK and Ireland) 265 *Communicating Deficiencies in Internal Control to Those Charged With Governance and Management* (ISA 265);
- ISA (UK and Ireland) 315 *Identifying and Assessing the Risks of Material Misstatement Through Understanding of the Entity and Its Environment* (ISA 315);
- ISA (UK and Ireland) 330 *The Auditor's Reponses to Assessed Risks* (ISA 330).

KEY TERMS AND DEFINITIONS FOR THIS CHAPTER

Blind Count   A blind count should happen when counting inventory. A blind count means that the individuals responsible for counting cannot see the volume that is expected, i.e. the volume per the perpetual records.

Computer Assisted Audit Techniques (CAATs)   CAATs involve the use of IT systems by an auditor to support his testing of financial statements. (A detailed discussion on CAATs can be found in **Chapter 9**, **Section 9.4**.)

Control Deviations   Control deviations are situations where actual events differ from those expected. For example, an auditor selects 200 invoices and traces them to customer-signed proof of delivery notes (PODs), but finds five deviations in that five of the customer PODs are not signed.

Exception Report   This is a report that is run from the client entity's computer system, highlighting unusual activity. For example, within payroll, an exception report might be run for overtime in excess of 10 hours.

Knowledge-based Systems   A knowledge-based system allows an auditor to design a questionnaire containing the most common questions related to a particular procedure and support this with troubleshooting information that can help to guide him with respect to best practice.

Master data   Also known as 'standing data', master data relates to the information held by an entity that supports transactions. Customers' names and their bank account details are examples of master data. The integrity of master data is of utmost importance to any entity.

Misappropriation   The dishonest use of the assets of the client entity, such as stealing inventory or abuse of a company phone.

Organisational Structure   The hierarchical arrangement of authority and rights and duties within an organisation.

Policies and Procedures   Policies outline the principles or rules that guide decisions within an organisation (e.g. it might be a company's policy to only accept return of goods within 28 days of sale). Procedures outline what action is to be taken or what steps are to be followed when performing a particular task (e.g. when a customer presents a return, the procedure might be to request a receipt or invoice and check that the date on the receipt or invoice is within 28 days; for returns over €100, contact a supervisor to approve the return).

System Control   A system control is one that is embedded into an entity's IT system. For example, the system can ensure the 'segregation of duty' control requirement is met by ensuring that only those individuals with credit control rights can approve the opening of a new customer account on credit.

Segregation of Duties   The division of key tasks in a transaction to ensure that no one individual can influence a transaction from beginning to end.

Terminated employee   A former employee of the client entity.

Tone at the Top   The 'tone at the top' relates to the words and actions of the directors and senior management of an organisation, in this case relating to internal controls and ethical values.

Walkthrough Test   The tracing of a single transaction from beginning to end to establish if it operates as described in the policies and procedures of the client entity.

8.1 INTRODUCTION

After the risks have been identified by the auditor, as discussed throughout **Chapter 7**, the auditor should gain an understanding of the controls over each financial cycle. ISA (UK and Ireland) 315 *Identifying and Assessing the Risks of Material Misstatement Through Understanding of the Entity and Its Environment* (ISA 315) states that:

"The auditor shall obtain an understanding of internal control relevant to the audit."(ISA 315, para 12)

The auditor uses his understanding of internal control to:

- identify types of potential misstatements;
- consider factors that may affect the risks of material misstatement; and
- design the nature, timing, and extent of further audit procedures.

The purpose of the above is to identify the existence of internal controls that mitigate the risk factors identified within each cycle.

In **Section 8.2** we will introduce the internal control system and discuss the components of the internal control system as laid down by the Committee of Sponsoring Organizations of the Treadway Commission (COSO). In this section we will also discuss the objectives of internal controls and their importance to the client entity.

Section 8.3 discusses the importance of the internal control system to the external auditor addressing the question, "Why is the auditor interested in the controls of the organisation?"

The auditor does not test the controls of the organisation in every instance. He must first determine whether he believes the control environment (or specific financial cycle controls) to be strong before testing. The stages involved in reviewing the internal controls of the client entity are the subject of discussion in **Section 8.4** and it is this section that sets the scene for **Sections 8.5–8.9**. In **Section 8.4** we explain the four-staged approach used to review controls. In **Sections 8.5–8.9** we apply this four-staged approach to specific financial cycles, namely: the revenue and receivables cycle; the purchases and payables and payroll cycle; the inventory cycle; the bank and cash cycle; and the investments cycle. It is essential to understand the generic application described within **Section 8.4** but more importantly, to be able to apply this process to individual financial cycles. Typical financial cycles processes are described in order to demonstrate the key control activities expected within each cycle, but the reader should be mindful that these can vary from company to company. There are a number of different methods used to describe the processes (for example, narratives and flowcharts), which are intended to give the reader an insight into the types of methods used by companies to describe their internal control environment.

Finally, in **Section 8.10** we discuss how the auditor communicates any deficiencies in the control environment to the client entity.

8.2 THE INTERNAL CONTROL SYSTEM

Before exploring the importance of the internal control system to the work of the auditor, it is important to first understand its importance to the entity or organisation.

The *UK Corporate Governance Code*[1] recommends that "the board should maintain a sound risk management and internal control system". Detailed advice on the application of a strong internal control system is provided by the Committee of Sponsoring Organizations of the Treadway Commission (COSO, formed in 1985 in order to sponsor the national commission on fraudulent reporting) in its *Internal Control–Integrated Framework*,[2] a document designed to provide detailed advice to companies on the application of a strong internal control system. COSO defines internal control as:

> "a process, effected by an entity's board of directors, management, and other personnel, designed to provide reasonable assurance regarding the achievement of objectives in the following categories:
> * Effectiveness and efficiency of operations.
> * Reliability and reporting.
> * Compliance with applicable laws and regulations." (p. 1, para 11)

---

[1] http://www.frc.org.uk/Our-Work/Codes-Standards/Corporate-governance.aspx
[2] *Internal Control–Integrated Framework* (Committee of Sponsoring Organizations of the Treadway Commission, 2011). See http://www.coso.org/documents/coso_framework_body_v6.pdf

Internal Control Objectives

The internal control system is not simply a fraud and error prevention activity, but rather a system that helps the orderly running of the business. The objectives of internal control, endorsed both by the FRC in its pronouncements and by the COSO guidelines, include:
- safeguarding of the company's assets;
- ensuring the accuracy and completeness of the accounting records;
- the timely preparation of financial information;
- the efficient conduct of the entity's business (including adherence to internal policies); and
- the prevention and detection of fraud.

Responsibilities for Internal Control

COSO states that "Everyone in an organization has responsibility for internal control" (p. 123, para 415). While the **chief executive officer** (CEO) holds ultimate responsibility for internal controls, there are a number of other groups in an organisation that will also impact on the effectiveness of any internal control system. **Management** is responsible for communicating, enabling and evaluating adherence to requirements defined by external laws, regulations, standards, internal policies and standards of conduct. **All employees** are responsible for performing their roles in compliance with set policies and procedures. **Internal auditors** are responsible for evaluating the system of internal controls, reporting on weaknesses and recommending courses of action to remedy these. While **external auditors** hold no direct responsibilities with regard to the internal control system of an organisation, "they provide another independent view on the reliability of the entity's external reporting".

Components of Internal Control

As outlined above, internal controls may be incorporated within computerised accounting systems. However, the internal control system extends beyond those matters relating directly to the accounting system. COSO outlines five components of internal control, which are outlined in **Figure 8.1** below.

The COSO components of internal control are recognised within the ISAs (UK and Ireland) in the form of Appendix 1 of ISA 315, which further explains the components of internal control as they relate to an audit of financial statements. These requirements are considered throughout the balance of this chapter.

Types of Internal Control

The auditor is required to consider how the design and implementation of internal controls **prevent** material misstatements from occurring and, if material misstatements did occur, how the system would **detect** and correct them. The auditor will assess the quality of these controls, which are usually broken down into **manual** and **automated** controls.

FIGURE 8.1: FIVE COMPONENTS OF INTERNAL CONTROL

Control Environment	Risk Assessment	Control Activities	Information Systems & Communication	Monitoring Activities
Management Integrity and Competence	Risk Identification Policy and Procedures	Segregation of Duties	Existence of strong General Controls relating to IT	Existence of Internal Audit
Tone at the Top	Risk Analyses and Action Plan Procedures	Physical Controls	Existence of Strong Application Controls	Response to Control Deviations / Weak Controls
Organisational Structure and Chart of Authority	Fraud Risk Assessment	Reviews and Authorisation	Communication of Objectives and Requirements with regard to IC's	
HR Policies and Procedures	Change Management	System Controls		
		Reconciliations		
Chapter 7	Chapter 7	Chapter 8	Chapter 9	Chapter 8/10

System of Internal Control (IC)

The foundation of any control system is its people ....

"Everyone in the organaisation has responsibility for Internal Control"

Manual Controls

These are controls carried out by employees in the organisation and can therefore be subject to **human error**. Examples of manual controls include:
- performance of bank reconciliations; and
- credit checks performed by the credit controller.

Such controls require that the assigned individual, first, performs the control periodically (i.e. daily, monthly, weekly, etc.) and, secondly, that he carries it out as described within the relevant policy and procedure. Human error can be minimised by the introduction of higher level (management) reviews to ensure timely and accurate performance.

Automated Controls

Automated controls are controls embedded within the client entity's computerised accounting system. Once the system is configured to deal with the control, it should occur automatically (i.e. once it is set up correctly to perform a certain control, it will behave in the same way every time). Examples of automated controls could include:
- systematic prevention of orders where the order will result in the customer exceeding their credit limit; or
- inability to input an order for an out-of-stock item.

Such controls work seamlessly, once they are properly set up in the system.

Detective Controls

These controls detect errors that have already occurred in the system, allowing their correction. An example of such a control would be the performance of a bank reconciliation, which should highlight any errors in posting or missing postings, etc.

Preventative Controls

These controls prevent an error occurring in the first place. For example, the inability to enter an order for a customer where the order will cause the customer to exceed their credit limits or where the customer account is overdue (this demonstrates an automated preventative control). It is important, however, to consider the ability to override the control. For example, as discussed in **Chapter 3**, Section 3.5, management are best positioned to override controls by either giving instruction to employees to enter transactions that are not valid, knowing staff are unlikely to question them, or by creating journal entries to smooth profits.

Automated controls are preferred over manual controls as they are not subject to human error once they have been properly configured in the system. Preventative controls are preferred over detective controls as they are intended to prevent occurrence of the error in the first place. However, it is never possible to eliminate manual and detective controls due to the complexity of business and the limitations of systems within each entity. Therefore, an auditor will always encounter a combination of the above controls.

8.3 WHY THE CONTROL SYSTEM IS SO IMPORTANT TO THE EXTERNAL AUDITOR

Introduction

Understanding and testing controls addresses the requirements of two key auditing standards:
- ISA (UK and Ireland) 315 *Identifying and Assessing the Risks of Material Misstatement Through Understanding of the Entity and Its Environment* (ISA 315); and
- ISA (UK and Ireland) 330 *The Auditor's Response to Assessed Risks* (ISA 330).

Meeting the requirements of ISA 315 (discussed throughout **Chapter 7**) will allow the auditor to gain a greater understanding of the client entity's operations and, ultimately, empower him to perform a more robust audit. With respect to ISA 330, the auditor's aim is to ensure that he appropriately addresses risks. When designing the nature, timing and extent of audit procedures, the auditor will often search for control activities that mitigate risks and therefore reduce the level of substantive audit procedures. An understanding of the client entity's controls therefore allows the auditor to perform a more effective and efficient audit.

Nature, Timing and Extent of Audit Procedures at the Assertion Level

ISA 330, paragraph 6, states:

"The auditor shall design and perform further audit procedures whose **nature, timing, and extent** are based on and are responsive to the assessed risks of material misstatement at the **assertion level**." (emphasis added)

Nature, Timing and Extent of Substantive Audit Procedures

The auditor is concerned with ensuring that he designs appropriate procedures with respect to the nature, timing and extent in order to ensure that all risks are addressed. However, he also needs to ensure that he does so in the most **efficient and effective** manner. 'Efficiency' in this context means the time the auditor spends on the audit; the more time he spends on the audit the more costs are incurred. 'Effectiveness' refers to the quality of the work performed; the auditor should never jeopardise quality and increase audit risk for the sake of efficiency (i.e. perform a more time-efficient test that does not meet the definition of sufficient appropriate audit evidence as discussed in **Chapter 6**, Section 6.2).

A systems-based (or controls-approach) audit means that the auditor understands and tests the system of controls operating within the client entity sufficiently to satisfy himself that these controls:
(a) mitigate risks;
(b) address the audit objectives; and
(c) worked effectively throughout the entire period under review.

In doing so he can rely on those systems of internal controls to reduce the nature, timing and extent of audit procedures and improve the overall efficiency of the audit while not negatively impacting on its quality. This is demonstrated in **Figure 8.2** below.

Tying Controls to Assertions

"In making risk assessments, the auditor may identify the controls that are likely to prevent, or detect and correct, material misstatements in specific assertions" (ISA 315, para A116). Application note A116 of ISA 315 reminds the auditor that: "Often, only multiple control activities, together with other components of internal control, will be sufficient to address a risk." Additionally, application note A118 reminds the auditor that controls "can be either directly or indirectly related to an assertion". We can consider this by way of **Example 8.1** below.

EXAMPLE 8.1: INDIRECT AND MULTIPLE CONTROL ACTIVITIES

For example, the existence of an 'organisational chart' and a 'chart of authority' act as **indirect control activities** to the purchases cycle. These documents are controlled by senior management. The organisation chart dictates hierarchy within an organisation and the chart of authority dictates who in the organisation can perform certain transactions and activities and to what value (e.g. it can list who in the organisation can place a purchase order and to what value, and who can approve purchase orders).

FIGURE 8.2: HOW EFFECTIVE CONTROLS INFLUENCE THE NATURE,
TIMING AND EXTENT OF SUBSTANTIVE AUDIT PROCEDURES

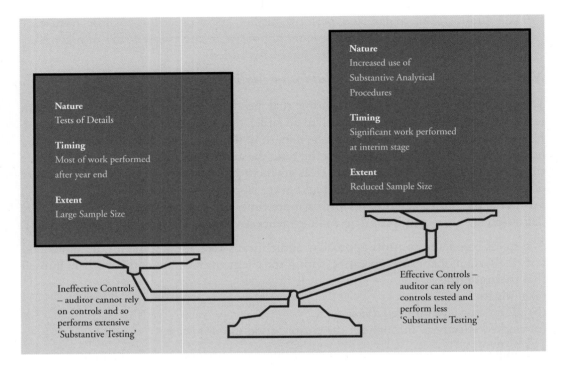

A **direct control activity** would include, for example, the inability of an employee to approve a purchase order in the system for which he is not authorised (this control activity covers the rights and obligations assertion). This control activity, however, cannot be effective without the existence of the organisational controls noted above (and therefore multiple control activities are required to cover one assertion).

Additionally, because control activities are parts of a system of controls, control activities can be further supported by the control component of the information systems.

Understanding and Testing the Entity's Entire Internal Control System

Due to the fact that control activities are often supported by other control components (see **Example 8.1** above), it is essential that the auditor gains assurance over the entire control system. The control environment was discussed in detail in **Chapter 7**; however, below at **Example 8.2**, you can see how the auditor would conclude on the effectiveness of the client entity's control environment. This type of working paper is used to record the accounting systems in a way that is sufficient for the purposes of complying with the auditing standards and relevant legislation.

EXAMPLE 8.2: WORKING PAPER SUPPORTING THE CONCLUSIONS DRAWN
BY THE AUDITOR ON THE ENTITY'S CONTROL ENVIRONMENT

Dairy Fresh Limited 31 December 2012 Control Environment – Audit Programme		Working Paper Reference		
Objective		To ascertain if the control environment is adequate to support the other control components.		
		Initials	Date	Date
	Prepared by:			
	Reviewed by:			

Working Paper Reference: P1

INTERNAL CONTROL ENVIRONMENT

The following aspects of the entity's operations provide an overview of its internal control environment:

List main factors of client's control environment, for example:
- Management are experienced and have been with the entity for an average of 10 years and hold qualifications respective to each of their disciplines (a copy of these qualifications can be found at working paper reference **P1A**).
- Finance Staff/Book-keeper has been with the entity seven years and a copy of his qualifications can be found at working paper reference **P1B**).
- The **organisational structure can be found at P1C**. It is not complex and management and directors are involved in the daily operations of the business.
- A chart of authority exists (see working paper reference **P1D**) and adequately addresses all types of transaction/activity and the related individual/s responsible for their approval.
- Human resources (HR) policies and procedures are in place and adequately address recruitment, retaining, training and discipline procedures. Full testing of same can be found at working paper reference **P1E**.

Management attitude to internal control is positive. Management demonstrate their attitude to internal controls by:
1. Ensuring adequate investment in information systems.
2. Imposing systematic controls (automated through the clients computer system) to ensure the adherence to the chart of authority. Tested at working paper reference **P1I**.
3. Ensuring multiple authorisations are required for transactions which are more susceptible to **misappropriation**/fraud (e.g. signatures of two officials for bank transfers).

4. Imposing of objectives on all employees related to their achievement of key business indicators (KBIs), which measure the application of internal controls (see copies of five employees' objectives at working paper reference **P1F**).
5. Actively communicate a **tone-at-the-top** document to all employees (see employee survey proving this at working paper reference **P1G**).
6. Follow through on disciplinary procedures with regard to non-adherence to internal control standards/instances of fraud (see review of such procedures applied to issues occurring in the period at **P1H**).

Conclusion: based on results of testing performed above as at 1 March 2013, we will rely on all of the controls above. Any control deficiencies have been discussed with management and any significant deficiencies have been communicated in writing to the directors.

You can see within each statement noted above that the auditor makes reference to where the documents are contained on his audit file that support his statement.

8.4 STAGES INVOLVED IN REVIEWING CONTROLS

Introduction

Up to this point we have discussed what an internal control system is and why it is so important to the client entity as well as to the auditor. Now we must consider how the auditor goes about using the client entity's system of internal control when carrying out his audit. There are a number of stages involved in reviewing a client entity's system of controls. We have already established that if the auditor tests the control system and finds it to be operating efficiently, that he can rely on this to reduce the level of substantive testing he needs to perform on the financial statements. However, testing the controls within a client entity may not always be the most efficient approach. The auditor will only test the controls if he believes that:

1. it will help to reduce substantive testing; and
2. the result of controls testing will show the controls to be effective.

It is important that the auditor follows a process to determine whether testing controls will make the overall audit more efficient. **Figure 8.3** below sets out the steps the auditor will take before commencing testing. Each step is discussed in detail below the figure.

Stage One: Identify Risks and Objectives within each Financial Cycle

Identifying Risks

As discussed in **Chapter 7**, the risks will have been identified during the planning stage and will be both specific to the client entity's current operating environment as well as some inherent risks, which are unavoidable.

FIGURE 8.3: STAGES INVOLVED IN SYSTEM-BASED (CONTROLS-APPROACH) AUDIT

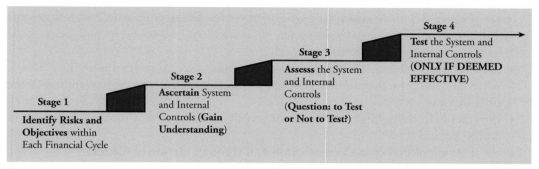

Identifying Financial Statement Assertions (Objectives)

When designing tests of controls, substantive analytical reviews and tests of details, the auditor must ensure that sufficient comfort has been obtained over **all** financial statement management assertions (audit objectives). It is therefore essential that the financial statement assertions or objectives are considered for **each transaction class and each account balance**.

> **Note**: it is important that you are familiar with the concept of financial statement assertions. A discussion on the assertions can be found in **Chapter 4**, Section 4.3.

Stage Two: Ascertain Internal Controls System

For each financial cycle, the auditor should identify the **principal business activities** and **key documents**. He should then determine the flow of documents and extent of controls relative to each risk and financial statement management assertion/audit objective by reviewing the client entity's policy and procedure documentation, as well as through discussions with management and the operational departments relative to the financial cycle being assessed.

Obtaining Information on Controls

The auditor can seek to gain an understanding of the client entity's systems of internal control in a number of ways:

- **Inquiry** – the auditor can inquire of management or the individuals who are responsible for operating the system.
- **Questionnaires** – in many cases, the audit firm will have developed a predetermined set of questions (usually in the form of knowledge-based systems) relative to each financial cycle, which, when answered, help the auditor to form an understanding of the process from beginning to end.

- **Flowcharts** – flowcharts are diagrammatic representations of the sequences of movements or actions in a particular transaction cycle. They depict certain aspects of processes. **Figure 8.5** in **Section 8.6**, later in this chapter, is an example of a flowchart within the purchases and payables cycle.

  Advantages to the auditor of using flowcharts:
  - they aid the understanding of the accounting and internal control system;
  - when drawn up by the auditor, they allow him to gain a better understanding of the organisation;
  - they can help to highlight strengths and weaknesses, as well as unnecessary steps, in a process; and
  - the drawing of flowcharts can be simplified through the use of **CAATs**.

  Disadvantages to the auditor of using flowcharts:
  - developing a flowchart can be time-consuming;
  - when dealing with more simple systems, narratives may be more appropriate;
  - preparing them requires experience; and
  - symbols can tend to mean different things to different people/organisations.

- **Narratives** – narratives are written documents that describe the connected events of a transaction in chronological order. **Example 8.4**, in **Section 8.5**, provides an example of a narrative within the revenue and receivables cycle.

  Advantages to auditors of narratives are that they:
  - are simple to prepare and do not require too much expertise; and
  - describe the process in detail.

  Disadvantages to auditors of narratives are that they:
  - do not highlight strengths and weaknesses as clearly as flowcharts do; and
  - can be lengthy to prepare and read.

Once the auditor has ascertained how the system of internal control is intended to operate, he should perform a **walkthrough** test (i.e. trace of one transaction of each type through the system), observing the operation of the controls as described in the client entity's policy and procedure documentation and described to him by management and staff. The purpose of the walkthrough is to determine if the systems observed by the auditor match those recorded in the client entity's policy and procedure documentation (i.e. staff members may tell the auditor what they should be doing rather than what they are actually doing).

EXAMPLE 8.3: A WALKTHROUGH

A **walkthrough** is a **test of a single transaction from beginning to end (cradle to grave) to prove or disprove the existence of the controls as documented by the client entity.**

The following is an example of a walkthrough that might be performed with respect to the receivables cycle.

Documented Control Activities Sales orders are entered into the computer system by a telesales clerk. Orders cannot be entered for customers where:

1. the order will result in the customer exceeding their credit limit;
2. the customer's account has been placed on hold; or
3. the goods are not in stock.

Pricing is predetermined in **master data** and cannot be amended by the telesales clerk. Orders are marked as dispatched only when the driver signs the Goods Dispatch Note (GDN). Orders are marked as invoiced only when the driver returns a signed Proof of Delivery (POD).

Performance of a Walkthrough The auditor would observe an order being taken by a telesales clerk, ensuring that no adjustments can be made to price (e.g. by requesting the telesales clerk to try to amend price, to see if it is possible). Record the name of the customer and order value. On completion of the observation, review the customer account to ensure that the order does not exceed the assigned customer credit limit and confirm with the credit controller that the customer account was not on hold. Trace the transaction through to dispatch and confirm that the date of the driver signature on the GDN matches the date it is marked as dispatched on the system. Trace the transaction through to invoicing, ensuring that the date the order was invoiced matches the date on the signed POD. Ensure all other details of all documents match.

The tracing of one transaction proves that the process operates as described. It does not, however, prove that it operates consistently in this manner throughout the entire period and this is why the auditor performs further 'tests of controls'.

Categories of Control Activities

Control activities can be categorised as follows:

TABLE 8.1: CATEGORIES OF CONTROL ACTIVITIES

Category of Control	Abbreviation
Organisational Control	OC
Segregation of Duties	SOD
Physical Control	PC
Reviews and Authorising	R&A
System Control	SC
Reconciliation	R

- **Organisational Controls** (OC) These encompass written policies and procedures, hiring and retaining of appropriately qualified personnel, and the existence of a **chart of authority**. A chart of authority outlines who in the organisation can approve which transactions and to what value. Similarly, an **organisational chart** indicates hierarchy within the organisation.

- **Segregation of Duties** (SOD) This control involves the separation of staff responsible for different tasks. For example, in the revenue cycle (see an example of a revenue cycle in **Example 8.4** below) the individuals responsible for taking orders should not be able to approve new customers or grant credit limits.
- **Physical Controls** (PC) These include safeguarding of items such as documentation and inventory, or imposing restricted access to physical locations and computer systems. This can be in the form of access cards for entry to different locations.
- **Reviews and Authorising** (R&A) This means double-checking of tasks performed and approval for transactions. For example, inventory picked in the warehouse based on an order should be checked prior to dispatch by someone independent of the picker, to ensure no errors have been made and that the order picked equals the order taken. Authorisation should be given for certain transactions, such as returned stock or bad debt write-offs.
- **System Controls** (SC) Such controls involve the configuration of systems to prevent invalid recordings. For example, during order entry, the system should prevent the order-entry clerk from taking an order that will result in a customer exceeding his credit limit or ordering items that are currently out of stock.
- **Reconciliations** (R) As a form of control, reconciliation involves the performance of reconciliations between two sources of data, e.g. reconciling of bank statement to bank balance per general ledger.

The most efficient way to get an overview of the controls in place in a client entity is to perform a walkthrough of the process as outlined above. The extent of documentation required will vary depending on the size, nature and complexity of the client entity and is a matter of professional judgement.

Stage Three: Assess the Internal Controls System

We have now reached stage three of a system-based (controls-approach) audit: the auditor's review of the client entity's controls. Having identified the risks and objectives relating to the cycle and obtained an understanding of how the controls relating to that cycle should operate, the auditor now needs to assess what he has learned so far in order to decide whether it is efficient to go ahead and test the controls.

The purpose of evaluating a system of internal control is to establish its reliability and formulate a basis for testing its effectiveness in practice. In completing stages one and two of a system-based (controls-approach) audit as outlined above, the auditor is now armed with knowledge of:
- related risks;
- related financial statement assertions; and
- documented internal control systems,

all of which will allow him to make an informed decision as to whether or not to test the related controls. **To test or not to test – this is the question the auditor must now answer.**

If tests conclude that the controls are effective, then the auditor need only carry out a reduced level of substantive procedures.

If tests conclude that the controls are ineffective, then more extensive substantive procedures are required.

While substantive testing must be performed regardless of the results of controls testing, a controls system which has been confirmed to be effective can reduce the level of substantive testing by reducing sample sizes or by the use of substantive analytical procedures rather than tests of detail, which can be more time-consuming. **Figure 8.4** below outlines the decision process of the auditor when deciding whether or not to test the internal controls and demonstrates that the decision is greatly influenced by the auditor's judgement of the situation.

It is essential that the auditor is confident that system tests will confirm that the controls are effective. If the auditor proceeds to the controls testing stage and the controls prove to be ineffective, the audit will be less efficient as the auditor will have wasted time testing the controls and then will still have to perform focused substantive testing anyway.

Stage Four: Test the Internal Controls System

Having reached the final stage of a system-based (controls-approach) audit, we are now going to test the controls, but only if the auditor has deemed the controls to be effective and decided that it is an efficient audit approach.

The audit objective is to select and perform tests designed to establish whether or not there is compliance with the system controls as documented by the client entity. The controls must be effective in practice and on paper.

Tests of controls are:
1. concerned only with those areas subject to effective controls;
2. concerned only with those controls mitigating risks and supporting management assertions/audit objectives (financial statement assertions);
3. a representative sample of transactions throughout the period; and
4. likely to cover a larger number of items than a walkthrough test.

In designing tests of controls, the auditor must ask himself:
• What tests of the operating effectiveness of controls (if any) will reduce the nature, timing and extent of substantive testing?
• What controls require testing because they cannot be tested substantively?

Typical tests of controls will involve:
• tracing samples;
• checking for authorisation;
• testing for sequential numbering;
• observing control activities taking place; and
• confirming performance of reconciliations.

FIGURE 8.4: WEIGHING UP THE DECISION TO TEST CONTROLS

8.5 CONTROLS AND THE REVENUE AND RECEIVABLES CYCLE

In **Section 8.4** we discussed the four stages involved in a system-based (controls-approach) audit. We will now apply this approach to each of the key financial cycles, starting with the revenue and receivables cycle.

Stage One: Identify Risks and Objectives within the Revenue and Receivables Cycle

Risks

The identification of risks is dealt with in detail in **Chapter 7**. However, listed below are risks that the auditor might consider with respect to revenue and receivables:

- **Previous experience with the client**   For example, where a significant risk existed in the past in relation to the recoverability of aged receivables balances (an example of an aged receivables listing can be found in **Chapter 13,** Example 13.1), the auditor will be alert to this in the current audit and may choose to perform focused substantive testing for this area.
- **Reliability of estimates**   Made by the client in the past, e.g. where the basis of the bad debt provision determined by the client in the past was deemed unreliable, resulting in adjustments by the auditor being necessary to fairly state the provision. The auditor will be alert for this in the current audit when performing tests in this area and again may perform focused substantive testing in this area.
- **Complexity of business**   For example, where recognition of a sale occurs only after a number of key stages have been completed or actions taken, then the auditor will remain alert to the possibility that revenue may have been recognised in the period which is not true revenue, i.e. revenue has been accounted for in the period but all the necessary stages resulting in revenue recognition have not been completed before the period end. In such an instance, the auditor may feel gaining a better understanding of how this is managed and testing its related controls will help to reduce substantive testing later.
- **Scope for fraud-related activity**   In relation to revenue and receivables, this could include:
  - creation of false customer accounts, resulting in overstated revenue figures and receivables balances; or
  - misappropriation of cash receipts where the business is cash-based.

Control Objectives

As introduced in **Chapter 4** and discussed continually throughout this textbook, each transaction class and balance tested by the auditor must address all the audit assertions (audit objectives). Before commencing, let us take a look at the specific audit objectives relevant for the revenue and receivables cycle.

TABLE 8.2: CONTROL OBJECTIVES WITHIN THE REVENUE AND RECEIVABLES CYCLE

Management Assertion/ Audit Objective	Control Objective for Transaction Class	Control Objective for Account Balance
	Revenue	**Receivables**
Existence or occurrence	• Recorded revenue transactions represent goods shipped. • Recorded cash receipts transactions represent cash received. • Recorded revenue adjustment transactions represent authorised discounts, returns, allowances and bad debts.	• Receivables balances represent amounts owed by customers at the balance sheet date.
Completeness	All revenue, cash receipts and revenue adjustment transactions that occurred have been recorded.	Receivables include all claims on customers at the balance sheet date.
Rights and obligations	The entity has rights to the receivables balance and cash resulting from recorded revenue transactions.	Receivables at the balance sheet date represent legal claims of the entity on customers for payment.
Accuracy, Classification and Valuation	All revenue, cash receipts and revenue adjustment transactions are correctly journalised, summarised and posted to the correct accounts.	• Receivables represent gross claims on customers at the balance sheet date and agree with the sum of the aged receivables ledger (refer to **Chapter 13**, Example 13.1 for an example of an aged receivables listing). • The provision for bad debts represents a reasonable estimate of the difference between gross receivables and their net realisable value (NRV).
Cut-off	All revenue, cash receipts and revenue adjustment transactions are recorded in the correct accounting period.	

Presentation and disclosure	The details of revenue, cash receipts and revenue adjustment transactions support their presentation in financial statements, including their classification and related disclosures.	• Receivables are properly identified and classified in the balance sheet. • Appropriate disclosures have been made concerning debts that have been factored or otherwise assigned.

Stage Two: Ascertain Internal Controls System for Revenue and Receivables

In **Section 8.4** we determined that at stage two of a system-based (controls-approach) audit, for each financial cycle, the auditor should identify the **principal business activities** and **key documents**. He should then determine the flow of documents and extent of controls relative to each risk and financial statement objective by reviewing the client policy and procedure documentation, as well as through discussions with management and the operational departments relative to the financial cycle being assessed. We will now consider this in relation to the revenue and receivables cycle.

Each step within the revenue and receivables cycle should feature a number of key controls in order to ensure the objectives at **Table 8.2** above are achieved. These controls also act to minimise the possibility of material misstatement due to fraud and error.

The components of a client entity's revenue cycle should comprise a number of key steps. **Example 8.4** demonstrates the types of controls that exist in a typical revenue and receivables cycle. (***Note***: this example demonstrates the cycle within an automated environment.) The control activity category is noted by its abbreviation beside each control. A summary of control activities categories, and their abbreviations, can be found above in **Table 8.1**.

EXAMPLE 8.4: NARRATIVE OF REVENUE AND RECEIVABLES CYCLE
(IN AN AUTOMATED ENVIRONMENT)

COMPANY PROFILE AND REVENUE POLICIES

Company: Dairy Fresh Ltd
Products: Dairy
Industry: Fast Moving Consumer Goods (FMCG)
Customer Profile: 70% Large wholesale and supermarket players, 20% Convenience (smaller convenience stores), 10% restaurants
Revenue Recognition: Revenue is recognised on delivery (within the industry the signed POD is largely recognised as proof of delivery).
Computer Environment: The company has an enterprise resource planning (ERP) system that is fully integrated, with the exception of the payroll package.
Customer Credit Terms: 30 days from last day of the month in which invoice was issued.

Ordering and Granting of Credit All customers order directly online using a user name and password (**System Control**) assigned to them on approval of their credit application form.

All new customers must complete a credit application form and sign:
1. the company's terms and conditions (T&Cs), and
2. a direct debit (DD) mandate.

The sales representative enters the details from the credit application form onto the company's internal system for review by the credit controller (**segregation of duties**). The form will not save for the revenue representative unless all fields are completed (**system control**). The credit controller reviews the application form, which must include two references. The credit controller contacts both references and reviews the prospective customer on credit check, i.e. to assess their creditworthiness and identify an appropriate credit limit (**review and authorisation**). When satisfied that the prospective customer is:
1. creditworthy,
2. has signed the T&Cs, and
3. has signed the DD mandate,

the credit controller approves the customer, assigning a credit limit (**review and authorisation**). The account is only activated after a credit limit has been assigned (**system control**). Only the credit controller has the ability to enter a credit limit (**segregation of duties and system control**). The system automatically generates a customer number, username and password, which are e-mailed directly to the customer, notifying them of their assigned credit limit. The customer is now free to place orders online.

Each customer is automatically assigned to the approved price list, which is signed off by the head of revenue and finance. The revenue teams are notified of all new customers being set up and can propose discounts from the agreed price list based on the proposed volume that the customer will generate. This proposal is completed via the ERP system and must be approved electronically by the head of finance before it becomes active on the customer account (**segregation of duties**)/(**review and authorisation**).

When the customer enters an online order, the system first checks:
1. that the customer is not entering an order that will result in them exceeding their credit limit (if so, the order is referred to a credit controller for approval) (**system control**);
2. that the customer is not on hold (*customers whose accounts are overdue are automatically placed on hold by the system* (**system control**)); and
3. that the goods are in stock. The order is automatically valued based on the price list assigned to that customer (**system control**).

The order is automatically assigned a sequential order number (**system control**). In the system the order is assigned a status of '**awaiting dispatch**'.

Dispatch and Invoicing All orders processed become visible to the warehouse the following morning. The warehouse 'picker' prints a manual copy of a goods dispatch note (GDN) from the system in duplicate form. The picker picks each order according to the printed sheets and stages them ready for collection by the driver, attaching the duplicate GDN signed by him.

The driver, on arrival, physically counts the goods to be delivered and compares the results to the GDN. Once satisfied that the two agree, he signs the duplicate GDN (**physical control**). The driver only has access to the staging area and not to the warehouse (**physical control**). He returns one copy to the office and takes one with him (**segregation of duties**)/(**physical control**)/(**reviews and authorisation**). On receipt of the GDN signed by the driver, the 'settlement clerk' marks the order as '**dispatched**' in the system. The system generates and prints a proof of delivery note (POD) in duplicate for the driver. *The stock now shows as in transit rather than in warehouse.*

On delivery of the goods the driver has the customer count the goods delivered and sign a copy of the POD as proof of delivery and acceptance of the goods in good condition. Any discrepancies with respect to volume/condition are marked on the POD and signed in duplicate by the driver and the customer. The driver returns to the office and gives a copy of the signed POD to the settlement clerk. The settlement clerk inspects the documentation (**reviews and authorisation**)/(**physical control**) and marks the order as delivered in the system (**segregation of duties**). The system now assigns a status of '**delivered not yet invoiced**' to the order. Each evening, before finishing, the settlement clerk runs a system activity (automated client computer system control) that bills all orders with a status of *delivered not yet invoiced*. This action causes the invoices to be generated (which are automatically e-mailed by the system to the customer) and creates the necessary entries in the books of first entry: DR Cost of Sales, CR Inventory; and DR Customer, CR Revenue. The order now has a status of '**complete**'.

Accounting In order to ensure that revenue is complete, the accounting department runs three exception reports (reports from the client entity's computer system highlighting unusual transactions):

1. Orders with a status of '**awaiting dispatch**' for more than 24 hours. This report is sent to the warehouse to investigate why/if orders have not been dispatched. This helps to highlight issues where goods were dispatched but not marked in the system as such.
2. Orders with a status of '**dispatched**' for more than 24 hours. This report is sent to the settlement department to investigate why/if a POD has not yet been returned by the driver. This helps to highlight issues where a POD was returned but not marked in the system as such and ensures timely follow-up of the driver.
3. Orders with a status of '**delivered not yet invoiced**' for more than 24 hours. This report is sent to the settlement department to investigate why/if the system activity was run to trigger invoicing.

These exception reports are signed off as reviewed by the financial controller and filed.

Most customers pay by DD. The accounts receivable team run a program in the computer system on the last working day of each month which highlights the amounts due from customers (based on pre-defined credit terms). The instruction for direct debits is approved by the credit controller prior to sending it to the bank (**segregation of duties**).

A few customers pay by cheque and for those: all post is opened by two individuals, a summary is made of all cheques received and signed by both individuals (**physical control**). The cheques are sent directly to the cash office (persons charged with lodging receipts who are independent from the accounts receivable department to avoid teeming and lading (a process of stealing a customer's cheque and delaying the posting of the receipt onto their GL account until a cheque comes in from another customer, which is used to post to the account of the customer from whom the cheque was stolen and so on) (**segregation of duties**). The summary of cheques along with remittance advices are sent to the accounts receivable department, which allocates the cheques to the related transactions as outlined in the remittance advice. The accounting department reconciles the bank daily, ensuring that the amount banked equals the amount posted to customer accounts (**reconciliation**)/(**segregation of duties**).

As part of the accounting end-of-period procedures, the following reconciliations are performed by the accounts assistant and reviewed and signed off by the financial controller (**reviews and authorisation**)/(**segregation of duties**):
• reconciliation of the aged list of receivables to the general (nominal) ledger; and
• bank reconciliation.

On notification from the accounting department that all activities have been processed for month end, the accounts receivable department a program in the client entity's computer system that automatically e-mails customer statements to all customers (**system control**). The system generates a report highlighting any exceptions/errors that occurred during the activity, which is signed off by a member of the accounting department (**system control**)/(**review and authorisation**).

All credit note requests are entered into the system by the credit claims department. Once entered they must be approved as follows:
• if price related – systematic (automated computer-approval process) approval by the sales and accounting departments (**segregation of duties**)/(**review and authorisation**); or
• if quality/quantity related – systematic approval by settlement department following physical inspection of POD (**physical control**)/(**segregation of duties**) (**review and authorisation**).

Every month the credit controller reviews the aged receivables listing and follows up on accounts that are overdue. The financial controller follows up on overdue accounts with the credit controller, signs off and files the review (**physical control**). Bad debts are proposed by the credit controller through the system, but only come off the customer account after systematic (automated computer) approval by the accounting and sales departments (**system control**)/(**segregation of duties**).

Stage Three: Assess the Internal Controls System for Revenue and Receivables

We have now reached stage three in the system-based (controls-approach) audit of revenue and receivables. Having identified the risks and objectives relating to the audit of the revenue and receivables cycle and obtained an understanding of how the controls should operate relating to that cycle, the auditor now needs to assess what he has learned so far in order to decide whether it is efficient to go ahead and test the controls.

Where the revenue figure and receivables balance are not material to the financial statements, limited testing of controls and substantive testing will be performed; however, revenue and receivables are normally material figures in the financial statements for most companies.

Where a significant audit risk has been identified in relation to the revenue and receivables cycle, the level of substantive testing to be performed will need to be increased and the testing of controls may become more important to help reduce the level of substantive testing. **Example 8.5** below demonstrates the type of working paper the auditor might use to assess the risks within the revenue and receivables cycle.

A key consideration when deciding whether or not to test controls will be the risk assessment made by the auditor on the client **and** the initial assessment of the control environment.

EXAMPLE 8.5: AUDIT WORKING PAPER EXTRACT:
RISK ASSESSMENT FOR REVENUE AND RECEIVABLES CYCLE

Dairy Fresh Limited 31 December 2012 Revenue and Receivables Risk Assessment		Working Paper Reference		R1
Objective		To summarise the risk assessment for the revenue and receivables cycle.		
		Initials	Date	Date
	Prepared by:			
	Reviewed by:			

Risk Assessment: Below is a list of the risks identified relating to revenue and receivables and the planned approach to address these risks.

Risk Identified	Level of Risk	Controls Testing	Response to Risk	Ref
Example Risks:	*H/M/L*	*Yes/No*		
Receivables may not be recoverable. Planning analytical review indicates that receivables have increased significantly.	High	No	We will review management's provision for bad debts. We will challenge the assumptions made and consider the outturn of last year's provision. We will ensure that we have sufficient provision for specific large receivables including Z Limited and Y Limited.	R11

| All **revenue** may not be recorded | Med | Yes | We will take a controls approach in relation to the completeness assertion by ensuring regular reviews are carried out by the organisation on goods ordered not yet delivered and goods delivered not yet invoiced. If these reports are reviewed regularly we will be able to rely on controls relating to the completeness assertion and therefore perform a reduced level of substantive testing. | R10 |

Stage Four: Test the Internal Controls System for Revenue and Receivables

Having reached the final stage of the system-based (controls-approach) audit of revenue and receivables, we are now going to test the internal controls relating to revenue and receivables (but only if the auditor has deemed the controls to be effective and decided that it is an efficient audit approach).

The audit objective is to select and perform tests designed to establish compliance with the system controls as documented by the client entity.

Once an understanding is obtained in relation to the revenue and receivables cycle, a testing plan can be designed based on the key controls that are in operation.

Note: the auditor will only proceed with testing the controls if he believes that the controls are strong and if walkthrough tests show that the client entity's procedures, as documented by its management, are operating exactly as documented. When designing such tests it is essential that the auditor remembers the assertions that must be addressed by the controls tests. He should further keep in mind that the objective of tests of controls is to obtain sufficient appropriate audit evidence that the control operated effectively throughout the entire period under review (thus, his samples should cover the entire period).

Specific tests connected to the revenue and receivables cycle are provided in **Example 8.6** below.

EXAMPLE 8.6: WORKING PAPER: REVENUE AND
RECEIVABLES CONTROLS AUDIT PROGRAMME

Dairy Fresh Limited 31 December 2012		Working Paper Reference		D1
Revenue and Receivables Controls Audit Programme				
Objective		**To ascertain if the Revenue and Receivables Cycle is adequately controlled by the entity with respect to all assertions.**		
		Initials	**Date**	**Date**
	Prepared by:			
	Reviewed by:			
	Audit Programme	**Assertion**	**Test**	**Ref to Test**

Ensure the audit plan is reflected in the following tests. The following steps are suggestions only and should be removed or added to as necessary to address the risks of material misstatement identified at the risk assessment stage.

Organisational and IT Controls

1	Lack of policies and procedures surrounding revenue and receivables area that may result in inconsistent application of policies and lack of adherence to desired procedures.	Valuation/ Occurrence/ Completeness/ Rights and Obligations/ Cut-off	Assess the appropriateness of the accounting policy and procedure documentation and the accounting estimates method for revenue and receivables. Ensure that the accounting policy is in accordance with accounting standards and applicable law.	
2	Inappropriate access may result in a lack of segregation of duties (SOD).	Valuation/ Occurrence/ Completeness/ Rights and Obligations	Obtain a report from the system outlining who in the organisation has access to which step in the revenue and receivables function. Review the report to ensure that no SOD issues exist (e.g. that no one has access to order entry and credit control).	

Ordering and Granting of Credit				
1	Customers with poor credit ratings may get deliveries of inventory, increasing risk of bad debts.	Valuation	Inspect a sample of customers set up in the period and confirm they were approved by the credit controller, a credit check was performed and a credit limit assigned and authorised.	
		Valuation	Run a report from the system and ensure no customers exist without a credit limit.	
2	Customers exceeding their credit limits or with overdue amounts may get deliveries of stock increasing the risk of bad debts.	Valuation	*** System check (test of one)** Attempt to enter in an order that will result in the customer exceeding their credit limit. Ensure the system does not permit you to enter the order.	
		Valuation	*** System check (test of one)** Attempt to enter an order for a blocked customer. Ensure the system does not permit you to enter the order.	
		Valuation	In Excel format obtain: (1.) a sample of aged receivables listing for a random number of months, and (2.) a copy of each customer's credit limit. Using Vlookup, compare the customer balances to the credit limits. For customers exceeding credit limit, ensure that they were approved by the credit controller.	
3	Invalid prices are entered at order entry stage.	Accuracy	Observe the order entry clerk entering an order and ensure they cannot amend pricing.	

Dispatch and Invoicing				
1	Not all goods delivered are invoiced.	Completeness	Randomly select 30 working days and obtain the signed review of the three **exception reports:** (1.) Orders awaiting dispatch >24hrs; (2.) Orders Dispatched >24 hrs; (3.) Orders Delivered not yet invoiced >24hrs. Inspect the document for evidence of review.	
			** Trace a sample of 100 customer orders to GDN, signed POD and invoice.	
2	Invoices are raised for goods not delivered or the invoice does not match the goods delivered.	Occurrence (Existence)/ Accuracy/Rights and Obligations	*** Trace a sample of invoices to customer-signed PODs and sales orders. Ensure Goods dispatch note (GDN) is signed by a driver. Match the details from the invoice to the signed customer POD/ GDN and sales order.	
3	Prices are incorrectly applied to the invoice or discounts may not be approved.	Occurrence/ Accuracy	* **System check (test of one)** Using test data, attempt to change the customer invoice price and ensure the system does not permit you to make the change. With assistance from IT department, inspect who has access to pricing master data (ensure no SOD issues).	
			** Select a sample of 100 invoices and compare the prices charged to the approved customer price list at that time.	

Accounting				
1	Credit notes are issued for invalid reasons.	Occurrence/ Accuracy	Trace a sample of credit notes to ensure they were approved. For 'quantity' credit notes, trace the credit note back to the signed POD to ensure quantity marked on the POD.	
2	Invoices may be recorded in the incorrect period.	Completeness	Obtain a copy of the review of the three **exception reports** at 31 Dec 2012. Inspect the document for evidence of review.	
		Cut-off	Select the last 30 invoices posted to the **general ledger** and trace them to signed PODs, ensuring that the date on the POD matches the invoice and posting date in the system.	
3	Customer balances may be written off without proper authorisation.	Occurrence/ Accuracy/Rights and Obligations	*** System check (test of one)** Observe the credit controller entering in a bad debt proposal. Ensure it is not activated onto the customer account until approved by the sales and finance functions.	
			** Select a sample of 50 bad debts written off in the period and trace to approval by the finance and sales functions.	
4	Trade receivables may be old and go uncollected.	Valuation	Obtain a copy of the review of the aged receivables listing balance for five random months. Ensure there is evidence of review.	

| 5 | Not all remittances are entered onto the customer's account. | Valuation | Select 100 random days and obtain a copy of the dual signed cheque receipts listing. Trace the amounts to the customers' accounts. Obtain a copy of the reconciliation of the bank statement for five random months to ensure that the amount lodged to the bank matched the amount entered onto customer accounts. | |

** Indicates an alternative testing method. Although those tests requiring lower sample sizes (because they cover a greater volume) or that are a system test of one are considered more efficient and effective.

* System check (test of one) – when a system test is carried out to determine the existence of a control, generally the auditor will only need to perform the test once, as once set up correctly the system should behave in the same way every time. The auditor need then only test for changes in configuration.

*** Note the change in the direction of this test (**general ledger** to **source** for completeness and **source** to **general ledger** for occurrence (existence)).

Conclusion

Subject to the matters noted for the reviewer, in my opinion the revenue and receivables are adequately controlled with respect to all assertions

Name:		**Accountant in Charge**
Date:		
Name:		**Reviewer**
Date:		

8.6 CONTROLS AND THE PURCHASES AND PAYABLES AND PAYROLL CYCLES

In **Section 8.4** we discussed the four stages of a system-based (controls-approach) audit. We have completed the four stages for revenue and receivables and will now discuss the four stages with reference to purchases and payables and payroll.

Stage One: Identify Risks and Objectives for Purchases and Payables and Payroll

As introduced in **Chapter 4**, and discussed continually throughout this textbook, each transaction class and balance tested by the auditor must address all the management assertions (audit objectives). First, let us take a look at the specific audit objectives relevant for the purchases and payables cycle and the payroll cycle.

Stage Two: Ascertain Internal Controls System (within Purchases and Payables)

In **Section 8.4** we determined that at stage two of a system-based (controls-approach) audit, for each financial cycle, the auditor should identify the **principal business activities** and **key documents**. He should then determine the flow of documents and the extent of controls relative to each audit risk and management assertion/financial statement assertion/audit objective by reviewing the client entity's policy and procedure documentation, as well as through discussions with management and the operational departments relative to the financial cycle being assessed. We will now consider this relevant to purchases and payables, and then the payroll cycle will be discussed.

When we looked at the four stages involved in a system-based (controls-approach) audit of revenue and receivables in **Section 8.5**, Example 8.4, we looked at an example of a narrative-description of the process. Below, at **Figure 8.5**, we obtain an understanding of the purchases and payables system using a flowchart.

There is a wide variety of control procedures that may be implemented by a business to mitigate risks of misstatement occurring in the financial statements. These can vary significantly, depending on specific circumstances unique to each business. However, there are a number of key control procedures that are common to the majority of businesses. The auditor will generally test the design, implementation and the operating effectiveness of these controls in order to reduce the level of substantive testing he must perform over purchases and trade payables/accruals.

In summary, the key controls over the purchases and payables cycle are:
- Segregation of Duties;
- Authorisation of Purchase Orders;
- Chart of Authority;
- Matching;
- Authorisation of Supplier Payments;
- Review of Supplier Statement Reconciliations; and
- Review of Exception Reports.

We will now discuss these in more detail below.

TABLE 8.3: CONTROL OBJECTIVES PURCHASES AND PAYABLES (INCLUDING PAYROLL)

Management Assertion/ Audit Objective	Control Objective for Transaction Class	Control Objective for Account Balance
	Purchases and Payroll Expenses	**Payables and Payroll Accruals**
Existence or Occurrence	• Recorded purchases transactions represent goods and services received. • Recorded payment transactions represent payments made to suppliers and payables. • Recorded payroll expenses relate to employee services received.	Recorded trade payables represent amounts owed by the entity at the balance sheet date. Accrued payroll liability balances represent amounts owed at the balance sheet date.
Completeness	• All purchases-payments transactions that occurred have been recorded. • Payroll expenses include all such expenses incurred.	• Trade payables include all amounts owed by the entity to suppliers of goods and services at the balance sheet date. • Accrued payroll liabilities include all amounts in respect of payroll and payroll deductions at the balance sheet date.
Rights and Obligations	Recorded purchases and payroll transactions represent the liabilities of the entity.	Trade payables and accrued payroll liabilities are liabilities of the entity at the balance sheet date.
Accuracy, Classification and Valuation	Purchases transactions, payments transactions and payroll transactions are correctly recorded in the accounting systems.	• Trade payables and accrued payroll liabilities are stated at the correct amount owed. • Related expense balances conform with applicable accounting standards.
Cut-off	All purchases, payments and payroll transactions are recorded in the correct accounting period.	
Presentation and Disclosure	The details of purchases, payments and payroll transactions support their presentation in the financial statements, including their classification and disclosure.	• Trade payables, accrued payroll liabilities and related expenses are properly identified and classified in the financial statements. • Disclosures pertaining to commitments, contingent liabilities and related party payables are adequate.

Segregation of Duties

In order to reduce the risk of fraudulent or erroneous purchases, it is common for an enforced **segregation of duties** to be built into the purchasing procedures whereby different members of staff are responsible for:
- raising purchase orders and accepting goods from suppliers;
- receiving goods from suppliers and recording purchase invoices on the purchase ledger; and
- raising purchase orders and processing payment.

We can see from **Figure 8.5** that none of these tasks is carried out by the same person (department). Generally, the ability to perform tasks is restricted in the system (i.e. an individual's access rights are determined centrally, restricting individuals to transactions which relate to their assigned function in the organisation), which allows the auditor to more easily test the control by testing the configuration of the system.

Authorisation of Purchase Orders

In order to mitigate the risk of unnecessary or fraudulent purchases, it is common for only a small number of experienced staff to have the authority to raise purchase orders (POs). (In **Figure 8.5** we can see that there is a purchasing department, which is separate from the requester, the approver and the accounts payable (AP) department.)

Chart of Authority

The value of purchases which a staff member can authorise often varies depending on their seniority and level of experience. This is outlined in a document called the 'chart of authority' (COA).

Matching

Where the process is automated, the PO is entered and approved within the system, the goods received note (GRN) is matched in the system to the PO and, finally, the invoice details are matched to the PO price and the GRN quantity. Where differences arise, the system will reject further processing outside a pre-determined threshold.

Authorisation of Supplier Payments

In order to mitigate the risk of fraudulent or erroneous payments being made to suppliers, it is common for only a small number of senior staff to be authorised to make supplier payments (i.e. in a computerised environment, through two separate automated approvals). In addition, prior to approving a payment the approver should sign off on back-up documentation supporting the payment (usually a supplier statement reconciliation).

Review of Supplier Statement Reconciliations

Where the client entity receives regular statements from its suppliers, it is common for these statements to be reconciled to the balance per the trade payables ledger and for any differences to be investigated.

Review of Exception Reports

In order to ensure that expenses occurred, are complete, accurate and pertain to the client entity, it is important for the client entity to regularly review two exception reports. First, the aged open PO report may highlight issues where goods were received but no GRN was raised in the system, meaning no accrual/expense was generated (completeness). Secondly, review of the aged 'goods received invoices not received' (GRIR) may highlight where goods were accrued in error as being received: these can be matched to supplier statements to see if: (a) the invoice got mislaid or was never received (accuracy); or (b) the goods were never received (occurrence).

Key Documents within the Purchases and Payables Cycle

The following are the key documents the auditor would expect to find in a typical purchases and payables cycle:
- purchase requisition;
- purchase order (PO);
- goods receipt note (GRN);
- purchase invoices;
- debit notes;
- aged payables listing; and
- payment summary/payment proposal.

The following provides a description for the symbols used in the flowchart overleaf.

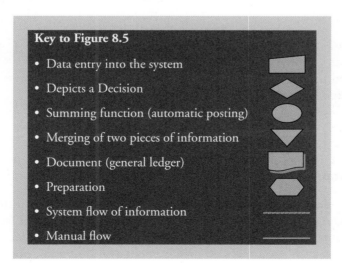

Key to Figure 8.5

- Data entry into the system
- Depicts a Decision
- Summing function (automatic posting)
- Merging of two pieces of information
- Document (general ledger)
- Preparation
- System flow of information
- Manual flow

FIGURE 8.5: FLOWCHART OF PURCHASES AND PAYABLES CYCLE (IN AN AUTOMATED ENVIRONMENT)

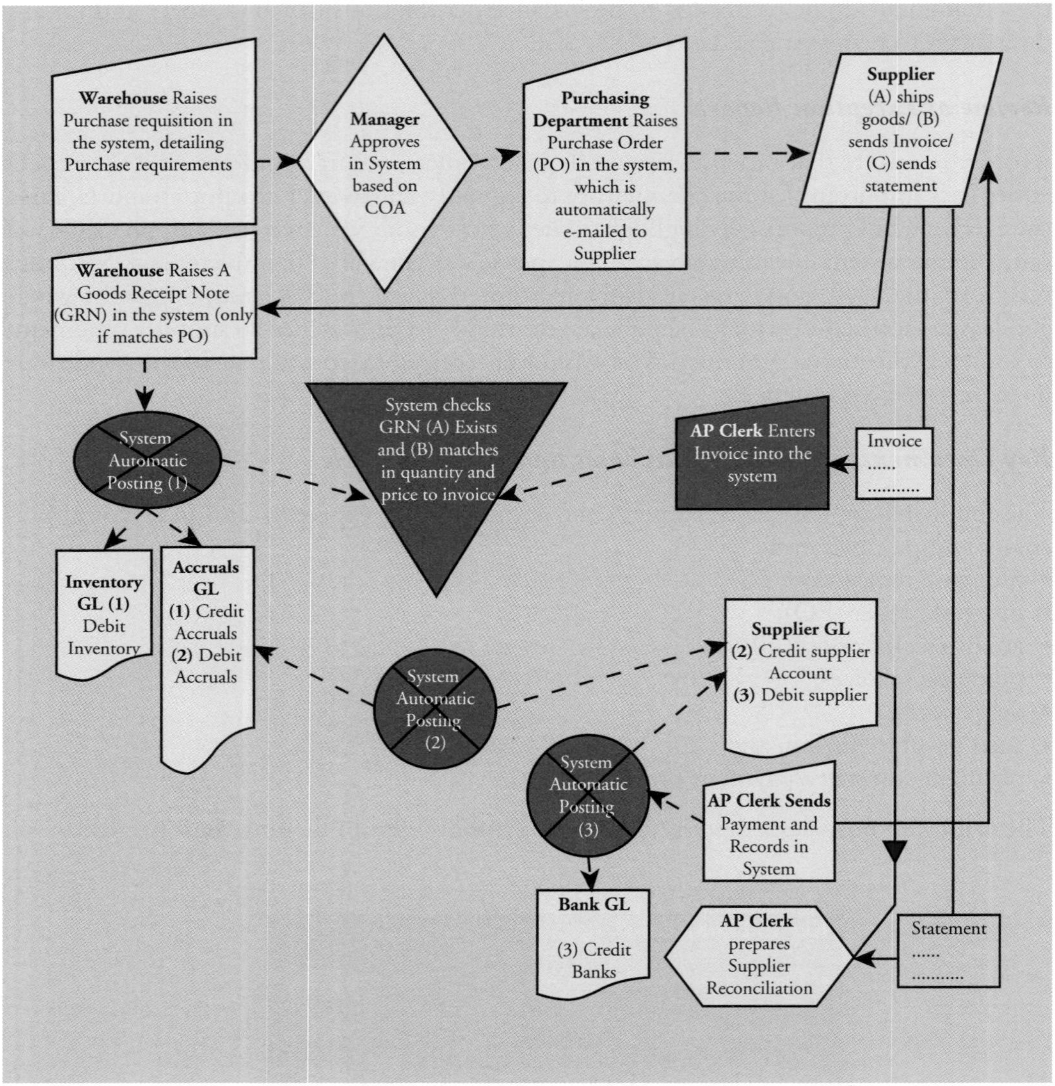

Stage Two: Ascertain Internal Controls System (within Payroll)

In **Section 8.4** we determined that at stage two in a system-based (controls-approach) audit, for each financial cycle, the auditor should identify the **principal business activities** and key documents. He should then determine the flow of documents and extent of controls relative to each audit risk and management assertion/audit objective/financial statement objective by reviewing the client entity's policy and procedure documentation, as well as through discussions with management and the operational departments relative to the financial cycle being assessed. We will now consider this relevant to payroll.

Below are the controls found over a typical payroll cycle within a computerised environment. The headings denote the principal business activities, which are then followed by the specific types of control activities the auditor would expect to find in a typical payroll cycle.

Hiring Employees

An 'employee authorisation' form should be completed for all new employees (signed by human resources (HR) and the hiring manager). This form includes employee **master data**, such as name, title, contracted hours, starting salary (rate per hour), Personal Public Service Number (PPS), (social security) number, start date, etc.

The HR department is responsible for entering the master data of an employee. No other department should have access to add new employees or edit employee master data.

Weekly/monthly (prior to processing of payroll) a person independent of the individual who inputs the master data should run an edit report from the system (showing all changes made to employee master data) and compare it to the employees' authorisation forms.

Key control: segregation of duties between the HR department and the payroll function with respect to employee master data and independent review of data entry.

Recording Hours Worked

Most large companies record hours worked using a clock-in system. A clock-in system allows the employee to record start and finish times. This information is stored and interfaced with the payroll program.

Salaried employees receive the same amount every month and as such salaried employees usually do not clock-in (a clock-in system for salaried staff can, however, be helpful to record days worked, sick days, holidays, etc. to maintain control).

Key control: the computerised transfer from the clock-in system provides a strong control of the occurrence assertion (i.e. the event took place, the employee worked the hours).

Recording Other Payroll Variables

Other payroll variables can include commission, bonuses, holidays, sick days, etc. and should be requested directly from the payroll clerk's manager. The payroll clerk should never enter any variables onto the system without authorisation forms being completed.

Key control: exception reports noted later (under accounting) allow the manager to validate the information entered by the payroll clerk, giving assurance over occurrence, accuracy and rights and obligations.

Calculating Payroll

The payroll department is responsible for calculating the payroll once all information regarding each employee has been collected. The following common controls exist relating to the required calculation.

- Most companies have a payroll package that calculates their payroll. Employee master data is input directly from the employee master data database (to which only HR has access) (SOD).
- Hours worked is input directly from the clock-in system.
- Payroll variables are entered directly by the payroll clerk.

This is demonstrated in **Figure 8.6** below.

Key control: automating the segregation of duties (SOD) protects the integrity of the master data and hence reduces the possibility of misstatements occurring.

Payroll Reports

Once the payroll calculations have been posted, a number of reports may be generated, all of which should be reviewed by appropriate personnel:

- **Gross to net reports** (which show the gross amount owed to employees and all deductions necessary to determine the figure paid to the employee). These should be reviewed and signed off by HR.
- **Exception reports** These can include number of bonus hours paid, number of holidays, number of sick days, value of bonuses paid, number of overtime hours paid, wages exceeding a certain value, employees with no clock-in hours (may indicate **terminated employee** that has not been terminated in the system, etc.). These should be reviewed and signed off by HR.
- **Departmental summary reports** These should be signed off by department heads (managers) to ensure that they are happy with the total number of employees and hours charged to their department, including overtime hours, bonus, etc. This ensures that only details they authorised the payroll clerk to input have been included.
- **Payroll control summary total** These are used by the finance department to reconcile amounts paid out of the bank and the journal entries posted to the accounting system.

Accounting

The finance department need to satisfy themselves that payroll related postings are correct. The following common controls exist relating to the accounting (finance) department review of payroll postings.

- Most payroll packages interface directly with the client entity's accounting package and so post the payroll transactions automatically.
- These postings should be reviewed by a member of the finance department and reconciled with the payroll control summary total report (a report that summarises all related payroll totals for accounting).
- The finance department should also reconcile the net payment according to the payroll control summary total report to the amount paid out of the bank account.

Key control: the review and sign-off of exception reports, summary reports and reconciliations are all essential controls and give assurance over occurrence, completeness, recording and rights and obligations.

Terminating Employees

- Managers should notify the HR department and the payroll function when an employee leaves the organisation.
- HR should be the only department that has access to the system to terminate an employee and should do so in a timely fashion to avoid the payment of employees after they cease to be employed by the organisation.
- The payroll function should ensure that the employee is no longer active on the payroll system.

FIGURE 8.6: SEGREGATION OF DUTIES WITHIN THE PAYROLL CYCLE

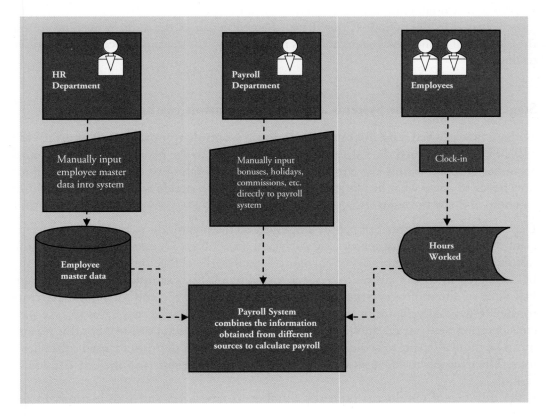

Stage Three: Assess the Systems and Internal Controls (within Purchases and Payables)

We have now reached stage three of a system-based (controls-approach) audit of the purchases and payables cycle. Having identified the risks and objectives relating to the purchases and payables cycle and obtained an understanding of how the controls relating to that cycle should operate, the auditor now needs to assess what he has learned so far in order to decide whether it is efficient to go ahead and test the controls.

The value for purchases and payables is usually material for most companies and, in addition, transactions are normally high in volume. For this reason it is normally more efficient for the auditor to test controls around the purchasing and payables cycle to assist in reducing substantive testing. Some of the factors that affect sample sizes are the values of the balances and the inherent and control risk assessment. With the values generally being material and there being inherent risks connected to purchases and payables, the sample sizes for substantive testing may be substantial and the substantive testing extremely time-consuming if controls are not tested as being efficient. However, if preliminary assessments of the purchases and payables cycle indicate that controls are not strong, or have not been effective throughout the entire period, a purely substantive approach may be the most efficient. In considering whether or not to test controls, the auditor will also take into account whether or not any changes to procedures or systems have occurred in the period. If they have, this will result in the auditor needing to test the old as well as the new system and this may not warrant the time saved on substantive testing.

Stage Three: Assess the Systems and Internal Controls (within Payroll)

We have now reached stage three in a system-based (controls-approach) audit of the payroll cycle. Having identified the risks and objectives relating to the payroll cycle and obtained an understanding of how the controls should operate relating to that cycle, the auditor now needs to assess what he has learned so far in order to decide whether it is efficient to go ahead and test the controls.

Depending on the number of people employed by the organisation, it may be more efficient to test payroll using substantive analytical procedures. Due to the fact that payroll normally has a limited number of changing variables, the charge for the year can usually be calculated to within a threshold of the actual figure (for example, by obtaining from HR a list of all employees' salaries and multiplying by 12, the auditor should get close to the annual salary figure in the financial statements, albeit he may need to take into consideration new starters and leavers in the period and time apportion). For this reason, it can be more efficient to avoid testing controls and instead perform focused substantive tests. The decision to move straight to focused substantive tests will include consideration of:
- the number of employees (and the number of new hires and terminations in the year);
- the number of changes in salary during the period, and whether changes were applied in one go across the organisation or ad hoc to some employees;
- the predictability of overtime; and
- the availability of information on headcount and changes from HR.

Stage Four: Test the Internal Controls System (within Purchases and Payables)

Having reached the final stage in a system-based (controls-approach) audit of the purchases and payables cycle, we are now going to test the internal controls relating to purchases and payables (if the auditor has deemed the controls to be effective and decided that it is an efficient audit approach).

The audit objective is to select and perform tests designed to establish compliance with the system controls as documented by the client entity.

The tests of controls will include testing of the operation of controls over a sample of transactions from the period and obtaining documentary evidence of the controls in operation. These can be seen in **Example 8.7** below.

EXAMPLE 8.7: WORKING PAPER: PURCHASES AND PAYABLES CONTROLS PROGRAMME

Dairy Fresh Limited 31 December 2012 Purchases and Payables Controls Audit Programme		Working Paper Reference		P1
Objective		To ascertain if the Purchases and Payables Cycle is adequately controlled by the entity with respect to all assertions.		
		Initials	Date	Date
	Prepared by:			
	Reviewed by:			
	Audit Programme			
		Assertion	Test	Ref to Test

The following steps are suggestions only and should be removed or added to as necessary to address the risks of material misstatement identified at the risk assessment stage.

Organisational and IT Controls

| 1 | Lack of policies and procedures surrounding purchases and payables functions that may result in inconsistent application of policies and lack of adherence to desired procedures. | Valuation/ Occurrence/ Completeness/ Rights and Obligations/ Cut-off | Assess the appropriateness of the accounting policy and procedure documentation and the accounting estimates method for purchases and payables. Ensure that the accounting policy is in accordance with accounting standards and applicable law. | |

2	Inappropriate system access may result in a lack of segregation of duties (SOD).	Valuation/ Occurrence/ Completeness/ Rights and Obligations	Obtain a report from the system outlining who in the organisation has access to which steps in the systems for purchasing and payable functions. Review the report to ensure that no SOD issues exist (e.g. those individuals with access to supplier master data do not have access to AP functionality).	
3	Purchases may be approved at an inappropriate level/ payments may be approved at an inappropriate level.	Valuation/ Occurrence/ Completeness/ Rights and Obligations	Obtain a copy of the company Chart of Authority and review to ensure authorisation levels are reasonable.	
Raising the PO				
1	Goods and services ordered are not properly authorised, increasing the risk of non-business purchases.	Rights and Obligations/ Occurrence	*****System check (test of one)** Observe the entry of a purchase requisition and ensure that a workflow approval is triggered (in accordance with the Chart of Authority (COA).	
			** Randomly select 200 POs raised and ensure they were approved in accordance with the COA.	
2	Unauthorised suppliers are used, increasing the risk of losing bulk discounts.	Rights and Obligations/ Occurrence	Obtain a report showing suppliers added to the system. Obtain tendering documents and approval of supplier set-up from the procurement department.	

			*** **System check (test of one)** Observe the PO entry process and ensure that the purchasing department cannot raise a PO with a supplier who is not contained within the approved supplier listing.	
			**¥ Select 200 supplier invoices posted to the system and ensure that: (1.) there is a related GRN and the quantity and price match (to within predefined tolerance); (2.) there is a related PO and the quantity and price match (to within predefined tolerance); (3.) there is a purchase requisition and the quantity and price match (to within predefined tolerance).	
Receiving the Goods				
1	Goods or services are physically received and accrued for that were **not ordered**.	Occurrence/ Accuracy/Rights and Obligations	*** **System check (test of one)** Observe the goods in process and request the warehouse operative to attempt to enter in a GRN for which there is no PO.	
			** ¥ See dual test above (at raising the PO, Point 2, Test 3).	
2	GRNs are raised in the system for goods that were **not received**.	Occurrence	Obtain a copy of the review of the open aged and the GRIR report for a randomly selected five months and ensure that there is evidence of review and follow-up.	
			** ¥ See dual test above (at raising the PO, Point 2, Test 3).	

3	**GRNs are not** raised in the system for goods received, resulting in incomplete accruals.	Completeness	Obtain a copy of the review of the aged open PO report for a randomly selected five months and ensure that there is evidence of review and follow-up.	
			Randomly select 50 supplier reconciliations from throughout the period and ensure there is evidence of review and follow-up.	
4	Invoices are received for goods not received or for goods in poor condition.	Occurrence/ Accuracy/Rights and Obligations	Observe the goods (at raising the PO, Point 2, Test 3) check-in area to ensure goods are being counted and physically inspected.	
			** ¥ See dual test above (at raising the PO, Point 2, Test 3).	
Accounting				
1	Payments are made to incorrect bank accounts.	Occurrence/ Accuracy/Rights and Obligations	Randomly select 200 supplier payments from throughout the period and ensure they were approved and that there is evidence that the back-up was reviewed prior to payment.	
			Ensure only the purchasing department can make changes to supplier bank account details and that personnel in the procurement department are: (1.) not cheque signatories; and (2.) not part of the AP function.	

| 2 | Payments may be made for goods or services not received. | Occurrence/ Accuracy/Rights and Obligations | See test at 1. above | |
| | | | Obtain five randomly selected months' bank reconciliations and ensure there is evidence of review and follow-up. | |

** Indicates an alternative testing method. Although those tests requiring the testing of a lower sample size (because they cover a greater volume of the population) or that are a system test of one are considered more efficient and effective (i.e. those requiring lower sample sizes are performed more quickly and those that are system checks require a test of one item only and therefore are more efficient).

When a system test is carried out, there is only ever one test (as, once set up correctly, the system should behave in the same way every time). The auditor need then only test for changes in configuration of the computer system.

*** Note the change in the direction of this test (**general ledger to source** for completeness and **source** to **general ledger** for occurrence (existence)).

¥ Dual test – the same test can be used to cover: (a) multiple assertions; (b) multiple risk; and/or (c) control and substantive testing.

Conclusion			

Subject to the matters noted for the reviewer, in my opinion the revenue and receivables are adequately controlled with respect to all assertions.		
Name:		**Accountant in Charge**
Date:		
Name:		**Reviewer**
Date:		

Stage Four: Test the Internal Controls System (within Payroll)

Having reached the final stage of a system-based (controls-approach) audit of the payroll cycle, we are now going to test the internal controls relating to the payroll cycle (if the auditor has deemed the controls to be effective and decided that it is an efficient audit approach).

The audit objective is to select and perform tests designed to establish compliance with the system controls as documented by the client entity. The tests of controls will include the testing of the operation of controls over a sample of transactions from the period and obtaining documentary evidence of the controls in operation. A typical working paper relating to controls testing over the payroll cycle can be found at **Example 8.8** below.

EXAMPLE 8.8: WORKING PAPER: PAYROLL CONTROLS PROGRAMME

Dairy Fresh Limited 31 December 2012		Working Paper Reference		P1
Payroll Controls Audit Programme				
Objective		To ascertain if the payroll cycle is adequately controlled by the entity with respect to all assertions.		
		Initials	**Date**	**Date**
	Prepared by:			
	Reviewed by:			
	Audit Programme	**Assertion**	**Test**	**Ref to Test**

The following steps are suggestions only and should be removed or added to as necessary to address the risks of material misstatement identified at the risk assessment stage.

Organisational and IT Controls

1	Lack of policies and procedures surrounding payroll area, which may result in inconsistent application of policies and lack of adherence to desired procedures.	Valuation/ Occurrence/ Completeness/ Rights and Obligations	Assess the appropriateness of the accounting policy and the accounting estimates method for payroll. Ensure that the accounting policy is in accordance with accounting standards and applicable law.	
2	Inappropriate system access may result in a lack of segregation of duties (SOD).	Valuation/ Occurrence/ Completeness/ Rights and Obligations	Obtain a report from the system outlining who in the organisation has access to which functions in the payroll system. Review the report to ensure that no SOD issues exist (e.g. those individuals with access to employee master data do not have access to payroll application).	

Hiring Employees/Amending Employee Master data			
1	Fictitious employees may be added or incorrect master data may be input (employees may not exist).	Occurrence/ Recording/ Rights and Obligations	Ensure only HR has access to add/edit employee master data.
			Obtain four random copies of the reviewed edit reports. Ensure: (a) there is evidence of review by someone who does not have access to employee master data; and (b) select three changes from each report and compare to employee authorisation forms.
Recording Payroll Variables and Calculating Payroll			
1	People may be paid for hours they did not work or bonuses or commission that was not approved.	Occurrence/ Recording/ Rights and Obligations/ Completeness	For five months' payroll, randomly selected, reconcile the hours worked per the clock-card system to the hours paid per the payroll system. Ensure an authorisation form exists for any changes made to clock-card information.
			Randomly select five months' department summary report reviews and confirm evidence of review.
2	Payroll may be calculated incorrectly.	Recording	**System check (test of one)** Check the mathematical accuracy of one payslip.
Accounting			
1	The amount paid to employees from the bank may not equal the amount calculated according to the payroll system.	Recording/ Completeness/ Occurrence	Randomly select five months and ensure that the amount paid from the bank account was reconciled to the amount per the payroll control summary report.

2	The amounts entered into the finance system may not equal the amounts calculated according to the payroll system.	Recording/ Completeness/ Occurrence	Randomly select five months and ensure that the journals posted to the accounting system were reconciled to the amount per the payroll control summary report.	
Terminating Employees				
	Individuals may be paid after they have been terminated.	Occurrence	Randomly select five months of department summary report reviews and confirm evidence of review.	
			For five months' payroll, reconcile the hours worked per the clock-card system to the hours paid per the payroll system. Ensure an authorisation form exists for any changes made to clock-card information.	
When a system test is carried out, there is only ever one test (as, once set up correctly, the system should behave in the same way every time). The auditor need then only test for changes in configuration.				
Conclusion				
Subject to the matters noted for the reviewer, in my opinion the payroll system is adequately controlled with respect to all assertions.				
Name:		**Accountant in Charge**		
Date:				
Name:		**Reviewer**		
Date:				

8.7 CONTROLS AND THE INVENTORY CYCLE

In **Section 8.4** we discussed the four stages involved in a system-based (controls-approach) audit involved in reviewing controls. We have applied this approach to revenue and receivables in **Section 8.5** and to purchase and payables and the payroll cycle in **Section 8.6** and we will now apply the four stages to the inventory cycle.

Stage One: Identify Risks and Objectives for Inventory

As introduced in **Chapter 4** and discussed continually throughout this textbook, each transaction class and balance tested by the auditor must address all the management assertions/audit objectives. Before commencing, let us take a look at the specific audit objectives relevant for the inventory cycle.

TABLE 8.4: CONTROL OBJECTIVES: INVENTORY

Management Assertion/ Audit Objective	Control Objective for Transaction Class	Control Objective for Account Balance
	Inventory Movements	**Inventory Balances**
Existence or Occurrence	Recorded purchase transactions represent inventory acquired, recorded transfers represent inventory transferred between locations or categories. Recorded revenue transactions represent inventory sold.	Inventory included in the balance sheet physically exist.
Completeness	All purchases, transfers and sales of inventory that occurred have been recorded.	Inventory includes all materials, products and supplies on hand at the balance sheet date.
Rights and Obligations	The entity has rights to the inventory recorded during the period.	The entity has rights to the inventory included in the balance sheet.
Accuracy, Classification and Valuation	The costs of materials purchased and of labour and overheads applied have been accurately determined and are in accordance with applicable accounting standards.	Inventory is properly stated at the lower of cost or NRV, determined in accordance with applicable accounting standards.
Cut-off	All purchases, transfers and sales of inventory is recorded in the correct account period.	
Presentation and Disclosure	Transactions relating to inventory have been properly identified and classified in the financial statements.	Inventory is properly identified and classified in the financial statements. Disclosures pertaining to the classification, basis of valuation and the pledging of inventory is adequate.

Stage Two: Ascertain Internal Controls System for Inventory

In **Section 8.4** we determined that at stage two in a system-based (controls-approach) audit, for each financial cycle, the auditor should identify the principal business activities and key documents. He should then determine the flow of documents and extent of controls relative to each audit risk and management assertion/audit objective/financial statement objective by reviewing the client entity's policy and procedure documentation, as well as through discussions with management and the operational departments relative to the financial cycle being assessed. We will now consider this relevant to the inventory cycle.

Due to the fact that the auditor normally attends the year-end physical inventory count as part of his substantive procedures, there is a more detailed discussion in **Chapter 12** on exactly what is expected from the client entity with respect to carrying out a physical inventory count.

Key documents within the Inventory Cycle

The following documents are the key documents the auditor would expect to find in a typical inventory cycle:
- inventory requisitions forms;
- goods receipt notes (GRNs);
- goods dispatch dockets (GDNs);
- inventory cards;
- inventory write-off forms;
- aged stock listing; and
- status stock listing.

Stage Three: Assess the Internal Controls System for Inventory

We have now reached stage three of a system-based (controls-approach) audit of the inventory cycle. Having identified the risks and objectives relating to the inventory cycle and obtained an understanding of how the controls should operate relating to that cycle, the auditor now needs to assess what he has learned so far in order to decide whether it is efficient to go ahead and test the controls.

In a non-manufacturing environment the movements of stocks are normally tested within the purchases and payables and revenue and receivables cycles and are not dealt with separately under 'inventory cycle' control documentation. In a manufacturing environment, a more in-depth understanding of stock movement controls needs to be gained by the auditor.

Many of the inventory tests of controls are in the form of dual-purpose tests in that they will also support substantive testing.

Before moving onto testing of the inventory system's controls, the auditor should ensure that testing the controls will be an efficient approach. If there are no manufacturing activities, then the likelihood is that it will be more efficient to perform focused substantive tests on the inventory balance as movements of stock will be covered under the purchases and payables and revenue and receivables cycles. Considering that the auditor will attend the inventory count at year end regardless of the results of controls testing, there is not much time to be saved by testing the controls in such a scenario.

Below we will consider the typical types of controls that would be required to be in place under key areas of inventory management, including:
- inventory status;
- inventory counts;
- inventory write-offs;
- standard costing review;
- inventory safeguarding; and
- inventory reconciliations.

These will now be discussed in more detail.

Inventory Status

Typical controls that would be required to be in place as part of inventory status management are as follows.
- Status of inventory should be known at all times, especially if consignment inventory is held or inventory is subject to retention of title (e.g. obsolete, damaged, third party, held on consignment) (**R&A**).
- Reviews of damaged, obsolete and slow-moving inventories should be carried out periodically throughout the year (**R&A**).
- Obsolete, damaged and short-dated inventory should be segregated from good inventory and the status of same recorded against the perpetual records, where possible (**PC**).

Inventory Counts

Physical inventory counts should be carried out periodically (at least once a year) as follows.
- The count should be carried out by personnel who are independent of the stores function (**SOD**).
- The count should be carried out in accordance with documented and predetermined inventory count procedures and instructions (**OC**).
- The count should be a blind count (i.e. the expected results of the count should not be known to counters), performed by two individuals who compare results and investigate differences (**R&A**) (**R**).
- The final count results should be compared to perpetual records (**R**).
- All differences between physical and perpetual records should be investigated (**R&A**).
- Unresolved differences between the physical count and perpetual records should be written off following authorisation from management (**R&A**).

Inventory Write-offs

Typical controls that would be required to be in place as part of inventory write-off management are as follows.
- Inventories identified for write-off should be appropriately authorised by relevant management personnel prior to being recorded in the system (**R&A**).
- Disposal of inventory should be based on informed decisions that are evidenced in writing (**R&A**).

Standard Costing Review

Typical controls that would be required to be in place as part of the management of the standard costing of inventory are as follows.
- Standard costs should be reviewed by management to ensure they relate to actual costs being incurred. Standard costs should be reviewed by management to ensure they are reliable and that costing is made on a consistent basis year on year (**R&A**).
- Standard cost variances should be reviewed by management periodically and differences investigated (**R&A**) (**R**).

Inventory Safeguarding

Typical controls that would be required to be in place as part of the management of the safeguarding inventory are as follows.
- Inventory should be held in an environment that prevents deterioration (**PC**).
- Access to stores should be restricted (e.g. access cards) (**PC**).

Inventory Reconciliations

The following reconciliations and reviews should be carried out by the finance department in order to ensure sub-ledgers are in line with the general ledger balances and that adequate provisions are in place.
- Inventory sub-ledgers should be reconciled to the general ledger periodically (**R**)
- Provisions for obsolete, damaged and short-dated inventory should be reviewed regularly by management (**R&A**).

Stage Four: Test the Internal Controls System for Inventory

Having reached the final stage of a system-based (controls-approach) audit of the inventory cycle, we are now going to test the internal controls relating to the inventory cycle (if the auditor has deemed the controls to be effective and decided that it is an efficient audit approach).

The audit objective is to select and perform tests designed to establish compliance with the system controls as documented by the client entity.

Example 8.9 shows the tests that the auditor can carry out to ensure that the control activities are operating effectively and efficiently throughout the period. Beside each control the management assertion/audit objective/financial statement assertion of the test is considered so as to ensure that the relevant member of the audit team understands that each test must cover an objective in order to support the reduction in substantive testing. *Note:* within this audit programme only the following are considered: inventory counts, inventory safeguarding, inventory write-offs and inventory reconciliations. The receipt and issue of inventory is considered within the purchases and payables cycle and the revenue and receivables cycle.

EXAMPLE 8.9: WORKING PAPER: INVENTORY CONTROLS PROGRAMME

Dairy Fresh Limited 31 December 2012 Inventory Controls Audit Programme		Working Paper Reference		I1
Objective		To ascertain if the Inventory Cycle is adequately controlled by the entity with respect to all assertions.		
		Initials	**Date**	**Date**
	Prepared by:			
	Reviewed by:			
	Audit Programme	**Assertion**	**Test**	**Ref to Test**

Ensure the audit plan is reflected in the following tests. The following steps are suggestions only and should be removed or added to as necessary to address the risks of material misstatement identified at the risk assessment stage.

Organisational and IT Controls

	Audit Programme	Assertion	Test	Ref to Test
1	Lack of policies and procedures surrounding the area of inventory, which may result in inconsistent application of policies and lack of adherence to desired procedures.	Valuation/ Occurrence/ Completeness/ Rights and Obligations/ Cut-off	Assess the appropriateness of the accounting policy and procedure documentation and the accounting estimates method for inventories. Ensure that the accounting policy is in accordance with accounting standards and applicable law.	
2	Inappropriate access may result in a lack of segregation of duties (SOD).	Valuation/ Occurrence/ Completeness/ Rights and Obligations	Obtain a report from the system outlining who in the organisation has access to which functions in the inventory system. Review the report to ensure that no SOD issues exist (e.g. individuals with access to physical inventory should not have access to perform inventory write-offs).	

Inventory status				
1	Inventory held may not belong to the client or may be obsolete or out of date.	Occurrence/ Valuation/ Rights and Obligations	During your attendance at the physical inventory count, identify damaged, obsolete and short-dated inventory, obtain a status inventory report and compare a sample to ensure appropriate status is recorded. Additionally, ensure that inventories held for third parties are segregated from the client entity's inventories.	
		Valuation	During your attendance at a physical inventory count, observe the segregation of damaged, obsolete and short-dated inventory.	
Inventory Counts				
1	Not all goods delivered are invoiced.	Existence and Valuation	Ensure stocktake instructions exist and are documented and attend a physical inventory count to ensure they are adhered to.	
			Select a random sample (see **Chapter 6**, Section 6.7 for calculation of sample sizes) of five months and request physical inventory count records to confirm physical inventory counts are taking place as prescribed and inspect reconciliations between count records and perpetual inventory records.	
Inventory Write-offs				
1	Stock may be written off without authorisation.	Occurrence and Accuracy	Select a sample (see **Chapter 6**, Section 6.7 for calculation of sample sizes) of write-offs of inventory to ensure they were adequately approved. Ensure disposal records exist for the selected inventory.	

Standard Costing				
1	Standard costing applied to inventory may not be reasonable.	Valuation	Request a sample (see **Chapter 6**, Section 6.7 for calculation of sample sizes) of standard cost variance reviews to ensure they are taking place periodically and to ensure there is evidence of management's investigation of differences.	
Inventory Safeguarding				
1	Inventory may be subject to misappropriation.	Existence	Observe physical securities.	
Inventory Reconciliations				
1	Inventory balances may be written off without proper authorisation.	Completeness/ Existence and Valuation	Request and inspect a sample (see **Chapter 6**, Section 6.7 for calculation of sample sizes) of five months' randomly selected reconciliations between the inventory sub-ledger and the general ledger.	
Conclusion				
Name:			**Accountant in Charge**	
Date:				
Name:			**Reviewer**	
Date:				

8.8 CONTROLS AND THE BANK AND CASH CYCLE

In **Section 8.4** we discussed the four stages involved in a system-based (controls-approach) audit. We have applied this approach to revenue and receivables in **Section 8.5**, to purchases and payables and the payroll cycle in **Section 8.6**, to the inventory cycle in **Section 8.7** and we will now apply the four stages to the bank and cash cycle.

Stage One: Identify Risks and Objectives for Bank and Cash

As introduced in **Chapter 4** and discussed continually throughout this textbook, each transaction class and balance tested by the auditor must address all the audit objectives (management assertions). Before commencing, let us take a look at the specific audit objectives relevant to the bank and cash cycle.

TABLE 8.5: CONTROL OBJECTIVES: BANK AND CASH

Management Assertion/ Audit Objective	Control Objective of Audit Evidence
Existence	To ensure that recorded bank and cash balances exist at the balance sheet date.
Completeness	To ensure that all bank and cash balances are recorded in the correct period and included in the financial statements.
Accuracy	To ensure bank and cash balances are accurately recorded in the financial statements.
Valuation	To ensure bank and cash balances are properly valued, and a provision has been made for any balances that may not be recoverable.
Cut-off	All transactions have been accounted for in the correct accounting period.
Rights and Obligations	To ensure the entity has the rights to all bank and cash balances shown at the balance sheet date.
Presentation and Disclosure	To ensure cash balances are properly classified and disclosed in the balance sheet and that lines of credit, loan guarantees and other restrictions on bank and cash balances are appropriately disclosed.

Stage Two: Ascertain Internal Controls System for Bank and Cash

In **Section 8.4** we determined that at stage two of a system-based (controls-approach) audit, for each financial cycle, the auditor should identify the **principal business activities** and **key documents**. He should then determine the flow of documents and extent of controls relative to each risk and management assertion/audit objective/financial statement objective by reviewing the client entity's policy and procedure documentation, as well as through discussions with management and the operational departments relative to the financial cycle being assessed. We will now consider this relevant to the bank and cash cycle.

The key control areas relevant to the bank and cash cycle should include the following:
• payments,
• receipts, and
• bank account.

Let us consider the individual control activities expected under each.

Payments

Typical controls that would be expected to be in place as part of the management of payments are as follows.

- Payments should be properly authorised (usually by two individuals) (**OC**) (**R&A**). Only authorised staff can make payments and this is ensured through the establishment of mandates with the bank. Where signatories on the account changed during the year, review the bank mandate form (document indicating who can sign-off on cheques or credit transfers) to ensure that this has been updated correctly.
- Payments should only be made in respect of legitimate liabilities (supporting documentation is reviewed by management prior to authorisation of payments) (**R&A**).
- Every payment run should be reviewed by management and matched to appropriate invoices (**R&A**).
- Reconciliations should be performed between the amounts appearing on bank statements and the amounts posted to the payables sub-ledger (**R**). The reconciliation should be performed by someone independent of the individuals who do the postings to the payables accounts (**SOD**).
- There should be segregation of duties between the personnel dealing with receipts and payments, those dealing with revenue transactions, those dealing with purchases transactions and the individuals authorising payments (**SOD**).
- Cheque books should be stored securely in a safe and only authorised personnel should have access to them (**PC**).

Receipts

Typical controls that would be expected to be in place as part of the management of receipts are as follows.

- Receipts should be collected and banked intact. (If receipts are received by post, post should be opened by two individuals and cheques sent directly to the cash office and remittances to the receivables department or accounting, depending on the purpose of the receipt, in order for the receipt to be reflected on the accounting system for later reconciling to the bank statement) (**PC**) (**SOD**).
- Reconciliations of amounts banked versus amounts posted should be performed by someone independent of the cash custodians and the individuals posting cash to the ledgers (**R**) (**SOD**).
- A cash to revenue reconciliation should be performed and reviewed by management (**R&A**).

Bank Accounts

Typical controls that would be expected to be in place as part of the management of bank accounts are as follows.

- Bank reconciliations should be performed and reviewed by management on a regular basis (**R**) (**R&A**).
- There should be restrictions on the opening and closing of accounts – only authorised staff or management should be authorised to open bank accounts (**OC**).

Key Documents within the Bank and Cash Cycle

Key documents within the bank and cash cycle are as follows:
- remittance advices (for cash received);
- payment run summaries (if paid by BACS);
- bank statements;
- bank reconciliations;
- cheque books;
- lodgment books; and
- bank mandates.

The most efficient way to get an overview of the controls in place is to perform a walk-through test.

Stage Three: Assess the Systems and Internal Controls for Bank and Cash

We have now reached stage three in the system-based (controls-approach) audit of the bank and cash cycle. Having identified the risks and objectives relating to the bank and cash cycle and obtained an understanding of how the controls should operate relating to that cycle, the auditor now needs to assess what he has learned so far in order to decide whether it is efficient to go ahead and test the controls.

Controls testing is normally carried out on bank and cash transactions to reduce substantive testing in the purchases and revenue cycles (as they interlink due to the payment of suppliers and receipt of cash from customers). However, cash and bank balances at year end are normally tested using focused substantive testing, as it is usually the most efficient way.

Stage Four: Test the Internal Controls System for Bank and Cash

Having reached the final stage of the system-based (controls-approach) audit of the bank and cash cycle, we are now going to test the internal controls relating to the bank and cash cycle (if the auditor has deemed the controls to be effective and decided that it is an efficient audit approach). The audit objective is to select and perform tests designed to establish compliance with the system controls as documented by the client entity.

Tests of controls for bank and cash include:
- inspection of the reconciliations between the bank balances per bank statements and the bank balances per the general ledger, ensuring that they have been prepared and reviewed regularly for all bank accounts;
- check the signatories on all the bank accounts (i.e. obtain copies of bank mandates currently in force for each account and ensure that they are up to date and only include current staff). Obtain a copy of the bank mandate which contains sample signatures of the authorised signatories;
- test the authorisation of opening and closure of bank accounts; and
- check that all bank accounts exist.

8.9 CONTROLS AND THE INVESTMENTS CYCLE

In **Section 8.4** we discussed the four stages involved in a system-based (controls-approach) audit. We have applied this approach to revenue and receivables in **Section 8.5**, to purchase and payables and the payroll cycle in **Section 8.6**, to the inventory cycle in **Section 8.7**, to the bank and cash cycle in **Section 8.8** and we will now apply the four stages to the investments cycle.

Stage One: Identify Risks and Objectives for the Investments Cycle

As introduced in **Chapter 4** and discussed continually throughout this textbook, each transaction class and balance tested by the auditor must address all the management assertions/audit objectives. Before commencing, let us take a look at the specific audit objectives relevant for the investments cycle.

TABLE 8.6: CONTROL OBJECTIVES: INVESTMENTS

Management Assertion/Audit Objective	Control Objective for Transaction Class	Control Objective for Account Balance
Existence or Occurrence	Recorded investment revenues, gains and losses are the result of transactions and events that occurred during the period.	Recorded investment balances represent investments that exist at the balance sheet date.
Completeness	All investment transactions and events are included in the statement of comprehensive income.	All investments are included in the balance sheet and classified as investment accounts.
Rights and Obligations		All recorded investments are owned by the client entity.
Accuracy, Classification and Valuation	Investment revenues, gains and losses are reported at the correct amounts.	Investments are stated on the balance sheet at valuation or at the lower of cost and NRV, as appropriate for particular types of investment.
Presentation and Disclosure	Appropriate disclosures in the financial statements are made concerning: 1. related party investments; 2. the bases for valuing investments; and 3. the pledging of investments as collateral.	Investment balances are properly identified and classified in the financial statements.

Stage Two: Ascertain Internal Controls System for the Investments Cycle

In **Section 8.4** we determined that at stage two in a system-based (controls-approach) audit, for each financial cycle, the auditor should identify the **principal business activities** and **key documents**. He should then determine the flow of documents and extent of controls relative to each audit risk and management assertion/audit objective/financial statement objective by reviewing the client entity's policy and procedure documentation, as well as through discussions with management and the operational departments relative to the financial cycle being assessed. We will now consider this relevant to the investments cycle.

Ideally, the following should be present in the control environment of the investments cycle.
- Authority and responsibility for investing activities should be given to an individual who is deemed to be a person of integrity and of sufficient knowledge and experience in dealing with investments.
- The information system in place should be one that is reliable and accurate at all times in the recording of the data required for accounting for the various categories of investments.
- Internal audit should closely monitor the effectiveness of controls over investing activities.
- Title to the investments (ownership documents), usually in the form of a share or debenture certificate, should be held in a secure location.

Key Documents

The auditor would expect to find the following key documents in a typical investments cycle (although investment ownership documents can take many forms):
- debenture certificates,
- shareholding certificates, and
- investment contracts.

Stage Three: Assess the Systems and Internal Controls for the Investments Cycle

We have now reached stage three in a system-based (controls-approach) audit of the investments cycle. Having identified the risks and objectives relating to the investments cycle and obtained an understanding of how the controls should operate relating to that cycle, the auditor now needs to assess what he has learned so far in order to decide whether it is efficient to go ahead and test the controls.

Depending on the number of investments, it may be more appropriate for the auditor to test the balance substantively (if this is the case, there is no need to continue with the tests of controls).

Stage Four: Test the Internal Controls System for the Investments Cycle

Having reached the final stage of a system-based (controls-approach) audit of the investments cycle, we are now going to test the internal controls relating to the investments cycle (if the auditor has deemed the controls to be effective and decided that it is an efficient audit approach). The audit objective is to select and perform tests designed to establish compliance with the system controls as documented by the client entity.

Tests of controls for the investments cycle include:
- inspection of controls over the custody of investments and obtaining a confirmation of investments from all custodians of investments;
- checking the authorised signatures;
- testing authorisation of additions and disposals of investments; and
- checking existence of all investments.

8.10 MANAGEMENT LETTERS

Throughout this text we have described how the auditor might go about gaining an understanding of the client entity's system of internal controls and, during the course of that exercise, he will discover weaknesses in the design, operation and consistent application of the client entity's system of internal controls. A management letter is a document used by the auditor to inform those charged with governance of the client entity about his findings relating to the system of internal controls.

ISA 265 *Communicating Deficiencies in Internal Control to Those Charged With Governance and Management* (ISA 265) states:
> "The auditor shall communicate in writing significant deficiencies in internal control identified during the audit to those charged with governance on a timely basis." (ISA 265, para 9)

When communicating to management, however, the auditor will consider if there are any reasons why it would be inappropriate to communicate certain deficiencies directly to those charged with governance (e.g. instances of suspected fraud, where those charged with governance are suspected to be connected to the suspected fraud). Additionally, the auditor may be alerted by third parties to matters of importance that he, in his professional judgement, feels merit highlighting to the management.

The management letter is a by-product of the audit and it is important that the auditor highlights to those charged with governance that the purpose of the audit was not to identify weaknesses in the audited entity's controls but to express an opinion on the financial statements. Therefore, the auditor should note that any weaknesses identified relate only to those controls reviewed as part of the audit procedures used to express an opinion on the financial statements and are not intended to be an exhaustive list of all possible control weaknesses in the entity's controls.

When preparing the management letter, the structure should be such that it clearly outlines for management a description of each deficiency and an explanation of its potential effects on the client entity's financial statements.

Application note A6 of ISA 265 outlines examples of matters that the auditor may consider for inclusion in a management letter and some of those are listed below:

- deficiencies that may lead to material misstatement in the financial statements;
- weaknesses that increase the susceptibility of the related asset or liability to loss or fraud; and
- weaknesses that are considered important to the financial reporting process (e.g. key organisational controls, or controls connected to the prevention and detection of fraud).

An example of a management letter can be found at **Example 8.10** below. You can see from Appendix 1 to this example that for each control weakness and its related risk, a remedial recommendation is included.

EXAMPLE 8.10: SAMPLE MANAGEMENT LETTER

Morris & Co
Chartered Accountants
Andy Place
Cork

Client reference: 56767

Management Letter

The Board of Directors
Dairy Fresh Ltd
Heath Road
Cork

Under international standards on auditing, auditors are encouraged to report on 'significant deficiencies' in internal control identified during the audit that, in the auditor's professional judgment, could adversely affect the entity's ability to record, process, and generate financial statements which are consistent with the management assertions.

In performing the audit of the financial statements of Dairy Fresh Ltd for the year ended 31 December 2012, we considered Dairy Fresh's internal control system in order to determine the nature, timing, and extent of our audit procedures. Our consideration of internal control did not entail an in-depth study and evaluation of any of its components and was not intended for the purpose of making detailed recommendations or evaluating the adequacy of internal controls to prevent or detect all errors and irregularities.

We remind you that Management is responsible for establishing and maintaining internal control. In fulfilling this responsibility, estimates and judgments by management are required to assess the expected benefits and related costs of internal control **policies and procedures**.

Although the purpose of our consideration of internal control was not to provide assurances thereon, matters came to our attention that in our professional opinion are of importance. These matters are discussed in Appendix 1.

We would be pleased to discuss the above noted matters with you and, as such, if you have any queries or concerns, please do not hesitate to contact us.

Kind regards,

Morris & Co
Andy Place
Cork

Appendix 1

Control Weakness	Risk	Recommendation
No authorisation is required for the credit controller to perform write-offs on a customer's account.	Monies which may be collectable may be written off.	The credit controller should only be permitted to perform write-offs of insignificant amounts (these amounts should be formalised). Any significant amounts should only be written-off after a member of the finance department and a member of the sales departments have authorised the write-offs. Another member of the finance department should review all write-offs to ensure adequate approval was obtained.

8.11 CONCLUSION

We must remember that auditing firms are profit-making organisations and as such try to make a maximum return on any audit, but never at the risk of increasing audit risk. This means that the auditor needs to perform the audit in the most efficient and effective manner possible. The most efficient way to audit can be to take a controls approach (system-based approach). A controls approach is where the auditor gains an understanding of the client entity's internal controls and tests those internal controls to prove that they worked consistently throughout the year and address the control objectives. By doing this the auditor gains some comfort over the occurrence and existence, completeness, recording, rights and obligations and classification of the figures in the financial statements. This comfort gained (known as assurance) allows the auditor to take a more relaxed approach with respect to substantive testing. While the auditor has increased the efficiency of the audit, he has in no way jeopardised its quality.

An essential consideration, however, is whether or not he believes the internal controls are effective. Prior to commencing controls testing, the auditor will gain an understanding of the internal control environment sufficient for him to decide if he feels the controls documented as being in place are sufficient to address the risks, otherwise it will not be worth his while testing them. If he proceeds with testing and the controls are not effective, the auditor will have wasted time testing the controls and gained no assurance to reduce substantive testing.

SUMMARY OF LEARNING OBJECTIVES

Learning Objective 1 Demonstrate a detailed knowledge of what makes up the internal control system.

The *UK Corporate Governance Code*, section C, recommends that "The board should maintain sound risk management and internal control systems". COSO provides advice on the application of a strong internal control system. The **Internal Control System** comprises five components: the control environment, risk assessment, control activities, information and communication systems and monitoring activities. Although ultimate responsibility for internal control lies with the directors, **everyone in the organisation has responsibility**.

Controls generally come in the form of manual or automated, and preventative or detective. Automated and preventative controls are preferred, although the auditor recognises that, due to the complexity of business, a combination of all four will be found.

Learning Objective 2 Appreciate the importance of client entity internal controls to the auditor.

The auditor is required, under ISA (UK and Ireland) 330 *The Auditor's Responses to Assessed Risks*, to design and perform procedures whose nature, timing and extent are responsive to address risk of material misstatement at the assertion level. Reviewing control systems (a) gives the auditor greater insight into the client entity's organisation and ultimately provides him with better knowledge on which to audit the entity; and (b) allows the auditor to perform a more efficient audit, as testing and relying on the control system will allow him to reduce the level of substantive testing he performs.

Learning Objective 3 Demonstrate a detailed knowledge of the stages involved in the review of the internal control system of the client entity by the external auditor.

There are four key stages involved in the review of controls by the auditor.
1. Identify risks and objectives within each financial cycle.
2. Ascertain the internal control system (generally by use of narratives and flowcharts).
3. Assess the internal control system – the auditor, at this stage, must decide whether it is an efficient approach to test the controls. He will test controls that address risks, cover financial statement assertions and that he believes are effective controls.
4. Test the controls (only if his assessment determines it is an efficient approach; if not, the auditor will proceed to focused substantive testing).

Learning Objective 4 Gain an understanding of the financial statement assertions (audit objectives) relative to each financial cycle.

The auditor's consideration of internal controls is intended to provide the auditor with assurance over the assertions for each account balance, transaction class and disclosures in the financial statements sufficient to reduce the level of substantive testing to be performed. As such he must first understand the assertions relative to each financial cycle and ensure that his control testing addresses these assertions. The assertions he seeks to prove in relation to each transaction class are: occurrence; completeness; rights and obligations; accuracy and classification; cut-off and presentation and disclosure. The assertions he seeks to prove in relation to each account balance are: existence; completeness; rights and obligations; valuation; and presentation and disclosure.

Learning Objective 5 Appreciate the control activities that should exist relative to each financial cycle.

Control activities generally fall into one or more of a number of categories outlined below:
* organisation controls (**OC**),
* segregation of duties (**SOD**),
* physical controls (**PC**),
* reviews and authorising (**R&A**),
* system controls (**SC**), and
* reconciliations (**R**).

While the specific control activities vary from cycle to cycle, they generally fall into one or more of the above.

Learning Objective 6 Gain an appreciation of when it is most efficient to test controls.

The auditor should only test controls that he has assessed to be strong either by initial review of his understanding of those controls or through the performance of a walkthrough test. Testing controls that are likely to fail is an inefficient use of the auditor's time.

Learning Objective 7 Be able to select and apply appropriate control tests to typical financial cycles, which address the financial statement assertions (audit objectives).

The audit objective is to select and perform tests designed to establish compliance with the system controls as documented by the entity. The controls must be effective in practice and on paper. Tests of control are:
1. concerned only with those areas subject to effective controls;
2. concerned only with those controls mitigating risks and supporting audit objectives (financial statement assertions);
3. a representative sample of transactions throughout the period; and
4. likely to cover a larger number of items than a walkthrough test.

Typical tests of controls will involve: tracing samples; checking for authorisation; testing for sequential numbering; observing control activities taking place; and confirming performance of reconciliations.

Learning Objective 8 Explain how the auditor communicates control deficiencies to the client entity.

A management letter is sent by the auditor to those charged with governance outlining to them significant deficiencies in internal controls that he noted while performing the audit. In the management letter the auditor will clearly outline that the purpose of the audit was to express an opinion on the financial statements and not to perform an extensive review of controls. The letter will describe each deficiency and its associated risk.

QUESTIONS

Self-test Questions

8.1   What is COSO?

8.2   According to COSO, who in the organisation is responsible for internal controls?

8.3   According to COSO, what are the five components of internal control?

8.4   Distinguish between detective and preventative controls.

8.5   How do controls impact on the nature, timing and extent of substantive audit procedures?

8.6   What are the stages involved in reviewing and testing controls?

8.7   Why is the decision whether or not to test controls so important to the auditor?

8.8   Name six categories of control activities.

8.9   What is the purpose of a narrative?

8.10 What is segregation of duties and why is it so important to the control of the organisation?

8.11 What types of control activities should exist around completeness of revenue?

8.12 What types of control activities should exist around valuation with respect to revenue?

8.13 What is a walkthrough test?

8.14 How might the auditor test the controls around valuation of revenue?

8.15 What control activities should exist to ensure the completeness of purchases?

8.16 What is a flowchart?

8.17 What key activities should be segregated in the payroll cycle?

8.18 What is the significance of an Organisational Chart and Chart of Authority with respect to the purchases function?

8.19 How might the auditor test the assertion 'occurrence' with respect to new employees?

8.20 Name five key controls that should exist around physical inventory counts.

8.21 How might the auditor test the 'occurrence' assertion with respect to inventory write-offs?

8.22 Name four key tests the auditor should perform when testing the bank and cash control cycle.

Review Questions

(See Suggested Solutions to Review Questions in **Appendix D**.)

Question 8.1

Where the controls process surrounding the revenue and receivables cycle is found to be weak, explain the impact of this on the audit plan for the auditor.

Question 8.2

Where the controls process surrounding the revenue and receivables cycle is found to be strong, explain the impact of this on the audit plan for the auditor.

Question 8.3

The following information has been gathered by an audit team carrying out fieldwork around the revenue and receivables cycle of Mac Apple Ltd:

- Business is predominantly cash orientated, with total weekly takings of approximately €100,000.
- Customer accounts do exist and represent approximately €30,000 of weekly takings.
- Over-the-counter cash sales take place on a daily basis.
- All sales are processed through front office sales and sales invoices are printed on process of every sale through the till.
- The company has three separate locations, head office and two further sites (a) and (b), from which cash sales are made.
- Tills at the three locations are not networked.
- Daily cash takings are agreed to daily Z reports printed from the till, however the client stopped keeping the reconciliations at the start of the financial year as they take up too much space.
- Cash takings are delivered to head office by an employee from locations (a) and (b) at the end of each trading week.
- One lodgement is made per week for all three locations.
- A manual cash lodgement book is not maintained by the client entity.
- Receipts received from customers are posted to the customers' accounts.
- As a manual cash received book is not maintained, the client is unable to provide an analysis of weekly lodgements split between cash sales, cheque sales and customer account receipts.
- The client requested that the audit firm did not perform a debtors' circularisation at the year-end as relations with customers are sensitive.

Requirement
(a) Explain the weaknesses in the above cycle and the impact on the auditor's ability to gain sufficient appropriate audit evidence over:
- cash sales;
- year-end receivables balance.
(b) Outline three changes that the client could make to the above cycle in order to improve controls operating around the revenue and receivables cycle.

Question 8.4

Barrow Ltd (Barrow) manufactures electrical components for use in various electronic applications worldwide. The company has been a client of your audit firm for many years. It is a significant local employer, with almost 400 permanent employees. It also recruits temporary staff at peak periods.

At the audit planning meeting you were informed that the company decided during the year to outsource its payroll function in order to cut costs. It has engaged Otter Ltd, a well-known payroll bureau, to carry out the payment functions. The results of your audit testing have identified a number of control weaknesses in the payroll and also in other financial statement areas, including fixed assets, bank and cash and accounts payable.

Requirement
(a) State, as part of your audit planning, what further information you need to obtain arising from Barrow's decision to outsource its payroll function.
(b) State what additional audit procedures you would carry out as a result of the decision taken during the year to outsource the payroll function.
(c) Set out five key considerations for the reporting of control weaknesses to the directors of the company.

Question 8.5

You are the audit senior for Hart & Ryan Auditors and are currently reviewing the working papers for Express Ltd, which employs in excess of 1,000 staff based in sites throughout Ireland and the UK. Due to the large number of employees, the volume of leavers and joiners is generally high. You receive the following process document with respect to payroll:

Joiners Individual managers, on hiring a new employee, forward a 'starter form' to HR. The starter form includes the employee's name, address, PPS/social security number, phone number, bank details, department, position and salary or wage rate. On receipt, HR notes in an Excel spreadsheet the details from the form. On a weekly basis HR then forwards the list of starters to Terry, the payroll supervisor, who enters the new employees onto the payroll package. Only Terry has access to add employees.

Leavers Individual managers complete a 'leaver form', which includes the employee's name, date of exit and holidays outstanding and, once complete, forward it to the HR department. HR marks on its employee spreadsheet the date that the employee exited and the number of days holidays due and forwards the leaver form to payroll. Only Terry has access to remove employees from payroll.

Recording of time

Salary – salaried employees do not have timesheets and are automatically paid the same amount each week.

Wages – wages are paid at an hourly rate. The individual managers record on a pre-defined Excel spreadsheet the following pieces of information:
• number of basic hours worked;
• number of overtime hours worked;
• commission due; and
• number of leave days taken.

James, the payroll assistant, enters all the details received by the managers into the payroll system.

Once all details are entered, Terry runs a 'gross to net report' and reviews this for anything that looks unusual. Once he is satisfied, he generates the payslips and sends the file to the bank for payment into employees' bank accounts.

Terry sends the summary payroll report to the accounts department, which uses it to reconcile to the bank and make the necessary entries into the accounting system.

The payroll system can print the following **exception reports**:
• new starters added that week;
• leavers terminated that week;
• number of basic hours per department (individual manager); and
• number of overtime hours per department (individual manager).

Each week Terry reviews these, signs them and files them in the payroll department.

Requirement

(a) Identify for your assistant five weaknesses of the payroll process described above. For each of the weaknesses identified you should note the risk connected to that weakness.
(b) List the controls you believe Express Ltd should introduce to mitigate each risk identified in Part A above.
(c) For each cycle listed below, identify one test you would perform to address the noted assertion.

	Cycle	Assertion	Suggested Test
A	Revenue	Occurrence	
B	Receivables	Valuation	
C	Fixed Assets	Existence	
D	Purchases	Completeness	

9

AUDITING IN A COMPUTERISED ENVIRONMENT AND E-COMMERCE

LEARNING OBJECTIVES

Having studied this chapter on auditing in a computerised environment and e-commerce you should:
1. understand the IT audit process, and the steps that should be taken when key controls are automated.;
2. understand the meaning of 'computer-assisted audit techniques' (CAATs);
3. be able to consider the cost–benefit relationship of applying CAATs; and
4. understand the impact e-commerce and cloud computing have on businesses and on the auditor

KEY TERMS AND DEFINITIONS FOR THIS CHAPTER

Application Controls   An 'application' is a specific computer program, such as the payroll programme used to calculate wages and salaries. 'Application controls' are the specific controls imbedded in the application to aim to ensure the integrity of input data, data processing and the output data. (Also known as '**IT application controls**'.)

Enterprise Resource Planning (ERP)   A system used by organisations to manage multiple aspects of the business.

General IT Controls (GITC)   General IT controls are those controls that support the entire IT system and, as such, if general IT controls are weak, this would impact on application controls.

Interface Controls   Controls designed to control the transfer of data from one system to another.

IT Controls   The terms 'IT controls' and '**computer controls**' are used interchangeably to describe controls operated by computers.

Logical Security   Logical security controls are the settings and configuration that can be applied to a system.

Real Time   Transactions that occur in 'real time' are those that are completed without any delay or requirement for manual intervention (i.e. systems that respond to input immediately).

Server Room   A room that houses mainly computer servers. Climate is one of the factors that affects the energy consumption and environmental impact of a server room and so access to this area should be restricted to maintain required levels of control.

Standby Facilities   Facilities available as a contingency should unforeseen events cause the normal place of business to become unworkable. The entity must ensure business continuity by ensuring premises are identified where day-to-day activities can continue to take place (e.g. taking customer orders, posting invoices, etc).

9.1 INTRODUCTION

Discussions on audit procedures thus far in this textbook have been relevant for both manual and computer-controlled environments. This chapter considers the specific advantages and disadvantages, as well as the challenges faced by the auditor, when the client uses IT systems to control the entity. As stated in the Key Terms table above, the terms 'IT controls' and 'computer controls' are used interchangeably to describe controls operated by computers.

Whether an auditor is auditing a small company or a large multinational, in today's world computers will have been used by the client entity in processing financial information (input transactions and accounting records).

While small companies tend to use readily available general accounting software that fulfils their requirements, larger companies will often have tailormade software to suit their needs. In many cases, these software solutions are full **enterprise resource planning (ERP)** systems. ERP systems are designed to cover all, or the majority of, the core functions of an enterprise, no matter what its business is.

The auditor will also have to consider the role of the entity's computer/IT systems and design the audit plan in order to assess the relevant IT controls. Regardless of the computer systems used, the audit objectives and approach will remain largely unchanged from that if the audit was being carried out in a non-computer environment.

- Audit objective – the **audit objective** will not change, as the auditor must obtain **sufficient appropriate audit evidence** to draw reasonable conclusions on which to base the **audit opinion**.
- Audit approach – the audit approach will not change as the auditor must continue to plan, ascertain, record and evaluate.
- Controls assessment – the requirement for and method of assessing controls will not change, as the normal procedures for control assessment used in a manual system will still exist in a computer controlled environment.

The normal elements of internal control discussed throughout **Chapter 8**, such as personnel, authorisation, monitoring, physical controls and appropriate segregation of duties, are just as important in a computer controlled system as they are in a manual system.

Section 9.2 of this chapter discusses the audit approach when the client entity operates in a computerised environment. **Section 9.3** then explains the types of controls the auditor would expect to see in such a computerised environment, concentrating on general IT controls and IT application controls.

The topic of **computer-assisted audit techniques (CAATs)** is introduced in **Section 9.4** and is a key learning point of this chapter. This section describes what CAATs are and how they might be used by the auditor to perform a more efficient and effective audit. The section also discusses the key considerations of the auditor prior to adopting procedures which involve the use of CAATs.

Finally, in **Sections 9.5** and **9.6** we discuss how the emerging computer technologies, specifically **e-commerce** and **cloud computing**, impact on the complexity of audit and, in turn, discuss the auditor's response to these technologies.

9.2 THE AUDIT APPROACH IN A COMPUTERISED ENVIRONMENT

Traditionally, auditors were focused on verifying that data was correctly input and generated by the computer. Often what happened **in** the computer itself was not fully assessed. This approach was called '**auditing around the computer**'. Audit activity was primarily focused on ensuring that the source documentation was processed correctly and the auditor would verify by checking source documentation to the output documentation.

Computers today are more complex. Many IT systems are now **real time** and hence there might be only a limited amount of documentation, paperwork; in addition, there may be a very large number of transactions, which makes auditing 'around the computer' far more difficult, at best, or even impossible, as there would be no paper trail.

Under these circumstances, where there is no paper trail and a very large number of transactions, the auditor will use an approach called 'auditing through the computer system'. This involves the auditor performing tests on the **IT controls** to evaluate if they are effective.

After performing these tests, if the auditor finds that the controls are effective, then he can go on to perform a reduced amount of **substantive procedures testing**. However, it must be borne in mind that a level of skill and experience is required in order to evaluate IT controls and this will often involve the use of IT audit specialists.

In light of the need for additional specialists and the complexity of the work involved, the auditor will need to decide if reliance should be placed on IT controls. In making this decision, a first step is to assess the entity's use of computer systems and the auditor should consider its use of computers under three headings:
- extent of use of IT systems by the client entity;
- importance of the IT system to the business; and
- complexity of the IT system.

In general, the greater the extent of the IT system used, its importance to the business and its complexity, the greater the need to assess IT controls. Furthermore, a computer system can become more complicated if there is a high degree of customisation or if it is not managed centrally.

When the auditor decides that there is a need to assess IT controls, the key focus will be to identify and evaluate the controls in place which ensure the **integrity**, **availability** and **confidentiality** of the data processed and stored by the computer systems. Typically, the auditor will ask:
- what controls are in place to prevent unauthorised changes to the data? (**integrity**);
- what measures are in place to ensure that the data is available when required? (**availability**); and
- what controls are available to ensure that only authorised personnel can access the data? (**confidentiality**).

The auditor will also need to consider some other key factors which will influence the effective application of controls within the IT system. Some of these factors include the following.
- Whether processing is **centralised** or **decentralised**:
  - in 'centralised' systems, where several processes, such as wages, sales and purchases, etc. are processed in the same computerised environment in one location, the auditor may opt to identify a small number of controls that will provide assurance over several areas of the entity's accounting system;
  - in a 'decentralised' environment there is often an increased level of effort required of the auditor to identify and evaluate the controls in place.

- The **complexity** and **level of customisation** of the IT system – in less complex systems the auditor may find that identifying and evaluating key controls requires fewer resources.
- The **availability of skilled and experienced audit staff** – testing IT controls requires members of the auditor's staff to be appropriately trained and technically competent.

All of the above considerations will help the auditor to decide whether it is efficient to test the IT system controls. If the auditor's initial assessment is that the IT/computer system is an integral part of the controls in the client entity, and that the auditor has sufficiently skilled audit staff to handle the complexities of the IT system in place, then they may decide to rely on those IT system controls to reduce the level of substantive testing to be performed on the financial statements.

9.3 CONTROLS IN A COMPUTERISED ENVIRONMENT

Introduction

Once a decision has been made to evaluate IT controls, there are two major types of controls in computerised systems to be considered.

1. **General controls** – these are controls over the environment in which the computer system operates. Broadly speaking, this type of control includes organisational controls, systems development controls, maintenance controls, access controls and other general controls.
2. **Application controls** – these are controls designed with the objective of ensuring the accuracy and completeness of data input controls, data processing controls and data output controls. Application controls are designed to detect errors before, during and after the processing of specific types of transaction.

Note: **these areas of control, specific to the computer environment, are a sub-set of all the entity's internal control system**. **Figure 9.1** below outlines the components of an entity's internal control system and, as we can see, IT systems support the internal control system. An IT system, in turn, has two layers: **general IT controls** and **IT application controls**. Extensive discussions are included below in this section about general IT controls (general controls) and IT application controls (or 'application controls').

If the auditor considers the general controls to be weak, then it is unlikely that the effectiveness of the application controls would be assessed as the IT application controls are a subset of the general IT controls. In this scenario, a wholly substantive approach would be considered.

Computer controls, as with all internal controls, can be divided into three categories:
- preventative controls;
- detective controls; and
- corrective controls.

Preventative controls are considered to be the strongest type of controls as they are intended to prevent errors from occurring in the first place.

FIGURE 9.1: INTERNAL CONTROL SYSTEM AND IT SYSTEM COMPONENTS

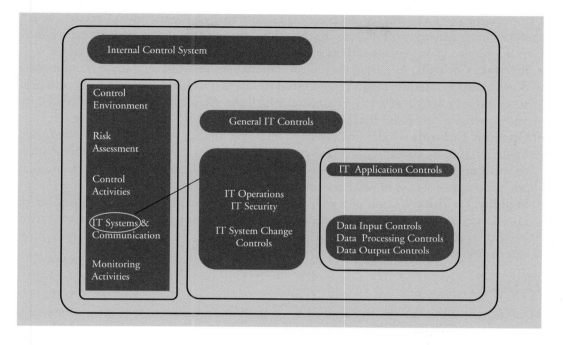

EXAMPLE 9.1: PREVENTION, DETECTION AND CORRECTION CONTROLS

In an entity, employee access to the IT system is managed as follows.
- When a new employee joins the entity, access is not granted to the IT system without authorisation from the line manager. This is an example of a **preventative control**.
- Once a month, the IT manager should review the list of individuals with IT access and compare it to an active employee report. This is an example of a **detective control**.
- Unnecessary IT access is regularly reviewed and removed. This is an example of a corrective control.

General Controls

As set out above, the key audit objective when reviewing general IT controls is to ensure that the integrity, availability and confidentiality of the data is appropriately controlled. In order to meet this objective, the auditor will look to identify and test relevant control activities under each of the general control categories as follows:
- IT operations;
- IT security; and
- IT system change controls.

Examples of control activities for each of the main general control areas are described below.

IT Operations

IT operations refers to the processes associated with management of the IT service, which should aim to deliver an IT system that has the right fit to the entity and operates effectively. IT service management activities can include the introduction of:

- **Interface Controls** As part of this control, measures should be in place to monitor data flows between systems to ensure that interfaces have operated as intended. The auditor should also look to review any procedures which the client entity has in place to identify and remediate data flows that fail to operate correctly.
- **Operator Controls** Under this category, responsibility for scheduling and monitoring operational tasks should be divided between employees (always giving consideration to segregation of duty requirements). Additionally, the client entity should ensure that adequate operators are in place to sufficiently meet the required workload.
- **Standby Facilities** In case of a catastrophic event occurring, the entity should make appropriate arrangements, either with other organisations who operate similar systems or with specialist service providers, so that processing can continue with minimum interruption.

IT Security

IT security is a level of security applied to computers and networks. It incorporates any level of security applied to the protection of:

- the computer equipment,
- information contained within the IT systems, or
- services associated with the IT system,

from unauthorised access, unauthorised change or destruction. IT security can include:

- **Logical Access Controls** Computer systems should be secured with the use of passwords and other suitable security parameters. These measures should be regularly reviewed to ensure that they remain effective.
- **User Access Management** Organisations should ensure that appropriate controls are in place to govern access to their computer systems. In particular, a process should be established to ensure that sufficient user access management controls are in place, i.e. that the granting of user access is appropriately approved and that accounts are removed when staff leave employment or change roles.
- **System Security** This control deals with making sure that antivirus software is up-to-date, and that there is adequate protection for the system through use of firewalls, etc. Entities should ensure that all employees who use the systems are provided with guidance and policies in relation to the use of e-mails, Internet access and other business tools.
- **Physical Security** In addition to good logical security settings, entities should also ensure that physical access to their computer systems is appropriately restricted, particularly with respect to the **server room**, where even the climate is of key importance to the operational effectiveness of the computer systems, therefore strict access controls are essential.

IT System Change Controls

It is essential that changes to the IT computer environment are regulated to ensure that they do not compromise existing computerised controls or, in themselves, prove inadequate in controlling the entity's data. As such, the following should be considered when making any changes to the IT system controls.

- **IT Systems Development Controls** These controls relate to the development of the IT system. There should be controls to ensure that users' needs are addressed and that all system changes are approved. Typically, this will involve co-ordination between users and management, and experts who will be implementing and developing the computer system. All changes to the IT system should be authorised by management.
- **System Change Documentation** There should be adequate documentation of the system, which usually consists of either flowcharts or narrative descriptions, or a combination of both. For all system changes, there should also exist examples of input documentation and output documentation. Details on organisation charts, job descriptions for personnel, details of the system hardware and the location of equipment on the premises should also be included with the above documentation to ensure a clear understanding of the change is communicated.
- **System Change Testing and Training** There should also be adequate testing and training. Individual programs should be tested to ensure that they are working properly. Typically, this will involve the use of test data. This also involves the testing of the actual hardware in the system to ensure that it is functioning properly. All staff should also be trained in their jobs to carry out the tasks that will be allocated to them. Additionally, there should be a process for user acceptance (i.e. a process whereby the end user acknowledges receipt of training and accepts that the applications being implemented are sufficient for them to carry out their tasks).
- **Segregation of duties** This is a very basic internal control and should ensure that there is adequate segregation between systems maintenance, operators, data preparation and the end users' department. Segregation of duties is particularly important in ensuring that those who are responsible for making changes to IT systems and developing IT systems do not have access to the production or live systems.
- **File controls** These controls will ensure that only correct files are taken for processing, that files are maintained in a library and only given to authorised persons. Electronic files should also be properly labelled, and logged in and out from the library.

Application Controls

Under this category, there are three groups of controls, namely:
- data input controls;
- data processing controls; and
- data output controls.

These controls exist to support the IT system controls and, in turn, a sound system of internal control for the entity. These controls also provide the auditor with comfort that the recording, processing and the reports generated by the computer system are performed properly.

Unlike general controls, application controls are specific to particular IT applications and generally operate differently for each application, depending on the specific application or system used. For example, the internal controls surrounding the payroll function will be considered separately from the purchasing system or the revenue system.

Set out below in **Figure 9.2** is a summary of the types of controls expected at each stage in the data processing cycle.

FIGURE 9.2: COMPUTERISED ENVIRONMENT CONTROLS

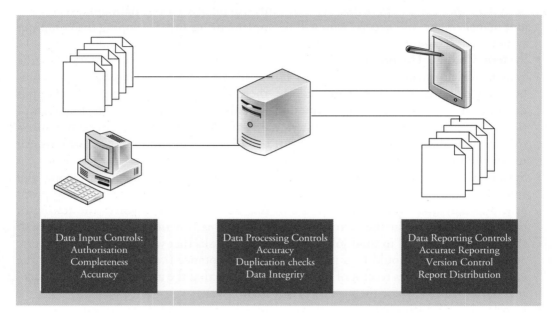

Data Input Controls:
Authorisation
Completeness
Accuracy

Data Processing Controls
Accuracy
Duplication checks
Data Integrity

Data Reporting Controls
Accurate Reporting
Version Control
Report Distribution

Data Input Controls

Input controls are extremely important as a lot of errors could occur at the input stage. These controls are designed to ensure that the input data has been authorised correctly, is complete, and accurate. If input errors are detected by the IT system, these need to be reviewed, corrected and resubmitted for inputting into the system again.

Approval workflows are often imbedded into the computer environment, whereby a request for approval is raised in the system and then the system, using a preconfigured approval strategy, routes the document to the individual in the organisation permitted to approve this type of transaction.

Authorisation

Each transaction should be properly authorised in accordance with management's instructions and general rules. Authorisation can occur and be evidenced in a number of ways, e.g. a password could be input into the system or a manual approval can occur through the stamping of a document or manual signature.

EXAMPLE 9.2: MANUAL VERSUS AUTOMATED APPROVAL

Take, for example, a bad debt request. The credit controller has put an uncollectable debt out to a debt-collection agency, which advises the credit controller that the organisation has gone into liquidation and no money is available to ordinary creditors. According to company policy, all bad debt write-offs should be approved by the head of sales and the CFO.

Manual Approval – the credit controller completes a manual bad debt write-off form, which she presents to the head of sales and CFO for physical sign-off. The credit controller then presents the approved form to the designated accounts receivable clerk, who applies the write-off to the customer's account on the system. Monthly, the credit controller compares the actual bad debts written off in the system to the approvals authorised by her, to ensure each write-off is complete, accurate and valid.

IT Automated Computerised Approval – the credit controller raises a bad debt request directly in the system. The system is configured to route the document to the head of sales and the CFO for approval. On log-in to the computer system, the head of sales and CFO are advised of a pending approval. Once both IT automated computerised approvals have been obtained, the bad debt write-off is automatically applied to the customer's account.

We can see from the above that the IT automated computerised approval: (a) reduces the number of steps involved in the process and so is more efficient; and (b) operates using all automated preventative controls, making it overall a more reliable process.

Data Accuracy and Completeness

These controls are designed to ensure that data being input to the IT application is complete and accurate. Specific controls include some of the following.

Control Name	Explanation	Example
Control Totals	Also known as 'batch check' totals. These controls include document or record counts (i.e. the number of documents or records to be processed).	A payroll clerk counts the number of overtime records to be entered and compares this to the actual number of overtime records input to the system.
Hash Totals	Hash totals are computed by adding together values that would not be typically added together, e.g. employee numbers, inventory code numbers, etc. These hash totals are only used for the purpose of control and for no other purpose.	Employee numbers are totalled before and after a payroll run in order to confirm that no employee records are missing.

| **Editing Checks** | These controls are intended to detect incorrect, unreasonable or incomplete data. They include the following:

• **Key Verification** – fields are restricted to certain data types.

• **Missing data check** – this ensures that all the data has been completely input, and that no fields are missing.

• **Check digit verification** Account numbers are verified using a predetermined mathematical calculation and matched to a check digit contained within the number. If it matches the check digit, the account number will be accepted as being a valid entry. | **Key verification** Data fields must be entered in a specified date format to avoid any incorrect data. When processing invoices, complete customer account codes, stock quotes, quantities, etc. are required.

Missing data check If any fields are missing, the input will be rejected for further review and follow-up. For example, you cannot complete an order without entering in the quantity of inventory.

Check digit verification Examples include credit card numbers, which include a check digit in order to recognise valid credit card numbers. |
| **Sequence Checks** | Checks sequentially numbered documents to ensure that there are no missing or duplicate sequence numbers. | Credit notes are processed in sequence and missing and duplicate sequence numbers are investigated. |

Data Processing Controls

Processing controls are designed to provide **reasonable assurance** that the computer processes have been performed as intended. They ensure that the transactions are not duplicated or lost or improperly changed in any way and that errors are identified and corrected on a timely basis.

These controls include the following.

- **Reasonableness checks** A reasonableness check will ensure that the item is reasonable, e.g. if customers usually order no more than six to eight items of a typical inventory item, and if the processed order is greater than eight, the computer will flag the order for follow-up to ensure it is a genuine and valid quantity.
- **Naming conventions** All files should follow a standard naming convention so that only the correctly named files are used in processing. For example, the file name may be matched to the operator's instructions before processing can start.
- **Before and after report** This report will show the number of entries that should be updated and the actual number of accounts that were updated. For example, if deliveries

were made to 100 different customers, the report will also show that 100 customer accounts were updated with invoices.
- **Control totals** – the computer checks that the sum of the totals of the input documents for each run matches the total processed amount in that run.

Data Output Controls

Data output (reporting) controls are designed to ensure that the processing has been correctly carried out, and the output reports are then distributed to authorised personnel only. These controls include the following:
- **Visual scanning** – this involves reading and scanning to see if the output looks reasonable, and could involve comparing actual results with estimated results and/or source documents being matched to output reports on a sample basis.
- **Reconciliation** – this involves the output totals being matched to input totals and processing totals by the various relevant departments within the organisation, for example, the user department and the computer department.

9.4 COMPUTER-ASSISTED AUDIT TECHNIQUES (CAATs)

Introduction

In **Section 9.3** the approach to identifying and testing relevant general and application-specific IT controls was discussed. Another area of consideration for the auditor is the use of computer software and computer techniques (computer-assisted audit techniques (CAATs)) to assist him in carrying out the audit of the financial statements.

Regardless of whether or not the auditor decides to test relevant IT controls, a decision may be made to use IT systems to support the testing of other areas of the audit. CAATs can impact on the audit procedures in two ways:

1. the auditor may wish to test the IT system controls to reduce the level of substantive testing; and
2. even if the IT System controls are not relied upon, the auditor may still call upon the support of IT applications (internal to the entity or external audit software) to help to carry out his focused substantive procedures. **Figure 9.3** below depicts this concept.

CAATs can be used to support the audit in a wide range of areas. In any area of the audit where there is a large volume of data, CAATs will provide a more comprehensive audit than the traditional methods of sampling or analytical review. Without CAATs, the auditor will usually select a sample of transactions for review; however, CAATs will allow for much greater coverage, and in many cases even 100% coverage. CAATs can even support the sample selection process by assisting with statistical sampling methods. The auditor, however, must consider the cost–benefit of using CAATs.

FIGURE 9.3: AUDITOR TESTING IN A COMPUTERISED ENVIRONMENT

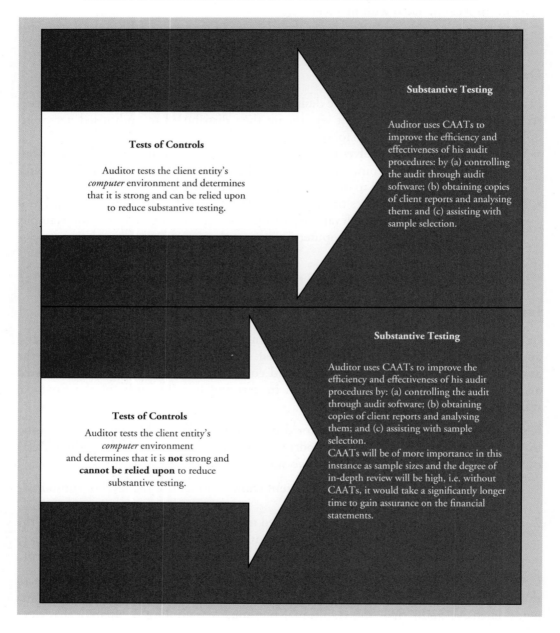

Tests of Controls

Auditor tests the client entity's *computer* environment and determines that it is strong and can be relied upon to reduce substantive testing.

Substantive Testing

Auditor uses CAATs to improve the efficiency and effectiveness of his audit procedures: by (a) controlling the audit through audit software; (b) obtaining copies of client reports and analysing them: and (c) assisting with sample selection.

Tests of Controls

Auditor tests the client entity's *computer* environment and determines that it is **not** strong and **cannot be relied upon** to reduce substantive testing.

Substantive Testing

Auditor uses CAATs to improve the efficiency and effectiveness of his audit procedures by: (a) controlling the audit through audit software; (b) obtaining copies of client reports and analysing them; and (c) assisting with sample selection.
CAATs will be of more importance in this instance as sample sizes and the degree of in-depth review will be high, i.e. without CAATs, it would take a significantly longer time to gain assurance on the financial statements.

Cost versus Benefit

Typically, CAATs are expensive to set up in the first year of the audit but are far more cost effective in the long run, as they can be used in future years (usually with only minor modifications). A key consideration for the auditor is the level of planning and preparation required, as it is critical that the use of CAATs is fully planned so that the software application used is correctly configured to conduct the necessary tests.

The **benefits** associated with CAATs generally far outweigh any cost, and include:

- CAATs can be used in the **assessment of the client entity's computer environment**. Audit software tools can be run to find various parameter settings that influence a client's security. These tools can then perform a comparison of the setting against the predefined security policy existing in that organisation.
- CAATs provide the auditor with the **ability to test the entire population** or a much greater part of the population than would be feasible using a manual sampling approach.
- **Common tests can be designed and programmed so that they can be repeated within the same audit entity or across the audits of different entities** and thus increase audit efficiency.
- The use of data analysis tools allows **scrutiny of transactions** and concentrated attention on erroneous and exceptional transactions, even when data volumes are huge. This can be done in a fraction of the time required for manual methods.
- Audit software can offer the auditor a **uniform, user-friendly interface** for performing audit testing, regardless of the data formats presented by the client entity's applications.
- The audit software can also **record exceptions existing in the audit process**, such as un-reviewed work, missing tests, etc. Additionally, advanced features of audit software can allow for certain routines (macros) to be programmed and therefore further improve audit effectiveness and efficiency.
- Attack and penetration testing can be performed by the auditor (particularly in an e-commerce environment) to detect vulnerabilities in networks.

Other Considerations in Using CAATs

In addition to carrying out a cost–benefit analysis, the auditor should also consider the following before he engages in the use of CAATs.

1. Maintaining Necessary Expertise

When using CAATs, the auditor would also need to consider the level of expertise needed among audit staff in performing the audit. While audit software encompasses many features, it cannot perform the audit on its own and relies on the inputs of the auditor in the same way that any computer system does. The designing of tests requires strong audit skills along with strong knowledge of the client entity, as well as expertise with the audit software.

2. Availability of the Necessary Information in a Useable Format

The auditor will need to inquire as to the downloadable formats available from the client entity to ensure that they can be used by the audit software or other application being used by the auditor. However, it should be noted that most CAATs packages can handle data in multiple formats and in most circumstances the software can be configured to handle available data.

3. Maintaining Sound Audit Software

Like any system implementation, the introduction of audit software is not without its complications. The client entity's IT staff may be reluctant to allow the auditor permission to access the production data being concerned that the audit software may interfere with the IT system. This is a valid concern for any IT department and the auditor needs to be confident that he has carried out the necessary testing and training on the audit software to minimise the risk of contaminating the client entity's IT system.

One common solution is for the auditor to work on a copy of the data instead of working in the live system, which greatly reduces the risk that data is contaminated and the risk of inadvertent changes to client IT system and/or data. Once implemented and operational, audit software, similar to any IT environment, will require maintenance and change management procedures to ensure it can be used year after year.

Substantive Testing

If the auditor determines.
- that the benefit of using CAATs outweighs the cost;
- that he has the necessary up-to-date expertise to use CAATs;
- that the client's environment and reports are suitable for CAATs; and
- if applicable, that he maintains sound audit software.

he may achieve significant efficiencies by using CAATs to assist with substantive testing.

In **substantive testing**, the auditor is trying to verify the truth and fairness of transactions and balances (completeness, accuracy, etc.) in the financial statements (see **Chapter 4**).

The amount of substantive testing that the auditor will perform will depend upon the results of the **tests of controls**. Where controls have been found to be ineffective or have not been tested, a greater level of substantive testing will be necessary.

There is a variety of ways in which CAATs can be used to support the audit approach and in this section we will discuss various types of substantive procedure that an auditor can perform using CAATs. For instance, in the audit of receivables, the auditor can extract a sample to be circularised and configure the program to print out the confirmation letters with the addresses and balances to be confirmed. The use of appropriate software provides the auditor with the ability to select a sample using an appropriate statistical approach, such as **monetary unit sampling** (MUS). (See also **Chapter 6**, Section 6.7.)

The CAATs software can also be configured to search for unusual items, such as large and unusual balances or credit balances in receivables balances. Other tests might include totalling the accounts receivable ledger and comparing it to the balance on the receivables account in the general ledger. In the review of receivables, the auditors may also use the audit software to *age* the receivables listing in order to help identify possible bad debts.

In the audit of payroll, the program could be used to recalculate the payroll cost for the year, which could then be agreed to the general ledger. It could identify employees who might have worked excessive hours for further follow-up by the auditor.

Some further examples of specific uses of CAATs in various financial cycles are provided below in **Figure 9.4**.

FIGURE 9.4: SPECIFIC USES OF CAATs – FURTHER EXAMPLES

Inventory	Non-current Fixed Assets	Purchases and Payroll
• Testing overhead allocations. • Checking the mathematical accuracy of the inventory records by multiplying the cost by the quantity. • Adding the total values of inventory items to come up with a total value of inventory included in the financial statements. • Identifying slow-moving items by comparing to sales records	• Analysing assets by different classes. • Re-performing depreciation calculations to ensure that they have been correctly calculated. • Verifying the mathematical accuracy of different asset classes and agree to the financial statements. • Selecting a sample of additions during the year for further testing. • Selecting a sample from the repairs and maintenance account for further testing to ensure that those items should not have been capitalised.	• Comparison of goods received with purchases orders as part of cut-off testing. • Identify any large or unusual purchases. • Identify any employees who are also suppliers. • Stratify purchases by month to detect unusual patterns.

9.5 E-COMMERCE

Introduction

Electronic commerce, or 'e-commerce', is the use of information systems and networks (such as the Internet) to conduct buying or selling activities. It has been one of the most significant business growth areas in recent years and it continues to expand and be an important source of business for many organisations.

A company selling products on its website is a commonly observed example of e-commerce. Other 'business-to-consumer' (B2C) examples of e-commerce include online banking, online booking systems and online advertising. In recent years, mobile technology is being used for e-commerce more frequently.

Many organisations also engage in 'business-to-business' (B2B) e-commerce. In addition to the examples given above, B2B e-commerce activities can also include electronic supply-chain management and electronic invoicing. For example, businesses may electronically submit orders to a supplier for goods, track fulfilment of their order and check the goods into inventory when they are delivered.

Key technology components of e-commerce are:
- websites or web applications;
- infrastructure (databases and servers) hosting web applications;
- browsers;
- networks (World Wide Web, wide-area networks and virtual private networks); and
- electronic funds transfer.

Considerations

When auditing a client entity that is involved in e-commerce, there are a number of important factors that the auditor should consider.

- **Complexity** In an online environment it is very likely that transactions will be much more complex than in a business that only engages in traditional trading techniques. The auditor will need to ensure that he is fully aware of the transaction flows in order to identify relevant risks and controls. He will also need to consider the existence of mobile technology-enabled trading.
- **Volume** For many e-commerce-enabled businesses, the volume of transactions is higher than traditional business channels. This can pose several difficulties for the auditor and may demand the use of CAATs or some such automated techniques in order to ensure appropriate coverage of the population.
- **Transaction Speed** In addition to the high volume of transactions, in the online environment transactions tend to be fully automated and completed in real-time or at a high speed. This usually means that the opportunity for manual intervention is limited, and controls must be fully automated. The auditor must rely on automated controls in order to obtain sufficient assurance.
- **Security** In an online environment, the need for appropriate security is vitally important. An e-commerce-enabled website is equivalent to a shop and should be secured appropriately. Businesses will typically be responsible for collecting sensitive information, such as credit card numbers and personal details, and will need to ensure that these are not lost or accessed by intruders. The Internet is fundamentally insecure and in addition to its responsibilities to its customers, the auditor will also need to ensure that the client entity has protected its own information assets.
- **Third Parties** In the e-commerce environment, there is increased use of third parties as outsourced partners to support the business. For example, many organisations rely on third parties to process payments on their behalf. In addition to considering the controls and practices at the client entity (auditee), the auditor may also need to understand and review the controls in place at relevant third-party organisations.
- **Systems Resilience** For many e-commerce organisations, the online channels of selling and purchasing are core to their business activities. A website being offline for a period of time is equivalent to a traditional organisation being forced to close a shop. Where systems stability issues exist, auditors should consider the impact that this will have on the client entity. Client entities that are reliant on technology must have appropriate disaster recovery and business continuity plans in place.

Auditing in an e-Commerce Environment

The approach taken to performing an audit of an entity that uses e-commerce is very similar to a standard IT audit approach. The primary difference is that the elements of the client entity's IT environment are accessed by external parties (customers, suppliers and other business partners). Rather than just facilitating and supporting the entity's business processes, these elements are core components.

When conducting the audit of an entity that uses e-commerce the steps outlined below should be consider by the audiotor.

- **Map Flow of Transactions and Data** As described above at **Section 9.3**, e-commerce can increase the complexity of processes. In order to identify key risks and controls, auditors should consider using process or data flow diagrams to map the flow of transactions.
- **IT General Controls (ITGCs)** Testing of ITGCs, as described above, should be completed for applications and infrastructures. Interfaces from externally facing websites and internal systems should be tested to obtain assurance that all data transferred is complete and accurate.
- **Application Controls** Data input controls are described above in **Section 9.3**, and are typical of the application controls that should be tested as part of an e-commerce audit.
- **Network Controls** With e-commerce, as key elements of the IT environment are externally facing, the auditor should consider engaging the services of information security technical specialists to perform a penetration test of websites and mobile applications. A 'penetration test' is where the actions of a computer hacker are simulated in order to identify security vulnerabilities or weaknesses. Firewalls are used by organisations to separate external Internet traffic from internal network traffic. The firewalls in place between externally facing technology and other internal systems are key controls. The processes in place for managing firewall rules should be tested as part of an e-commerce audit.

Electronic Data Interchange (EDI)

Electronic data interchange (EDI) is a system often used to support business B2B e-commerce by facilitating the transmission of data between partner organisations. Data files (such as orders or invoices) are exported from the business applications systems used by the organisation, translated into a pre-agreed standardised format and uploaded to a value added network (VAN) used by the group of business partners. A number of checks can be performed on the files being transmitted, including: field validation (to confirm, for example, that alphabetic characters are not included in a numeric field, such as phone number); order number sequence checks; duplication checks; and delivery checks.

When auditing a company that is involved in EDI, there are some important factors that the auditor should consider.

- **Lack of a 'paper trail'** Electronic data exchange results in the reduction of a paper trail, or 'hard copy' documentation, which means the auditor must test the controls of the system to gain sufficient appropriate audit evidence. It is unlikely, due to the large volume of transactions, that every transaction can be audited; thus, the auditor tests the internal controls to identify the possibility of instigating unauthorised transactions.

- **Uncontrolled changes** Uncontrolled changes could be ruinous to any system using electronic data exchange because of the absence of an adequate paper trail and, therefore, no physical document examination by management. The very characteristics that make EDI appealing because of improved efficiencies cause the auditor concern if the audited entity has not established effective controls over the whole EDI system. Auditors may seek to establish whether all changes have been authorised by management and that there is a paper trail of all changes, which has been inspected by management. If the auditor detects any evidence that uncontrolled changes have taken place, he might want to record that information in his letter to management and advise management that any uncontrolled changes can impact on the financial information.

9.6 CLOUD COMPUTING

Introduction

Cloud computing is an emerging technology in commercial computing. It enables distribution of computing tasks to a shared pool of resources, which can be accessed quickly with a minimal amount of effort for management. Cloud computing provides easy access to information systems services by combining information systems infrastructure and applications that can be retrieved through the Internet. There are five essential characteristics of cloud computing as shown in **Figure 9.5** below and discussed in detail thereafter.

On Demand Self-service This is the availability of cloud services on demand. The users can individually access services at times convenient to them. In such an environment, the user accesses the cloud services in question via an online control panel.

FIGURE 9.5: FIVE CHARACTERISTICS OF CLOUD COMPUTING

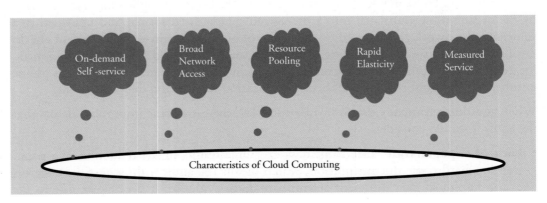

Broad Network Access Services are accessible over the Internet through a range of platforms, such as laptops, smart phones and personal digital assistants (PDAs (tablets)).

Resource Pooling The provider pools resources to serve multiple clients, which are configured to meet clients' individual needs.

Rapid Elasticity The provider can swiftly scale up and rapidly release services and resources.

Measured Service The use of resources by clients can be monitored, controlled and reported on by the provider.

Audit Considerations

When auditing a company that is involved in cloud computing, there are three important factors that the auditor should consider.

1. **Access** The auditor should test the controls used by the company to restrict access to authorised individuals only. He should consider how management uses authentication and authorisation methods to control access (e.g. if management uses passwords, the auditor must consider who controls the issuing of the passwords, how often they are reset and how strong the passwords are).
2. **Data Protection** The auditor must consider if a breach in data protection has occurred, and whether that breach affected the audited entity's financial performance, its reputation and whether the breach impacted on regulatory requirements. The auditor will examine the policies and procedures developed by the client to protect data stored by a third party.
3. **Technology Risks** Due to technologies constantly evolving, with a lack of standardised rules in how they should integrate, the auditor must consider if the client entity's technology has become obsolete or if it requires substantial investment to be updated. The auditor must also consider management's use of monitoring tools and the use of period back-ups.

9.7 CONCLUSION

In this chapter, we have seen that auditing in a computerised environment is very similar to auditing in a manual environment in that the auditor still needs to obtain sufficient and appropriate audit evidence to support his opinion.

Though the basic approach is very similar, the auditor will have to ensure that staff are properly trained and have the knowledge to be able to audit in a computerised environment.

The nature of the tests, i.e. **tests of controls** and **substantive tests**, is also similar to performing an audit in a non-computerised environment. The major difference is that the auditor has to use the computer in performing his tests, in both tests of controls and substantive tests.

SUMMARY OF LEARNING OBJECTIVES

Having studied this chapter on auditing in a computerised environment and e-commerce you should:

Learning Objective 1 Understand the IT audit process, and the steps that should be taken when key controls are automated.

Organisations are increasingly reliant on IT systems. Systems can vary in size and complexity, from off-the-shelf accounting systems to customised **ERP** systems. The auditor will be required to consider the role of the computer systems used by their clients and design the audit plan in order to evaluate the relevant controls in information systems.

The IT audit approach is **risk-based** in nature. Auditors should review processes to identify risks and key control activities. Due to the lack of a paper trail, the auditor needs to **audit through the computer instead of around it**, which means that he will require a greater understanding of the internal controls of information systems.

General IT controls areas include: IT security; user access; IT operations; and change control. They relate to the IT computerised systems in their entirety and not just to a specific IT application. **Application controls** are specific aspects of functionality of process steps. If the auditor believes that general controls in the IT computerised system are weak, he is unlikely to test application controls and instead will take a wholly substantive approach.

Learning Objective 2 Understand the meaning of 'computer-assisted audit techniques (CAATs).

While CAATs can be used to improve the coverage and efficiency as well as the effectiveness of audits, there is a cost incurred when implementing them. The use of CAATs at the substantive stage becomes more important to the auditor when he deems the controls around the computer environment to be weak, as he will be required to perform more substantive testing, which will increase the size of the samples.

Learning Objective 3 Be able to consider the cost–benefit relationship of applying CAATs.

Typically, CAATs are expensive to set up in the first year of the audit, but are far more cost-effective in the longer term as they can be used in future years (usually with only minor modifications). The main benefits to be derived from the use of CAATs is that they can save time and produce more accurate testing results, and thus support the auditor's aim to perform efficient and effective audits.

Learning Objective 4 Understand the impact e-commerce and cloud computing has on businesses and on the auditor.

The IT audit approach can be used when assessing controls in an e-commerce environment. Elements of the IT environment will be externally facing and accessible from the Internet (or other networks), and this increases the risk profile of those systems. Businesses involved in e-commerce cause specific difficulties for the auditor due, primarily, to the lack of a paper trail and reduced security when doing business on the Internet. The area of e-commerce has expanded further in recent years with the increased use of electronic data interchange (**EDI**) and the more recent explosion of **cloud computing**.

QUESTIONS

Self-test Questions

9.1 Distinguish between general IT controls and application controls.

9.2 What are the benefits associated with using CAATs?

9.3 What important factors does the auditor need to consider when auditing a company that is involved in e-commerce?

9.4 When classifying the extent of the client entity's use of computer system, what three areas might you consider?

9.5 What are the main objectives that should be considered in relation to the audit of a data processing environment?

9.6 List the three computer control categories.

9.7 List three controls that might be used to confirm the accurate conversion of data from one system to another.

9.8 List some relevant tests where CAATs might be used in the testing of inventory.

Review Questions

(See Suggested Solutions to Review Questions in **Appendix D**.)

Question 9.1

You are the audit senior working on the audit of Complex Computers Ltd, a technology company involved in the development of computer software and the manufacture of IT hardware. The company relies heavily on its IT systems to manage and operate the business. It has just implemented a new accounting system, which is used to support and record all of its financial transactions.

At a recent meeting with the company's chief financial officer (CFO), your audit partner informed the CFO that this year an IT audit would be conducted.

Requirement

(a) The CFO has asked you for a short overview of the key aims and objectives of an IT audit.

(b) As part of your discussions at the meeting, you mentioned that there are three main areas on which an IT audit would focus. The CFO would like you to list these three areas again and outline the key risks and controls for one of those areas listed.

(c) The audit partner has also noted that the team will use computer-assisted audit techniques (CAATs) as part of this year's audit and would like you to briefly describe the
benefits of using CAATs.

Question 9.2

The incumbent auditor of Large Company Ltd (Large Company) has reached retirement
age and the directors are planning to appoint a new auditor to take over the appointment.
The directors of Large Company have decided to put the audit out to tender and your
firm, Smith & Smith, is interested in being considered.

The directors have told you that they require an auditor who can demonstrate clear, jargon-free knowledge of the most modern auditing techniques. In particular, one of the
non-executive directors has told the Board how the auditor of his own company uses computer-assisted audit techniques (CAATs). The directors of Large Company have requested
you to give them an authoritative definition of CAATs and a jargon-free explanation of
how you, as a potential auditor, might use CAATs specifically in relation to the substanti-
ation of Large Company's year-end receivables balance.

The directors have provided you with the following details regarding receivables.
1. The directors regard inventory as one of their most important assets. Accounting for
   inventory is carried out through a bespoke software package that is three years old. The
   package has been trouble-free and the directors are very happy with it. The package is
   fully integrated with the general ledger.
2. Large Company analyses its inventory accounts as follows:

	€000
Raw materials and consumables	9,320
Work in progress	12,530
Finished goods and goods in transit	27,924
	49,774

The directors regard any amount greater than €1 million as material.

Requirement On the assumption that your firm has been appointed auditors, draft a letter to the Board of Directors of Large Company explaining how you would apply CAATs
to the inventory ledger of the company. Your letter should deal with each of the following
issues:
(a) the general application of CAATs; and
(b) the application of CAATs in the specific circumstances of Large Company.

Question 9.3

Application controls in a computer system may be classed as either 'input', 'processing' or
'reporting' (output) controls. Such controls, together with general IT controls, help ensure
the completeness, integrity and accuracy of information in a computer system.

Requirement

(a) Define the terms 'input controls', 'processing controls' and 'reporting (output) controls' and give one example of each.
(b) Outline the key areas that should be considered when assessing general IT security controls.

Question 9.4

In most organisations a significant amount of accounting information is held on computers in various electronic formats, including spreadsheets and databases. Poor controls may lead to sensitive commercial information ending up in the hands of unauthorised personnel.

Requirement

(a) Explain, in relation to computer systems, what is meant by:
  • physical access controls; and
  • logical access controls.
(b) Set out examples of controls that might be used within a computer system program to ensure that only valid changes are made to computer systems.
(c) Give three examples of controls that might be deployed in a computer system to detect any unauthorised access.

Question 9.5

Auditors use computer-assisted auditing techniques (CAATs) as an economical way of carrying out substantive tests for large audit clients.

Requirement Give two different examples of CAATs that could be used to make substantive testing more efficient and effective in respect of the audit of each of the following areas for a large audit client:

(a) Sales and trade receivables;
(b) Inventories;
(c) Purchases and trade payables;
(d) Wages and salaries;
(e) Fixed assets (PPE).

Question 9.6

You are the audit senior engaged on the audit of the Silver Birch Hotel, a client of your firm of Chartered Accountants & Registered Auditors.

The Silver Birch Hotel is owned by a partnership of individuals who have employed a general manager to operate the hotel on their behalf. The partnership meets on a quarterly basis to review the hotel's performance. It is a four-star hotel, which opened for the first time in April 1999, and comprises 60 bedrooms, a leisure centre, a function room, a lounge, a bar and a restaurant. The accounting system is a state-of-the-art integrated point-of-sale system, with electronic recording of reservations, food and drink sales, bedroom sales, telephone and laundry.

The General Manager has informed you that, despite the significant impact on operations arising from the economic downturn and the slowdown in tourist traffic, the hotel's performance was satisfactory and he is confident about current and future trading prospects.

You are provided with the following information:

	Year Ended 30 April 2012 €000	Year Ended 30 April 2011 €000
Revenue		
Rooms	220	120
Bar	380	400
Restaurant	510	550
Other	75	80
	1,185	1,150
Gross Profit	408 (34%)	318 (28%)
Depreciation	560	500
Marketing Expenditure	120	250
Payroll costs – management	120	150
Security and other building-related costs	40	50
Other costs	65	80
	905	1,030
Net loss	(497)	(712)

Requirement

(a) With regard to the Silver Birch Hotel, set out the risks and benefits associated with the use of a computerised system for the recording and processing of the following transactions:
- bedroom revenue;
- bar and restaurant revenue.
(b) Set out three areas where computer-assisted audit techniques (CAATs) could be used on the audit of the Silver Birch Hotel and explain clearly the benefits of using each of the techniques you have outlined.

Question 9.7

IT systems require continuous upgrade and improvement. Most companies have spent significant funds on IT and now rely heavily on IT to support all aspects of their business, including the financial systems. The maintenance of these business systems is a key function of any IT department. Furthermore, as software and hardware products are upgraded and improved to later and newer versions, the process of change needs to be carefully managed.

Elegant Ltd is a client of the firm of Chartered Accountants and Registered Auditors in which you work. You have just had a phone call from the Managing Director, informing you that he believes information may have been lost as a result of a recent upgrade to the IT systems.

As a result of this issue, he has decided to initiate a review of IT development and maintenance and is seeking your advice.

Requirement
(a) Advise the Managing Director on each of the following matters:
  (i) the controls that should be put in place for the maintenance of computer systems;
  (ii) the steps which you, as auditor, would take in order to carry out a review of the IT development controls.
(b) On hearing of this issue, the audit partner had also asked you to review the operational controls in the company. What are the main headings under which you would report?

Question 9.8

Pal Pay Ltd (Pal Pay) has been a client of your firm since its establishment two years ago. Pal Pay sells a range of products online and offers all of its products in an e-commerce environment.

Requirement
(a) The audit partner has asked if you could provide an outline of the key areas that should be considered as part of the audit in this e-commerce environment.
(b) You have also been asked to provide the finance director with an overview of the key control considerations that should be implemented as part of the delivery of services online. In particular, the finance director has asked about security considerations.

10

USING THE WORK OF OTHERS

LEARNING OBJECTIVES

Having studied this chapter on the auditor's use of the work of others you should:
1. understand the external auditor's responsibility when using the work of others;
2. understand the options open to the auditor to gain an understanding of controls in place at service organisations which impact on the entity's financial statement transactions;
3. understand the difference between internal and external audit;
4. understand the work of the internal auditor;
5. be able to identify independence issues connected to the internal auditor; and
6. understand the audit procedures that the external auditor must carry out with respect to the work of others.

CHECKLIST OF RELEVANT STANDARDS

The relevant standards covered in this chapter are:
- ISA (UK and Ireland) 315 *Identifying and Assessing the Risks of Material Misstatement Through Understanding of the Entity and Its Environment* (ISA 315);
- ISA (UK and Ireland) 330 *The Auditor's Responses to Assessed Risks* (ISA 330);

- ISA (UK and Ireland) 402 *Audit Considerations Relating to an Entity Using a Service Organisation* (ISA 402);
- ISA (UK and Ireland) 610 *Using the Work of Internal Auditors* (ISA 610);
- ISA (UK and Ireland) 620 *Using the Work of an Auditor's Expert* (ISA 620).

KEY TERMS AND DEFINITIONS FOR THIS CHAPTER

Auditor's Expert   If expertise in a field other than accounting or auditing is necessary to obtain sufficient appropriate audit evidence, the auditor shall determine whether to use the work of an auditor's expert.

Complementary User Entity Controls   Controls that the service organisation assumes, in the design of its service, will be implemented by user entities in the description of its systems.

Governance   The combination of processes and structures implemented by the board to inform, direct, manage and monitor the activities of the organisation toward the achievement of its objectives.

Internal Audit   The process designed, implemented and maintained by **those charged with governance**, management and other personnel to provide **reasonable assurance** about the achievement of an entity's objectives with regard to reliability of financial reporting, effectiveness and efficiency of operations and compliance with applicable laws and regulations. The term 'control' refers to any aspect of one or more components of internal control.

Internal Audit Activity   "A department, division, team of consultants or other practitioner(s) that provides independent, objective assurance and consulting services designed to add value and improve organisations' operations. The internal audit activity helps an organisation accomplish its objectives by bringing a systematic, disciplined approach to evaluate and improve the effectiveness of governance, risk management and control procedures."[1]

Internal Audit Independence   "The freedom from conditions that threaten the ability of the internal audit activity to carry out internal audit responsibilities in an unbiased manner."[2]

Service Auditor   An auditor who, at the request of the **service organisation**, provides an assurance report on the controls of that organisation.

Service Organisation   A third-party organisation (or element of a third-party organisation) that provides services to user entities that are part of those entities' information systems relevant to financial reporting.

---

[1] Source: Institute of Internal Auditors, *International Standards for the Professional Practice of Internal Auditing Standards*, October 2010.
[2] *Ibid.*

> **User Auditor** An auditor who audits and reports on the financial statements of a **user entity**.
>
> **User Entity** A client entity is referred to as a user entity when it outsources a key function impacting on the financial statements (for example, when a client entity outsources its payroll function it is known as a user entity).

10.1 INTRODUCTION

The auditor cannot be expected to be an expert in all matters related to the financial statements and, in some instances due to proximity or time, he may need to call on 'the work of others'. For example:

- When reviewing the inventory of an art gallery, the auditor cannot be expected to competently value the associated works of art and as such he may call on an expert's help.
- When faced with a service organisation providing services to the client entity, and that service represents controls that relate to the client entity's financial statements, the auditor will need to look to the service organisation to obtain the information needed to support his audit procedures. This may involve using a third party to confirm the sound operation of those controls.
- When auditing the financial statements of a client entity that has an internal audit function, the auditor may find that he can use the work of the internal auditor to reduce his own work or, alternatively, use the services of one of the internal audit members to assist him with his work.

Before considering the auditor's use of the work of others, it is important to remember that the auditor has sole responsibility for the audit opinion expressed and that responsibility is not reduced by the auditor's use of another's work. The standards dealt with in this chapter outline the degree to which the auditor can rely on the use of the work of others but in no way diminish the responsibility of the auditor in the expression of an opinion.

Section 10.2 discusses the auditor's approach when the entity uses a '**service organisation**' for a key task that impacts on the financial statements. Guidance on this topic is covered by ISA (UK and Ireland) 402 *Audit Considerations Relating to an Entity Using a Service Organisation* (ISA 402).

In **Section 10.3** we will consider how the external auditor might use the '**internal audit**' department in place at the client entity, as well as discuss what is required of the external auditor when considering whether to use the work of the internal audit department. Guidance on this topic is provided by ISA (UK and Ireland) 610 *Using the Work of Internal Auditors* (ISA 610).

Finally, in **Section 10.4** we will discuss the provisions of ISA (UK and Ireland) 620 *Using the Work of an Auditor's Expert* (ISA 620), which provides guidance for the external auditor on the use of an '**auditor's expert**'.

10.2 ENTITY'S USE OF SERVICE ORGANISATIONS

Introduction

ISA (UK and Ireland) 315 *Identifying and Assessing the Risks of Material Misstatement Through Understanding of the Entity and Its Environment* (ISA 315, para 12) and ISA (UK and Ireland) 330 *The Auditor's Responses to Assessed Risks* (ISA 330, para 8) both address the need for the auditor to obtain an understanding of the entity, including internal control relevant to the audit, sufficient to identify and assess the risks of material misstatement and for designing and performing further audit procedures responsive to those risks.

An issue arises for the auditor, however, **where certain procedures are not carried out by the entity but instead by a service organisation employed by the entity.** ISA 402 "deals with the user auditor's responsibility to obtain sufficient appropriate audit evidence when a user entity uses the services of one or more service organizations" (ISA 402, para 1).

Understanding Services Provided by a Service Organisation

ISA 402, paragraph 9, outlines the requirements of the auditor when gaining an understanding of a service organisation in use by the entity, which include:
(a) the 'nature' and 'significance' of services provided, including their effect on the user entity's internal control;
(b) the "nature and materiality of the transactions processed or … affected by the service organisation";
(c) the "degree of interaction between the activities of the service organisation and those of the user entity";
(d) the nature of the relationship between the two parties and the contractual terms that govern the activities undertaken by the service organisation;
(e) the impact on the auditor's working arrangements where the client entity's accounting records are maintained by the service organisation.

The management of the entity that is using the service organisation must satisfy itself as to the effectiveness of the design and implementation of the service organisation's controls that are relevant to its operations, in the same way in which it satisfies itself with respect to its own internal controls. The auditor should then assess the entity's documented procedures with respect to the service organisation. Should he be unable to obtain this understanding from the **user entity**, ISA 402, paragraph 12, advises the following activities:
• obtaining a 'Type 1' or 'Type 2' report – see below;
• directly contacting the service organisation to gain the necessary understanding;
• visiting the service organisation and applying similar audit procedures to those performed on the entity itself to obtain necessary information about the relevant controls; or
• using a third-party auditor to provide the necessary information.

Type 1 and Type 2 Reports

If the auditor is to rely on the controls in place at the service organisation, which support transactions and balances in the client entity's financial statements, then he is going to: (a) need to obtain an understanding of those controls; and (b) should he wish to test them, he is going to need a method of doing so.

Type 1 and Type 2 reports form audit evidence to support the **user auditor's** understanding about the design and implementation of controls at the service organisation.
- **Type 1 Report** This involves the use of a **service auditor** to report on the description and design of the service provider's controls with respect to the entity.
- **Type 2 Report** The use of a service auditor to report on the description, design **and operating effectiveness** of the service provider's controls with respect to the entity.

Before relying upon a Type 1 or Type 2 report, the auditor **must be satisfied as to the service auditor's professional competence and independence from the service organisation** as well as give consideration to the adequacy of the standards under which the Type 1 or Type 2 report was issued.

Responding to the Assessed Risks of Material Misstatement

Should the auditor be unable to obtain sufficient appropriate audit evidence in the records held at the client's premises to support the relevant financial statement assertions, then *he* should review the records of the service organisation or have another auditor perform those procedures on his behalf.

Where the testing of controls is necessary, and records are held at the service organisation, and the auditor cannot carry out that testing himself, then the auditor will require a **Type 2 report**. The principal auditor remains responsible for the opinion provided on the financial statements and for this reason he **must be satisfied that the Type 2 report constitutes sufficient appropriate audit evidence with respect to the competence and professionalism of its preparer and its form and content**.

Should the auditor be unable to obtain **sufficient appropriate audit evidence** with regard to service organisations, then he shall modify his report as appropriate in accordance with ISA (UK and Ireland) 705 *Modifications to the Opinion in the Independent Auditor's Report – Revised October 2012* (ISA 705) (see also **Chapter 19**).

10.3 USING THE WORK OF INTERNAL AUDITORS

Introduction

The *UK Corporate Governance Code* (the Code) emphasises the need for an **audit committee,** stating:

> "The board should establish an audit committee of at least three, or in the case of smaller companies two, independent non-executive directors." (Provision C.3.1)[3]

---

[3] Financial Reporting Council, *The UK Corporate Governance Code*, September 2012.

- Provision C.3.2 of the Code outlines a number of key responsibilities with respect to audit committees, two of which are relevant to our discussion on internal audit: "to review the company's internal financial controls and, unless expressly addressed by a separate board risk committee composed of independent directors, or by the board itself, to review the company's internal control and risk management systems;
- to monitor and review the effectiveness of the company's internal audit function."

The audit committee is therefore responsible for the activities of the **internal audit** function. Provision C.3.6 of the Code advises that,

> "The audit committee should monitor and review the effectiveness of the internal audit activities. Where there is no internal audit function, the audit committee should consider annually whether there is a need for an internal audit function and make a recommendation to the board, and the reasons for the absence of such a function should be explained in the relevant section of the annual report."

Those acting within the internal audit function are not required to obtain qualifications in internal audit and often are appointed due to their expertise in a particular area. Individuals can, however, seek to obtain a qualification in internal audit through the Institute of Internal Auditors, which is the internationally recognised authority and a principal educator with respect to internal audit.

Before proceeding, consider **Table 10.1**, which highlights the key differences between internal auditors and external auditors:

TABLE 10.1: KEY DIFFERENCES BETWEEN INTERNAL AUDITORS AND EXTERNAL AUDITORS

	Internal Auditors	External Auditors
Report to:	Management (audit committee).	Shareholders.
Objective:	Varies, depending on type of assignment which can include: • value for money assignments (3Es – economy, efficiency and effectiveness); • audit of IT systems; • financial audit; • **Sarbanes–Oxley (SOX) audit**; and • operational assignments.	To issue an opinion on the truth and fairness of the financial statements in accordance with an applicable financial reporting framework.
Report format:	Varies, depending on assignment type.	Independent auditor's report.
Status:	Usually an employee of the entity (although could be an outsourced function).	Independent of the entity.

| Governed by: | Institute of Internal Audit (although an internal auditor may operate without any qualifications). | Irish Auditing and Accounting Supervisory Board (IAASA)/ Financial Reporting Council (FRC)/ Companies Acts (in order to act as auditor, the individual must have prescribed qualifications and be a member of an approved recognised accounting body, e.g. ICAI). |

Activities Undertaken by Internal Auditors

As more fully discussed in **Chapter 8**, 'Controls and Controls Testing', advice on the application of a strong internal control system is provided by the Committee of Sponsoring Organizations of the Treadway Commission (COSO), which has outlined five key components of internal control and the importance of the internal audit department is evident throughout all of the components. These five components are:
- the control environment;
- the risk assessment process;
- the control activities;
- IT systems and communication; and
- monitoring activities.

Typical activities in which an internal auditor engages include:
- observation and reporting on risk assessment exercises;
- participation in and the planning of internal audit engagements;
- forming recommendations on improvements to weaknesses within the entity;
- participating in the implementation of recommended procedures;
- involvement in the identification and monitoring of key performance indicators (KPIs);
- participation in the annual audit planning process; and
- preparation of materials for and attendance at audit committee meetings.

The Importance of Internal Audit

As defined by the European Confederation of Institutes of Internal Audit (ECIIA):
"Internal auditing is an independent, objective assurance and consulting activity designed to add value and improve an organisation's operations. It helps an organisation accomplish its objectives by bringing a systematic, disciplined approach to evaluate and improve the effectiveness of risk management, control and governance processes."[4]

---

[4] European Confederation of Institutes of Internal Auditing (ECIIA). See http://www.eciia.eu/about-us/vision-and-mission-0

Risk information gathered by external auditors is usually limited to financial reporting risks and does not include information on the way senior management and the board/audit committee are managing/monitoring the entity's strategic, business and compliance risk. Additionally, the European Commission's argument for reform (as expressed in its Green Paper on corporate governance in financial institutions), highlighted in the ECIIA's magazine *European Governance*, argues: "while corporate governance did not directly cause the crisis, 'the lack of effective control mechanisms contributed to excessive risk-taking on the part of financial institutions.' Moreover, it says, the crisis revealed that boards of directors and their regulators 'rarely comprehended either the nature or scale of the risks they were facing'."[5] For this reason internal audit is better placed to make these assessments.

The Institute of Internal Auditors' (IIA) "Position Paper: The Three Lines of Defense in Effective Risk Management and Control" (January 2013) describes how internal audit is regarded as the last line of defence in effective risk and management control. The first line of defence, naturally, is that of operational management, which has ownership, responsibility and accountability for directly assessing, controlling and mitigating risk. The second line of defence consists of the activities covered by the components of the control environment (see **Chapter 8**, Section 8.2) and essentially oversees the activities of the first line of defence. Internal audit is then considered the third line of defence. The independence and risk-based approach provided by the internal audit department provide comfort to the board of directors with respect to the entity's management of risk and the effectiveness of the first and second lines of defence.

In addition to the above, the internal audit activity adds value to the organisation by providing objective and relevant **assurance**. The internal audit department also contributes to effective and efficient governance, risk-management and control processes.

From our discussion of fraud in **Chapter 3**, and specifically the fraud cases over the last decade included at **Table 3.2**, one can see that fraud is on the rise. Internal audit is in a unique position with respect to its access to and in-depth knowledge of the organisation, including its financial information, and, as illustrated in the WorldCom scandal of 2002, which was uncovered by an internal auditor, can play an instrumental role in the detection of fraud.

The Independence of Internal Audit

Chapter 2 outlined the importance of the independence of the external auditor, and the ethical code that governs internal auditors requires similar levels of independence from the internal auditor.

The IIA's **Code of Ethics** provides principles relevant to the profession and practice of internal auditing, and **Rules of Conduct** that describe behaviour expected of internal auditors. The Code of Ethics applies to both individuals and entities that provide internal audit services, the purpose being to promote an ethical culture in the global profession of internal auditing.

---

[5] Baker, N "Reforming Governance", *European Governance*, (2011) Issue 20, pp.5-8

Being independent, however, is somewhat more difficult for the internal auditor due to his direct employment by the entity. If we consider **Chapter 2**, where we identified the threats to external auditor independence, we can apply these to the independence issues facing the internal auditor. This is considered in **Table 10.2** below.

TABLE 10.2: THREATS TO THE INTERNAL AUDITOR'S INDEPENDENCE

Self-interest Threat	The internal auditor has his remuneration package agreed within the organisation. Quite often, the individual to whom the internal auditor reports will influence, if not dominate, the performance reviews of the internal auditor. For this reason it is essential that the head internal auditor reports directly to the audit committee. Consider a situation where the internal auditor reports directly to, *say*, the CFO and identifies a control failing or even a fraud with respect to the CFO or his department. A **self-interest threat** arises due to the internal auditor's concern for his remuneration or possibly his job should he report failings with respect to his superior.
	Two key considerations need to be addressed: 1. the internal audit department's line of reporting; and 2. the bonus targets imposed (which should not be based on a reduced number of findings, as this could encourage the wrong behaviour).
Self-review Threat (usually brought on through longevity of association)	A **self-review threat** can arise in two key instances with respect to the internal audit function. 1. the auditor has worked as internal auditor in the organisation for a number of years and finds an error or fraud which has existed for many years and gone undetected by the internal audit department. The internal auditor may be reluctant to highlight the issue due to fear he will be reprimanded for not identifying it earlier; or 2. the internal auditor throughout his time has contributed to the recommendation and implementation of controls and, on occasion, has offered advice to various departments on the execution of their duties. He now finds a control weakness in a process designed and implemented by himself. Will he report it, considering he is partially to blame for its existence?
Familiarity Threat	It is difficult to work in any organisation and not become familiar and even friendly with one's colleagues. On identification of an error or fraud connected to a close colleague, will the internal auditor disclose it?
	It is important either to rotate the heads of internal audit around the group or, alternatively, impose internal independent audit reviews of the work performed by the local internal audit department.

Intimidation Threat	The head of internal audit will often sit on the line of authority below that of senior management and his superiors may intimidate him into not reporting certain instances of fraud or error.
	The audit committee should ensure the entity enforces the availability of a whistleblowing hotline to permit the anonymous reporting of concerns over fraud or error.

Current Issues Surrounding Internal Audit

The Sarbanes–Oxley Act (SOX)

The Enron and WorldCom scandals in the USA (both companies were listed on the New York Stock Exchange) resulted in the introduction of the Sarbanes–Oxley Act in 2002, and specifically section 404. This Act required **those charged with corporate governance** to formally declare (in an annual report) that they believe adequate accounting controls are in place in the organisation and declare any material deficiencies in the company's internal controls. In order to gain this comfort, they needed to perform **'SOX' audits** (which involve the documentation, evaluation, testing and monitoring of their internal controls over financial reporting). In order to carry out such a task, many organisations have turned to their internal audit departments (or introduced one to tackle the issue where no internal audit department existed). The attestation made by the directors must be audited by an independent external auditor. This requirement only exists for companies listed on the New York Stock Exchange or subsidiaries of such listings.

UK Corporate Governance Code

With a close eye on governance, general public interest in this area has been on the rise following the economic downturn and the loss of confidence in certain banks' and directors' ability to operate with integrity, which means the role of the internal audit department is becoming increasingly important. Additionally, the volume of large-scale company collapses is driving the question: where were internal audit in all of this and how much of the failure lies at their doorstep? While the internal audit department already features in the *UK Corporate Governance Code*, there is no doubt we will see increased provisions directly associated with the internal audit function.

ECIIA Findings

The European Confederation of Institutes of Internal Auditing (ECIIA) has carried out a review of corporate governance codes in its member bodies and identified the following key issues for internal auditors.
- **Presence** To date, 90% of EU Member States now either require or recommend the presence of an internal audit function in listed companies, with it being compulsory within the financial institutions sector.

- **Regulation**, however, continues to be loose with regard to the effectiveness of the audit function and also with regard to essential requisites, such as independence and scope.
- **Slashed resources** Cost-cutting is a priority for most organisations; unfortunately, too often management sees internal audit as a non-value-adding function and as such has slashed resources in this area.

Protection of the Whistleblower

In Ireland, the Prevention of Corruption (Amendment) Act 2010 ('the 2010 Act') aims to improve the strength of anti-corruption legislation while providing specific '**protection for the whistleblower**'. Throughout the world, people are generally afraid of being penalised by their employers if they 'blow the whistle'. Generally speaking, those who are most aware, or likely to be aware, of fraud are those in the internal audit department, therefore such protection will be welcomed by them. The Act, however, currently only covers whistleblowing relating to public sector offices/departments; thus, for now at least, the internal audit departments of private or listed companies will have to comply with the IIA's Code of Ethics, trusting that no retribution is sought by aggrieved management.

External Auditor Considerations with Respect to the Internal Audit Function

Quite often the activities of the internal audit department can be used by the external auditors to form part of their audit evidence. ISA (UK and Ireland) 610 *Using the Work of Internal Auditors* (ISA 610) provides guidance to the external auditor on the use of the work of the internal auditor. Before relying on the work of the internal auditor, the external auditor must establish whether or not the work of the internal auditor is adequate for the purposes of the audit. If it is deemed adequate, he must plan the nature timing and extent of audit procedures that are impacted upon by the work of the internal auditor. In deciding whether or not to use the work of the internal auditor, the external auditor will take into consideration the following:

- the existence of an internal audit charter, which defines the internal audit functions purpose, authority and responsibility;
- whether or not the results of the internal audit activity's work achieve the purpose and responsibility included in the internal audit charter;
- whether or not the internal audit function conforms with the definition of internal auditing or performs some other activities;
- the existence of quality communication between the internal audit function and those charged with governance (accurate, objective, clear, concise, constructive, complete and timely);
- the existence of adequate documentation to support conclusions and engagements results;
- whether individuals operating within the internal audit department demonstrate conformance with the IIA's Code of Ethics; and
- whether the internal auditors have the technical competence to carry out the internal audit role.

ISA 610 outlines the following audit procedures that may be carried out by the external auditor prior to relying on the work of an internal audit team. These include:
- Examination of items already examined by the internal auditors;
- Examination of other similar items; and
- Observation of procedures performed by the internal auditors." (ISA 610, para A6)

Such procedures will validate the quality of the work carried out by the internal auditors and therefore provides the external auditor with a greater degree of assurance.

The external auditor may also obtain direct assistance from the internal audit team. For example, he may actually request members of the internal audit team to carry out parts of the external audit. When doing so, however, the auditor should obtain written representations from the active members (members of the internal audit team being used for external audit tasks), outline their role to the head of internal audit, directly supervise and review their work and ensure that they are not involved in anything which would pose a **self-review threat** (i.e. work on auditing anything that they themselves have prepared).

10.4 USING THE WORK OF AN AUDITOR'S EXPERT

Introduction

ISA 620, paragraph 7, states:
> "If expertise in a field other than accounting or auditing is necessary to obtain sufficient appropriate audit evidence, the auditor shall determine whether to use the work of an auditor's expert."

As noted at the start of this chapter, the auditor must remember that he holds sole responsibility for the audit opinion expressed and that while he might deem it necessary to obtain expert advice, he does so knowing he must obtain **sufficient appropriate audit evidence** with respect not only to the subject matter but also to the calibre of the expert himself.

Nature, Timing and Extent of Audit Procedures

When designing the nature, timing and extent of the audit procedures, the auditor will take into consideration the **materiality** of the matter requiring expert advice, the risk of material misstatement of the matter and the significance of the expert's work to the overall audit. Additionally, before engaging the work of the expert, the auditor is responsible for evaluating the necessary qualifications, competence, capabilities and objectivity of the expert.

The nature, scope and objectives of the audit engagement (in which the expert is to be involved), the respective roles and responsibilities, as well as the nature, timing and extent of communication, should be documented and agreed in writing between the expert and the auditor. This document should also require the expert to observe confidentiality requirements regarding any information disclosed.

Evaluating the Adequacy of the Work of the Auditor's Expert

Once the expert has concluded on the matter at hand, the auditor needs to ensure that the conclusion appears relevant, reasonable and consistent with other audit evidence. Additionally, should the use of assumptions have been required by the expert, the auditor should assess the relevance and reasonableness of these assumptions in the given circumstances. Should source data have been required in concluding on the work assigned, the auditor should validate its completeness and accuracy.

Expert's Scope of Work

The scope of the expert's work will vary, depending on the particular assignment type. The scope of the expert's work should be documented in the form of written instructions, maintained on the independent audit file, and should include:
- the objectives and scope of the expert's work;
- a general outline of specific matters the report is to cover;
- the intended use;
- the extent of the expert's access to records and files;
- clarification of the expert's relationship to the client entity (to ensure he is independent);
- requirements regarding the confidentiality of client information; and
- the assumptions and methods to be used by the expert.

Assessing the Work of the Auditor's Expert

In assessing the expert's work, the auditor should ensure that the substance of the expert's findings are properly reflected in the financial statement assertions. The auditor must also consider:
- the source of the data used (was it generated by the client entity or by some other external source?);
- the assumptions and methods used;
- when the work was carried out;
- reasons for any changes in assumptions and methods; and
- the result of the expert's work in light of the auditor's knowledge of the business and the results of other audit procedures.

The auditor is not the expert and therefore cannot judge all assumptions and methods used; however, he should seek to obtain an understanding of these to consider their reasonableness. This will involve discussions with the expert as well as with the client to ensure that explanations, assumptions and methods are not contradictory to other evidence obtained.

10.5 CONCLUSION

While the auditor may call on various sources to assist him in concluding on his opinion, he holds **sole responsibility for that opinion**. For that reason, he makes no reference to the use of the work of auditors of service organisations, internal auditors or auditors' experts in his audit report, as doing so would be perceived as an attempt to diminish his own responsibility with respect to the conclusion he has drawn.

Therefore, when using the work of others, the auditor must be satisfied as to the adequacy of the qualifications, expertise and competence of individuals involved, as well as the reasonableness, accuracy, relevance and completeness of the conclusions drawn by others.

SUMMARY OF LEARNING OBJECTIVES

Having studied this chapter on using the work of others you should:

Learning Objective 1   Understand the external auditor's responsibility when using the work of others.

The auditor has sole responsibility for the **audit opinion** expressed and that responsibility is not reduced by the auditor's use of another's work. The auditor must seek to satisfy himself with regard to the expert's qualifications and competency to carry out the task in question, as well as review the work and conclusions drawn by that expert.

Learning Objective 2   Understand the options open to the auditor to gain an understanding of controls in place at service organisations that impact on the entity's financial statement transactions.

Entity's Use of Service Organisations – ISA 402 When an entity uses a service provider that may impact on material transactions in the financial statements, the auditor, in line with ISA 315 and ISA 330, is required to obtain an understanding of the internal controls relevant to the audit, sufficient to identify and assess risks of material misstatement.

This can be done in two ways:
* getting the information **directly** from the service provider; or
* obtaining a 'Type 1 report', which is a report on the description and design of the service provider's controls with respect to the entity.

If the controls need to be tested surrounding the service organisation, the auditor can either test them himself, if permitted and practicable, or alternatively obtain a 'Type 2 report', which provides information on the description and design of the internal controls relevant to the entity, as well as reporting on their **operating effectiveness**.

Learning Objective 3   Understand the difference between internal and external audit.

The external auditor's objective is to issue an independent opinion on the truth and fairness of the financial statements. This opinion is included in the independent auditor's report, which is addressed to the shareholders of the client entity. The external auditor must be independent of the client entity and must be a member of a RAB/RSB (e.g. ICAI). Strict rules exist around who can act as an external auditor.

An internal auditor, on the other hand, is employed directly by the client entity (often as an employee, though the function can be outsourced) and is responsible for the recommendation and review of the systems of control in the client entity. The scope and report format of their work can vary and is driven by the directors of the organisation (usually the **audit committee**). Professional internal auditors are usually members of the IIA, but can operate without any qualifications.

Learning Objective 4   Understand the work of the internal auditor.

External Auditor's Use of the Work of Internal Auditors – ISA 610   Viewed as an independent and objective assurance provider around the areas of risk and control, the internal audit function should report directly to the audit committee of the organisation. The internal audit department is also value-adding, making the control environment as efficient and effective as possible.

An Institute of Internal Auditors' (IIA) *Position Paper* (January 2013) outlines how internal audits are regarded as 'the last line of defence' in effective risk and management control.

While the external auditor may use the work of the internal audit department, he must be satisfied with regard to the competency of the department and adequately assess their work before relying on it. Additionally, the external auditor may use the services of the internal auditors to assist him in his work, but must adequately supervise and review their work and obtain written representations from any internal auditor involved, as well as ensuring they do not engage in any self-review activities.

Learning Objective 5   Be able to identify independence issues connected to the internal auditor.

While internal auditors can be subject to the same types of independence threats as those faced by external auditors, these threats can present themselves in a different way. Members of the IIA are subject to a Code of Ethics similar to that of external auditors (i.e. work on auditing anything that they themselves have prepared).

Learning Objective 6   Understand the audit procedures that the external auditor must carry out with respect to the work of others.

Auditor's Experts – ISA 620   "If expertise in a field other than accounting or auditing is necessary to obtain sufficient appropriate audit evidence, the auditor shall determine whether to use the work of an auditor's expert." (ISA 620, para 7)

Before engaging the work of the expert, the auditor is responsible for evaluating the necessary qualifications, competence, capabilities and objectivity of the expert. Any conclusions reached by the auditor's expert require audit procedures as to their reasonableness and consistency with other audit evidence.

QUESTIONS

Self-test Questions

10.1 Can the auditor refer to the work of an auditor's expert in his audit report?

10.2 How might the auditor gain an understanding of the controls in place in a service organisation?

10.3 What options does the auditor have if he wishes to rely on the controls in place in a service organisation where those controls impact on transactions of the client entity?

10.4 What are the key differences between external and internal auditors?

10.5 What are the benefits to the organisation of the internal audit department?

10.6 What current issues face the internal auditing profession?

10.7 What must the auditor check in relation to an auditor's expert whose work he intends to use for the purpose of an audit?

Review Questions

(See Suggested Solutions to Review Questions in **Appendix D**.)

Question 10.1

Your audit client, Elite Ltd, has recently hired an internal auditor to deal with Sarbanes–Oxley (SOX) requirements (they are a subsidiary of a company quoted on the New York Stock Exchange). He has indicated that he believes the presence of this internal auditor will dramatically reduce the work that your audit firm will need to perform and he expects to see the impact of this on the audit fee.

Requirement The audit engagement partner is concerned about this request and asks you to draft him an e-mail indicating, with bulletpoints, where (if at all) you will be able to reduce your audit testing due to the existence of the newly-appointed internal auditor. The audit engagement partner has indicated that your report should include the audit requirements imposed by ISA 610 on using the work of the internal auditor at Elite Ltd.

Question 10.2

You and your colleague have recently become managers of the audit firm in which you both trained. You have both been assigned to your first engagements as audit managers. As part of the training for new managers, you are reminded of your responsibility to control the timing of audits: 'they must be efficient notwithstanding the need for effectiveness'. There has been concern that many audits have been running over their budgeted times and reducing the margins being achieved. Your colleague is determined not to run over his allotted time and discusses with you his plans to perform the audit in the budgeted time or less.

First, he knows that his audit client has an internal audit department and he is going to obtain a copy of their audit work on controls and use this to support a reduced level of substantive testing.

Secondly, the company uses a service organisation to perform a significant amount of work that impacts directly on the financial statements, so he is going to get a 'Type 1 report' (third party confirmation) from their auditors to reduce the need for him to do any work on this area.

Finally, the property has been revalued and he is going to get an independent valuer to review the valuation received by the company. This will mean he can also avoid doing any work on the valuation.

Requirement You are concerned about your colleague's plans to reduce the hours spent on this audit. Prepare an informal e-mail to him outlining your concerns.

Question 10.3

The Institute of Internal Auditors' (IIA) *Position Paper* from January 2013 outlines how internal audits are regarded as the last "line of defense" in effective risk and management control.[6]

Requirement The above being true, how important is the independence of the internal auditor? Your answer should make reference to at least **two** independence threats to which an internal auditor may be subject.

---

[6] IIA Position Paper: *The Three Lines of Defense in Effective Risk Management and Control* (Institute of Internal Auditors, January 2013) See https://na.theiia.org/standards-guidance/Public%20 Documents/PP%20The%20Three%20Lines%20of%20Defense%20in%20Effective%20Risk%20 Management%20and%20Control.pdf

CHALLENGING QUESTIONS FOR PART II

(Suggested Solutions to Challenging Questions are available through your lecturer.)

These challenging questions aim to test your knowledge of **Chapters 4–10,** and the topics they discuss. For each question, you are presented with a case study on which you are asked to deliver on a number of requirements intended to test practical application of what you have learned in Part II: The Audit and Assurance Process: Planning and Controls.

Question II.1

You are an audit manager for Smith & Reilly, a long-established accounting practice. Smith & Reilly has been approached by Large Company Limited (Large) to conduct its audit. The previous auditors have resigned due to the size of the fee charged to Large Company Limited relative to the firm's total fee income. Large Company Limited has shared the Statement of Circumstances from the previous auditors, which corroborates this. It is June 2012 and the year end of Large Company Limited is 31 December. The directors of Large Company Limited have provided you with an overview of their business, at Appendix 1. Your Company, Smith & Reilly, currently provides other services to Large Company Limited in the form of payroll and tax advice. They also provided you with a listing of directors and the non-executive director name rings a bell with you. You remember reading an article about him in the newspaper some months back (see Appendix 2, regarding Fred Afternoon). Large has felt that the audit has taken up a huge amount of time in the past, so have requested that the audit commence at the end of January and be finished by mid-February. This concerns you as Large is the largest company Smith & Reilly has ever audited and you are unlikely to have enough resources to complete the engagement in this timeframe. The directors of Large have offered €200 vouchers for each member of the engagement team should this request be met. The partners of Smith & Reilly have recently promoted a new partner, and he will take responsibility with regard to the role of 'ethics partner'.

Requirements
(a) You are asked to prepare a recommendation on whether or not to proceed with the engagement for Large for this new partner to review.
(b) In preparation for the potential acceptance of this client, the partners have asked you to draft a letter to the directors on the requirement for them to sign an engagement letter, outlining the purpose of the engagement letter and some of the contents therein.

APPENDIX 1 – COMPANY BACKGROUND

Principal activities and review of the business The company's principal activity is the manufacture of furniture. The directors expect revenue to increase by in excess of 30% (from €198.5 million in 2011). The directors believe that this trend will continue for the foreseeable future as a new line of furniture has effectively broken into the luxury market. Demand for this range has also introduced sales in foreign countries, with an expected

€40 million increase in revenue being attributable to exports. All other ranges are selling successfully and are expected to do so for the balance of the year and into the future.

Research and development The company is involved in the development of two new ranges of furniture for future commercial production. These ranges are the 'Authentic Mexican Pine' range and the 'Mahogany Cast Iron' range. An additional employee has been employed to investigate these designs and to develop accompanying accessories. He is sourcing the accessories from China due to the low cost, albeit he notes they are not of a high quality and do not comply with EU regulations.

APPENDIX 2: EXTRACT FROM NEWSPAPER ARTICLE

Tooling with the Accounts

The directors of ToolRUs are being questioned in connection with the overstating of closing inventory in order to increase profits. The company was set to be taken over by a US company and falling profits threatened that proposition. The directors overstated inventory values by claiming that they had modified some of the tools and hence charged labour and consumable tools to inventory items. No modifications were found to have taken place and the tools were, in fact, as originally purchased. Fred Afternoon, an executive director, claims he had no knowledge of this activity and places full blame on the shoulders of the CFO, stating, "*I know nothing of accounting and am not involved in any way with the production of accounts. My expertise lies in the sourcing of quality tooling equipment. I am appalled by what I have learned.*" While no connection has been made between the fraudulent accounting records and Mr Afternoon, suspicion still lies at his door due to the value he received for his shares when the takeover ultimately took place.

Question II.2

The audit engagement for Large has been accepted, with all recommendations laid down by you having been followed. You are the assigned audit manager on the engagement and have recently conducted the planning meeting with the directors. The minutes of that meeting are included at Appendix 1 below.

Requirements
(a) The audit partner requests that you send him a copy of the minutes and outline your opinion for him on:
   (i) the inherent and controls risks identified by you at this meeting along with the proposed audit approach to deal with these risks (i.e. detection risk);
   (ii) whether or not you believe a controls approach should be taken; and
   (iii) how you believe you should deal with the more risky areas identified.

(b) Considering the size of the new client and risks identified, the audit partner asks you to prepare a memo to the engagement staff outlining their requirement to collect sufficient appropriate audit evidence as well as an explanation on what is sufficient appropriate audit evidence.

(c) The audit senior assigned to this job has never worked on an initial engagement and asks you to outline Smith & Reilly's responsibility with regard to the opening balances of Large Company Limited.

APPENDIX 1: LARGE COMPANY LIMITED PLANNING MEETING

LARGE COMPANY LIMITED

PLANNING MEETING

21 OCTOBER 2012

In attendance: *John Doe – Audit Manager, Smith & Reilly*
James McCarthy – Audit Partner, Smith & Reilly
Thomas Hogan – Chairperson, Large Company Limited
Mark Hogan – Managing Director, Large Company Limited
Kevin Byrne – Finance Director, Large Company Limited
Kate Louis – CFO, Large Company Limited

Company Background

The company's principal activity is the manufacture of furniture. The directors expect revenue to increase by in excess of 30% (from €198.5 million in 2011). The directors believe that this trend will continue for the foreseeable future as a new line of furniture has effectively broken into the luxury market. Demand for this range has also introduced sales in foreign countries, with an expected €40 million increase in revenue being attributable to exports. All other ranges are selling successfully and are expected to do so for the balance of the year and into the future. This demand has resulted in the opening of a branch in the UK and a branch in Northern Ireland, which means they are dealing with the consolidation of branch accounts and foreign exchange for the first time.

The company employs 1,000 employees throughout the company, most of who are employed in production. The head of production, credited with the recent development of the luxury products, left the company last month.

The company had just five people employed in finance, but this has increased due to the increased work around consolidation and foreign exchange and the need to analyse revenue by geographical area and product to produce better management accounts. While the increase in staffing has helped, the systems need to be updated to cope with the increased volume of transactions and added complexity with the introduction of the branches. An accountant is employed in each branch and they have implemented their own controls within each branch.

Due to the training of the new accounts staff, the company is behind on the reconciliation of account balances, but hopes to catch up on this before the year end.

Kate Louis outlines the following with regard to specific balances:

Non-current Assets

The value of non-current assets has reduced in the period due to a deficit on revaluation of freehold land and buildings.

Inventory

- Inventory includes raw materials, WIP and finished goods.
- An inventory count has not taken place since June, and Kate is worried that the physical inventory held will be different from that in the perpetual records.

Trade Receivables

Kate has always been an advocate of ensuring receivables balances are regularly followed up and believes controls in this area to be strong. For this reason she spends time with the credit controller each month, understanding the aging of receivables (although with the recent increase in business overseas, she has not had as much time for this).

Available-for-sale Investments

The directors have concerns over the value of investments.

Payables and Accruals

The purchases and payables system is probably the most closely controlled, with this function being overseen by a very strong manager who has implemented excellent controls. The branches do not purchase anything directly themselves; all purchasing and payables are managed centrally.

PART III

THE AUDIT AND ASSURANCE PROCESS: SUBSTANTIVE PROCEDURES

THE AUDIT AND ASSURANCE PROCESS

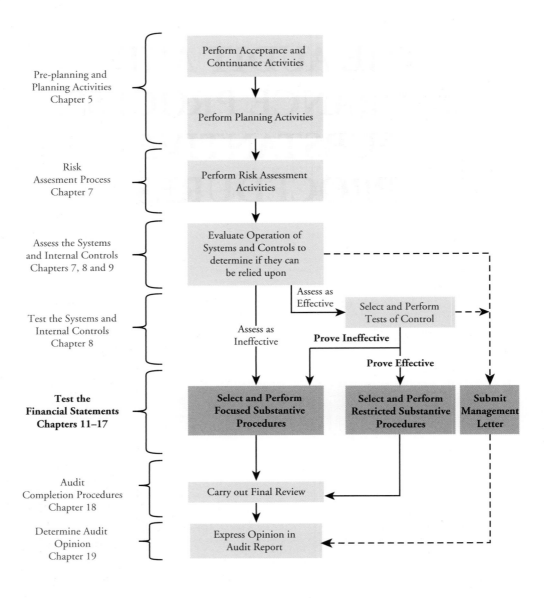

Pre-planning and
Planning Activities
Chapter 5

Perform Acceptance and
Continuance Activities

Perform Planning Activities

Risk
Assesment Process
Chapter 7

Perform Risk Assessment
Activities

Assess the Systems
and Internal Controls
Chapters 7, 8 and 9

Evaluate Operation of
Systems and Controls to
determine if they can
be relied upon

Test the Systems and
Internal Controls
Chapter 8

Assess as
Effective

Select and Perform
Tests of Control

Assess as
Ineffective

Prove Ineffective

Prove Effective

**Test the
Financial Statements
Chapters 11–17**

**Select and Perform
Focused Substantive
Procedures**

**Select and Perform
Restricted Substantive
Procedures**

**Submit
Management
Letter**

Audit
Completion Procedures
Chapter 18

Carry out Final Review

Determine Audit
Opinion
Chapter 19

Express Opinion in
Audit Report

11

THE AUDIT OF PROPERTY, PLANT AND EQUIPMENT

LEARNING OBJECTIVES

Having studied this chapter on the audit of property, plant and equipment you should:
1. understand what is included in the audit of property, plant and equipment (PPE);
2. be able to identify the risks and audit objectives applicable to PPE;
3. be able to determine an appropriate audit strategy for PPE, taking into consideration the specific risks and audit objectives (assertions);
4. be able to develop an audit programme that addresses all the audit objectives (assertions) for PPE;
5. be able to describe and apply specific substantive testing procedures relating to the audit of PPE;
6. understand the role CAAT's can play when auditing PPE; and
7. understand the auditor's approach relating to the disclosures of PPE.

CHECKLIST OF RELEVANT STANDARDS

The relevant standards covered in this chapter are:
- ISA (UK and Ireland) 315 *Identifying and Assessing the Risks of Material Misstatement Through Understanding of the Entity and its Environment* (ISA 315)
- ISA (UK and Ireland) 330 *The Auditor's Responses to Assessed Risks* (ISA 330)
- ISA 500 *Audit Evidence* (ISA 500)
- ISA (UK and Ireland) 510 *Initial Audit Engagements – Opening Balances* (ISA 510)
- ISA (UK and Ireland) 520 *Analytical Procedures* (ISA 520)
- ISA (UK and Ireland) 530 *Audit Sampling* (ISA 530)
- ISA (UK and Ireland) 540 *Auditing Accounting Estimates, Including Fair Value Accounting Estimates, and Related Disclosures* (ISA 540)
- ISA (UK and Ireland) 620 *Using the Work of an Auditor's Expert* (ISA 620)
- IAS 16 *Property, Plant and Equipment* (IAS 16)
- IAS 17 *Leases* (IAS 17)
- IAS 36 *Impairment of Assets* (IAS 36)

KEY TERMS AND DEFINITIONS FOR THIS CHAPTER

Fixed Asset Register (FAR)   An accounting technique used to gain control over the fixed assets (PPE) of a client entity.

Lead Schedule   The lead schedule acts as a summary of the balances and transactions to be audited relating to a particular class of transactions and balances. It allows the auditor to control his procedures by referencing each balance or transaction to the location in the audit file at which testing has taken place.

Substantive Analytical Procedure   Also known as a '**proof in total**', a substantive analytical procedure is an audit procedure that is generally more efficient than a **test of details** and is permitted where a low level of inherent and control risk exist. It involves the auditor developing an independent calculation (expectation) of the balance being audited and comparing it with the actual balance as per the financial statements. If the auditor's independent expectation is within a threshold from the actual figure, then no further testing is required by the auditor in relation to the balance (Some other assertions, however, such as valuation may still need to be considered.)

Title Deeds   Legal documents that verify a person's legal right or title to property.

Vehicle Registration Certificate   A legal document verifying the ownership of a motor vehicle.

11.1 INTRODUCTION

This chapter outlines the requirements of the international accounting standard IAS 16 *Property, Plant and Equipment* ('IAS 16') with respect to property, plant and equipment (PPE) and then considers how the auditor:

(a) identifies audit risks and audit objectives (management assertions) for property, plant and equipment;

(b) develops an audit plan for PPE and refines this into an audit programme;

(c) designs specific tests associated with property, plant and equipment; and

(d) ensures adequate presentation and disclosure in the financial statements relating to property, plant and equipment.

Finally, the chapter considers how computer-assisted audit techniques (CAATs), considered in detail in **Chapter 9**, can assist with the audit of PPE.

11.2 WHAT IS PROPERTY, PLANT AND EQUIPMENT?

Property, plant and equipment (PPE) are those assets that are retained for use in the entity's operations and not consumed in the year of purchase or held for resale.

IAS 16, paragraph 7 states:

"The cost of an item of property, plant and equipment shall be recognised as an asset if, and only if:

(a) it is probable that future economic benefits associated with the item will flow to the entity; and

(b) the cost of the item can be measured reliably."

If you refer to **Appendix C**, Large Company Limited, Note 13, you will see that property, plant and equipment can include assets such as freehold land and buildings, plant and machinery or motor vehicles. On the face of the statement of financial position, the **net book value** (NBV) (cost less accumulated depreciation) is disclosed and this is expanded upon in a note to the financial statements.

The note in the financial statements needs to disclose:

• the opening cost (or valuation) of each category of PPE;

• changes to each category of PPE, which can include additions, disposals, retirements, revaluations, and impairments;

• the closing cost (or valuation) of each category of PPE at the end of the period;

• the opening depreciation of each category of PPE;

• changes to depreciation on each category of PPE, which can include additions, disposals, retirements, revaluations and impairments;

• the closing depreciation on each category of PPE at the end of the period; and

• opening and closing NBV of each category of PPE.

The property, plant and equipment note should also include details such as security held on any assets, details of revaluation, assets held under finance lease or hire purchase, and details of capitalised interest costs.

With respect to the statement of comprehensive income, when it comes to PPE the auditor is concerned with the charge for depreciation in the year and ensuring that it ties back to the note in the financial statements.

11.3 RISKS ASSOCIATED WITH PROPERTY, PLANT AND EQUIPMENT

Throughout **Chapter 7** (which addresses the requirements of ISA (UK and Ireland) 315 *Identifying and Assessing the Risks of Material Misstatement Through Understanding of the Entity and Its Environment* and ISA (UK and Ireland) 330 *The Auditor's Responses to Assessed Risks*) we discussed the topic of 'risk' and considered how the auditor should go about detecting risks. We also discussed how the auditor should consider these risks when designing the nature, timing and extent of further audit procedures relative to each financial cycle. As such, before developing the audit plan, the auditor needs to consider a number of risks that may be associated with property, plant and equipment. Risks associated with PPE can include:

- **Rights and obligations** The client entity may not actually **own** the PPE included in the financial statements.
- **Existence** The PPE included in the financial statements might not actually **exist**.
- **Valuation (impairment)** The valuation of **PPE** may be overstated in the financial statements, e.g. the value of the tangible assets may have fallen to less than their current NBV.
- **Valuation (depreciation rate)** The depreciation rate applied to PPE may be too low.
- **Obsolescence** PPE may have become obsolete (e.g. due to technological advancement).
- **Overstatement** The client entity may have failed to record disposals of PPE.
- **Overstatement (repairs and maintenance)** Revenue items may have been charged in error to capital expenditure on PPE.
- **Data integrity** Control over PPE may be poor and fixed asset registers may not have been kept up-to-date.

11.4 AUDIT OBJECTIVES/MANAGEMENT ASSERTIONS FOR PROPERTY, PLANT AND EQUIPMENT

As discussed in **Chapter 6** (which addressed ISA 500 *Audit Evidence*), it is necessary for the auditor to seek appropriate audit evidence to satisfy all of the audit objectives and to eliminate the possibility of any of the risks outlined above in **Section 11.3** going undetected. In **Chapter 4** we introduced audit objectives (management assertions) and explained their generic meanings; we then reintroduced this topic again throughout **Chapter 8**, making management assertions specific to each financial cycle. In **Tables 11.1** and **11.2**, we remind you of the audit objectives as they relate to property plant and equipment.

Table 11.1 addresses the management assertions (audit objectives) as they relate to the transactions and events occurring during the period relating to PPE.

Table 11.2 addresses the management assertions (audit objectives) as they relate to the balances associated with PPE.

TABLE 11.1: PROPERTY, PLANT AND EQUIPMENT AUDIT OBJECTIVES FOR TRANSACTIONS AND EVENTS DURING THE PERIOD

Transactions and Events During the Period	
Management Assertion/ Audit Objective	**Objective of Gathering Audit Evidence**
Occurrence	• To ensure recorded additions represent PPE acquired during the period under review. • To ensure recorded disposals represent property, plant and equipment sold, transferred or scrapped during the period under review.
Completeness	To ensure that all additions and disposals that occurred during the period under review have been recorded.
Accuracy	To ensure that all additions and disposals have been correctly recorded.
Cut-off	To ensure all additions and disposals have been recorded in the correct period.
Rights and Obligations	To ensure the entity holds the rights to all property, plant and equipment resulting from recorded purchase transactions.
Classification	To ensure all additions to and disposals of PPE have been recorded in the correct ledger accounts and adequately support their classification in the financial statements.

TABLE 11.2: PROPERTY, PLANT AND EQUIPMENT AUDIT OBJECTIVES FOR ACCOUNT BALANCES AT YEAR END

Account Balances at Year End	
Management Assertion/ Audit Objective	**Objective of Gathering Audit Evidence**
Existence	To ensure that recorded PPE represent productive assets that are in use at the reporting date.
Rights and Obligations	To ensure the entity holds the rights to all recorded PPE at the reporting date.
Completeness	To ensure that all PPE that exists at the year end is recorded in the PPE balance (i.e. the balance is complete and no assets are ommitted).
Valuation and Allocation	To ensure that PPE are included in the financial statements at appropriate figures for cost or valuation less accumulated depreciation at the reporting date.

Presentation and Disclosure	To ensure PPE are correctly disclosed in the financial statements at the reporting date. This includes disclosing: • cost/revaluation, accumulated depreciation and NBV; • disposals and the related profit or loss on disposal; • depreciation, including the total depreciation charged, the depreciation method and useful economic life or depreciation rate. Where assets are held under finance lease and/or hire-purchase contracts, separate disclosure should be made of the depreciation charged in the reporting period on these assets; and • the pledging of property, plant and equipment as collateral; • details regarding revaluations; • details of capitalised interest.

Now that we understand the objectives of the auditor with regard to PPE, in the following sections we will consider how the auditor addresses these objectives through substantive testing.

11.5 DEVELOPING AN AUDIT PLAN FOR PROPERTY, PLANT AND EQUIPMENT

Before the audit of property, plant and equipment is undertaken, an assessment of the audit risk must be completed. As discussed in detail in **Chapter 7**, audit risk is made up of three components: inherent risk; control risk; and detection risk. We will examine these components specifically as they relate to PPE.

$$\text{Audit Risk} = \text{Inherent Risk} + \text{Control Risk} + \text{Detection Risk}$$

Inherent Risk

Inherent risk can vary, depending on the types of property, plant and equipment in question. Inherent risk for the existence assertion of a manufacturing company may be high as there is a risk that scrapped or old machinery may not be taken off the fixed asset register or that small tools or equipment used in production may have been stolen. Alternatively, inherent risk for the existence assertion of a sole trader (e.g. a dentist) may be low as plant and equipment are not normally vulnerable to theft because of the type of equipment held (i.e. is not easily resold).

Control Risk and Detection Risk

Control risk can also vary, depending on the type of asset class. Fixtures and fittings may have a lower assessed level of control risk as these are sometimes processed as routine purchase transactions. On the other hand, land and buildings will be subject to separate controls, such as capital budgeting and specific authorisation by the board of directors.

Because fixed asset transactions are infrequent and high in monetary value, a predominantly **substantive audit approach** (as discussed throughout **Chapter 8**) is normally adopted for PPE and, as a result, the planned level of detection risk (discussed in **Chapter 7**) is low, i.e. focused substantive procedures are required because no reliance is placed on controls.

In summary, because transactions involving PPE are infrequent, and are usually for **material** amounts, auditors rarely test controls over fixed asset transactions but instead adopt a substantive audit approach. This approach is discussed in detail in **Section 11.7** below.

11.6 KEY DOCUMENTS RELATING TO PROPERTY, PLANT AND EQUIPMENT

The main safeguard over property, plant and equipment is the preparation of a **fixed asset register** (FAR). The fixed asset register records all movements relating to PPE. The fixed asset register should be maintained by the client entity and the individual responsible (within the client entity) should be independent of those actually using the assets. In order for this register to be relied on, the auditor should perform the following procedures:

- select a sample of a number of assets listed on the register and physically inspect the items;
- reconcile the fixed asset register to the various nominal ledger accounts associated with PPE, e.g. additions, disposals, depreciation, etc., and investigate any differences arising; and
- ascertain the insurance cover on each class of asset and compare it to the cost or net book value (carrying value) of the asset.

If a fixed asset register is not maintained or is subject to error (due, for example, to poor controls over the fixed asset register, e.g. unauthorised access), control risk will increase and the auditor may need to extend his substantive tests.

11.7 SUBSTANTIVE AUDIT PROGRAMME FOR PROPERTY, PLANT AND EQUIPMENT

An **audit programme** records the specific details of tests to be performed by the auditor. The audit programme becomes a guide to the **audit engagement team** as to the work to be done in a particular area. As work is completed, a reference is included on the audit programme showing the location on the audit file where details of the tests performed are included. While the audit programme for any cycle will vary from entity to entity, in **Example 11.1** below we consider the typical types of test the auditor would include in the audit programme for PPE.

EXAMPLE 11.1: SUBSTANTIVE TESTING AUDIT PROGRAMME FOR
PROPERTY PLANT AND EQUIPMENT (LARGE COMPANY LIMITED)[1]

Large Company Limited 31 December 2012 Property, Plant and Equipment			
	Audit Materiality		**€3,642,500**
	Performance Materiality		**€2,731,875**
		Initials	**Date**
	Prepared by:		
	Reviewed by:		
Audit Programme	**Assertion Covered**	**Reference to Work**	**Initials and Date**
Ensure that the audit plan is reflected in the following tests. The following tests are suggestions only and should be removed or added to as necessary to address the risks of material misstatement identified at the risk-assessment stage.			
Accounting Policy			
Assess the appropriateness of the accounting policy and the accounting estimates method for this area. Ensure that the accounting policy is in accordance with accounting standards and applicable law, and that the methods used for making the accounting estimates are appropriate.	Existence, Completeness, Rights and Obligations, Accuracy/ Valuation and Classification		
Initial Procedures			
Obtain or prepare a lead schedule, agree to balance sheet and provide sufficient audit trail: (a) agree to nominal ledger; (b) agree opening balances to last year's accounts; and (c) prepare a commentary explaining the composition of the fixed asset balance and comparing the balance with prior periods and with expectations.	Existence, Occurrence, Accuracy and Classification		

---

[1] Source: based on *Procedures for Quality Audit 2010* (© Chartered Accountants Ireland, 2010), E1.

Property, Plant and Equipment Movements in the Period			
Obtain or prepare separate schedules of: (a) additions within each category; and (b) disposals within each category. Vouch as appropriate a sample of the additions and disposals.	Occurrence, Completeness, Accuracy and Classification Occurrence, Accuracy, Rights and Obligations		
Ensure additions meet the client's capitalisation policy.	Accuracy and Classification		
Obtain a copy of the capital expenditure budget of the entity and vouch additions to it to confirm authority to purchase.	Occurrence, Rights and Obligations		
Consider the accounting treatment of any self-built assets.	Occurrence, Existence, Accuracy, Rights and Obligations		
Consider possible unrecorded disposals (e.g. assets scrapped).	Completeness		
Enquire if any fixed assets have been improved or constructed during the period and ensure capitalised or expensed as appropriate.	Completeness		
Review nominal ledger accounts for repairs and renewals (or similar) for items which should have been capitalised.	Completeness		
Depreciation			

(a) Consider reasonableness of provision of all depreciation with regard to:
     (i) estimated useful lives; and
     (ii) residual value.
(b) Test-check depreciation calculations (either via a sample or a substantive analytical procedure).
(c) Agree total to statement of comprehensive income charge.
(d) Challenge estimates made by management.
	Accuracy and Classification		

Asset Balances			
Ascertain location of title deeds and inspect or confirm details with third party. If these are inspected on a rotational basis, check and note the last year that these were inspected.	Existence, Rights and Obligations		
Inspect vehicle registration documents and agree details to company records and ensure that vehicles are registered in the company's name.	Existence, Rights and Obligations		
Physically inspect a sample of items contained in fixed assets and document on file.	Existence (indications of impairment and therefore valuation)		
Other Considerations			
Revaluations – Ensure that all revaluations are accounted for correctly. Ensure that historical cost information is available for disclosure purposes.	Valuation, Presentation and Disclosure		
Impairment – Enquire of management whether or not they have considered carrying out an impairment review. Consider whether assets are impaired in value and whether an impairment review is required.	Valuation		
Leases – Obtain or prepare a schedule of net book value and depreciation of assets held under hire-purchase contracts and finance leases.	Occurrence, Completeness, Accuracy and Classification, Presentation and Disclosure		
Leases – Review lease costs expensed and consider whether the accounting treatment is correct.	Occurrence, Completeness, Accuracy and Classification, Presentation and Disclosure		

Capital Commitments – Review relevant documentation to ensure that any capital commitments have been identified (e.g. board minutes, after-date review, and enquiries).	Presentation and Disclosure		
Ensure financial statements comply with the appropriate legislation and applicable accounting standards.	Presentation and Disclosure		
Conclusion Subject to the matters noted for the reviewer, in my opinion sufficient audit assurance has been obtained to enable us to conclude that Property, Plant and Equipment are not materially misstated.			
Name:	Accountant in Charge		
Date:			
Name:	Reviewer		
Date:			

11.8 SUBSTANTIVE TESTING PROCEDURES FOR PROPERTY, PLANT AND EQUIPMENT

In this section, we will discuss in more detail some of the procedures outlined in the substantive audit programme above. We will start with **initial procedures**, which include:
- opening balances;
- mathematical accuracy of schedules;
- the lead schedule; and
- analytical reviews.

Initial Procedures

Opening Balances

Initially, evidence must be obtained as to the accuracy of the opening balances and the ownership of the assets comprising the balances. This can be completed as follows:
- Agree the opening balances to the prior-year working papers and signed financial statements. This may highlight an opening balance in the current year's accounts that does not agree to the closing balance per the prior-year's financial statements. In this instance, a change would be made to the opening balance of the current year, which would impact the closing balance of the current year. This usually arises due to final adjustments in the prior year that are not reflected in the actual accounts (nominal and general ledgers).
- Inspect the permanent audit file (file containing long-standing documents that do not change every year) for details of title deeds and registered charges, such as mortgages.

- If this is the first year of the audit engagement, the auditor will still need to establish that the opening balances are materially correct, which can pose a difficulty for him if either the client entity was exempt from audit in the prior year or a predecessor auditor carried out the audit. The audit of opening balances in such instances is discussed in detail in **Chapter 6**, Section 6.8, which addresses the requirements of ISA (UK and Ireland) 510 *Initial Audit Engagements – Opening Balance*.

Mathematical Accuracy of Schedules

All schedules (e.g. in the case of fixed assets, the **fixed asset register**) provided by the client entity should be totalled and cross-totalled to ensure their mathematical accuracy. Additionally, they should be agreed to the financial statements balances and transactions that they support.

Prepare Lead Schedules

The **lead schedule** acts as a summary of the balances and transactions to be audited relating to a particular class of transactions and balances. It allows the auditor to control his procedures by referencing each balance or transaction to the working paper that records the audit tests performed. For property, plant and equipment, the lead schedule is similar to the PPE note in the financial statements (as can be seen in **Appendix C**, Note 13). An example of a lead schedule is included below at **Example 11.2**.

As with any audit working paper, the standard headings apply with regard to: company name; year end; materiality; performance materiality and preparer and reviewers of the document. Also included as standard is the audit working paper title, which in this instance is: 'Property, Plant and Equipment Lead Schedule'. What follows is a summary of the balances that make up the property, plant and equipment balance. This now acts a checklist for the auditor, allowing him to ensure that he audits all aspects that make up the balance and the movements in the period leading to that balance. As he tests each item contained in the lead schedule, he notes a reference directly on the lead schedule to where testing is contained in the audit file.

EXAMPLE 11.2: LEAD SCHEDULE FOR PROPERTY, PLANT AND EQUIPMENT
(LARGE COMPANY LIMITED)[2]

Large Company Limited			
31 December 2012	**Audit Materiality**		**€3,642,500**
	Performance Materiality		**€2,731,875**
		Initials	**Date**

---

[2] Source: Based on *Procedures for Quality Audit 2010* (© Chartered Accountants Ireland, 2010), E-.

Property, Plant and Equipment Lead Schedule			Prepared by:		
			Reviewed by:		

	Freehold Land and Buildings €000	Plant and Machinery €000	Motor Vehicles €000	Total €000
Cost/Valuation:				
1 January 2012	400,000	113,625	28,800	542,425
Additions	0	82,250	35,000	117,250
Revaluation	(355,000)	0	0	(355,000)
Disposals	0	(49,000)	(14,655)	(63,655)
31 December 2012	**45,000**	**146,875**	**49,145**	**241,020**
Depreciation:				
1 January 2012	319,800	61,725	20,400	401,925
Provided during the year	18,000	48,705	14,500	81,205
Revaluation	(337,800)	0	0	(337,800)
Disposals	0	(29,000)	(5,360)	(34,360)
31 December 2012	**0**	**81,430**	**29,540**	**110,970**
Net book value:				
31 December 2012	**45,000**	**65,445**	**19,605**	**130,050**
31 December 2011	**80,200**	**51,900**	**8,400**	**140,500**

Analytical Review

An **analytical review** (covered under **Chapter 5**, Section 5.4, which addresses the requirements of ISA 520 *Analytical Procedures*) is usually performed at the start of each substantive procedure relating to each balance or class of transactions. Calculating ratios and analysing results against industry information, prior-year results, budgets, etc., allows the auditor to get a feel for the movements in the year and make comparisons against norms, thereby enabling him to better prepare the audit programme. The following example shows the types of ratios and comparisons the auditor might perform in relation to PPE. An analytical review is similar to a preliminary analytical procedure, which focuses the auditor on movements and key ratios, equipping him with additional insight prior to commencing his substantive procedures. At the close of his substantive procedures, he aims to ensure that he can comment on all movements and key ratios, with supporting explanations. If the auditor cannot explain any element, then this will highlight for him the need to perform additional substantive procedures. The analytical review performed here differs from a substantive analytical procedure in that the auditor's aim is not to substantiate the balance (i.e. prove the assertions), but rather to ensure that he understands the movements and relationships to assist him in performing substantive procedures.

EXAMPLE 11.3: INITIAL PROCEDURES – ANALYTICAL REVIEW AND COMMENTARY ON PROPERTY, PLANT AND EQUIPMENT

Analysis	2012 €000	2011 €000	Movement	Commentary
Return on PPE	Revenue ÷ PPE = €280,250 ÷ €130,050 = 215%	Revenue ÷ PPE = €198,500 ÷ €140,500 = 141%	+74%	This rise in return on PPE is partially driven by the deficit on revaluation which is masking some of the additions in the period. Additionally, revenue, due to a move into the luxury market, is significantly up on the prior year.
PPE NBV year-on-year comparison	€130,050	€140,500	(€10,450)	While the figure for fixed assets has decreased overall, additions of €117,250,000 occurred in the period, which are being masked by the high depreciation charge of €81,205,000 as well as the deficit on revaluation of freehold buildings and some small disposals. The new assets are helping to drive the revenue number.

Property, Plant and Equipment Movements in the Period

Having performed the initial procedures, let us now consider the specific audit procedures the auditor might carry out in relation to the movements of PPE in the period, which essentially includes:

- additions;
- disposals;
- consideration of the repairs and maintenance in the period; and
- depreciation.

Additions (purchase of new PPE in the period)

In order to audit the additions to PPE in the period, the auditor needs to establish: (a) what was purchased (which he should be able to see on the fixed asset register); (b) what was the cost of the asset purchased; (c) if the asset is permitted to be capitalised under IAS 16; and (d) that all additions have been recorded.

As stated in IAS 16, at paragraph 16:
"The cost of an item of property, plant and equipment comprises:
(a) its purchase price, including import duties and non-refundable purchase taxes, after deducting trade discounts and rebates.
(b) any costs directly attributable to bringing the asset to the location and condition necessary for it to be capable of operating in the manner intended by management.
(c) the initial estimate of the costs of dismantling and removing the item and restoring the site on which it is located ...".

The following procedures should be performed in relation to **additions** to PPE:
- The auditor should obtain a copy of the fixed asset budget of the entity for the year under review. This document not only confirms authority to purchase but will also highlight any significant variances between actual and budgeted purchases. In addition, a review of budgeted expenditure not yet incurred will indicate if the entity has adequate funds and working capital to finance such additions. Budget approval should be verified through a review of the board approving minutes.
- An understanding of the client entity's capitalisation policy must be obtained. This gives an understanding of the client's policy for deciding whether a purchase is a capital item or whether it should be expensed to the statement of comprehensive income. Broadly speaking, most companies set a monetary value below which, regardless of their nature, purchases are expensed. The auditor must ensure that this policy is consistent year-on-year.

EXAMPLE 11.4: CAPITALISATION OF EXPENDITURES

A client entity's capitalisation policy is to capitalise all items greater than €1,000 which are of a capital nature.

Included in the fixed asset additions are the following:

Description	Cost
Laptop	€1,200
Memory keys	€400

The client has correctly capitalised the laptop in line with its capitalisation policy, as the asset is of a capital nature and it cost more than €1,000. However, the client has incorrectly capitalised the memory keys, as capitalisation of these items is not in line with its policy. (Although the assets are of a capital nature, the memory keys cost less than €1,000.)

The cost of additions must be verified, which can be completed on a test sample basis if there are a large number of additions (sampling is covered in **Chapter 6,** Section 6.7, which addresses the requirements of ISA 530 *Audit Sampling*). This is done by tracing the amount capitalised as per the **additions schedule** to the supporting purchase invoice. A number of items on the invoice must be agreed:

1. The date of the invoice must be within the accounting period under review.
2. The invoice must be addressed to the client being audited.
3. The cost per the invoice must be agreed to the amount capitalised, as stated in the additions schedule.
4. VAT must have been properly accounted for (i.e. if the client is registered for VAT, then the VAT is reclaimable, the assets must be capitalised at cost excluding the VAT element; if the client is not registered for VAT, then the assets are capitalised at cost including the VAT element).
5. Ensure all costs capitalised are allowable under IAS 16 (as noted above):
   (a) For major additions, the assets should be physically inspected. It is important, on physical inspection, to ensure that details of the asset are agreed to the invoice and to the capitalised amount (e.g. serial number, description, etc.).
   (b) When a client entity internally manufactures its PPE, the auditor should verify that all costs have been properly classified, including cost of materials, labour, borrowing costs and overheads, if applicable. There is potential for **inherent risk** (see **Chapter 7**, Section 7.2) in this area and the auditor needs to evaluate company controls and perform substantive procedures, as necessary, to ensure costs are genuine, accurate and complete.

Repairs and Maintenance

As stated in IAS 16, paragraph 12:

"an entity does not recognise in the carrying amount of an item of property, plant and equipment the costs of the day-to-day servicing of the item. Rather, these costs are recognised in profit or loss as incurred."

Thus, repairs and maintenance costs are not capitalised but instead are expensed to the statement of comprehensive income ('profit and loss account') as they are incurred. It is important to look out for this when auditing the costs capitalised. The auditor must also review the repairs and maintenance accounts to ensure items of a capital nature have not been incorrectly expensed to the statement of comprehensive income.

Disposals

The second key type of movement relating to PPE is the disposal of assets. The auditor commences his audit of disposals by requesting a list of disposals during the period under review from the client (alternatively, these should be recorded in the fixed asset register). To ensure that all disposals have been accounted for, the auditor must confirm all such disposals with management, re-analyse any miscellaneous income that may relate to the sale of PPE and reconcile the results of a physical count of relevant PPE to the general ledger, as this may highlight any possible omissions.

Supporting documentation should be obtained and inspected for sales and trade-ins of PPE. This documentation should include cash remittance advices and/or sales agreements. These are examined to determine the accuracy of the accounting records, including the recognition of any related gain or loss. The gain or loss on disposal of a fixed asset is re-calculated by the auditor to ensure its accuracy. Proceeds received should be traced to bank statements to confirm receipt and that the profit or loss on disposal was calculated correctly.

Depreciation

The client entity's depreciation methods must be reviewed to ensure that they are reasonable and consistent with the prior year. It is also important to ensure the depreciation policy used by the client entity is in agreement with the depreciation policy as outlined in the financial statements. The auditor will use one of two methods to verify the accuracy of the depreciation charge:

1. **Test of Details** In this method, the auditor verifies the accuracy of the depreciation charge by recalculation. This can be completed on a sample basis. First, the auditor needs to obtain a schedule of depreciation charged by asset and agree this schedule to the charge in the financial statements. He then selects a sample of assets and re-computes the depreciation charge for each asset selected, and agrees the charge calculated to the client's charge as per the lead schedule. The use of CAATs may mean that the auditor can easily test 100% of the population due to the ability to repeat formula in applications such as Excel (see **Chapter 9**).
2. **Substantive Analytical Procedure** (covered under **Chapter 5,** Section 5.4, which addresses the requirements of ISA 520 *Analytical Procedures*). A **substantive analytical procedure** (also known as a '**proof in total**') is a widely used method for auditors to validate the depreciation charge in the financial statements. This involves computing the depreciation by class on an overall basis. **Example 11.5** below illustrates how to test depreciation on a reasonableness basis.

EXAMPLE 11.5: SUBSTANTIVE ANALYTICAL PROCEDURE ON DEPRECIATION

In the 'Depreciation' section of the Statement of Accounting Policies in **Appendix C**, relating to Large Company Limited, the company's policy with respect to expected useful lives is outlined. The auditor can use this to prepare a substantive analytical procedure (proof in total) on depreciation. It also states that the company charges a full year of depreciation in the year of purchase and a full year's depreciation in the year of disposal.

This information, along with elements of the fixed asset note and fixed asset register (which indicates that €60,000,000 of the plant and machinery is fully depreciated), allows the auditor to calculate an expected deprecation charge as follows:

Freehold Land and Buildings According to Note 13, property, plant and equipment, €15,000,000 of the €400,000,000 relates to freehold land, which means that €385,000,000 is depreciable (remember: under IAS 16, land is not depreciable). Therefore €385,000,000 charged as straight-line depreciation over 22 years would require an annual depreciation charge of €17,500,000.

Plant and Machinery According to the Statement of Accounting Policies, 'Property, Plant Equipment', plant and machinery has a useful life of three years, a full year's depreciation is charged on additions and on disposals, and the straight-line method is used to calculate depreciation. Furthermore, the fixed asset register indicates that €60,000,000 of plant and machinery is fully depreciated. The auditor's calculation would look something like this:

	Cost €000s	NBV €000s	Useful Life (Years)	Expected Charge €000s
Balance at 1 January 2012	113,625	N/A	3	37,875
Less Fully Depreciated	(60,000)	0		(20,000)
Additions	82,250	N/A	3	27,417
				45,292

Motor Vehicles Also according to Large Company's Statement of Accounting Policies, motor vehicles have a useful life of four years, a full year's depreciation is charged on additions and disposals and the straight-line method is used to calculate depreciation. Thus, the auditor's calculation would be as follows:

	Cost €000s	NBV €000s	Useful Life (Years)	Expected Charge €000s
Balance at 1 January 2012	28,800	N/A	4	7,200
Additions	35,000	N/A	4	8,750
				15,950

Comparison of Expected Depreciation to Actual Depreciation	€000s
Total Expected Depreciation (17,500 + 45,292 + 15,950)	78,742
Actual Depreciation Charged	81,205
Difference	2,463

This difference would be compared to a threshold (tolerable error) calculated by the auditor. If the difference was within the threshold, the depreciation charge would be accepted as not being materially misstated. If the difference was outside of the threshold, the auditor would have to perform further substantive procedures in order to be satisfied as to the accuracy of the depreciation figure. The tolerable error will take into account: materiality, risk and the value of the balance being tested.

Considering that the performance materiality for Large Company Limited is €2,731,875 (see **Example 11.2** above), it is likely that the above difference would be above a calculated threshold and therefore further audit procedures would be performed.

Further audit procedures may include either performing tests of details or querying with management why they believe the expected depreciation charge based on your calculation differs from that of the actual charge in the financial statements. The difference would be noted on the auditor's error schedule.

Assessing Reasonableness of Useful Lives It important that the auditor considers the reasonableness of the useful lives applied by the entity. It is not enough to compare the useful life in the depreciation calculation with that stated in the depreciation section of the statement of accounting policies detailed in the financial statements; the auditor must also consider if the estimate of useful life is appropriate. The three years' depreciation period for plant and machinery appears quite low, although it may be adequate for the type of equipment in this industry, and considering that, as per **Example 11.2**, the PPE additions are 78% and disposals 43% off opening balance, this may well be reasonable. Additionally, charging a full year's depreciation in the year of addition as well as the year of disposal seems aggressive, and management should be queried in relation to this.

Property, Plant and Equipment Balances

Having obtained evidence for the management assertions related to the movements with property, plant and equipment, the auditor must then be satisfied as to the continued existence of the PPE balances. Existence can be determined in a number of ways, and three key methods of determining existence are discussed below:

1. **Physical inspection** The auditor should request to view (physically inspect) a sample of assets to confirm their existence. This will also give him the opportunity to inspect their condition and confirm that they are actually in use. Assets that appear unused (indicating obsolescence and impairment) should be queried with management to ensure that their valuation is recorded accurately in the financial statements.
2. **Ownership documentation** The physical presence of an asset does not prove that it actually belongs to the client; thus, by inspecting ownership documents, such as title

deeds, vehicle registration certificates, etc., the auditor confirms the rights and obligations assertion.

3. **Insurance documentation** Reviewing insurance documentation will also provide evidence of existence and rights and obligations, as the client entity will only insure assets that it owns. The insurance value of assets will also give some indication of valuation.

Other Considerations

Having performed the substantive procedures relating to PPE movements and PPE balances, there are some other matters that the auditor must consider before he has adequately completed his substantive procedures relating to PPE. These include:
- an **impairment** review;
- consideration of any **revaluations** of PPE; and
- substantive procedures for **leases** (where applicable to the entity).

We will consider each of these in turn.

Impairment Review

The client entity is required to carry out an impairment review where there is any indication that an individual asset or class of assets may be impaired. The auditor's job in this context is twofold:
1. he must ensure that the client has adequately considered the possibility of impairment; and
2. then, where impairment reviews have taken place, the auditor must ensure that these are in line with IAS 36 *Impairment of Assets*.

1. The client entity's consideration of impairment The auditor's first task is with regard to the client entity's consideration of impairment. An **impairment review** is required by the client entity at the end of the first financial year following the purchase of an asset, and annually where an asset's useful life exceeds 20 years or is indefinite. IAS 36 recognises that an impairment review should be carried out when there is some indication that impairment has occurred. Impairments generally arise when there has been an event or change in circumstances, such as:
- something has happened to the asset (e.g. physical damage); or
- there has been a change in the economic environment in which the asset is used (e.g. taxes on assets with high emissions may render those assets uneconomical to use going forward and they may have become impaired); or
- there has been a change in the demand for the product which the asset is used to produce (e.g. a move away from carpets to laminate flooring, rendering carpet looms impaired).

2. Ensuring client's impairment reviews are in line with IAS 36 As required by IAS 36, the auditor must ensure that the **carrying value** of property, plant and equipment does not exceed the greater of their **net realisable value** (sales price less cost to sell) or **value in use** (**net present value** (NPV), of a cash flow or other benefits that an asset generates for a specific owner under a specific use. This can be tested by completing the following:
- reviewing the client entity's workings on the impairment (how have they calculated the impaired value?);

- reviewing the reasonableness of the assumptions used in the calculation of the impairment. (The auditor would inquire of management about any potentially overvalued assets. Obsolete and damaged assets should be physically inspected and compared to values included in financial statements.);
- determining if any assets of the client entity are held that relate to discontinued activities.

The audit of estimates was discussed in **Chapter 6**, Section 6.9, which covers the requirements on the auditor when auditing estimates under ISA 540 *Auditing Accounting Estimates, Including Fair Value Accounting Estimates, and Related Disclosures*.

Revaluation of Property, Plant and Equipment

The client entity may decide to revalue PPE so as to reflect a more accurate value in the statement of financial position. A revaluation of an asset should reflect the 'real' conditions surrounding the asset of the client entity based on actual market conditions. According to IAS 16:

"If an item of property, plant and equipment is revalued, the entire class of property plant and equipment to which that asset belongs shall be revalued." (para 36)

Thus, the auditor needs first to consider if the client entity has properly considered the entire class of PPE where one asset within that class has been revalued.

Also required by IAS 16:

"Revaluations shall be made with sufficient regularity to ensure that the carrying amount does not differ materially from that which would be determined using fair value at the end of the reporting period." (para 31)

This requires the auditor to ensure that if a policy of revaluation exists, then the client entity considers the revalued amount regularly to ensure that it is reflected at its fair value. The auditor can make inquiries of management as to their approach to these considerations and should review any exercises carried out by management which demonstrate that their consideration of the fair value of the revalued assets, even in years where no revaluation has taken place.

If assets are revalued during the period under review, the auditor must obtain a copy of the valuer's report as per ISA (UK and Ireland) 620 *Using the Work of an Auditor's Expert* (see **Chapter 10**). Before considering this report of the expert, the auditor should first consider the calibre of the expert by reviewing his experience in the subject area and his qualifications. The auditor should also consider his relationship to the client entity in order to ensure that the report is not subject to bias.

In assessing the expert's work, the auditor should ensure that the substance of the expert's findings are properly reflected in the financial statement assertions. The auditor must also consider:

- the source of the data used (was it generated by the client entity or by some other external source?);
- the assumptions and methods used;
- when the work was carried out;
- the reasons for changes in assumptions and methods; and

- the result of the expert's work in light of the auditor's knowledge of the business and the results of other audit procedures (i.e. is the expert's work corroborated by other evidence found?).

As discussed in **Chapter 10**, Section 10.4, the auditor is not the expert and therefore cannot judge all assumptions and methods used. However, he should seek to obtain an understanding of these to consider their reasonableness. This will involve discussions with the expert as well as with the client to ensure that explanations, assumptions and methods are not contradictory to other evidence obtained.

Leases

Leases may be classified as either **finance leases** (capitalised under PPE) or **operating leases** (charged to the statement of comprehensive income). For PPE held under lease agreements, it is important that the auditor obtains a copy of each lease agreement and ensures they are correctly classified in line with IAS 17 *Accounting for Leases* (IAS 17). For assets held under finance leases, these assets should be included in the client entity's **fixed asset register**. The cost of assets held under finance leases should be verified by comparison with purchase invoices. This cost should also be agreed to the cost as stated in the finance lease agreement. IAS 17, paragraph 20, states that, at the commencement of the lease term, finance leases should be recorded as an asset and a liability at the lower of the fair value of the asset and the present value of the minimum lease payments (discounted at the interest rate implicit in the lease, if practicable, or else at the enterprise's incremental borrowing rate). The auditor needs to obtain a copy of the lease agreement and ensure that all conditions of the lease are recorded correctly and comply with the requirements of IAS 17.

11.9 USE OF COMPUTER-ASSISTED AUDIT TECHNIQUES FOR PROPERTY, PLANT AND EQUIPMENT

The purpose of computer-assisted audit techniques (CAATs) and their generic uses are discussed in detail in **Chapter 9**, Section 9.4. We will now consider the primary use of CAATs when auditing the area of property, plant and equipment, which include the following:
- **Preparation of the lead schedule** Frequently, the auditor will use audit software that will read the client entity's trial balance and prepare the PPE **lead schedule**, which will assist the auditor to control the performance of the audit.
- **Preparation of depreciation expectation** Often, off-the-shelf programs, such as Excel, are used to help to perform the **proof in total (substantive analytical procedure)** on depreciation due to its ability to deal with formula.
- **Tests of details on depreciation** The auditor can obtain a copy of the client entity's assets by class, including their individual cost, accumulated depreciation and NBV. By converting the data into Excel, for example, the auditor can insert formulas to recalculate the depreciation of each individual asset and then make a comparison to the client entity's calculation. When using a tool like Excel, the auditor has the ability to

test 100% of the population, as the formula can be easily copied and hence provide an efficient and accurate calculation.
- **Interrogation of the computerised fixed asset register** This can help the auditor identify material additions and disposals.

11.10 DISCLOSURE REQUIREMENTS

Finally, with regard to PPE the auditor will consider the adequacy of the disclosures. Disclosure requirements relating to PPE for most companies entail inclusion of the 'Fixed Asset Note', as discussed many times throughout this chapter. However, the auditor needs to consider the requirements of IAS 16 to ensure that all disclosures are:
- complete (no PPE-related disclosures are missing – the auditor can use IAS 16 as a checklist);
- accurate (reflect the actual transactions and information relating to events surrounding PPE);
- related to events that actually occurred; and
- properly presented (i.e. in a manner expected by IAS 16).

The disclosure requirements are included in IAS 16, paragraphs 73–79 and include requirements relating to:
- restrictions on title;
- contractual commitments;
- details of revaluations;
- details of finance leases; and
- details of borrowing costs capitalised.

The auditor must fully understand these requirements in order to adequately review the adequacy of the client entity's disclosures.

11.11 CONCLUSION

While property, plant and equipment can represent a material balance in the financial statements and, for some classes of assets, be inherently risky, the auditor frequently takes a focused substantive approach. The reason for this is due to the fact that the volume of transactions relating to movements on fixed assets accounts is normally low and 100% (or at least a high percentage coverage) is normally possible; therefore, the auditor can efficiently test PPE using a substantive approach.

When auditing the area of PPE, the auditor needs to pay special attention to the existence management assertion by physically inspecting the asset and ownership documents. Additionally, care must be taken when assets are revalued to assess, not just the calculation presented by a valuer (auditor's expert) but also the experience, qualifications and expertise of the valuer himself.

Significant disclosure requirements exist in the area of PPE and the auditor should dedicate sufficient time to ensuring the completeness and accuracy of all PPE disclosures in the financial statements.

Summary of Learning Objectives

Having studied this chapter on the audit of property, plant and equipment you should now:

Learning Objective 1 Understand what is included in the audit of property, plant and equipment.

IAS 16 *Property, Plant and Equipment* governs the accounting treatment of PPE, which can include assets such as freehold land and buildings, plant and machinery, or motor vehicles. On the face of the statement of financial position the net book value (cost less accumulated depreciation) is disclosed and this is expanded upon in a note to the financial statements. The auditor must audit the management assertions relating to the figures that appear on the face of the statement of financial position as well as the disclosure notes that support them.

Learning Objective 2 Be able to identify the risks and audit objectives applicable to PPE.

The primary risks associated with PPE relate to the risks of:
• Existence – do the assets actually exist and are they in use?
• Valuation – are the assets worth the carrying value included in the financial statements (are they impaired due to obsolescence, damage, etc.)?; and
• Have only items capitalisable under IAS 16 been capitalised?

Audit Objectives/Management Assertions for PPE All assertions are relevant for PPE on the transactions side (additions and disposals). The auditor will seek to ensure that the transactions occurred, are complete, properly classified (according to IAS 16) and pertain to the company. Additionally, the auditor will seek to ensure the accuracy of the depreciation figure included in the income statement. With respect to the PPE balance, the auditor will seek to ensure that all PPE exists and is complete, that the entity has the rights to ownership and that all PPE is appropriately valued.

Learning Objective 3 Be able to determine an appropriate audit strategy for PPE, taking into consideration the specific risks and audit objectives (assertions).

Developing the Audit Plan for PPE Generally, the volume of PPE purchased in the period is relatively low and so the auditor will normally take a substantive approach when testing PPE (i.e. not test and rely on controls to reduce substantive testing).

Learning Objective 4 Be able to develop an audit programme that addresses all the audit objectives (assertions) for PPE.

Key Documents when Auditing PPE The 'fixed asset register' is the key document of interest to the auditor. Other documents which may form audit evidence connected to PPE include:
• additions invoices;
• certificates of destruction;

- title deeds;
- vehicle registration certificates;
- accounting policy documents connected to PPE.

Key Substantive Testing Procedures Connected to PPE
- **Depreciation** The auditor normally conducts **substantive analytical procedures** when testing depreciation.
- **Valuation** The auditor will consider indications of impairment of assets; for assets revalued in the period the auditor will seek evidence not only on the valuation provided by the valuer but also on the expertise and competence of the valuer himself (known as an auditor's expert).
- **Existence** The auditor will seek to prove existence by: (a) physical inspection of the asset; and (b) inspecting ownership documentation.
- **Additions and Disposals** The auditor will trace the transactions to source documentation to prove their occurrence.
- **Repairs and Maintenance** The auditor will review the repairs and maintenance general ledger account to ensure that no items included therein are of a capital nature (**completeness**). Additionally, he will review the assets capitalised to ensure none is of repairs and maintenance nature (**classification**).

Learning Objective 5 Be able to describe and apply specific substantive testing procedures relating to the audit of PPE.

Specific procedures relating to the audit of PPE, other than relating to the standard audit of additions, disposals, depreciation and year-end balances, include the consideration of: impairment reviews; revaluations of PPE; and leases.

Learning Objective 6 Understand the role CAATs can play when auditing PPE.

The auditor may use a combination of audit software, data analysis tools and other applications, such as Excel, when auditing the area of PPE.

Learning Objective 7 Understand the auditor's approach relating to the disclosures of PPE.

The auditor needs to consider the requirements of IAS 16 to ensure that all necessary PPE disclosures are: complete and in line with IAS 16; accurate; relate to events that actually occurred; and are properly presented.

QUESTIONS

Self-test Questions

11.1 When should the cost of an item of PPE be recognised as required by IAS 16?

11.2 What is a fixed asset register and who should maintain it?

11.3 What are the benefits of performing an analytical review?

11.4   What should the costs of an item of PPE comprise of? (Refer to IAS 16.)

11.5   Where should the costs of repairs and maintenance of PPE be recognised?

11.6   Describe the two methods an auditor uses to verify the accuracy of the depreciation charge.

11.7   List three ways that the existence of PPE can be verified.

11.8   What circumstances may give rise to impairment of PPE?

11.9   When using the work of an auditor's expert, what should the auditor consider?

Review Questions

(See Suggested Solutions to Review Questions in **Appendix D**.)

Question 11.1

Outline the audit procedure that is most likely to detect the incorrect capitalisation of an expense to fixed assets.

Question 11.2

When auditing non-current fixed assets (PPE), why might the auditor decide to assess control risk as high and therefore perform predominantly substantive testing?

Question 11.3

Builder Limited ('Builder') is a new client of your audit firm. Builder is an engineering company. You are the audit senior. The accounts clerk in Builder has provided you with the draft accounts, which show the following tangible fixed assets (PPE) for the year ended 31 March 2013.

	Freehold Land and Buildings €000	Plant and Machinery €000	Motor Vehicles €000	Total €000
Cost				
At 1 April 2012	1,231	679	423	2,333
Additions	122	242	147	511
Disposals	–	(125)	(162)	(287)
At 31 March 2013	**1,353**	**796**	**408**	**2,557**
Depreciation				
At 1 April 2012	674	333	267	1,274
Charge for year	54	80	82	216
Disposals	–	(99)	(138)	(237)
At 31 March 2013	**728**	**314**	**211**	**1,253**

Requirement The manager on the engagement has asked you to prepare a memorandum for the assistant assigned to the audit, setting out the work programme that the assistant should carry out in the audit of the tangible fixed assets (PPE) in Builder.

Question 11.4

Handitel Limited ('Handitel') manufactures a range of mobile phones and operates a cellular phone network. You are audit senior on Handitel and have been provided with the following reconciliation of Handitel's fixed assets (PPE) for the year ended 31 December 2012.

RECONCILIATION OF FIXED ASSET REGISTER TO THE NOMINAL LEDGER

	Notes	€000
Balance as per fixed asset register at 31 December 2012		14,802
Less		
Plant held on operating lease	1	(357)
Repairs posted to fixed asset register	2	(174)
Assets purchased 5 January 2012	3	(1,400)
Add		
Assets excluded from fixed asset register	4	589
Adjustment for capitalisation of interest	5	73
Asset constructed internally	6	3,061
		16,594

1. This piece of plant was leased in August 2012 for a six-month term.
2. The clerk responsible for maintaining the fixed asset register was on maternity leave for six months from March to September 2012. A placement student was taken on to carry out her duties while on leave. On review of the fixed asset register, the accountant uncovered two revenue expense items that were posted to the register in April 2012.
3. This vehicle was ordered in November 2012 and delivered on-site on 15 December 2012. A 20% deposit was paid at the time of the order with the balance paid on 5 January 2013.
4. Assets received in September 2012 but not posted to the fixed asset register until January 2010.
5. Handitel decided to change its accounting policy on capitalisation of interest and now opts to capitalise all interest payments.
6. This asset was brought into use in October 2012, with the most significant construction cost being Handitel's own labour.

Requirement Prepare the audit programme in respect of the fixed asset (PPE) reconciliation above, detailing the specific audit tests you would perform on each reconciling item.

THE AUDIT OF INVENTORY

LEARNING OBJECTIVES

Having studied this chapter on the audit of Inventory you should:
1. understand what is included in the audit of inventory;
2. be able to identify the risks and audit objectives applicable to inventory;
3. be able to determine an appropriate audit strategy for inventory, taking into consideration the specific risks and audit objectives (management assertions);
4. be able to develop an audit programme that addresses all the audit objectives (management assertions) for inventory;
5. be able to describe and apply specific substantive testing procedures relating to the audit of inventory; and
6. understand the role CAATs can play when auditing inventory.
7. understand the auditor's approach relating to the disclosures of inventory.

CHECKLIST OF RELEVANT STANDARDS

The relevant standards covered in this chapter are:
- ISA (UK and Ireland) 315 *Identifying and Assessing the Risks of Material Misstatement Through Understanding of the Entity and Its Environment* (ISA 315)
- ISA (UK and Ireland) 330 *The Auditors Responses to Assessed Risks* (ISA 330)
- ISA (UK and Ireland) 500 *Audit Evidence* (ISA 500)
- ISA (UK and Ireland) 501 *Audit Evidence – Specific Considerations for Selected Items* (ISA 501)
- ISA (UK and Ireland) 510 *Initial Audit Engagements – Opening Balances* (ISA 510)
- ISA (UK and Ireland) 520 *Analytical Procedures* (ISA 520)
- ISA (UK and Ireland) 530 *Audit Sampling* (ISA 530)
- ISA (UK and Ireland) 540 *Auditing Accounting Estimates, Including Fair Value Accounting Estimates, and Related Disclosures* (ISA 540)
- ISA (UK and Ireland) 620 *Using the Work of an Auditor's Expert* (ISA 620)
- IAS 2 *Inventories* (IAS 2)
- IAS 11 *Construction Contracts* (IAS 11)

KEY TERMS AND DEFINITIONS FOR THIS CHAPTER

Aged Inventory Listing   An entity's aged inventory listing depicts the total inventory balance, broken down by the length of time that inventory has been in the entity's books.

Bill of Material (BOM)   This is a list of all components required to make a particular item of inventory, including quantities of each item needed to manufacture a finished product.

Cycle Counts   Cycle counts are when an entity performs ongoing counts of its inventory throughout the year instead of performing a full inventory count at the year end.

Final Inventory Sheet   The final inventory sheet breaks down the inventory balance in the financial statements by inventory item, along with the quantity and unit price per inventory item. Its total should represent the carrying value of inventory in the financial statements.

Roll-forward or Roll-back Procedures   When the auditor is unable to attend the physical inventory count at year end, he may attend an earlier or later physical inventory count and, internal control procedures permitting, he can perform a roll-forward or roll-back to determine the existence of inventory at year end.

12.1 INTRODUCTION

Sections 12.2 to **12.8** of this chapter outline the requirements of IAS 2 *Inventories* (IAS 2) with respect to inventories and then consider how the auditor:
(a) identifies audit risks and audit objectives (management assertions) for inventory;
(b) develops an audit plan for inventory and refines this into an audit programme;
(c) designs specific tests associated with inventory; and
(d) ensures adequate presentation and disclosure in the financial statements relating to inventory.

In **Section 12.9** we consider how computer-assisted audit techniques (CAATs) (considered in detail in **Chapter 9**) can assist with the audit of inventory.

Finally in **Section 12.10** we consider the auditor's approach when auditing the reasonableness of disclosures relating to inventory.

12.2 WHAT IS 'INVENTORY'?

IAS 2 is the International Accounting Standard governing the requirements for inventories and the auditor shall seek to ensure that inventories are recorded in compliance with this standard.

Inventory is commonly referred to as 'stock'. In a manufacturing company, inventory consists of three elements: raw materials, work in progress (WIP) and finished goods. For example, in the car-manufacturing business, one of the raw materials is steel, a component of WIP might be a chassis, and finished goods would be the finished car, which will be the final product for sale. However, in a retail company there will only be goods for sale.

Inventory may be verified by a physical count (inventory count), most commonly at the year-end or recorded on a continuous 'rolling' system (basis). In either case, extensive tests of control must be performed over both the recording of inventory and the maintenance of inventory records in order to "obtain sufficient appropriate audit evidence regarding the existence and condition of inventory" (ISA (UK and Ireland) 501 *Audit Evidence – Specific Considerations for Selected Items* (ISA 501, paragraph 3). ISA 501, at paragraph 6, states that if the auditor is unable to attend the physical inventory counting due to unforeseen circumstances, the auditor should observe some physical counts on an alternative date and perform audit procedures on intervening transactions. For example, his non-attendance may have arisen due to his perception that the location did not hold material inventory values or because he was not aware of the location at the time of the count.

12.3 RISKS ASSOCIATED WITH INVENTORY

Throughout **Chapter 7** (which addresses the requirement of ISA (UK and Ireland) 315 *Identifying and Assessing the Risks of Material Misstatement Through Understanding of the Entity and Its Environment* (ISA 315) and ISA (UK and Ireland) 330 *The Auditor's Responses to Assessed Risks* (ISA 330) we discussed the topic of 'risk' and we considered how the auditor should go about detecting risks. We also discussed how the auditor should consider these risks when designing the nature, timing and extent of further audit procedures relative to each financial cycle. As such, before developing the audit plan, the auditor needs to consider a number of risks that may be associated with inventory. Risks associated with inventory can include:

- The reliability of the inventory recording system – see details of **cycle counting** below.
- The volume of transactions that have occurred during the year, i.e. sales, purchases and transfers. If this is high, then there is a greater chance of misstatements occurring.
- The saleability of products is constantly affected by demand and competition, and therefore valuation is always at risk (lower of cost and net realisable value (NRV).
- Valuation allocations relating to materials, labour and overheads, accounting for scrap and obsolescence, joint product costs, etc.
- Timing of inventory counts and reliability of **roll-forward procedures** in place if the inventory count is not held at the year end. Roll-forward procedures include tracking movements in and out of inventory between the count and the period end. The assessment of controls surrounding the movements of inventory is critical in determining whether a count can be performed pre-year end.
- Location of inventory, as often inventory may be stored in multiple locations or with a third party.
- Physical controls over inventory and its susceptibility to theft. Susceptibility to theft will take into consideration such factors as: (a) how easy it is to sell in a black market economy; (b) how moveable the product is; and (c) the value of the product. Examples of inventory items susceptible to theft include:
  - cigarettes (demand on the black market due to high retail price, small in size, easy to transport and a reasonable value can be obtained due to high retail value);
  - mobile phones (for the same reasons as above, though the transfer of mobile phones is becoming increasingly difficult due to built-in technology that disables stolen phones or built-in tracking devices); and
  - phone-credit cards (again, small and easy to transport and high retail value-making them easy to sell on the black market, which is why they no longer exist in card form and now are run off system only on purchase).
- The degree of fluctuation in inventory levels.
- The nature of the inventory and the requirement of specialist knowledge, e.g. valuing mining activities or works of art may require specialist knowledge (i.e. the use of an auditor's expert as covered in **Chapter 10**, Section 10.4, which addresses the requirements of ISA (UK and Ireland) 620 *Using the Work of an Auditor's Expert* (ISA 620).
- Susceptibility of the inventory to obsolescence. This is more prevalent in some industries than others (e.g. the shelf-life in the supermarket department of a store versus the clothing department, where inventory is not perishable, however an issue still arises in the clothing department due to items going out of fashion).
- Risks associated with goods sold on a sale or return basis.
- Risks due to fraud, which include:
  - false sales;
  - movement of inventory between different locations with inventory counts on different days (entity may move inventory from one location to the other to increase inventory in both locations);

- application of inappropriate estimation techniques (e.g. inappropriate allocation of overheads);
- altered inventory count sheets; and
- additional inventory count records being added to those prepared during the count.

The auditor will focus less on those risk factors which he determines will not have a material impact on the financial statements.

12.4 AUDIT OBJECTIVES/MANAGEMENT ASSERTIONS FOR INVENTORY

As discussed in **Chapter 6** (which addressed the requirements of ISA (UK and Ireland) 500 *Audit Evidence* (ISA 500)), it is necessary for the auditor to seek appropriate audit evidence to satisfy all of the audit objectives and to eliminate the possibility of any of the risks outlined in **Section 12.3** going undetected. In **Chapter 4** we introduced audit objectives (management assertions) and explained their generic meanings and then we reintroduced this topic again throughout **Chapter 8**, making management assertions specific to each financial cycle. In **Table 12.1** we remind you once more of the audit objectives/management assertions as they relate to inventory.

Table 12.1 addresses the management assertions (audit objectives) as they relate to the transactions and events occurring during the period relating to inventory.

TABLE 12.1: INVENTORY AUDIT OBJECTIVES FOR
TRANSACTIONS AND EVENTS DURING THE PERIOD

Management Assertion/ Audit Objective	Objective of Audit Test
Existence	To ensure all purchase and sales transactions represent inventories acquired and sold during the year. To ensure that all transfers between locations and categories are correctly recorded.
Completeness	To ensure all purchases, sales and transfers of inventory above have been recorded.
Accuracy/valuation	To ensure all materials, labour and overheads have been accurately calculated for each class of inventory.
Cut-off	To ensure that all purchases, sales and transfers of inventory have been recorded in the correct accounting period.
Ownership	To ensure that all inventory held during the period is the property of the entity.
Classification, Presentation and Disclosure	To ensure that all inventory transactions have been properly classified in the financial statements in accordance with applicable accounting standards.

Table 12.2 below addresses the management assertions (audit objectives) as they relate to the balances associated with inventory.

TABLE 12.2: INVENTORY AUDIT OBJECTIVES FOR ACCOUNT BALANCES AT YEAR END

Management Assertion/Audit Objective	Objective of Audit Test
Existence	The inventory amounts in the balance sheet exist at the year-end date.
Completeness	All inventories have been recorded in the financial statements at the year-end date.
Accuracy	Inventory items have been accurately identified, measured and recorded at the lower of cost and net realisable value
Valuation	Inventories are properly valued, making provisions for damaged, slow-moving or obsolete inventory.
Cut-off	All transactions relating to the movements of inventory have been recorded in the correct accounting period.
Ownership	All inventory items in the statement of financial position are owned by the client.
Disclosure	Inventories have been properly classified and disclosed in the financial statements.

Now that we understand the objectives of the auditor with regard to inventory, in the following sections we will consider how the auditor addresses these objectives through substantive testing.

12.5 DEVELOPING THE AUDIT PLAN FOR INVENTORY

Before the audit of inventory is undertaken, an assessment of audit risk must be completed. As discussed in detail in **Chapter 7**, audit risk is made up of three components: inherent risk (discussed under **Section 12.3**); control risk (discussed under **Section 12.4**); and detection risk, which is determined by the auditor based on his assessment of inherent and control risk. We will consider these components specifically as they relate to inventory in order to determine the type of audit approach the auditor might take. Remember, as discussed in **Chapter 7**, the auditor's assessment of the required detection risk will determine the nature, timing and extent of further audit procedures.

Audit Risk = Inherent Risk + Control Risk + Detection Risk

An entity's inventory may or may not have a large number of inherent risks, depending on the inventory type, industry and economic environment. These are considered in **Section 12.3** above. With regard to the **control environment**, the auditor may have already tested a significant amount of controls for inventory while testing purchases and revenue (purchases will relate to the goods inwards of inventory and revenue will relate to the goods out of inventory).

The auditor is required to attend the physical inventory count of the client entity regardless of controls in place in the entity. As such, testing the controls cannot reduce this task to any large extent other than to reduce sample sizes reviewed during the observation of the inventory count. In a non-manufacturing environment, the auditor may decide that it is not efficient to test inventory controls and instead take some reliance received (through controls testing) over revenue and purchases to support some inventory assertions and for the balance perform focused substantive testing. Remember: the controls in the revenue and receivables cycle relate to the sale of inventory, and the controls in the purchases and payables cycle relate to the purchase of inventory and, as such, testing the controls here provides supporting evidencefor the movement of inventory in and out of the warehouse.

In a manufacturing environment, however, the volume of testing using a wholly substantive (focused substantive approach) may be too onerous and the auditor may find it more efficient and effective just to test the controls surrounding inventory. When testing the controls in a manufacturing environment, the auditor may get the benefit of dual tests (tests which support the control objectives but also support substantive testing objectives), particularly in the area of standard costing. For example, during controls testing an understanding of the approach used to allocate overheads to individual items of inventory would need to be ascertained by the auditor and this information will assist the auditor when testing the cost of the inventory item at the substantive stage.

12.6 KEY DOCUMENTS RELATING TO INVENTORY

The following outlines the key documents relating to inventory that the auditor will require during his audit of inventory.

Aged Inventory Listing

The entity's **aged inventory listing** depicts the total inventory balance, broken down by the length of time that inventory has been held. The aged inventory listing allows the auditor to query items of inventory that have been held for long periods of time and are either: (a) not moving, such as inventory item 'Chair C' in **Example 12.1** below; or (b) have subsequent movement in later periods, such as inventory items 'Table C' or 'Wood Type C' in **Example 12.1** below.

With regard to finished goods 'Chair C', because no other inventory is recorded for this item other than that held for more than 120 days, it may lead the auditor to believe that this inventory item is obsolete (no longer saleable). With regard to finished goods 'Table C', the entity appears to be building up large inventories of this item and the auditor might query why it continues to produce this item when a large inventory holding already exists. For raw material 'Wood Type C', the auditor might ask why new inventory items have been purchased in the last 60 days when there was €200,000 worth of inventory that was 120 days old. This inventory may be damaged and unusable, causing the entity to buy new batches. All of the above can be used to help with supporting the valuation assertion (i.e. answering the question: will the product sell for more than cost?).

EXAMPLE 12.1: AN AGED INVENTORY LISTING (FOR LARGE COMPANY LIMITED)

Inventory Description	Class	Total Value €000s	Current €000s	30–60 days old €000s	60–90 days old €000s	90–120 days old €000s	>120 days old €000s
Table A	FG	1,200	1,200				
Table B	FG	5,200	4,000	1,000	200		
Table C	FG	11,700	5,000	5,000	1,000	700	
Chair A	FG	1,164	1,164				
Chair B	FG	900	800	100			
Chair C	FG	400					400
Stool A	FG	2,400	2,400				
Stool B	FG	2,610	2,610				
Stool C	FG	2,350	2,000	350			
		27,924	19,174	6,450	1,200	700	400
Batch of Table A	WIP	5,130	5,130				
Batch of Chair A	WIP	1,615	1,000	615			
Batch of Stool C	WIP	5,785	5,785				
		12,530	11,915	615	–	–	–
Wood Type A	RM	200	200				
Wood Type B	RM	300	200	100			
Wood Type C	RM	1,500	1,000	300			200
Metal A	RM	1,600	1,600				
Metal B	RM	2,400	2,000	400			
Metal C	RM	3,320	2,000	1,200			120
		9,320	7,000	2,000	–	–	320
Total		49,774	38,089	9,065	1,200	700	720
		100%	76.5%	18.2%	2.4%	1.4%	1.5%

FG – Finished Goods
WIP – Work in Progress
RM – Raw Materials

Final Inventory Sheets

A **final inventory sheet** breaks down the inventory balance in the financial statements by inventory item along with the quantity and unit price per inventory item. The final inventory sheets are used to compare (cross-reference) to physical inventory count sheets when confirming the completeness and existence of inventory items. This document also supports the testing of cost, as the auditor can verify unit price of raw materials to supporting purchase invoices or standard costing workings. A detailed discussion of its use is contained at 'Inventory Balance' in **Section 12.8** below.

EXAMPLE 12.2: A FINAL INVENTORY SHEET FOR LARGE COMPANY LIMITED

Inventory Description	Category	Quantity	Per Price (Cost) Unit	Total Value
		Units	€	€
Table A	Finished Goods	4,000	300	1,200,000
Table B	Finished Goods	8,000	650	5,200,000
Table C	Finished Goods	12,000	975	11,700,000
Chair A	Finished Goods	12,000	97	1,164,000
Chair B	Finished Goods	9,000	100	900,000
Chair C	Finished Goods	2,000	200	400,000
Stool A	Finished Goods	8,000	300	2,400,000
Stool B	Finished Goods	8,700	300	2,610,000
Stool C	Finished Goods	4,700	500	2,350,000
				27,924,000
Batch of Table A	WIP	19,000	270	5,130,000
Batch of Chair A	WIP	19,000	85	1,615,000
Batch of Stool C	WIP	12,856	450	5,785,200
				12,530,200
Wood Type A	Raw Materials	2,000	100	200,000
Wood Type B	Raw Materials	3,000	100	300,000
Wood Type C	Raw Materials	5,000	300	1,500,000
Metal A	Raw Materials	8,000	200	1,600,000
Metal B	Raw Materials	8,000	300	2,400,000
Metal C	Raw Materials	8,300	400	3,320,000
				9,320,000
			Total	**49,774,200**

Physical Inventory Count Sheets

A physical inventory count sheet is a sheet used by the client entity employees to record the physical inventory counted during the physical inventory count. A client entity may have several different warehouses and within each warehouse there may be separate locations, in which case the client entity may have a physical inventory count sheet at a warehouse level or individual sheets which relate to locations within the warehouse. Each client entity inventory location that is physically counted should have two count sheets. This is to facilitate a more accurate 'blind count'. A blind count requires two individuals to independently count the inventory using their own count sheets that are not pre-populated with expected volumes per inventory system records (i.e. what is recorded in the client entity's accounting records). When they have completed their independent counts, they then compare their results and investigate any differences. (Examples of physical inventory count sheets are included below.) Once the comparison is made and the counters are satisfied they have an accurate count, the auditor selects a sample from:

1. the inventory floor (i.e. physical location where inventory is held) to the physical inventory count sheet to test for completeness; and
2. the physical inventory count sheet to the inventory floor to test for existence.

Copies of the physical inventory count sheets are taken and **then compared** to the final inventory sheets at the audit fieldwork stage. A full discussion of the physical inventory count and the auditor's procedures with respect to same is included at 'Evidence on Quantity – Attending Entity Inventory Year-end Count' in **Section 12.8** below.

EXAMPLE 12.3: PHYSICAL INVENTORY COUNT SHEETS FOR LARGE COMPANY LIMITED

Location	Dublin Road Premises
Stores Type	Raw Material Stores
Counter 1	John Duffy

	Quantity Counted
Wood Type A	200
Wood Type B	200
Wood Type C	1,000
Metal A	1,600
Metal B	2,000
Metal C	2,000

Location	Dublin Road Premises	
Stores Type	Raw Material Stores	
Counter 2	Carl Ryan	
	Quantity Counted	Agreed to Counter 1
Wood Type A	200	Yes
Wood Type B	200	Yes
Wood Type C	1,000	Yes
Metal A	1,600	Yes
Metal B	2,000	Yes
Metal C	1,800	No – further investigation revealed an area missed by counter 2, so 2,000 is confirmed quantity.

Signed

Counter 1	John Duffy
Counter 2	Carl Ryan

12.7 SUBSTANTIVE AUDIT PROGRAMME FOR INVENTORY

An audit programme records the specific details of tests to be performed by the auditor. The audit programme becomes a guide to the audit engagement team as to the work to be performed in a particular area. As work is completed, a reference is included on the audit programme showing the location on the audit file where details of the tests performed are included. The audit programme for any cycle will vary from entity to entity and below we consider the typical types of test the auditor would include in the audit programme for inventory.

EXAMPLE 12.4: AUDIT PROGRAMME FOR INVENTORY[1]

Large Company Limited **31 December 2012**			
	Audit Materiality		€3,642,500
	Performance Materiality		€2,731,875
		Initials	**Date**
	Prepared by:		
Inventory	**Reviewed by:**		

---

[1] Source: based on *Procedures for Quality Audit 2010* (© Chartered Accountants Ireland, 2010), G1.

Audit Programme	Assertion Covered	Reference to Work	Initials and Date
Ensure the audit plan is reflected in the following tests. The following steps are suggestions only and should be removed or added to as necessary to address the risks of material misstatement identified at the risk-assessment stage.			
Accounting Policy			
Assess the appropriateness of the accounting policy and the accounting estimates method for this area. Ensure that the accounting policy is in accordance with accounting standards and applicable law, and that the methods used for making the accounting estimates are appropriate.	Existence, Completeness, Rights and Obligations, Accuracy/ Valuation and Classification		
Initial Procedures			
Obtain or prepare lead schedules. 1. Distinguish between raw materials and consumables, work in progress, and finished goods and goods for resale. 2. Agree to balance sheet.	Completeness and Existence		
Prepare commentary explaining the composition of inventory balances and comparing them with prior periods and our expectations. Investigate significant changes in inventory levels and values.	Completeness and Existence		
Inventory Balances – Attendance at the Entity Year End Inventory Count			
Refer to full audit programme (see **Example 12.6** below)	Completeness and Existence, Valuation: through physical inspection of condition.		

Inventory Balances – Valuation			
Test check pricing of final inventory sheets by vouching a sample to purchase invoices or costing records.	Valuation		
Ascertain and record basis of valuation of work in progress.	Valuation		
Test check valuation of work in progress and ensure that: 1. material costs are correctly recorded; 2. the allocation of labour hours is correct; 3. the allocation of overheads is correct; and 4. the accounting for turnover and attribution of profit in long-term work in progress is appropriate.			
Consider treatment of slow-moving and obsolete inventory. Ensure that provisions are adequate and consistent. Challenge the estimation techniques used by management in the calculation of the provision. Consider the outturn of the provision in previous years.	Valuation		
Ensure that inventory and work in progress are valued at the lower of cost and net realisable value. In reviewing NRV, consider: 1. the saleability of inventory; 2. overall inventory levels and levels of key items; 3. post year-end sales of key inventory items.	Valuation		

Other Considerations			
Where inventory is held by third parties on behalf of the company, obtain confirmations where amounts are material. (ISA 501, para 8)	Existence		
Where the company holds inventory on behalf of third parties, such items are excluded from inventory. Where material, consider confirmation from the third party.	Rights and Obligations		
Cut-off			
Review the documentation obtained at the period end physical inventory counting relating to the last goods movements (in and out) in the period.	Cut-off		
Agree this documentation to purchase and sales invoices recorded in the nominal ledger. Ensure that these purchases and sales are recognised in the same period as the inventory movement to which they relate.	Cut-off		
In addition, consider material purchase and sales invoices posted pre- and post-period end. Agree these invoices to goods receipt and dispatch documentation. Ensure that these sales and purchases are recorded in the correct periods.	Cut-off		
Contracts			
Ascertain the nature of contracts, i.e. short term or long term, and ensure that these are appropriately categorised.			

Short-term Contracts Select a sample of contracts from the accounting records and discuss the state of progress with the person in charge. Vouch costs incurred to supporting documents, e.g. invoices, timesheets, etc.	Occurrence/ Existence and Accuracy/ Valuation		
Review the allocation of overheads to contracts to ensure the basis is reasonable and consistent.	Valuation		
Review the progress on these contracts post-period end and evaluate whether the contract is being valued at the lower of cost and NRV.	Valuation		
Review the level of provisions to ensure they are adequate.	Valuation		
Long-term contracts Select a sample of contracts from the accounting records and discuss the state of progress with the person in charge. Vouch amounts included in turnover to appropriate supporting documents, e.g. surveyors' certificates as being the value of work done.	Occurrence/ Existence and Accuracy/ Valuation.		
Vouch costs incurred to supporting documents, e.g. invoices, timesheets, etc. ensuring they are correctly allocated between current and future periods.	Valuation		

Review the allocation of overheads to contracts to ensure the basis is reasonable and consistent.	Valuation		
Vouch amounts invoiced on account to the revenue ledger and ensure the balance/excess on payments to account is correctly calculated and treated.	Accuracy/ Valuation		
Compare the costs to date against the estimated budgeted cost to the same stage of completion and consider the requirement for a provision.	Accuracy/ Valuation		
Ensure that any provisions/ accruals for foreseeable losses are treated appropriately and consider the need for any further provision.	Accuracy/ Valuation		

Conclusion

Subject to the matters noted for the reviewer, in my opinion sufficient audit assurance has been obtained to enable us to conclude that Inventories are not materially misstated.

Note: a separate substantive audit programme is included at (see Example 12.6) which covers substantive procedure for attendance at the entity's physical inventory count.

Name:	Accountant in Charge
Date:	
Name:	Reviewer
Date:	

12.8 SUBSTANTIVE TESTING PROCEDURES FOR INVENTORY

Below we are going to discuss in more detail some of the procedures outlined in the substantive audit programme above at **Example 12.4**.

We will start with initial procedures, which include: opening balances; mathematical accuracy of schedules; the lead schedule; and analytical reviews.

Initial Procedures

Opening Balances

Before commencing further audit procedures, evidence must be obtained as to the accuracy of the opening balances of inventory. The reason for this is twofold: first, it confirms that the comparative figures in the financial statements (which must be included in the current year's financial statements) agree to the final accounts of the prior year; and, secondly, it highlights any final entries (last-minute adjusting journal entries) of the prior year not correctly carried forward, which may indicate an error in the current year's financial statement figures. The auditor tests opening balances as follows:

- Agree the opening balances to the prior-year working papers and signed financial statements. This may highlight an opening balance in the current year's accounts that does not agree to the closing balance per the prior year's financial statements. In this instance a change would be made to the opening balance of the current year, which would impact the closing balance of the current year. This usually arises due to final adjustments in the prior year that are not reflected in the actual accounts (nominal and general ledgers).
- If this is the first year of the audit engagement, the auditor will still need to establish that the opening balances are materially correct, which can pose difficulty for him if either the client entity was exempt from audit in the prior year or a predecessor auditor carried out the audit. The audit of opening balances in such instances is discussed in detail in **Chapter 6**, **Section 6.8** which addresses the requirements of ISA (UK and Ireland) 510 *Initial Audit Engagements – Opening Balances* (ISA 510).

Mathematical Accuracy of Schedules

The auditor obtains the **final inventory sheets** and **aged inventory listing** of the entity and tests their mathematical accuracy. The value of the aged inventory listing is agreed to the inventory balances in the statement of financial position and the inventory note in the financial statements.

Prepare Lead Schedules

The **lead schedule** acts as a summary of the balances and transactions to be audited relating to a particular class of transactions and balances. It allows the auditor to control his procedures by referencing each balance or transaction to the working paper that records the audit tests performed.

The auditor prepares a lead schedule that agrees to the inventory note in the financial statements. The lead schedule should provide a summary of current and prior year inventory balances broken into raw materials, work in progress and finished goods. An example of an inventory lead schedule is included at **Example 12.4** below.

EXAMPLE 12.4: INVENTORY LEAD SCHEDULE[2]

Large Company Limited			
31 December 2012	**Audit Materiality**		**€3,642,500**
	Performance Materiality		**€2,731,875**
		Initials	**Date**
	Prepared by:		
Inventory	**Reviewed by:**		
	31 December 2012	**31 December 2011**	
	€000	**€000**	
Raw materials and consumables	9,320	7,770	
Work in progress	12,530	10,750	
Finished goods and goods for resale	27,924	16,500	
	49,774	35,020	

Analytical Review (Initial)

An analytical review (covered under **Chapter 5**, Section 5.4, which addresses the requirements of ISA (UK and Ireland) 520 *Analytical Procedures* (ISA 520) is usually performed at the start of each substantive procedure relating to each balance or class of transactions. Calculating ratios and analysing results against industry information, prior-year results, budgets, etc., allows the auditor to get a feel for the movements in the year and make comparisons against norms, thereby enabling him to better prepare the audit programme. The following example shows the types of ratio and comparison the auditor might perform in relation to inventory. An analytical review is similar to preliminary analytical procedures and focuses the auditor on movements and key ratios that equip him with additional insight prior to commencing his substantive procedures. At the close of his substantive procedures, the auditor aims to ensure that he can comment on all movements and key ratios with supporting explanations. If the auditor cannot explain any element then this will highlight to him the need to perform additional substantive procedures.

---

[2] Source: based on *Procedures for Quality Audit 2010* (© Chartered Accountants Ireland, 2010), G-.

The analytical review performed here differs from a substantive analytical procedure in that the auditor's aim is not to substantiate the balance (i.e. prove the assertions), but rather to ensure that he understands the movements and relationships, to assist him in performing substantive procedures.

A standard analytical review for the audit of inventories would include:
- reconciling changes in inventory quantities from the beginning to the end of the year to purchases, sales and production records;
- comparing quantities and amounts of inventories in their various categories to those at the prior-year balance sheet date and to the current period's sales and purchases;
- comparing gross profit and inventory turnover ratios year-on-year;
- obtaining industry comparisons and trends; and
- calculation of key ratios, such as inventory turnover, gross margin, etc.

An example of the type of analytical procedures carried out at the initial stages of substantive testing by the auditor is included at **Example 12.5** below.

EXAMPLE 12.5: ANALYTICAL REVIEW CARRIED OUT AS PART OF INITIAL SUBSTANTIVE PROCEDURES

	31/12/2012 €	31/12/2011 €	Movement €	Commentary
Raw materials and consumables	9,320	7,770	1,550	
Work in progress	12,530	10,750	1,780	
Finished goods and goods for resale	27,924	16,500	11,424	
	49,774	**35,020**	**14,754**	
			42%	
Inventory turnover (Cost of sales ÷ inventory)	=140,250 ÷ 49,774	=120,800 ÷ 35,020		
	2.82 times	3.45 times		

While inventories have increased by 42%, inventory turnover has decreased by only 18%, indicating that the increase in inventory is supporting the increase in revenue.

Inventory Balance

Having performed the initial procedures, now let us consider the specific audit procedures the auditor might carry out in relation to the inventory balance, which essentially includes the auditor obtaining evidence with regard to: the quantity of inventory at year end; and the price used to value inventory.

The inventory is essentially made up of two key variables: **quantity** and **price**. Consider the final inventory sheet at **Example 12.2** above. The auditor, having received this, would first re-calculate the total and ensure its mathematical accuracy and then he would trace the total value to the statement of financial position and the inventory note. Once satisfied that it agrees, he must then obtain sufficient appropriate audit evidence over the quantity and price that makes up the total value. He does this by: (a) attending the entity's inventory count; and (b) vouching price (cost per unit) back to supporting purchase invoices or standard costing records and by assessing if there are any indicators that the net realisable value (NRV) may be less than cost.

Let us discuss this in more detail, starting with how the auditor obtains evidence with regard to inventory quantities.

Evidence on Quantity – Attending Entity Inventory Year-end Count

Attending the entity's year-end inventory count enables the auditor to inspect the inventory, observe compliance with the operation of management's procedures for recording and controlling the results of the count and provide audit evidence as to the reliability of management's procedures. There are three steps involved: planning; attending; and completing the inventory count. The responsibilities of the auditor are detailed in the following audit programme in **Example 12.6**.

EXAMPLE 12.6: AN AUDIT PROGRAMME FOR ATTENDANCE
AT YEAR-END INVENTORY COUNT[3]

Large Company Limited 31 December 2012			
	Audit Materiality		**€3,642,500**
	Performance Materiality		**€2,731,875**
		Initials	**Date**
Inventory – attendance Substantive Tests	**Prepared by:**		
	Reviewed by:		
Test	**Assertion Covered**	**Reference to Work**	**Initials and Date**
Planning the Inventory Count			

---

[3] Source: based on *Procedures for Quality Audit 2010* (© Chartered Accountants Ireland, 2010), G2.

Obtain and evaluate details of the client's planned inventory count procedures (ISA 501, para 4). Review and confirm that: 1. client staff are properly briefed; 2. proper controls have been set up to cover inventory movements and cut-off; and 3. the overall procedures are adequate and will result in the accurate recording of inventory and work in progress.	Completeness, Existence, Rights and Obligations and Valuation		
Review the prior period's audit file and/or the audit planning memorandum for major inventory lines held, their location and any special knowledge required for identifying inventory, its condition, etc.	Existence and Valuation		
Attending the Inventory Count			
Attend the client's physical inventory counting of sites where inventory held is material, unless impractical. Note conclusions drawn from observing count, as to: 1. care taken by client staff; 2. accuracy of recording results; 3. the execution of the count and the manner in which instructions were followed; 4. control of inventory movements; 5. control over issue of count sheets and their return, including ruling off of inventory sheets after last item and cancellation of issued but unused sheets; 6. recording of damaged, obsolete or slow-moving goods; and 7. control over counting to ensure that inventory is not double counted or omitted and the manner in which problems were cleared.	Accuracy, Completeness, Existence and Valuation		

Select a sample of items from the inventory on hand and: 1. count items and trace to the count sheets, note and reconcile any differences; 2. if an item looks obsolete or damaged, ensure a note is made to this effect; and 3. check that enough detail is recorded on the test schedule to ensure that the item can be traced to the final inventory sheets.	Existence and Valuation		
Select a sample of items from the count sheets and: 1. check to physical inventory, note and reconcile any differences; 2. if an item looks obsolete or damaged, ensure a note is made to this effect; and 3. check that enough detail is recorded on the test schedule to ensure that the item can be traced to the final inventory sheets.	Completeness and Valuation		
Review procedures taken to record the current stage of completion of work in progress and confirm that these are being followed.	Accuracy and Valuation		
Inspect inventory area, and make enquiries of the staff to determine if there are slow-moving or obsolete items of inventory. In particular, enquire about and document items stored in relatively inaccessible areas, dirty or damaged items and items with previous year's inventory tickets still attached.	Valuation		

Where the client uses numbered goods inward and outward dockets, note the last numbers used before the count commences. Where these are not in use consider and document what other cut-off controls exist. (See cut-off items immediately below.)	Cut-off		
Obtain a list of completed despatch documents for goods not despatched at the inventory count date and ascertain whether these were included in the inventory count.	Cut-off		
Determine whether items in the goods inward area are included in the inventory count.	Cut-off		
Note the numbers of the count sheets used to ensure that none is added or removed at a later date.	Completeness and Existence		
Non-attendance at Year-end Inventory Count			
If the physical counting is conducted at a date other than the date of the financial statements, perform additional audit procedures to obtain audit evidence about whether changes in inventory between the count date and the date of the financial statements are properly recorded. (ISA 501, para 5)	Completeness and Existence		
If unable to attend physical inventory counting make or observe some physical counts on an alternative date and perform audit procedures on intervening transactions. (ISA 501, para 6)	Completeness and Existence		
If attendance at the physical inventory counting is impracticable, perform alternative procedures to obtain sufficient appropriate audit evidence regarding the existence and condition of the inventory. (ISA 501, para 7)	Completeness and Existence		

Agreeing Outcome of Inventory Count to Final Inventory Sheets				
Obtain final inventory sheets and test check additions and extensions.	Existence and Completeness			
Complete physical inventory audit programme and Trace all items tested during the inventory count from rough inventory sheets (obtained during the inventory count) to the final inventory sheets.	Completeness			
Select a sample of items from the final inventory sheets and trace back to the rough inventory sheets (obtained during inventory count).	Existence			
Consider the extent and implication of goods in inventory subject to reservation of title.	Rights and Obligations			
Conclusion				
Subject to the matters noted for the reviewer, in my opinion sufficient audit assurance has been obtained to enable us to conclude that the inventory count was adequately performed.				
Name:			**Accountant in Charge**	
Date:				
Name:			**Reviewer**	
Date:				

The above audit programme relates to an inventory count that occurs at the year end. It is the auditor's attendance at the inventory count that provides him with evidence to support the existence assertion (audit objective). Difficulty arises for the auditor, however, in two instances as follows:

- where the client entity performs **cycle counts**; and
- where the physical inventory count **occurs either before or after the year-end**.

Below we consider these instances in more detail.

Cycle Counts

Some companies do not carry out a full inventory count at year end but perform ongoing counts of their inventory throughout the year. These ongoing counts are commonly known as **cycle counts**. This proves less disruptive to the operations of the business and also ensures that any discrepancies noted in the inventory quantities held can be identified and investigated on an ongoing basis. Cycle counts also ensure that companies can meet tight year-end reporting deadlines.

When cycle counting is in place, the auditor will not have a full inventory count report to rely on to cover the existence assertion. As such, the book quantities held at year end must be relied on. Therefore, the auditor must be confident that the inventory system is reliable (by testing the related controls). The following are factors that the auditor can assess in this regard:

1. Reliable internal controls over inventory.
2. Properly planned programme of continuous counting:
    (a) clear responsibility for the count;
    (b) detailed count plans to ensure all items are counted at least once, with high value items counted on a more regular basis;
    (c) segregation of duties, i.e. independence of counters from storekeepers.

Physical Inventory Count occurs Before or After the Year End

If the physical inventory count takes place before or after the year end, the auditor needs to consider how he can test the existence assertion for the volume of inventory included in the financial statements at year end. The counting of inventory may occur before or after the year end for various reasons. For audit purposes, this is deemed acceptable, provided records of inventory movements in the intervening periods are maintained such that the movements can be examined and substantiated. Difficulties in performing this calculation should be lessened provided a well-developed system of internal control exists and satisfactory inventory records are kept. The physical count should ideally occur no more than three months before or after the year end. The auditor should still attend this count to validate the physical inventory counted (using the same audit programme noted above at **Example 12.4**). His audit procedures thereafter, however, will be reconciling the physical inventory at the time of the count to the physical inventory that existed at the year end. He will do this by vouching the inventory movements (e.g. sales of inventory out and purchases of inventory in) that support the reconciliation.

ISA 315 states that tests of controls or substantive testing may be performed at an interim date and inventory counts are an example of an audit procedure sometimes performed at an interim date. Attending an inventory count before year end may facilitate an entity with tight reporting deadlines.

When considering whether to rely on inventory counts performed before or after the year end, the auditor should consider:
- the control environment;
- risks over inventory;
- when relevant information is available, i.e. when the client entity's physical inventory count takes place;
- reliability of the inventory control system;
- length of period between the inventory count and the year end; and
- materiality of inventory figures.

If the physical inventory count is performed at an interim date, **roll-forward procedures** must be completed in order to agree the quantities counted to the inventory listing at year end (if the count takes place after the year end, the auditor performs roll-back procedures). The following are examples of roll-forward procedures:

- Testing the completeness of raw material receipts between the physical inventory count and the year end. This may be tested through testing the sequence of goods received notes (GRNs) and tracing a sample of the GRNs to the raw material sub-ledger.
- Testing the completeness of the transfer in to work in progress (WIP) from raw materials (RM) and the transfer out of work in progress to finished goods (FG). This may be completed by testing a sample of journal entries for transfers of RM to WIP, and WIP to FG.
- Checking the completeness of dispatches of FG. This should be tested by checking the sequence of dispatch notes and tracing a sample of items in sales reports to the FG sub-ledger.

(*Note*: sampling is covered in **Chapter 6**, Section 6.7, which addresses the requirements of ISA (UK and Ireland) 530 *Audit Sampling* (ISA 530).)

While some audit procedures relating to inventory can occur before or after the year end, other audit procedures relating to inventory can only be performed at the year end (for example, cut-off) as the risk only occurs at the year end.

We now know how the auditor obtains evidence relating to the existence assertions so let us address how he obtains evidence relating to the valuation assertion which involves the auditor obtaining audit evidence relating to the cost of inventory and then comparing this cost to the likely net realisable value of the related inventory (i.e. comparison of cost versus NRV).

Evidence on Price (Value) – Vouching Cost and Testing Cost versus NRV

IAS 2 defines **cost** as "all costs of purchase, costs of conversion and other costs incurred in bringing the inventories to their present location and condition". (IAS 2, para 10).

The cost of inventory may be stated at actual cost (conventional method) or at a standard cost (**standard costing** method). Cost should be calculated for each category of inventory and not for inventory as a whole. A standard costing system involves the company setting a budget/standard cost for inventory items at the beginning of the year. The standard is then used to price the inventory as it passes through the company's costing system. Any difference from the standard results in variances, i.e. when the cost of purchasing the goods is more/less than the standard. These purchase price variances are then allocated to cost of sales/inventory as appropriate.

Closing inventory should be valued using **FIFO (first in first out)**, unit cost or weighted average. **LIFO (last in first out)** and replacement cost approaches are not acceptable. When examining the value at which inventory is recorded, the auditor should ascertain the prices at which finished goods have been sold post-year-end, as this will highlight any items that may need to be reduced to below cost. The auditor should ensure that the selling price takes into account any trade discounts allowed and whether such selling price has been reduced by disposal costs. This adjusted selling price should then be compared to the **carrying value** of the finished goods.

The auditor should also review post year-end sales of inventory to establish whether or not the sales price (and therefore the NRV) is achievable. A provision may be required for slow-moving or obsolete inventory based on this review.

The auditor should determine the client entity's policy for the valuation of inventory and ensure that it is in line with IAS 2, which states that inventory must be valued at the lower of cost and net realisable value (NRV). **Net realisable value** is the selling price less the cost to completion, less selling, marketing and distribution costs. It may also be defined as the value the inventory would achieve in the open market based on its present condition. An example of how to test that the inventory is costed correctly would be to obtain a sample of invoices to support the cost of a sample of inventory and obtain a copy of the most recent sales invoice to support the selling price. Compare the selling price to the cost and ensure it is valued at the lower of both.

To summarise the above discussion, there are two stages involved in validating the price used to value inventory:
1. validating cost by vouching to original purchase invoices/standard costing records; and then
2. ensuring that inventory is valued at the lower of cost and NRV.

Validating Cost by Vouching to Original Purchase Invoices/Standard Costing Records

Validating Raw Material Cost Price

As introduced above, when validating the original cost of inventories the auditor may be faced with two types of costing systems: a '**conventional costing system**', which refers to 'goods bought for resale' (e.g. in the retail business the goods are sold as purchased with no alternations to the product); or a '**standard costing system**', where inventory purchased represents raw materials that need to be converted into finished goods. Along with the raw materials, other costs will be incurred in turning raw materials into finished goods, such as: production wages and salaries; equipment depreciation; and overheads to cover light, heat and rent of the production area. The following considers the auditor's approach with regard to validating the 'cost' assigned to the client entity's inventory using both methods of costing:
- *Conventional Costing System* The auditor needs to determine that the inventory is stated at the lower of cost and NRV. This can be tested by verifying the cost used by the client entity to value the inventory at the year end to a purchase invoice.
- *Standard Costing System* The auditor must satisfy himself that the standard cost approximates closely to the actual cost. This can be verified through agreeing the standard to a supporting purchase invoice for a sample of raw materials. Also, the purchase price variances which arise should be reviewed as they indicate the reasonableness of the standard (i.e. if large variances occur between the standard cost and the actual costs incurred for production, then the standard cost may not be an accurate reflection of the actual costs to make the finished goods item). Furthermore, in order for the auditor to adequately

review the accuracy of the standard costs, he must first gain a good understanding of the standard costing system and the process for developing standard costs. The auditor should also consider how often the standards are revised and who sets them, i.e. are the standards set annually/quarterly and how attainable are they? If standards are attainable, the level of variances should be low. Also, the procedures for setting standards should be reviewed by the auditor for reasonableness.

Validating Work in Progress/Finished Goods (Short-term Contracts)

Work in progress (WIP) includes both short-term WIP and long-term WIP. Short-term WIP is considered here. WIP and finished goods (FG) will contain an element of labour and overheads that have brought the raw materials to the WIP/FG stage. The cost collection of these elements is usually captured on a **bill of material** (BOM). Remember, as defined at the outset of this chapter, the BOM is a list of all components required to make a particular item of inventory, including quantities of each item needed to manufacture a finished product.

The following audit procedures should be carried out by the auditor in relation to the validation of WIP and finished goods for short-term contracts:
- *Raw Material Element* Cost accounting records should be cross-checked to accounting records and vice versa. In order to test the materials component, a BOM should be obtained and the raw materials input should be tested as outlined above. All documentation should be properly authorised and any variances investigated.
- *Labour Element* The labour element of a BOM should be tested by comparing the labour content to job sheets/time sheets and compare the labour rate to payroll records. The auditor should:
  - reconcile financial and cost accounting records;
  - ensure the wage rate indicated on the job sheet agrees to wage rates determined by social security documentation, etc., and that the total time indicated on the job sheet is the actual labour cost allocated to the job; and
  - ensure that idle time has not been charged to the job, and is instead charged to overhead expenses.
- *Overhead Element* An understanding should be gained of how overheads are allocated to inventory items, i.e. machine hours or labour hours. The basis for allocating overheads should be broadly in line with the prior year and based on normal production levels in the company. All overheads relating to abnormal activity levels should be written off to the income statement, e.g. idle time when machinery is being repaired. The overhead absorption calculation should then be re-performed through agreeing the relative factors to underlying documentation, e.g. machine hours to production schedule, labour hours to time sheets. All related supporting documentation should be examined.

Validating Work in Progress/Finished Goods (Construction Contracts – IAS 11)

Long-term WIP, often relating to construction contracts, can cover many accounting periods and often proves to be a problematic area for auditors to review. The auditor may have to exercise judgement and involve an expert valuer. The auditor should:

- examine contracts to determine timescales and penalty clauses;
- ascertain which costing system was used and determine whether it can be relied on, given the nature of the contract;
- ensure that costs incurred are accurate, genuine and complete;
- assess the stage of completion and ensure that costs are properly charged to the item based on the stage reached;
- inquire into the qualifications, etc., of the expert valuer certifying the completed work;
- ensure that all profits realised are eliminated from WIP (IAS 2 does not allow elements of profit to be included in WIP); and
- identify any losses on contracts as these have to be recognised in the valuation.

Standard Costing – Treatment of Variances

As previously mentioned, the auditor should compare actual and standard costs of items included in the year-end valuation. Due to the nature of **standard costing**, differences will always arise between the standard and the actual cost of production. These variances may be as a result of differences relating to the price of raw materials, differences in the cost of labour or differences in the cost of overheads related to the product. During the audit, the level of variances should be analysed, which would provide an indication of the reliability of the standards. Attainable standards will not give rise to large variances as the standard will approximate cost. As a rule, variances which relate to inefficiencies and are not as a result of a poorly set standard should be expensed to the statement of comprehensive income. However, if the standards are not set accurately, the variances that arise should be apportioned between cost of sales and inventory appropriately. The auditor should ascertain the last time the standards were reviewed and determine whether the current standards are still relevant in light of changes in general prices, production methods and product specification. Any changes in standards should be properly authorised.

EXAMPLE 12.7: DEMONSTRATING THE AUDIT PROCEDURES USED
FOR VALUATION OF DIFFERENT CLASSES OF INVENTORY

If we look back at **Example 12.2** (final inventory sheet), we can see that the unit cost price for inventory item 'Wood Type A' is priced at €100 per unit. Wood Type A is a raw material, so the auditor can validate this by simply obtaining a recent purchase invoice for Wood Type A and vouching that the €100 represents the price paid.

Inventory item Table A has a unit cost price €300. Table A is a finished good. The auditor can validate this by reference to standard costing, which could be made up of items such as those contained in the bill of materials (BOM) below. For the raw material items, the auditor can perform the same test as that noted for raw materials above (vouch to purchase invoice). For the labour and overhead allocations, the auditor needs to test the standard costing assumptions for reasonableness as follows:
- Validating the total number of labour hours available in a year and the total cost of direct labour for a year (both of which could be obtained through testing of payroll).

The total cost divided by the total number of hours available should be close to €25. The total labour hours for the year should be that operating in the normal environment.
- Validating the total expected cost of direct overheads in the year (which again should be based on normal capacity) and the total number of labour hours in a period (as per above). The total direct overheads divided by the total number of labour hours should be close to €15.
- The auditor can validate the reasonableness of the depreciation by reference to his testing of non-current fixed assets.

Table A: BOM for batch of 100

	Units	Unit Cost €	Total €
Raw Material – Wood type A	99	100	9,900
Raw Material – Metal A	99	200	19,800
Labour (per hour)	6.75	25	169
Overhead (per labour hour)	6.75	15	101
Depreciation (Plant Item A)	6.75	5	34
Cost to produce batch of 100			**30,004**
Cost to Produce 1 unit			300

The same type of exercise can be performed for work in progress by estimating its stage of completion to the above.

Ensuring Inventory is Valued at the Lower of Cost and NRV

The auditor must be alert to indications that NRV may be lower than cost. Examples of when NRV is likely to be less than cost include when there has been:
- an increase in costs and a decrease in selling price (indicated in tests of details of samples selected above and sales invoices in the new period);
- physical deterioration of inventory or obsolescence (indicated by observation during attendance at the physical inventory count);
- a marketing decision to sell below cost (indicated in management meeting minutes or through inquiry of management);
- errors in production or purchasing (indicated by high returns of customer product in the new period); or
- a fall-off in sales of the inventory item (indicated by zero/minimal orders of the inventory item in the order book in the new period).

Other Considerations

Having performed the substantive procedures relating to inventory movements and inventory balances, there are some other matters the auditor must consider before he has adequately completed his substantive procedures relating to inventory. These include considerations relating to: inventory provisions; the cut-off of inventory; and the ownership of inventory. These are discussed below.

Inventory Provisions

The auditor should ensure that slow-moving, damaged and obsolete inventory is provided for in the accounts, and review the reasonableness of the inventory provision. This requires the auditor to review the estimate for the inventory provision (Estimates are covered in **Chapter 6**, Section 6.9, which addresses the requirements of ISA (UK and Ireland) 540 *Auditing Accounting Estimates, Including Fair Value Accounting Estimates, and Related Disclosures* (ISA 540).)

Inventory held at the current year end should be compared to that held at the prior year end to identify any non-moving items. Records of the physical inventory counts should be reviewed for items noted of an unsaleable condition.

In relation to WIP, the auditor reviews the records for any WIP items which have no expenses charged in recent months. This may highlight items that have not been worked on recently, where the WIP has been cancelled. This may also be completed through reviewing the ageing of the inventory provision. The auditor should also test the ageing of the aged inventory report through agreeing a sample of inventory to their related goods received notes (GRNs), to determine how old the inventory is, and agreeing the age of the inventory to the **aged inventory listing**. In reviewing the inventory provision, the auditor may also review the physical inventory count report for details of obsolete inventory and testing the controls over identification of obsolete inventory. Some companies may perform monthly/quarterly reviews of obsolete inventory, which will determine amounts to be written off and amounts to be provided for.

Cut-off

Cut-off testing ensures that all movements of inventory are recorded in the correct period. In order to test this assertion, a review should be made of goods received notes (GRNs) and dispatch dockets around the period end to ensure they are sequential, and any missing numbers should be investigated. Further, a sample of goods in/out on either side of year end should be selected for testing to ensure they are recorded in the correct period. The last GRN and dispatch docket numbers should have been obtained during the attendance at the year-end inventory count and these should be used as evidence of the last goods in and the first goods out.

In order to guarantee accurate cut-off, the auditor should ensure that management:
- allocate the responsibility to a certain individual for ensuring cut-off details are accurate;
- ensure there is no movement in and out of inventory while the inventory count is being performed;
- ensure that, if movements are occurring, records are being kept of all movements and goods inward are being held in a separate location until the count has ceased.

Ownership

Inventory items belonging to third parties should be identified and excluded from the final inventory summary. Also, the auditor must ensure that inventories awaiting dispatch, which have been included in sales, are excluded from inventory figures.

The following situations often pose problems for auditors when reviewing inventory and WIP:

1. **The ownership of goods bought near the year end** This relates to goods purchased, but not yet delivered to the entity at the balance sheet date. The auditor must ascertain whether legal title has passed, based on the terms of the individual contract. The auditor must also determine whether the goods in question have been correctly or incorrectly included in the financial statements at the balance sheet date. An adjustment may be required based on his findings.

2. **The ownership of goods sold near the year end** This relates to goods sold, but which are still on the client's premises at the balance sheet date. The auditor must ensure that these goods are not included in inventory in the financial statements.

3. **Consignment inventory** This relates to goods that are not owned by the client, but are held on consignment or under a franchise agreement, until a specified condition is met. These items should not form part of the inventory figure at the balance sheet date. The auditor should also ensure that the opposite is also the case, where inventory owned by the client which is held on consignment or under a franchise agreement by a third party is included in the closing inventory figure at the balance sheet date. In this case, the auditor should physically inspect the inventory where possible. If this is not permitted, he should request confirmation from the third party as to the quantities and condition of items held or perform other audit procedures that will provide sufficient appropriate audit evidence as to the existence and condition of the inventory.

12.9 USES OF COMPUTER-ASSISTED AUDIT TECHNIQUES WHEN AUDITING INVENTORY

The purpose of computer-assisted audit techniques (CAATs) and their generic uses are discussed in detail in **Chapter 9**, Section 9.4. Some of the uses of CAATs by the auditor when auditing the area of inventory include:

- manipulating client entity schedules to highlight negative inventory balances (simple sort in Excel for example or through the use of audit software);
- stratifying inventory balances in order to ensure the most material balances are considered while still ensuring the total population is audited (stratification is discussed in more detail in **Chapter 6**, Section 7.
- re-performing the ageing of inventory using a programme such as Excel or audit software;
- re-totting the aged inventory listing for comparison to the financial statements;
- identifying slow-moving or obsolete inventory;
- quickly identifying items below re-order level; or
- comparing inventory cost to purchase ledger records in the new year when testing for cost versus NRV.

12.10 DISCLOSURE REQUIREMENTS FOR INVENTORY

Finally, with regard to inventory, the auditor will consider the adequacy of the disclosures. When considering the adequacy of the disclosures relating to inventory the auditor needs to consider the requirements of IAS 2, paragraph 36, to ensure that all disclosures are:
- complete (no inventory related disclosures are missing. The auditor can use IAS 2 as a checklist);
- accurate (reflect the actual transactions and information relating to the events surrounding inventory);
- relate to events that actually occurred or exist at the year end; and
- are properly presented (in a manner expected by IAS 2).

IAS 2, paragraphs 36–39 details the disclosures required for inventory which include:
- accounting policies used to value inventory, including the cost formula used;
- details of inventories valued at NRV;
- ensuring the correct classification of inventory between, raw materials, work in progress, and finished goods;
- ascertaining the value of inventory sold under retention of title clauses and ensure adequate disclosure. Retention of title, otherwise known as reservation of title, relates to where the supplier retains title of the goods sold until he has been paid;
- ensuring correct disclosure of inventory pledged as security for liabilities of the client or third parties;
- details of the write-down of inventory expensed during the year;
- if a reversal of a write-down occurred, a description of the circumstances which caused this; and
- details of long-term contracts.

The auditor must fully understand these disclosure requirements in order to properly review the adequacy of the client entity's disclosures.

12.11 CONCLUSION

When the auditor has performed controls testing, substantive analytical review and substantive tests of details, he must consider if sufficient appropriate audit evidence has been obtained over inventory, which gives the appropriate level of comfort required over the management assertions/audit objectives stated at the outset, these being:
- completeness;
- valuation;
- existence/occurrence;
- cut-off;
- valuation; and
- rights and obligations.

The auditor must also consider if the testing performed has appropriately addressed any key risks identified by the auditor surrounding the inventory cycle and reduced the risk of material misstatement arising as a result of key risks to a suitably low level.

When testing the area of inventory the auditor is most concerned with the completeness and existence assertions, which he ascertains through his attendance at the physical inventory count, and with the valuation assertion, for which he remains alert to indications of events that may give rise to cost being greater than NRV.

The auditor must consider the impact on the audit opinion of the results of his testing in the area of inventory. He does so by considering whether any misstatements, found either individually or in aggregate (when combined with other misstatements detected throughout the audit) will result in the financial statements being materiality misstated. As such, all misstatements found are taken to the auditor's errors schedule for consideration at the audit completion stage (discussed in detail in **Chapter 18**). The auditor's report on financial statements is considered in detail in **Chapter 19**, 'Audit Reports'.

SUMMARY OF LEARNING OBJECTIVES

Learning Objective 1   Understand what is included in the audit of inventory.

IAS 2 *Inventories* is the International Accounting Standard that governs inventories and the auditor will seek to ensure that inventories are recorded in compliance with this standard.

Inventory is commonly referred to as stock. In a manufacturing company inventory consists of three elements: raw materials, work in progress and finished goods.

Learning Objective 2   Be able to identify the risks and audit objectives applicable to inventory.

Risks Associated with Inventory The primary risks associated with inventory relate to:
• the volume of transactions and the reliability of internal controls in tracking them;
• the risk of inventory items being worth less than cost;
• the complicated accounting associated with standard costing;
• the susceptibility of inventory to theft;
• degree of fluctuations in inventory levels; and
• inventory's susceptibility to obsolescence.

Audit Objectives/Management Assertions for Inventory With respect to the movements of inventory in the period, the auditor is predominantly interested in the occurrence, accuracy and completeness of transactions.

Learning Objective 3   Be able to determine an appropriate audit strategy for inventory, taking into consideration the specific risks and audit objectives (management assertions).

When auditing the inventory balance, the auditor is seeking to ensure existence and completeness (the inventory actually exists at the year end and all inventories that exist are included) and that the inventory is appropriately valued (lower of cost and NRV as per IAS 2).

Learning Objective 4   Be able to develop an audit programme that addresses all the audit objectives (management assertions) for inventory.

Developing the Audit Plan Generally speaking, in a non-manufacturing environment the auditor will not seek to test and rely on controls as the majority of movements of inventory will have been tested within revenue and receivables and purchases and payables. Additionally, the auditor must attend the physical inventory count at year end regardless of controls and, as such, the controls approach is rarely the efficient approach to take. In a manufacturing environment the auditor may choose to test the controls around valuation (standard costing).

Learning Objective 5   Be able to describe and apply specific substantive testing procedures relating to the audit of inventory.

Key Documents when Auditing Inventory The aged inventory listing and physical inventory count sheet are the key documents of interest to the auditor. Other documents with may form audit evidence connected to inventory include:

- Bills of Material (BOM);
- Inventory Purchase Invoices.

Key Substantive Testing Procedures Connected to Inventory With regard to the transactions, generally speaking, the auditor will have tested these through his testing of revenue and receivables and purchases and payables. With respect to the manufacturing environment the auditor will be primarily interested in the accuracy of the bill of material.

For inventory balances the auditor will seek to:
- attend the **physical inventory count** to validate existence and completeness of inventory. Taking some physical inventory sheets from the count and comparing to the final inventory listing provided to him at the time of audit fieldwork;
- ensure that inventory is **valued** at the **lower of cost and NRV** by validating cost by reference to purchase invoices (or BOM) and considering any reasons why the sale value would be less than the validated cost; and
- with respect to rights and obligations consider the existence of **third-party inventory** on the premises of the entity or entity **inventory on the premises of a third party**. Also consider inventory **sold on a sale or return basis**.

Learning Objective 6   Understand the role CAATs can play when auditing inventory.

CAATs and Inventory the auditor may use a combination of audit software, data analysis tools and other applications, such as Excel, when auditing the area of inventory.

Learning Objective 7   Understand the auditor's approach relating to the disclosures of inventory.

The auditor needs to consider the requirements of IAS 2 to ensure that all necessary inventory disclosures are: completed in line with IAS 2; accurate; relate to events that actually occurred; and are properly presented.

QUESTIONS

Self-test Questions

12.1   Define inventory.
12.2   List seven risks relating to inventory.
12.3   Outline the documents that support the auditor when testing costs.
12.4   Describe a blind count.
12.5   List four standard analytical review procedures for the audit of inventories.
12.6   What conclusions should an auditor draw from observing an inventory count?
12.7   Which assertions are tested when a sample of items from the inventory and count sheets are selected?
12.8   What procedures must an auditor perform if he is unable to attend the year-end inventory count?
12.9   How does IAS 2 state that inventory must be valued?
12.10   What circumstances lead to NRV being lower than cost?
12.11   How is cut-off testing performed?

Review Questions

(See Suggested Solutions to Review Questions in **Appendix D**.)

Question 12.1

Castelyons Ltd ('Castelyons') is a long-established audit client of your firm. The company has had moderate success over the years, but in recent years trading has deteriorated. Castlelyons sells assembled components to mechanical manufacturers. It can also sell some of the unassembled components separately.

The audit for the year ended 30 June 2013 is to commence in two weeks. In advance of the audit, the audit file has been delivered. You are reviewing the client entity's inventory schedule, which is in the same format as for the last number of years.

Product No.	Cost per Item €	Quantity	Total €
Z110	2,100	25	52,500
Z111*	3,200	40	128,000
Z112	1,110	30	33,300
Z114	4,333	8	34,664
Z115	2,000	9	18,000
Z116*	5,100	21	107,100
Z117*	5,420	40	216,800
Z118	1,000	52	52,000
Z120	900	54	48,600
Z121*	3,450	34	117,300
			808,264

* = components can be sold separately.

Management have asserted that the inventory amount of €808,264 will be included in current assets in the financial statements.

Requirement
(a) Assuming the quantities of the components are correct, outline what further audit work you would perform on the inventory schedule provided.
(b) As the audit commences, the financial controller informs you that there was an error in the inventory count. Outline the audit procedures you would perform to handle this situation.
(c) Outline the implicit and explicit assertions of management reporting the inventory figure of €808,264 in current assets in the financial statements.

Question 12.2

Your firm is the auditor of Tulla Wholesalers Limited. Each month a physical inventory count is undertaken when all high-value inventory is counted. Other inventory is counted at least every four months to ensure that all inventory is counted at least three times in the year. You are to attend a physical inventory count on 15 December. The year end is 31 December. No physical inventory counts will take place at the year end date. The inventory quantities per the system are being relied on at year end by management.

Requirement
(a) Detail the procedures you should perform when you attend the physical inventory count on 15 December.
(b) Detail the checks you will perform over cut-off at the date of the physical inventory count and at the year end.
(c) Detail how you will verify that inventory quantities used in the valuation of inventory at year end are correct.

13

THE AUDIT OF REVENUE AND RECEIVABLES

LEARNING OBJECTIVES

Having read this chapter on the audit of revenue and receivables you should:
1. understand what is included in the audit of revenue and receivables;
2. be able to identify the risks and audit objectives applicable to revenue and receivables;
3. be able to determine an appropriate audit strategy for revenue and receivables, taking into consideration the specific risks and audit objectives (management assertions);
4. be able to develop an audit programme that addresses all the audit objectives (management assertions) for revenue and receivables;
5. be able to describe and apply specific substantive testing procedures relating to the audit of revenue and receivables;
6. understand the role CAATs can play when auditing revenue and receivables; and
7. understand the auditor's approach relating to the disclosures of revenue and receivables.

CHECKLIST OF RELEVANT STANDARDS

The relevant standards covered in this chapter are:
- ISA (UK and Ireland) 315 *Identifying and Assessing the risks of Material Misstatement Through Understanding of the Entity and its Environment* (ISA 315)
- ISA (UK and Ireland) 330 *The Auditor's Responses to Assessed Risks* (ISA 330)
- ISA (UK and Ireland) 500 *Audit Evidence* (ISA 500)
- ISA (UK and Ireland) 510 *Initial Audit Engagements – Opening Balances* (ISA 510)
- ISA (UK and Ireland) 505 *External Confirmations* (ISA 505)
- ISA (UK and Ireland) 520 *Analytical Procedures* (ISA 520)
- ISA (UK and Ireland) 530 *Audit Sampling* (ISA 530)
- ISA (UK and Ireland) 540 *Auditing Accounting Estimates, Including Fair Value Accounting Estimates, and Related Disclosures* (ISA 540)
- IAS 1 *Presentation of Financial Statements* (IAS 1)
- IAS 18 *Revenue* (IAS 18)

KEY TERMS AND DEFINITIONS FOR THIS CHAPTER

Aged Receivables Listing   This is a full list of individual customer balances that can be reconciled to the receivables figure in the financial statements. The balance for each customer is broken down by the length of time it has been outstanding (usually due within 30 days, 60 days, 90 days and greater than 90 days).

Doubtful Debt Provision   A credit balance set against receivables, representing the estimate of uncollectable amounts included in the trade receivables listing. The auditor will evaluate the adequacy of the doubtful debt provision when considering the valuation of receivables.

Receivables Circularisation   This is a letter sent to the client entity customers by the auditor with the objective of obtaining independent evidence as to the existence and accuracy of the receivables balance in the financial statements. The auditor must receive permission from the client entity before circularising its customers.

13.1 INTRODUCTION

Sections 13.2–13.8 of this chapter outline the requirements of the IAS 18 with respect to revenues and IAS 1 *Presentation of Financial Statements* with respect to classification of assets as 'current', and then considers how the auditor:
(a) identifies audit risks and audit objectives (management assertions) for revenue and receivables;
(b) develops an audit plan for revenue and receivables and refines this into an audit programme;

(c) designs specific tests associated with revenue and receivables; and

(d) ensures adequate presentation and disclosure in the financial statements relating to revenue and receivables.

In **Section 13.9** we consider how **computer-assisted audit techniques** (CAATs) – considered in detail in **Chapter 9** – can assist with the audit of revenue and receivables.

Finally, in **Section 13.10**, we consider the auditor's approach when auditing the reasonableness of disclosures relating to revenue and receivables.

13.2 WHAT IS 'REVENUE AND RECEIVABLES'?

In the financial statements of an entity, the revenue figure represents the income earned by the business in return for the passing of title on goods or services. The auditor needs to be sure that revenue is recognised in line with IAS 18 *Revenue*. The receivables balance arises as a result of sales made and represents money due to the business from customers for those sales. The auditor will consider IAS 1 *Presentation of Financial Statements* in order to consider the classification of items as 'current assets'.

The value of total sales generated (revenue) in the period under review and the value of period-end receivables is material to the financial statements in most businesses, which is why the testing to be performed on this area by the auditor is so important.

As discussed in **Chapter 6**, ISA (UK and Ireland) 500 *Audit Evidence* states the need for the auditor to obtain **sufficient appropriate audit evidence** over classes of transactions (revenue) and accounts balances (receivables).

We will now consider the steps the auditor takes when performing an audit on revenue and receivables.

13.3 RISKS ASSOCIATED WITH REVENUE AND RECEIVABLES

Throughout **Chapter 7** (which addresses the requirement of ISA (UK and Ireland) 315 *Identifying and Assessing the risks of Material Misstatement Through Understanding of the Entity and its Environment* and ISA 330 (UK and Ireland) *The Auditor's Responses to Assessed Risks*), we discussed the topic of 'risk' and considered how the auditor should go about detecting risks. We also discussed how the auditor should consider these risks when designing the nature, timing and extent of further audit procedures relative to each financial cycle. So, before developing the audit plan the auditor needs to consider a number of risks that may be associated with **revenue and receivables**. The auditor should consider and take into account the following with regard to identifying risks associated with revenue and receivables:

• previous experience with the client entity, e.g. where a significant risk existed in the past in relation to recoverability of receivables balances, the auditor will be alert to this in the current audit when performing testing in this area;

- reliability of estimates made by the client in the past, e.g. where the basis of the **doubtful debt provision** determined by the client in the past was deemed unreliable, resulting in adjustments by the auditor being necessary to fairly state the provision, the auditor should be alert for this in the current audit when performing testing in this area;
- robustness of the client entity's accounting system, e.g. where cut-off errors were discovered in a prior audit as a result of sales invoices being posted to the system in the incorrect period around the period end date, the auditor will remain alert for this when performing testing in this area in the current period;
- complexity of the business, e.g. where recognition of a sale occurs only after a number of key stages have been completed or actions taken, then the auditor will remain alert to the possibility that sales may have been recognised in the period which are not true sales, i.e. sales have been accounted for in the period but all the necessary stages resulting in revenue recognition earned have not been completed before the period end;
- scope for fraud-related activity, which in relation to revenue and receivables could include:
  - creation of false customer accounts, resulting in overstated revenue figures and receivables balances; or
  - misappropriation of cash receipts where the business is cash-based.
- indication of risks associated with certain revenue transactions (e.g. recognition of goods sold on a sale-or-return basis or recognition of revenue connected to work in progress)

13.4 AUDIT OBJECTIVES/MANAGEMENT ASSERTIONS FOR REVENUE AND RECEIVABLES

As discussed in **Chapter 6** (which addressed the requirements of ISA (UK and Ireland) 500 *Audit Evidence*), it is necessary for the auditor to seek appropriate audit evidence to satisfy all of the audit objectives and to eliminate the possibility of any of the risks outlined above in **Section 13.3** going undetected. In **Chapter 4**, we introduced **audit objectives (management assertions)** and explained their generic meanings; we then re-introduced this topic throughout **Chapter 8**, making management assertions specific to each financial cycle. In Tables 13.1 and 13.2 below we remind ourselves of the audit objectives as they relate to revenue and receivables.

Table 13.1 addresses the management assertions (audit objectives) as they relate to the **transactions and events** occurring during the period relating to revenue and receivables.

Table 13.2 addresses the management assertions (audit objectives) as they relate to the **account balances** associated with revenue and receivables.

When designing **tests of controls**, **substantive analytical review** and **tests of details**, the auditor must ensure that sufficient comfort has been obtained over all of the assertions noted in those tables. This is usually achieved through designing an audit testing plan that includes all or a combination of the types of testing outlined above.

TABLE 13.1: REVENUE AND RECEIVABLES AUDIT OBJECTIVES
FOR TRANSACTIONS AND EVENTS DURING THE PERIOD

Assertion	Objective of Audit Evidence
Completeness	To ensure that all transactions that should have been recorded, have been recorded.
Occurrence	To ensure all transactions and events have been recorded and pertain to the entity.
Accuracy	To ensure that all transactions have been recorded correctly.
Cut-off	To ensure transactions and events have been recorded in the correct period.
Presentation and disclosure	To ensure that all amounts are properly disclosed and presented in the financial statements.

TABLE 13.2: REVENUE AND RECEIVABLES AUDIT OBJECTIVES
FOR ACCOUNT BALANCES AT THE YEAR END

Assertion	Objective of Audit Evidence
Existence	To ensure that all receivables in year-end statement of financial position exist.
Completeness	To ensure that all receivables that should have been recorded, have been recorded.
Rights and Obligations	To ensure the entity holds the rights to the receivables and has obligations.
Valuation and Allocation	To ensure that all receivables are included in financial statements at correct valuation and in the correct account.
Cut-off	To ensure transactions and events have been recorded in the correct period.
Presentation and disclosure	To ensure that all amounts relating to receivables are properly disclosed and presented in the financial statements.

Having discussed the objectives of the auditor with regard to revenue and receivables, we now consider how the auditor addresses these objectives through **substantive testing**.

13.5 DEVELOPING THE AUDIT PLAN FOR REVENUE AND RECEIVABLES

Before the audit of revenue and receivables is undertaken, an assessment of the audit risk must be completed. As discussed in detail in **Chapter 7**, audit risk is made up of three components: inherent risk; control risk; and detection risk. We will examine these components specifically as they relate to revenue and receivables.

Audit Risk = Inherent Risk + Control Risk + Detection Risk

The inherent risks associated with revenue and receivables are discussed in **Section 13.3** above, and in **Chapter 8**, 'Controls and Controls Testing', which gives a description of a typical revenue system and outlines the specific controls the auditor would expect to find, as well as how to test those controls. **Chapter 8** also discusses whether or not controls should be tested. Remember: where the revenue and receivables balances are not **material** to the financial statements, limited controls and substantive testing will be performed. However, revenue and receivables are usually a material figure and transactions tend to be high in volume; for this reason, the auditor usually takes a **controls approach** when testing revenue and receivables in order to reduce the level of detailed **substantive testing** required.

The general rules the auditor should consider when deciding on the audit approach relating to revenue and receivables include:
- where the revenue figure and receivables balance are not material to the financial statements, limited controls and substantive testing will be performed;
- where a significant risk has been identified in relation to the revenue and receivables cycle, the level of substantive testing to be performed will be more rigorous;
- where a strong control environment has been identified, the extent of substantive testing to be performed will be much less than the level of substantive testing to be performed in an entity where a weak control environment has been identified.

Generally, a controls approach is the most productive (effective and efficient) approach when testing the area of revenue and receivables. Remember, however, that the auditor can decide to take a controls approach in relation to only certain assertions and then perform focused substantive testing on the other assertions. With respect to **valuation**, quite often the auditor will choose to take a wholly substantive approach when auditing this assertion, due to the risks associated with it.

13.6 KEY DOCUMENTS RELATING TO REVENUE AND RECEIVABLES

Before commencing substantive testing procedures, it is important that the auditor becomes familiar with documents associated with the revenue and receivables cycles. The primary document of interest to the auditor is the **aged receivables listing**, which provides the following for the auditor:
- a full list of all the individual customer balances that exist at the date of statement of financial position which can be reconciled to the receivables figure in the financial statements;
- an ageing of each customer's debt, which allows the auditor to better analyse the collectability of balances at the year end;
- a list from which to select a sample for details testing or to perform receivables circularisation (discussed in more detail at **Section 13.8**) below;
- if received in Excel, the list can be manipulated by the auditor to show top-value customers' balances, credit balances, nil balances, etc., which may highlight risks; and
- a list against which credit limits can be compared to assist with the valuation assertion.

As discussed above, the aged receivables listing is probably the most important document used by the auditor during the audit of revenue and receivables and an example of one is included at **Example 13.1** below. As can be seen from this example, the listing includes all customers, total amount owing by each customer and then this total amount is broken down into categories representing the age of the debt. If you refer to **Appendix C** of this textbook, Large Company Limited, Note 17, you will see that the totals at the end of the aged receivables listing agree to the ageing per the note in the financial statements (i.e. total receivables: €3,750,000; current: €3,100,000; 30–60 days: €420,000; 60–90 days: €150,000; and greater than 90 days old: €80,000). The auditor must confirm this before he commences any testing on the aged receivables listing.

EXAMPLE 13.1: EXAMPLE OF AN AGED RECEIVABLES LISTING (LARGE COMPANY LIMITED)

Customer Name	Credit Limit	Total Value €000s	Current €000s	30–60 days old €000s	60–90 days old €000s	Greater than 90 days old €000s
Customer A	150	100	100			
Customer B	20	39	39			
Customer C	650	596	490		55	51
Customer D	400	364	364			
Customer E	150	90	70	20		
Customer F	10	4				4
Customer G	25	18	18			
Customer H	20	14	10	4		
Customer I	500	400	375	25		
Customer J	800	650	650			
Customer K	200	15	15			
Customer L	900	785	810	–	(25)	
Customer M	15	20	20			
Customer N	40	30	20	10		
Customer O	28	25	25			
Customer P	100	50	44	6		
Customer Q	250	400	–	255	120	25
Customer R	200	150	50	100		
		3,750	**3,100**	**420**	**150**	**80**
			83%	11%	4%	2%

13.7 SUBSTANTIVE AUDIT PROGRAMME FOR REVENUE AND RECEIVABLES

An **audit programme** records the specific details of tests to be performed by the auditor. The audit programme becomes a guide to the **audit engagement team** as to the work to be performed in a particular area. As work is completed, a reference is included on the audit programme showing the location on the audit file where details of the tests performed are included. While the audit programme for any cycle will vary from entity to entity, in **Example 13.2** below we consider the typical types of test the auditor would include in the audit programme for revenue and receivables.

EXAMPLE 13.2: SUBSTANTIVE TESTING AUDIT PROGRAMME FOR
REVENUE AND RECEIVABLES (LARGE COMPANY LIMITED)[1]

Large Company Limited				
31 December 2012	**Audit Materiality**			**€3,642,500**
	Performance Materiality			**€2,731,875**
			Initials	**Date**
	Prepared by:			
Revenue and Receivables	**Reviewed by:**			
Audit Programme	**Assertion Covered**		**Ref to Work**	**Initials and Date**
Accounting Policy				
Assess the appropriateness of the accounting policy and the accounting estimates method for this area. Ensure that the accounting policy is in accordance with accounting standards and applicable law, and that the methods used for making the accounting estimates are appropriate.	Existence, Completeness, Rights and Obligations, Accuracy/Valuation and Classification			

---

[1] Source: based on *Procedures for Quality Audit 2010* (© Chartered Accountants Ireland, 2010), H1.

Initial Procedures			
Agree opening balances to prior year working papers.	Presentation and Disclosure		
Obtain the aged receivables and ensure its mathematical accuracy, agree totals to the figures in the financial statements.	Completeness, Occurrence and Existence, Accuracy		
Obtain or prepare an aged analysis of trade receivables and test its reliability.	Valuation and Classification		
Obtain or prepare lead schedules and agree to balance sheet.	Existence, Occurrence, Accuracy and Classification		
Prepare a commentary explaining the composition of debtor balances. Compare balances and debtor days with prior years and with your expectations. Note any significant changes in the ratio of overdue accounts. Obtain explanations of any variations and consider implications for the doubtful debts provision.	Existence, Completeness, Accuracy, Valuation		
Revenue Transactions			
Obtain or prepare a schedule of revenue: Check mathematical accuracy of the schedule, then select a sample and: 1. Trace the sample from the general ledger to the source document (signed customer purchase order delivery) confirming, date, name, quantity and value matches the invoice and general ledger posting.	Occurrence and Accuracy		
2. Trace a sample of Customer sales orders through to general ledger.	Completeness and Accuracy		
Repeat the above for deductions from revenue (i.e. trace from general ledger to source to test occurrence and from source to general ledger to test completeness).	Occurrence, Accuracy and Completeness		
			continued overleaf

Receivables Balance			
Obtain or prepare a schedule of trade receivables: Select a sample and: 1. circularise trade receivables, or explain why circularisation is not appropriate; 2. verify against post year-end receipts and other evidence of the existence of the debtor; 3. examine correspondence about disputed balances; 4. enquire into all significant credit balances; 5. examine after-date sales credit notes; and 6. re-analyse amounts due from parent, subsidiary and associated undertakings, directors and employees. In the case of each non-response to a receivables confirmation letter, perform alternative audit procedures to obtain relevant and reliable audit evidence. (ISA 505, para 12) If it is determined that a response to a receivables confirmation request is necessary to obtain sufficient appropriate audit evidence, alternative audit procedures will not provide the audit evidence required. If such confirmation cannot be obtained, determine the implications for the audit and the auditor's opinion in accordance with ISA 705 (UK and Ireland). (ISA 505, para 13)	Existence/ Occurrence, Completeness, Rights and Obligations		
Collectability of Receivables Balance	Valuation		
Identify any outstanding receivables in breach of contract and/or late payment regulations. Ensure potential interest is quantified.			

Discuss bad and doubtful debts with management and review the entity's provisions. Discuss with the client any debts which are outside the terms of trade and unpaid. Evaluate explanations given for not providing against long-term outstanding balances. Examine correspondence where available and always corroborate management assertions. Challenge the estimation techniques used by management in the calculation of the provisions. Consider the outturn of the provision in previous years. Identify and verify provisions made for reasons other than the age of debt.			
Other Considerations			
Test check invoices immediately prior to and after year end: 1. to ensure they are entered in correct accounting period; and 2. to ensure inventory movement is in correct period.	Cut-off		
Enquire into and verify correct treatment of inventories dispatched on sale or return.	Cut-off		
Enquire into any material receivable balances cleared by journal entry after the period end.	Cut-off		
Obtain or prepare a schedule of **prepaid expenses** and: 1. compare with previous period; 2. vouch material items to source documentation; and 3. consider the reasonableness of other items.	Existence and Completeness		
			continued overleaf

Extract as necessary and agree **intra-group or related company balances** to the other party's accounts, or obtain written confirmation of agreement between the companies, and ensure disclosed. Obtain financial statements for group and related companies. Confirm by reference to the financial statements that intra-group or related company balances are recoverable. Obtain alternative confirmations or audit evidence if the financial statements show deficits or other difficulties in repaying the loans. Consider the adequacy of this evidence.	Existence, Completeness and Presentation and Disclosure		
Confirm that intra-group or related company balances are properly presented in the correct part of the balance sheet.	Presentation and Disclosure		
Identify any **loans due from directors** and ensure adequate disclosure of these is made in the financial statements. (In respect of the Republic of Ireland: specifically consider compliance with the relevant sections of the Companies Act 1990 and the possible requirement to report in accordance with the Company Law Enforcement Act 2001.)	Presentation and Disclosure		

Name:	Accountant in Charge
Date:	
Name:	Reviewer
Date:	

13.8 SUBSTANTIVE TESTING PROCEDURES FOR REVENUE AND RECEIVABLES

Substantive procedures are used to gather evidence in order to substantiate account balances, i.e. receivables and classes of transactions, e.g. revenue. They are designed to address the risk of **material misstatement** at the financial statement (entity) assertion level. As discussed in **Chapter 6,** 'Gathering Audit Evidence', substantive testing includes **substantive analytical review** and **substantive tests of details**.

Initial Procedures

We will now discuss in more detail some of the procedures outlined in the substantive audit testing programme above. We will start with **initial procedures**, which include:
• opening balances and mathematical accuracy of schedules;
• lead schedules; and
• analytical reviews.

Opening Balances and Mathematical Accuracy of Schedules

The auditor should obtain the detailed aged receivables listing for the entity, gain comfort over its mathematical accuracy and then perform the following:
• agree the current period's opening balance to the closing audited balances in the prior year's audit working papers or signed financial statements;
• agree the balance per the aged receivables listing to the balance per the trial balance. Reconciling items should be tested in order to obtain the desired level of assurance and agreed to supporting documentation;
• review the aged receivables listing for any unusual balances, such as large balances, credit balances and old balances;
• test the reliability of the aged receivables listing by selecting one customer and agreeing ageing to original invoice dates;
• obtain a copy of the sales general ledger, test its mathematical accuracy and vouch it to the financial statements – review its contents for any unusual items.

The auditor will also need to give consideration to the approach of auditing opening balances where he is performing an initial engagement; this is considered in **Chapter, 6**, Section 6.8, which addresses the requirements of (ISA (UK and Ireland) 510 *Initial Audit Engagements – Opening Balances*).

Lead schedules

Lead schedules can be prepared to summarise all trade and other receivables both within and greater than one year. This will allow the auditor to ensure that he obtains evidence for all balances during the audit, thus providing some control over the performance of audit procedures. A typical lead schedule of the receivables area is included below in **Example 13.3** (relating to Large Company Limited – see **Appendix C**).

EXAMPLE 13.3: RECEIVABLES LEAD SCHEDULE (LARGE COMPANY LIMITED)[2]

Large Company Limited
31 December 2012

Audit Materiality		€3,642,500
Performance Materiality		€2,731,875
	Initials	Date
Prepared by:		
Reviewed by:		

Receivables

Receivables – Amounts falling due within one year

	31 December 2012 €000	31 December 2011 €000
Trade Receivables	3,750	4,850
Provision for Doubtful Debts	(500)	(750)
Loan Notes	1,500	1,500
Other receivables	750	600
Prepayments and accrued income	1,000	1,050
	6,500	7,250

Receivables – Amounts falling due after one year

	31 December 2012 €000	31 December 2011 €000
Loan Notes	6,000	8,000
Called-up share capital not paid	685	875
Prepayments and accrued income	0	0
Pension prepayment	65	25
Other prepayments	1,950	1,350
	8,700	10,250

---

[2] Source: based on *Procedures for Quality Audit 2010* (© Chartered Accountants Ireland, 2010), H-

Prepayments and accrued income

	31 December 2012	31 December 2011
	€000	€000
Insurance	200	500
Rent	500	0
Supplier Prepayment (Bespoke Goods)	300	550
	1,000	1,050

Movement in Doubtful Debt Provision

	31 December 2012	31 December 2011
	€000	€000
Opening Balance	750	700
Increase / (Decrease) in Provision	(450)	150
Doubtful Debt Write off	(700)	(100)
Closing Balance	500	750

Trade Receivables Aged Analysis

	31 December 2012	31 December 2011
	€000	€000
Current (within credit terms)	3,100	4,250
30–60 days	420	350
60–90 days	150	140
Greater than 90 days	80	110
	3,750	4,850

Analytical Review

An **analytical review** (covered under **Chapter 5**, Section 5.4, which addresses the requirements of ISA (UK and Ireland) 520 *Analytical Procedures*) is usually performed at the start of each substantive procedure relating to each balance or class of transactions. Calculating ratios and analysing results against industry information, prior-year results, budgets, etc., allows the auditor to gain a better understanding for the movements in the year and make comparisons against norms, thereby enabling him to better prepare the audit programme.

Example 13.4 below shows the types of ratios and comparisons the auditor might perform in relation to revenue and receivables. An analytical review is similar to preliminary analytical procedures and focuses the auditor on movements and key ratios that equip him with additional insight prior to commencing his substantive procedures. At the close of his substantive procedures he aims to ensure that he can comment on all movements and key ratios with supporting explanations. If the auditor cannot explain any element, then this will highlight to him the need to perform additional substantive procedures. The analytical review performed here differs from a substantive analytical procedure in that the auditor's aim is not to substantiate the balance (i.e. prove the assertions) but rather ensure that he understands the movements and relationships, to assist him in performing substantive procedures.

While this procedure will not provide any further comfort over financial statement assertions, it will provide an overview of the reasons for the movements in balances and should corroborate the auditor's findings noted through performance of substantive procedures (also outlined at **Example 13.4** below).

The analytical review, performed as part of initial substantive procedures, can include calculations such as:
- receivables days ratio (receivables/credit sales × 365);
- number of day sales in trade receivables versus previous year;
- aged receivables versus the previous years in order to identify increased receivables ageing;
- wherever a change in relationships cannot be readily obtained or an unusual pattern is uncovered, auditors should seek explanations from management and corroborate the explanation received by performing additional tests of details.

As mentioned, an example of an analytical review now follows, which demonstrates some of the items discussed above relating to revenue and receivables.

EXAMPLE 13.4: INITIAL PROCEDURES ANALYTICAL REVIEW
AND COMMENTARY ON REVENUE AND RECEIVABLES

Trade Receivables

	31/12/2012		31/12/2011	
	€000		**€000**	
Trade Receivables	3,750		4,850	
Provision for Doubtful Debts	−500	−13%	−750	−15%
	3,250		4,100	

Revenue Analysis (Obtained from the client)

	31/12/2012		31/12/2011	
	€000		**€000**	
Revenue (Cash Sales)	237,750	85%	129,500	65%
Revenue (Credit Sales)	42,500	15%	69,000	35%
	280,250	100%	198,500	100%

Trade Receivables Aged Analysis

	31/12/2012		31/12/2011	
	€000		**€000**	
Current (within credit terms)	3,100	83%	4,250	88%
30–60 days	420	11%	350	7%
60–90 days	150	4%	140	3%
Greater than 90 days	80	2%	110	2%
	3,750	100%	4,850	100%

Receivables Days	= (3,750 ÷ 42,500)	= (4,850 ÷ 69,000)	
	× 365	× 365	
(trade receivables ÷ credit sales × 365)	32.2	25.7	**+6.5 days**

Total revenue has increased by €81,750,000 (41%) due to a new line of furniture that has broken into the luxury market, as well as an increase in foreign sales. Both of these factors pose increased inherent risks and have been taken into account in the audit strategy and the audit plan. While cash sales have increased by 84%, reducing the level of credit sales to just 15% of revenue compared to 53% of revenue in the prior year, the collectability of debtors appears to be reducing, with receivables days increased by approximately 6.5 days. The increase in cash sales has increased inherent risk, which has to be taken into account in the audit strategy and the audit plan.

Having performed the initial procedures, the auditor must then commence more specific audit procedures relating to revenue and receivables (i.e. to test the classes of transactions and balances in the current year), starting with the audit procedures normally carried out in relation to revenue (class of transactions).

Testing of Revenue and Revenue Deductions through Tests of Details

As discussed at the outset of this chapter, 'revenue' represents sales made by the entity during the period by way of the supply of goods or services. If the auditor has tested the revenue and receivables controls in place in the entity and they were found to be effective, resulting in a low **control risk**, he may test the revenue figure using a substantive analytical procedure. This method of testing usually takes less time to carry out than substantive tests of details. However, if controls have proved to be weak, the auditor is required to perform substantive tests of details.

We will first consider the testing of recorded revenue using tests of details.

Testing Recorded Revenue through Tests of Details

In this context, tests of details involve the selection of a sample from the total revenue population (sampling is discussed **Chapter 6**, Section 6.7, which addresses the requirements of ISA (UK and Ireland) 530 *Audit Sampling*) and the vouching of that sample to supporting documentation. This type of testing covers the following assertions:
- Existence/Occurrence;
- Accuracy; and
- Completeness.

When testing total revenue recorded by the client entity in the period, the auditor should consider/perform the following:
- verifying that a sales invoice was issued for each sales amount recorded;
- verifying that the sale was accurately posted to the correct customer's account on the receivables ledger;
- testing the mathematical accuracy of sales invoices;
- testing the selling price of items on an invoice by agreeing the amounts to the client's price list/sales catalogue and validating that any discount allowed has been authorised by the appropriate person; and
- verifying that output VAT has been calculated properly on sales invoices.

Furthermore, the auditor should consider performing testing around the actual delivery of sales orders to gain assurance around the existence of the sale. He should select delivery documentation (e.g. goods delivery notes (GDNs)) and perform the following:
- tracing delivery documentation (e.g. delivery docket) to sales invoices and agreeing the quantity delivered to the quantity recorded on the invoice (inspecting customer acknowledgement signatures as evidence of receipt of goods, i.e. basis for proof of delivery if there is a subsequent dispute);
- if delivery dockets are raised in a sequential order, verifying the numerical sequence on a test basis; and

- obtaining explanations for and corroborating where necessary significant adjustments made in sales accounts throughout the year.

Testing Revenue Returns through Tests of Details

When testing revenue, the auditor needs to also consider revenue returns. Returns represent goods returned by the client entity's customers that have been refunded. As with recorded revenue (above), tests of details of revenue returns covers the following assertions:
- Existence/Occurrence;
- Accuracy; and
- Completeness.

When testing total sales returns recorded by the client in the period, the auditor should consider/perform the following:
- testing the mathematical accuracy of sales returns credit notes;
- testing pricing by checking credit notes to sales invoices;
- ensuring that the credit note was approved by an individual authorised to issue credit notes;
- ensuring that the credit note has been correctly posted to the receivables ledger and the customer's account; and
- verifying that output VAT has been calculated properly on sales returns credit notes.

Testing Revenue Discounts through Tests of Details

Revenue discounts relate to discounts offered to the client entity's customers. The auditor will mainly be concerned with the **authorisation** of discounts. Again, tests of details will cover the following assertions:
- Existence/Occurrence;
- Accuracy; and
- Completeness.

Where the client issues discounts to customers, the auditor should perform testing to validate the following:
- that any sales discount has been approved by an individual authorised to do so;
- that where the discount has been issued due to damaged inventory, the facts surrounding the discount should be validated through inspection of appropriate information held on file by the client; and
- that the granting of discounts complies with company policy.

Receivables Balance

Having tested the classes of transactions that make up 'revenue', the auditor must then focus on the receivables balance. The most common method of testing the receivables balance is by way of **circularisation**. Other typical methods include review of post year-end cash/bank receipts and substantive analytical procedures. We will discuss these in more detail below.

Circularisations

Circularisations cover the following assertions for the auditor:
- Existence/Occurrence; and
- Rights and Obligations.

ISA 500 *Audit Evidence* states that the reliability of audit evidence is influenced by its source and nature, and is dependent on the individual circumstances under which it is obtained. It can be concluded, therefore, that audit evidence obtained independently from third parties can reduce the risk of **material misstatement** surrounding the particular account balance to an acceptably low level. With regard to accounts receivables balances, the performance of a **receivables circularisation** is a means of obtaining independent third-party confirmation of the accuracy and existence of the year-end balance on the receivables ledger. Through performance of this substantive test, the auditor seeks confirmation directly from customers as to whether they are in agreement with the balance per the client entity's receivables ledger at the year end.

The use of receivables circularisations to test the year-end receivables balances has a number of **advantages** for the auditor, including:
- direct external, third-party evidence that provides evidence over the existence and ownership of the debt and also the accuracy of the recorded amount due;
- confirmation of the effectiveness of the system of internal control in operation within the client entity;
- assistance in determining cut-off procedures by identifying invoices in transit over the year end; and
- providing evidence of items in dispute where the amount stated by the customer differs from the amount recorded in the books of the client entity.

Using such circularisations also has its **disadvantages**, however, which include the following:
- where the client entity's customers are small businesses or private individuals, they are less likely to maintain accurate ledger balances to provide a reliable response;
- customers are less likely to admit to owing more than is shown on the confirmation letter;
- many trivial differences are likely to be reported as a result of cash/goods in transit; and
- the non-response rate may be high.

Two methods of confirming receivables balances exist, namely:

1. **Negative Circularisation** Such circularisations request the customer to respond only if they are not in agreement with the balance stated.

   The problem with this is that it may be impossible to tell whether the customer agrees with the year-end balance stated or whether there is simply a failure on their part to reply. It can be concluded that negative confirmations provide less persuasive audit evidence than positive confirmations.

ISA 505, at paragraph 15, permits the use of negative confirmations (as the sole substantive procedure). However the auditor should use this method only when he is satisfied that: internal controls are operating effectively; risk of material misstatement is low; the population subject to confirmation consists of a large number of small account balances; very few exceptions are expected; and the auditor has no reason to believe the recipients of the letters will disregard the confirmation request. This form of circularisation is rarely used due to the risks connected to it.

2. **Positive Circularisation** Here the customer is asked to reply whether they agree with the balance or not. In some cases, customers are asked to supply the balance themselves.

    The positive form is used when planned **detection risk** is low or individual customer balances are relatively large, and generally produces statistically valid evidence, as long as non-responses are verified by other means. While positive circularisation tends to be the favoured method over negative circularisation, a combination of the two may be used in a single engagement.

    The following should be considered when performing a receivables circularisation:
    (a) **Control of external confirmation process** The auditor must remain in control of the external confirmation process, meaning that he must select the customers to be contacted, prepare and send the confirmation requests and ensure that responses are sent directly to the auditor and not through the client.
    (b) **Timing in sending external confirmations** The receivables circularisation process should be carried out a suitable length of time prior to the commencement of the audit fieldwork in order to allow customers time to respond.
    (c) **Stratification of ledger to ensure sufficient value of the ledger is circularised** The auditor should target high-value balances on the year-end receivables ledger in order to gain high assurance over the total balance. *Do not, however, omit nil balances, credit balances or accounts written off in the period.*
    (d) **Investigation into differences between responses and client balances** For responses returned that are not in agreement with the balance per the client's receivables ledger, appropriate investigation into the differences arising should be conducted by the auditor with appropriate journal adjustments proposed, if necessary, in order to correct the balance per the client's ledger.
    (e) **Non-responses** Where responses are not returned, the auditor should ordinarily consider contacting the customer by telephone in order to obtain a response; in the scenario where a response still cannot be obtained, alternative procedures should then be performed to confirm the year-end balance per the receivables ledger (alternative procedures are discussed below).
    (f) **Management refusal to permit circularisation** Where management requests that the auditor does not perform a receivables circularisation, the auditor must consider if there are valid grounds for such a request and obtain audit evidence to support the validity of management's request. If the auditor agrees to management's request and does not perform a receivables circularisation, the auditor should apply alternative audit procedures in order to obtain **sufficient appropriate audit evidence**

regarding the year-end receivables balance (discussed below). If the auditor does not accept the validity of management's request and is prevented from carrying out the confirmations, there has been a **limitation on the scope** of the auditor's work and he should consider the possible impact on the auditor's report.

(g) **Application of professional scepticism** When considering the reasons provided by management not to circularise the receivables, the auditor should apply **professional scepticism** and consider if it raises any questions surrounding the integrity of management or possible instances of fraudulent behaviour within the business.

(h) **Responses received by the client** Where responses are returned to the client directly, these cannot be accepted by the auditor on the grounds that the client may have manipulated the response.

When the auditor receives responses from the receivables circularised, the following should then be considered:

- **Collectability** Where the customer confirms the balance due to the client entity, this confirms the accuracy of the balance for the auditor but it does not confirm the collectability and the valuation of the balance, i.e. is recoverability of the balance likely? The auditor must consider this further when testing the allowance for doubtful debts (see below).

- **Customer disagrees with balance** Where the customer is not in agreement with the balance due per the client's records, work must be performed by the auditor in order to reconcile the difference. Differences arising can be due to the following:
  - timing differences, for example:
    - the customer has sent a cheque payment to the client but the client has not received the payment at the time of preparation of receivables circulars; or
    - the client has credited the customer account with a discount for prompt payment but the customer has not yet received the credit note and updated their system;
  - permanent differences, for example:
    - the client has posted an invoice incorrectly to the customer account, either at the wrong amount or to the wrong customer account entirely; or
    - the customer has not posted a legitimate invoice to their system.

The auditor must carry out appropriate work to reconcile any differences arising.

The auditor must summarise findings from the receivables circularisation in a suitable manner. The working paper should list each account selected for confirmation and the results obtained from each request, cross-referenced to the actual confirmation response. Differences should be investigated and discussed with management when deemed to be material. A possible means of documenting audit work is shown in **Example 13.5** below.

EXAMPLE 13.5: RECEIVABLES CIRCULARISATION SUMMARY

Customer Name	Customer Code	Balance per Client Entity Ledger	Balance Confirmed by Customer	Difference Arising	Further Audit Work Performed on difference Arising
Customer I	I001	€400,000	€375,000	€25,000	Confirmed that client entity had posted three invoices totalling €25,000 to Customer I in error; invoices should have been posted to Customer L. Inspected invoices and confirmed that they were in the name of 'Customer L' and not Customer I.
Customer C	C001	€596,000	€550,000	€46,000	This relates to cash in transit that was received and banked on 2 January 2013.
Customer D	D001	€364,000	€364,000	€0	
Customer F	F001	€4,000	No Response	N/A	Followed up on non-response to discover customer is gone into liquidation. This is, however, included in doubtful debt provision.
Customer N	N001	€30,000	No Response	N/A	Alternative procedures performed at working paper Reference [XX].

In the case where no responses are received, **alternative procedures** should be performed by the auditors. The two main alternative procedures are as follows:
- examining post year-end cash/bank receipts; and
- vouching unpaid invoices and supporting documentation,

which we will discuss in more detail below.

Receivables Balance (Post Year-end Cash Receipts Testing)

Testing post year-end cash/bank receipts can be used as a first choice in testing the receivables balances or as an alternative testing procedure where a receivables circularisation letter is either: (a) not returned; (b) compromised; or (c) does not agree with the balance per the aged receivables listing.

The most logical way to confirm **money outstanding** (i.e. a **receivables balance**) at the year end is to see if it was paid after year end. The performance of post year end cash receipts testing will cover the following management assertions (audit objectives):
- Existence/Occurrence;
- Completeness; and
- Valuation.

In order to perform this test correctly, the following should be considered:
- Obtaining a detailed breakdown of the sales invoices that make up the year end balance per the receivables ledger for each customer of the client entity.
- Obtaining details of cash received from selected customers post year end with details of the sales invoices to which the receipts relate.
- Vouching cash receipts to remittances or bank statements.
- Where cash has not been received post year end from the customer, the auditor should vouch the year-end receivables balance to supporting documentation, such as invoices, proof of delivery notes, goods dispatch notes and customer orders, in order to confirm the occurrence of the sale.
- It is important to determine the invoices outstanding at the year end in order to confirm that post year-end cash payments relate to invoices that have been included on the ledger at the year end. If post year-end cash receipts are discovered that relate to pre year-end invoices which are not outstanding on the ledger, a **cut-off error** has occurred and the receivables ledger is understated. It will be necessary to propose an adjusting journal to correct for material pre year-end sales invoices not included on the receivables ledger.

Revenue and Receivables Balances (Substantive Analytical Procedures)

Thus far, we have discussed only the tests of details approach to substantively testing revenue and receivables. The other type of substantive testing frequently used for revenue and receivables (particularly when the controls environment is strong) is **substantive analytical procedures**. This type of substantive procedure covers the following assertions for the auditor:

- Existence/Occurrence;
- Completeness;
- Valuation; and
- Cut-off.

Substantive analytical procedures can be used as the main test for revenue or receivables or they can be used in conjunction with substantive tests of details. If the controls surrounding revenue and receivables have been tested and a strong control environment exists, the auditor can use substantive analytical procedures and avoid tests of details relating to the above assertions. (The background to the approach of the performance of substantive analytical procedures has been discussed in **Chapter 6**.)

Performing Substantive Analytical Procedures Relating to Receivables

As outlined in **Chapter 6**, when performing substantive analytical procedures, the following four steps should be considered by the auditor:

1. an expectation (which represents a calculation by the auditor where the objective is to calculate what the auditor would expect the receivables balance to be) for current year results, with the basis of expectation being explained and the reliability of the data used being assessed;
2. a threshold level, which represents the maximum tolerable monetary value the auditor is willing to accept when he compares his expected result to the actual result. The threshold calculation is usually based on performance materiality;
3. calculation of the deviation occurring between actual results and the expected results; and
4. performance of further substantive testing where the deviation from expectation is greater than the threshold established.

Performing Substantive Analytical Procedures Relating to Revenue

The auditor can use the following when developing an independent expectation for current period revenue:

- results for the prior period;
- current period revenue budget as developed by management (provided that the budgetary process has been tested by the auditor and is found to be robust);
- market expectations for the industry within which the business operates.

When developing an independent expectation for current period results, the auditor must consider if any significant changes have taken place within the operations of the business during the period under review, compared to the prior period, which have impacted on the revenue level for the current period. Consideration should be given to the following:

- Is the duration of the period under review in line with the duration of the prior period?
- Have any new divisions opened (e.g. a new store) during the period under review?
- Have any divisions been discontinued during the period under review?
- Have any new products been introduced?
- Have products been discontinued?
- Has the competitive environment changed for the business?
- Has the macroeconomic environment changed, e.g. have consumer spending habits altered?

- Have new sales personnel been employed during the period under review impacting on the trading results?
- Have selling prices been increased during the period under review?
- How does current period gross margin compare to prior period margin?
- After review, how do daily/weekly/monthly revenue figures for current period compare to the same period in the prior year?

Depending on the answers to the questions above, the auditor must then consider how these will impact on the development of an expectation for current period revenue, obtain relevant, reliable substantive evidence to support and/or quantify the known changes, and build in the effects of such changes on revenue within the current period expectation.

We have considered above the approach relating to revenue, so let us now consider the approach to performing a substantive analytical procedure on the receivables balance. With the exception of expectations for the market, developing an independent expectation for the period-end receivables balance is similar to that for current period revenue:

- prior period results; and
- the current period budget as developed by management of the entity (provided that the budgetary process has been tested and is found to be robust).

When developing an independent expectation for the receivables balance, the auditor must consider if any significant changes have taken place within the operations of the business during the period under review (compared to the prior period) which have impacted on the period-end receivables balance. Considerations should be given to the following:

- Has the company expanded significantly, resulting in increased revenue and a corresponding increase in the period-end receivables balance?
- Has the company reduced operations significantly resulting in reduced revenue and a corresponding decrease in period end receivables balance?
- Have normal payment terms for customers been changed during the period, e.g. from 30 days to 45 days, i.e. a change in the receivables days ratio?
- Have any one-off sales contracts been taken on and completed during the period and remain due at the period end?
- Has the macroeconomic environment changed, e.g. have consumer spending habits changed?

Depending on the answers to the questions above, the auditor must then consider how these will impact on the development of an expectation for period-end receivables balance and build in the effects of the known changes within the current period expectation.

When expectations are developed, the auditor must compare the expectation calculated to the actual balance in the financial statements. Where the deviation is below the threshold amount established for further investigation, no additional substantive testing is necessary. However, where the deviation is greater than the threshold, the auditor must perform further substantive testing to provide appropriate evidence around the unexpected deviation.

Example 13.6 below demonstrates the above discussion by way of example.

EXAMPLE 13.6: WORKED EXAMPLE – SUBSTANTIVE ANALYTICAL
PROCEDURES FOR REVENUE AND RECEIVABLES

You are undertaking the revenue and receivables sections of the audit for your client, Holiday Heaven Ltd. You are at the phase of the audit where substantive analytical procedures are being performed. You have ascertained the following information from the work carried out by the audit team to date:

(a) Revenue levels for existing products have remained reasonably in line with the prior period.
(b) No products have been discontinued in the period.
(c) Two new sales contracts have been won during the period, these are one-off contracts, details as follows as agreed to signed contracts:
    (i) Contract 1 commenced 1 February 2012, contracting the client to produce and supply the customer with goods totalling €100,000 (sales value) per month;
    (ii) Contract 2 commenced 1 October 2012, contracting the client to produce and supply the customer with goods totalling €45,000 (cost price) per month. Gross profit margin on this contract is expected to be 40%.
(d) The selling price for all items (except new contracts in the year) increased by 5% on 1 September 2012 – corroborated through inspection of a letter sent out to customers outlining the above in August 2012.
(e) Normal credit terms have increased from 30 days in the prior period to 35 days in the current period – corroborated through inspection of a letter sent out to credit customers stating this in January 2012.
(f) A dispute is ongoing with one customer for payment of €300,000, which is nine months outstanding at the period end. This was a new customer accepted in the period under review. The audit team inspected invoices issued to the customer and letters sent to it demanding payment. The dispute is confirmed as now being with the legal representatives.

Other required information:
• Current period: 12 months to 31 December 2012
• Current period revenue: €6,690,000
• Period-end receivables balance: €930,000
• Threshold for further investigation: 75% of planning materiality of €25,000, i.e. €18,750
• Prior period: 15 months to 31 December 2011
• Prior period revenue: €6,575,000
• Prior period-end receivables balance: €540,410.

Using the information above, a substantive analytical review of revenue can be performed:

1. Develop expectation:
Prior period revenue   = €6,575,000 over 15 months
Prior period monthly revenue   = €6,575,000/15
                                 = €438,333

continued overleaf

Expected revenue for current period using prior period

$$\begin{aligned} \text{monthly revenue value} &= (\text{€}438{,}333 \times 8) + (\text{€}438{,}333 \times 1.05 \times 4)\ \text{W1} \\ &= \text{€}3{,}506{,}667 + \text{€}1{,}840{,}999 \\ &= \text{€}5{,}347{,}666 \end{aligned}$$

Adjustment for additional revenue won during the year:
Additional revenue from Contract 1 = €1,100,000 (W2)
Additional revenue from Contract 2 = €225,000 (W3)

Total expected revenue for current period = €6,672,666 (5,347,666 + 1,100,000 + 225,000)

2. Outline deviation for further investigation:
From information above, deviation threshold is €18,750

3. Compare actual result to expectation and calculate deviation:

Actual revenue	= €6,690,000
Total expected revenue for current period	= €6,672,666
Deviation from expectation	= €17,334

4. Perform further investigation where deviation is above threshold for further investigation.
As deviation is below the threshold for further investigation no further work is deemed necessary.

W1: Being eight months' revenue at the average month revenue of the prior period + 4 months' revenue adjusted for 5% price increase in September 2012.
W2: Being €100,000 per month over 11 months (100,000 × 11).
W3: Being revenue of €75,000 over 3 months.

Cost price =	€/£45,000
Gross margin =	40%
Cost price =	60%
Revenue =	100% being (€45,000/60) × 100 = €75,000 per month

Contract Value = (75,000 × 3mths) = 225,000.

Using the information above, a receivables substantive analytical review can be performed:

1. Develop expectation:
Expectation to be developed using the information ascertained in relation to debtor credit terms and ongoing dispute with customer – assuming that sales are spread evenly throughout the year.

Credit terms are 35 days, as corroborated above.
Actual sales are €6,690,000.
Expectation can be developed using this information and the receivables days ratio: (assuming sales are spread evenly throughout the year):

$$\frac{\text{Receivables}}{\text{Revenue}} \times 365 = \text{Receivables days}$$

$$\frac{Receivables}{€6,690,000} \times 365 = 35$$

Receivables   = (35/365) × €6,690,000
                    = €641,507

Add increase in period-end receivables due to customer dispute:
€300,000

Expected receivables = €941,507 (€641,507 + €300,000)

2. Outline deviation for further investigation:
From information above deviation threshold is €18,750

3. Compare actual result to expectation and calculate deviation
Expected receivables   = €941,507
Actual receivables   = €930,000
Deviation from expectation   = €11,507

4. Perform further investigation where deviation is above threshold for further investigation
As the deviation is below threshold for further investigation, no further work is deemed necessary.

Other Considerations

Having performed audit procedures on the revenue-related figures and on the receivables balance, the auditor will then have to consider:
- the reasonableness of the provision for doubtful debts (which confirms the valuation assertion for the receivables balance);
- cut-off procedures relating to revenue and receivables; and
- post year-end returns.

These are discussed in turn below.

Reasonableness of the Provision for Doubtful Debts Testing

On the face of the statement of financial position, the figure for receivables is net of the **doubtful debts provision**. As such, in confirming that the valuation of the receivables number is correct, the auditor must consider the reasonableness of the provision for doubtful debts. The audit of estimates was discussed in **Chapter 6,** Section 6.9, which covers the requirements on the auditor when auditing estimates under ISA 540 *Auditing Accounting Estimates, Including Fair Value Accounting Estimates, and Related Disclosures.*

Most entities determine the doubtful debts provision by:
- making a general provision, which is usually determined by applying a percentage to balances overdue by more than a specified period; or
- making a specific provision, which involves identifying customers that are known to be in financial difficulties or where payment is in dispute.

The doubtful debt provision is an estimate; ISA 540 therefore applies. The auditor is required to adopt one or more of the following approaches:
- reviewing and testing the process used by management;
- using an independent estimate;
- reviewing subsequent events.

The first approach, usually adopted for verifying general provisions, is to:
- obtain client entity's procedures for determining the doubtful debts provision estimate and consider the reliability and reasonableness of these procedures;
- ensure that the procedures have been followed and have been appropriately approved;
- consider the reasonableness of assumptions used in the calculation of the doubtful debts provision; and
- check calculations and consider the reliability of prior-year provisions.

Approaches usually adopted when considering specific doubtful debt provisions include examining correspondence from customers, reviewing customer credit reports and financial statements, and discussing collectability of debts with management.

The risk of doubtful debts occurring is a common risk for most businesses. The auditor must exercise caution and assess the ageing of the balances outstanding on the year-end receivables ledger and consider if the balance has been provided for by the client and, if not, he must consider if a provision is necessary. This assessment is crucial for the overall valuation of the receivables balance included within the financial statements.

The auditor should also consider the following:
- the adequacy of the system of internal controls relating to approval of credit terms and follow-up of overdue debts;
- the period of credit allowed and taken;
- whether balances have been settled post year end;
- whether an account is made up of specific items or not, e.g. customer paying amounts on account such as round sum amounts off his total balance rather than paying specific invoices, as this could indicate that the customer has cash flow difficulties and is potentially a doubtful debt;
- whether an account is within the maximum credit limit approved;
- reports on major receivables from collectors, agencies, etc.; and
- any legal proceedings and the legal status of receivables, e.g. customers in liquidation are unlikely to be able to pay amounts owed to their suppliers.

The auditor should perform the following:
- review the aged receivables listing for debts aged 60–90 days and older. The auditor should also at this point review a sample of sales invoices included on the period-end ledger to assess the reasonableness of the ageing of the invoices by the system on the period-end ledger;
- confirm and verify if such balances have been paid post year end;
- where balances have not been settled post year end, the auditor should inquire from management if there are any circumstances surrounding the non-payment of the

balance, such as a dispute between the customer and the entity, the customer being declared bankrupt or experiencing cash flow difficulties;
- where receipt of the balance outstanding on the aged listing at the year end is deemed unlikely after the above testing is performed, the auditor should consider if the client has provided for the balance; and
- where the client has not provided for the balance and the auditor deems that a provision is necessary, then an adjusting journal should be proposed.

The doubtful debt provision created by the client is known as an **accounting estimate**, as the final payment amount that will be received from the customer is not known with certainty. It is the role of the auditor to assess the facts surrounding the aged balances and to determine if the provision appears reasonable based on what is known.

Where the client entity has included a general provision in the accounts, (i.e. a provision which is general in nature and not established in respect of a specific customer and balance), the auditor should understand the basis of the provision and inspect corroborating information to determine the reasonableness of the provision.

Cut-off Procedures Relating to Revenue and Receivables

Cut-off ensures that items sold (and having met the revenue recognition criteria) in the first few days of the new period are not recorded in the year-end revenue. Additionally, cut off ensures that items sold (and having met the revenue recognition criteria) in the period prior to the year end are not recorded in the revenue of the next period. Cut-off, therefore, also helps to address the Completeness and Occurrence audit objectives.

In summary, cut-off errors can arise when either of the following occurs:
- a pre year-end dated sales invoice is not posted to the receivables ledger until post year end;
- a post year-end dated sales invoice is posted to the receivables ledger before the year-end date.

When either of the above occurs, the sale in question will have been recorded in the incorrect period in the financial statements of the company.

In order to determine whether the client has undertaken appropriate cut-off procedures at the year end, the auditor should perform appropriate tests. The following should be considered:

- the auditor should assess the high-risk period, i.e. the dates around the year end where the risk of a cut-off error occurring is deemed greatest – this could be the final week of trade pre year end and the first week of trade post year end;
- the auditor should target invoices posted to the receivables ledger during the high risk periods; and
- he should inspect the chosen sales invoices and the corresponding delivery documents in order to confirm that the sales have been recorded in the correct period.

Post Year-end Returns

It is important for the auditor to consider post year-end credit notes issued by the client in order to ensure that no major sales values need to be reversed due, say, to faulty goods being dispatched throughout the final month of the year. The auditor should consider the following:

- any significant post year-end credit notes raised and if they have been accounted for in the correct period, i.e. if a credit note has been raised post year end in relation to a pre year-end sales invoice then the credit note has not been accounted for in the correct period and an adjusting journal will be necessary;
- the level of credit notes raised post year end. Where there are unusual amounts of high value credit notes issued early in the new accounting period in relation to pre year-end sales invoices, the auditor should consider the legitimacy of the sales invoices issued pre year-end and consider the possibility of a cut-off error arising;
- the reason for the returns and the credit notes being issued; and
- journal adjustments should be proposed to correct for post year-end credit notes raised relating to pre year-end invoices.

13.9 USES OF CAATs WHEN AUDITING REVENUE AND RECEIVABLES

The purpose of **computer-assisted audit techniques** (CAATs) and their generic uses are discussed in detail in **Chapter 9**, Section 9.4. We will now consider the primary use of CAATs when auditing the area of revenue and receivables.

CAATs can provide considerable advantages when testing the area of revenue and receivables. Examples of the use of CAATs when testing the area of revenue and receivables are included below:

- **Audit Software** To prepare lead sheets and control the performance of the audit.
- **Knowledge-based Software** To prepare questionnaires and suggest testing steps based on answers to the questionnaires.
- **Data Analysis Software** By obtaining a copy of the client's outstanding invoice listing (including customer name and invoice date) at year end, the auditor can use data analysis software to:
  - categorise the invoices by customer;
  - stratify the receivables listing by value;
  - sort the listing in order of value and then ensure adequate testing is given to larger balances, credit balances, round sum balances;
  - tot the ledger to facilitate comparison to the financial statements;
  - merge of the aged receivables listing with credit limit data to identify customers who are exceeding their credit limit.

Example 13.7 below is a worked example of how CAATs can be used by the auditor to make his audit more efficient and more effective by assisting with the stratification of the receivables balance (the topic of **stratification** is considered in **Chapter 6**, Section 6.7.)

EXAMPLE 13.7: STRATIFICATION OF THE RECEIVABLES
BALANCE (LARGE COMPANY LIMITED)

Taking the aged receivables listing, the auditor can use CAATs to stratify the balances into categories below, the aged receivables listing of Large Company Limited is stratified below according to the value owing by each customer. This allows the auditor to ensure he tests highest values and in doing so reduces the materiality of the remaining balance and therefore reduces the sample size required in the remaining balance, i.e. instead of calculating a sample size on €3,750,000, the auditor fully tests the three customers at a value of €2,031,000 (54% of the total balance is now validated), and then calculates a sample size on the remaining value of €1,719,000. This provides the auditor with a more efficient (*in that the ultimate number of items tested will be reduced*) and effective (*in that a larger percentage of the total value will be covered*) method of auditing.

	>€500 000s	>€99<€500 000s	<€100 000s	Total 000s
Total Balance €000s	2,031	1,414	305	3,750
No of Accounts	3	5	10	18
% of Total Balance	54%	38%	8%	100%
% of No of Accounts	17%	27%	56%	100%

13.10 DISCLOSURE REQUIREMENTS FOR REVENUE AND RECEIVABLES

Finally, with regard to revenue and receivables, the auditor will consider the adequacy of the disclosures. The auditor needs to consider the requirements of IAS 18 and IAS 1 to ensure that all disclosures are:
- complete (i.e. no revenue- and receivables-related disclosures are missing – the auditor can use IAS 18 and IAS 1 as a checklist);
- accurate (reflect the actual transactions and information relating to events surrounding revenue and receivables);
- relate to events that actually occurred; and
- are properly presented (i.e. in a manner expected by IAS 18 and IAS 1).

Specific disclosure considerations relating to revenue and receivables include:
- auditors must be aware of the disclosure requirements for trade receivables and revenue under the applicable financial reporting framework;
- distinguish between receivables amounts due within one year and those falling due after one year;

- review of receivables ledger may indicate amounts owed from employees, officers, other group companies and related parties, which should be specifically disclosed if found to be material;
- credit balances included in the receivables ledger may, if found to be material, require reclassification to current liabilities;
- evidence of other activities requiring disclosure may be obtained through the review of minutes from board of directors' meetings and from inquiry of management; and
- obtain management's representations on these matters in writing in a representation letter.

13.11 CONCLUSION

When the auditor has performed controls testing, substantive analytical review and substantive tests of details, it must be considered if sufficient appropriate audit evidence has been obtained over revenue and receivables, which give the appropriate level of comfort required over the assertions stated at the outset, these being:

- Completeness;
- Valuation;
- Existence/Occurrence;
- Cut-off; and
- Rights and obligations.

The auditor must also consider if the testing performed has appropriately addressed any key risks identified by the auditor surrounding the revenue and receivables cycle, and reduced the risk of material misstatement arising as a result of key risks to a suitably low level.

The auditor must consider the impact on the **audit opinion** of the results of his testing in the area of revenue and receivables. He does so by considering whether any misstatements, found either individually or in aggregate (when combined with other misstatements detected throughout the audit), will result in the financial statements being materially misstated. As such, all misstatements found are taken to the auditor's errors schedule for consideration at the audit completion stage (discussed in detail in **Chapter 18**). The auditor's report on financial statements is considered in detail in **Chapter 19**, 'Audit Reports'.

SUMMARY OF LEARNING OBJECTIVES

Learning Objective 1   Understand what is included in the audit of revenue and receivables.

What is Revenue and Receivables? In the financial statements of an entity, the revenue figure represents the income earned by the business in return for the passing of title on goods or services. The receivables balance arises as a result of sales made and represents money due to the business from customers for those sales.

Learning Objective 2   Be able to identify the risks and audit objectives applicable to revenue and receivables.

Risks Associated with Revenue and Receivables The primary risks associated with revenue and receivables relate to:
1. existence of trade receivables balances; and
2. collectability of receivables.

Learning Objective 3   Be able to determine an appropriate audit strategy for revenue and receivables, taking into consideration the specific risks and audit objectives (management assertions).

Audit Objectives/Management Assertions for Revenue and Receivables With respect to revenue, the auditor seeks to prove that revenue recorded in the financial statements relates to events that occurred and that it has been recorded accurately and only relates to transactions where risks and rewards of items have passed to the buyer.

When auditing the receivables balance, the auditor seeks to confirm their existence and the entity's right to collect receivables (rights and obligations) and to gain assurance over the collectability of the receivables balance (i.e. valuation). He also seeks to prove that they are properly classified and disclosed in the financial statements.

Learning Objective 4   Be able to develop an audit programme that addresses all the audit objectives (management assertions) for revenue and receivables.

Developing the Audit Plan Where the revenue and receivables balances are not material to the financial statements, limited controls and substantive testing will be performed. However, revenue and receivables are usually material figures and transactions tend to be high in volume; for this reason the auditor usually takes a controls approach when testing revenue and receivables in order to reduce the level of detailed substantive testing.

Learning Objective 5   Be able to describe and apply specific substantive testing procedures relating to the audit of revenue and receivables.

Key Documents when Auditing The aged receivables listing is the key document of interest to the auditor. Other documents that may form part of audit evidence connected to revenue and receivables include:

- sales invoices;
- goods dispatch notes (GDNs);
- proof of delivery notes (PDNs);
- customer statements; and
- customer remittances.

Key Substantive Testing Procedures Connected to Revenue The auditor may carry out detailed testing of the revenue balance by vouching transactions included in the revenue general ledger to source documents, confirming their occurrence and accuracy. Additionally, he will seek to gain comfort over completeness by tracing from documents of first entry to entries in the revenue ledger.

Alternatively, if controls have tested strong and reduced substantive procedures are being performed the auditor may carry out substantive analytical procedures (**proof in total**).

For the revenue and receivables balances the auditor will seek to:

- Circularise customers to confirm that the balance exists and is accurately recorded at year end (or apply alternative procedures such as substantive analytical procedures or tracing of receivables to post year-end receipts in the bank statement).
- Review valuation by reference to a review of the doubtful debt provision set by management and by reviewing the aged receivables listing and post year-end receipts.
- The auditor will also assess the adequacy of disclosure notes relating to revenue and receivables.

Learning Objective 6   Understand the role CAATs can play when auditing revenue and receivables.

CAATs and Revenue and Receivables The auditor may use a combination of audit software, data analysis tools and other applications, such as Excel, when auditing the area of revenue and receivables.

Learning Objective 7   Understand the auditor's approach relating to the disclosures of revenue and receivables.

The auditor should seek to ensure that all disclosures relating to receivables are complete, accurate, pertain to the entity and adequately presented in line with applicable international reporting standards.

QUESTIONS

Self-test Questions

13.1 What benefits are derived from an aged receivables listing?

13.2 Discuss an audit procedure that should be performed to test the receivables balance.

13.3 How might the auditor use substantive analytical procedures in the audit of revenue and receivables?

13.4 Which procedures should an auditor perform while testing total revenue?

13.5 List the two methods of confirming receivables balances, and discuss the benefits of each method.

13.6 Explain the advantages and disadvantages relating to receivables circularisation.

13.7 Explain the four steps an auditor should consider when performing substantive analytical procedures.

13.8 How do most entities determine the provision for doubtful debt?

13.9 Why must an auditor review the aged receivables listing for debts aged 60–90 days and older?

13.10 What procedures will an auditor perform to test cut-off?

Review Questions

(See Suggested Solutions to Review Questions in **Appendix D**.)

Question 13.1

You are given the following information regarding total revenue for Football Crazy Ltd:

	FY 2012 (1 Jan–31 Dec 2012) €000	FY 2011 (1 Jan–31 Dec 2011) €000	
DVDs	335	227	(a) and (b)
Sweatshirts	55	37	(c)
Magazines	178	198	(d)
	568	462	

(a) Five new DVDs have been brought to the market during the financial year to 2012, details as follows:

DVD	Month of Introduction to Market	Selling Price	Budgeted Monthly Sales Volume (Units)
1	Feb 2012	€10	250
2	April 2012	€17	300
3	July 2012	€12	485
4	September 2012	€15	245
5	November 2012	€22	165

(b) Two DVDs were discontinued in January 2012 due to poor revenue in prior year, details as follows:

DVD	Selling Price	Prior Year Annual Sales Volume (Units)
1	€22	565
2	€19	500

(c) The sweatshirt range for adults has remained the same, however a new range for children was introduced during the 2012 financial year, details as follows:
  • new sweatshirt range introduced for children for the final two months of the 12-month period under review;
  • selling price range of sweatshirts on sale is €12–€15;
  • based on market research, expected monthly sales of sweatshirts is 650 per month.

(d) During financial year 2012 the company was forced to reduce magazine selling prices due to growing competition from competitors:

Magazine	Prior Year Selling Price	Prior Year Sales Volume	Prior Year Sales Revenue	New Reduced Price	Month of Price Cut
1	€2.50	20,000	€50,000	€2.30	Jan 12
2	€2.00	13,500	€27,000	€1.80	Jan 12
3	€4.75	10,000	€47,500	€4.45	March 12
4	€3.50	11,000	€38,500	€3.10	Jan 12
5	€1.25	28,000	€35,000	€1.10	June 12
			€198,000		

Requirement
(a) Use the information above to develop an expectation for total sales revenue for the 2012 financial year, showing the overall expectation and an expectation for each individual revenue stream.
(b) Outline for each particular sales component what additional information you would require in order to determine the reliability of the information used when developing the expectation above.
(c) Explain briefly the remaining three parts of the four-step approach which should be considered by the auditor when performing substantive analytical procedures.

Question 13.2

Quad Tec Engineering Ltd has a doubtful debt provision of €253,000 at the year end.

Requirement
(a) Outline what your approach to the audit of this provision would be in order to gain comfort over the valuation of year-end accounts receivables balance.
(b) List three other accounting estimates that can be included in financial statements and briefly describe the audit approach which should be adopted for these estimates.

Question 13.3

Ballycane Metals Ltd is a new audit client for your audit firm. The engagement partner and audit manager attended a preliminary meeting with the directors and the financial director of the company in the past few days. Audit fieldwork is due to commence in one week. The audit manager noted the following from the meeting:

1. in recent months the company has experienced severe competition and as a result has increased its payment terms for customers in order to attract new customers and maintain current customers;
2. receivables days ratio has moved from 35 days in prior year to 60 days in current year;
3. the client is contemplating introducing a 3% discount for payment within credit terms;
4. on review of the aged receivables listing half of the year-end receivables balance is aged greater than 90 days.

Requirement
(a)   As audit senior of the team, draft a memorandum to your audit team outlining how the team will approach the audit of receivables balances aged greater than 90 days old on the aged receivables listing at the year end. The memorandum should include general and specific guidance.
(b)   If the client decides to implement a 3% discount for prompt payment, explain how in future years the audit team could develop an independent expectation for total discount allowed during the performance of substantive analytical procedures.

Question 13.4

Explain how an audit team should approach the audit of credit balances on the receivables ledger.

Question 13.5

As audit team manager you are considering carrying out a receivables circularisation on year-end trade receivables for one of your audit clients where the trade receivables balance is material to the financial statements.

Requirement
(a)   Outline how you will perform the receivables circularisation.
(b)   Give three circumstances where it is not necessary to perform a receivables circularisation.
(c)   Where receivables circularised do not respond to your audit request, explain the alternative audit procedures that should be performed to gain comfort over these balances.

Question 13.6

Describe and discuss three potential risks surrounding the trade receivables balance and link these risks to the relevant financial statement assertions. Suggest testing which the auditor can perform to mitigate these risks.

Question 13.7

You have just been promoted to a senior associate at your audit firm, CPD Chartered Accountants, and you have been asked by your manager to act as audit senior on the audit of Tiser Ltd ('Tiser').

Tiser Ltd has a year end of 31 December 2012 and the company publishes a monthly homewares directory, which provides customers with the best homewares places to shop throughout Ireland.

Extracted income statement amounts for the year ended 31 December 2012 are presented below:

Revenue   €28,525,000

Revenue and receivables

Approximately 85% of Tiser's revenue is derived from advertising from those retailers and businesses that choose to include advertising campaigns in the directory. The remaining 15% of Tiser's revenue is generated from subscription fees from businesses that choose to list their business in Tiser's directory. Individual advertisements range from:

- €1,000 (1/4 page)
- €1,500 (1/2 page)
- €2,500 (full page)
- €4,500 (double page)

Each directory has 750 pages of advertisements. The advertisements are generally comprised of:

- 30% 2-page spreads
- 30% 1-page ads
- 25% ½- page ads
- 15% ¼-page ads

Discounts are given to 2-page spread purchases and range between 10% and 20%. Your audit junior, through other testing, has identified the average discount given to be 16%.

Business listings carry a standard subscription fee of €200 per monthly issue. Currently there are 1,800 subscribers (this number has been consistent throughout the year).

Requirement On the basis of the information presented above on revenue and receivables:
- (a) Conduct substantive analytical procedures to establish the reasonableness or otherwise of advertising revenue for the year ended 31 December 2012. You have already calculated a threshold of €300,000.
- (b) A risk has been identified with respect to the valuation of receivables. Outline, for your audit junior on the engagement, a plan on how to test the valuation of receivables.
- (c) Outline two appropriate substantive audit procedures to test the occurrence of the subscriptions revenue. You should make reference specifically to proving how 'subscriptions revenue' occurred.

14

THE AUDIT OF BANK AND CASH

LEARNING OBJECTIVES

Having read this chapter on the audit of bank and cash you should be able to:
1. understand what is included in the audit of bank and cash;
2. be able to identify the risks and audit objectives (management assertions) applicable to bank and cash;
3. be able to determine an appropriate audit strategy for bank and cash, taking into consideration the specific risks and audit objectives (management assertions);
4. be able to develop an audit programme that addresses all the audit objectives (assertions) for bank and cash;
5. be able to describe and apply specific substantive testing procedures relating to the audit of bank and cash;
6. understand the role CAATs can play when auditing bank and cash; and
7. understand the auditor's approach relating to the disclosures of bank and cash.

CHECKLIST OF RELEVANT STANDARDS

The relevant standards covered in this chapter are:
- ISA (UK and Ireland) 315 *Identifying and Assessing the Risks of Material Misstatement Through Understanding of the Entity and Its Environment* (ISA 315)
- ISA (UK and Ireland) 330 *The Auditor's Responses to Assessed Risks* (ISA 330)
- ISA (UK and Ireland) 500 *Audit Evidence* (ISA 500)
- ISA (UK and Ireland) 505 *External Confirmations* (ISA 505)
- ISA (UK and Ireland) 510 *Initial Audit Engagements – Opening Balances* (ISA 510)
- ISA (UK and Ireland) 530 *Audit Sampling* (ISA 530)
- IAS 7 *Statement of Cash Flow* (IAS 7).

KEY TERMS AND DEFINITIONS FOR THIS CHAPTER

Bank and Cash   Bank and cash represents the bank balances and cash on hand included within current assets and the bank overdrafts and bank loans included within the entity's current and non-current liabilities.

Bank Confirmation   This is a letter requested by the auditor and sent directly from the bank to the auditor, which discloses cash on deposit, loans and details of all accounts in the name of the client entity at the balance sheet date.

Bank Reconciliation   The bank reconciliation is performed by the client and reconciles the balance per the bank statement to the balance per the ledger (accounting records).

'Window Dressing'   A strategy used by management near the year end to manipulate the appearance of the financial statements (e.g. where profit has performed poorly in the year, management might overinflate the revenue by including some of January's sales in December's revenue).

14.1 INTRODUCTION

Sections 14.2 to **14.8** of this chapter consider how the auditor addresses the substantive testing of bank and cash. In doing so this chapter deals with how the auditor:
(a) identifies audit risks and audit objectives (management assertions) for bank and cash;
(b) develops an audit plan for bank and cash and refines this into an audit programme;
(c) designs specific tests associated with bank and cash; and
(d) checks the adequate presentation and disclosure in the financial statements relating to bank and cash.

In **Section 14.9** we consider how computer-assisted audit techniques (CAATs) considered in detail in **Chapter 9**, can assist with the audit of bank and cash.

Finally, in **Section 14.10** we consider the auditor's approach when auditing the reasonableness of disclosures relating to bank and cash.

14.2 WHAT IS BANK AND CASH?

Bank and cash represents the bank balances and cash on hand included within current assets, and the bank overdrafts and loans included within current and non-current liabilities. Bank and cash also incorporates balances relating to cash on deposit.

The auditor is predominantly concerned with the existence and completeness of all bank and cash balances.

The auditor will need to ensure that debit and credit balances relating to bank and cash are not netted against one another, but instead disclosed separately under assets and liabilities as appropriate

14.3 RISKS ASSOCIATED WITH BANK AND CASH

Throughout **Chapter 7** (which addresses the requirements of ISA (UK and Ireland) 315 *Identifying and Assessing the Risks of Material Misstatement Through Understanding of the Entity and Its Environment* (ISA 315) and ISA (UK and Ireland) 330 *The Auditor's Responses to Assessed Risks* (ISA 330)) we discussed the topic of 'risk' and we considered how the auditor should go about detecting risks. We also discussed how the auditor should consider these risks when designing the nature, timing and extent of further audit procedures relative to each financial cycle. As such, before developing the audit plan, the auditor needs to consider a number of risks that may be associated with bank and cash. Risks associated with bank and cash can include:
- the reliability of the entity's cash-recording system;
- the frequency of bank reconciliations (i.e. how often does the client entity receive bank statements and when are the reconciliations prepared?);
- physical controls over cash and its susceptibility to theft;
- risk due to fraud: false bank accounts, fraudulent or erroneous payments, rights over bank accounts (i.e. whether the entity being audited owns the account or does it belong to another company within the group?) and whether the company has rights to all of the cash in the bank account (directors of companies may have personal cash in company accounts);
- cut-off (i.e. whether the payments and receipts have been recorded in the correct period); and
- whether other transactional risks exist that could result in a material misstatement if not mitigated, e.g. credit card transactions.

14.4 AUDIT OBJECTIVES/MANAGEMENT ASSERTIONS FOR BANK AND CASH

As discussed in **Chapter 6** (which addressed the requirements of ISA (UK and Ireland) 500 *Audit Evidence* (ISA 500)) it is necessary for the auditor to seek appropriate audit evidence to satisfy all of the audit objectives and to eliminate the possibility of any of the risks outlined in **Section 14.3** going undetected. In **Chapter 4** we introduced audit objectives (management assertions) and explained their generic meanings, and then we re-introduced this topic again throughout **Chapter 8**, making management assertions specific to each financial cycle. In **Table 14.1** below we remind you once more of the audit objectives, as they relate to bank and cash.

Table 14.1 addresses the management assertions (audit objectives) as they relate to the balances associated with bank and cash. The movements in bank and cash in the year and captured during the testing of other substantive areas (such as revenue and receivables, which will cover the receipt of cash, and purchases and payables, which will cover the payment of cash).

Now that we understand the objectives of the auditor with regard to bank and cash, in the sections to follow let us consider how he addresses these objectives through substantive testing.

TABLE 14.1: CONTROL OBJECTIVES FOR BANK AND CASH
FOR ACCOUNT BALANCE AT YEAR END

Management Assertion/ Audit Objective	Objective of Audit Test
Existence	To check that recorded bank and cash balances exist at the balance sheet date.
Completeness	To check that all bank and cash balances are recorded in the correct period and included in the financial statements.
Accuracy	To check bank and cash balances are accurately recorded in the financial statements.
Valuation	To check bank and cash balances are properly valued, and a provision has been made for any balances that may not be recoverable.
Cut-off	To check that all transactions have been accounted for in the correct accounting period.
Rights and Obligations	To check the entity has the rights to all bank and cash balances shown at the balance sheet date.
Presentation and Disclosure	To check that bank and cash balances are properly classified and disclosed in the balance sheet and that lines of credit, loan guarantees and other restrictions on bank and cash balances are appropriately disclosed.

14.5 DEVELOPING THE AUDIT PLAN FOR BANK AND CASH

Before the audit of bank and cash is undertaken, an assessment of the audit risk must be completed. As discussed in detail in **Chapter 7**, audit risk is made up of three components: inherent risk; control risk; and detection risk. We will consider these components specifically as they relate to bank and cash.

Audit Risk = Inherent Risk + Control Risk + Detection Risk

Inherent Risks

Cash is inherently risky because it is liquid (and is highly susceptible to theft), so if the client entity operates a cash business, this will be considered an **inherent risk**.

Controls and Detection Risk

Generally, when it comes to cash and cash equivalents, the most efficient method of testing is focused substantive procedures. All bank accounts must be tested substantively, regardless of the outcome of controls testing, which usually means the auditor will not test the controls unless to gain a greater understanding of the management and control of cash in a predominantly cash business (e.g. retail business, where all customer transactions are in cash).

14.6 KEY DOCUMENTS OF INTEREST TO THE AUDITOR WHEN AUDITING BANK AND CASH

Before commencing substantive procedures it is important for the auditor to have an appreciation for the key documents related to bank and cash. When it comes to **bank and cash**, the auditor is interested in two key documents:
1. **Bank Reconciliation** The bank reconciliation is performed by the client entity and reconciles the balance per the bank statement to the balance per the ledger (accounting records).
2. **Bank Confirmation** As part of the audit of bank and cash the auditor should obtain a bank confirmation, which will provide the auditor with independent reliable audit evidence (see **Chapter 6**). The bank confirmation should disclose cash on deposit, loans and details of all accounts in the name of the client entity at the balance sheet date.

The confirmation can be subdivided into two categories: one which should detail standard information (e.g. the bank balances); and the other which should detail supplementary information relating to trade finance and derivative and commodity trading. The bank confirmation request letters should:
• confirm all bank accounts the entity has with the bank – this should also include nil balances and accounts opened/closed during the year);
• credit limits/overdraft facilities;
• terms of loans/other borrowings;

- outstanding charges and interest accrued;
- outstanding bills of exchange, guarantees, acceptances, etc.;
- foreign currency contracts;
- hire-purchase/leasing agreements; and
- items held in safe custody or as security for borrowings.

14.7 SUBSTANTIVE AUDIT PROGRAMME FOR BANK AND CASH

An audit programme records the specific details of tests to be performed by the auditor. The audit programme becomes a guide for the audit engagement team as to the work to be done in a particular area. As work is completed, a reference is included on the audit programme showing the location on the audit file where details of the tests performed are included. The audit programme for any cycle will vary from entity to entity, but below we consider the typical types of test the auditor would include in the audit programme for bank and cash.

EXAMPLE 14.1: AUDIT PROGRAMME FOR BANK AND CASH[1]

Large Company Limited				
December 2012	Audit Materiality			€3,642,500
	Performance Materiality			€2,731,875
			Initials	Date
	Prepared by:			
Bank Balances and Cash in Hand	Reviewed by:			
Audit Programme	Assertion Covered		Reference to Work	Initials and Date
Initial Procedures				
Assess the appropriateness of the accounting policy and the accounting estimates method for this area. Ensure that the accounting policy is in accordance with accounting standards and applicable law, and that the methods used for making the accounting estimates are appropriate.	Existence, Completeness, Rights and Obligations, Valuation, Presentation and Disclosure			
Agree opening balances to prior-year working papers.	Presentation and Disclosure			

---

[1] Source: based on *Procedures for Quality Audit 2010* (© Chartered Accountants Ireland, 2010) I1.

Obtain or prepare a lead schedule and agree to balance sheet.	Completeness, Existence and Accuracy		
Bank Reconciliation			
Obtain or prepare reconciliations of all accounts held. Check outstanding items to post period-end bank statements. Enquire into any items un-presented for a significant period of time.	Completeness, Existence, Valuation and Presentation and Disclosure		
Bank Confirmations			
Obtain standard bank confirmation and check to reconciliations as per ISA 505: 1. in the case of each non-response, perform alternative audit procedures to obtain relevant and reliable audit evidence (ISA 505, para 12); 2. if it is determined that a response to a bank confirmation request is necessary to obtain sufficient appropriate audit evidence, alternative audit procedures will not provide the audit evidence required. If such confirmation is not obtained, determine the implications for the audit and the auditor's opinion in accordance with ISA 505 (para 13).	Completeness, Existence, Valuation and Presentation and Disclosure		
Other Considerations			
Consider whether **window dressing** has taken place. In particular: 1. check that all payments recorded prior to the period end were dispatched before that date; 2. review cash book and statements for significant movements around the year end; and 3. verify any significant reconciling items reversed in the subsequent period.	Completeness, Existence, Valuation, Presentation and Disclosure		

Where possible, verify material amounts of **cash in hand**. Consider whether there have been significant cash movements in the period and what further verification work is needed. Review cash book during the period and highlight significant and unusual entries. Investigate any such items found. Consider checking analysis.	Occurrence and Existence, Accuracy and Valuation		
Ensure that disclosure is made of all bank security. (a) Review covenants in place in relation to bank facilities. Document situations where these have been breached in the period, commitments and security given and implications for the audit. (b) Ensure adequate disclosure of commitments, security and covenants in place, including any breach of covenants noted.	Occurrence and Existence, Rights and Obligations		
Name:		Accountant in Charge	
Date:			
Name:		Reviewer	
Date:			

14.8 SUBSTANTIVE TESTING PROCEDURES FOR BANK AND CASH

Below we are going to discuss in more detail some of the procedures outlined in the substantive audit programme above (at **Example 14.1**).

We will start with initial procedures, which include: opening balances; mathematical accuracy of schedules; the lead schedule; and analytical reviews.

Initial Procedures

Opening Balances

Before commencing further audit procedures, evidence must be obtained as to the accuracy of the opening balances of bank and cash. The reason for this is twofold: first, it confirms that the comparative numbers in the financial statements (which must be included in the current year's financial statements) agree to the final accounts of the prior year; and, secondly, it highlights any final entries (last-minute adjusting journal entries) of the prior year not correctly carried forward, which may indicate an error in the current year's financial statement figures. The auditor verifies opening balances as follows:

- Agree the opening balances to the prior-year working papers and signed financial statements. This may highlight an opening balance in the current year's accounts that does not agree to the closing balance per the prior year's financial statements. In this instance a change would be made to the opening balance of the current year, which would impact the closing balance of the current year. This usually arises due to final adjustments in the prior year that are not reflected in the actual accounts (nominal and general ledgers).
- If this is the first year of the audit engagement, the auditor will still need to establish that the opening balances are materially correct, which can pose difficulties for him if either the client entity was exempt from audit in the prior year or a predecessor auditor carried out the audit. The audit of opening balances in such instances is discussed in detail in **Chapter 6**, Section 6.8, which addresses the requirements of ISA (UK and Ireland) 510 *Initial Audit Engagements – Opening Balances* (ISA 510).

Mathematical Accuracy of Schedules

All bank reconciliations should be tested for their mathematical accuracy and should be agreed to the schedule of bank balances that tie-in with the financial statements.

Prepare Lead Schedules

The **lead schedule** acts as a summary of the balances and transactions to be audited relating to a particular class of transaction and balances. It allows the auditor to control his procedures by referencing each balance or transaction to the working paper that records the audit tests performed. An example of a lead schedule for bank and cash is included below at **Example 14.2**.

As with any audit working paper, the standard headings apply with regard to: company name; year-end; materiality; performance materiality; and preparer and reviewers of the document. Also included as standard is the audit working paper title, which in this instance is 'Bank and Cash Lead Schedule'. What follows is a summary of the balances that make up the bank and cash balance. This now acts as a checklist for the auditor, allowing him to ensure he audits all aspects that make up the balance and the movements in the period leading to that balance. As he tests each item contained in the lead schedule, he notes a reference directly on the lead schedule to where testing is contained in the audit file.

EXAMPLE 14.2: BANK AND CASH LEAD SCHEDULE
(LARGE COMPANY LIMITED)[2]

Large Company Limited 31 December 2012		
	Audit Materiality	**€3,642,500**
	Performance Materiality	**€2,731,875**

[2] Source: based on *Procedures for Quality Audit 2010* (© Chartered Accountants Ireland, 2010) I-.

Bank Balances and Cash in Hand	Initials	Date
	Prepared by:	
	Reviewed by:	
	31/12/2012	31/12/2011
	€000s	€000s
Receivables Balances: Bank and Cash		
Current account	9,199	20,528
Deposit account	95,000	85,000
Petty cash	1	2
	104,200	105,530
Payables Balances: Amounts payable within one year		
Current		
Galway Bank Loan	1,000	1,000
Dublin Bank Loan	3,250	8,650
	4,250	9,650
Amounts payable after one year		
Non-current Eurobond	3,750	350
Galway Bank Loan	14,000	15,000
Dublin Bank Loan	2,600	12,210
	20,350	27,560
Total Bank Loans	**24,600**	**37,210**

Analytical Review

An analytical review is usually performed at the start of each substantive testing of a balance or class of transactions. Calculating ratios and analysing results against industry information, prior-year results, budgets, etc. allows the auditor to better understand the movements in the year and make comparisons against norms, therefore enabling him to better prepare his audit programme. **Example 14.3** below shows the types of ratio and comparison the auditor might perform in relation to bank and cash.

EXAMPLE 14.3: INITIAL PROCEDURES: ANALYTICAL REVIEW AND
COMMENTARY ON BANK AND CASH (LARGE COMPANY LIMITED)

Receivables Balances: Bank and Cash

	2012 €000	2011 €000	Change €000	
Current account	9,199	20,528	(11,329)	
Deposit account	95,000	85,000	10,000	Cash reserves have decreased due to repayment of loans.
Petty cash	1	2	(1)	
	104,200	105,530	(1,330)	

Payables Balances: Amounts Payable within One Year

	2012 €000	2011 €000	Change €000	
Current	4,250	9,650	(5,400)	Both short- and long-term borrowing has decreased due to the repayment of the Dublin loan facilitated by the significant surge in cash revenue.
Amounts payable after one year	20,350	27,560	(7,210)	
Total Bank Loans	**24,600**	**37,210**	(12,610)	

			Change	
Interest Cover (EBIT ÷ interest)	= 73,400 ÷ 550 = 133	= 24,610 ÷ 550 = 45	88	Although one would have expected interest costs to decrease due to the repayment of the Dublin loan, it was not repaid until the year end, meaning that similar interest charges were incurred. With the improvement in profit, interest cover has improved greatly.

Bank Account Balances

Having performed the initial procedures, now let us consider the specific audit procedures the auditor might carry out in relation to the bank and cash balances, which essentially includes: the examination of bank reconciliations; review of bank confirmation request letters; and the review of cash balances.

Examination of Bank Reconciliations

The client entity should prepare bank reconciliations for every bank account included within the bank and cash balances on the financial statements. The auditor is required to review all of these bank reconciliations by performing the following:

- Obtaining a copy of all bank reconciliations in respect of all bank accounts held at the balance sheet date and obtaining explanations for large or unusual reconciling items.
- Agreeing the total as per the reconciliation to the bank/cash account in the nominal ledger, the bank confirmation request letter and the bank statements.
- Recalculating the totals in the reconciliation to ensure their mathematical accuracy.
- Tracing any outstanding cheques at the balance sheet date to post year-end bank statements. In the case of outstanding cheques taking a longer than expected time to clear after the year end, obtain explanations as to the delay and ensure that the cheques were actually issued by the client prior to the balance sheet date and not after the balance sheet date. Depending on the number of outstanding cheques and lodgements, a sample of outstanding items may be tested. (Sampling is covered in **Chapter 6**, Section 6.7 which addresses the requirements of ISA (UK and Ireland) 530 *Audit Sampling* (ISA 530).)
- Tracing outstanding lodgements to post year-end bank statements.
- Agreeing a sample of lodgements from the bank statements to the lodgement book.
- For a sample of receipts and payments taken from the cash receipts / cheque payments book, the auditor should ensure that items selected are either included on the bank statements prior to year-end or included on the list of outstanding lodgements/cheques.
- Examining the cash receipts book for evidence of reversals of lodgements subsequent to the year-end.
- Reviewing the bank statements, cash receipts book and cheque payments book for any large or unusual items.
- Ensuring interest payable on loans is properly accrued and included in the financial statements.
- For a sample of items included within outstanding cheques and lodgements, the auditor should test to ensure that the items have been treated appropriately in year-end receivables and payables, i.e. items included in outstanding lodgements have been removed from the receivables ledger, and items included within outstanding cheques have been removed from the payables ledger.
- Obtaining post year-end bank statements and tracing all prior-year dated cheques to outstanding cheques listed on the bank reconciliation (this could assist in finding prior-year cheques not included as outstanding on the bank reconciliation).

If uncleared cheques are material, it could indicate '**window dressing**' – where cheques are written on the last day of the year but not mailed for several weeks until there are funds in the account to meet these payments. The entity will not usually delay in lodging cheques received and as such the auditor should expect outstanding lodgements on the bank reconciliation to clear the bank within one week of the year end. Make inquiries of management if the delay in presentation of cheques is greater than two weeks.

• Tracing deposits in transit on the bank reconciliation to deposits on the post year-end bank statement (these should be one of the first items shown on the post year-end bank statement, if not, inquire into the reason for the time lag and corroborate explanation – significant delays in depositing receipts could indicate fraudulent practice of teeming and lading). Scan the statement for unusual items, such as unrecorded bank debits/ credits, bank errors and corrections.

Bank Confirmation Letters (Bank Confirmations)

In **Chapter 6**, Section 6.5 we introduced external confirmations (ISA (UK and Ireland) 505 *External Confirmations* (ISA 505)) . Here we will discuss an external confirmation relating to bank and cash. When auditing bank accounts, agreeing the bank reconciliation to the bank statement is not sufficient. The auditor needs to obtain a confirmation from the bank (known as a bank confirmation request letter), which confirms not only the bank balance but other key pieces of information which support both the figures on the face of the primary statements as well as the disclosures in the financial statements.

The bank confirmation letter should be sent by the auditor on the auditor's letterhead and clearly identify all of the information required. It is important that the auditor maintains complete control over the process. The bank confirmation is a very important part of the audit of bank and cash as it provides the auditor with **independent third-party audit evidence** (see **Example 14.4** below for a sample of a bank confirmation).

ISA 505, paragraph 7, states:
> "When performing confirmation procedures, the auditor shall maintain control over the external confirmation request, including:
> (a) Determining the information to be confirmed or requested;
> (b) Selecting the appropriate confirming party;
> (c) Designing the confirmation requests, including determining that requests are properly addressed and contain return information for responses to be sent directly to the auditor; and
> (d) Sending the requests; including follow-up requests when applicable, to the confirming party."

The confirmation of other arrangements with the banks should also be conducted through the bank confirmation process. When returned, the bank confirmation should confirm: guaranteed loans to third parties; bills discounted with recourse; details of any contingent liabilities of which the bank may be aware; details of the existence of any other banking relationships with the company of which the recipient bank may be aware; and any unused facilities (e.g. bank overdrafts). The bank confirmation should be signed or stamped by the bank and it should be obtained by the auditor directly from the bank.

It is important to note that bank confirmation request letters cannot be relied upon entirely. Such confirmations include a disclaimer in favour of the bank and, in essence, the bank cannot be held liable if it provides incomplete/inaccurate information.

EXAMPLE 14.4: BANK CONFIRMATION REQUEST LETTER[3]

STANDARD FORM OF REQUEST

The Manager   Auditor: Smith and Smith
Worldwide Bank   Date: 1 February 2013
123 Main Street   Our Ref: 1234
Ennis

Co. Clare

Customer/Client Name – Large Company Limited

Account Number: 20506025
Sort Code: 900150

Dear Sir,

I/We have read this document and I/we authorise you to provide the information requested herein in respect of the accounts of the above-named customer and also to disclose the number of joint accounts, if any, to which the above-named customer is party. An account number has been included above to assist with identification.

Please send this information to our auditor(s)

Mr Joe O'Connor
Smith and Smith
123 Market Street
Kilkenny

Yours faithfully,

....

Authorised Signature(s)

Note: the above forms the first page sent to the bank, which essentially represents the request to the bank to complete the bank confirmation request letter attached. The bank would complete the attached form and return it directly to the auditor. The bank confirmation request letter that the bank would return is included below:

Dear Sir,

We report that at the close of business on 31/12/2012 the record of this branch showed:

---

[3] Source: http://www.ibf.ie/gns/publications/formsguides/bankaudit.aspx

1. BANK ACCOUNTS

Description of accounts (including deposit accounts)	S/SX Note A	Date of last letter outlining terms/conditions of borrowing	Balance	Dr/ Cr	Amounts accrued but not posted at above date (Note B)	
					Estimated interest Dr/Cr	**Est. Current Account Fees and other charges**
			€		€	€

Note A: where a specific letter of set-off for principal exists affecting any of the above accounts, please indicate this by adding S to the account title. If the set-off refers to accounts other than those being reported on, use SX. (Other set-offs may arise either at law or on foot of a bank security document.)

Note B: the provision of this information may entail work and costs. If the information is not essential this request should be deleted.

2. FULL TITLES AND DATES OF CLOSURE OF ALL ACCOUNTS CLOSED DURING PERIOD: From 01/01/20XX to 31/12/20XX.

3. CUSTOMER'S ASSETS Nature of security held directly from customer (e.g. deeds, stocks, shares, etc.). Amount only of any guarantees held for the benefit of the customer.

4. CONTINGENT LIABILITIES All known contingent liabilities.

	Date(s)	Amount €

(a) Total of bills discounted for your customer, with recourse:

(b) Amounts and dates of each guarantee, (excluding acceptances) bond or indemnity given to you by the customer:

(c) Amounts and dates of each guarantee (excluding acceptances), bond or indemnity given by you on behalf of your customer:

(d) Total of bills drawn on and accepted by the bank on behalf of the customer (excluding (f) hereunder):

(e) Total forward foreign exchange contracts:

(f) Total of outstanding liabilities under documentary credits:

(g) Others – please give details:

The information available at the branch contained herein is given in confidence for your use only, in your capacity as auditor(s) and without responsibility on the part of the bank or any of its officials.

Note: no information can or will be given which would disclose confidential information regarding other customers.

Signed .... Manager

  .... Date

Branch Brand

Cash Balances

Above we have dealt with the audit of bank balances and we now need to consider how the auditor goes about substantively testing cash balances included within the financial statements.

Where cash transactions are significant and therefore **inherent risk** is high, the auditor should:

- Consider if internal controls surrounding cash receipts and payments are sufficient.
- Where the balance sheet cash balance is **material**:
  - review the operation of the cash system (how cash is collected, reconciled to till receipts, lodged and reconciled to the bank account);
  - count the cash either at the year end or by performing a surprise cash count at a randomly selected point during the audit;
  - during the cash count, ensure that full control exists over all cash simultaneously to prevent cash from being swapped from one count to another, perform the count in the presence of independent client personnel (not those in regular custody of cash); list details of notes and coins and ensure IOUs are recorded and collectible and that they are made according to the client entity's policy guidelines.
- Reconcile the cash counted to the petty cash records, and investigate any differences.
- Have the cashier perform and initial the reconciliation as evidence of agreement.

Other Considerations

Having performed the substantive procedures relating to bank and cash balances, there are some other matters the auditor must consider before he has adequately completed his substantive procedures relating to bank and cash. These are discussed below:

- **Auditing the valuation assertion for bank and cash** – the auditor should review relevant loan agreements or board minutes to determine whether there are any restrictions on the availability or use of bank balances or cash.
- **Auditing the ownership assertion for bank and cash** – the auditor should:

- obtain sufficient audit evidence in relation to bank balances from bank confirmation request letters; and
- check that all bank statements are in the name of the client entity.
- **Auditing the completeness assertion for bank and cash** – the auditor should:
  - carry out an analytical review of the balances and obtain explanations for any large or unusual variations;
  - review the bank confirmation request letters, minutes of board meetings and inquire of management if any new accounts were opened during the period;
  - investigate whether separate bank accounts exist for the payment of payroll or petty cash, and ensure that all bank accounts are included at the balance sheet date.
- **Auditing the statement of cash flows** – the movement in the balance of cash and cash equivalents for the period is shown in the statement of cash flows, which summarises the effect of the operating, investing and financing cash movements. The statement of cash flows is one of the primary statements within the financial statements. It shows how cash and cash equivalents have flowed in and out of the entity by category: operating, investing, and finance over the reporting period. The auditor should obtain sufficient appropriate audit evidence to support the figures included on the statement of cash flows and ensure they are consistent with the other primary statements in the financial statements. Additionally the auditor should ensure that all disclosures, as required by IAS 7 *Statement of Cash Flows* (IAS 7), are included in the notes to the financial statements. Financial ratios that employ cash flow measures can be used to evaluate the company's going concern assumption and therefore the auditor should seek to use the information contained in the statement of cash flows to evaluate the client entity's liquidity status and abilities.

14.9 CAATs AND BANK AND CASH

The purpose of CAATs and their generic uses are discussed in detail in **Chapter 9**, Section 9.4. The primary use of CAATs when auditing bank and cash would be around the preparation of **lead schedules** and the performance of bank reconciliations using a programme such as Excel. Other uses include:
- The automatic preparation of bank confirmation request letters. A mailout programme can be used to prepare multiple letter templates. These would only be useful in instances where a large number of letters need to be prepared.
- The use of audit software to prepare lead schedules and control the performance of the audit.
- The use of data analysis software to analyse electronic versions of the client entity's bank account transactions. This analysis could include:
  - searching for duplicate amounts;
  - searching for payments over a certain value; or
  - searching for transactions within a specific period or date.

The auditor may also request access to the client entity's online banking facility to trace certain bank transactions or to download the transactions for further analysis.

14.10 DISCLOSURE REQUIREMENTS FOR BANK AND CASH

Finally, with regard to bank and cash, the auditor will consider the adequacy of the disclosures in the client entity's financial statements. In doing so, the auditor aims to ensure that disclosures relating to bank and cash are:
- complete (no bank-related disclosures are missing);
- accurate (reflect the actual transactions and information relating to events surrounding bank and cash);
- relate to events that actually occurred or existed at the year-end; and
- are properly presented in line with international financial reporting standards.

The bank confirmation request letter is the key document that the auditor will use to assist him with supporting some of the above requirements. The bank confirmation request letter will:

- indicate to the auditor the existence of contingent liabilities (discussed further in **Chapter 18**) that may need to be disclosed;
- provide the auditor with details of interest (charged by the bank for lending money) which may need to be disclosed; and
- facilitate the preparation of notes relating to monies due within one year and after more than one year.

14.11 CONCLUSION

When the auditor has performed controls testing (see **Chapter 8**) and all the substantive procedures discussed above, it must be considered if sufficient appropriate audit evidence has been obtained over bank and cash balances to give the appropriate level of comfort required over the assertions stated at the outset, these being:
- Completeness;
- Valuation;
- Existence/occurrence;
- Cut-off;
- Rights and obligations; and
- Presentation and disclosure.

The auditor must also consider if the testing performed has appropriately addressed any key risks identified by him surrounding bank and cash and has reduced the risk of material misstatement arising as a result of key risks to a suitably low level.

When testing the area of bank and cash, the auditor is most concerned with the **completeness** assertion (for liabilities) and the **existence** assertion (for positive bank balances). Additionally, the auditor is concerned with the correct classification of bank and cash and ensuring that there is no netting of positive and negative balances. Finally, the auditor is interested in possible holds on assets connected to loans (the details of which he will obtain through the **bank confirmation request letter**).

The auditor must consider the impact on the **audit opinion** of the results of his testing in the area of bank and cash. He does so by considering whether any misstatements found, either individually or in aggregate (when combined with other misstatements detected throughout the audit), will result in the financial statements being materially misstated. All misstatements found are taken to the auditor's errors schedule for consideration at the audit completion stage (discussed in detail in **Chapter 18**). The auditor's report on financial statements is considered in detail in **Chapter 19**, 'Audit Reports'.

Summary of Learning Objectives

Learning Objective 1 Understand what is included in the audit of bank and cash.

Bank and cash represent the bank balances and cash on hand included within current assets and the bank overdrafts and loans included within current and non-current liabilities.

Learning Objective 2 Be able to identify the risks and audit objectives (management assertions) applicable to bank and cash.

The primary risks associated with bank and cash relate to:
• physical controls over cash/susceptibility to theft;
• fraud; and
• cut-off.

Learning Objective 3 Be able to determine an appropriate audit strategy for bank and cash, taking into consideration the specific risks and audit objectives (management assertions).

The auditor seeks to gain assurance that the bank and cash balances exist and are accurate; that all bank and cash balances are included and appropriately classified, presented and disclosed on the statement of financial position.

Learning Objective 4 Be able to develop an audit programme that addresses all the audit objectives (management assertions) for bank and cash.

Due to the fact that all bank and cash balances need to be validated by the auditor, he will rarely rely on the controls in place in the organisation and, he will perform focused substantive testing.

Learning Objective 5 Be able to describe and apply specific substantive testing procedures relating to the audit of bank and cash.

Key Documents when Auditing Bank and Cash The bank confirmation request letter, bank statements and bank reconciliations are the key documents of interest to the auditor. Other documents which may form part of audit evidence connected to bank and cash include:

- bank mandates;
- loan agreements; and
- covenants.

Key Substantive Testing Procedures Connected to Bank and Cash The main audit procedures surrounding bank and cash relate to:

- **bank confirmations** – which cover existence, valuation, rights and obligations and completeness of bank and cash balances;
- re-performance/review of **bank reconciliations**;
- reviews to ensure **window dressing** has not taken place; and
- attendance at the physical count of cash balances (where material).

Learning Objective 6 Understand the role CAATs can play when auditing bank and cash.

The auditor may use a combination of audit software, data analysis tools and other applications, such as Excel, when auditing the area of bank and cash.

Learning Objective 7 Understand the auditor's approach relating to the disclosures of bank and cash.

The auditor needs to consider the disclosure requirements necessary for bank and cash by ensuring they are: complete; accurate; relate to events that actually occurred; and are properly presented in line with applicable international reporting standards.

QUESTIONS

Self-test Questions

14.1 What audit benefits are derived from a bank confirmation request letter?

14.2 Why is it important to check outstanding cheques at the year end?

14.3 What steps should the auditor take if there is evidence of 'window dressing' at the year end?

14.4 List three key risks associated with the audit of the bank and cash balances.

14.5 List the four key financial statement assertions associated with the bank and cash balances.

14.6 For each of the financial statement assertions mentioned in Self-test Question 14.5 above, list at least one audit procedure that the auditor should perform in order to address each of the assertions.

14.7 As part of the audit of bank and cash, what should the auditor prepare and send in order to obtain independent reliable audit evidence about a company's year-end bank balances?

Review Questions

(See Suggested Solutions to Review Questions in **Appendix D**.)

Question 14.1

Outline briefly the audit procedures you would perform in relation to gaining assurance over the balance included under bank loans in the financial statements.

Question 14.2

You are the manager in charge of the external audit of Green Ltd (Green), which operates a chain of retail outlets throughout Ireland. Green has an established internal audit function, which undertakes monitoring procedures at head office and outlets. All outlets have electronic point-of-sale systems, which record the sale of an item and update the inventory records. All takings are required to be banked daily.

Requirement In order to determine whether you can reduce the amount of detailed testing on bank and cash, set out the monitoring procedures you would expect the internal auditors to have conducted.

Question 14.3

Why is it important for the auditor to confirm all bank accounts held and operated by the entity during the year?

Question 14.4

What steps can the auditor take to ensure that all bank accounts have been confirmed at the balance sheet date?

Question 14.5

Explain the benefits to the company, in addition to the maintenance of its borrowing facility, of having a full audit.

15

THE AUDIT OF INVESTMENTS

LEARNING OBJECTIVES

Having read this chapter on the audit of investments you should:
1. understand what is included in the audit of investments;
2. be able to identify the risks and audit objectives applicable to investments;
3. be able to determine an appropriate audit strategy for investments, taking into consideration the specific risks and audit objectives (assertions);
4. be able to develop an audit programme that addresses all the audit objectives (assertions) for investments;
5. be able to describe and apply specific substantive testing procedures relating to the audit of investments;
6. understand the role CAATs can play when auditing investments; and
7. understand the auditor's approach relating to the disclosures of investments.

CHECKLIST OF RELEVANT STANDARDS

The relevant standards covered in this chapter are:
- ISA (UK and Ireland) 315 *Identifying and Assessing the Risks of Material Misstatement Through Understanding the Entity and Its Environment* (ISA 315)
- ISA (UK and Ireland) 330 *The Auditor's Responses to Assessed Risks* (ISA 330)
- ISA (UK and Ireland) 500 *Audit Evidence* (ISA 500)
- ISA (UK and Ireland) 505 *External Confirmations* (ISA 505)
- ISA (UK and Ireland) 510 *Initial Audit Engagements – Opening Balances* (ISA 510)
- ISA (UK and Ireland) 520 *Analytical Procedures* (ISA 520)
- ISA (UK and Ireland) 550 *Related Parties* (ISA 550)
- IAS 27 *Consolidated and Separate Financial Statements* (superseded by IAS 27 (2011), IFRS 10 and IFRS 12, which are effective for annual reporting periods beginning on or after 1 January 2013 (IAS 27, superseded)
- IAS 27 *Separate Financial Statements* (issued in May 2011 and effective for annual reporting periods beginning on or after 1 January 2013) (IAS 27)
- IAS 28 *Investments in Associates* (superseded by IAS 28 (2011) and IFRS 12, which are effective for annual reporting periods beginning on or after 1 January 2013) (IAS 28, superseded)
- IAS 28 *Investments in Associates and Joint Ventures* (issued in May 2011 and effective for annual reporting periods beginning on or after 1 January 2013) (IAS 28)
- IAS 31 *Interests in Joint Ventures* (superseded by IFRS 11 and IFRS 12, which are effective for annual reporting periods beginning on or after 1 January 2013) (IAS 31, superseded)
- IAS 32 *Financial Instruments: Presentation* (superseded by IFRS 9, which is applicable for annual periods beginning 1 January 2013, with early adoption from 2009) (IAS 32, superseded)
- IAS 39 *Financial Instruments: Recognition and Measurement* (IAS 39)
- IFRS 7 *Financial Instruments: Disclosures* (IFRS 7)
- IFRS 10 *Consolidated Financial Statements* (IFRS 10)
- IFRS 12 *Disclosure of Interests in Other Entities* (IFRS 12)

KEY TERMS AND DEFINITIONS FOR THIS CHAPTER

Amortised   Refers to the reduction in the value of an intangible asset over its useful life.

Debentures   Debt instrument in the form of an unsecured loan issued by a company, which is generally backed by the issuer's creditworthiness rather than by physical assets.

Diminution in Value   The decrease (impairment) in the value of an asset. For example, economic conditions cause some investments to devalue and the client entity is required to measure the value lost in the asset.

15.1 INTRODUCTION

Sections 15.2 to **15.8** of this chapter outline the requirements of IFRS 7 *Financial Instruments: Disclosures* (IFRS 7); IAS 39 *Financial Instruments: Recognition and Measurement* (IAS 39); IAS 32 *Financial Instruments: Presentation* (IAS 32); ISA (UK and Ireland) 315 *Identifying and Assessing the Risks of Material Misstatement Through Understanding the Entity and Its Environment* (ISA 315); ISA (UK and Ireland) 330 *The Auditor's Responses to Assessed Risks* (ISA 330); IAS 28 *Investments in Associates* (IAS 28); IFRS 10 *Consolidated Financial Statements* (IFRS 10); IAS 27 *Separate Financial Statements* (IAS 27); and IAS 28 *Investments in Associates* (IAS 28) with respect to the audit of investments by the external auditor. These sections consider how the auditor:
(a) identifies audit risks and audit objectives (management assertions) for investments;
(b) develops an audit plan for investments and refines this into an audit programme;
(c) designs specific tests associated with investments; and
(d) ensures adequate presentation and disclosure in the financial statements relating to investments.

In **Section 15.9** we consider how computer-assisted audit techniques (CAATs) (see **Chapter 9**) can assist with the audit of investments.

Finally, in **Section 15.10** we consider the auditor's approach when auditing the reasonableness of disclosures relating to investments.

15.2 WHAT ARE INVESTMENTS?

Investment balances constitute ownership of securities issued by other entities and these may be in the form of certificates of deposit, shares, **debentures** or government bonds. When an entity invests money in an asset, it does so with the expectation of capital appreciation or dividend returns or both. An entity generally holds investments for a long period of time (greater than one year). Money held on deposit does not constitute an investment from an audit testing point of view and instead would be covered under bank and cash (dealt with in **Chapter 14**). Investments broadly relate to two categories: financial instruments, and those investments requiring consideration of consolidation, both of which are discussed below.

Investments requiring Consolidation Considerations

A special type of investment is one held for the purpose of acquiring influence or control over the investee entity. Such entities must be classified as subsidiaries, associates or joint ventures (accounted for under IAS 27, IAS 28 or IAS 31 (or, for periods beginning on or after 1 January 2013, IFRS 10, IAS 27 (amended to be single entity only) or IAS 28, as amended)). Investments in such entities require consideration of consolidation. The main audit considerations related to consolidated financial statements are explained at the end of this chapter (see **Section 15.8**). Investments that do not take the form of a subsidiary, associate or joint arrangement are therefore refered to as 'investment interests', which are dealt with under IAS 39.

When the auditor is dealing with a client entity that is a parent, then he will need to consider the requirements for group audits, which are covered in **Chapter 20**, 'Group Audits'.

Financial Instruments

Investments in financial instruments represent financial assets in the hands of the entity that owns them. The accounting requirements for such investments are determined by IFRS 7, IAS 39 and IAS 32.

Investments are initially measured at cost, but should be subsequently re-measured. The accounting requirements for subsequent measurement (IAS 39 outlines the requirements for the recognition and measurement of financial assets) of the four categories of financial assets as defined by IAS 39 are:

1. **loans and receivables not held for trading:** amortised cost using the effective interest method subject to impairment.
2. **held to maturity investments:** amortised cost using the effective interest method subject to impairment.
3. **financial assets measured at fair value through profit or loss:** fair value, with value changes recognised through profit or loss.
4. **available-for-sale assets and others not falling into any of the above categories:** measured at fair value in the statement of financial position, with value changes recognised in other comprehensive income as an unrealised gain or loss, subject to impairment testing. If the fair value cannot be reliably measured, the asset is carried at cost.

15.3 RISKS ASSOCIATED WITH THE AUDIT OF INVESTMENTS

Throughout **Chapter 7** (which addresses the requirements of ISA 315 and ISA 330) we discussed the topic of 'risk' and we considered how the auditor should go about detecting risks. We also discussed how the auditor should consider these risks when designing the nature, timing and extent of further audit procedures relative to each financial cycle. As such, before developing the audit plan, the auditor needs to consider a number of risks that may be associated with investments.

According to ISA 315, the auditor should use professional judgement to assess the risk of material misstatement. Risk factors relating to investments include:
- the reliability of the investment recording system;
- physical controls over investments held and the susceptibility to theft of investments physically held by the client entity or by an independent custodian. If the investment certificates are held by the client entity, the auditor should ensure that they are adequately stored (i.e. in a securely locked safe);
- risk due to fraud: false investments and rights over investments (the auditor must check whether the investments are in the client entity's name or held in the name of a director

or another entity). Does the entity hold the risks and rewards relating to the investments recognised in its financial statements?;

- risk due to complicated accounting treatment involved in consolidations, which may lead to errors or be seen as an opportunity to conceal fraud; and
- risk of diminution in value not being adequately recorded in the financial statements.

15.4 AUDIT OBJECTIVES/MANAGEMENT ASSERTIONS FOR INVESTMENTS

As discussed in **Chapter 6** (which addressed the requirements of ISA (UK and Ireland) 500 *Audit Evidence* (ISA 500)), it is necessary for the auditor to seek appropriate audit evidence to satisfy all of the audit objectives and to eliminate the possibility of any of the risks outlined in **Section 15.3** going undetected. In **Chapter 4** we introduced audit objectives (management assertions) and explained their generic meanings and then we reintroduced this topic throughout **Chapter 8**, making management assertions specific to each financial cycle. In **Table 15.1** we remind you once more of the audit objectives as they relate to investments.

Table 15.1 addresses the management assertions (audit objectives) as they relate to the balances associated with investments.

TABLE 15.1: INVESTMENTS: AUDIT OBJECTIVES
FOR ACCOUNT BALANCES AT YEAR END

Management Assertion/ Audit Objective	Objective of Audit Evidence
Existence	To ensure that recorded investments exist at the balance sheet date.
Completeness	To ensure all investments have been included in the financial statements.
Accuracy	To ensure all investments are properly recorded and included in the financial statements.
Cut-off	To ensure all additions and disposals of investments have been accounted for in the correct accounting period.
Valuation	To ensure investments have been accurately valued and provision has been made for any investments whose carrying value exceeds realisable value.
Rights and Obligations	To ensure the entity has the rights to all investments recorded at the balance sheet date.
Presentation and Disclosure	To ensure investments are properly classified and disclosed in the balance sheet.

15.5 DEVELOPING THE AUDIT PLAN FOR INVESTMENTS

Before the audit of investments is undertaken, an assessment of the audit risk must be completed. As discussed in detail in **Chapter 7** (which addresses the requirements of IAS 315 and IAS 330), audit risk is made up of three components: inherent risk; control risk; and detection risk. We will consider these components specifically as they relate to investments.

$$\text{Audit Risk} = \text{Inherent Risk} + \text{Control Risk} + \text{Detection Risk}$$

Inherent Risk

Investment transactions and balances are inherently risky due to their complicated accounting treatment.

Control Risk

Due to the fact that the purchases and sales of investments are often processed separately from all other purchases and sales, entities that hold substantial investments often adopt specific control procedures over investments. The volume of transactions, however, is generally low and so the auditor will usually take a focused substantive approach and will not test the controls. Where, however, the investment relates to entities requiring consideration of consolidation, the auditor will need to consider the need for a group audit, which is discussed in detail in **Chapter 20**.

Detection Risk

A focused substantive approach is generally taken with regard to the audit of financial instruments because they are inherently risky; dedicated controls do not usually exist in the client entity relating to investments and the number of transactions tends to be low. With regard to investments constituting consolidation, the auditor needs to consider the audit of a group (see **Chapter 20**).

15.6 KEY DOCUMENTS RELATING TO INVESTMENTS

Before the auditor can plausibly audit the area of investments, he must first familiarise himself with the types of documents held by the entity relating to its investments. The type of investment documents held by entities varies depending on the type of investment in question. If they relate to bonds or deposits, the investment certificates will be requested by the auditor as evidence to support testing. Alternatively, the auditor will seek any ownership document that can prove occurrence/existence and valuation. Some companies that hold large volumes of investments will have investment schedules that will identify the investment type (listed, unlisted or other, and subsidiary, joint venture, associate or other).

The primary document of interest to the auditor will be the investment schedule. This schedule will provide him with a summary of investments (which he will agree to the financial statements) that need to be audited. He will, however, require further documents to support the audit objectives relating to existence and valuation. Documents which can provide evidence for such assertions relating to investments include, for example, share certificates or government bond certificates.

15.7 SUBSTANTIVE AUDIT PROGRAMME FOR INVESTMENTS

An audit programme records the specific details of tests to be performed by the auditor. The audit programme becomes a guide to the audit engagement team as to the work to be done in a particular area. As work is completed a reference is included on the audit programme, showing the location on the audit file where details of the tests performed are included. The audit programme for any cycle will vary from entity to entity and, as such, in **Example 15.1** below we consider the typical types of test the auditor would include in the audit programme for investments.

EXAMPLE 15.1: AUDIT PROGRAMME FOR INVESTMENTS[1]

Large Company Limited 31 December 2012			
	Audit Materiality		**€3,642,500**
	Performance Materiality		**€2,731,875**
		Initials	**Date**
	Prepared by:		
Investments	**Reviewed by:**		
Audit Programme	**Assertion Covered**	**Ref to Work**	**Initials and Date**
Accounting Policy			
Assess the appropriateness of the accounting policy and the accounting estimates method for this area. Ensure that the accounting policy is in accordance with accounting standards and applicable law, and that the methods used for making the accounting estimates are appropriate.			

[1] Source: based on *Procedures for Quality Audit 2010* (© Chartered Accountants Ireland, 2010), F1.

Initial Procedures			
Vouch **Opening balances** to prior-year working papers	Presentation and Disclosure		
Obtain or prepare lead schedules and agree to balance sheet, distinguishing between: 1. investments listed on a stock exchange; 2. other investments; and 3. unlisted investments. Ensure that the schedule also correctly distinguishes subsidiaries, associated companies and joint ventures and that it provides a sufficient audit trail. Agree to nominal ledger.	Existence and Completeness		
Obtain or prepare separate schedules of additions and disposals and vouch as appropriate, confirming that recognition has taken place in the correct period.	Existence and Completeness		
Test Valuation			
Obtain and disclose market value at balance sheet date of all listed investments. Agree valuation of investments to an authoritative source. Confirm that the book value/carrying value of **unlisted** investments is not stated in excess of net realisable value. Obtain supporting evidence for the carrying value by obtaining and reviewing recent financial statements for the investment. Consider permanent diminution in value of investments.	Valuation		
Other Considerations			
Check with an authoritative source that all bonus and rights issues have been accounted for.	Completeness		

Vouch profits and losses on disposals, confirming that recognition has taken place in the correct period.	Occurrence, Cut-off and Accuracy		
Consider completeness of investment income and that cut-off has been correctly applied.	Completeness and Cut-off		
Examine share certificates to ensure good title (and test a sample, if appropriate). Obtain confirmation (ISA 505) from third parties holding certificates of title, details of joint venture arrangements, etc.	Existence		
Ensure investments are correctly analysed between current and non-current asset investments.	Presentation and Disclosure		
Name:	Accountant in Charge		
Date:			
Name:	Reviewer		
Date:			

15.8 SUBSTANTIVE TESTING PROCEDURES FOR INVESTMENTS

Below we are going to discuss in more detail some of the procedures outlined in the substantive audit programme in **Example 15.1** above.

We will start with initial procedures, which include: opening balances; mathematical accuracy of schedules; the lead schedule; and analytical reviews.

Initial Procedures

Opening Balances

Before commencing further auditor procedures, evidence must be obtained as to the accuracy of the opening balances of investments. The reason for this is twofold: first, it confirms that the comparative numbers in the financial statements (which must be included in the current year's financial statements) agree to the final accounts of the prior year; and, secondly, it highlights any final entries (last-minute adjusting journal entries) of the prior year not correctly carried forward, which may indicate an error in the current year's financial statements' figures. The auditor checks opening balances as follows.

- Agree the opening balances to the prior-year working papers and signed financial statements. This may highlight an opening balance in the current year's accounts that does not agree with the closing balance per the prior year's financial statements. In this instance a change would be made to the opening balance of the current year, which would impact the closing balance of the current year. This usually arises due to final adjustments in the prior year that are not reflected in the actual accounting records (nominal and general ledgers).
- If this is the first year of the audit engagement, the auditor will still need to establish that the opening balances are materially correct, which can pose difficulties for him if either the client entity was exempt from audit in the prior year or a predecessor auditor carried out the audit. The audit of opening balances in such instances is discussed in detail in **Chapter 6**, Section 6.8, which addresses the requirements of (ISA (UK and Ireland) 510 *Initial Audit Engagements – Opening Balances* (ISA 510)).

Mathematical Accuracy of Schedules

- All schedules, for example, in the case of investments, the investment schedule, provided by the client entity should be totalled and cross-totalled to ensure their mathematical accuracy. Additionally, they should be agreed to the financial statements' balances and transactions that they support. The auditor should review the activity in the investment-related accounts to identify entries that are unusual.

Lead Schedules

Prepare or obtain from the audited entity a lead schedule that agrees to the investments (financial assets) note in the financial statements. The lead schedule should provide a summary of the:

- cost at the start of the year, movements in cost (including additions, disposals and **diminution in value**) and cost at the end of the period; and
- NBV (carrying amount) of investments (financial asset) at the start and end of the year.

An example of an investments lead schedule is included at **Example 15.2** below.

EXAMPLE 15.2: INVESTMENTS LEAD SCHEDULE (LARGE COMPANY LIMITED)

Large Company Limited			
31 December 2012	**Audit Materiality**		**€3,642,500**
	Performance Materiality		**€2,731,875**
		Initials	**Date**
	Prepared by:		
Investments	**Reviewed by:**		

	Investment Properties €000	Available-for-sale Investments €000	Total €000
Cost			
1 January 2012	100,000	10,500	110,500
Additions	0	23,700	23,700
Diminution in value	(20,000)	0	(20,000)
Disposals	0	(1,700)	(1,700)
31 December 2012	**80,000**	**32,500**	**112,500**
Provision for diminution in value			
1 January 2012	0	300	300
Additions	0	0	0
Disposals	0	0	0
31 December 2012	**0**	**300**	**300**
Net book value			
31 December 2012	**80,000**	**32,200**	**112,200**
31 December 2011	100,000	10,200	110,200

Analytical Review (Initial)

The auditor will perform an analytical review (covered under **Chapter 5**, Section 5.4, which addresses the requirements of ISA (UK and Ireland) 520 *Analytical Procedures* (ISA 520)) to ensure completeness and obtain explanations for any material variances. Analytical procedures can be applied in comparing receipts of interest and dividends to investment balances. Unexpected differences should be investigated as they could indicate misstatements. An example of an analytical review the auditor might carry out is included at **Example 15.3**.

EXAMPLE 15.3: ANALYTICAL REVIEW OF INVESTMENTS (LARGE COMPANY LIMITED)

	2012 €000	2011 €000	Movement €000
Investment Properties	80,000	100,000	(20,000)
Available-for-sale Investments	32,200	10,200	22,000
Income from Investment Properties	10	9	1
Income from Available-for-sale Investments	210	209	1

Return on Investment Properties	0.01%	0.01%	0%
Return on Available-for-sale Investments	0.65%	2.05%	(1%)

Neither category of investments yields a large return and the return on available-for-sale investments fell by over 50%. Discussions with management reveal that these are strategic investments and are not currently held for immediate returns. The fall in investment properties relates to a diminution in value.

Substantive Testing of Movements of Investments in the Period

Having performed the initial procedures, now let us consider the specific audit procedures the auditor might carry out in relation to the movements of investments in the period, which essentially involves: additions and disposals; and investment income.

Additions and Disposals

Where investments have been acquired or disposed of during the year, the auditor should:
- ensure additions and disposals of investments have been authorised and approved;
- agree the cost of investments to supporting documents (contract notes or similar documentation);
- for listed investments, check the market value to the stock exchange daily list as reported in the *Financial Times* or some other reliable pricing source;
- for unlisted investments, if the valuation has been undertaken by the directors, discuss the basis of valuation with the client in order to ascertain whether the valuation has been made on the basis of reasonable criteria. The auditor may consider the need to acquire the advice of an expert;
- agree disposals of investments to contract notes, ensuring disposals have been officially authorised and approved; and
- check the profits or losses on the disposals of a sample of investments and ensure they have been correctly posted.

Investment Income

The auditor should perform a check of investment income to the schedule of investments to ensure that all income due has been recorded and received. The list of investments should act as a checklist for the auditor, allowing him to ensure that all investment income that he would expect to be received has been received. The auditor can do this by vouching dividend/interest receipts to remittance advices that accompany each payment. Additionally, he should recalculate the interest received by multiplying the par value of the debt by the interest rate to ensure all interest has been received. Alternatively, the auditor could confirm the amount of the interest receipt with the issuer. Finally, with respect to investment income, the auditor should view the investees' financial statements in order to verify the dividends received.

To ensure correct classification (as either interest/dividends, or profit/loss on disposal), the auditor should also check the posting of income to the correct account in the nominal ledger.

Investment Balance

Having obtained evidence for the management assertions related to the movements of investments, the auditor must then satisfy himself as to the continued existence of the investments and their valuation included in the statement of financial position.

When it comes to auditing the investment balance the auditor is predominantly interested in validating ownership, existence and valuation. Ownership and existence are normally covered in the same tests.

Ownership and Existence

Where securities are held at the audited entity's premises, these should be inspected and counted at the same time as the auditor performs the cash count (if applicable). The auditor should ensure: the custodian of the securities is present at the time of the inspection and count; that a receipt is signed when the securities are returned; and that the securities are adequately safeguarded until the inspection and count are complete.

Where securities are held by the bank for safekeeping, ensure the bank seals the boxes on the date of the inspection and count, and obtain confirmation from the bank that there will be no access to the box (other than by the auditors) until the inspection and count has been completed. This will ensure there was no adding/removing of documents during inspection. Where the inspection and count take place on a date other than the balance sheet date, a reconciliation should be prepared between the date of the inspection and count and the balance sheet date. All movements between these dates should be reviewed by the auditor.

When inspecting securities, the following points should be observed:
* the certificate number on the document and agree it to the investment register;
* the name of the owner to ensure they pertain to the entity;
* the description of the security to ensure it agrees to the investment register and to ensure it is adequately disclosed in the financial statements;
* the number of shares/debentures and agree to the investment register;
* the face value of shares/debentures and agree to the investment register; and
* the name of the issuer.

Further procedures that should be carried out by the auditor include:
* Obtaining direct third-party confirmation of investments held on behalf of the client and inspect the documents of title.
* Obtaining confirmation of securities held by outsiders for safekeeping, which outlines the securities held by that entity at the year-end date. This confirmation should be by way of third-party confirmation (and follow the guidance of ISA (UK and Ireland) 505 *External Confirmations* (ISA 505), as discussed in **Chapter 6**, Section 6.5). The mailing of these third-party confirmations must be under the control of the auditor and responses must be made directly to the auditors.
* Reviewing board minutes and obtaining representations from management to ascertain whether investments have been pledged as collateral or security for liabilities.

- Obtaining direct third-party confirmation from borrowers in respect of loans made to them by the client entity.

Valuation

Having obtained evidence relating to existence and rights and obligations relating to investment balances, the auditor now must obtain evidence relating to the valuation assertion, which requires him to do the following.

- Consider whether the value of any investments should be reduced to recognise a permanent diminution in value. The auditor should discuss any such diminution with management and obtain independent information to support the revaluation of investments.
- If an investment was written down in previous years and the reasons for the write-down no longer apply, the auditor should check that the write-down has been reversed.
- For financial assets valued on the basis of amortised cost, consider recalculation tests based on cash flows and interest rate used to discount the cash flows. Consider the appropriateness of the discount factor used. Also, consider the need for adjustments because of the diminished recoverability of the asset and other factors that give rise to impairment.
- Audited financial statements of the entity in which the investments are held can be used to assist in the valuation of unquoted shares, debentures and similar investments.
- Check that the basis of the valuation is consistent with the basis used in previous years. If there are any changes in the basis of the valuation, the auditor should discuss this with management, and ensure that the basis of valuation is reasonable and in line with the appropriate laws and regulations.
- Check market value calculations for listed investments to published prices, e.g. prices published by the *Financial Times*, Bloomberg, Reuters or prices obtained from independent stockbrokers. For infrequently traded securities, it may be necessary to seek advice from an independent stockbroker as to the estimated market value at the balance sheet date.
- Confirm that directors' valuations of unlisted investments are reasonable. For each valuation the auditor should obtain independent support or written representations from management to support their valuations.
- Obtain evidence about the ability of the entity to hold onto the investments on a long-term basis. Written representations from management indicating their intention to hold onto the investments on a long-term basis must be obtained.
- Review post-balance sheet events to identify any changes in circumstances surrounding investments which may impact on the disclosure of such investments at the year end.
- In respect of investments in the form of loans, check that repayments are being made on time and that interest payments are being made.
- Discuss with management the recoverability of the loans and obtain independent confirmation from the entities to which the loans have been made of the value of and repayments on the loans.

Other Considerations

Having performed the substantive procedures relating to investment movements and investment balances, there are some other matters the auditor must consider before he has adequately completed his substantive procedures relating to investments. These include: investments held in foreign currencies; cut-off; and consolidation. Let us consider these in turn.

Investments held in Foreign Currencies

For investments held in foreign currencies, ensure that the translations into the domestic currency are correct. This can be done by independently obtaining appropriate foreign exchange rates and recalculating the translations, ensuring there is not a material difference in the rates used.

Cut-off

For a sample of additions and disposals during the period, check that they are accounted for in the correct accounting period.

Consolidation

The individual accounts of a parent company do not adequately present its real economic activities and financial position. As such, consolidated financial statements are required where a parent entity controls another entity. Control is defined by the ability of the parent entity to direct power over the accounting and financial policies of another entity. The parent entity that controls one or more other entities must prepare consolidated financial statements in line with IFRS 10. A single consolidation model has been designed by the International Accounting Standards Board (IASB) in order to address the differences applied in practice when approaching consolidations. This single consolidation model (IFRS 10) is supported by a suite of standards designed to address the treatment of all types of business combination. These standards include:

- IAS 27 *Separate Financial Statements* (IAS 27) (this standard used to be Consolidated and Separate Financial Statements, but consolidation is now dealt with under a separate standard);
- IAS 28 *Investments in Associates and Joint Ventures* (IAS 28) (this standard used to deal with investments in associates only);
- IFRS 10 *Consolidated Financial Statements* (IFRS 10);
- IFRS 11 *Joint Arrangements* (IFRS 11);
- IFRS 12 *Disclosure of Interests in Other Entities* (IFRS 12) (Disclosure requirements used to be detailed within the standard relating to the particular investment type, however disclosure requirements are now dealt with under one standard: IFRS 12).

Part V of Ciaran Connolly's, *International Financial Accounting and Reporting,* 4th Edition (Chartered Accountants Ireland, 2013), provides an excellent overview of the accounting for business combinations. This textbook is not intended to assist with the study of consolidations but instead addresses how the auditor considers whether the requirements laid down in the relevant standards have been adhered to by the client entity when preparing its financial statements.

In order to review the adequacy of the presentation of the financial statements relating to consolidation, the auditor must first understand the 'control' relationship between the parent entity and the entity in which it holds an interest. Under the old accounting standards, control was defined by reference to the percentage ownership held. The new accounting standards (outlined above) require a more complex assessment when determining whether one entity controls another or not. Control under IFRS 10 can exist when an investor holds power over an investee, which can present itself in a number of ways. The auditor must ask, "Does the parent entity have the rights to direct the relevant activities of the investee?". If the answer is "Yes", then the parent entity must present its investment by way of consolidation (i.e. the investee is a subsidiary of the parent company). If an investee is not a subsidiary, it must be defined as either: an 'associate interest'; a 'joint arrangement'; or an 'investment interest' (i.e. a 'financial instrument' under IAS 39).

The audit of consolidated accounts is a complex task and is discussed in more detail in **Chapter 20**, 'Group Audits'.

15.9 COMPUTER-ASSISTED AUDIT TECHNIQUES AND INVESTMENTS

The purpose of CAATs and their generic uses are discussed in detail in **Chapter 9**, Section 9.4. We will now consider the primary use of CAATs when auditing the area of investments. Some of the uses of CAATs by the auditor when auditing the area of investments include:
1. Using audit software to:
   (a) control the audit by preparing documents such as lead schedules;
   (b) produce questionnaires through knowledge-based software (quite often built into audit software). The auditor can use this to probe the client entity with respect to investments. Quite often the auditor will be less familiar with the area of investments as they do not always feature in the financial statements of client entities. As such, the use of knowledge-based software to produce questionnaires can ensure that the auditor is prompted to ask the right questions and to respond adequately to the answers to those questions.
2. Using data-analysis software to review investment schedules provided by the client entity. Usually an investment schedule does not have many line items and can be easily reviewed and analysed. However, if the list is extensive, the auditor can use data-analysis software to highlight high-value investments, nil value investments (investments held without an associated value due to diminution), etc.
3. Using applications such as Excel to:
   (a) calculate expected returns on investments;
   (b) translate foreign investments; and
   (c) calculate the totals in investment schedules.

In the case of group audits, CAATs will play a significant role with respect to the control of consolidation.

15.10 DISCLOSURE REQUIREMENTS

Finally, with regard to investments, the auditor will consider the adequacy of the disclosures. The auditor needs to consider the requirements of IFRS 12 *Disclosure of Interests in Other Entities* (IFRS 12) and IFRS 7 *Financial Instruments: Disclosures* (IFRS 7) to check that all disclosures are:

- complete (no investment-related disclosures are missing; the auditor can use IFRS 12 and IFRS 7 as a checklist);
- accurate (reflect the actual transactions and information relating to events surrounding investments);
- relate to events that actually occurred; and
- are properly presented (in a manner expected by: IAS 27; IAS 28; IAS 32; IAS 39; IFRS 7; IFRS 9; IFRS 10; IFRS 11; and IFRS 12).

The investment-related disclosure requirements are included in IFRS 12 and IAS 39 and include requirements relating to:

> "• … information about significant judgements and assumptions it has made (and changes in those judgements and assumptions) in determining:
> (a) that it has control of another entity …
> (b) that it has joint control of an arrangement or significant influence over another entity; and
> (c) the type of joint arrangement (i.e. joint operation or joint venture) when the arrangement has been structured through a separate vehicle." (IFRS 12, para 7);

- information about interests in subsidiaries sufficient to enable the users of consolidated financial statements to, for example, understand the composition of the group (IFRS 12, para 10);
- information about interests in unconsolidated subsidiaries (where exceptions to consolidation are invoked) (IFRS 12, para 19A);
- information about interests in joint arrangements and associates, such as the nature, extent and financial effects of such interests (IFRS 12, para 20);
- significance of financial instruments (IFRS 7);
- information about hedge accounting (IFRS 7); and
- nature and extent of exposure to risks arising from financial instruments (IFRS 7).

The auditor will also need to consider the requirements of ISA (UK and Ireland) 550 *Related Parties* (ISA 550), which is covered in more detail in **Chapter 18**.

15.11 CONCLUSION

Once the auditor has completed his substantive testing, he must consider whether sufficient appropriate audit evidence has been obtained for the investment balances and transactions, which give the appropriate level of assurance required over the assertions stated at the outset, these being:

- completeness;
- valuation;

- existence/occurrence;
- cut-off;
- valuation; and
- rights and obligations.

The auditor must also consider if the testing performed has appropriately addressed any key risks identified by the auditor surrounding investments and reduced the risk of material misstatement arising as a result of key risks to a suitably low level.

When testing the area of investments, the auditor is most concerned with the valuation assertion due to the risk associated with diminution in value.

The auditor must consider the impact on the audit opinion of the results of his testing in the area of investments. He does so by considering whether any misstatements found, either individually or in aggregate (when combined with other misstatements detected throughout the audit), will result in the financial statements being materially misstated. As such, all misstatements found are taken to the auditor's errors schedule for consideration at the audit completion stage (discussed in detail in **Chapter 18**). The auditor's report on financial statements is considered in detail in **Chapter 19**, 'Audit Reports'.

SUMMARY OF LEARNING OBJECTIVES

Learning Objective 1 Understand what is included in the audit of investments.

Investment balances constitute ownership of securities issued by other entities and these may be in the form of certificates of deposit, shares, debentures or government bonds. Such securities represent financial assets in the hands of the entity that owns them. Investments can take the form of subsidiary investments, investments in associates, joint arrangement investments or investment interests.

Learning Objective 2 Be able to identify the risks and audit objectives applicable to investments.

The primary risks associated with investments relate to:
- diminution in value;
- reliability of investment recording system;
- complications surrounding consolidation and other complex accounting treatments; and
- validating fair value (where the investment is not listed).

Learning Objective 3 Be able to determine an appropriate audit strategy for investments, taking into consideration the specific risks and audit objectives (management assertions).

The auditor seeks to ensure that the investment balances exist and are accurate; that all investment balances are included and appropriately classified, presented and disclosed on the statement of financial position.

Learning Objective 4 Be able to develop an audit programme that addresses all the audit objectives (management assertions) for investments.

The volume of transactions is generally low and so the auditor will usually take a focused substantive approach and not test the controls. This will not be the case where the investment requires consolidation, which is considered in more detail in **Chapter 20**, 'Group Audits'.

Learning Objective 5 Be able to describe and apply specific substantive testing procedures relating to the audit of investments.

Key Documents when Auditing Investments Documents of interest to the auditor could include:
- investment schedules;
- share certificates;
- saving certificates; and
- bond certificates.

Key Substantive Testing Procedures Connected to Investments The main audit procedures surrounding investments relate to:
- confirming the existence of investments to authoritative sources;
- confirming the valuation of investments to authoritative sources;
- considering the requirement for consolidation; and
- considering permanent diminution in value.

Learning Objective 6 Understand the role CAATs can play when auditing investments.

The auditor may use a combination of audit software, data analysis tools and other applications, such as Excel, when auditing the area of investments.

Learning Objective 7 Understand the auditor's approach relating to the disclosures of investments.

The auditor has a wide range of disclosure requirements to consider relating to investments and so he should dedicate sufficient time to this area where significant investments are held. His aim is to check that disclosures are complete, accurate, pertain to the entity and that the financial statements are adequately presented in line with applicable international reporting standards.

QUESTIONS

Self-test Questions

15.1 List five ways in which fraud could be committed in respect of investments.

15.2 What valuation method should be used for trade investments?

15.3 Why is it important to inspect original supporting documentation for investments?

15.4 Identify the main steps an auditor adopts in order to assess the risk of a material misstatement in the investments balance.

Review Questions

(See Suggested Solutions to Review Questions in **Appendix D**.)

Question 15.1

Meridian Ltd is a large company with a number of financial investments in entities in Ireland and internationally. You have been assigned to the investments section of the audit engagement and a member of the client entity's finance team has provided you with the following schedule:

Name of Investment	Investment €000	Market Value €000
Rainbow	1,243	1,721
Lilly	936	1,321
Golden	1,654	1,320
Yellow	1,111	300
Grenadier	1,879	2,012
Total Investments	**6,823**	**6,674**

The following information has also been offered:
- the investment in Rainbow was acquired during the year, and the Yellow investment was sold before the year end for €300,000.
- the investments' total balance in the draft financial statements is €6,823,000. Meridian Ltd has a policy of recognising its investments at cost with any gains/losses only recognised on disposal.

Requirement
(a) Describe the general and specific audit work that you would plan in order to enable you to form an opinion on the investment account balance of Meridian.
(b) From the information above, list the potential audit issues in Meridian and state the additional audit work that you would perform.
(c) Assuming the information included in the schedule is correct and the client has no further information to provide, outline the adjustments to the investment balance that you would recommend to your audit partner.

Question 15.2

You have been assigned to the audit of Wilcox Ltd, a successful property development company. The audit area for which you will have direct responsibility is that of current assets. Your audit manager has informed you that the prior-year audit file did not contain a detailed audit plan for current assets, but that he would like one prepared prior to the commencement of the current year's audit. You note from the prior-year audit file that the audit materiality figure was €100,000 and that the current assets at the previous year end were made up as follows:

	€000
Trade investments (listed)	500
Trade investments (unlisted)	800
Prepayments	100
Bank balances	950
Cash balances	100
	2,450

Requirement Set out the procedures that you would adopt in order to obtain the required assurance concerning the standard audit objectives for the current assets detailed above. You should assume that the current asset balances for the current year are expected to be at a similar level to those of the prior year.

16

THE AUDIT OF PURCHASES AND PAYABLES

LEARNING OBJECTIVES

Having studied this chapter on the audit of purchases and payables you should:
1. understand what is included in the audit of purchases and payables;
2. be able to identify the risks and audit objectives (management assertions) applicable to purchases and payables;
3. be able to determine an appropriate audit strategy for purchases and payables, taking into consideration the specific risks and audit objectives (management assertions);
4. be able to develop an audit programme that addresses all the audit objectives (assertions) for purchases and payables;
5. be able to describe and apply specific substantive testing procedures relating to the audit of purchases and payables;

6. understand the role CAATs can play when auditing purchases and payables; and
7. understand the auditor's approach relating to the disclosures of purchases and payables,

CHECKLIST OF RELEVANT STANDARDS

The relevant standards covered in this chapter are:
- ISA (UK and Ireland) 315 *Identifying and Assessing the Risks of Material Misstatement Through Understanding of the Entity and its Environment* (ISA 315)
- ISA (UK and Ireland) 330 *The Auditor's Responses to Assessed Risks* (ISA 330)
- ISA (UK and Ireland) 500 *Audit Evidence* (ISA 500)
- ISA (UK and Ireland) 505 *External Confirmations* (ISA 505)
- ISA (UK and Ireland) 510 *Initial Audit Engagements – Opening Balances* (ISA 510)
- ISA (UK and Ireland) 520 *Analytical Procedures* (ISA 520)
- ISA (UK and Ireland) 530 *Audit Sampling* (ISA 530)
- IAS 37 *Provisions, Contingent Liabilities and Contingent Assets* (IAS 37)
- IAS 1 *Presentation of Financial Statements* (IAS 1)

KEY TERMS AND DEFINITIONS FOR THIS CHAPTER

Aged Payables Listing   This is a full list of individual supplier balances that can be reconciled to the payables figure in the financial statements and analysed to assess the existence of supplier balances. It shows each supplier by reference to the length of time the payable balance has existed (usually broken down into payable within 30 days, 60 days, 90 days, and greater than 90 days).

Earnings Management   The use of certain techniques to produce financial statements that portray a desired (rather than **true and fair**) picture of an entity's statement of comprehensive income.

Search for Unrecorded Liabilities   Techniques used by the auditor to identify understatement of liabilities.

Supplier Reconciliation   When a company reconciles the balance on the supplier's statement to the supplier's balance per the client entity's ledger.

16.1 INTRODUCTION

Sections 16.2–16.8 of this chapter outline the requirements of the international accounting standards with respect to the recording of purchases and payables and then consider how the auditor:

(a) identifies audit risks and audit objectives (management assertions) for purchases and payables;

(b) develops an audit plan for purchases and payables and refines this into an **audit programme**;

(c) designs specific tests associated with purchases and payables; and

(d) ensures adequate presentation and disclosure in the financial statements relating to purchases and payables.

In **Section 16.9** we consider how computer-assisted audit techniques (CAATs) (considered in detail in **Chapter 9**) can assist with the audit of purchases and payables.

Finally, in **Section 16.10** we discuss the auditor's approach when auditing the reasonableness of disclosures relating to purchases and payables.

16.2 WHAT ARE PURCHASES AND PAYABLES?

Every business incurs costs in the process of generating goods and services, which it subsequently sells to its customers. For example, an entity involved in the manufacture of shoes will have to purchase leather in order to make its shoes and might employ the services of an advertising agency to promote its finished products. When such transactions are not settled immediately by cash payments, they give rise to **trade payables**. Such trade payables meet the definition of liabilities as set out in IAS 37 *Provisions, Contingent Liabilities and Contingent Assets,* which at paragraph 10 states:

"A liability is a present obligation of the entity arising from past events, the settlement of which is expected to result in an outflow from the entity of resources embodying economic benefits."

It is the auditor's duty to gain assurance that both purchases and trade payables have been reflected appropriately in the company's year-end financial statements. In simple terms, all goods and services that a company has received during the financial year should be recorded within their financial statements as purchases in the statement of comprehensive income. Where amounts due to suppliers relating to purchases have not been settled at the year end, they should be recorded as **liabilities** in the statement of financial position. These are included either within trade payables, where an invoice has been received, or within accruals when the goods or services have been received but the invoice was not received from the supplier before the year end.

16.3 RISKS ASSOCIATED WITH PURCHASES AND PAYABLES

Throughout **Chapter 7** (which addresses the requirement of ISA (UK and Ireland) 315 *Identifying and Assessing the risks of Material Misstatement Through Understanding of the Entity and its Environment* and ISA 330 *The Auditor's Responses to Assessed Risks*) we discussed the topic of 'risk' and considered how the auditor should go about detecting risks. We also discussed how the auditor should consider these risks when designing the nature, timing and extent of further audit procedures relative to each financial cycle. As such, before developing the audit plan, the auditor needs to consider a number of risks that may be associated with **purchases and payables**. Risks associated with purchases and payables can include:

- inappropriate/fraudulent payments recorded in the purchases ledger due to weaknesses in internal controls in the purchases system (see **Chapter 8**, 'Controls and Controls Testing' for a full discussion of internal controls);
- misstatement of year-end payables and accruals due to incorrect **cut-off** procedures being applied (i.e. transactions occurring pre year end not being recorded until the following period and, conversely, transactions occurring post year end being incorrectly recorded in the current period);
- understatement of year-end payables and accruals due to failure to record all outstanding liabilities because of fraud or error.

The auditor must consider the internal controls within the organisation/client entity in determining how much substantive testing should be carried out on purchases and payables. The results of **inherent** and **control risk** assessments will help to establish the extent of substantive testing required.

16.4 AUDIT OBJECTIVES/MANAGEMENT ASSERTIONS FOR PURCHASES AND PAYABLES

Having established the risks associated with purchases and payables, the auditor must now ascertain the related audit objectives (management assertions). As discussed in **Chapter 6** (which addressed the requirements of ISA (UK and Ireland) 500 *Audit Evidence*), it is necessary for the auditor to seek appropriate audit evidence to satisfy all of the audit objectives and to eliminate the possibility of any of the risks outlined in **Section 16.3** going undetected. In **Chapter 4**, we introduced audit objectives (management assertions) and explained their generic meanings; we then reintroduced this topic throughout **Chapter 8**, making management assertions specific to each financial cycle. In **Table 16.1** below, we remind ourselves of the audit objectives as they relate to purchases and payables.

Having discussed the objectives of the auditor with regard to purchases and payables, we now consider how the auditor addresses these objectives through **substantive testing**.

16.5 DEVELOPING THE AUDIT PLAN FOR PURCHASES AND PAYABLES

Before the audit of purchases and payables is undertaken, an assessment of the 'audit risk' must be completed. As discussed in detail in **Chapter 7**, audit risk is made up of three components: inherent risk; control risk; and detection risk. We will consider these components specifically as they relate to purchases and payables.

Audit Risk = Inherent Risk + Control Risk + Detection Risk

TABLE 16.1: PURCHASES AND PAYABLES/ACCRUALS AUDIT OBJECTIVES

Management Assertion/ Audit Objective	Transactions and Events During the Period (purchases)	Account Balances at Year End (payables/accruals and related payroll balances)
Existence or Occurrence	• Recorded purchases transactions represent goods and services received. • Recorded payment transactions represent payments made to suppliers of goods and services.	Recorded trade payables represent amounts owed by the entity at the statement of financial position date.
Completeness	All purchases and payments transactions that occurred have been recorded.	• Trade payables include all amounts owed by the entity to suppliers of goods and services at the statement of financial position date. • Accrued payroll liabilities include all amounts in respect of payroll and payroll deductions at the statement of financial position date.
Rights and Obligations	Recorded purchases transactions represent the liabilities of the entity.	Trade payables are liabilities of the entity at the statement of financial position date.
Accuracy Classification and Valuation	Purchases transactions and payments transactions are correctly recorded in the accounting systems.	• Trade payables and accrued liabilities are stated at the correct amount owed. • Related expense balances conform with applicable accounting standards.
Cut-off	All purchases and payments transactions are recorded in the correct accounting period.	
Presentation and Disclosure	The details of purchases and payments transactions support their presentation in the financial statements, including their classification and disclosure.	• Trade payables, accrued liabilities and related expenses are properly identified and classified in the financial statements. • Disclosures pertaining to commitments, contingent liabilities and related party payables are adequate.

Chapter 8 discusses whether or not controls should be tested surrounding purchases and payables. Remember: where the purchases and payables balances are not material to the financial statements, limited controls testing and substantive testing will be performed. However, purchases and payables are usually a material figure and transactions tend to be high in volume and for this reason the auditor usually takes a controls approach when testing this area in order to reduce the level of detailed substantive testing.

When developing the audit plan relating to purchases and payables, a few general rules can be applied as follows:
- Where the purchases figure and payables balance are not material to the financial statements, limited controls testing and substantive testing will be performed.
- Where a significant risk has been identified in relation to the purchases and payables cycle, the level of substantive testing to be performed will be higher.
- Where a strong control environment has been identified, the level of substantive testing to be performed will be much lower than the level of substantive testing to be performed in an entity where a weak control environment has been identified.

Generally, a **controls testing** approach is the most productive (effective and efficient) approach when testing the area of purchases and payables. Remember: as detailed in **Chapter 8**, Section 8.6, the auditor can decide to take a controls approach in relation to only certain assertions and then perform focused substantive testing on the other assertions. With respect to the **completeness** assertion, the auditor will quite often choose to take a wholly substantive approach due to the risks associated with auditing it (i.e. he will perform focused substantive procedures (substantive tests of details) around the **search for unrecorded liabilities**).

16.6 KEY DOCUMENTS RELATING TO PURCHASES AND PAYABLES

Before commencing substantive testing procedures, the auditor should be familiar with the key documents associated with purchases and payables, in order for him to carry out an efficient and effective audit.

The primary document of interest relating to purchases and payables is the **aged payables listing**, which provides the following for the auditor:
- a full list of all individual supplier balances that exist at the date of the statement of financial position, which can be reconciled to the payables figure in the financial statements;
- an ageing of each supplier's amount due, which allows the auditor to better analyse the existence of the suppliers' balances (if a balance is outstanding for a lengthy period of time without proceedings for collection, it may be an indication that it does not exist. It may also be an indication of liquidity problems, i.e. the client entity might be delaying payment because it does not have the cash);
- a list from which to select a sample to perform substantive tests of details or perform reviews on **supplier reconciliations**; and
- if received in Excel (or a similar format), the list can be manipulated by the auditor to show top-value supplier balances, debit balances, round-sum balances and nil balances

(nil balances are of interest in the search for unrecorded liabilities), which may highlight risks.

The aged payables listing is similar in form to the aged receivables listing at **Example 13.1** in **Chapter 13**, 'The Audit of Revenue and Receivables', except in that it depicts suppliers rather than customers.

Also of interest to the auditor will be the supplier reconciliations, which can support the following management assertions (audit objectives):
- Completeness,
- Existence; and
- Accuracy.

16.7 SUBSTANTIVE AUDIT PROGRAMME FOR PURCHASES AND PAYABLES

An **audit programme** records the specific details of tests to be performed by the auditor. It becomes a guide to the **audit engagement team** as to the work to be done in a particular area. As work is completed, a reference is included on the audit programme, showing the location on the audit file where details of the tests performed are included. While the audit programme for any cycle will vary from entity to entity, in **Example 16.1** below we consider the typical types of test the auditor would include in the audit programme for purchases and payables.

EXAMPLE 16.1: SUBSTANTIVE TESTING: AUDIT PROGRAMME FOR
PURCHASES AND PAYABLES (LARGE COMPANY LIMITED)[1]

Large Company Limited 31 December 2012			
	Audit Materiality		€3,642,500
	Performance Materiality		€2,731,875
		Initials	**Date**
	Prepared by:		
Purchases and Payables	**Reviewed by:**		
Audit Programme	**Assertion Covered**	**Ref to Work**	**Initials and Date**
Accounting Policy			
Assess the appropriateness of the accounting policy and the accounting estimates method for this area. Ensure that the accounting policy is in accordance with accounting standards and applicable law, and that the methods used for making the accounting estimates are appropriate.	Existence, Completeness, Rights and Obligations, Accuracy/ Valuation and Classification		

---

[1] Source: Based on Procedures for Quality Audit 2010 (© Charted Accountants Ireland, 2010)

Initial Procedures			
Vouch **opening balances** to prior-year working papers.	Presentation and Disclosure		
Obtain or prepare **lead schedules** showing amounts falling due within one year and after more than one year. Prepare a **commentary** explaining the composition of payables balances and comparing them with prior periods and auditor expectations.	Existence, Occurrence, Accuracy and Classification		
Obtain a copy of the purchases general ledger and agree cost of sales and other expenses to the financial statements (lead schedule). Check **mathematical accuracy** of the document and review its contents for any **unusual items**.	Existence, Completeness, Accuracy		
Purchases Transactions			
Tests of Details Select a sample of transactions from the purchases ledger and trace to supplier invoice, goods receipt note and approved purchase order.	Occurrence, Accuracy, Rights and Obligations		
Alternatively, where controls environment has been tested as effective, perform **substantive analytical procedure** on purchases.	Occurrence, Completeness, Accuracy, Rights and Obligations		
Payables Balance			
Obtain or prepare a list of trade payables: 1. extract a sample from the payables ledger accounts and **reconcile balances to supplier statements**. Where supplier statements are not available, test for understatement by an alternative means, such as by circularisation (ISA 505, para 7); 2. investigate significant **debit balances**;	Existence, Occurrence, Accuracy and Classification		
3. check after-date invoices and credit notes for additional provisions; 4. investigate and explain amounts outstanding for an unusually long period; and 5. re-analyse amounts due from parent, subsidiary and associated undertakings.			

If necessary, evaluate whether the results of the external confirmation procedures provide relevant and reliable audit evidence, or whether further evidence is necessary (ISA 505, para 16).	Existence, Occurrence, Accuracy and Classification		
Obtain or prepare a **control account** where a purchase ledger is maintained: 1. test check extraction and addition of ledger balances, agree list to control account; 2. check the addition of the control account and check the balance to the list of payables balances and lead schedule; and 3. examine and vouch reconciling entries, adjustments and journal entries. Ensure there is an adequate explanation for each of them.	Existence, Occurrence, Accuracy and Classification		
Search for Unrecorded Liabilities			
Review **post-period-end** cash book, bank payments, purchase invoices and vouchers to identify any un-provided payables and/or accruals.	Completeness		
Review **open purchase orders** report and query aged items. Review goods received, invoices not received and report and query any aged items.	Completeness and Existence		
For the period after the statement of financial position date to the end of the fieldwork, scrutinise the following for payables omitted: 1. purchase day book or invoice listing; 2. invoices in the process of being passed for payment; 3. cash book; 4. correspondence with suppliers and inquire of the client entity's staff.	Completeness		
Ensure that any reconciling items noted in the trade payables reconciliations to payables statements are accrued where necessary.	Completeness		
Test cut-off procedures to ensure a liability is recorded for all inventory items received on credit (whether or not an invoice has been received).	Cut-off		
Other Considerations			
Sale or Return Enquire into correct treatment of inventory held on sale or return.	Occurrence, Completeness		

Directors' Loans and Shareholders' Loans Prepare detailed schedules of movements on directors' loan accounts and shareholders' loan accounts. Obtain directors'/shareholders' own written confirmation of movements and balances.	Existence, Presentation and Disclosure		
VAT 1. Review the VAT returns and reconcile a sample to the accounting records. 2. Test check recording of VAT when testing sales and purchases. 3. Test to ensure VAT returns are completed correctly and accurately and submitted in a timely manner. Review most recent return to ascertain whether returns are up to date. 4. Consider whether any interest or penalties may be due and that they have been correctly recorded. 5. Review any correspondence with customs and excise authorities. 6. Reconcile the period end VAT figure. 7. Test for payment or receipt of the balance post period end. 8. Agree revenue payments/refunds to ROS records (RoI).	Existence, Completeness and Accuracy		
Accruals 1. Obtain or prepare a schedule of accruals. 2. Compare with previous year's schedule. 3. Vouch material items. 4. Consider the reasonableness of other items. 5. Vouch any material other payables to supporting documentation.	Occurrence, Completeness and Accuracy/ Valuation		
Inter-company balances Extract as necessary and agree group or inter-company balances to the other party's accounts, or obtain written confirmation of agreement between the companies.	Presentation and Disclosure		
Confirm that group or inter-company balances shown as due after more than one year are subject to at least 12 months' notice of repayment.			

Capital commitments Identify, schedule and check disclosure of capital commitments not provided for and which: 1. are contracted for; and 2. are committed but not contracted. (See also the PPE Audit Programme, in **Example 11.1** in **Chapter 11**).	Presentation and Disclosure		
Name:		Accountant in Charge:	
Date:			
Name:		Reviewer:	
Date:			

16.8 SUBSTANTIVE TESTING PROCEDURES FOR PURCHASES AND PAYABLES

We will now discuss in more detail some of the procedures outlined in the substantive audit testing programme for purchases and payables outlined above. We will start with **initial procedures,** which include:
- opening balances;
- mathematical accuracy of schedules;
- lead schedules; and
- analytical reviews.

Initial Procedures

Opening Balances

Before commencing further audit procedures, the auditor must obtain evidence as to the accuracy of the opening payables balance. The reason for this is twofold:
1. it confirms that the comparative numbers in the financial statements (which must be included in the current year's financial statements) agree to the final accounts of the prior year; and
2. it highlights any final entries (last-minute adjusting journals) of the prior year not correctly carried forward, which may indicate an error in the current year's financial statements' figures.

The auditor checks opening balances as follows:
- Agree the opening balances to the prior-year working papers and signed financial statements. This may highlight an opening balance in the current year's accounts that does not agree to the closing balance per the prior year's financial statements. In this instance, a change would be made to the opening balance of the current year, which would impact the closing balance of the current year. This usually arises due to final

adjustments in the prior year that are not reflected in the actual accounts (nominal and general ledgers).
- If this is the first year of the audit engagement, the auditor will still need to establish that the opening balances are materially correct, which can pose a difficulty for him if either the client entity was exempt from audit in the prior year or a predecessor auditor carried out the audit. The audit of opening balances in such instances is discussed in detail in **Chapter 6,** Section 6.8, which addresses the requirements of (ISA (UK and Ireland) 510 *Initial Audit Engagements – Opening Balances*).

Mathematical Accuracy of Schedules

The auditor should obtain the detailed aged payables listing, gain comfort over its mathematical accuracy and then perform the following:
- agree the balance per the aged payables listing to the balance per the trial balance and the balance per the statement of financial position. Reconciling items should be investigated by the auditor in order to obtain the desired level of assurance and agree to supporting documentation;
- review the aged payables listing for any unusual balances, such as large balances, debit balances, old balances, nil balances and round-sum balances.
- test the reliability of the aged payables listing by selecting one supplier and agreeing ageing to the original invoices' dates.

Lead Schedules

The **lead schedule** can be used to summarise all trade and other payables due both within one year and after more than one year. This will allow the auditor to ensure that he obtains evidence for all balances during the audit and therefore provide some control over the performance of audit procedures. A typical lead schedule of the payables area is included in **Example 16.2** below (relating to Large Company Limited).

EXAMPLE 16.2: PAYABLES LEAD SCHEDULE (LARGE COMPANY LIMITED)[2]

Large Company Limited 31 December 2012			
	Audit Materiality		€3,642,500
	Performance Materiality		€2,731,875
		Initials	**Date**
	Prepared by:		
Payables	**Reviewed by:**		

---

[2] Source: based on *Procedures for Quality Audit 2010* (© Chartered Accountants Ireland, 2010), J-.

Important Note: this lead schedule is for general guidance only. It will need to be amended as necessary to reflect the circumstances of the individual audit assignment.

Payables – Amounts falling due within one year	31/12/2012 €000	31/12/2011 €000
Bank and other loans (**Tested in Bank and Cash Lead Schedule**)	4,250	9,650
Obligations under finance leases and hire-purchase contracts (**Tested under PPE**)	2,500	4,000
Derivative Financial Instruments	120	80
Trade payables	109,320	114,650
Tax Payables	2,690	2,740
Other Payables	16,300	10,730
Accruals and deferred income	500	750
	135,680	142,600
Note: *amounts included in trade payables where suppliers claim reservation of title.*	20,000	21,000

Payables: *amounts falling due after more than one year.*

Note: *all Payables greater than one year for Large Company Ltd relate to areas captured under other lead schedules, such as Bank and Cash and Investments.*

Analytical Review

An analytical review (covered under **Chapter 5**, Section 5.4, which addresses the requirements of ISA (UK and Ireland) 520 *Analytical Procedures*) is usually performed at the start of substantive testing in each audit area. Calculating ratios and analysing results against industry information, prior-year results, budgets, etc. allows the auditor to understand the nature of the movements during the year and make comparisons against norms, thereby enabling him to better prepare his audit programme. **Example 16.3** shows the types of ratio and comparison the auditor might perform in relation to trade payables and accruals, including the commentary he might make with respect to same.

EXAMPLE 16.3: INITIAL PROCEDURES: ANALYTICAL REVIEW AND COMMENTARY ON PAYABLES (LARGE COMPANY LIMITED)

Large Company Limited
31 December 2012

Audit Materiality		€3,642,500
Performance Materiality		€2,731,875
	Initials	**Date**
Prepared by:		
Reviewed by:		

Payables

Payables – Amounts falling due within one year

	31/12/2012 €000	31/12/2011 €000	Change €000	Change %
Bank and Other Loan Notes	4,250	9,650	(5,400)	(56)
Obligations under Finance Leases and HP contracts	2,500	4,000	(1,500)	(38)
Derivative Financial instruments	120	80	40	50
Trade payables	109,320	114,650	(5,330)	(5)
Tax Payables	2,690	2,740	(50)	(2)
Other Payables	16,300	10,730	5,570	52
Accruals and Deferred Income	500	750	(250)	(33)
	135,680	142,600	(6,920)	(4.9)

Note: bank loans are tested under bank and cash testing area.
Obligations under finance leases and HP contracts are considered under non-current fixed assets.

Commentary on movement following investigation

The rent accrual has been omitted, resulting in the 33% decrease in accruals (this has been taken to the error schedule). Other payables include a €5 million settlement provision set aside for a legal case won by a customer in late December 2012 and payable by 31 January 2013, this represents the majority of the 52% increase. A discussion of the fall in relation to payables is included below.

Key Ratios

Trade Payables Days	= (109,320 ÷ 140,250) × 365	= (114,650 ÷ 120,800) × 365	
(trade payables ÷ cost of sales × 365)	284.5	346.4	– 61.91 days

From discussions with management it was noted that the trade payables number includes plant and machinery purchased in December for €82,250 and €85,600 for 2012 and 2011, respectively. Below are the payables days recalculated, excluding PPE, related payables. The credit terms being taken were excessive in 2011 and suppliers had threatened to cease supply if improvements were not made, resulting in a reduction in payables days in 2012.

Trade Payables Days			
(trade payables ÷ cost of sales × 365)	=((109,320 − 82,250) ÷ 140,250) × 365	= ((114,650 − 85,600) ÷ 120,800) × 365	
	70.4	87.8	−17.4 days

Having carried out the initial procedures, the auditor must commence testing of movements during the period (i.e. purchases figures in the statement of comprehensive income and payments made throughout the period) and balances (i.e. payables and accruals balances). We will first consider the substantive testing of the transaction classes relating to purchases.

Substantive Testing of Purchases Transactions in the Period

We have already established in **Section 16.2** what constitutes **purchases**, in that every business incurs costs in the process of generating goods and services, which it subsequently sells to its customers. For example, an entity will purchase goods for resale or raw materials to use in the manufacturing process (i.e. cost of sales purchases). Additionally, 'purchases' include all expense type items relating to light and heat, rent, wages and salaries (be it production, sales or administration related), consultancy expenses, etc. Having learnt about the audit objectives in **Table 16.1** when it comes to the audit of the classes of transactions relating to purchases and payables, we now consider the types of substantive audit procedures the auditor might use to address these audit objectives. These procedures include **tests of details** and **substantive analytical procedures**, and we will discuss them in turn below.

Tests of Details over Purchases

Tests of details over purchases are audit procedures used to substantiate the purchases figure in the financial statements. They are used to obtain audit evidence regarding certain assertions. In the case of purchases, they are used to gain audit evidence over the following management assertions (audit objectives):
- Existence/Occurrence;
- Accuracy; and
- Completeness.

Where the auditor does not feel that sufficient audit evidence over purchases can be obtained from substantive analytical procedures alone, he may choose, additionally, to perform substantive tests of details to gain assurance over the existence and accuracy of purchases. These substantive tests of details will involve agreeing a sample (sampling is covered in **Chapter 6,** Section 6.7, which addresses the requirements of ISA (UK and Ireland) 530 *Audit Sampling*) of reported purchases transactions to supporting documentation, such as purchase orders, goods received notes (GRNs) and supplier invoices, confirming that the amounts recorded are accurate and are recorded within the correct period. It is also important to test the numerical sequence of purchase orders and GRNs and to trace them to purchase invoices and trade payables to confirm completeness. The auditor will often use a sampling tool (also discussed in **Chapter 6**) as a method of generating an appropriate sample size.

Additional assurance over the completeness of purchases can be obtained from the performance of **unrecorded liabilities** testing, which is discussed below.

Substantive Analytical Procedures in Testing Purchases

Substantive analytical procedures (covered in **Chapter 5,** Section 5.4, which addresses the requirements of ISA 520 *Analytical Procedures*) are designed to substantiate predictable relationships among both financial and non-financial data. They are mostly applicable to large volumes of transactions that tend to be predictable over time.

Within the context of the audit of purchases, substantive analytical procedures are most suitable in order to gain audit evidence over the purchases figure in the financial statements. The purchases figure consists of a large volume of routine transactions that tend to be predictable over the course of a financial year. (Tests of details are more commonly used within the audit of trade payables and accruals balances.)

When performing substantive analytical procedures, it is necessary for the auditor to review his understanding of the entity in order to establish whether changes to the purchases figure are to be expected. Significant changes in amounts between the current year and the prior year should be identified. Ratios, such as the gross profit margin ratio, should be calculated, and trends identified and analysed.

The auditor will develop an expectation of the level of purchases in the year based upon key factors affecting the performance and operation of the business in that period. This could include:
- prior-year volumes of purchasing;
- movements in cost prices of key supplies;
- inflation; and
- movements in levels of demand for the finished goods produced by the entity.

The auditor will seek to quantify and substantiate the effects of each of these factors through obtaining documentary and other evidence, where available. For example, prior-year purchase and sales volumes could be verified to prior-year audit working papers; movements in cost prices of key supplies could be verified by comparing current-year and prior-year supplier invoices; and movements in demand levels for finished goods could be verified by comparing current-year and prior-year sales reports.

Once the auditor has developed his expectation for the current year purchases figure, he will compare this to the actual figure reported in the financial statements. He will gain comfort over the completeness, existence and accuracy of the purchases figure by confirming that his original expectation is within a pre-defined acceptable range (tolerable error or threshold) of the actual figure reported in the financial statements. Though this acceptable range is a matter of judgement, a commonly used range is a reported purchases figure within 5% of that expected.

Analysis of expense accounts is also important. This is usually undertaken by comparing the ratio of each expense to sales in the current and prior period. An unusually low expense may indicate unrecorded liabilities. Wherever a change in relationships cannot be readily explained, the auditor must seek an explanation from management and corroborate it, usually by conducting additional tests.

Substantive Testing of Trade Payables and Accruals Balances

Where purchase transactions are not settled immediately through cash payments, they give rise to **trade payables**.

Specific substantive testing over trade payables and accruals will tend to vary, depending upon the nature of the client entity's operations. However, there are a number of key substantive tests that are common to the audit of the majority of client entities. These will generally take the form of substantive tests of details rather than substantive analytical procedures, and they are summarised below.

Re-performance of Supplier Statement Reconciliations (Completeness, Existence and Accuracy)

Where the client entity receives monthly supplier statements from its suppliers, the auditor will seek to gain audit evidence over the completeness, existence and accuracy of the trade payables balance by reconciling amounts appearing on year-end supplier statements to corresponding balances appearing on the payables ledger.

The supplier statements are evidence that is generated external to the client entity and therefore they provide reliable audit evidence as to the accuracy of year-end supplier balances. Photocopied or faxed copies of supplier statements should not be used in testing; instead, the auditor should request a copy of the statement from the supplier or confirm the balance directly with the supplier.

In selecting the supplier account balances for testing, the focus should not centre on the year-end supplier balance (or the highest value balances), but instead should centre on those suppliers with which the entity has had the greatest volume of business during the year, as the auditor's concern is that the recorded payables balance might be understated.

Differences between supplier statements and the recorded year-end trade payables balances should be investigated. The main reasons for differences can be attributed to goods in transit and cash in transit, and also amounts in dispute between the two parties to the transaction.

Accruals

An accrual is an amount set aside for a specific liability, i.e. where expenditure has been incurred in the period but for which no invoice has been received. Key audit procedures include:
- determining how the client entity identifies all accruals required to be made – discover and test the procedures; and
- checking the schedule of accruals for arithmetical accuracy.

Confirming Trade Payables (All Assertions)

The auditor may choose to request confirmation from suppliers regarding the balance outstanding from them to the client entity. External confirmations are covered under ISA 505, which is discussed in detail in **Chapter 6,** Section 6.5. However, confirmation of trade payables is not often a method adopted by the auditor because:
- it offers no assurance that unrecorded liabilities will be discovered; and
- external evidence, such as invoices/supplier statements, should be available to substantiate the balances.

It is recommended to confirm trade payables through circularisation of suppliers only when:
- the level of detection risk is low; and
- the suppliers being confirmed are those with which the company engaged in a substantial level of business and do not issue monthly statements and/or the statement is not available at the date of the statement of financial position.

If confirmations obtained through **circularisation** of suppliers are used to confirm trade payables, the auditors must be in control of the preparation and of the mailing of the requests. They must also ensure they receive the responses directly from the suppliers.

The positive form of the circularisation letter should be used (positive and negative confirmations are discussed in **Chapter 13**, Section 13.8) in making the confirmation request and the amount due at the reporting date should not be stated on the request – the supplier should specify the amount due to them as recorded in their own records. The supplier should also be requested to provide details regarding purchase commitments and any collateral for the amount due.

Confirming the trade payables balance provides only a limited amount of evidence relating to the completeness assertion due to the high probability that the test may fail to identify suppliers with which the entity has unrecorded liabilities.

Search for Unrecorded Liabilities (Completeness)

The search for **unrecorded liabilities** is a fundamental substantive test of detail over the completeness of trade payables and accruals common to almost every audit. The objective of the test is to gain assurance that all of a client entity's liabilities that were in existence at the year end were recorded in the statement of financial position.

Intentional understatement of year-end liabilities is a key technique that could be used by client entities engaging in '**earnings management**', i.e. by recording current year expenditure in the following period, current year costs are reduced with the result that profits are overstated. The auditor searches for unrecorded liabilities by examining various sources of evidence to identify pre year-end transactions where goods or services have been received by the client entity before the year end. The auditor then checks that any such pre year-end transactions are appropriately included in the year-end financial statements. The main sources of evidence are:

- post year-end payments identified from bank statements (payments made in January usually relate to purchases of an earlier period);
- post year-end invoices received (invoices received in January usually relate to purchases of an earlier period);
- goods received notes which have not been matched to invoices at the year end;
- open purchase orders – significantly aged purchase orders indicate that items for which a purchase order was raised may have been received but not recognised as being received in the accounting records and as such no accrual would be recognised for the related expense (nor would the inventory (if an inventory related purchase) have been included in the accounting record); and
- cut-off tests.

For example, for a client entity with a 31 December year end the auditor may identify, from a review of post year-end bank statements, a significant payment of €100,000 made on 10 January. Upon investigation, he ascertains that this payment relates to an invoice that was received on 3 January. On further examination, the auditor finds that this invoice has been matched to a goods received note dated 31 December. As the goods were received pre year end and included in inventory, the transaction should be recorded in the current year's purchases and accruals. If this is not the case, the purchases and year-end accruals figures will be understated.

Substantive analytical procedures may also help identify unexpected differences between the current and prior year's liability figures, which could indicate the presence of unrecorded liabilities.

An examination of **contractual commitments** may also indicate the existence of unrecorded liabilities, such as progress payments on long-term contracts. In addition, the performance of a subsequent events and contingent liabilities review may also contribute to uncovering unrecorded liabilities.

Performance of Purchases Cut-off Testing (Completeness, Existence and Accuracy)

Another key test performed in almost every audit of purchases is the performance of purchases cut-off testing in respect of the purchase of goods. The objective of this test is to ensure that purchases close to the year end are recorded in the appropriate accounting period.

Unlike sales, it may take several weeks for transactions that have occurred before the statement of financial position date to be invoiced by suppliers. Many entities do not have sufficient controls in place to ensure accurate distinction between the recording of transactions before and after the statement of financial position date.

Purchases cut-off testing is generally performed by examining goods received notes (GRNs) arising close to the year end and confirming that they are appropriately recorded in the financial statements. Remember: a liability is recognised once an event takes place that may result in the passing of economic benefits (requirement to pay for the goods/service received) which requires the entity to record the accrual at the time of receiving the goods/service and not at the time the invoice arrives.

GRNs issued in the days prior to the statement of financial position date may be traced to purchase journal entries or purchase accruals, to ensure they have been recorded pre year end.

In addition, goods received notes raised after the statement of financial position date will be traced to suppliers' invoices to ensure they are recorded after the year end.

The number of GRNs to be examined is again a matter of judgement; however, typically the auditor will examine the last 10 pre year-end GRNs and the first 10 post year-end GRNs. He will also obtain details of the last pre year-end GRNs at the time of attendance at the year-end inventory count and can then identify the first post year-end GRNs by following the numerical sequence.

Other Considerations

Re-calculation of a Sample of Year-end Accruals (Existence and Accuracy)

The auditor can gain audit evidence over the existence and accuracy of year-end accruals by recalculating a sample of accruals appearing on the year-end schedule of accruals. These calculations can be performed with the help of supporting documentation used by the client entity in its calculation. For example, for an entity with a 31 December year end, there may be an accrual for electricity costs for December when the previous bill related to the quarter ending 30 November and the next expected bill covers the period 1 December to 28 February. The auditor may recalculate the year-end accrual by dividing the previous quarterly bill by three.

Comparison of Year-end Accruals to Prior-year Accruals (Completeness, Existence and Accuracy)

Generally, accruals relate to similar items within a business year-on-year, e.g. rent, rates, electricity, etc. It is possible to gain audit evidence over the completeness, existence and accuracy of accruals by comparing items and amounts on the prior-year accruals listing to those on the current year listing and identifying and examining any unusual omissions or additions.

In addition, the auditor should perform an analytical review of expenses included in the statement of comprehensive income to highlight any inconsistencies that could relate to under- or over- accruals.

16.9 COMPUTER-ASSISTED AUDIT TECHNIQUES AND PURCHASES AND PAYABLES

The purpose of **computer-assisted audit techniques** (CAATs) and their generic uses are discussed in detail in **Chapter 9**, Section 9.4. We will now consider the primary use of CAATs when auditing the area of purchases and payables.

CAATs can provide considerable advantages when testing the area of purchases and payables. Examples of the use of CAATs when testing the area of purchases and payables are included below:

- **Audit Software** The auditor can use audit software to prepare **lead schedules** and control the performance of the audit.
- **Knowledge-based Software** The auditor can use knowledge-based software to prepare questionnaires and suggest testing steps based on answers to the questionnaires.
- **Excel** The auditor can use Excel to prepare substantive analytical procedure calculations.
- **Data Analysis Software** By obtaining a copy of the client entity's unpaid invoice listing at the year end (including supplier names and invoice dates) the auditor can use data analysis software to:
  - categorise the invoices by supplier;
  - stratify the payables listing by value;
  - sort the listing in order of value and then ensure adequate testing is given to larger balances, debit balances, round-sum balances and nil balances;
  - total the listing to facilitate comparison to the financial statements; and
  - cross-check for instances of employee names or bank account numbers (or employee-related businesses) appearing as suppliers.

16.10 DISCLOSURE REQUIREMENTS

Finally, with regard to purchases and payables, the auditor will consider the adequacy of the disclosures. Disclosures relating to liabilities are covered throughout the international accounting standards, although particular attention should be paid to IAS 1 *Presentation*

of Financial Statements and IAS 37 *Provisions, Contingent Liabilities and Contingent Assets.*
The auditor aims to ensure that all disclosures are:

- complete (no purchases- or payables-related disclosures are missing. The auditor can use IAS 1 and IAS 37 as a checklist);
- accurate (reflect the actual transactions and information relating to events surrounding purchases and payables);
- relate to events that actually occurred; and
- are properly presented (in a manner expected by international accounting standards).

The auditor should assess the purchases and payables disclosure requirements as follows:

- obtain an understanding of the disclosure requirements for trade payables and purchases under the applicable financial reporting framework;
- review the payables ledger, which may indicate amounts owed to employees, directors, other group companies and related parties – these should be specifically disclosed if they are material;
- identify debit balances included in the payables ledger that may, if found to be material, require reclassification to current assets;
- review minutes from board of directors' meetings and from inquiries of management to identify any contingent liabilities that may need to be provided for or disclosed;
- review management meeting minutes, open purchase orders, significant contracts and post year-end events to identify capital commitments or other material purchase commitments that may require disclosure.

16.11 CONCLUSION

When the auditor has performed controls testing, substantive analytical review and substantive tests of details, it must be considered if **sufficient appropriate audit evidence** has been obtained over purchases and payables, which gives the appropriate level of comfort required over the assertions stated at the outset, these being:

- Completeness;
- Valuation;
- Existence/Occurrence;
- Cut-off; and
- Rights and obligations.

The auditor must also consider if the testing performed has appropriately addressed any key risks identified by him surrounding the purchases and payables cycle, and reduced the risk of **material misstatement** arising as a result of key risks to a suitably low level.

When testing the area of purchases and payables, the auditor is most concerned with the **completeness** assertion due to the risk associated with fraudulent activity to reduce payables, resulting in an increase in profit.

The auditor must consider the impact on the **audit opinion** of the results of his testing in the area of purchases and payables. He does so by considering whether any misstatements found, either individually or in aggregate (when combined with other misstatements detected throughout the audit,) will result in the financial statements being materially misstated. As such, all misstatements found are taken to the auditor's errors schedule for consideration at the audit completion stage (discussed in detail in **Chapter 18**). The auditor's report on financial statements is considered in detail in **Chapter 19**, 'Audit Reports'.

SUMMARY OF LEARNING OBJECTIVES

Having studied this chapter on the audit of purchases and payables you should:

Learning Objective 1 Understand what is included in the audit of purchases and payables.

Every business incurs costs in the process of generating the goods and services, it subsequently sells to its customers. Where such transactions are not settled immediately through cash payments, they give rise to **trade payables**. Such trade payables meet the definition of liabilities as set out in IAS 37 *Provisions, Contingent Liabilities and Contingent Assets,* paragraph 10.

Learning Objective 2 Be able to identify the risks and audit objectives (management assertions) applicable to purchases and payables.

Risks Associated with Purchases and Payables The primary risks associated with purchases and payables relate to:
* completeness of payables; and
* inappropriate and fraudulent payments.

Learning Objective 3 Be able to determine an appropriate audit strategy for purchases and payables, taking into consideration the specific risks and audit objectives (management assertions).

Management Assertions (Audit Objectives) for Purchases and Payables With respect to purchases, the auditor seeks to prove that the purchases recorded in the financial statements relate to events that occurred and are recorded accurately, completely and only relates to transactions that pertain to the entity.

When auditing the payables balance, the auditor seeks to confirm their existence and accuracy (valuation) as well as their completeness. The auditor will also seek to ensure they are appropriately classified and disclosed.

Learning Objective 4 Be able to develop an audit programme that addresses all the audit objectives (management assertions) for purchases and payables.

Developing the Audit Plan Purchases and payables are usually a material figure and transactions tend to be high in volume; thus, the auditor usually takes a **controls approach** when testing this area in order to reduce the level of detailed substantive testing.

Learning Objective 5 Be able to describe and apply specific substantive testing procedures relating to the audit of purchases and payables.

Key Documents when Auditing Purchases and Payables The **aged payables listing** is the key document of interest to the auditor. Other documents that may form part of audit evidence connected to purchases and payables include:

- supplier statements and reconciliations;
- supplier invoices;
- open purchase order listing;
- Goods Received Invoice Not Received Report (GRIR);
- purchase orders (PO); and
- signed customer proof-of-delivery (POD) notes.

Key Substantive Testing Procedures Connected to Purchases and Payables Regarding purchases, the auditor seeks to prove that recorded purchases in the financial statements relate to events that occurred and that it has been recorded accurately and only relating to transactions where risks and rewards of items have passed to the buyer. The auditor will also seek to ensure that all purchase transactions are recorded (completeness).

When auditing the payables balance, the auditor seeks to confirm their existence, accuracy (valuation) and completeness by re-performing or reviewing supplier reconciliations. The auditor will pay particular attention to the **completeness assertion** by performing a number of audit procedures connected to the **search for unrecorded liabilities** (including post year-end payments, review of open PO reports, etc.). The auditor will also seek to ensure the **completeness of accruals** by performing **substantive analytical procedures** (comparing with prior-year accruals to identify under-accruals).

Learning Objective 6 Understand the role CAATs can play when auditing purchases and payables.

CAATs and Purchases and Payables The auditor may use a combination of audit software, data analysis tools and other applications, such as Excel, when auditing the area of purchases and payables.

Learning Objective 7 Understand the auditor's approach relating to the disclosures of purchases and payables.

The auditor aims to ensure that the disclosures relating to purchases and payables are complete, accurate, pertain to the entity and are adequately disclosed in line with related international accounting standards.

QUESTIONS

Self-test Questions

16.1 Define liabilities as set out in IAS 37, paragraph 10.

16.2 What benefits can be derived from an aged payables listing?

16.3 What are the key audit risks for the auditor associated with purchases and payables?

16.4 List the key audit procedures performed to test accruals.

16.5 When is it recommended that an auditor should confirm trade payables? Also, discuss the method that should be used.

16.6 Explain why an auditor performs the search for unrecorded liabilities.

16.7 Discuss four methods the auditor might use to search for unrecorded liabilities.

16.8 Generally, how does an auditor test cut-off for purchases?

Review Questions

(See Suggested Solutions to Review Questions in **Appendix D**.)

Question 16.1

You are the audit senior on the audit of Kopite Cabinets, a manufacturer of trophy display cabinets, for the year ended 31 December 2012. You have instructed your junior to review the file of post-year-end invoices received. From the review, your junior has identified the following:

1. An invoice dated 1 January 2013 for timber with a value of €12,000. The goods received note for the timber is also dated 1 January 2013. The invoice is not recorded in payables or accruals at the year end.

2. An invoice dated 7 January 2013 for glass with a value of €9,000. The goods received note for the glass is dated 31 December 2012. The invoice is not recorded in payables or accruals at the year end.

3. An invoice dated 2 January 2013 for glue with a value of €5,000. The goods received note for the glue is dated 2 January 2013. The invoice is found to be included in year-end accruals.

4. An invoice dated 1 January 2013 for nails with a value of €50. The goods received note is dated 31 December 2012. The invoice is not included in year-end payables or accruals.

Requirement What action would you take as audit senior in respect of each of these items including, where appropriate, relevant audit differences? (*Note*: audit materiality for the engagement has been set at €5,000.)

Question 16.2

Lactic Ltd ('Lactic') is a client of your firm. You are the audit senior on the audit for the year end 31 May 2013. Your assistant is responsible for the audit of the accounts payable and she has asked you to review, and provide guidance on, the following creditor reconciliation that she is about to audit.

Lactic Ltd – Accounts Payable Reconciliation

	€000	€000	€000
Balance per accounts payable listing			1,490
Balance per supplier's statement 28 May 2013			2,620
Difference			1,130
Reconciling items:			
– Payments made not on statement		(720)	
– Invoices on statement not on ledger			
24/05/2013 No. 14255	540		
27/05/2013 No. 15105	650		
28/05/2013 No. 15385	760		
		1,950	
			1,230
			100

The financial controller has noted that, in general, the audit fieldwork has always run smoothly, but there was a delay each year in the completion of the statutory accounts. The financial controller has indicated that a better understanding of the key financial statement completion steps would benefit Lactic's finance department in supporting the audit process.

Requirement Assuming that your assistant has not performed any audit work on the Lactic reconciliation, outline briefly the audit work to be performed and any queries she should consider.

Question 16.3

B Ltd ('Bistro') is a confectionery distributor that has been in business for the last 20 years and is managed by J Bistro. Your audit firm has been the auditor of this company since its incorporation. The audit partner is new to the engagement, following a required rotation. The company has performed well during the year ended 31 March 2013, with revenue (€2,565,000) and profit before tax (€100,000) running at approximately 10% higher than prior-year performance.

The fieldwork for the 2013 audit is complete and the partner has asked you to assess the analytical review of operating expenses. The following is the schedule of analytical review work performed by the audit assistant on the operating expenses:

Description	2013 €000	2012 €000	Comments
Insurance	20	10	The increase is due to rising insurance charges (J. Bistro)
Administration salaries	113	98	The increase is attributable to the cost of hiring a temporary accounts clerk to cover maternity leave (J. Bistro)
Depreciation	12	10	Appears reasonable
Distribution costs	322	182	The company had a policy of splitting distribution costs between cost of sales and operating expenses 50:50 ratio, but in 2012 all distribution costs have been charged to operating expenses (J. Bistro)
Repairs and maintenance	32	4	There were significant improvements made to the warehouse in 2012 (J. Bistro)
Computer costs	9	8	Appears reasonable
Accountancy	12	11	Appears reasonable based on prior-year fee
Rent and rates	15	11	The local authority increased rates during the year (J. Bistro)
Total:	535	334	

Requirement

(a) Define the term 'substantive analytical procedures'.

(b) Draft a memorandum to the partner on this engagement, highlighting what further work should be performed on the analytical review of operating expenses.

(c) J. Bistro has just phoned you about an article he has read in an accountancy journal on CAATs. He has asked you to describe, briefly, the ways in which CAATs could be used in the audit of Bistro.

THE AUDIT OF SHARE CAPITAL AND RESERVES

LEARNING OBJECTIVES

Having studied this chapter on the audit of share capital and reserves you should:
1. understand what is included in the audit of share capital and reserves;
2. be able to identify the risks and audit objectives applicable to share capital and reserves;
3. be able to determine an appropriate audit strategy for share capital and reserves, taking into consideration the specific risks and audit objectives (management assertions);
4. be able to develop an audit programme that addresses all the audit objectives (management assertions) for share capital and reserves;
5. be able to describe and apply specific substantive testing procedures relating to the audit of share capital and reserves;
6. understand the role CAATs can play when auditing share capital and reserves; and
7. understand the auditor's approach relating to the disclosures of share capital and reserves.

CHECKLIST OF RELEVANT STANDARDS

The relevant standards covered in this chapter are:
- ISA (UK and Ireland) 315 *Identifying and Assessing the Risks of Material Misstatement Through Understanding of the Entity and its Environment* (ISA 315)
- ISA (UK and Ireland) 330 *The Auditor's Responses to Assessed Risks* (ISA 330)
- ISA (UK and Ireland) 500 *Audit Evidence* (ISA 500)
- ISA (UK and Ireland) 505 *External Confirmations* (ISA 505)
- ISA (UK and Ireland) 510 *Initial Audit Engagements – Opening Balances* (ISA 510)
- ISA (UK and Ireland) 520 *Analytical Procedures* (ISA 520)
- ISA (UK and Ireland) 530 *Audit Sampling* (ISA 530)
- IAS 32 *Financial Instruments: Presentation* (IAS 32)
- IAS 33 *Earnings Per Share* (IAS 33)
- IFRS 2 *Share-based Payment* (IFRS 2)

KEY TERMS AND DEFINITIONS FOR THIS CHAPTER

Articles of Association A legal document that controls the internal management of the business, and the policies made to guide the execution of the objects as set out in the memorandum.

Memorandum of Association A legal document that defines the capacity of a company's activities and governs the relationship between the company and the outside world. It includes such items as: company name; type of company (e.g. limited or private); company objective; and intended powers of the company.

Trust Deeds A legal document that transfers to a trustee the title to property.

Share Register A list of all the current shareholders of a company updated on an on going basis.

17.1 INTRODUCTION

Sections 17.2 to **17.8** of this chapter outline the requirements of the international accounting standards, including, specifically, the requirements of IFRS 2 *Share-based Payment* (IFRS 2) and IAS 33 *Earnings Per Share* (IAS 33) with respect to share capital and reserves and then considers how the auditor:
(a) identifies audit risks and audit objectives (management assertions) for share capital and reserves;
(b) develops an audit plan for share capital and reserves and refines this into an audit programme;
(c) designs specific tests associated with share capital and reserves; and

(d) checks adequate presentation and disclosure in the financial statements relating to share capital and reserves.

In **Section 17.9** we consider how computer-assisted audit techniques (CAATs), considered in detail in **Chapter 9**, can assist with the audit of share capital and reserves.

Finally, in **Section 17.10** we consider the auditor's approach when auditing the reasonableness of disclosures relating to share capital and reserves.

17.2 WHAT IS SHARE CAPITAL AND WHAT ARE RESERVES?

Share capital is the investments made in the entity by its shareholders (i.e. the company's owners) at the time(s) the shares were issued. Both called-up share capital and called-up share capital not paid must be disclosed on the statement of financial position.

Reserves are the profits retained in the business and not distributed to the shareholders. Reserves include, for example, retained earnings and revaluation reserves. The Companies Acts 1963–2012, UK/NI Companies Act 2006, require disclosure of the following categories of reserves:
- profit and loss account;
- share premium account;
- revaluation reserve; and
- other reserves, e.g. capital redemption reserve.

17.3 RISKS ASSOCIATED WITH SHARE CAPITAL AND RESERVES

Throughout **Chapter 7** (which addresses the requirement of ISA (UK and Ireland) 315 *Identifying and Assessing the Risks of Material Misstatement Through Understanding of the Entity and its Environment* (ISA 315) and ISA (UK and Ireland) 330 *The Auditor's Responses to Assessed Risks* (ISA 330)) we discussed the topic of 'risk' and we considered how the auditor should go about detecting risks. We also discussed how the auditor should consider these risks when designing the nature, timing and extent of further audit procedures relative to each financial cycle. As such, before developing the audit plan, the auditor needs to consider a number of risks that may be associated with share capital and reserves.

The risks associated with share capital and reserves mainly revolve around presentation and disclosure. Although, in practice, this section of the audit usually requires the least amount of time, it should be noted that it is an important part of the audit. It is good practice for the auditor to carry out a search on the company through either the 'Companies House' or the 'Companies Registration Office' in order to verify information such as the existence of the company, its shareholders and directors. This facility is operated by the 'Companies House' for companies registered in the UK/NI and by the 'Companies Registration Office' for companies registered in the Republic of Ireland.

17.4 AUDIT OBJECTIVES/MANAGEMENT ASSERTIONS FOR SHARE CAPITAL AND RESERVES

As discussed in **Chapter 6** (which addressed the requirements of ISA (UK and Ireland) 500 *Audit Evidence* (ISA 500)), it is necessary for the auditor to seek appropriate audit evidence to satisfy all of the audit objectives and to eliminate the possibility of any of the risks outlined in **Section 17.3** going undetected. In **Chapter 4** we introduced audit objectives (management assertions) and explained their generic meanings, and then we re-introduced this topic again throughout **Chapter 8**, making management assertions specific to each financial cycle. In **Table 17.1** below we remind you once more of the audit objectives as they relate to share capital and reserves.

Table 17.1 addresses the management assertions (audit objectives) as they relate to the balances associated with share capital and reserves.

TABLE 17.1: AUDIT OBJECTIVES/MANAGEMENT ASSERTIONS
FOR SHARE CAPITAL AND RESERVES

Audit Objective/ Management Assertion	Objective of Audit Evidence
Existence	To ensure the company is in existence and is operating in line with its Memorandum and Articles of Association.
Completeness	To ensure any movement in the share capital account has been recorded in the year under review.
	To ensure opening reserves are accurately stated and tie into the prior-year closing reserves as per the last audited balance sheet.
Valuation and Allocation	To ensure share capital is included in the financial statements at the correct value, often shares are allotted at a premium.
Presentation and Disclosure	To check that reserves are correctly disclosed in the financial statements and that provisions in the Articles of Association are adhered to.
	To check that share capital is appropriately disclosed in the financial statements. This includes disclosing: • authorised share capital; • issued share capital; and • directors' and company secretary's interests in the share capital of the company or parent undertaking.
	To check that share capital is presented correctly in the financial statements. In accordance with IAS 32, each class of shares must be appropriately disclosed as equity or a financial liability.
	To check that dividends are not paid from capital.

17.5 DEVELOPING THE AUDIT PLAN FOR SHARE CAPITAL AND RESERVES

Before the audit of share capital and reserves is undertaken, an assessment of the audit risk must be completed. As discussed in detail in **Chapter 7**, audit risk is made up of three components: inherent risk; control risk; and detection risk. The auditor will rarely test controls around share capital and reserves and instead will adopt a wholly substantive approach. This is because, usually, there are a limited number of transactions relating to share capital and reserves and normally corroborating evidence has been obtained during other substantive procedures which support balances in the share capital and reserves accounts (e.g. revaluation of property and movement disclosed in the statement of comprehensive income).

17.6 KEY DOCUMENTS OF INTEREST TO THE AUDITOR WHEN AUDITING SHARE CAPITAL AND RESERVES

Before commencing his audit of share capital and reserves, the auditor should familiarise himself with the key documents associated with the area. Normally, with respect to share capital and reserves, the auditor is predominantly concerned with the examination of documentation pertaining to rights, preferences or restrictions that may be imposed by various authorities, agreements or legal requirements. Documents of interest to the auditor include:
- ordinary and preference share registers;
- Memorandum and Articles of Association;
- trust deeds;
- ordinary share certificates;
- preference shares certificates;
- documents pertaining to rights to acquire share capital (share options); and
- company search from the Companies Registration Office (CRO) in the Republic of Ireland or the Companies House in Northern Ireland/UK.

17.7 SUBSTANTIVE AUDIT PROGRAMME FOR SHARE CAPITAL AND RESERVES

An audit programme records the specific details of tests to be performed by the auditor. The audit programme becomes a guide to the audit engagement team as to the work to be done in a particular area. As work is completed, a reference is included on the audit programme showing the location on the audit file where details of the tests performed are included. The audit programme for any financial cycle will vary from entity to entity and, as such, in **Example 17.1** below we consider the typical types of test the auditor would include in the audit programme for share capital and reserves.

Example 17.1 below shows a sample audit programme for share capital and reserves.

EXAMPLE 17.1 AUDIT PROGRAMME FOR SHARE CAPITAL & RESERVES[1]

Large Company Limited 31 December 2012	Audit Materiality		€3,642,500
	Performance Materiality		€2,731,875
		Initials	Date
	Prepared by:		
Share Capital and Reserves	Reviewed by:		

Audit Programme	Assertion Covered	Reference to Work	Initials and Date
Ensure the audit plan is reflected in the following. The following steps are suggestions only and should be removed or added to as necessary to address the risks of material misstatement identified at the risk assessment stage.			
Agree authorised share capital with up-to-date Memorandum of Association and any special resolutions.	Existence and Valuation		
Agree issued share capital with register of members.	Existence and Valuation		
Prepare schedule of directors' interest in shares. *(For Republic of Ireland companies, include company secretary's interests).*	Presentation and Disclosure		
Prepare schedule of share capital issued during the period, detailing the date of issue, the consideration and, if required, the reason for issue.	Occurrence, Accuracy		
Prepare schedules for all classes of reserves, detailing movements during the period.	Existence, Completeness		
Prepare schedule of dividends paid and proposed giving dates of payment and check disclosure in Directors' Report where necessary. Confirm dividends are all paid out of distributable reserves.	Occurrence and Accuracy		
Name:	Accountant in Charge		
Date:			
Name:	Reviewer		
Date:			

---

[1] Source: based on *Procedures for Quality Audit 2010* (© Chartered Accountants Ireland, 2010), M1

17.8 SUBSTANTIVE TESTING PROCEDURES FOR SHARE CAPITAL AND RESERVES

Below we are going to discuss in more detail some of the procedures outlined in the substantive audit programme above at **Example 17.1.**

We will start with initial procedures, which include: opening balances; mathematical accuracy of schedules; the lead schedule; and analytical reviews.

Initial Procedures

Opening Balances

Evidence must be obtained as to the accuracy of the opening balances and the ownership of the assets comprising the balances. This can be completed as follows:
- agree the opening balances to prior-year working papers and signed financial statements. This will highlight any adjustments relevant to the prior-year financial statements that need to be carried forward into the current year's opening balances;
- if this is the first year of the audit engagement, a copy of the previous auditor's working papers (if possible) is obtained and opening balances are agreed to these working papers along with the prior-year signed financial statements. See **Chapter 6**, Section 6.8, which addresses the requirements of (ISA (UK and Ireland) 510 *Initial Audit Engagements – Opening Balances* (ISA 510)).

Mathematical Accuracy of Schedules

All schedules, e.g. in the case of share capital and reserves, the share register, provided by the client entity should be totalled and cross-totalled to check their mathematical accuracy. Additionally, they should be agreed to the financial statements, balances and transactions that they support.

Prepare Lead Schedules

The lead schedule acts as a summary of the balances and transactions to be audited relating to a particular class of transactions and balances. It allows the auditor to control his procedures by referencing each balance or transaction to the working paper that records the audit tests performed. For share capital and reserves the lead schedule is similar to the share capital and reserves note in the financial statements (as can be seen in **Appendix C**, Note 28). An example of a lead schedule is included below at **Example 17.2.**

EXAMPLE 17.2: SHARE CAPITAL AND RESERVES LEAD
SCHEDULE (LARGE COMPANY LIMITED)[2]

Large Company Limited 31 December 2012	Audit Materiality		€3,642,500
	Performance Materiality		€2,731,875
		Initials	Date
	Prepared by:		
Statutory Matters, Share Capital and Reserves	Reviewed by:		
Important Note – this lead schedule is for general guidance only. It will need to be amended as necessary			

	31/12/2012 €000	31/12/2011 €000
Authorised:		
100,000,000 Ordinary shares of €1 each	100,000	100,000
5,000,000 10% redeemable preference shares of €1 each	5,000	5,000
Allotted, called up and fully paid:		
84,050,000 (2011: 78,160,000) Ordinary shares of €1 each	84,050	78,160
3,000,000 10% redeemable preference shares of €1 each	3,000	3,000

Note: a similar schedule would be created for reserves.

Analytical Review

An analytical review (covered under **Chapter 5**, Section 5.4 which addresses the requirements of ISA (UK and Ireland) 520 *Analytical Procedures* (ISA 520)) is usually performed
at the start of each substantive procedure relating to each balance or class of transactions.
Calculating ratios and analysing results against industry information, prior-year results,
budgets, etc., allows the auditor to get a feel for the movements in the year and make
comparisons against norms, thereby enabling him to better prepare the audit programme.
The following example shows the types of ratio and comparison the auditor might perform in relation to share capital and reserves. An analytical review, similar to preliminary
analytical procedures, focuses the auditor on movements and key ratios, which equip him

---

[2] Source: based on *Procedures for Quality Audit 2010* (© Chartered Accountants Ireland, 2010), M1

with additional insight prior to commencing his substantive procedures. At the close of his substantive procedures he aims to ensure that he can comment on all movements and key ratios, with supporting explanations. If the auditor cannot explain any element, then this will highlight to him the need to perform additional substantive procedures. The analytical review performed here differs from a substantive analytical procedure in that the auditor's aim is not to substantiate the balance (i.e. prove the assertions), but rather to ensure that he understands the movements and relationships, to assist him in performing substantive procedures.

Specific ratios of interest to the auditor in relation to share capital and reserves might include:
- earnings per share (EPS);
- dividend yield;
- price/earnings (P/E) ratio; and/or
- debt to equity ratio.

Share Capital and Reserves Movements in the Period

Having performed the initial procedures, the auditor will then seek to audit the movements in share capital and reserves. Movements in share capital can include, for example, sale of additional shares or redemption of shares. Movements in reserves can include, for example: finance costs associated with share issue; profit for the year; dividends distributed in the year; or revaluation of property, plant and equipment (PPE). Below we consider the auditor's approach to auditing some of these movements.

Share Capital Movements

Obtain a copy of the share capital and share premium general ledger accounts and agree the movements to the difference between opening and closing balances on the financial statements. Once the above is validated, the auditor should:
- scan the activity in the share capital and share premium account for large or unusual transactions;
- confirm the total number of shares issued, dividends paid or payable, and other pertinent information directly with the independent registrar or transfer agent; and
- vouch transfers to the share register and share transfer forms.

For dividends declared/paid on share capital (or a component) that is classified as a financial liability, the auditor should check that the dividend is recognised as an expense in the profit and loss account.

Share Capital and Reserves Balances

Having completed initial procedures, as well as procedures relating to movements in the period, the auditor then needs to perform substantive procedures on the balances included within share capital and reserves.

Reserves

The audit of reserves is completed as follows:

1. Check that the prior-year closing reserves as stated in the signed financial statements tie into the current year opening reserves (i.e. reserves prior to inclusion of the current year profit/loss). This is a simple audit procedure but, is of the utmost importance as it provides assurance that the prior-year audit adjustments have been posted.
2. Prepare or obtain a schedule from the client detailing all reserve movements during the year. The auditor should vouch material movements to supporting documentation (e.g. board approving minutes) and check compliance with legal regulations. Such reserve movements need to be disclosed in the financial statements.

Share Capital

Share capital is primarily audited by obtaining third-party confirmations:

- Request a copy of the company search from the Companies Registration Office (CRO) in the Republic of Ireland or the Companies House in Northern Ireland/UK. The company search details all the documents filed and available on public record for the company.
- Once the search has been obtained, review all documents filed during the period under review and, where necessary, request copies of the documents filed. The most common documents include the annual return, change of registered office amendments or changes to the Memorandum and Articles of Association, changes in directors or company secretary and any changes to the share capital.
- It is important to check that any changes reflected in these documents are verified to board approving minutes and correctly updated and disclosed in the financial statements.
- The company search will give details of any changes to the share capital. Such changes include the issuing of shares, the redemption of shares, bonus shares, options taken up or issued, share splits and rights issues. It is important to check that these transactions are appropriately disclosed in the financial statements.
- The auditor should check the consideration received for any shares issued and agree amounts called up but not paid. In addition, the legality of any share repurchases should be investigated. The auditor also needs to determine whether a provision for premiums payable on redemption is required.
- The authorised and issued share capital must be agreed to the company's annual return. The authorised share capital should also be agreed to the Memorandum and Articles of Association.
- The Memorandum and Articles of Association must be reviewed to gain an understanding of the rights attaching to each class of share. As per IAS 32 *Financial Instruments: Presentation,* consideration must be given to how equity instruments are treated, i.e. as liabilities or equity. Authorised and issued share capital should be analysed in the financial statements by each class of shares. The auditor should examine significant shareholdings, in particular, the register of members should be vouched to issued share capital, and the auditor should check that correct disclosure of the directors' shareholdings has been made.

The critical feature in differentiating a financial liability from an equity instrument is the existence of a contractual obligation of one party to the financial instrument to either deliver cash or another financial asset to the other party or to exchange another financial instrument with the holder under conditions that are potentially unfavourable. Put simply:
- if a contractual obligation exists, the instrument is a financial liability;
- if the instrument is redeemable at the option of the holder it is a financial liability;
- if no contractual obligation exists, it is an equity instrument; and
- if the instrument is redeemable at the option of the company, it is considered an equity instrument.

Examples 17.3 and **17.4** below consider the classification under a financial liability and under equity.

EXAMPLE 17.3: CLASSIFICATION UNDER FINANCIAL LIABILITY

Company A has issued preference shares which carry rights to cumulative fixed net dividends and repayment of share price on redemption (redeemable at the option of the holder). Should this be classed as a liability or equity?

Look at the substance of the arrangement:

Two obligations are attached to the preference shares **and** they are redeemable at the option of the holder, therefore they are classified as a financial liability.

EXAMPLE 17.4: CLASSIFICATION UNDER EQUITY

Company B has issued redeemable shares. Company B may redeem all or part of the shares at any time; holders are not entitled to payment of a dividend.

Look at the substance of the arrangement:

No obligations are attached to the preference shares **and** they are redeemable at the option of the company, therefore they are classified as equity.

Minutes of shareholder meetings are also reviewed during the audit. It is a requirement under company law that companies hold shareholder meetings and maintain minutes. Any changes to the Memorandum and Articles of Association should also be reviewed by the auditor. As discussed above, the auditor should examine documentation pertaining to rights, preferences or restrictions that may be imposed by various authorities, agreements or legal requirements, including:
- trust deeds;
- voting rights;
- preference shares and other preferences;
- dividend arrears; and
- rights to acquire share capital.

17.9 COMPUTER-ASSISTED AUDIT TECHNIQUES AND SHARE CAPITAL AND RESERVES

Above we have considered how the auditor might go about testing the assertions relating to share capital and reserves. Now we will consider how CAATs might aid him in his testing. The purpose of CAATs and their generic uses are discussed in detail in **Chapter 9**, Section 9.4. The primary use of CAATs with respect to share capital and reserves will involve the auditor using audit software to:

1. control the audit by preparing documents such as lead schedules; and
2. produce questionnaires through knowledge based software, which is quite often built into audit software. The auditor can use this to probe the client entity's records with respect to share capital and reserves. Knowledge based software can be used to produce standard questionnaires relating to share capital and reserves and can ensure that the auditor is prompted to ask the right questions and respond to the results of those questions adequately.

17.10 DISCLOSURE REQUIREMENTS

Finally, with regard to share capital and reserves, the auditor will consider the adequacy of the disclosures. The auditor needs to consider the requirements of international accounting standards to ensure that all disclosures are;

- complete (no share capital- and reserves- related disclosures are missing);
- accurate (reflect the actual transactions and information relating to events surrounding share capital and reserves);
- relate to events that actually occurred; and
- are properly presented (in line with applicable international accounting standards).

When auditing the adequacy of presentation and disclosure of share capital and reserves, the auditor will:

- check that directors' and company secretary's interests in shares of the company disclosed in the directors' report agree with the information extracted from the register of directors' interests during the performance of the share capital and reserves work;
- check that each class of share is appropriately presented as equity and/or a financial liability in accordance with the requirements of accounting standards;
- check that proper disclosures are made of the accounting policies and methods adopted for equity instruments;
- consider whether disclosure of non-distributable reserves is required in order to give a true and fair view;
- inquire from management as to the name of the entity's controlling and, if different, its ultimate controlling party and agree details to the register of shareholdings and other corroborating evidence; and
- check that EPS has been appropriately disclosed in accordance with IAS 33.

17.11 CONCLUSION

When the auditor has completed his substantive tests in the area of share capital and reserves, he must consider whether or not sufficient appropriate audit evidence has been obtained over share capital and reserves balances and transactions, which give the appropriate level of comfort required over the audit objectives/management assertions stated at **Table 17.1**, these being:

- Completeness;
- Existence/occurrence;
- Cut-off;
- Valuation and allocation;
- Rights and obligations; and
- Presentation and disclosure.

Additionally, the auditor must consider if the audit testing performed has appropriately addressed any key risks surrounding share capital and reserves that were identified by him during the course of the audit. He must also consider whether the risk of material misstatement arising as a result of key risks has been reduced to a suitably low level.

When testing the area of share capital and reserves, the auditor is most concerned with the presentation and disclosure of audit objectives/management assertions due to the regulatory requirements relating to this area.

The auditor must consider the impact on the audit opinion of the results of his testing in the area of share capital and reserves. He does so by considering whether any misstatements found, either individually or in aggregate (when combined with other misstatements detected throughout the audit), will result in the financial statements being materially misstated. As such, all misstatements found are taken to the auditor's errors schedule for consideration at the audit completion stage (discussed in detail in **Chapter 18**). The auditor's report on financial statements is considered in detail in **Chapter 19**, 'Audit Reports'.

SUMMARY OF LEARNING OBJECTIVES

Learning Objective 1 Understand what is included in the audit of share capital and reserves.

Share capital is the amount paid into the company by the shareholders (i.e. the owners) at the time(s) the shares were issued. Both called-up share capital and called-up share capital not paid must be disclosed on the statement of financial position.

Reserves are the profits retained in the business and not distributed to the shareholders.

Learning Objective 2 Be able to identify the risks and audit objectives applicable to share capital and reserves.

The risks associated with share capital and reserves revolve mainly around presentation and disclosure.

Learning Objective 3 Be able to determine an appropriate audit strategy for share capital and reserves, taking into consideration the specific risks and audit objectives (management assertions).

The auditor seeks to ensure that: the share capital and reserves balances exist and are accurate; all share capital and reserve balances are included and appropriately classified, presented and disclosed on the statement of financial position.

Learning Objective 4 Be able to develop an audit programme that addresses all the audit objectives (management assertions) for share capital and reserves.

The auditor will rarely test controls around share capital and reserves and instead will adopt a wholly substantive approach.

Learning Objective 5 Be able to describe and apply specific substantive testing procedures relating to the audit of share capital and reserves.

Key Documents when Auditing Share Capital and Reserves Documents of interest to the auditor include:
- ordinary and preference share registers;
- Memorandum and Articles of Association;
- trust deeds;
- ordinary share certificates;
- preference shares certificates;
- documents pertaining to rights to acquire share capital (share options); and
- company search and inspection of annual return.

Key Substantive Testing Procedures Connected to Share Capital and Reserves The main audit procedures surrounding share capital and reserves relate to confirming the existence of shares by reference to share registers and ensuring the adequate disclosure and presentation of share capital and reserves in the financial statements. The auditor should also test the movements of share capital and reserves in the period. For share capital this will involve testing the additions and disposals of shares in the period.

Learning Objective 6 Understand the role CAATs can play when auditing share capital and reserves.

The auditor may use a combination of audit software, data analysis tools and other applications, such as Excel, when auditing the area of share capital and reserves.

Learning Objective 7 Understand the auditor's approach relating to the disclosures of share capital and reserves.

The auditor must consider if the disclosures included in the entity's financial statements are complete, accurate, pertain to the entity and are adequately disclosed in line with applicable international accounting standards.

QUESTIONS

Self-test Questions

17.1 What is the difference between share capital and reserves?

17.2 List four categories of reserves.

17.3 List seven key documents of interest to the auditor when auditing share capital and reserves.

17.4 Explain how the audit of reserves is performed.

17.5 Discuss how a company search can benefit an auditor.

17.6 Explain what determines whether a financial instrument is classified as either a liability or as equity.

Review Questions

(See Suggested Solutions to Review Questions in **Appendix D**.)

Question 17.1

You are the audit senior on XYZ Limited for the year ended 31 March 2013. On receipt of the financial statements, you notice ordinary share capital has increased from €100,000 in financial year FY 2012 to €200,000 in FY 2013.

Requirement Outline the audit procedures you would undertake to audit the increase in share capital.

Question 17.2

You are the audit senior on Printer Limited (Printer) for the year ended 31 December 2012. Following your review of the company search and the documents filed during the year, you note that 50 shares were issued at €2 each during the year. The nominal price of the shares is €1. The issue of the shares has not been reflected in the draft financial statements provided to you by Printer Limited.

Requirement Outline the audit procedures you would undertake to audit the above.

CHALLENGING QUESTIONS FOR PART III

These Challenging Questions aim to test your knowledge of **Chapters 11–17**. The challenging questions are intended to test your practical application of what you have learned in these chapters and so you are presented with a case study on which you are asked to deliver on a number of requirements.

(Suggested solutions to Challenging Questions are available through your lecturer.)

Question III.1

You are a member of the engagement team on the audit of Large Company Limited. It is February 2013 and you have been assigned the area of non-current assets and have been provided with the following:

- the non-current assets note as per the draft financial statements (see **Appendix C**, Note 13);
- Mastersons & Associates carried out the revaluation on the freehold land and buildings based in Dublin city centre. Mastersons & Associates are a UK company. Management has the document, prepared by Mastersons & Associates, outlining the findings and recommended valuation.
- the non-current asset value as per the statement of financial position in the draft financial statements is €140,500, the value per the Non-current Asset Register is €145,500 (the non-current asset register which includes accumulated depreciation charges to date and date of purchase/disposal is available in Excel).
- the non-current asset additions listing was received in Excel. A junior member of the audit team checked the mathematical accuracy of these schedules, which showed additions of €75,500,000 relating to plant and machinery and €35,000,000 relating to motor vehicles. The listing was sorted according to value and the following were the items purchased for the lowest values:

Plant and Machinery Additions

	€	€	€
Pallet Count Reader	500		
Fittings to Repair Line 1	1,200		
New Conveyor Belt		5,000	
Improvement to Line 2	5,800		
New Fork Lift		11,500	
New Fork Lift		15,000	
New Palletiser		16,000	
Additions to Line 3		22,000	
			38,000

Motor Vehicle Additions

	€	€	€
Install of 5 Car Phone Kits		1,200	
Volkswagen Passat (05D21256)	8,900		
Toyota Avensis (06D21587)	9,200		
			19,300

- The company's accounting policies with regard to property, plant and equipment are included in the draft accounts of Large Company Limited (see **Appendix C**, Statement of Accounting Policies).
- The audit team performed controls testing on the non-current assets area at the interim audit carried out in November and found the controls around non-current assets to be effective.

Requirement

(a) Your audit manager, John Doe, wants to be confident that you know how to sub-stantively test the area of non-current assets. As such, he asks you to send him a memo outlining:

   (i)   the initial audit procedures you intend to perform on non-current assets. He notes that you should include at least **three** initial procedures **and** identify any **immediate issues noted** from the information obtained to date.

   (ii) the substantive audit procedures you intend to perform on additions, giving **specifics** relevant to the information obtained to date.

(b) You are running short of time and so are delegating the audit of depreciation and the revaluation to a more junior member of the audit team. You advise him to choose the most efficient method of testing depreciation. Your audit junior asks for clarification on the methods open to him to test depreciation and how one can be more efficient than the other. You are therefore required to:

   (i)   draft an e-mail to the audit junior, outlining for him two substantive testing procedures that he could use to audit depreciation;

   (ii) critique each method with regard to its efficiency; and

   (iii) outline two tests for the audit junior to carry out with regard to the revaluation carried out by Mastersons & Associates.

Question III.2

You are a member of the engagement team on the audit of Large Company Limited. It is February 2013 and you have been assigned the area of receivables and have been provided with the following:

- Appendix 1: Extract from the Receivables Lead Schedule prepared by the audit manager.
- Appendix 2: Extract from the Aged Receivables Listing showing the make-up of the greater than 90 days figure of €80,000.
- Appendix 3: Extract from a meeting held with the credit controller.

Requirement

(a) Your audit manager has asked you to:

   (i)   Perform a review of the bad debt provision performed by management. He asks you to prepare this in working paper format, noting any items that you believe should be taken to the error schedule; and

   (ii) outline any further audit procedures you believe are necessary to conclude on the valuation of receivables.

(b) Appendix 4 shows an analytical review carried out by a junior member of the audit engagement team. She is unsure how to create the correction journal entry that would be necessary to correct the omissions of accruals, **you are therefore required to prepare the correction journal entry for her**.

(c) The audit partner feels, with so much having been omitted from accruals, there is a high risk that there are further unrecorded liabilities and asks **you to outline further audit procedures to be carried out by the audit junior in order to conclude on the completeness assertion for payables and accruals**.

APPENDIX 1: EXTRACT FROM RECEIVABLES LEAD SCHEDULE

Large Company Limited   **H**

31 December 2012			
	Audit Materiality		€3,642,500
	Performance Materiality		€2,731,875
		Initials	Date
	Prepared by:	MM	15/02/2013
Receivables	Reviewed by:		

Receivables – Amounts falling due within one year

	31 December 2012 €000	31 December 2011 €000
Trade Receivables	3,750	4,850
Provision for Bad Debts	(500)	(750)
Loan Notes	1,500	1,500
Other receivables	750	600
Prepayments and accrued income	1,000	1,050
	6,500	7,250

Movement in Bad Debt Provision

	31 December 2012 €000	31 December 2011 €000
Opening Balance	750	700

Increase/(decrease) in Provision	450	150
Bad Debt Write off	(700)	(100)
Closing Balance	500	750

Trade Receivables Aged Analysis

	31 December 2012	31 December 2011
	€000	€000
Current (within credit terms)	3,100	4,250
30–60 days	420	350
60–90 days	150	140
Greater than 90 days	80	110
	3,750	4,850

Appendix 2: Extract From Aged Receivables Listing

Customer	Name	Location	Total	Current	30–60	60–90	>90
			€000	€000	€000	€000	€000
1256325	Dow ns Ltd	UK	1	–	–	–	1
1256325	Marks Ltd	RoI	1	–	–	–	1
1256358	Avondale Ltd	UK	8	3	2	2	1
1258945	Tuffy's Ltd	RoI	64	49	13	–	2
1259687	Bons Ltd	NI	18	–	–	15	3
1259865	AFG Ltd	RoI	185	80	60	40	5
1254587	Dunner Ltd	RoI	7	–	0	0	7
1254875	Hogan Ltd	UK	8	–	–	–	8
1254786	Bernstein Ltd	UK	18	10	-2	-2	12
1256985	Jack Ltd	NI	45	35	10	-15	15
1256489	Josh Ltd	RoI	25	–	–	–	25
			3,750	3,100	420	150	80

APPENDIX 3: MINUTES OF MEETING REGARDING BAD DEBT PROVISION

Minutes of Meeting with Jean Kelly (Credit Controller) and Kate Louis (CFO)

In attendance   **John Keane (Smith & Reilly)**

                         Jean Kelly (Large Company Ltd)

                         Kate Louis (Large Company Ltd)

Re: **Bad debt provision**

John Keane – I see the bad debt provision is €500,000, yet the amount owing for more than 90 days is only €80,000. What makes up most of the provision?

Kate Louis – In November a very large customer (Gone Ltd) went into liquidation owing us €450,000. At present we are unsure if any of this is collectable as there is no indication how much creditors will receive. We expect to get nothing of this €450,000.

John Keane – This means that just €50,000 is assigned to all other balances?

Kate Louis – That is correct.

John Keane – The provision in the prior year was €750,000. Why was it so high?

Kate Louis – A similar situation arose at the end of last year, except the amount owing was €500,000, none of which we collected. Additionally, we had a lot of really old balances dating back a few years that we wrote off during the period on the advice of the debt-collection agency. In total, bad debts written off were €700,000 and we increased the provision by €450,000 to account for the large bad debt at the end of 2012.

John Keane – Is the rest of the provision made up of 90+ debts?

Kate Louis – Yes, we haven't provided for Josh because although they've gone into liquidation and there is nothing available for unsecured creditors, one of our directors knows the liquidator and he is going to make sure we get the €25,000 back; he's doing the same for a big retailer who went into liquidation owing €300,000 from December 2012 (Away Ltd). We also haven't provided for AFG – the €5,000 relates to goods they say we didn't deliver. We can't find the POD, but we know the name of the person who the driver gave them to, so we are not letting this one go. We've provided for all the other balances > 90 days old as these have all either gone out of business or are likely to.

John Keane – Have you considered the possibility of debt less than 90 days being uncollectable?

Kate Louis – No, we only review them when they hit 90 days.

John Keane – The Jack Ltd debt appears to have been paid but just not allocated, is this correct?

Jean Kelly – Yes, that's correct, I forgot to allocate that.

Kate Louis – But it will just cover something else in case we've missed anything.

APPENDIX 4: ANALYTICAL REVIEW CARRIED OUT BY JUNIOR MEMBER OF THE AUDIT ENGAGEMENT TEAM

Accrual Item	2012	2011	Comment
Rent	€000 150	€000 350	*Rent for Dublin premises is under accrued by €200,000 and rent of UK and NI offices has been omitted (being €200,000)*
Electricity	90	100	*Reviewed post year-end invoice – accrual reasonable*
Phone	30	30	*Reviewed post year-end invoice – accrual reasonable*
Repair of Building	150	0	*Not applicable in prior year*
Expenses Not yet Claimed	70	60	*Reviewed payroll expenses claimed – reasonable*
Unused Holidays	10	60	*The €10,000 represents unused holidays outstanding since 2011, no provision has been made for holidays outstanding from 2012 which are estimated to be approx €70,000*
Bonuses Due for 2012 (payable 2013)	0	150	*Bonus accrual was omitted and is expected to be approx. €150,000 for 2012.*
	500	750	

PART IV

THE AUDIT AND ASSURANCE PROCESS: CONCLUSION AND REPORTING

THE AUDIT AND ASSURANCE PROCESS

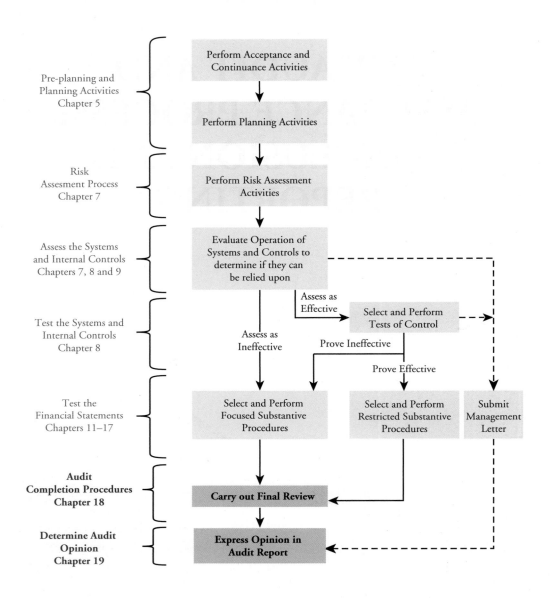

18

AUDIT WORK CONCLUSIONS

LEARNING OBJECTIVES

Having studied this chapter you should:
- have a clear understanding of final analytical procedures and their importance in the conclusion of an audit;
- be able to consider the misstatements taken to the schedule of unadjusted errors when concluding on whether the financial statements are materially misstated;
- understand the auditor's responsibility regarding subsequent events for the different time periods highlighted in ISA (UK and Ireland) 560 *Subsequent Events*;
- be able to discuss the requirements of the auditor regarding the assessment of the going-concern assumption;
- understand the role that written representations play as well as their content;
- understand the auditor's approach to reviewing the classification of provisions, contingent assets and contingent liabilities;
- understand the importance of the final review of the audit working papers;
- be able to discuss the form of other reports directed at 'those charged with governance'; and
- understand the considerations of the auditor relating to related parties.

CHECKLIST OF RELEVANT STANDARDS

ISA (UK and Ireland) 260 *Communication with Those Charged With Governance* (ISA 260)

ISA (UK and Ireland) 320 *Materiality in Planning and Performing an Audit* (ISA 320)

ISA (UK and Ireland) 450 *Evaluation of Misstatements Identified During the Audit* (ISA 450)

ISA (UK and Ireland) 501 *Audit Evidence – Specific Considerations for Selected Items* (ISA 501)

ISA (UK and Ireland) 520 *Analytical Procedures* (ISA 520)

ISA (UK and Ireland) 550 *Related Parties* (ISA 550)

ISA (UK and Ireland) 560 *Subsequent Events* (ISA 560)

ISA (UK and Ireland) 570 *Going Concern* (ISA 570)

ISA (UK and Ireland) 580 *Written Representations* (ISA 580)

IAS 2 *Inventories* (IAS 2)

IAS 10 *Events after the Reporting Period* (IAS 10)

IAS 37 *Provisions, Contingent Liabilities and Contingent Assets* (IAS 37)

KEY TERMS AND DEFINITIONS IN THIS CHAPTER

Going Concern The going concern assumption focuses on the client entity being able to continue in business for the foreseeable future without an intention to liquidate or cease the entity, or that there are no conditions that might not allow it to continue (e.g. a changing business environment or significant litigation that could impact on the future of the business).

Management "The person(s) with executive responsibility for the conduct of the entity's operations. For some entities in some jurisdictions management includes some or all of those charged with governance, for example, executive members of a governance board, or an owner manager." (ISA 260, para 10)

Subsequent Events Events occurring between the date of the financial statements and the date of the auditor's report, and facts that become known to the auditor after the date of the auditor's report.

Written Representation A written statement by management provided to the auditor to confirm certain matters or to support other audit evidence. Written representations in this context do not include financial statements, the assertions therein, or supporting books and records.

18.1 INTRODUCTION

As the audit draws to a conclusion, the auditor performs audit procedures to obtain further audit evidence in order to draw conclusions and finalise the audit process. He will perform the following when concluding on an entity's financial statements:
1. final analytical procedures;
2. evaluation of misstatements identified during the audit;
3. subsequent events review/events after the reporting period;
4. evaluation of the going concern assumption;
5. management representations (letter of representation);
6. review of provisions, contingent liabilities and contingent assets;
7. final review of working papers;
8. communicating with those charged with governance.
9. concluding on related parties.

These are discussed in turn in the sections below.

18.2 FINAL ANALYTICAL PROCEDURES

Introduction

As stated above, in concluding on the audit work performed, the auditor should complete final analytical procedures to form an overall opinion on the financial statements. ISA (UK and Ireland) 520 *Analytical Procedures*, at paragraph 6 states:
> "The auditor shall design and perform analytical procedures near the end of the audit that assist the auditor when forming an overall conclusion as to whether the financial statements are consistent with the auditor's understanding of the entity."

Performing final analytical procedures allows the auditor not only to see if the financial statements 'make sense' and if any unusual or unexpected relationships exist but also whether the results are consistent with other information obtained by the auditor.

The Benefits of Final Analytical Procedures

The following benefits will arise if the auditor performs **analytical procedures** at the end of the audit:
- During the course of the audit a previously unidentified risk of material misstatement may arise. Final analytical procedures will help reduce the **detection risk** by providing the auditor with an opportunity to ensure he understands all movements in the financial statements.
- Unusual fluctuations or unexpected results that are inconsistent with other audit evidence will be highlighted.
- Final analytical procedures will ensure conclusions formed by the auditor during the audit of the financial statements can be supported.
- The auditor can conclude on the reasonableness of the financial statements with added assurance and support.

Identification of New Risks during Final Analytical Procedures

In concluding on the final analytical procedures at the completion stage of the audit, if the auditor identifies new risks, it may be necessary to re-evaluate the audit procedures performed. Prior to conducting additional procedures, the auditor should evaluate the misstatements identified and assess whether these misstatements have a material impact on the financial statements. In making this assessment, he should consider the possibility of similar undiscovered misstatements that may require further investigation. ISA 520, at paragraph 7 states:

> "If analytical procedures performed in accordance with this ISA (UK & Ireland) identify fluctuations or relationships that are inconsistent with other relevant information or that differ from expected values by a significant amount, the auditor shall investigate such differences by: (a) enquiring of management and obtaining appropriate audit evidence relevant to management's responses; and (b) performing other audit procedures as necessary in the circumstances."

Final analytical procedures are similar to the preliminary analytical procedures performed at the planning stages of the audit covered in **Chapter 5,** Section 5.3, and again in **Chapter 7** by **Example 7.1.** They allow the auditor to review the financial statements in their entirety in order to highlight any unusual balances or relationships (gross profit movements) that may not have been noted in the audit.

Use of Benchmarks

Final analytical procedures may be performed by comparing current-year figures to prior-year financials or through **using external knowledge sources as a benchmark.** Based on the auditor's understanding of the client entity and its market, the auditor should identify an accurate and **comparable benchmark.** For example, if the client entity is a medium-sized hardware store, a large multinational hardware store should not be used for comparison purposes. It is important to remember to use **an appropriate benchmark** when performing final analytical procedures. The following are examples of instances of the use of benchmarks during final analytical procedures:

- customer acquisition – use the benchmark to compare how many new customers have been acquired during the financial year;
- customer retention – again using the benchmark, compare how many customers have been retained during the financial year;
- sales growth – compare sales growth to the benchmark during the financial year;
- selling and marketing activities – compare selling and marketing activities to the benchmark;
- determine the key performance measures that capture the business activities so that the actual key performance figures can be benchmarked against those budgeted.

In summary, final analytical procedures conducted by the auditor supplement the other audit procedures conducted by the auditor during the course of the audit of the client entity. They provide a comparison to the market and an overall assessment of the client's performance. However, it is important to stress that final analytical procedures **supplement** other audit procedures and are not effective in any way on their own.

18.3 EVALUATION OF MISSTATEMENTS IDENTIFIED DURING THE AUDIT

Introduction

At the final stages of the audit the auditor needs to summarise all misstatements found during the course of the audit. This is referred to as the **summary of unadjusted differences** (or is more commonly known as 'the error schedule').

ISA (UK and Ireland) 200, *Overall Objectives of the Independent Auditor and the Conduct of an Audit in Accordance with International Standards on Auditing*, at paragraph 3 states:
"The purpose of an audit is to enhance the degree of confidence of intended users of the financial statements. This is achieved by the expression of an opinion by the auditor on whether the financial statements are prepared, in all material respects, in accordance with an applicable financial reporting framework."

During the course of the audit, the auditor may note **misstatements** in the accounts of the client entity that were not corrected by **management** and that may need to be brought to the **summary of unadjusted differences** (error schedule) if, after discussions with management, they are to remain uncorrected. It is important to consider **materiality** and **tolerable error** when examining audit differences. Once these have been set, the auditor should evaluate the effect of the uncorrected misstatements, both individually and in aggregate, on the financial statements.

Materiality is set at the **planning stage** of the audit. However, it should be reassessed throughout the audit. Generally, materiality is set on either a percentage of revenues or net assets. A lower level of materiality is often used in practice when bringing misstatements to the summary of unadjusted differences. A full discussion of the calculation and use of materiality is contained in **Chapter 5,** Section 5.4. The auditor should take into account any uncorrected misstatements from the prior period as this may increase the risk of the current period financial statements being materially misstated. **The overall materiality level (rather than performance materiality) is then used to decide which adjustments need to be posted to the client's accounts**. (**Performance materiality**, as introduced in **Chapter 5,** Section 5.4,[1] is used throughout the performance of the audit to provide a margin of error for the auditor in ensuring that all potential material misstatements are captured; now the auditor is at the completion stage, he compares all misstatements brought to the error schedule against overall materiality.)

Misstatements Requiring Adjustment

Qualitative factors must also be taken into account when posting adjustments, for example classification errors which, if not rectified, could be in contravention of a financial reporting standard (e.g. mis-classification of goods for resale as fixed assets is in contravention of IAS 2). A discussion is held with management regarding the posting of adjustments to

---

[1] Discussing ISA (UK and Ireland) 320 *Materiality in Planning and Performing and Audit.*

the accounts and, if the client refuses to adjust, the auditor must consider the effect on the auditor's report.

Set out below are **examples** of reasons why adjustments may be required:

- a mistake in gathering or processing information from which the financial statements are prepared;
- the exclusion of an amount or disclosure, e.g. if a new asset was purchased during the year and not included in the **fixed asset register**;
- an incorrect accounting estimate arising from overlooking or clearly misinterpreting facts, e.g. if the accountant has omitted significant details that may impact on a provision in the accounts; or
- management's judgements concerning accounting estimates or the selection and application of accounting policies, which the auditor considers unreasonable or inappropriate.

An adjustment in itself may not be material; however, a culmination of misstatements noted by the auditor could result in an overall material difference. The auditor should record a summary of errors in his working papers during the course of the audit. During the final phase of the audit, he must conclude on the cumulative effect of misstatements and the impact they have on the financial statements of the entity. An example of a summary of errors is set out below at **Figure 18.1**.

Example 18.1 below is a worked example of the preparation of the **summary of unadjusted differences** and the auditor's review of same. This example goes through the types of misstatement that the auditor may have come across throughout the performance of the audit. Remember: misstatements will have been taken to the summary of unadjusted differences, whether material or not, so that the auditor can consider if the aggregate effect of misstatements constitutes an overall material misstatement in the financial statements. He does so by preparing a summary of misstatements found and assessing their aggregate impact on the financial statements.

FIGURE 18.1: FORMAT OF SUMMARY OF ERRORS ('ERROR SCHEDULE')

		Adjusted (Yes/No)	Statement of Financial Position		Statement of Comprehensive Income	
			Dr €	Cr €	Dr €	Cr €
Dr	Capital Expense				X	
Cr	Fixed Assets			X		
(being the write off of incorrectly capitalised assets).						

EXAMPLE 18.1: EVALUATION OF MISSTATEMENTS BROUGHT TO THE SUMMARY OF UNADJUSTED DIFFERENCES

It is May 2013 and you are auditing Rapid Ltd for year ended 31 December 2012. Rapid Ltd is a logistics company based in the Republic of Ireland but who distribute throughout Europe. You have asked a member of the audit team to compile a list of all issues noted. The following is what you have been provided with:

- The bad debt provision provided by the directors is a general provision of €100,000 relating to all debtors greater than 90+ days, plus two specific provisions relating to Chairs.com and Sofa Express Ltd for €25,000 and €30,000 respectively. The general provision has been tested as adequate; however, your junior heard on the radio on his way to work this morning that Sofa Express have gone into liquidation with insufficient funds to pay creditors. Sofa Express Ltd owed €75,000 at 31 December 2012 and has paid €15,000 year-to-date 2013. The dispute with respect to Chairs.com, which relates to damage of property while being delivered costing €25,000, is on going.
- On auditing depreciation, it was noted that it was understated by €100,000.
- The solicitor's confirmation letter (which is covered under ISA 505 *External Confirmations*) returned from the solicitor outlines the likely value of a claim relating to an employee accident to be €75,000; the client's accounts, however, have no provision relating to this.
- A payment of €150,000 made to a supplier in 2013 was recorded as being made in 2012.
- Cut-off tests revealed that a delivery that occurred in 2013, valued at €15,000, was included in the revenue for 2012. The client, however, has adjusted for this.

Requirement (a): Prepare an error schedule summarising all of the unadjusted errors noted throughout the audit.

The error schedule is set out below in a manner that shows the adjustments required to the statement of financial position (SOFP) and the statement of comprehensive income (SOCI), which facilitates a more effective and accurate review of whether the financial statements are materially misstated.

	Statement of Financial Position		Statement of Comprehensive Income	
	Dr	Cr	Dr	Cr
	€	€	€	€
Dr Bad debt provision movement in SOCI			30,000	
Cr Bad debt provision on SOFP		30,000		

Being correction of bad debt provision understatement				
Dr Depreciation charge on the SOCI			100,000	
Cr Depreciation on SOFP		100,000		
Being correction of depreciation understatement				
Dr Claims provision movement SOCI			75,000	
Cr Provision for legal claims on SOFP		75,000		
Being correction of legal claim understatement				
Dr Bank (SOFP)	150,000			
Cr Payables (SOFP)		150,000		
Being correction classification error on bank and payables				
Summary	150,000	355,000	205,000	-
Net Impact on the SOCI				**205,000 (Dr)**

(*Note*: the cut-off error was adjusted by the client and does not get brought to the error schedule.)

Workings					€
1	Beds Express				
	Owed at year end				75,000
	Paid				15,000
	Still outstanding at time of liquidation				60,000
	Required bad debt provision				60,000
	Actual bad debt provision				30,000
	Understatement of bad debt provision				**30,000**

Requirement (b): Considering that overall materiality is €270,000, are these accounts materiality misstated?

Yes, these accounts are materially misstated. While the statement of comprehensive income remains under the €270,000 overall materiality, the liabilities on the statement of financial position in aggregate are €355,000 understated. Errors must be considered both individually and in aggregate. While no one error is material, when all are considered together, a material error exists.

Requirement (c): If the client were to amend the classification error of €150,000 between payables and bank, would these financial statements be materially misstated?

No, correcting this error would result in the aggregate error being as follows:

	Statement of Financial Position		Statement of Comprehensive Income	
	Dr	Cr	Dr	Cr
	€	€	€	€
Summary	–	205,000	205,000	–
Net Impact on the SOCI		205,000	205,000	

This means that a material misstatement would not exist within any individual account balance or when considered in aggregate if this adjustment is made.

In conclusion, the auditor must document the significance and severity of the misstatements. The documentation of a **summary of errors** allows the auditor to consider the **cumulative effect of the errors** and the impact they have on the financial statements. Remember: the misstatements listed are not necessarily individually material but may be material when aggregated with other misstatements. At the point of completion, the auditor must conclude on the cumulative effect of the errors and consider whether, collectively, the errors will have a material impact on the financial statements. Where *unadjusted* material misstatements exist, the auditor should consider the implications for his report (see **Chapter 19**).

Should management decide not to adjust for material errors, the auditor should seek a written representation from **those charged with governance** explaining their reasons for non-adjustment and that they believe the uncorrected misstatements are immaterial to the financial statements.

18.4 SUBSEQUENT EVENTS REVIEW

Introduction

The auditor must consider whether events that occur after the reporting date have an impact on the financial statements. The auditor's responsibility with regard to subsequent events varies depending on the timing of the event.

ISA (UK and Ireland) 560 *Subsequent Events* ('ISA 560') defines **subsequent events** as:
    "Events occurring between the date of the financial statements and the date of the auditor's report, and facts that become known to the auditor after the date of the auditor's report."

The standard also states that:
    "Financial statements may be affected by certain events that occur after the date of the financial statements. Many financial reporting frameworks specifically refer to

such events. Such financial reporting frameworks ordinarily identify two types of events:

(a) Those that provide evidence of conditions that existed at the date of the financial statements.

(b) Those that provide evidence of conditions that arose after the date of the financial statements." (IAS 10, para 3)

IAS 10 *Events After the Reporting Period* outlines conditions pertaining to adjusting or non-adjusting events. It also states that, ideally, the date the financial statements are signed by the board of directors and the date the auditor's report is issued should be the same date.

The auditor must ensure that there are no events post year end that will materially impact the financial statements:

"The auditor shall perform audit procedures designed to obtain sufficient appropriate audit evidence that all events occurring between the date of the financial statements and the date of the auditor's report that require adjustment of, or disclosure in, the financial statements are appropriately reflected in those financial statements." (ISA 560, para 6)

Table 18.1 below outlines the key dates defined by ISA 560, and shows that the auditor's responsibilities regarding the detection, review and consideration of subsequent events varies depending on the timing of the event. The time periods and auditor obligations are summarised in the Table and then discussed further in detail below.

Let us now consider the approach of the auditor within each time period.

1. Events Occurring between Date of the Financial Statements and Date of the Auditor's Report

The auditor has an active role in understanding management's approach to identifying **subsequent events** as well as a role to perform audit procedures in order to identify subsequent events. In doing so the auditor should:

- obtain an understanding of any procedures management have established to ensure that subsequent events are identified;
- inquire of management as to whether subsequent events have occurred which might affect the financial statements;
- read the minutes of meetings held after the date of financial statements and inquire about matters discussed at any such meetings for which minutes are not available;
- read the interim financial statements to see if there are any indications of events that may impact the year-end financial statements (e.g. a large customer balance write-off).

TABLE 18.1: DEFINITION OF 'KEY DATES' AS PER ISA 560

Key Date	Date Definition	Responsibility of Auditor *Between* these Dates
Time Period 1		
Date of the financial statements	The date of the end of the latest period covered by the financial statements.	
Date of approval of the financial statements	The date on which all the statements that comprise the financial statements, including related notes, have been prepared and those with the recognised authority have asserted that they have taken responsibility for those financial statements.	**Events occurring between date of financial statements and date of auditor's report:** the auditor has an active role in understanding management's approach to identifying subsequent events, as well as a role to perform audit procedures in order to identify subsequent events.
Time Period 2		
Date of the auditor's report	The date the auditor signs the report on the financial statements in accordance with ISA 700.	**Events after the date of the auditor's report but before the date the financial statements are issued:** the auditor need only consider the impact of facts/events that become known to him (i.e. he does not have any obligation to perform further audit procedures regarding subsequent events).
Date the financial statements are issued	The date that the auditor's report and audited financial statements are made available to third parties.	
Time Period 3		

After the financial statements have been issued: the auditor need only consider the impact of facts/events that become known to him (i.e. he does not have any obligation to perform further audit procedures regarding subsequent events).

2. Events after the Date of the Auditor's Report but before the Date the Financial Statements are Issued

The auditor need only consider the impact of facts/events that become *known* to him subsequence to the date of the auditor's report (i.e. he does not have any other obligation to perform further audit procedures regarding subsequent events). If an event/fact becomes known that would have resulted in a modified audit opinion, then the auditor should:

- discuss it with management;
- determine if the financial statements should be amended;
- inquire if management intend to amend the misstatement deriving from the subsequent event:
  - if an amendment is made, it should be restricted to the subsequent event and the auditor should perform audit procedures to gain **sufficient appropriate audit evidence** on the amendment and issue a new report if necessary;
  - if no amendment is made by the management, the auditor instructs management not to issue the financial statements in their present form and includes a modified opinion reports (i.e. qualifying his opinion); or
  - if no amendment is made and the auditor's instruction to management not to issue the financial statements is ignored, the auditor will then take appropriate action to prevent reliance on the auditor's report.

3. After the Financial Statements have been Issued

After the financial statements have been issued, the auditor has no obligation to perform any audit procedures regarding such financial statements.

If, however, the auditor becomes aware of an event that would have required an amendment to the financial statements, he should discuss the issue with management and inquire how they intend to address it. If the financial statements are amended and reissued, the auditor shall perform audit procedures on the amendment to satisfy himself that the audit report is still appropriate and, if it is not, issue an amended audit report.

If no amendment is made to the financial statements by the management, the auditor should seek to prevent reliance on the auditor's report.

Adjusting and Non-adjusting Events

Once the auditor determines that an event has taken place subsequent to the date of the financial statements, he needs to consider if it is an adjusting or non-adjusting event. This will determine whether or not a misstatement exists in the financial statements.

Adjusting events provide evidence of conditions that existed at the year-end date and allow a more accurate valuation of balances and events at that date. These events must be reflected in the financial statements of the entity. Examples of such events are as follows:

- the settlement of a court case that confirms the entity has a present obligation at the reporting date;
- the receipt of information after the balance sheet date which indicates an asset was impaired at the balance sheet date;

- the determination after the balance sheet date of the cost of assets purchased or proceeds of assets sold before such balance sheet date;
- details of fraud or errors which mean that the financial statements are incorrect.

Non-adjusting events are not required to be reflected in the financial statements of the entity as they do not provide additional evidence of events that existed at the reporting date. However, there are many non-adjusting events that *do* need to be disclosed by way of note to the financial statements due to their materiality. For example:
- the discontinuing of an operation after the reporting date;
- major restructuring plans;
- a major business combination after the balance sheet date;
- an issue of shares after the balance sheet date.

(See IAS 10 *Events after the Reporting Period*, paras 21–22 for further examples.)

Audit Procedures to Identify Subsequent Events

Between the date of the financial statements and the date of signing of the auditor's report, the auditor has an active role in identifying subsequent events that may provide evidence of conditions that existed at the reporting date. This active role can be discharged by performing some of the following audit procedures:
- reading original signed minutes of meetings held by management, shareholders and those charged with governance;
- inquiring of the client's legal counsel;
- inquiring of management about the following:
  - new commitments or borrowings entered into;
  - major sales or acquisitions planned;
  - any increase in capital or debt instruments;
  - any assets appropriated or destroyed by fire, flood, etc.;
  - any developments in risk areas or where contingent liabilities were identified;
  - whether any events call into question the appropriateness of the accounting policies utilised;
- reviewing latest management accounts, budgets, cash flows, etc., for unusual trends;
- investigating risk areas and contingencies arising from the nature of the business;
- calculating the current cash position and comparing it to the overdraft limit and cash flow forecast and analysing movements since the year end;
- following up on any matters cleared tentatively or on the basis of inconclusive information during the detailed fieldwork;
- investigating unusual transactions occurring shortly before or after the year-end date;
- reviewing journal entries to ensure that material adjusting events have been properly processed;
- agreeing details of material non-adjusting events with the notes to the financial statements.

For any subsequent events that have been identified, the auditor should ensure that they have been appropriately disclosed and accounted for by management. If management are unwilling to amend the financial statements for the effect of a material and/or pervasive subsequent event, the auditor must consider the potential impact on their audit opinion. This will be discussed further in **Chapter 19**, 'Audit Reports'.

18.5 GOING CONCERN

Introduction

The going concern assumption focuses on the client entity being able to continue in business for the foreseeable future, without an intention to liquidate the entity or that there are no conditions that might not allow it to continue (e.g. a changing business environment or significant litigation that could impact on the future of the business).

As introduced in **Chapter 5,** ISA (UK and Ireland) 570 *Going Concern,* at paragraph 9, states that one of the objectives of the auditor is to "obtain sufficient appropriate audit evidence regarding the appropriateness of management's use of the going concern assumption in the preparation of the financial statements."

The primary responsibility for assessing the appropriateness of the **going concern** assumption (i.e. the basis on which the financial statements are prepared) rests with the directors (**those charged with governance**) of the entity. The auditor has a secondary responsibility in respect of the going concern assumption used in the preparation of the financial statements in that he must ensure the validity of management's assumptions. During the audit work conclusion stage, the auditor must reconsider and revise, if necessary, his initial assessment of the going concern basis for the preparation of the financial statements. It is recommended that there are early meetings between the management and the auditor to discuss the assessment of going concern and any relevant disclosures.

The going concern assumption is a fundamental principle in the preparation of the financial statements. As such, the auditor must ensure that the financial statements have been presented on a going concern basis only if assessments indicate that the entity will in fact continue in its present capacity for the foreseeable future (usually 12 months from the date of the Audit Report).

While going concern is considered initially at the planning stage, it is during the completion stage of the audit that the auditor makes a final decision on the going concern assumption of the entity. In order to conclude on whether the entity is a going concern, the auditor will consider:
*   the factors impacting the judgement of going concern;
*   the assessment period for going concern; and then
*   specific substantive audit procedures in assessment of the going concern assumption.

These are considered in turn below.

Factors Impacting the Judgement of Going Concern

The auditor should remain alert to factors that may raise any doubts over the entity's ability to continue as a going concern. According to ISA 570, paragraph 5, the following factors are relevant to the auditor's judgement in relation to going concern:

- The degree of uncertainty associated with the outcome of an event or condition increases significantly the further into the future a judgement is being made about the outcome of an event or condition.
- "The size and complexity of the entity, the nature and condition of its business, and the degree to which it is affected by external factors affect the judgment regarding the outcome of events or conditions."
- Any judgement about the future is based on information available at the time at which the judgement is made. Subsequent events can contradict a judgement which was reasonable at the time it was made.

During the course of the audit the **audit engagement team** will gain an understanding of the organisation, and through the performance of control and substantive procedures may obtain audit evidence which suggests that the entity may not be able to continue as a going concern. The engagement partner and engagement manager must ensure that the members of the engagement team are mindful of the factors outlined above so that they alert the engagement manager as to their existence. This will ensure that all factors are considered at a senior level within the engagement team.

Assessment Period for Going Concern

Generally, the auditor will assess going concern for a period from one year from the date of approval of the financial statements. Where the period under consideration is less than one year, the auditor should consider disclosing the following in the financial statements:
- the time period being considered by **management**, e.g. seven months; and
- the reasons why they believe the period being considered is appropriate.

Specific Substantive Audit Procedures Regarding Going Concern

Audit Procedure 1 – Considering Management's Assessment of Going Concern

It is the auditor's responsibility to consider the appropriateness of management's (or those charged with governance) going concern assumption in the preparation of the financial statements (ISA 570, para 6). This is usually done by:
- evaluating the means by which directors (including management) have satisfied themselves that the going concern basis of preparation is appropriate;
- judging the adequacy of the length of the period directors (including management) have assessed and the systems by which they have identified warnings of future risks and uncertainties;
- examining all appropriate audit evidence utilised in making the assumption, e.g. reviewing board minutes, cash flows, loan agreements, budgets, management accounts and other reports of recent activities, etc.;
- assessing the sensitivity of the audit evidence to events and conditions both inside and outside the control of the entity;
- concluding on whether or not the auditor is of the same opinion as the directors (including management) based on evidence available and reasonable assumptions about the outcome of future events;

- assessing the directors' (including management) plans for resolving any matters on the going concern assumption;
- assessing management's consideration of future periods.

Audit Procedure 2 – The Auditor's Assessment of Going Concern

In considering the entity's ability to continue as a going concern, the auditor should be mindful of the following:
- the auditor's knowledge of the client entity and its operating characteristics, e.g. its business, products, competitors, environment, etc.;
- the industry and the economic conditions which surround it;
- discussing with the client entity's principal officers their assessment of its ability to continue as a going concern;
- the possibility of any legal cases involving the entity;
- any undisclosed arrangements or events which may hinder the entity's ability to continue as a going concern;
- any events or conditions that, individually or collectively, may have an impact on the going concern of the entity.

Table 18.2 below provides examples of events or conditions that may indicate that an entity does not have the ability to continue as a going concern. These events or conditions are considered under three categories: Financial, Operational and Other.

TABLE 18.2: EXAMPLES OF EVENTS OR CONDITIONS THAT MAY HAVE
AN IMPACT ON THE GOING CONCERN STATUS OF AN ENTITY

Financial	Operational	Other
• Entity has not met necessary borrowing agreements.	• Loss of key management or staff.	• Non-compliance with capital or other statutory requirements.
• Indication of the withdrawal of financial support by creditors.	• Labour difficulties and a shortage of key suppliers.	• Changes in legislation or government policy which may adversely affect the business.
• Unable to pay creditors on the appropriate due dates.	• Loss of a major market or a loss of a key supplier.	
• Entity sells substantial non-current fixed assets when it has no intention of replacing the assets.	• Fundamental changes in the marketplace or in technology to which the entity cannot respond.	
• Non-compliance with capital or other statutory requirements.	• Excessive dependence on a few products where the market is depressed.	• Pending legal claims against the company which cannot be met.
• Legislative changes that will adversely impact the entity.		
• Inability to finance new products and product development.		
• Substantial operating losses.		

Audit Procedure 3 – Conclude on Going Concern Assumption

Finally, the auditor should prepare appropriate documentation which shows the **audit evidence and conclusions** reached on the going concern assumption and consider implications for the **audit report** based on circumstances presented to him, which could include:

1. The auditor concurs with management's assessment that the entity is a going concern – no modification of the audit opinion is required regarding going concern.
2. The auditor considers that there are uncertainties connected to the going concern assumption that will not be known until the occurrence of future events. However, he is satisfied that the all necessary provisions and disclosures are made based on the evidence available at the time of the fieldwork (this will be reassessed in line with his responsibilities connected with subsequent events as outlined in **Section 18.4** above). In this instance, the auditor will not qualify his opinion but may include an **emphasis of matter** paragraph in his report to draw attention to the disclosure note in the financial statements outlining the significance of the outcome of the future event. (Emphasis of matter is dealt with in detail in **Chapter 19**, Section 19.3.)
3. The auditor considers that there are uncertainties connected to the going concern assumption that will not be known until the occurrence of future events and is not satisfied that all necessary provisions and disclosures are made based on the evidence available at the time of the fieldwork (this will be reassessed in line with his responsibilities connected with subsequent events, as outlined in **Section 18.4** above). In this instance, the auditor disagrees with the financial statements and may issue a modified ('except for') opinion on the financial statements due to disagreement over the adequacy of disclosures.
4. The auditor disagrees with the going concern assumption and as such disagrees with the financial statements, and issues an **adverse opinion**. An adverse opinion is generally the outcome of a disagreement on going concern due to the gravity of the misstatement, be it financial or non-financial (i.e. disclosure-related).

A summary of the above discussion is included at **Table 18.3** below.

The auditor should also always include a note with respect to going concern in the **management representation letter**, which will require the directors to confirm their assumptions and, if necessary, their understanding of uncertain events and their possible impact.

Audit Procedure 4 – Subsequent Events and Going Concern Uncertainties

Where, under items 2. and 3. above, there are uncertain future events that may provide evidence of conditions which existed at the reporting date, then the auditor should, prior to the signing of the financial statements, consider if any further evidence is available that will provide a more accurate picture of necessary provisions and disclosures relating to going concern.

Concluding on a Going Concern Uncertainty Disclosure Note

When concluding on the adequacy of, or requirement for, a financial statement disclosure related to uncertainties as to the continued existence of the entity as a going concern, the auditor considers whether the financial statements:

- adequately describe the principal events or conditions that give rise to the significant doubt on the entity's ability to continue in operation and management's plans to deal with these events or conditions; and
- state clearly that there is a material uncertainty related to events or conditions which could cast significant doubt on the entity's ability to continue as a going concern and, therefore, that it may be unable to realise its assets and discharge its liabilities in the normal course of business (ISA 570, para 18).

Table 18.3 below summarises the types of opinion that the auditor may issue when concluding on going concern, taking into account the different types of concerns that may arise relating to going concern as well as considering management's response to those concerns.

(See **Chapter 19**, 'Audit Reports', for further details, and **Appendix 19.3**, which depicts the decision-making process undertaken by the auditor when considering the reporting implications for going concern.)

18.6 WRITTEN REPRESENTATIONS

Introduction

The auditor will hold a number of meetings with the management of the client entity throughout the audit, and during those meetings management will make a number of oral representations regarding various matters in connection with the financial statements. **Written representations** represent audit evidence that the management acknowledges its responsibility for the fair presentation of the financial statements in accordance with the applicable financial reporting framework and has approved the financial statements. Additionally, written representations allow the auditor to solidify the oral representations made by management by summarising these and having management sign the document acknowledging the accuracy of the statements made.

ISA (UK and Ireland) 580 *Written Representations*, at paragraph 6, requires the auditor to "obtain written representations from management and, where appropriate, those charged with governance that they believe that they have fulfilled their responsibility for the preparation of the financial statements and for the completeness of the information provided to the auditor".

Written representations are recognised as being an appropriate method of obtaining audit evidence. By receiving such evidence in writing, the auditor ensures that there is no conflict as to what was originally said and leaves little room for misinterpretation or misunderstanding.

TABLE 18.3: GOING CONCERN UNCERTAINTY AND AUDIT REPORTS

Types of Disclosure	Types of Audit Report
Adequate evidence exists regarding an '**uncertainty**' (*i.e. auditor does not conclude that entity is not a going concern, but that an uncertainty exists, which cannot be concluded upon right now, which may indicate that the entity will not continue in business*) concerning the going concern assumption. This uncertainty has been fully disclosed by management in the financial statements by way of a disclosure note.	An **unqualified opinion**, including an explanatory '**emphasis of matter**' paragraph in the 'basis of opinion' section.
Adequate evidence is available to the auditor, yet '**uncertainty**' exists over the going concern assumption, which is ***not*** fully disclosed by the directors in financial statements.	A **qualified opinion** of an 'except for' type, due to disagreement over adequacy of disclosures.
The directors have not fully considered the going concern assumption for at least one year following the approval of the financial statements.	If full disclosures of facts concerning the period under review are provided by the directors and the auditor has no concerns regarding going concern, then no reference to the matter is made in the audit report. If inadequate disclosures are made, then the period reviewed should be noted in the 'basis of opinion' section of the report, noting the period of going concern considered by the directors. The auditor report, however, will not be qualified unless the auditor disagrees that the client entity is a going concern.
Financial statements are found to be prepared on a going concern basis, however, audit evidence suggests that the entity is not a going concern.	An **adverse opinion** should be issued as the financial statements do not give a **true and fair** view.

These representations are an important source of evidence to the auditor as not only do they confirm oral representations previously given by management but they also complement other audit procedures, e.g. going concern review. Matters relating to representations made by management should be material in nature and should not deter the auditor from seeking all other evidence to support his conclusions (i.e. written representations are not a substitute for other evidence that the auditor could reasonably expect to be available).

Written representations do not take the place of other audit procedures available to auditors, but rather serve to corroborate other evidence (albeit it being recognised that in some instances written representations may be the only source of audit evidence available to the auditor).

The auditor should assess the reasonableness of the representations on material matters by:
- obtaining corroborative evidence from inside or outside the entity;
- assessing the representations for inconsistency with other evidence obtained; and
- considering whether those who made the representations can be expected to be well-informed on the matter.

General and Specific Representations

Written representations can be either general or specific. **General representations** are a matter of course (generic) and are included in all representation letters. The auditor may in some instances require additional **specific representations** to corroborate other audit evidence and ensure that evidence obtained is complete. Examples of both general and specific representations are included in **Table 18.4**, below.

Other Issues Relating to Written Representations

Preparation

It is generally the auditor who drafts the representations on behalf of the entity. However, the directors (and management) should be encouraged to participate in drafting the written representations. The auditor should not leave it until the end of the audit process to draft the **letter of representation**; he should instead note any matters that may warrant inclusion in the letter in his working papers throughout the audit work. The letter must be on the entity's own letterhead, signed and dated by an appropriate member of management and approved on a date as close as possible to that of the audit report, and after the post-balance sheet events (subsequent events – see above **Section 18.4**) review has been concluded.

Refusal by Management to Sign the Written Representations

In some circumstances, management may refuse to co-operate in providing the necessary written representations. In such cases, the auditor should discuss the matter further with the management or the audit committee. The integrity of management must be evaluated and the effect of their refusal to sign on the sufficiency and appropriateness of audit evidence should be considered. The auditor may conclude that he has not obtained all the information deemed necessary, which constitutes a **limitation of scope**. Should the client entity management refuse to sign any representations (including those in paragraphs 10 and 11 of ISA 580) then auditor would always issue a disclaimer of opinion.

TABLE 18.4: GENERAL AND SPECIFIC WRITTEN REPRESENTATIONS

General Representations

- All transactions have been recorded and are reflected in the financial statements.
- Management have fulfilled their responsibility for preparing and presenting the financial statements as set out in the audit engagement letter, and the financial statements are prepared and presented in accordance with the applicable financial reporting framework.
- Management have provided the auditor with all relevant books, records and information as agreed in the audit engagement letter and as required by the Companies Acts 1963–2012 (RoI) and Companies Act 2006 (UK/NI).
- Management acknowledges its responsibility for the design and implementation of internal control to prevent and detect error; and
- Management believes that the effects of those uncorrected misstatements found by the auditor during the audit are immaterial, both individually and in aggregate, to the financial statements taken as a whole. A summary of such items should be included in or attached to the written representations.
- All subsequent events to the approval of the financial statements requiring adjustment or disclosure have been adjusted or disclosed.
- All information relating to related-party relationships and transactions is complete and has been accounted for and disclosed.
- The selection and application of accounting policies is appropriate.

Specific Representations

- Any subsequent events are noted and their effect on the business.
- The basis of estimates or provisions where evidence to support the estimate or provision is not considered sufficient and the amounts included in the financial statements are based on management's judgements or averages.
- The goodwill of the entity is considered to be impaired and the value has been written down.
- A legal claim has been settled and management does not anticipate any further action in this instance.

Or any other specific representations as are relevant to the particular audit, e.g. inventory obsolescence or bad/doubtful debts provisions.

18.7 PROVISIONS, CONTINGENT LIABILITIES AND CONTINGENT ASSETS

At the final stage of the audit, the auditor must also give consideration to the **adequacy and completeness of provisions, contingent assets and contingent liabilities**. We will consider his approach in relation to each of these below.

Provisions

IAS 37 *Provisions, Contingent Liabilities and Contingent Assets* states that a provision should only be recognised when an entity has a present obligation, legal or constructive, as a result of a past event and it is probable that a transfer of economic benefits will be required to settle the obligation and a reliable estimate can be made of the amount of the obligation.

Essentially, a provision is recognised when the entity deems it likely to have to pay amounts as a result of an event that occurred prior to (or at) the reporting date. The entity must be able to reliably estimate the value of the amount to be transferred in the future. This amount is then included under liabilities within the statement of financial position.

The auditor will measure the provision by reference to the guidance above. Additionally, the auditor must ensure that the disclosure of a provision is adequate to allow the user of the financial statements understand:
• the nature of the obligation;
• the expected timing of any resulting transfers of economic benefits; and
• the uncertainty surrounding the amount and timing of any transfers.

When auditing the estimate of the provision provided by the entity, the auditor will refer to ISA (UK and Ireland) 540 *Auditing Accounting Estimates, including Fair Value Accounting Estimates, and Related Disclosures*. The requirements of the auditor under ISA 540 are discussed in **Chapter 6**, Section 6.9.

If the event does not meet the criteria for a provision (i.e. there is no present obligation, no probable transfers of economic benefits and it is not possible to evaluate the timing and amount of the obligation), it may, however, be classified as a **contingent liability**.

Contingent Liabilities sand Contingent Assets

A 'contingency' is a possible asset or liability that arises from past events and whose existence will be confirmed only by the occurrence or non-occurrence of one or more uncertain future events not wholly within the control of the entity.

Contingent liabilities are more of a concern for auditors than contingent assets because management may not be inclined to disclose them in the financial statements and because the events generally lie outside the accounting period. Examples of these include pending litigations, disputes, etc.

When performing his final audit procedures, the auditor should be searching for any undisclosed liabilities. The most common way to obtain such information is to:
- review subsequent and post-balance sheet events up to the date of approval of the financial statements;
- inquire of management of any unresolved legal disputes and obtain an estimate of claims to be paid (this information should also be disclosed in the **letter of representation**);
- inquire of the entity's legal counsel and banks;
- review the entity's solicitor's fees on their supplier account;
- review bank letters and other related correspondence;
- review original signed minutes of board and management meetings;
- review contracts and loan agreements entered into by the entity;
- review current and previous years' tax returns;
- request written confirmation from the entity's solicitors, etc., of any known existing, pending or expected contingent liabilities.

ISA (UK and Ireland) 501 *Audit Evidence – Specific Considerations for Selected Items,* at paragraph A21 states that:
> "direct communication with the entity's external legal counsel assists the auditor in obtaining sufficient appropriate audit evidence as to whether potentially material litigation and claims are known and management's estimates of the financial implications, including costs, are reasonable."

Having reviewed all evidence available, the auditor must assess whether or not a contingent liability or a contingent asset exists. The entity should not recognise a monetary amount in the statement of comprehensive income or the statement of financial position regarding a contingent asset or liability. As such, it is essential that the auditor ascertains the nature of matters with respect to management's treatment as a provision or contingent liability.

A matter subsequently treated as a contingent liability may be recognised as a provision only when:
- it can be reliably measured;
- it is probable the future event will occur; and
- the transfer of economic benefits is probable.

If none of these characteristics exists, the auditor must disclose the contingent liability, which must therefore be disclosed in the notes to the financial statements, providing the following information:
- an estimate of its financial effect;
- an indication of uncertainties relating to the amount or timing of the outflow of economic benefits; and
- the possibility of reimbursement.

If the uncertainty identified is adequately disclosed, an **unqualified audit report** should be issued. If the uncertainty identified is considered significant, the auditor should disclose such information in the '**emphasis of matter**' paragraph of his audit report without qualifying his audit opinion. However, where the auditor considers that the disclosure made by management is insufficient, he must qualify his opinion ('except for disagreement') or issue an adverse audit report. Again, this will be discussed further in **Chapter 19**, 'Audit Reports'.

18.8 FINAL REVIEW OF AUDIT WORKING PAPERS

Introduction

The file is now ready for review by the **audit engagement partner**. The partner examines the working papers and the information gathered over the course of the audit. The objective of the audit review is to evaluate the evidence obtained during the course of the audit and whether it constitutes '**sufficient appropriate audit evidence**', as well as evaluating the conclusions reached by the person preparing the working papers.

Whether "sufficient appropriate audit evidence has been obtained to support the conclusions reached and for the auditor's report to be issued" will depend on a number of factors:
- significance of the potential misstatement in the assertion and the likelihood of its having a material effect, individually or aggregated with other potential misstatements, on the financial statements;
- effectiveness of management's responses and controls to address the risks;
- experience gained during previous audits with respect to similar potential misstatements;
- results of audit procedures performed, including whether such audit procedures identified specific instances of fraud or error;
- source and reliability of the available information;
- persuasiveness of the audit evidence;
- understanding of the entity and its environment, including its internal control.

In reviewing the audit work, the partner thus ensures that:
- sufficient appropriate audit evidence has been obtained in each area of the audit process;
- the work performed by the auditor and the final financial statements are in compliance with statutory requirements (e.g. Companies Acts 1963–2012 (RoI), Companies Act 2006 (UK/NI)), with accounting and auditing standards (e.g. IASs/IFRSs, ISAs, etc.) and with other relevant regulations (e.g. the *UK Corporate Governance Code*);
- the nature, timing and extent of the audit procedures performed are in compliance with the applicable accounting reporting framework;
- the work completed by audit staff is accurate, thorough and in accordance with the audit programme;
- the judgements exercised by audit staff during the course of the audit were reasonable and appropriate and have been properly documented;
- all audit work has been completed in accordance with the conditions and terms specified in the **letter of engagement**;
- the audit staff have properly resolved any significant accounting, auditing and reporting questions raised during the audit;

- the audit work is properly performed, documented in working papers and supports the audit opinion (see **Chapter 19**);
- accounting policies adopted are in accordance with the applicable financial reporting framework, are appropriate to the entity and are applied consistently;
- the presentation of the final financial statements is appropriate in form, content and manner; and
- finally, the review should ensure that the audit working papers have been documented in accordance with the International Standards on Auditing and that the firm's quality control policies and procedures have been met (see the discussion on International Standard on Quality Control (UK and Ireland) 1 *Quality Control for Firms that Perform Audits and Reviews of Financial Statements, and other Assurance and Related Services Engagements* (ISQC 1) in **Chapter 2**, Section 2.8).

Paragraph 14 of ISA (UK and Ireland) 230 *Audit Documentation* notes that: "the auditor shall assemble the audit documentation in an audit file and complete the administrative process of assembling the final audit file on a timely basis after the date of the auditor's report". Paragraph 15 also states that: "after the assembly of the final file has been completed, the auditor should not delete or discard audit documentation before the end of its retention period".

Checklists are common practice for ensuring that all aspects of the financial statements are covered, not only by the engagement partner, but also by the audit staff and audit manager. Not only do they facilitate the review of the audit work performed, they act as evidence in showing a review has been carried out. The final analytical procedures and going concern analysis performed at the final phase of the audit will allow the auditor to make an informed conclusion on financial statements produced by the entity.

18.9 COMMUNICATION WITH THOSE CHARGED WITH GOVERNANCE

The final step the auditor should undertake before formulating his opinion is to communicate to the entity and to management any significant issues identified during the audit process which have impacted on the audit process and procedures (ISA (UK and Ireland) 260 *Communication with Those Charged with Governance*). These can include:

- difficulties in carrying out audit procedures, e.g. incomplete books and records (**limitation of scope**);
- views on accounting policies, estimates and financial statement disclosures;
- material unadjusted misstatements;
- summary of representations to be agreed by management;
- review of the going concern assumption and any related concerns;
- expected modifications to the audit report; or
- any fraudulent activities identified or non-compliance with regulations.

TABLE 18.5: COMMUNICATION OF AUDIT ISSUES

Level of Matter Identified	Communicating Body
Significant	Written and verbal communication to audit committee or governing body.
Less significant	Verbal discussion with management with authority to take appropriate action.

Table 18.5 above shows the reporting treatment of matters identified based on their level of significance.

The **management letter** is generally provided to **those charged with governance** at the end of the audit. A full discussion on management letters is included in **Chapter 8, 'Controls and Control Testing'**, at Section 8.9.

18.10 RELATED PARTIES

Another task at the final stage of the audit is concluding on related parties. The auditor pays particularly close attention to related parties due to the fact that fraud may be more easily committed through related parties. Additionally the opportunity for collusion is greater between related parties.

ISA (UK and Ireland) 550 *Related Parties* (ISA 550), paragraph 3, states that "the auditor has a responsibility to perform audit procedures to identify, assess and respond to the risks of material misstatement arising from the entity's failure to appropriately account for or disclose related party relationships, transactions or balances in accordance with the requirement of the framework".

Related party relationships arise due to the existence of a control relationship or a common control relationship between the client entity and another party. ISA 550, paragraph 10, offers a more extensive definition of what constitutes a related party.

During his risk assessment, discussed in **Chapter 7**, the auditor will have designed procedures to obtain information relevant to identifying the risks of material misstatement arising from related parties. In order to gain an understanding of related parties the auditor should: inquire of management; maintain alertness for related party information when reviewing records or documents; and share related party information with the engagement team to ensure all members are aware of which related party relationships exist.

Should the auditor, during the course of the audit, identify related parties not previously disclosed to him by management, this may indicate intentional concealment to hide instances of fraud. In such cases the auditor should:

- promptly communicate it to the engagement team;
- inform management and request that they identify all transactions and balances relating to the newly identified related party;

- inquire of management why the internal controls of the entity did not identify the related party;
- perform appropriate audit procedures on the newly identified related party;
- consider the risk that further unidentified related parties exist; and
- consider whether the omission by management is intentional or unintentional. If considered intentional the auditor should consider the implications for the audit.

Where the auditor identifies significant transactions and balances that are outside the normal course of business he should obtain the underlying contracts and/or agreements that support the transactions. He should then ensure that he understands the terms of the transactions therein and that they are appropriately accounted for and disclosed in the financial statements. If management account for and disclose related party transactions as occurring in the normal course of business (arm's length transaction) the auditor should obtain sufficient appropriate audit evidence to support this assertion.

When concluding on related party relationships, transactions and balances the auditor should conclude whether or not they have been appropriately accounted for and disclosed and ensure that they do not prevent the fair presentation of the financial statements. Finally the auditor should obtain written representations from management stating that they have disclosed all related party relationships and transactions of which they are aware and that they have been appropriately accounted for.

18.11 CONCLUSION

The auditor has now reached the audit reporting stage. He has completed the planning activities, performed controls assessment and testing, where applicable, concluded on all substantive testing and, finally, as discussed throughout this chapter, he has performed all concluding activities required to enable him to form an opinion on the financial statements.

The audit procedures discussed throughout this chapter cover areas not contained within specific financial cycle testing and are intended to allow the auditor to:
- Address issues that cannot be concluded on until the end of the audit, including:
  - concluding on going concern, for which he will have been gathering evidence throughout the audit;
  - satisfying himself that no subsequent events have occurred that need further substantive procedures; and
  - concluding on the classification of provisions, contingent assets and contingent liabilities.
- Reflect on the audit evidence collected through the:
  - performance of final analytical procedures;
  - performance of a final review of the working papers; and
  - evaluation of misstatements taken to the schedule of unadjusted errors in order to conclude on whether or not a material misstatement exists in the financial statements.
- Obtain written representations from management to confirm statements they have made both implicitly and explicitly.

Next, the auditor considers the implications of his conclusions for his **audit report** and this will be the focus of the next chapter, **Chapter 19**, 'Audit Reports'. The auditor must examine details of evidence obtained and ensure that the following are appropriately addressed:

1. disagreement over amount of an account value or relating to the adequacy of a disclosure;
2. limitation of scope, where evidence ought reasonably to be available to the auditor but is unavailable;
3. significant uncertainty, where the auditor is required to make a professional judgement based on evidence available.

Summary of Learning Objectives

Learning Objective 1 Have a clear understanding of final analytical procedures and their importance in the conclusion of an audit.

The auditor performs final analytical procedures in order to ensure that he fully understands all relationships and movements in the financial statements, and that he can comment on these relationships and movements, which he has supported by obtaining audit evidence throughout the audit.

Learning Objective 2 Be able to consider the misstatements taken to the schedule of unadjusted errors when concluding on whether the financial statements are materially misstated.

An adjustment in itself may not be material; however, a culmination of misstatements noted by the auditor could result in an overall material difference. The auditor should record a summary of errors in his working papers during the course of the audit. During the final phase of the audit the auditor must conclude on the cumulative effect of misstatements and the impact they have on the financial statements of the entity.

Learning Objective 3 Understand the auditor's responsibility regarding subsequent events for the different time periods highlighted in ISA (UK and Ireland) 560 *Subsequent Events*.

The auditor has an active role in identifying subsequent events up to the point that he signs the audit opinion. After the date of signing of the financial statements, the auditor has no active role in identifying adjusting subsequent events. However, should he become aware of events that impact on conditions that existed at the balance sheet date, then he needs to discuss with management whether the accounts are to be amended:
- If amended – the auditor reviews the amendment and confirms that his audit opinion remains appropriate.

- No amendment – the auditor disagrees with financial statements and issues modified/adverse audit opinion.

Learning Objective 4 Be able to discuss the requirements of the auditor regarding the assessment of the going concern assumption.

The primary responsibility for assessing the appropriateness of the going concern assumption in which the financial statements are prepared rests with management and the directors. The auditor has a secondary responsibility in respect of the going concern assumption used in the preparation of the financial statements in that he must ensure the validity of management's assumptions.

When concluding on the adequacy of or requirement of a financial statement disclosure related to uncertainties as to the continued existence of the entity, the auditor considers whether the financial statements:
- adequately describe the principal events or conditions that give rise to the significant doubt on the entity's ability to continue in operation and management's plans to deal with these events or conditions; and
- state clearly that there is a material uncertainty related to events or conditions that could cast significant doubt on the entity's ability to continue as a going concern and, therefore, that it may be unable to realise its assets and discharge its liabilities in the normal course of business (ISA 570, para 18).

Learning Objective 5 Understand the role that written representations play as well as their content.

ISA 580 requires the auditor to "request written representations from management with appropriate responsibilities for the financial statements and knowledge of the matters concerned".

Management representations are not a substitute for audit procedures (audit evidence) available to the auditor, but rather serve to corroborate such evidence and eliminate any misunderstandings in oral representations that may have been made by management.

Learning Objective 6 Understand the auditor's approach to reviewing the classification of provisions, contingent assets and contingent liabilities.

The client must ensure that matters are adequately classified as provisions or contingent liabilities and contingent assets, as outlined in IAS 37. A liability can only be recognised in the accounts if there is a probable transfer of economic benefits that can be reliably measured and is probable to occur.

Learning Objective 7 Understand the importance of the final review of the audit working papers.

Checklists are common practice in ensuring that all aspects of the financial statements are covered, not only by the reporting partner but also by the audit staff and audit manager. Not only do they facilitate the review of the audit work performed but they act as evidence in showing a review has been carried out.

Learning Objective 8 Be able to discuss the form of other reports directed at 'those charged with governance'.

Before formulating his opinion, the auditor is required to communicate to the entity and to management any significant issues identified during the audit process which impacted on the audit process and procedures (ISA (UK and Ireland) 260 *Communication with Those Charged with Governance*).

Learning objective 9 Understand the considerations of the auditor relating to related parties.

The auditor should aim to ensure that all related parties have been identified and appropriately accounted for and disclosed. If accounted for as 'arm's length transactions' then the auditor should obtain sufficient appropriate audit evidence to support this.

QUESTIONS

Self-test Questions

18.1   What are the benefits of performing final analytical procedures?

18.2   What key document is used by the auditor when evaluating the misstatements identified during the audit?

18.3   What is the purpose of the summary of unadjusted differences?

18.4   What are the three key time periods relevant to the auditor when considering subsequent events?

18.5   What are the auditor's responsibilities with regard to subsequent events occurring between the date of financial statements and date of the auditor's report?

18.6   Name five audit procedures the auditor might carry out to identify subsequent events.

18.7   What is meant by the term 'going concern'?

18.8   Name two financial, two operational and two other examples of events that may have an impact on the going concern of a client entity?

18.9   What is a written representation?

18.10 Name five things that the auditor might include in a written representation.

18.11 What is a contingent liability?

Review Questions

(See Suggested Solutions to Review Questions in **Appendix D**.)

Question 18.1

What audit procedures should normally be followed to obtain details of subsequent events?

Question 18.2

What is the period with which the auditor is normally concerned with regard to events after the reporting period?

Question 18.3

Is it possible for each individual item in financial statements to be fairly stated and for the financial statements as a whole to be misleading?

Question 18.4

Why, at the end of an audit, should an auditor review all audit working papers?

Question 18.5

How are final analytical review procedures useful to the auditor?

Question 18.6

You are the audit senior on Monitor Ltd ('Monitor') a security company. This is one of your firm's largest and most successful clients, with annual fee income (audit, tax and other services) in excess of €150,000 in each of the last three years.

The company, established in 1978, is owned 50:50 by Mike Greenwood and Dominic Clarke, who are the two directors of the company. You have been informed that Dominic Clarke is the brother-in-law of one of the tax partners in your firm, but that taxation services are provided by a different partner in the firm.

The 2012 audit fieldwork was completed one month ago, but the financial statements have not yet been approved by the directors due to the absence on leave of one of the directors. You understand that the financial statements are now due to be signed at the end of the week and arranged a meeting with the Financial Controller. At the meeting the Financial Controller informed you of the following matters:
- one of the customers covered by the doubtful debts provision has gone into liquidation. However, Monitor had ceased trading with this customer just after the year end and the debt due at the year end had been provided for in full;

- subsequent to the audit fieldwork, the company has changed all its banking arrangements to another bank, which was offering lower overdraft rates. You are informed that, in the current difficult trading environment, the company is undertaking a review of all of its significant contracts;
- the company is considering a sale and leaseback of its premises to raise finance to repay certain commitments;
- it is hoped to pay the final balance of 20% of the previous year's audit fee within the next two months, with the current year's fee to be paid when the re-financing is put in place.

Requirement Draft a file note, under the heading 'Subsequent Events Procedures', which outlines the matters that have come to your attention since the completion of the audit fieldwork. The note should address each of the following:
- further verification work required;
- any other procedures which, based upon the above information, you consider may need to be carried out.

Question 18.7

Your audit of Santa Ltd has uncovered the following:
1. Prepayments of €50,000 have been included within the trade payables balance in the trial balance, due to a mis-posting by the accountant.
2. Your payroll testing has identified bonus payments, in respect of the financial year, of €175,000 paid to staff subsequent to the year end. However, the year-end bonus accrual was only €25,000.
3. You have recalculated the depreciation charge as €364,000, which compares with the balance of €320,000 included in the accounts.
4. You were unable to agree the opening revenue reserves in the trial balance to the opening revenue reserves in the financial statements. This has been explained to you as being adjustments, which were processed through the prior year's financial statements, but which were posted into the accounting system in the current year.

The above matters have been brought to the attention of your client. However, no adjustments have been made to the accounts.

Requirement
(a) State what further audit work (if necessary) you would carry out in respect of each of the above matters.
(b) Draft the schedule of unadjusted differences (errors schedule) in respect of the above matters for review by the audit partner.
(c) Set out the factors that should be taken into account by the audit partner in his review of the schedule of unadjusted differences.

Question 18.8

It is May 2013 and you are auditing Express Ltd, for year ended 31 December 2012. Express Ltd is a logistics company based in the Republic of Ireland but distribute throughout Europe.

You are at the close of the audit and, as audit senior, you are performing a final review of all audit working papers and issues noted. While you review the working papers, you have asked a member of the audit team to compile a list of all issues noted. You have been provided with the following:

- The bad debt provision provided by the directors is a general provision of €100,000 relating to all debtors greater than 90+ days, plus two specific provisions relating to Sofas.com and Beds Express Ltd for €25,000 and €30,000 respectively. The general provision has been tested as adequate, however your junior heard on the radio on his way to work this morning that Beds Express Ltd has gone into liquidation with insufficient funds to pay creditors. Beds Express Ltd owed €75,000 at 31 December 2012 and has paid €15,000 year to date 2013. The dispute with respect to Sofas. com, which relates to damage of property while being delivered costing €25,000, is ongoing.
- On auditing depreciation, it was noted that it was understated by €100,000.
- The solicitor's letter returned outlines the likely value of a claim relating to an employee accident to be €75,000. The clients' accounts, however, have no provision relating to this.
- A payment of €150,000 made to a supplier in 2013 was recorded as being made in 2012.
- Cut-off tests revealed that a delivery that occurred in 2013, valued at €15,000, was included in revenue of 2012. The client, however, has adjusted for this.

During your review of the working papers you note that all assertions with respect to payables have been covered except completeness. You additionally note that while the calculations and assumptions for the revaluation of property has been adequately performed and found to be reasonable, you do not see any information with respect to the valuer.

Requirement

(a) Using the template provided below prepare an error schedule summarising all of the unadjusted errors noted throughout the audit.
(b) Considering that materiality is €270,000,
  (i)   are these accounts materially misstated?
  (ii) If the client did not want to make too many changes to the financial statements, what single adjustment could be made to bring the errors within materiality?
(c) Outline two other types of adjusting post balance sheet events (subsequent events).
(d) Name two matters that the auditor should confirm with respect to the valuer who provided a valuation on the property.

Matter	Statement of Financial Position		Statement of Comprehensive Income	
	Dr €	**Cr** €	**Dr** €	**Cr** €
[Journal Narrative]				

Question 18.9

(a) Going concern is one of the key principles on which a set of financial statements are based:

    (i) outline the directors' and auditor's responsibilities with respect to going concern. Your answer should include the basic steps required by the auditor under ISA (UK and Ireland) 570 *Going Concern*;

    (ii) list three financial **and** three operational events that may impact on the going concern assumption;

    (iii) if during an audit you note that there is a future event that could result in the company no longer being a going concern, what type of audit opinion would you issue:

        • where **full disclosure** of the event and its possible outcome is included in the financial statements?

        • where no disclosure of the event and its possible outcome is included in the financial statements?

(b) The completeness assertion is always the most difficult to prove for the auditor, particularly when it comes to provisions and contingent liabilities. Outline how the auditor might search for unrecorded liabilities.

APPENDIX 18.1: ILLUSTRATIVE REPRESENTATION LETTER[2]

[Entity's Letterhead]

(To Auditor)

(Date)

This representation letter is provided in connection with your audit of the financial statements of ABC Company for the year ended 31 December 20X2 for the purpose

---

[2] Source: based on Appendix 2 to ISA (UK and Ireland) 580 *Written Representations*.

of expressing an opinion as to whether the financial statements are presented fairly, in all material respects (or *give a true and fair view*), in accordance with International Financial Reporting Standards.

We confirm that, to the best of our knowledge and belief, having made such inquiries as we considered necessary for the purpose of appropriately informing ourselves:

Financial Statements

- We have fulfilled our responsibilities, as set out in the terms of the audit engagement dated [insert date], for the preparation of the financial statements in accordance with International Financial Reporting Standards; in particular the financial statements are fairly presented (or *give a true and fair view*) in accordance therewith.
- Significant assumptions used by us in making accounting estimates, including those measured at fair value, are reasonable. (ISA 540)
- Related-party relationships and transactions have been appropriately accounted for and disclosed in accordance with the requirements of International Financial Reporting Standards. (ISA 550)
- All events subsequent to the date of the financial statements and for which International Financial Reporting Standards require adjustment or disclosures have been adjusted or disclosed. (ISA 560)
- The effects of uncorrected misstatements are immaterial, both individually and in the aggregate, to the financial statements as a whole. A list of the uncorrected misstatements is attached to the representation letter. (ISA 450)
- [Any other matters that the auditor may consider appropriate (see paragraph A10 of ISA 580).]

Information Provided

- We have provided you with:
    - access to all information of which we are aware that is relevant to the preparation of the financial statements, such as records, documentation and other matters;
    - additional information that you have requested from us for the purpose of the audit; and
    - unrestricted access to persons within the entity from whom you determined it necessary to obtain audit evidence.
- All transactions have been recorded in the accounting records and are reflected in the financial statements.
- We have disclosed to you the results of our assessment of the risk that the financial statements may be materially misstated as a result of fraud. (ISA 240)
- We have disclosed to you all information in relation to fraud or suspected fraud that we are aware of and that affects the entity and involves:
    - management;
    - employees who have significant roles in internal control; or

- others where the fraud could have a material effect on the financial statements. (ISA 240)
- We have disclosed to you all information in relation to allegations of fraud, or suspected fraud, affecting the entity's financial statements communicated by employees, former employees, analysts, regulators or others. (ISA 240)
- We have disclosed to you all known instances of non-compliance or suspected non-compliance with laws and regulations whose effects should be considered when preparing financial statements. (ISA 250)
- We have disclosed to you the identity of the entity's related parties and all the related-party relationships and transactions of which we are aware. (ISA 550)
- [Any other matters that the auditor may consider necessary (see paragraph A11 of ISA 580).]

Management

19

AUDIT REPORTS

LEARNING OBJECTIVES

After studying this chapter you should:
1. be able to describe the principles underpinning the form and content of audit reports, with reference to the relevant standards and legislation;
2. be able to explain the different types of audit reports, including the impact of different types of opinion on the auditor's report itself.
3. be able to identify and assess typical scenarios in which audit reports might need to be modified.
4. understand the auditor's responsibility with regard to comparative information, other information and the directors' report included with the financial statements; and
5. understand the other issues relating to audit reports.

CHECKLIST OF RELEVANT STANDARDS

ISA (UK and Ireland) 450 Evaluation of Misstatements Identified During the Audit (ISA 450)

ISA (UK and Ireland) 570 *Going Concern* (ISA 570)

ISA (UK and Ireland) 700 *The Auditor's Report on Financial Statements* (Revised) (issued October 2012) (ISA 700)

ISA (UK and Ireland) 705 *Modifications to the Opinion in the Independent Auditor's Report* (Revised) (issued October 2012) (ISA 705)

ISA (UK and Ireland) 706 *Emphasis of Matter Paragraphs and Other Matter Paragraphs in the Independent Auditor's Report* (Revised) (issued October 2012) (ISA 706)

ISA (UK and Ireland) 710 *Comparative Information – Corresponding Figures and Comparative Financial Statements* (ISA 710)

ISA (UK and Ireland) 720 – Section A *The Auditor's Responsibilities Relating to Other Information in Documents Containing Audited Financial Statements* (ISA 720A)

ISA (UK and Ireland) 720 – Section B *The Auditor's Statutory Reporting Responsibility in Relation to Directors' Reports* (ISA 720B)

APB (FRC) Bulletin 2010/02 *Compendium of Illustrative Auditor's Reports on UK Private Sector Financial Statements for Periods Ended on or After 15 December 2010* (Revised) (APB (FRC) Bulletin 2010/02)

APB (FRC) Bulletin 1(I) *Compendium of Illustrative Auditor's Reports on Irish Financial Statements* (APB (FRC) Bulletin 1(I))

KEY TERMS AND DEFINITIONS IN THIS CHAPTER

Adverse Opinion   An adverse opinion is given when, due to an uncorrected disagreement on a material and pervasive matter, the auditor concludes that the financial statements do **not** give a **true and fair view**.

Disagreement   When audit evidence proves that there is a **material misstatement** in the financial statements and the directors will not make a correction.

Disclaimer Opinion   A **disclaimer opinion** is given when, due to a limitation in relation to a matter which is **material and pervasive**, the auditor cannot determine whether the financial statements give a true and fair view.

Emphasis of Matter Paragraph   This is a paragraph included in the auditor's report referring to a matter appropriately presented and disclosed in the financial statements that, in the auditor's judgement, is of such importance that it is fundamental to users' understanding of the financial statements.

Limitation of Scope   Inability to obtain sufficient appropriate information on which to conclude an opinion.

Modified Opinion   The auditor shall modify the opinion in the auditor's report when: 1. the auditor concludes that, based on the audit evidence obtained, the financial statements as a whole are not free from material misstatement; or 2. the auditor is unable to obtain sufficient appropriate audit evidence to conclude that the financial statements as a whole are free from material misstatement.

Other Matter Paragraph   "A paragraph included in the auditor's report that refers to a matter other than those presented or disclosed in the financial statements that, in the auditor's judgement, is relevant to users' understanding of the audit, the auditor's responsibilities or the auditor's report." (ISA 706, para 5(b))

Pervasive   A term used, in the context of **misstatements**, to describe the effects on the financial statements of misstatements or the possible effects on the financial statements of misstatements, if any, that are undetected due to an inability to obtain sufficient appropriate audit evidence.

Qualified Audit Opinion   Where either: 1. a material misstatement occurs due to disagreement; or 2. a limitation of scope has been imposed on a matter that is material but, while material, the matter is not pervasive and so a **qualified (except for) opinion** is issued (i.e. the auditor's opinion of the financial statements is that they give a true and fair view *except for* an isolated material matter).

Unqualified Opinion   A 'clean' audit opinion, i.e. the financial statements give a true and fair view.

19.1 INTRODUCTION

Chapter 19, 'Audit Reports' is very technical in content, but at the same time very logical. For a good understanding of the material it is essential to carefully study both the technical guidance and the examples given.

Initially we set the scene by examining the requirements of the Companies Acts 1963–2012, and the Companies Act 2006 that lay down mandatory conditions that must be met. We then consider the actual contents of an audit report, section by section, which is prescribed by ISA (UK and Ireland) 700 *The Auditor's Report on Financial Statements (Revised) (issued October 2012)* (ISA 700). Each section is fully discussed.

At this stage it is important to look at examples of actual audit reports so that the various aspects of the report's contents can be visualised. We therefore provide an example of a standard audit report for RoI and for UK/NI.

Technical complications may arise when the auditor has significant/material issues relating to the financial statements he is auditing. To help in gaining an understanding of the complications that may arise, we use decision trees dealing with, for example, types of audit opinion, to guide your thought process. We then provide examples of the audit opinions that deal with different significant/material circumstances. It is important to note that the auditor's opinion is on the current and comparative period information in the financial statements. Possible issues arising from this fact are discussed.

An important point to note, and one that is frequently confused, is the auditor's responsibility for reports which are included with the auditor's report and the audited financial statements but that the auditor is not reporting upon, e.g. the chairperson's report. ISA (UK and Ireland) 720 – Section A *The Auditor's Responsibilities Relating to Other Information in Documents Containing Audited Financial Statements* (ISA 720A) and ISA (UK and Ireland) 720 – Section B *The Auditor's Statutory Reporting Responsibility in Relation to Directors' Reports* (ISA 720B) deal with these responsibilities and they are discussed in this chapter.

Finally, the end product of the audit process is the auditor's report. Companies, ideally, would like an unqualified ('clean') audit report and for the vast majority of companies, this is the case. In certain circumstances, however, this may not be possible and a qualified audit report may be issued. A qualified audit report will only be issued after due consultation with the client entity's management and careful consideration by the auditor.

ISA 700 states, at paragraph 8:
"The auditor's report on the financial statements shall contain a clear written expression of opinion on the financial statements taken as a whole."

The auditor's primary task is to report to the shareholders on the truth and fairness of the financial statements prepared by the management of the entity.

The independent auditor's report, as discussed below, is the key end result from any audit engagement. It contains the auditor's opinion on the financial statements, an opinion that is based on the auditor's overall assessment and takes into account evidence gained during each phase of the audit process (as described in the earlier chapters of this textbook). The auditor's report is, in simple terms, the 'end product' of the audit engagement, to which users of the financial statements will look for assurance about the contents of an entity's financial statements.

The auditor can provide a number of different forms of opinion in his report, namely:
- an **unqualified opinion**, where the auditor is of the opinion that the financial statements show a true and fair view;
- a **modified opinion** is issued, where the auditor disagrees with a matter that gives rise to a material misstatement or where the scope of his work has been limited.

Audit reports are governed by a number of International Standards on Auditing for the UK and Ireland (ISAs), issued by the Financial Reporting Council (FRC), as well as by company law.

There are essentially six key international auditing standards specifically dedicated to audit reports. The first three of these ISAs deal with the format and opinion of the audit report and include:
- ISA (UK and Ireland) 700 *The Auditor's Report on Financial Statements (Revised) (issued October 2012)* (ISA 700);
- ISA (UK and Ireland) 705 *Modifications to the Opinion in the Independent Auditor's Report* (Revised) (issued October 2012) (ISA 705); and
- ISA (UK and Ireland) 706 *Emphasis of Matter Paragraphs and Other Matter Paragraphs in the Independent Auditor's Report (Revised) (issued October 2012)* (ISA 706).

The Republic of Ireland adopted the new ISA 700, ISA 705 and ISA 706 in 2012, resulting in their application to Irish audits for periods commencing on or after 1 October 2012. Therefore, from this date these standards will be applicable to both the UK and Ireland for the first time.

The last three remaining auditing standards are dedicated to the auditor's responsibility with respect to the comparative information, other information and the directors' report, and they are:

- ISA (UK and Ireland) 710 *Comparative Information – Corresponding Figures and Comparative Financial Statements* (ISA 710);
- ISA (UK and Ireland) 720 – Section A *The Auditor's Responsibilities Relating to Other Information in Documents Containing Audited Financial Statements* (ISA 720A); and
- ISA (UK and Ireland) 720 – Section B *The Auditor's Statutory Reporting Responsibility in Relation to Directors' Reports* (ISA 720B).

We will start our discussion with the requirements of company law and its impact on the auditor's report.

19.2 COMPANY LAW

In both the UK and the Republic of Ireland company law requires the auditor to provide an opinion as to whether the financial statements of the entity being audited have been prepared in accordance with the requirements of company law. Company law in both jurisdictions imposes similar requirements relating to the auditor, which include:
- the auditor shall carry out all audits with professional integrity;
- the auditor of a company shall make a report to its members and this shall be read at the annual general meeting (AGM);
- the auditor shall be entitled to attend and be heard at the AGM;
- the auditor has the right to access all books and records and any information or explanation that is necessary for the performance of his role (breach of this, such as making a false statement to an auditor, is an indictable offence);
- the auditor must specify the individual accounts subject to audit and the applicable financial reporting framework;
- the auditor shall state whether accounts have been prepared in accordance with the relevant company law;
- the auditor must include a statement with respect to the truth and fairness of the financial statements ('true and fair view'); and
- the auditor's report shall be signed and dated by the auditor (audit firm).

Company law also imposes more specific requirements with respect to the audit report and these are summarised in **Table 19.1** below. The Table considers the requirements of the Companies Acts in both jurisdictions as they relate to the auditor's report.

The Companies Acts requirements are quite similar in both jurisdictions in relation to: the adequacy of information obtained by the auditor; maintenance of proper books and

TABLE 19.1: COMPANY LAW REPORTING REQUIREMENTS
(REPUBLIC OF IRELAND AND NORTHERN IRELAND)

Republic of Ireland Companies Act 1963–2012 Other Matters Paragraph	Northern Ireland Companies Act 2006 (UK/NI) Other Matters Paragraph
If the auditor has obtained all the information and explanations which he considers necessary for the purposes of his audit.	If the auditor has obtained all the information and explanations which he considers necessary for the purposes of his audit.
If proper books of account have been kept by the entity.	Whether adequate accounting records have been kept.
If the financial statements are in agreement with the books of account.	If the financial statements are not in agreement with the accounting records (i.e. by exception).
Whether the information given in the directors' report is consistent with the financial statements.	N/A
If at the balance sheet date there exists a financial situation requiring the convening of an extraordinary general meeting.	N/A
If disclosures of directors' remuneration and transactions specified by law are not made – by exception in Other Matters paragraph.	If disclosures of directors' remuneration and transactions specified by law are not made – by exception in Other Matters paragraph.

accounts; adequacy of directors' remuneration disclosures; and whether the financial statements are in agreement with the books of account (although in the UK, the latter is by exception only). The Companies Acts in the Republic of Ireland also require the auditor to report on whether the information given in the directors' report is consistent with the financial statements and whether a situation exists that requires the convening of an extraordinary general meeting. In both jurisdictions instances of inadequacy of the directors' remuneration disclosures are required to be reported in the 'Other Matters' paragraph in the auditor's report.

The above discussion shows that the auditor needs to be mindful not only of the requirements contained within international standards on auditing but also of company law as it relates to the auditor's report. Company law is enforced by the Office of the Director of Corporate Enforcement (ODCE) in the Republic of Ireland (see http://www.odce.ie/), under UK company law that power is invested in the Department for Business Innovation and Skills (BIS), which does so through The Insolvency Service (see http://www.bis.gov.uk/insolvency/companies/company-investigation).)

19.3 BASIC CONTENTS OF THE AUDIT REPORT

Introduction

The auditing standards are prescriptive with respect to the contents of audit reports. ISA 700 establishes standards on the form and content of the auditor's report. **Figure 19.1** below demonstrates the broad framework imposed by the auditing standards and company law on the format and contents of audit reports. **Figure 19.1** is based on ISA 700, paragraphs 12–26, which list the basic elements that should appear in the auditor's independent audit report. All elements of this figure are essential requirements, including the title and addressee at the outset of the figure and the date, location and auditor's signature at the end. Each element is followed by a reference to where it is discussed in detail in the narrative below the figure.

FIGURE 19.1: OUTLINE OF AN AUDIT REPORT[1]

Title **(a)**

Addressee **(a)**

- Introductory Paragraph **(b)**

- Respective Responsibilities of Those Charged with Governance and Auditors **(c)**

- Scope of the Audit of the Financial Statements **(d)**

- Opinion on the Financial Statements **(e)**

- Opinion in Respect of an Additional Financial Reporting Framework **(f)**

- Requirement Specific to Public Sector Entities where an Opinion on Regularity is given (***not covered in this text***)

- Opinions on Other Matters **(g)**

Date of the Report
Auditor's Address

Auditor's Signature

---

[1] Source: based on ISA (UK and Ireland) 700 *The Auditor's Report on Financial Statements (Revised) (issued October 2012)*, paragraphs 12–26.

(a) Title and Addressee

The required title is 'Independent Auditor's Report'. Using the word 'independent' distinguishes the independent auditor's report from other reports issued and included with the financial statements.

The independent auditor's report, referred to here as the auditor's report, is usually addressed to the entity's shareholders (members) in both the UK and Ireland, as the audit is undertaken on their behalf.

(b) Introductory Paragraph

The introductory paragraph identifies the entity whose financial statements have been audited and:
• states that the financial statements have been audited;
• identifies the title of each of the financial statements that comprise the complete set of financial statements;
• refers to the summary of significant accounting policies and other explanatory notes; and
• specifies the date and period covered by the financial statements.

Where supplementary information is presented, the auditor needs to ensure it is either clearly covered by the **audit opinion** or clearly differentiated as not being covered.

(c) The Respective Responsibilities of those Charged with Governance and Auditors

It is important that the reader of the financial statements understands the respective responsibilities of those involved in the financial statements (i.e. management and the auditor). As such, the auditor under this paragraph outlines the responsibilities of both parties.

Within this paragraph of the audit report, ISA 700, at paragraph 15 requires:
"The auditor's report shall include a statement that those charged with governance are responsible for the preparation of the financial statements and a statement that the responsibility of the auditor is to audit and express an opinion on the financial statements in accordance with applicable legal requirements and International Standards on Auditing (UK and Ireland)."

The auditor must also state that he is required to comply with the Financial Reporting Council's (FRC's) Ethical Standards for Auditors (discussed throughout **Chapter 2**).

(d) Scope of the Audit of the Financial Statements

The auditor's report is required to describe the scope of the audit by stating that the audit was conducted in accordance with International Standards on Auditing (UK and Ireland). This outlines to the reader the regulatory environment used to determine the auditor's approach.

The auditor has three options with regard to the completion of this paragraph, he may:

1. cross-refer to the applicable version of a "Statement of the Scope of an Audit" that is maintained on the FRC website[2];
2. cross-refer to a "Statement of the Scope of an Audit" that is included elsewhere in the financial statements; or
3. include the actual wording of a statement of the scope of the audit of the financial statements (see **Examples 19.1** and **19.2** below).

(e) Opinion on the Financial Statements

Within the opinion paragraph the auditor must clearly state the financial reporting framework used to prepare the financial statements. The opinion paragraph must then clearly state whether, in the auditor's opinion, the financial statements give a true and fair view (in all material respects) in accordance with stated financial reporting framework. Once again, it should be noted that only matters material to the financial statements are considered by the auditor.

As stated, within this paragraph the auditor is required to "**Clearly state the auditor's opinion**". If the opinion is **unqualified**, the auditor must clearly state that "**the financial statements give a true and fair view**".

Additionally, the auditor must state whether the:

• financial statements are prepared in accordance with the Companies Acts 1963–2012 (for RoI); or
• financial statements have been properly prepared in accordance with the requirements of the Companies Act 2006 (for UK/NI).

(f) Opinion in Respect of an Additional Financial Reporting Framework

Should the auditor be engaged to express an opinion on the compliance of the financial statements with an additional financial reporting framework (e.g. IFRS as adopted by the European Union), then that second opinion shall be clearly separated from the first opinion under this heading.

(g) Opinions on Other Matters

Additionally, if the auditor is required to report on certain matters by exception (e.g. in the UK the auditor only makes reference to the financial statements' agreement with the accounting records if financial statements **are not** in agreement with accounting records, i.e. by exception), then these should also be included in a separate section and suitably concluded upon. ISA 706, paragraph 8 states that:

"If the auditor considers it necessary to communicate a matter other than those that are presented or disclosed in the financial statements that, in the auditor's judgement, is relevant to users' understanding of the audit, the auditor's responsibilities or the auditor's report and this is not prohibited by law or regulation, the auditor shall do so in a paragraph in the auditor's report, with the heading 'Other Matter'."

---

[2] www.frc.org.uk/audit-scope-ireland

Examples of other matters that might exist include:
- non-disclosure of certain items;
- inconsistencies between directors' report and financial statements;
- adequate accounting records have not been kept;
- returns adequate for the audit have not been received from branches not visited by the auditors;
- the company's individual accounts are not in agreement with the accounting records and returns; and
- certain disclosures of directors' remuneration specified by law are not made.

See the paragraphs called "Matters on which we are required to report by exception" in **Example 19.1** (Republic of Ireland) and **Example 19.2** (United Kingdom) below.

Illustrative Examples of a Standard Unqualified Audit Report

As outlined above, the form and content of an auditor's report is standard, as dictated by legislative and regulatory requirements. **Example 19.1** (Republic of Ireland) and **Example 19.2** (United Kingdom) are illustrative examples of standard 'Unqualified Audit Opinions'.

EXAMPLE 19.1: ILLUSTRATIVE AUDITOR'S REPORT (REPUBLIC OF IRELAND)[3]

INDEPENDENT AUDITOR'S REPORT TO THE MEMBERS OF LARGE COMPANY LIMITED

We have audited the financial statements of Large Company Limited for the year ended 31 December 2012, which comprise the Statement of Financial Position, the Statement of Comprehensive Income, the Statement of Cash Flows and the Statement of Changes in Equity and the related notes 1–35. The financial reporting framework that has been applied in their preparation is Irish law and International Financial Reporting Standards (IFRS) as adopted by the European Union.

This report is made solely to the company's members, as a body, in accordance with section 193 of the Companies Act 1990. Our audit work has been undertaken so that we might state to the company's members those matters we are required to state to them in an auditor's report and for no other purpose. To the fullest extent permitted by law, we do not accept or assume responsibility to anyone other than the company and company's members as a body, for our work, for this report, or for the opinions we have formed.

Respective Responsibilities of Directors and Auditor As explained more fully in the Statement of Directors' Responsibilities, the directors are responsible for the preparation of the financial statements giving a true and fair view. Our responsibility is to audit and express an opinion on the financial statements in accordance with applicable law and

---

[3] The Republic of Ireland example is based on APB Bulletin 1(I): *Compendium of Illustrative Auditors' Reports on Irish Financial Statements, Example 5*, and adapted to reflect a clean audit opinion for 'Large Company Limited' (see **Appendix C** of this textbook).

International Standards on Auditing (UK and Ireland). Those standards require us to comply with the Financial Reporting Council's Ethical Standards for Auditors.

Scope of the audit of the financial statements An audit involves obtaining evidence about the amounts and disclosures in the financial statements sufficient to give reasonable assurance that the financial statements are free from material misstatement, whether caused by fraud or error. This includes an assessment of: whether the accounting policies are appropriate to the company's circumstances and have been consistently applied and adequately disclosed; the reasonableness of significant accounting estimates made by the directors; and the overall presentation of the financial statements. In addition, we read all the financial and non-financial information in the Large Company Limited annual report to identify material inconsistencies with the audited financial statements. If we become aware of any apparent material misstatements or inconsistencies, we consider the implications for our report.

Opinion on financial statements In our opinion the financial statements:
- give a true and fair view, in accordance with IFRS as adopted by the European Union, of the state of the company's affairs as at 31 December 2012 and of its profit for the year then ended; and
- have been properly prepared in accordance with the requirements of the Companies Acts 1963–2012.

Separate opinion in relation to IFRS as issued by the IASB As explained in the financial statements in the statement of accounting policies under the 'Basis of Preparation' paragraph, the company, in addition to applying IFRS as adopted by the European Union, has also applied IFRS as issued by the International Accounting Standards Board (IASB).

In our opinion the financial statements comply with IFRS as issued by the IASB.

Opinions on other matters prescribed by the Companies Acts 1963–2012:
- We have obtained all the information and explanations which we consider necessary for the purposes of our audit.
- In our opinion, proper books of account have been kept by the company.
- The financial statements are in agreement with the books of account.
- In our opinion, the information given in the directors' report is consistent with the financial statements.
- The net assets of the company, as stated in the balance sheet, are more than half of the amount of its called-up share capital and, in our opinion, on that basis there did not exist at 31 December 2012 a financial situation which, under section 40(1) of the Companies (Amendment) Act 1983, would require the convening of an extraordinary general meeting of the company.

Matters on which we are required to report by exception We have nothing to report in respect of the provisions in the Companies Acts 1963–2012 which require us to report to you if, in our opinion, the disclosures of directors' remuneration and transactions specified by law are not made.

John Smith   **31/03/2013**   13 The Crescent, Dublin 2.

John Smith
for and on behalf of ABC & Co.

Example 19.2 now shows an illustrative example of a standard 'Unqualified Audit Opinion' (UK).

EXAMPLE 19.2: ILLUSTRATIVE AUDITOR'S REPORT (UK)[4]

INDEPENDENT AUDITOR'S REPORT TO THE MEMBERS OF LARGE COMPANY LIMITED

We have audited the financial statements of Large Company Limited for the year ended 31 December 2012, which comprise the Statement of Financial Position, the Statement of Comprehensive Income, the Statement of Cash Flows, the Statement of Changes in Equity and the related notes 1 to 35. The financial reporting framework that has been applied in their preparation is applicable law and International Financial Reporting Standards (IFRSs) as adopted by the European Union.

Respective responsibilities of directors and auditor

As explained more fully in the Statement of Directors' Responsibilities, the directors are responsible for the preparation of the financial statements and for being satisfied that they give a true and fair view. Our responsibility is to audit and express an opinion on the financial statements in accordance with applicable law and International Standards on Auditing (UK and Ireland). Those standards require us to comply with the Financial Reporting Council's Ethical Standards for Auditors.

Scope of the audit of the financial statements A description of the scope of an audit of financial statements is provided on the APB's website at www.frc.org.uk/apb/scope/private.cfm.

Opinion on financial statements In our opinion, the financial statements give a true and fair view of the state of the company's affairs as at 31 December 2012 and of its profit for the year then ended. They have been properly prepared in accordance with IFRSs as adopted by the European Union; and have been prepared in accordance with the requirements of the Companies Act 2006.

Separate opinion in relation to IFRSs as issued by the IASB As explained in the financial statements in the statement of accounting policies under 'Basis of Preparation' paragraph, the company in addition to applying IFRSs as adopted by the European Union, has also applied IFRSs as issued by the International Accounting Standards Board (IASB). In our opinion the financial statements comply with IFRSs as issued by the IASB.

Opinion on other matters prescribed by the Companies Act 2006 In our opinion: the information given in the Directors' Report for the financial year for which the financial statements are prepared is consistent with the financial statements.

---

[4] The UK example is based on APB Bulletin 2010/02 (Revised), *Compendium of Illustrative auditors' reports on UK private sector financial statements for periods ended on or after 15 December 2010, Example 4* and adapted to reflect a clean audit opinion for Large Company Limited (see **Appendix C** of this textbook).

Matters on which we are required to report by exception We have nothing to report in respect of the following:

Under the Companies Act 2006 we are required to report to you if, in our opinion:
- adequate accounting records have not been kept, or returns adequate for our audit have not been received from branches not visited by us; or
- the financial statements and the part of the Directors' Remuneration Report to be audited are not in agreement with the accounting records and returns; or
- certain disclosures of directors' remuneration specified by law are not made; or
- we have not received all the information and explanations we require for our audit.

John Smith   **31/03/2013**   13 The Estate, Belfast.

John Smith
for and on behalf of ABC & Co.

To review unqualified audit reports, please refer to:
- *Compendium of Illustrative Auditors' Reports on United Kingdom Private Sector Financial Statements for periods ended on or after 15 December 2010 (Revised), Examples 1-36);*[5]
- APB (FRC) Bulletin 1(I), *Compendium of Illustrative Auditors' Reports on Irish Financial Statements* (APB (FRC) Bulletin 1(I)), Examples 1–23.[6]

19.4 THE AUDIT OPINION

Introduction

In **Chapter 18**, the auditor performed his concluding procedures in order to conclude on his opinion. ISA 700, paragraphs 8–11, contain guidance on forming an audit opinion on the financial statements. Below we will consider the types of audit opinion that the auditor may reach.

There are essentially two types of opinion that an auditor can issue: '**modified**' and '**unqualified**'.
1. An unqualified opinion is a clean audit opinion, essentially stating that "the financial statements give a true and fair view".
2. A modified opinion indicates that a material misstatement exists (or could exist) in the financial statements, which has either arisen as a result of:
   (a) **disagreement**; or
   (b) **limitation of scope**.

---

[5] APB Bulletin 2010/02 *(Revised) Compendium of Illustrative auditors' reports on UK private sector financial statements for periods ended on or after 15 December 2010,* http://www.frc.co.uk/Our-Work/Publications/APB/Bulletin-2010-2-Compendium-of-Illustrative-Auditor.aspx.

[6] APB Bulletin 1(I): *Compendium of Illustrative Auditors' Reports on Irish Financial Statements* http://www.frc.co.uk/Our-Work/Publications/APB/Bulletin-1(I)-Compendium-of-Illustrative-Auditor-s.aspx

FIGURE 19.2: TYPES OF AUDIT OPINION

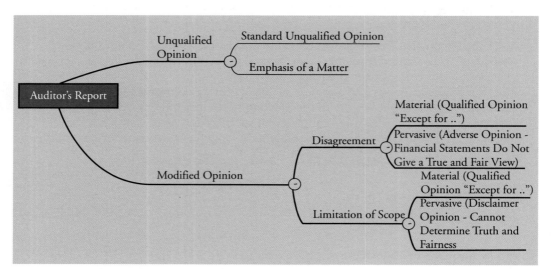

Figure 19.2 above outlines the types of audit opinion that can be issued by the auditor. These are dealt with in detail below.

Unqualified Opinion – Standard Unqualified Opinion

A standard unqualified opinion is the desired opinion of the audited entity, as it is a 'clean audit opinion': 'the financial statements give a true and fair view'. **Example 19.1** and **Example 19.2** above illustrate 'clean audit opinions' where no modifications are required. There are however two types of unqualified opinion. A standard unqualified opinion (which is unmodified) and a modified unqualified opinion. We will consider the latter below.

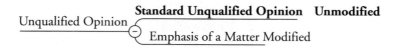

Unqualified Opinion – Emphasis of a Matter

An **emphasis of a matter** arises where, in the auditor's opinion, the matter in question is **not materially misstated** and is **adequately presented and disclosed** in the financial statements, but is of such significance that the attention of the users of the financial statements should be drawn to it. The auditor does not qualify his opinion with respect to the matter as he has gained sufficient appropriate audit evidence that the matter is not materially misstated and he is satisfied that it is adequately presented and disclosed in the financial statements.

Unqualified Opinion
  Standard Unqualified Opinion   Unmodified
  Emphasis of a Matter Modified

As outlined above, an **emphasis of a matter paragraph** is a paragraph included in the auditor's report that refers to a matter appropriately presented and disclosed in the financial statements that, in the auditor's judgement, is of such importance that it is **fundamental to users' understanding** of the financial statements.

The emphasis of a matter paragraph is included immediately after the **opinion paragraph** in the auditor's report and is headed 'Emphasis of Matter'. The paragraph should clearly state:

(a) that the auditor's **opinion is not qualified in respect of the matter** being emphasised; and

(b) make clear reference to the **location of the disclosure note** in the financial statements that makes reference to the significant matter being emphasised.

ISA 706, paragraph A1 provides the following as examples of matters which may give rise to an emphasis of matter paragraph:

• "An uncertainty relating to the future outcome of exceptional litigation or regulatory action.

• Early application (where permitted) of a new accounting standard (for example, a new International Financial Reporting Standard) that has a pervasive effect on the financial statements in advance of its effective date.

• A major catastrophe that has had, or continues to have, a significant effect on the entity's financial position."

An illustrative example is included at **Example 19.3** below, demonstrating how the 'Emphasis of Matter' paragraph would be included in the auditor's report. (This example is based on Note 34 to the financial statements of Large Company Limited, which can be found in **Appendix C** of this textbook.) As you can see, management has included a note relating to a contingent liability and we will assume that the auditor feels that this disclosure is adequate to address the issue. As such the auditor feels that the issue is adequately presented in the financial statements but feels that it is very important to the readers of the financial statements and therefore draws the users' attention to the note using the 'Emphasis of Matter' paragraph.

Should an adequate note not be presented in the financial statements, then the auditor will disagree with the treatment of the item and issue a modified opinion (i.e. he does not feel that the financial statements contain adequate disclosures and, on those grounds, he would issue a modified audit opinion in the form of a 'qualified opinion: except for'). These types of modifications are considered further below.

EXAMPLE 19.3: EXTRACT FROM THE REPORT OF THE INDEPENDENT AUDITOR
OF LARGE COMPANY LIMITED ILLUSTRATING 'EMPHASIS OF MATTER'

INDEPENDENT AUDITOR'S REPORT TO THE MEMBERS OF LARGE COMPANY LIMITED (EXTRACTS)

Opinion on financial statements (no change to that of an unqualified opinion).

Emphasis of Matter – Possible Outcome of a Lawsuit In forming our opinion on the financial statements, **which is not modified**, we have considered the adequacy of the disclosure made in Note 34 to the financial statements concerning the possible outcome of a lawsuit alleging the sale of faulty furniture resulting in an injury incurred on a customer's premises. The ultimate outcome of the matter cannot presently be determined, and no provision for any liability that may result has been made in the financial statements based on the advice of the company's solicitors that the action is unlikely to succeed. A successful outcome for the plaintiff, however, could cost up to €6 million, which is 8.2% of 2012 profit before tax.

Opinions on other matters prescribed by the Companies Acts 1963–2012 We have obtained all the ...

To review further illustrative examples of audit reports, including an emphasis of matter, please refer to:
- for Republic of Ireland Audit Reports: APB (FRC) Bulletin 1(I), Appendix 4, Examples 24 and 25;[7]
- for UK/Northern Ireland Audit Reports: APB (FRC) Bulletin 2010/02, Appendix 5, Examples 12 and 13;[8]
- see also, Chapter 8, Section 8.3 of Louise Kelly's, *Advanced Auditing and Assurance*.[9]

Modified Opinion

We have covered unqualified opinions above and now we will consider the types of modified opinion that result in qualifications. A modified opinion can be damaging to an audited entity as the readers are advised of an issue contained in the financial statements or pertaining to the auditor's ability to complete the audit. As such, normal assurance provided by the external auditor's report is not possible and could affect the decisions of the users of the financial statements.

---

[7] Bulletin 1(I) *Compendium of Illustrative Auditors' Reports on Irish Financial Statements.*
[8] *Compendium of Illustrative Auditors' Reports on United Kingdom Private Sector Financial Statements for periods ended on or after 15 December 2010 (Revised).*
[9] Chartered Accountants Ireland, 2013.

ISA 705 gives the auditor guidance on the expression of modified opinions on the financial statements. It aims to ensure that the auditor's assessment giving rise to the modified audit opinion is appropriate and that a modified opinion is expressed when:

(a) **disagreement** arises: "The auditor concludes, based on the audit evidence obtained, that the financial statements as a whole are not free from material misstatement" (ISA 705, para 4(a)); or

(b) there has been a **limitation of scope**: "The auditor is unable to obtain sufficient appropriate audit evidence to conclude that the financial statements as a whole are free from material misstatement." (ISA 705, para 4(b)).

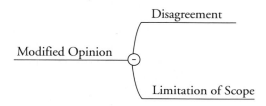

Once the auditor has determined that there is a **misstatement** (or a potential misstatement due to **limitation of scope**) and he concludes that the misstatement is **material**, he then needs to determine how material the misstatement is/could be. A material misstatement can either be:

1. material but not pervasive – while the item is material, it is **not** so material that the entire set of financial statements does not give a true and fair view; or

2. material and pervasive – the item is so material and pervasive that the entire set of financial statements does not give a true and fair view.

These are now considered in detail below.

ISA 705, paragraph 5(a) states that "pervasive effects on the financial statements are those that, in the auditor's judgement:

(i)   are not confined to specific elements, accounts or items of the financial statements" (e.g. efforts have been made to increase profit by applying incorrect cut-off to revenue, by understating accruals and by omission of contingent liabilities);

(ii)   "If so confined, represent or could represent a substantial proportion of the financial statements" (e.g. the value of the misstatement is 50% of profit); or

(iii)   "In relation to disclosures, are fundamental to users' understanding of the financial statements" (e.g. the directors have failed to include a note with respect to the possible outcome of a legal claim that, while not requiring provision in the accounts has the potential to result in a significant settlement that could pose cash flow problems for the entity and therefore impact on its ability to continue as a going concern).

Essentially, pervasive effects are not isolated, are well in excess of materiality or relate to the inadequacy of disclosures seen to be fundamental to the user of the financial statements. It is important that the auditor adequately assesses the level of materiality as being either material and not pervasive or material and pervasive as very different opinions are issued based on the assessed level of pervasiveness.

Once material, a modified opinion will be required; however, the level of materiality will further impact on the type of modification (see below). Also, to further support your understanding, refer to **Appendix 19.1** of this chapter, which illustrates the decision-making process of the auditor when deciding on the type of audit opinion that he will issue.

Modified Opinion – Disagreement

A **disagreement** arises when the auditor concludes that a material misstatement exists in the financial statements and the client entity is not willing to correct it.

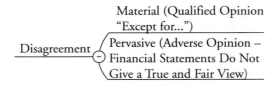

ISA (UK and Ireland) 450 *Evaluation of Misstatements Identified During the Audit* (ISA 450) defines a **misstatement** as:

"a difference between the amount, classification, presentation, or disclosure of a reported financial statement item and the amount, classification, presentation, or disclosure that is required for the item to be in accordance with the applicable financial reporting framework." (ISA 450, para 4(a))

ISA 705 outlines what circumstances might give rise to a material misstatement, including:

1. **The appropriateness of the selected accounting policies** The auditor needs to ask:
   (a) Are the selected accounting policies in line with applicable financial reporting framework?
   (b) Do the transactions and events that underlie the financial statements achieve fair presentation when selected accounting policies are applied?
   (c) Are changes in accounting policies in line with applicable financial reporting framework?
2. **The application of the selected accounting policies** The auditor needs to consider:
   (a) Are all transactions and events applied in line with selected accounting policies?
   (b) Have the accounting policies been applied consistently?
3. **The appropriateness or adequacy of disclosures in the financial statements** The auditor needs to ask:
   (a) Have all necessary disclosures been included in line with applicable financial reporting framework?
   (b) Are all disclosures that are included in the financial statements in line with applicable financial reporting framework?
   (c) Are the disclosures made sufficient to achieve fair presentation?

As outlined above once the auditor has determined that a disagreement has occurred, he must then determine:

1. if it is material; and
2. if it is material, how material is it?

Once he determines that it is material, the auditor must issue a **qualified opinion**. However, there are **two types of qualified opinion relating to disagreement** and the auditor determines which one to apply based on the level of materiality, as follows:

1. material but not pervasive – while the item is material, it is not so material that the entire set of financial statements does not give a true and fair view. In this case the auditor will issue a '**modified/qualified opinion, except for**'.
2. material and pervasive – the item is so material and pervasive that the entire set of financial statements does not give a true and fair view. In this case the auditor will issue a '**modified/adverse opinion**'.

Example 19.4 is a worked example of the auditor's decision in relation to a disagreement that arises. It assesses the auditor's consideration of the level of materiality to be applied and the form of the audit opinion. An extract of the auditor's report is shown below **Example 19.4**, to demonstrate how the audit opinion would impact on the form and content of the auditor's report.

EXAMPLE 19.4: ASSESSMENT OF LEVEL OF MATERIALITY AND
TYPE OF QUALIFICATION SCENARIO A: DISAGREEMENT …
MODIFICATION … 'QUALIFICATION EXCEPT FOR …'

Materiality for Large Company Limited is €3,642,500 (i.e. Overall Materiality determined in **Chapter 5**, Section 5.4).

Scenario A

A cut-off error occurred in relation to two transactions around the year end. The transactions related to the manufacture of luxury furniture for an overseas customer. According to the contract, the customer took rights to the furniture on delivery to the customer's premises in Japan. The transactions were recognised as sales when dispatched on 31 December 2012. The furniture was not signed for by the customer until arrival in Japan on 15 February 2013. The value of the transactions was €3,715,200. The balance of cut-off testing showed that all other transactions were appropriately accounted for in the correct accounting period.

What type of opinion will the auditor issue if the client does not correct the financial statements?

This gives rise to a **disagreement** as the treatment of these two transactions is not in line with IAS 18 *Revenue* because revenue on these two transactions is recognised before the transfer of significant risks and rewards to the buyer.

continued overleaf

The item is material because it exceeds the performance materiality of €3,642,500. However, it is not pervasive – it does not impact on the *entire* set of financial statements. One could say that '**the financial statements give a true and fair except for these two transactions**'.

The auditor would issue a '**qualification – except for**'.

The correction of this error would require the following journal entry:

	Dr €	Cr €
Revenue	3,715,200	
Receivables		3,715,200
VAT Payable		–
Income Tax		464,400
Tax Payable	464,400	
	4,179,600	4,179,600

Being correction of cut-off error

Note: there is no VAT on non-domestic revenue; assumes an income tax rate of 12.5%.

Below is an extract from the auditor's report (relative to the Republic of Ireland), which illustrates how the above example would be presented in the independent auditor's report.

Extract from Auditor's Report to reflect above Qualification (Republic of Ireland)

INDEPENDENT AUDITOR'S REPORT TO THE MEMBERS OF LARGE COMPANY LIMITED (EXTRACTS)

Basis for Qualified Opinion on Financial Statements

*Included in the revenue shown in the statement of comprehensive income is an amount of €3,715,200 relating to two transactions which occurred in 2013. This does not comply with IAS 18 Revenue in that, according to the contract, risks and rewards did not transfer to the buyer until delivery to the buyer's premises, which did not occur until February 2013. Accordingly, receivables and revenue should be reduced by €3,715,200 **and** tax should be reduced by €464,400, resulting in a reduction of profit and retained earnings of €3,250,800.*

Qualified Opinion on Financial Statements In our opinion, *except for the effects of the matter described in the 'Basis for Qualified Opinion' paragraph, the financial statements:*
* give a true and fair view of the state of the company's affairs as at 31 December 2012 and of its profit for the year then ended;

- have been properly prepared in accordance with International Financial Reporting Standards (IFRSs) as adopted by the European Union.
- have been prepared in accordance with the requirements of the Companies Act 1963–2012.

Opinions on Other Matters Prescribed by the Companies Acts 1963–2012
We have obtained all information and explanations, which ...

Matters on which we are required to report by exception (unchanged from unqualified report)

Below is an extract from the auditor's report (relative to the UK), which illustrates how the above example would be presented in the independent auditor's report.

Extract from Auditor's Report to Reflect above Qualification (NI/UK)

INDEPENDENT AUDITOR'S REPORT TO THE MEMBERS OF LARGE COMPANY LIMITED (EXTRACTS)

Basis for Qualified Opinion on Financial Statements Included in the revenue shown on the statement of comprehensive income is an amount of £3,715,200 relating to two transactions which occurred in 2013. This does not comply with IAS 18 *Revenue* in that, according to the contract, risks and rewards did not transfer to the buyer until delivery to the buyer's premises, which did not occur until February 2013. Accordingly, receivables and revenue should be reduced by £3,715,200 **and** tax should be reduced by £464,400, resulting in a reduction of profit and retained earnings of £3,250,800.

Qualified Opinion on Financial Statements In our opinion, except for the effects of the matter described in the 'Basis for Qualified Opinion' paragraph, the financial statements:
- give a true and fair view of the state of the company's affairs as at 31 December 2012 and of its profit for the year then ended;
- have been properly prepared in accordance with International Financial Reporting Standards (IFRSs) as adopted by the European Union;
- have been prepared in accordance with the requirements of the Companies Act 2006.

Opinions on Other Matters Prescribed by the Companies Act 2006
In our opinion the information given in the Directors' Report for the financial year for which the financial statements are prepared is consistent with the financial statements.

Matters on which we are Required to Report by Exception We have nothing to report in respect of ...

How to Read/Use the above Extracts from Independent Auditor's Reports

The above extracts demonstrate only those elements (paragraphs) of the auditor's report that change as a result of the modification, i.e. prior to the 'Basis of Qualified Opinion Paragraph' the report is the same as a standard unqualified (unmodified) audit opinion. Otherwise:

- the 'Basis of Opinion' and 'Opinion' paragraphs change to reflect the modified opinion';
- the 'Emphasis of Matter' paragraph, if required, will remain (i.e. issuing a modified (qualified) opinion does not negate the need to include the emphasis of matter paragraph if it is deemed required);
- 'Opinion on Other Matters prescribed by the Companies Acts' remain unchanged from the unqualified audit opinions; **and**
- the 'Other Matters' (report by exception) paragraph remains unchanged for Republic of Ireland but has a slight amendment for UK/NI.

Below at **Example 19.5**, we will now consider a similar example to that of **Example 19.4**, but where the facts lead to the auditor reaching an 'Adverse Opinion'. As outlined above an adverse opinion means that, in the auditor's opinion, the financial statements 'do not give a true and fair view'. An extract demonstrating the form and content of an adverse opinion is included directly below **Example 19.5** (in relation to the Republic of Ireland and the UK).

EXAMPLE 19.5: ASSESSMENT OF LEVEL OF MATERIALITY AND TYPE OF QUALIFICATION SCENARIO B: DISAGREEMENT … ADVERSE OPINION

Materiality for Large Company Limited is €3,642,500 (i.e. Overall Materiality determined in **Chapter 5**, Section 5.4).

Scenario B

Cut-off testing has revealed that the **client entity** applied inappropriate revenue recognition rules in that all furniture sales revenue was recognised on dispatch rather than on delivery (according to the contract with the customers, ownership passed on arrival of the furniture in the customer's premises). Seven transactions that occurred prior to the year end, while dispatched in 2012, did not arrive to customers until 2013. The value of these transactions was €77,982,800.

Additionally, in December the client commenced a new sales strategy with all domestic customers whereby the customers could buy on a sale-or-return basis. The sale-or-return term was for a period of 30 days. Five customers took up the offer and took delivery of the goods between 20 and 30 December 2012. The value of these transactions was €27,200,600.

In this scenario, do the transactions constitute a material but not pervasive situation or is it material and pervasive?

The above scenario would be considered pervasive due to the value of the error. The combined error is €105,183,400, which is 144% of profit, meaning its correction would result in a pre-tax loss of €32,333,400. In this instance, it is correct to say that **the financial statements do not give a true and fair view**.

The auditor would issue an **adverse opinion**.

The correction of this error would require the following journal entry:

	Dr €	Cr €
Revenue	105,183,400	
Receivables		110,895,526
VAT Payable	5,712,126	
Income Tax		13,147,925
Tax Payable	13,147,925	
	124,043,451	124,043,451

Being correction of incorrect application of revenue recognition rules under IAS 18

Note: VAT is assumed at a rate of 21% and applies only to domestic revenue; assumed income tax rate of 12.5%.

We will now consider how the above would be reflected in the auditor's report by way of an illustrative example relating to the Republic of Ireland.

Extract from Auditor's Report to Reflect above Qualification (Republic of Ireland)

INDEPENDENT AUDITOR'S REPORT TO THE MEMBERS OF LARGE COMPANY LIMITED

Basis for Adverse Opinion on Financial Statements *Incorrect revenue recognition has been applied to a number of transactions. Revenue of €77,982,000 was recognised for goods where risks and rewards had not yet transferred to the buyer, which is not in line with IAS 18 Revenue. A further €27,200,600 was recognised in relation to goods sold on a sale-or-return basis where the return period had not ceased prior to the year end; this is not in line with IAS 18. If revenue recognition had been applied according to IAS 18, the effect would have been to reduce receivables, VAT and income tax by €110,895,526, €5,712,126 and €13,147,925, respectively, on the Statement of Financial Position. The effect on the Statement of Comprehensive Income would result in a reduction of €105,183,400 and €13,147,925 to revenue and income tax, respectively, resulting in a reduction in profit for the year and retained earnings of €92,035,475.*

Adverse Opinion on financial statements *In our opinion, because of the significance of the matter described in the Basis for Adverse Opinion Paragraph, the financial statements do not give a true and fair view, in accordance with International Financial Reporting Standards (IFRSs) as adopted by the European Union, of the state of the company's affairs as at 31 December 2012 and of its profit for the year then ended.*

continued overleaf

In all other respects, in our opinion the financial statements have been properly prepared in accordance with the requirements of the Companies Acts 1963–2012.

Opinions on other matters prescribed by the Companies Acts 1963–2012
Notwithstanding our adverse opinion on the financial statements: We have obtained all the …

Matters on which we are Required to report by Exception We have nothing to report in respect of …

We will now consider how the above would be reflected in the auditor's report by way of an illustrative example relating to the UK.

Extract from Auditor's Report to Reflect above Qualification (UK/NI)

INDEPENDENT AUDITOR'S REPORT TO THE MEMBERS OF LARGE COMPANY LIMITED (EXTRACTS)

Basis for Adverse Opinion on Financial Statements *Incorrect revenue recognition has been applied to a number of transactions. Revenue of £77,982,000 was recognised for goods where risks and rewards had not yet transferred to the buyer, which is not in line with IAS 18 Revenue. A further £27,200,600 was recognised in relation to goods sold on a sale-or-return basis where the return period had not ceased prior to the year end; this is not in line with IAS 18. If revenue recognition had been applied according to IAS 18, the effect would have been to reduce receivables, VAT and income tax by £110,895,526, £5,712,126 and £13,147,925, respectively, on the Statement of Financial Position. The effect on the Statement of Comprehensive Income would result in a reduction of £105,183,400 and £13,147,925 to revenue and income tax, respectively, resulting in a reduction in profit for the year and retained earnings of £92,035,475.*

Adverse Opinion on financial statements *In our opinion, because of the significance of the matter described in the 'Basis for Adverse Opinion' paragraph, the financial statements do not give a true and fair view* of the company's affairs as at 31 December 2012 and of its profit for the year then ended, and have not been properly prepared in accordance with International Financial Reporting Standards (IFRSs) as adopted by the European Union.

In all other respects, in our opinion the financial statements have been properly prepared in accordance with the requirements of the Companies Acts 2006.

Emphasis of Matter – Possible Outcome of a Lawsuit In forming our opinion on the financial statements, ***which is modified but not with respect to this matter,*** …

Opinions on Other Matters Prescribed by the Companies Act 2006 *Notwithstanding our adverse opinion on the financial statements,* in our opinion the information given in the Directors' Report for the financial year for which the financial statements are prepared is consistent with the financial statements.

Matters on which we are Required to Report by Exception We have nothing to report in respect of …

For further review of modifications relating to 'disagreement', refer to:
- for Republic of Ireland Audit Reports: APB (FRC) Bulletin 1(I), Appendix 5, Examples 26, 27 and 28 and Appendix 6, Examples 31 and 32;[10]
- for UK/Northern Ireland Audit Reports: APB (FRC) Bulletin 2010/02, Appendix 13, Examples 37, 38 and 39 and Appendix 14, Examples 42 and 43;[11]
- see also, Chapter 8, Section 8.4.2 of Louise Kelly's, *Advanced Auditing and Assurance*.[12]

The above extracts demonstrate only the elements of the auditor's report that change as a result of the modification (i.e. prior to the 'Basis of Adverse Opinion on the Financial Statements' paragraph the report is the same as a standard unqualified (unmodified) audit opinion. The 'Basis of Opinion' and 'Opinion' paragraphs change. However the 'Emphasis of Matter' paragraph, if required, will remain.

How to Read/Use the above Extracts from Independent Auditor's Reports

The above extracts demonstrate only those elements of the auditor's report that change as a result of the modification, i.e. prior to the 'Basis of Qualified Opinion' paragraph the report is the same as a standard unqualified (unmodified) audit opinion. Otherwise:
- the 'Basis of Opinion' and 'Opinion' paragraphs change from that of an unqualified report, to reflect the modifications resulting from the disagreement;
- the 'Emphasis of Matter' paragraph, if required, will remain unchanged from that of an unqualified (modified) audit opinion;
- 'Opinion on Other Matters prescribed by the Companies Acts' has a slight amendment to reflect the fact that financial statements are not in line with books of accounts; and
- the 'Other Matters' (report by exception) paragraph remains unchanged for Republic of Ireland but has a slight amendment for Northern Ireland/UK.

Let us now summarise the specific inclusions by the auditor in the extracts above.

From the extracts from the independent auditor's report shown above in **Examples 19.4** and **19.5**, one can see:
- that the auditor is required to outline a clearly headed 'Opinion' paragraph' which immediately indicates to the reader whether the opinion is qualified and what form the qualification takes;
- an example of the financial effects and a brief description of the matter giving rise to the disagreement in the 'Basis for Qualified Opinion /Adverse Opinion' paragraph; and
- for omitted disclosures, include the **omitted information where practicable** (i.e. the information is available and not too **lengthy** for the auditor's report).

---

[10] APB (FRC) Bulletin 1(I) *Compendium of Illustrative Auditor's Reports on Irish Financial Statements*, http://www.frc.co.uk/Our-Work/Publications/APB/Bulletin-1(I)-Compendium-of-Illustrative-Auditor-s.aspx

[11] APB (FRC) Bulletin 2010/02, *Compendium of Illustrative Auditor's Reports on UK Private Sector Financial Statements for Periods Ended on or After 15 December 2010* (Revised), http://www.frc.co.uk/Our-Work/Publications/APB/Bulletin-2010-2-Compendium-of-Illustrative-Auditor.aspx

[12] Chartered Accountants Ireland, 2013.

> ***Note:*** even though the opinion was qualified/adverse in the scenarios above, this does not exclude the need to include an '**Emphasis of a Matter**' paragraph where required.

Before concluding on the area of disagreement, let us consider **Table 19.2** below, which provides further examples of situations that could give rise to a disagreement leading to a qualification (except for) or adverse opinion being issued by the auditor. The table considers disagreements at different materiality levels (material but not pervasive, material and pervasive) which give rise to the two types of opinion relating to disagreement.

TABLE 19.2: FURTHER EXAMPLES OF SITUATIONS THAT
COULD GIVE RISE TO DISAGREEMENT

Examples of Situations where Qualification (except for) or Adverse Opinions Could be Issued Relating to Disagreement	
Wording of report	**Examples where it might apply**
'Except for' – issues are material but not pervasive Adverse opinion	• Inadequate provision for doubtful debts. • Non-disclosure in accounts of going concern problems. • Disagreement over the value of some part of inventory. • Failure to comply with Companies Acts, accounting standards, etc., without acceptable reason. • Significant concern about the company's ability to continue as a going concern. • Significant uncertainties regarding the existence, ownership, valuation or recording of assets and liabilities.

Modified Opinion – Limitation of Scope

We have covered the first category of modified opinions above (i.e. disagreement) we will now consider the second category, being limitation of scope.

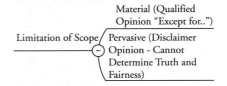

A **limitation of scope** (also referred to as a limitation on the scope of an audit) arises where the auditor fails to obtain sufficient appropriate audit evidence, which prevents him from concluding on the truth and fairness of a particular matter **or** on the truth and fairness of the entire set of financial statements. ISA 705, paragraph A8, outlines three instances which may give rise to a limitation of scope:

(a) "Circumstances beyond the control of the entity" (e.g. the entity's records got destroyed in a fire or the entity's controls are ineffective and the auditor determines that performing substantive procedures alone is not sufficient to conclude on an opinion);

(b) "Circumstances relating to the nature or timing of the auditor's work" (e.g. the auditor was appointed after the year-end date and was unable to attend the physical counting of inventories, no alternative audit procedures were available to the auditor); or

(c) "Limitations imposed by management" (e.g. management prevent the auditor from circularising the bank or customers).

The Requirement on the Auditor to Identify Alternative Audit Procedures

It is important to note at this point that where a limitation of scope is imposed, the auditor should seek to apply alternative audit procedures, and if other procedures are not considered adequate, he should consider the implications for his audit report. For example, where a limitation is imposed on the attendance at the physical inventory count (i.e. the entity refuses to allow the auditor to attend), then the auditor should attempt to count the stock at a later date and perform a **roll-back** to the year end, provided the controls in the organisation are such that this would be practicable and reliable. Limitations imposed by management may have other implications for the audit, such as the auditor's assessment of fraud risks and consideration of audit continuance (ISA 705, para A9).

Determining Level of Materiality

Once a limitation of scope arises, the auditor must then ask if the limitation of scope relates to a **material** matter. If not, then he will consider the possible **misstatement** impact when aggregated with other misstatements and, if it remains immaterial, then he will issue an **unqualified opinion**. If, however, the scope limitation is related to a material balance or transaction, then a **qualified opinion** will be issued by the auditor.

The level of materiality will determine what type of limitation of scope qualification to issue, as follows:

(a) material but not pervasive – while the item is material, it is not so material that the auditor must disclaim his opinion on the entire financial statements. In this case the auditor will issue a '**modified/qualified opinion, except for …**'; or

(b) material and pervasive – the item is so material and pervasive that the entire set of financial statements taken as a whole does not give a true and fair view. In this case, the auditor will issue a '**modified/disclaimer opinion**'.

A modified opinion that is 'qualified except for' means that except for the items which are material but not pervasive, the financial statements give a true and fair view. However, a modified opinion that is a 'disclaimer of opinion' (relating to material and pervasive matter(s)), represents the auditor's assessment of the situation as being that 'he is unable to form an opinion on the financial statements due to the limitation on the scope of the audit'. The auditor does not know if the financial statements give a true and fair view or not because he cannot carry out the work he deems necessary to form an opinion.

Let us consider limitation of scope by way of an example. **Example 19.6** first considers a matter where the auditor's scope is limited but where the matter in question is material but not pervasive, and so gives rise to a modified opinion in the form of a 'qualified opinion, except for'.

EXAMPLE 19.6: ASSESSMENT OF LEVEL OF MATERIALITY AND TYPE OF QUALIFICATION
SCENARIO A: LIMITATION OF SCOPE … MODIFIED/QUALIFIED OPINION 'EXCEPT FOR … '

Materiality for Large Company Limited is €3,642,500 (i.e. Overall Materiality determined in **Chapter 5,** Section 5.4).

Scenario A

The auditor was not made aware of one of the locations where a physical inventory count took place at 31 December 2012. The value of inventory held on the premises not attended by the auditor was €3,972,500. The auditor has exhausted other audit procedures but, due to a lack of controls, cannot carry out alternative procedures to determine the existence or condition and the quantity of inventory in question at the year end.

What type of opinion will the auditor issue?

This will give rise to a limitation of scope imposed by management, resulting in the auditor being unable to obtain **sufficient appropriate audit evidence** relating to the existence of an element of inventory at 31 December 2012.

The item is material because it exceeds the materiality of €3,642,500. However, it is not pervasive; it does not impact on the entire set of financial statements. One would say that the financial statements give a true and fair view **except for** this matter.

The auditor would issue an '**except for qualification**'.

Below is an illustrative extract of an auditor's report (relating to the Republic of Ireland), which demonstrates the form and content of the audit report that would be issued relating to the above example.

Extract from Auditor's Report to Reflect the above Qualification (Republic of Ireland)

INDEPENDENT AUDITOR'S REPORT TO THE MEMBERS OF LARGE COMPANY LIMITED (EXTRACTS)

Basis of Qualified Opinion on Financial Statements *With respect to a quantity of inventory having a carrying amount of €3,972,500, the audit evidence available to us was limited because we did not observe the physical inventory count as at 31 December 2012, since the management did not make us aware of its existence at the time of physical* *counting. Owing to the nature of the company's records, we were unable to obtain sufficient appropriate audit evidence regarding the inventory quantities and condition by using other audit procedures.*

Qualified Opinion on Financial Statements In our opinion, *except for the effects of the matter described in the 'Basis of Qualified Opinion' paragraph,* the financial statements:

- give a true and fair view, in accordance with IFRS as adopted by the European Union, of the state of the company's affairs as at 31 December 2012 and of its profit for the year then ended; and
- have been prepared in accordance with the requirements of the Companies Act 1963–2012.

Opinions on Other Matters Prescribed by the Companies Acts 1963–2012 *In respect solely of the limitation on our work relating to inventory, described above:*

- we have *not* obtained all the information an explanations that we consider necessary for the purpose of our audit; and
- *we were unable to determine whether proper books of account have been kept;*
- the financial statements are in agreement with the books of account;
- in our opinion, the information given in the directors' report is consistent with the financial statements; and
- the net assets of the company, as stated in the statement of financial position, are more than half of the amount of its called-up share capital and, in our opinion, on that basis there did not exist at 31 December 2012 a financial situation which, under section 40(1) of the Companies (Amendment) Act 1983, would require the convening of an extraordinary general meeting of the company.

Matters on which we are Required to Report by Exception We have nothing to report in respect of ...

Below is an illustrative extract of an auditor's report (relating to the UK) that demonstrates the form and content of the auditor's report that would be issued relating to the above example.

Extract from Auditor's Report to Reflect the above Qualification (UK)

INDEPENDENT AUDITOR'S REPORT TO THE MEMBERS OF LARGE COMPANY LIMITED (EXTRACTS)

Basis of Qualified Opinion on Financial Statements *With respect to a quantity of inventory having a carrying amount of £3,972,500 (being 8% of total carrying value of inventory of £49,774,000), the audit evidence available to us was limited because we did not observe the physical inventory count as at 31 December 2012, since the management did not make us aware of its existence at the time of physical counting. Owing to the nature of the*

continued overleaf

company's records, we were unable to obtain sufficient appropriate audit evidence regarding the inventory quantities and condition by using other audit procedures.

Qualified Opinion on Financial Statements In our opinion, *except for the effects of the matter described in the 'Basis of Qualified Opinion' paragraph,* the financial statements:
- give a true and fair view of the state of the company's affairs as at 31 December 2012 and of its profit for the year then ended;
- have been properly prepared in accordance with International Financial Reporting Standards (IFRSs) as adopted by the European Union; and
- have been prepared in accordance with the requirements of the Companies Act 2006.

Opinions on other matters prescribed by the Companies Act 2006
In our opinion the information given in the directors' report for the ...

Matters on which we are Required to Report by Exception *In respect solely of the limitation on our work relating to inventory described above:*
- *we have not obtained all the information and explanations that we considered necessary for the purpose of our audit; and*
- *we were unable to determine whether adequate accounting records had been kept.*

We have nothing to report in respect of ...

How to Read/Use the above Extracts from Independent Auditor's Reports

The above extracts demonstrate only those elements of the auditor's report that change as a result of the modification, i.e. prior to the 'Basis of Qualified Opinion' paragraph, the report is the same as a standard unqualified (unmodified) audit report. Otherwise:
- the 'Basis of Opinion' and 'Opinion' paragraphs change from that of the unqualified opinion, reflecting the modification resulting from the limitation of scope;
- the 'Emphasis of Matter' paragraph, if required, will remain unchanged from that of an unqualified (modified) opinion;
- the 'Opinion on Other Matters prescribed by the Companies Acts' paragraph remains unchanged; and
- the 'Other Matters' (report by exception) paragraph remains unchanged for the Republic of Ireland but has a slight amendment for the UK/NI.

Let us consider the meaning of 'limitation of scope' by way of an example. **Example 19.7** considers a matter where the auditor's scope is limited and the matter in question is material and pervasive and so gives rise to a modified opinion in the form of a 'Disclaimer of Opinion' paragraph.

EXAMPLE 19.7: ASSESSMENT OF LEVEL OF MATERIALITY AND TYPE OF
QUALIFICATION SCENARIO B: LIMITATION ON SCOPE … DISCLAIMER OPINION

Materiality for Large Company Limited is €3,642,500 (i.e. Overall Materiality determined in **Chapter 5**, Section 5.4).

Scenario B

Management of the client entity refused to allow the auditor to attend at the physical inventory count (inventory for Large Company Limited is €49,774,000) or to permit circularisation to confirm customer balances (trade receivables for Large Company Limited is €3,250,000). No explanations were provided by management for the imposed limitations.

What type of opinion will the auditor issue?

The above scenario gives rise to a **limitation of scope** imposed by management. The scenario would be considered as **pervasive** due to the level of the error and the fact that it is not confined to specific balances in the financial statements. The combined balance represents €53,024,000 (13%) of the Statement of Financial net asset Position.

The auditor would issue a 'disclaimer opinion' – **he cannot determine the truth and fairness of the financial statements due to the limitations imposed on audit scope.**

Below is an extract of the auditor's report which reflects the above example (relative to the Republic of Ireland).

Extract from Auditor's Report to Reflect the above Qualification (Republic of Ireland)

INDEPENDENT AUDITOR'S REPORT TO THE MEMBERS OF LARGE COMPANY LIMITED (EXTRACTS)

Respective Responsibilities of Directors and Auditor As explained more fully in the Directors' Responsibilities Statement page [XX], the directors are responsible for the preparation of the financial statements giving a true and fair view. Our responsibility is to audit and express an opinion on the financial statements in accordance with applicable law and International Standards on Auditing (UK and Ireland). Those standards require us to comply with the Financial Reporting Council's Ethical Standards for Auditors.

Because of the matters described in the 'Basis for Disclaimer of Opinion' paragraph, however, we were unable to obtain sufficient appropriate audit evidence to provide a basis for an audit opinion.

continued overleaf

Scope of the Audit of the Financial Statements (unchanged from unqualified)

Basis for Disclaimer of Opinion on Financial Statements *The audit evidence available to us was limited because we were unable to observe the counting of the physical inventory, having a carrying value of €49,774,000 and send confirmation letters to trade receivables having a carrying value of €3,250,000, due to limitations placed on the scope of our audit work by the directors of the company. As a result of this, we have been unable to obtain sufficient appropriate audit evidence concerning both inventory and trade receivables.*

Disclaimer Opinion on Financial Statements

Because of the significance of the matters described in the, Basis of Disclaimer Opinion on Financial Statements, paragraph, we have not been able to obtain sufficient appropriate audit evidence to provide a basis for an audit opinion. Accordingly, we do not express an opinion on the financial statements.

Opinions on Other Matters Prescribed by the Companies Acts 1963–2012 *Arising from the limitation of our work referred to above:*
- *we have not obtained all the information and explanations that we consider necessary for the purpose of our audit;*
- *we were unable to determine whether proper books of account have been kept; and*
- *we have been unable to form an opinion as to whether there did or did not exist at 31 December 2012 a financial situation which, under section 40(1) of the Companies Act 1983, would require the convening of an extraordinary general meeting of the company.*

Notwithstanding our disclaimer of an opinion on the financial statements:
- the financial statements are in agreement with the books of account; and
- in our opinion the information given in the Directors' Report is consistent with the financial statements.

Matters on which we are Required to Report by Exception We have nothing to report in respect of …

Below is an extract of the auditor's report, which reflects the above example (relative to the UK).

Extract from Auditor's Report to Reflect the above Qualification (UK/NI)

INDEPENDENT AUDITOR'S REPORT TO THE MEMBERS OF LARGE COMPANY LIMITED

Respective Responsibilities of Directors and Auditor As explained more fully in the Directors' Responsibilities Statement, page [XX], the directors are responsible for the preparation of the financial statements giving a true and fair view. Our responsibility is to audit and express an opinion on the financial statements in accordance with applicable law and International Standards on Auditing (UK and Ireland). Those standards require us to comply with the Financial Reporting Council's Ethical Standards for Auditors.

Because of the matters described in the 'Basis for Disclaimer of Opinion' paragraph below, however, we were unable to obtain sufficient appropriate audit evidence to provide a basis for an audit opinion.

Scope of the Audit of the Financial Statements (*no change – same as unqualified*)

Basis for Disclaimer of Opinion on Financial Statements *The audit evidence available to us was limited because we were unable to observe the counting of the physical inventory, having a carrying value of £49,774,000, and we were unable to send confirmation letters to trade receivables, having a carrying value of £3,250,000, due to limitations placed on the scope of our audit work by the directors of the company. As a result of this, we have been unable to obtain sufficient appropriate audit evidence concerning both inventory and trade receivables.*

Disclaimer Opinion on Financial Statements *Because of the significance of the matters described in the 'Basis of Disclaimer Opinion on Financial Statements' paragraph, we have not been able to obtain sufficient appropriate audit evidence to provide a basis for an audit opinion. Accordingly, we do not express an opinion on the financial statements.*

Emphasis of Matter – Possible Outcome of a Lawsuit In forming our opinion on the financial statements, *which is modified but not with respect to this matter,* ...

Opinions on Other Matters Prescribed by the Companies Act 2006 Notwithstanding our disclaimer of an opinion on the financial statements, in our opinion the information given in the Directors' Report for the financial year for which the financial statements are prepared is consistent with the financial statements.

Matters on which we are Required to Report by Exception *Arising from the limitation of our work referred to above:*
- *we have not obtained all the information and explanations that we consider necessary for the purpose of our audit; and*
- *we were unable to determine whether proper books of account have been kept.*

We have nothing to report in respect of the following matters where the Companies Act 2006 requires me to report to you if, in my opinion:

- returns adequate for my audit have not been received from branches not visited by me; or
- the financial statements are not in agreement with the accounting records and returns; or
- certain disclosures of directors' remuneration specified by law are not made.

Table 19.3 provides further examples of situations which could give rise to a limitation of scope, leading to an audit qualification or disclaimer of opinion being issued by the auditor. This table provides examples of limitation of scope relating to different levels of materiality and then shows which type of audit opinion would be issued by the auditor in each case.

TABLE 19.3: FURTHER EXAMPLES OF SITUATIONS WHERE
A LIMITATION OF SCOPE MAY ARISE

Examples of Situations where 'qualification except for' or 'disclaimer of opinion' relating to limitation of scope could arise	
Wording of Report	**Examples where it Might Apply**
'Except for' – limitation of scope	• Limited evidence available for cash purchases, which are material but not pervasive. • Some records lost due to accidental flooding.
Disclaimer of opinion – limitation of scope	• Appointed as auditors after year end and unable to attend physical inventory count where inventory is a material balance in the financial statements. • Directors deny access to information regarding significant claims against the company. • No cash flow forecasts/cash budgets prepared, so the going concern assumption cannot be considered.

For further review of modifications relating to limitation of scope, refer to:
• for Republic of Ireland Audit Reports: APB (FRC) Bulletin 1(I), Appendix 5, Examples 29 and 30, Appendix 7, Examples 33 and 34;[13]
• for UK/Northern Ireland Audit Reports: APB (FRC) Bulletin 2010/02, Appendix 13, Examples 40 and 41, and Appendix 15, Examples 44 and 45;[14]
• see also, Chapter 8, Section 8.4.2 of Louise Kelly's, *Advanced Auditing and Assurance*.[15]

Withdrawal from Engagement – Limitation of Scope

There may be instances where, due to a limitation of scope imposed, the auditor deems it necessary to withdraw from the engagement.

---

[13] Republic of Ireland Audit Reports – FRC Bulletin 1(I), *Compendium of Illustrative Auditor's Reports on Irish Financial Statements*, Appendix 5, Examples 29 and 30, Appendix 7, Examples 33 and 34. http://www.frc.co.uk/Our-Work/Publications/APB/Bulletin-1(I)-Compendium-of-Illustrative-Auditor-s.aspx

[14] UK/Northern Ireland Audit Reports – APB Bulletin 2010/2 (Revised), *Compendium of Illustrative Auditor's Reports on United Kingdom Private Sector Financial Statements for period ended on or after 15 December 2010 (Revised)*, Appendix 13, Examples 40 and 41, and Appendix 15, Examples 44 and 45 http://www.frc.co.uk/Our-Work/Publications/APB/Bulletin-2010-2-Compendium-of-Illustrative-Auditor.aspx.

[15] Chartered Accountants Ireland, 2013.

ISA 705, paragraph13(b) states that:

"If the auditor concludes that the possible effects on the financial statements of undetected misstatements, if any, could be both material and pervasive so that a qualification of the opinion would be inadequate to communicate the gravity of the situation, the auditor shall:

(i) Withdraw from the audit, where practicable and possible under applicable law or regulation; or

(ii) If withdrawal from the audit before issuing the auditor's report is not practicable or possible, disclaim an opinion on the financial statements."

Should the auditor decide to withdraw from the engagement, before doing so, he is required to "communicate to those charged with governance any matters regarding misstatements identified during the audit that would have given rise to a modification of the opinion" (ISA 705, para 14)

A decision tree is included at **Appendix 19.2** as an aid to understanding the auditor's decision-making process when considering a **limitation of scope**.

Figure 19.2 is re-presented below to remind us what we have covered:

Audit opinions can be:

• unqualified – standard unqualified opinion (financial statements give a true and fair view);

• unqualified with 'Emphasis of Matter' paragraph (financial statements give true and fair view, but contain a very serious matter that is highlighted by the auditor by reference to the adequate disclosure note that addresses the situation);

• modified:

  ◆ disagreement – financial statements are not in accordance with applicable financial reporting framework:

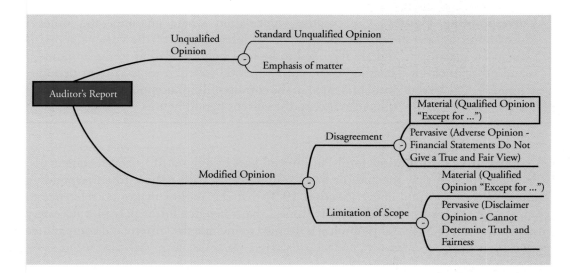

- ○ 'Qualified Except for' paragraph – except for the particular material matter with which the auditor disagrees, the financial statements give a true and fair view (material but not pervasive),
- ○ 'Adverse Opinion' paragraph – the financial statements do not give a true and fair view (material and pervasive);
- ◆ Limitation of Scope - auditor's work has been limited in some way:
  - ○ 'Qualified Except for' paragraph – except for the particular material matter to which the auditor's scope has been limited, the financial statements give a true and fair view (material but not pervasive),
  - ○ 'Disclaimer' paragraph – due to limitation of scope, the auditor cannot determine whether the financial statements give a true and fair view or not (material and pervasive).

19.5 COMPARATIVE INFORMATION – CORRESPONDING FIGURES

In line with IAS 1 *Presentation of Financial Statements* (IAS 1), prior year comparative figures are required to be included in a set of financial statements and therefore they form part of the financial statements. As such, the auditor cannot express an opinion on the financial statements without obtaining assurance over the comparative figures. ISA 710 offers the auditor guidance with regard to his review of comparative information.

Before we discuss the contents of ISA 710, we will first consider the key definitions provided by the standard, as set out below:

KEY TERMS DEFINED IN ISA 710

Comparative Information   The amounts and disclosures included in the financial statements in respect of one or more prior periods in accordance with the applicable financial reporting framework.

Corresponding Figures   Comparative information where amounts and other disclosures for the period are included as an integral part of the current period financial statements, and are intended to be read only in relation to the amounts and other disclosures relating to the current period (referred to as 'current period figures'). The level of detail presented in the corresponding amounts and disclosures is dictated primarily by its relevance to the current period figures.

As **comparative information** forms an integral part of any set of financial statements, it is not surprising that the auditor has a responsibility with respect to corresponding figures. We can see from above (**Section 19.3**) that the auditor makes no reference to comparative figures in his audit report (unless that reference forms part of a necessary modification); nonetheless, his opinion is deemed to include the current and comparative period figures).

With regard to prior period financial statements audited by a predecessor auditor, ISA 710, at paragraph A7-1, states that:

" … the incoming auditor does not refer to the predecessor auditor's report on the corresponding figures in the incoming auditor's report for the current period. The incoming auditor assumes audit responsibility for the corresponding figures only in the context of the financial statements as a whole. The incoming auditor reads the preceding period's financial statements and, using the knowledge gained during the current audit, considers whether they have been properly reflected as corresponding figures in the current period's financial statements."

This means that for entities where an auditor did not audit the financial statements in the prior period, he still needs to gain assurance over the comparative figures.

Once the auditor has carried out audit procedures relating to comparative figures he may find that material misstatements exist with regard to comparative figures. It may be necessary, therefore, for the auditor to modify his audit opinion or include an 'Other Matter' paragraph in relation to comparative figures where:

- The prior year was qualified and that qualification has not yet been resolved (e.g. where a provision for a legal claim which the audited entity's solicitors determine it is likely to materialise continues to be omitted from the financial statements).
- The client entity was audit exempt in the prior year and so the corresponding figures are unaudited (ISA (UK and Ireland) 510 *Initial Audit Engagements – Opening Balances* (ISA 510) provides the auditor with guidance in these circumstances, however, ISA 710, paragraph19, states: "If the prior period financial statements were not audited, the auditor shall state in an Other Matter paragraph that the comparative financial statements are unaudited. Such a statement does not, however, relieve the auditor of the requirement to obtain sufficient appropriate audit evidence that the opening balances do not contain misstatements that materially affect the current period's financial statements").
- During the course of the audit, the auditor discovers a material misstatement that relates to the corresponding figures (e.g. if the auditor determines that an asset in use in the prior year has not been depreciated and management continue not to depreciate, then the auditor would qualify the auditor's report referring to both prior and current year figures.
- Referring to the example above, if management have properly stated the corresponding figures and corrected the error in the current year, meaning that depreciation is now correct, then the auditor may refer to the matter in relation to the prior-year error in an **emphasis of matter paragraph**.

19.6 THE AUDITOR'S RESPONSIBILITIES RELATING TO OTHER INFORMATION AND THE DIRECTORS' REPORT

ISA 720A "deals with the auditor's responsibilities relating to other information in documents containing audited financial statements and the auditor's report thereon. In the absence of any separate requirement in the particular circumstances of the engagement, the auditor's opinion does not cover other information and the auditor has no specific responsibility for determining whether or not other information is properly stated. However, the auditor reads the other information because the credibility of the audited financial statements may be undermined by material inconsistencies between the audited financial statements and other information" (ISA 720A, para 1). ISA 720B "deals with the auditor's statutory reporting responsibility in relation to directors' reports." (ISA 720B, para 1).

For private companies the term 'Annual Report and Accounts' will typically include the 'Directors' Report', the 'Directors' Statement of Responsibilities', the 'Independent Auditor's Report' and the 'Audited Financial Statements' (including the statement of accounting policies). For public companies, public interest bodies, charities, etc. the term 'Annual Report and Accounts' will usually mean the inclusion of additional reports regarding the activities of the entity and governance issues.

As introduced above, the auditor needs to read the other information, and the directors' report to determine if there are any inconsistencies with the audited financial statements.

Inconsistent Other Information – ISA 720A

Before we discuss the contents of ISA 720A, we will first consider the key definitions provided by the standard, as set out below:

Key Terms Defined in ISA 720A

Inconsistency   Other information that contradicts information contained in the audited financial statements. A **material** inconsistency may raise doubt about the audit conclusions drawn from audit evidence previously obtained and possibly about the basis for the auditor's opinion on the financial statements.

Misstatement of Fact   Other information that is unrelated to matters appearing in the audited financial statements is incorrectly stated or presented. A material misstatement of fact may undermine the credibility of the document containing audited financial statements.

Other Information   Financial and non-financial information (other than the financial statements and the auditor's report thereon) that is included either by law, regulation or custom, in a document containing audited financial statements and the auditor's report thereon.

ISA 720A requires auditors, before signing the audit report, to read the other information contained in the annual report for material inconsistency with the audited financial statements and for material misstatements of fact.

As we can see from the definitions above:
• a **material inconsistency** may cause a user to doubt the reliability of the information contained in the audited financial statements and the reliability of the audit opinion.

- a **material misstatement** of fact might undermine the credibility of the document containing the audited financial statements.

Where the auditor becomes aware of an inconsistency between the audited financial statements and the other information contained in the annual report, it is necessary to consider whether it is the financial statements themselves or the other information which requires revision, and the matter should be discussed with **management**. If it happens to be the financial statements that require revision and management refuse to make the necessary revisions, a **qualified 'except for' opinion** or **adverse opinion** should be expressed, depending on how material and pervasive the matter is.

If it is the other information that requires revision and management refuse, the auditor should consider including an '**emphasis of matter**' paragraph to describe the material inconsistency or use his right to address shareholders at the annual general meeting. Before doing this, the auditor should seek legal advice as to the possible consequences of taking such actions. As a last resort the auditor should resign and use the required statement issued on resignation to inform the shareholders (as required by section 185 of the Companies Act 1990 for the Republic of Ireland and by sections 522 to 525 of the Companies Act 2006 for the UK).

Under UK and Irish company law, if the directors' report is inconsistent with the financial statements, the auditor must make reference to these inconsistencies in his audit report. The audit report should be modified, without qualifying the audit opinion, by modifying the opinion on the directors' report.

Inconsistent Other Information: ISA 720B

Similar to ISA 720A, as outlined above, under ISA 720B the auditor is required to read the information in the directors' report and assess whether it is consistent with the financial statements. Should inconsistencies exist, the auditor should try to resolve them with management. If unresolved and the matter is a material inconsistency, the auditor should describe the inconsistency in the audit report. Similar to the above, if the inconsistency relates to a material error in the financial statements, the auditor should consider the need for a qualified or adverse opinion, as appropriate.

19.7 COMMUNICATION WITH THOSE CHARGED WITH GOVERNANCE

The auditor has now formed an opinion and considered all comparative figures in the financial statements, as well as the consistency of information contained in other reports and, specifically, in the directors' report. In practice, while he has performed the audit on behalf of the shareholders, he does not now issue the report without first discussing it with the client entity's management (those charged with governance). This gives the entity an opportunity to influence the report by making necessary amendments to the financial statements or removing any limitation imposed on the audit scope.

Prior to issuing the audit opinion, the auditor should make it clear to **those charged with governance** of the intended opinion and provide them with the proposed wording of the modified opinion. This should clearly demonstrate to management the reasons or circumstances giving rise to the modification. The auditor should confirm agreement with management of the circumstances giving rise to the limitation of scope or confirm matters of disagreement. By informing management of the above, management has an opportunity to either:

1. remove the limitation of scope (if practicable); or
2. correct the material misstatement giving rise to the disagreement.

19.8 OTHER REPORTING MATTERS

Qualified Audit Reports and Dividends

Where a qualified audit opinion has been given on the previous year's annual financial statements, the company's ability to make a distribution by reference to those financial statements could be in doubt unless it receives a statement from its auditor, in accordance with section 49(3) of the Companies Act 1983, concerning the company's ability to make a distribution.

Electronic Publication of Financial Statements

APB's Bulletin 2001/1 *The electronic publication of auditors' reports,* although withdrawn from the Financial Reporting Council's Standards and Guidance, prescribes useful guidance to the auditor where a company makes its annual accounts available on its website. Such matters include:

- where the financial statements are published in a format other than PDF, the auditor's report must identify the audited financial statements by name and date instead of using page numbers;
- references to financial reporting and to auditing standards should specify the relevant nationality;
- documents loaded to the Internet must be identical to the hard-copy version; and
- hyperlinks should not inappropriately link the auditor's report to unaudited information.

Although the Bulletin has been removed, these points remain important and should be considered by the auditor.

Subsequent Events and Revised Accounts

Where a material misstatement is discovered after the financial statements and auditor's report have been issued, revised financial statements may have to be issued, in which case the auditors should issue a new audit report on the revised financial statements.

Summary Financial Statements, Interim Reports and Preliminary Announcements

Auditors may be involved in issuing other report, such as summary financial statements, which are issued in some countries by large quoted companies. Some listed companies may also issue interim financial statements and may request the auditors to carry out a review of the interim financial information and provide a conclusion on it. The auditor has no statutory responsibility for the interim financial reports. However, the FRC has issued an International Standard for Review Engagements (ISRE) (UK and Ireland) 2410, which applies to the auditor reviewing interim financial information issued by the entity.

Where management of an audited entity wishes to announce preliminary results, the auditors are required to communicate their consent to the publication.

19.9 EFFECT OF A QUALIFIED AUDIT OPINION

Generally, auditors believe that modifying their report is a last resort. In order to avoid having to issue a modified opinion, they will discuss the issues at great length with the client entity's management. In most cases, directors are prepared to adjust the financial statements for any material errors or omissions that auditors have brought to their attention, as they would be keen to ensure the accuracy of the financial statements.

The directors will also be aware that a modified opinion can have serious consequences for the company:
• it could affect shareholders' confidence in the company and its management;
• it could discourage potential investors;
• it could affect the willingness of lenders to continue offering a facility to the company; and
• it could affect the company's creditworthiness with its suppliers.

However, if the auditor feels a **modified opinion** is appropriate he must be able to justify the basis for the qualification and be able to explain this in the audit report.

The auditor must use his professional judgement to decide how serious the issues involved are, as this will influence which form of qualification will be included in the audit report.

The auditor must decide how seriously the issue/issues affect the truth and fairness of the financial statements.

19.10 CONCLUSION

The auditor's report is the key end result from any audit engagement. It contains the auditor's opinion on the financial statements, an opinion that is based on the auditor's overall assessment and taking into account evidence gained during each phase of the **audit process**.

The audit opinion is contained in a separate paragraph within the body of the auditor's report. Guidance on what is required to be included in this report is found within six specific International Standards on Auditing (UK and Ireland) (ISAs), as well as within the Companies Acts in force in each jurisdiction.

ISA 700 outlines the basic format of a 'clean' (unqualified) audit opinion. ISA 705 and 706 deal with modifications to the standard audit report. Additionally, there are three other standards, ISA 710, ISA 720A and ISA 720B, which cover the auditor's responsibility in relation to comparative information, other information and the directors' report. While the UK adopted the provisions of ISA 700 in 2010, the Republic of Ireland has recently adopted it for accounts commencing on or after 1 October 2012. ISA 705 and ISA 706 were also revised in 2012.

Together with the ISAs, the auditor is required to comply with company law requirements with regard to audit reports. Within the Republic of Ireland, this takes the form of the Companies Acts 1963–2012 and related legislation, for the UK refers to the Companies Act 2006.

Before concluding on the opinion, the auditor should be confident that he has carried out the **audit conclusion** tasks as outlined in **Chapter 18**, so that he is confident he is issuing an appropriate opinion.

SUMMARY OF LEARNING OBJECTIVES

Leaning Objective 1 Be able to describe the principles underpinning the form and content of audit reports with reference to the relevant standards and legislation.

There are six key standards which deal directly with the auditor's opinion/auditor's report including:
- ISA (UK and Ireland) 700 *The Auditor's Report on Financial Statements* (Revised) (issued October 2012);
- ISA (UK and Ireland) 705 *Modifications to the Opinion in the Independent Auditor's Report* (Revised) (issued October 2012);
- ISA (UK and Ireland) 706 *Emphasis of Matter Paragraphs and Other Matter Paragraphs in the Independent Auditor's Report* (Revised) (issued October 2012);
- ISA (UK and Ireland) 710 *Comparative Information – Corresponding Figures and Comparative Financial Statements*;
- ISA (UK and Ireland) 720 – Section A *The Auditor's Responsibilities Relating to Other Information in Documents Containing Audited Financial Statements*;
- ISA (UK and Ireland) 720 – Section B *The Auditor's Statutory Reporting Responsibility in Relation to Directors' Reports.*

ISA 700 and the Companies Acts 1963–2012 in the Republic of Ireland ISA (UK and Ireland) 720 – Section B and the Companies Act 2006 in the UK prescribe the form and content of an audit report which must include the following:
- title,
- addressee,

- introductory paragraph,
- respective responsibilities of those charged with governance and the auditor paragraph,
- scope of audit paragraph,
- opinion paragraph,
- opinion in respect of additional financial reporting framework,
- requirement specific to public sector entities where an opinion on regularity is given,
- opinions on other matters,
- date of report,
- location of auditor's offices, and
- signature of auditor.

Learning Objective 2   Be able to explain the different types of audit reports, including the impact of different types of opinion on the auditor's report itself.

Where the auditor believes the financial statements give a true and fair view, he issues an '**unqualified**' audit opinion.

ISA 706 deals with instances where the auditor believes the financial statements give a true and fair view, but feels that a particular matter which is **not materially misstated** and is **adequately presented and disclosed** in the financial statements, is of such significance that the users' attention should be drawn to it. In these instances he issues an 'unqualified' audit opinion with an '**emphasis of a matter**' paragraph, which makes reference to the disclosure note describing the circumstances surrounding the issue.

ISA 705 deals with modifications to the opinion in the independent auditor's report. If the auditor's opinion is that the accounts do not give a true and fair view, or that something has prevented him from forming an opinion on all or part of the financial statements, the client will receive a '**modified/qualified audit report**'.

Learning Objective 3   Be able to identify typical scenarios in which audit reports might need to be modified.

There are two main types of modified audit report:
- '**limitation on scope**' where the auditor is unable to form an opinion on the financial statements due to a limitation being imposed on his work:
  - '**qualification – except for**' where the limitation relates to a specific account balance and the auditor can form an opinion on the financial statements except for that balance;
  - '**disclaimer**' where the limitation is so material or pervasive that it prevents the auditor from forming any opinion on the financial statements;
- '**disagreement**' where the auditor disagrees with the financial statements prepared by the client:

- ◆ '**qualification – except for**' where the disagreement relates to a specific account balance and the auditor can form an opinion on the financial statements except for that balance;
- ◆ '**adverse**' where the effects of the disagreement are so material or pervasive that the auditor concludes that an 'except for' opinion is not adequate to disclose the misleading or incomplete nature of the financial statements.

Learning Objective 4   Understand the auditor's responsibility with regard to comparative information, other information and the directors' report included with the financial statements.

ISA 710 outlines the auditor's responsibility with respect to corresponding figures and comparative information in the financial statements and states that while the audit report does not make any specific reference to the corresponding figures in the financial statements, his opinion is deemed to include both years.

ISA 720 Sections A and B require the auditor to read all **other information**, including the **directors' report**, which are presented along with the financial statements to ensure that there are no material inconsistencies between other information and the audited financial statements. Where a material inconsistency exists and is uncorrected by management, the auditor will consider the impact for the auditor's report.

Learning Objective 5   Understand the other issues relating to audit reports.

When concluding on an audit opinion, it is essential that **those charged with governance are kept aware** of the decision and the contents of the audit report to (a) confirm their agreement with the situation, and (b) give them the opportunity to change the outcome, should it be practicable.

Other issues relating to audit reports include:
- impact on distribution of **dividends**;
- considerations for **electronic publication** of financial statements; and
- involvement in **summary financial statements, interim reports** and **preliminary announcements**.

While the consequences of an incorrect modification are grave, so too are the consequences of an unqualified opinion where a modified one was warranted and, as such, the auditor needs to be confident that he has carried out all the steps outlined in **Chapter 18**, 'Audit Work Conclusions', so that he is satisfied he has sufficient and appropriate audit evidence to support his opinion.

QUESTIONS

Self-test Questions

19.1 What governs the contents of an audit report?

19.2 Which standards cover the contents of the auditor's report?

19.3 In relation to the Republic of Ireland, what do the Companies Acts 1963–2012 require to be included in the audit report?

19.4 In relation to Northern Ireland/UK, what does the Companies Act 2006 require to be included in the audit report?

19.5 What are the key contents of an audit report?

19.6 What is the difference between an unqualified and a qualified audit opinion?

19.7 What is meant by the term 'disagreement' with respect to auditors' reports?

19.8 What is meant by the term 'limitation of scope' with respect to auditors' reports?

19.9 If a limitation of scope exists in relation to a material matter, which two types of opinion might the auditor issue?

19.10 If a disagreement exists in relation to a material matter, which two types of opinion might the auditor issue?

19.11 What is an 'emphasis of matter'?

19.12 Name three instances where an auditor might include an emphasis of matter paragraph.

19.13 What are the key paragraphs that are impacted by a modification resulting from an 'except for' qualification relating to limitation of scope?

19.14 What are the key paragraphs that are impacted by a modification resulting from an 'except for' qualification relating to disagreement?

19.15 Name four types of instances that might give rise to a Disclaimer of Opinion.

19.16 Name four types of instances that might give rise to an Adverse Opinion.

19.17 What is the auditor's responsibility with regard to other information included with a set of financial statements?

19.18 What is the auditor's responsibility with regard to the directors' report?

19.19 Where would the auditor report on a material inconsistency between other information or the directors' report and the audited financial statements?

Review Questions

(See Suggested Solutions to Review Questions in **Appendix D**.)

Question 19.1

Merlin Ltd ("Merlin") is an established client of your audit firm. A broad range of professional services are provided to Merlin. The audit fieldwork for the year ended 31 March 2013 was completed recently. Your firm's Cumulative Audit Knowledge and Experience (CAKE) is that there are relatively few audit issues. However, the following points have been noted from the audit:

1. A repairs provision of €500,000 is included on the balance sheet for future repairs of the distribution warehouse. No contracts have been signed.
2. From the Information Technology General Controls (ITGC) review, a number of weaknesses with regard to infrastructure security were noted.
3. A consultancy payment of €10,000 to the brother of the Managing Director of Merlin was made during the year; this item has not been disclosed in the financial statements.
4. From a review of the fixed asset (PPE) additions, the full salary costs of €100,000 relating to two employees have been capitalised. From discussions with management you have ascertained that 50% of the employees' time was spent on a related development project.
5. A management bonus of €225,000 is provided for in the accounts. This is not due to be paid until July 2013, at which time the accounts will have been signed. The bonus is €75,000 higher than in the prior year without any significant improvement in the performance of the company during the year.

The draft financial statements, which do not contain any adjustments or disclosures relating to the matters above, show the following:

	€000
Revenue	24,568
Profit before tax	1,609
Net current liabilities	(4,802)
Net assets	2,114

Requirement

(a) (i) For each of the points noted from your review, set out in bullet point format the potential audit report implications of each situation if treated individually. (**Note:** *your answer should explain briefly the reason for each of your opinions.*)

    (ii) In addition, outline and explain the overall audit opinion that you would provide, if no further adjustments or disclosures were made for the points noted. (**Note:** *no sections of the audit report are to be drafted.*)

(b) Outline briefly how an auditor would audit salary costs that have been capitalised as part of a development project.

(c) Prepare the accounting adjustments that you would recommend for the repairs provision and the capitalised employee costs for inclusion in the schedule of unadjusted differences.

Question 19.2

Denark Ltd ('Denark') is a client of your firm. You are audit senior on the assignment and the audit fieldwork for the year ended 31 December 2012 has just been completed. The following figures have been extracted from the draft financial statements.

	Year Ended 31 December	
	2012	2013
	€000	€000
Revenue	11,650	16,540
Profit before tax	331	590
(Loss)/profit after tax	(445)	540
Dividends proposed	(220)	(220)
(Loss)/profit for the year	(665)	320
Profit forward	810	490
Retained profit	145	810
Net assets	7,420	7,980

Audit Issues:

1. On 6 December 2012 the creditors ledger system unexpectedly crashed. As a result, all transactions posted to the creditors ledger on 6 December were lost. The accounts payable team re-posted these transactions on 7 December 2012 once the system error had been corrected. The re-posting exercise was successful and proved to be reliable.
2. In January 2013, one of Denark's customers went into liquidation owing the company €350,000 at that point. Denark made sales of €100,000 to the customer in January 2013. The directors have indicated that the full debt will be provided for in the financial statements for the year ended 31 December 2013.
3. Bonus costs of €7,500 paid to two directors of the company have not been disclosed in the financial statements of Denark. This information is commercially sensitive and the Finance Director has indicated that they are not willing to disclose the bonus costs.

Requirement

(a) Set out, in bullet point format, the potential implications for the audit report of Denark for the year ended 31 December 2012 arising from the audit Issues 1–3 noted above. (*You may assume that Denark is not willing to make changes to its draft financial statements.*)
(b) In respect of ISSUE 2 alone, draft any changes to the audit report that you deem necessary.

Question 19.3

Worldglobal Ltd (Worldglobal) is a client of your firm. The company has experienced significant trading difficulties in recent years. The audit fieldwork for the year ended 31 December 2012 has been completed and the following matters have been noted.

1. Worldglobal was in breach of its bank covenant arrangements at the year end. Management have indicated that a meeting has been held with the company's bankers, at which they received assurances from the bank that none of the financing facilities

of the company would be withdrawn. Worldglobal has a five-year term loan of €1.2 million and an overdraft facility of €500,000.

2. The company has a financial investment of €100,000 in a company called Horizon Ltd ("Horizon"). The investment does not qualify Horizon to be treated as a subsidiary of Worldglobal. The client is unable to provide evidence to support the carrying value of the investment.

The results of Worldglobal for the year ended 31 December 2012 show revenue of €16.2 million, a loss before tax of €200,000 and net assets of €5.5 million. There were no other matters noted from the audit work performed.

Requirement

(a) Draft a memorandum to the audit partner, setting out the audit evidence you would seek to obtain in respect of the matters noted and outlining their potential impact on the auditor's report.

(b) Assuming that the financial investment issue cannot be resolved, draft the qualification paragraph(s) required for the situation described.

(c) At the planning meeting for this engagement, the audit partner noted that the standard of audit reports being drafted by the audit seniors was poor. List a number of checks that should be performed on audit reports prior to signing.

APPENDIX 19.1: AUDIT OPINION DECISION TREE

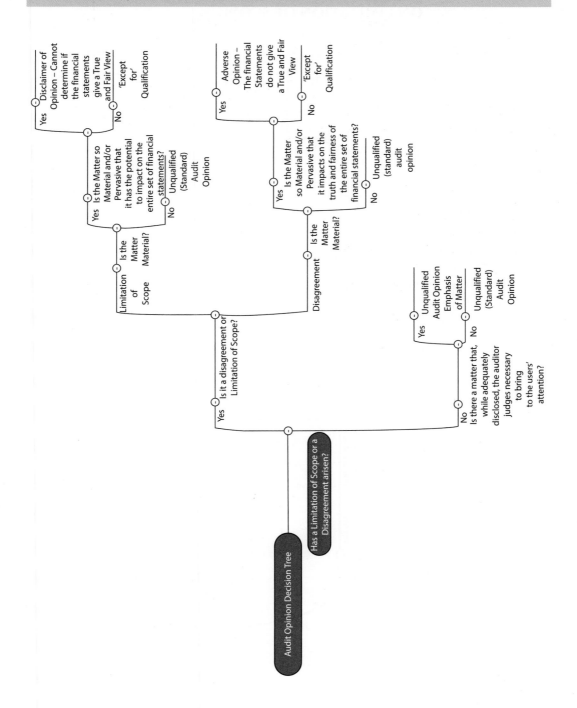

APPENDIX 19.2: DECISION TREE FOR CONCLUDING ON LIMITATION OF SCOPE

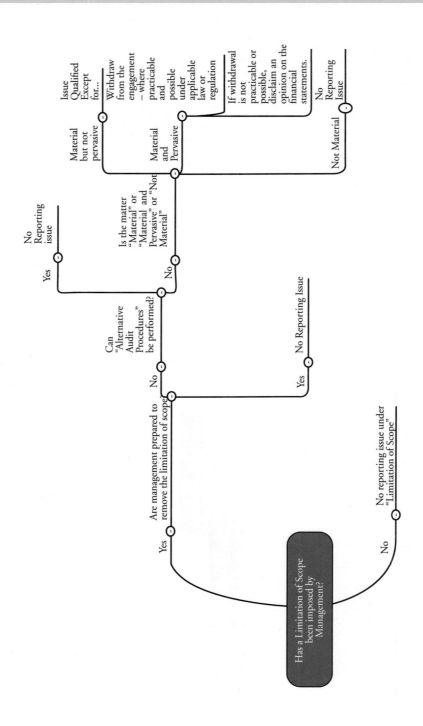

APPENDIX 19.3: DECISION TREE FOR CONCLUDING ON GOING CONCERN

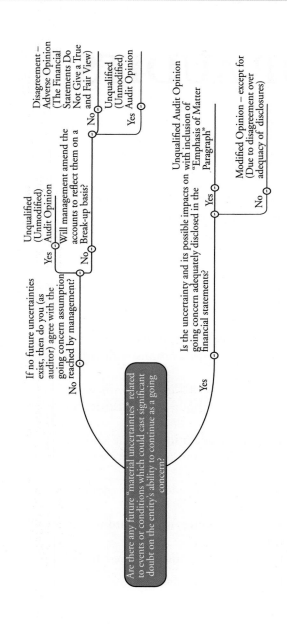

20

GROUP AUDITS

LEARNING OBJECTIVES

Having studied this chapter on group audits you should:
1. understand the additional considerations with regard to acceptance and continuance of group audits;
2. understand the requirements of ISA 600 with regard to risk assessment procedures and communication of group audit instructions with regard to component auditors;
3. be able to identify the considerations of the auditor with regard to group components, component auditors and materiality when performing an audit of group financial statements;
4. understand the importance of adequately scoping in and out significant and non-significant components;
5. know the auditor's responsibilities with regard to materiality when auditing group financial statements;
6. understand the concluding activities required by the group auditor prior to the issue of an opinion.

CHECKLIST OF RELEVANT STANDARDS

ISA (UK and Ireland) 220 *Quality Control for an Audit of Financial Statements* (ISA 220)

ISA (UK and Ireland) 600 *Special Considerations – Audits of Group Financial Statements (Including the Work of Component Auditors)* (ISA 600)

IAS 27 *Separate Financial Statements* (*Note*: this standard used to be *Consolidated and Separate Financial Statements* but consolidation is now dealt with under a separate standard);

IAS 28 *Investments in Associates and Joint Ventures* (*Note*: this standard used to deal with *Investments in Associates* only)

IAS 31 *Interests in Joint Ventures*

IFRS 3 *Business Combinations*

IFRS 10 *Consolidated Financial Statements*

IFRS 11 *Joint Arrangements*

IFRS 12 *Disclosure of Interests in Other Entities* (*Note*: disclosure requirements used to be held within the standard relating to the particular investment type, but they are now dealt with under one standard, i.e. IFRS 12.

KEY TERMS AND DEFINITIONS IN THIS CHAPTER

Component   "An entity or business activity for which group or **component management** prepares financial information that should be included in the group financial statements." (ISA 600)

Component Auditor   "An auditor who, at the request of the group audit engagement team, performs work on financial information related to a **component** for the group audit." (ISA 600)

Component Management   "Management responsible for the preparation of the financial information of a component." (ISA 600)

Component Materiality   "The materiality for a component determined by the group engagement team."

Group Audit   "The audit of group financial statements." (ISA 600)

Group Auditor vs. Component Auditor   The group auditor (also referred to as the principal auditor, or the parent company auditor) has responsibility for reporting on the group financial statements. The component auditor has responsibility for reporting on an individual component of the group.

Significant Component   "A component identified by the group engagement team: (i) that is of individual financial significance to the group; or (ii) that, due to its specific nature or circumstances, is likely to include significant risks of **material misstatement** of the group financial statements." (ISA 600)

Scoping   A term used to describe the exercise carried out to determine which components will undergo full audit procedures (scoping in) and which will be considered insignificant and therefore undergo a reduced level of testing (scoping out).

20.1 INTRODUCTION

This chapter outlines the requirements for a group audit and describes the audit process involved. (**Note**: **joint audits** are not discussed in this chapter as the audit process involved is similar to any audit, except in that the audit is carried out jointly by two audit firms and they give a joint audit opinion – two firms sign the audit report.)

The principal matters and issues discussed in the chapter are as follows:
- the circumstances in which a group audit is required and its unique features;
- the role and responsibilities of the group auditor and the component auditor;
- the importance of risk assessment;
- the group audit process;
- group auditor engagement acceptance considerations;
- risk-assessment strategy and materiality;
- communications in a group audit;
- group audit conclusion.

International Financial Reporting Standards (IFRS/IAS) and company law require the preparation and audit of consolidated (group) financial statements when a group exists. A group is deemed to exist when a parent company owns one or more subsidiaries and/or holds investments in associates and joint ventures.

It is important to note that the principles of auditing a group are the same as the audit of a single entity and that all of the ISAs are relevant to a group audit, with particular reference necessary to ISA (UK and Ireland) 600 *Special Considerations – Audits of Group Financial Statements (Including the Work of Component Auditors)* (ISA 600).

There are a number of unique features relating specifically to group audits, such as:
- the requirement for complicated consolidation adjustments;
- the need to ensure compliance with a number of complex financial reporting standards;
- the entities that comprise the group (the components) may be audited by firms of auditors other than the principal auditor (group auditor);
- the planning and organising of a group audit is usually complex, as the components are frequently based in several different countries.

When group financial statements are required to be audited, it is common for the **group auditor** (the principal auditor named on the audit engagement document) to require the assistance of other auditors, referred to as **component auditors**. As, for example, the larger Irish corporates, such as Kerry Group Plc (audited by Deloitte) or CRH Plc (audited by Ernst & Young) continue to expand into more far-reaching geographical areas, the complexity of the financial statements, and thus the audits thereon, also become increasingly challenging.

Regarding terminology in this area of audit, and as defined above, the various elements that are consolidated to make up the group financial statements are referred to as '**components**' and the auditors engaged to audit components, are referred to as '**component auditors**'.

The roles, responsibilities and competencies of the group auditors and component audit-ors involved in a group audit are clearly stated in ISA 600, of paragraph 4:

"the group engagement partner is required to be satisfied that those performing the group audit engagement, including component auditors, collectively have the appro-priate competence and capabilities. The group engagement partner is also respons-ible for the direction, supervision and performance of the group audit engagement."

This inevitably places a significant amount of responsibility and risk on the **group audit engagement partner** (and the related firm), thus requiring the audit partner to have an active part in communicating with the audit client the whole year round.

We have already discussed **audit risk** in detail (see **Chapter 7**) and appreciate that it relates to the risk that:

(a) the financial statements contain a material error; and

(b) the auditor does not detect that material error.

When dealing with groups, audit risk becomes more complicated as it relates to the risk that:

(a) the financial statements contain a material error; and

(b) the component auditor fails to detect that material error; and

(c) the group auditor fails to detect that the component auditor failed to detect the material error.

Remember: ultimate responsibility lies with the group auditors and hence they have to be satisfied as to the competence of the component auditor so as to reduce the risk they are taking in relying on that component auditor's work.

In practical terms, when an audit firm engaged in the audit of a group requires the use of component auditors, they will usually look to member affiliates of their firm. For instance, when Deloitte and Ernst & Young engage with Kerry Group Plc and CRH Plc, they tend to engage the services of overseas affiliates of their own firms. When, due to the need for additional expertise or geographical or jurisdictional constraints, they engage the services of non-affiliated firms, their emphasis on component auditor quality will tend to increase. This arises because the group auditor may not be familiar with the quality of that com-ponent audit firm's work.

20.2 THE GROUP AUDIT PROCESS

Figure 20.1 below shows how the process of auditing the group financial statements is very similar to a single entity audit. As stated above, the principles of auditing a group are the same as the audit of a single entity and all of the ISAs are applicable to a group audit. However, the key differences arise in relation to the planning, monitoring, supervision and review required by the group auditors in ensuring **sufficient appropriate audit evidence** has been obtained at a group level to support the audit opinion of the group auditor.

Figure 20.1 sets out a comparison of the typical audit process for a single entity (per-formed by a component auditor) and the additional features of the group audit process.

FIGURE 20.1: THE GROUP AUDIT PROCESS

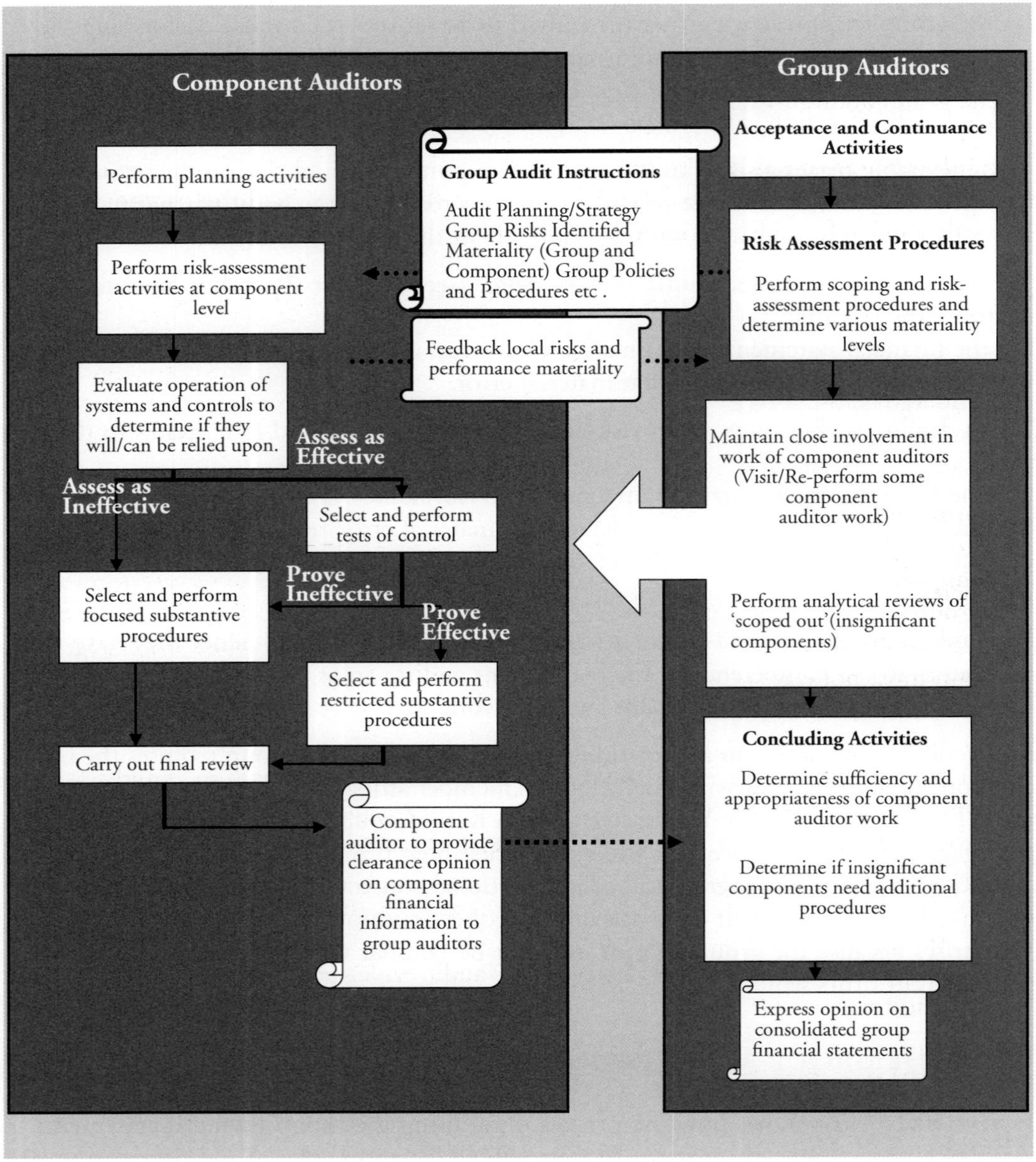

You will see that the group audit instructions are a significant additional aspect of the group audit. There is particular emphasis placed on risk assessment and the determination of materiality for the group and the component auditors. The close involvement between the group auditor and the component auditors manifests itself particularly in relation to the systems and substantive testing of the operations and controls in the components.

The extent of involvement depends on the significance to the group results of any particular component and the outcome of the 'scoping exercise' carried out by the group auditor (discussed below).

At the conclusion of the audit process, each component auditor must formally report to the group auditor, giving an opinion on the financial information of the component which is being consolidated into the group financial statements. This opinion is in the form of a **clearance opinion** stating, where applicable, that there are no material matters affecting the component financial information or, if there are, then the component auditor will provide full information relating thereto.

20.3 GROUP AUDIT FIRM ACCEPTANCE CONSIDERATIONS

In **Chapter 5**, we outlined the acceptance and continuance considerations that an auditor will undergo before accepting any audit engagement. When considering whether to accept or continue a group audit engagement, the group audit engagement partner will have some additional considerations, including:

1. **Considerations relating to adequacy of firm resources to complete a 'group audit'**
   Along with the standard acceptance and continuance considerations, as discussed in **Chapter 5**, the group auditor needs to ask: 'Do I/we have the necessary resources (group engagement team) to competently perform the audit of the group to the extent necessary to obtain sufficient appropriate audit evidence?' Remember: the engagement team must not only perform audit procedures on their own assigned components but also perform audit procedures:
   (a) on the competence of the component auditors; and
   (b) on a portion of the component auditor's work in order to minimise audit risk.
2. **Considerations as to the adequacy of the group auditor's internal policies and procedures to sufficiently address the requirements of ISA 600 relating to:**
   (a) the assessment of risks for the group;
   (b) the assignment of instructions/communication with component auditors;
   (c) the consolidation process; and
   (d) the evaluation of the sufficiency of the audit evidence obtained from component auditors.

20.4 GROUP AUDIT FIRM SCOPING AND RISK ASSESSMENT

Scoping and Risk-assessment Considerations

Having accepted the engagement for the group audit, the engagement team now has a number of additional considerations, including:
1. **Considerations relating to 'group components':**
   (a) 'Have I/we got a sufficient understanding of the group, its components, their environments and the consolidation process?' This will be necessary to identify the risk of material misstatement of the group financial statements.

(b) What components make up the group? **Components** may be operational or financial reporting structures and not necessarily that of a legal structure.

(c) What are the significant and insignificant components of the group and who will perform the audit engagement activities on those components?

(d) 'How will I/we deal with the more insignificant (immaterial) components?'

2. **Considerations relating to 'component auditors':**

(a) 'Do I/we have sufficient understanding as to the competence of the component auditors?' Considering the importance of the role they play and the onus on the group audit partner with regard to their opinion, understanding the component auditor is a key requirement.

(b) Do the component auditors possess an understanding of auditing and other standards applicable to the group audit?

(c) Do the component auditors comply with the ethical requirements that are relevant to the group audit?

(d) What regulatory environment does the component auditor operate within? Are the standards of regulation acceptable to the group auditor?

(e) Have there been any negative regulatory investigation findings against the component auditor?

(f) 'How much will I/we need to get involved in the work of the component auditors?'

(g) 'What will 'I/we' have to communicate to the component auditors in order for them to audit the assigned component?'

3. **Considerations relating to 'materiality':**

(a) What will group materiality be set at?

(b) What will component materiality be set at?

(c) Will different materiality levels be required for certain transactions or balances that are considered more risky?

(d) What level of error will be considered as clearly trivial to the group financial statements?

Scoping of Significant and Insignificant Components

There may be hundreds of components that make up the financial statements of a large group. The auditor does not have to perform focused substantive procedures on all components due to their insignificance to the group as a whole. Should some components:

(a) be individually financially insignificant; and

(b) pose no significant risks of material misstatement due to specific nature or circumstances, then they are considered '**insignificant**'.

For insignificant components, the auditor can perform **analytical procedures** at the group level. It may be the case, however, that even though they individually meet the criteria above, the aggregate effect of all insignificant components is too material to warrant their exclusion. For this reason, some seemingly insignificant components will need to be scoped back in for more focused substantive procedures in order to gain **sufficient appropriate audit evidence** on the group as a whole. This is explained further by way of **Example 20.1** below.

EXAMPLE 20.1: SCOPING IN/OUT OF COMPONENTS

A group audit engagement team have identified components with revenue of €10 million or less as being **insignificant** (provided no specific risks have been identified within those components). The group audit is required to perform greater than 90% coverage of all revenue. A group audit partner is reviewing the scoping exercise (Scoping Exercise 1) performed by the group audit engagement team. He determines that while all components scoped out do meet the laid down criteria, the coverage required to obtain sufficient appropriate audit evidence for revenue is not achieved, if all insignificant components are scoped out. Therefore, Scoping Exercise 2 is performed.

Component Number	Revenue €000s	Scoping Exercise 1	Scoping Exercise 2
1	70,000	Scope in	Scope in
2	25,000	Scope in	Scope in
3	10,000	Scope out	Scope in
4	15,000	Scope out	Scope in
5	2,000	Scope out	Scope out
6	1,000	Scope out	Scope out
7	80,000	Scope in	Scope in
8	2,000	Scope out	Scope out
9	3,000	Scope out	Scope out
10	2,000	Scope out	Scope out
11	1,000	Scope out	Scope out
12	500	Scope out	Scope out
13	1,000	Scope out	Scope out
14	3,000	Scope out	Scope in
15	2,000	Scope out	Scope out
16	2,500	Scope out	Scope out
17	200	Scope out	Scope out
18	500	Scope out	Scope out
19	700	Scope out	Scope out
Total Group Revenue	221,400		
Total Scoped In		175,000	203,000
Total Scoped Out		46,400	18,400
% Scoped In		79%	92%

For demonstration purposes the scoping is based on revenue only, in practice it will include an assessment of other key balances in the financial statements of the component.

Understanding the Environment of the Group and its Components

In order to gain an understanding of the group, the group audit engagement team performs similar activities to those discussed in **Chapter 6,** 'Gathering Audit Evidence' and **Chapter 7,** 'The Risk Assessment Process'. Gathering audit evidence and engaging in the risk process is an integral part of the group audit engagement team's activities. Based on the results of their findings, they will issue '**Group Audit Instructions**' to the component auditors. The group audit instructions will deal principally with such matters as the following:

- the financial reporting standards applicable to the financial statements of the component to be audited;
- group accounting policies – which should be consistent throughout the group;
- foreign currency exchange rates, which should be applied consistently throughout the group;
- risks identified at the group level that relate to the group as a whole or are component-specific (e.g. a component operating in a poorly regulated economy will be deemed to have a higher risk of fraud than other components);
- related parties identified at a group level for the purpose of disclosing related-party year-end balances and transactions during the year;
- guidance with regard to the role of internal audit (usually relating to the requirements of the Sarbanes–Oxley Act 2002 (SOX) work on internal controls); this is discussed in **Chapter 2**, Section 2.9. Where the company is required to be SOX-compliant, a significantly increased amount of work will be required on the area of fraud – particularly for companies listed on the New York Stock Exchange, where compliance with the Foreign Corrupt Practices Act (FCPA) will be required to be considered;
- procedures for reconciling and confirming intercompany balances between the parent and components and between components;
- the need for component compliance with additional laws and regulations (that may not be in operation in the local component environment).

Other additional detailed instructions include:

- a template error schedule, which will capture all errors noted on the component audit;
- a template for disclosure deficiencies, which will assist the component auditor to report to the group auditor any additional disclosures required for consolidation purposes;
- a template for control deficiencies, which will assist the component auditor to report to the group auditor any internal control weaknesses that need to be brought to the attention of those charged with governance.

Practically speaking, such instructions can be quite extensive for large complex groups. Thus, their preparation (and information-gathering in order to prepare them) can be an ongoing task for the group audit engagement team.

Obligations on the Component Auditor to Follow Group Audit Instructions

The effectiveness and efficiency of the group audit consolidation process depends very much on the co-operation of component auditors. Hence, the planning and guidance/ instructions given to component auditors must be clear, unambiguous and precise.

The group audit engagement team will have issued a strict set of deadlines by which information must be supplied to them.

The group audit engagement team will have issued a 'pack' for completion by each component auditor. The pack will include such matters as:

- component auditor confirmation of performance of the component audit by reference to group financial reporting policies;
- component auditor response to all risks identified by the group audit engagement team – if those risks apply to the component;
- component auditor to communicate any additional risks identified at a local level only;
- component auditor to confirm details of relevant related parties' disclosure information;
- the extent of use (if any) of internal audit by the component management;
- component auditor to inform the group audit engagement team of any breaches of laws and regulations by the component;
- component auditor to inform the group audit engagement team of any evidence of management bias in the financial reporting by the component;
- completed schedules to be provided to the group audit engagement team (e.g. unadjusted errors schedule, disclosure of internal control deficiencies, etc.;
- an audit clearance report (the component auditor's opinion on the component audited financial information for consolidation in the group financial statements).

Materiality

Figure 20.2 below depicts the complexity involved in setting materiality when dealing with the audit of a group. A **group materiality figure** will be set, which represents the value at which an item's omission or inclusion will impact materially on the decisions of users of

FIGURE 20.2: SETTING OF MATERIALITY FOR A GROUP

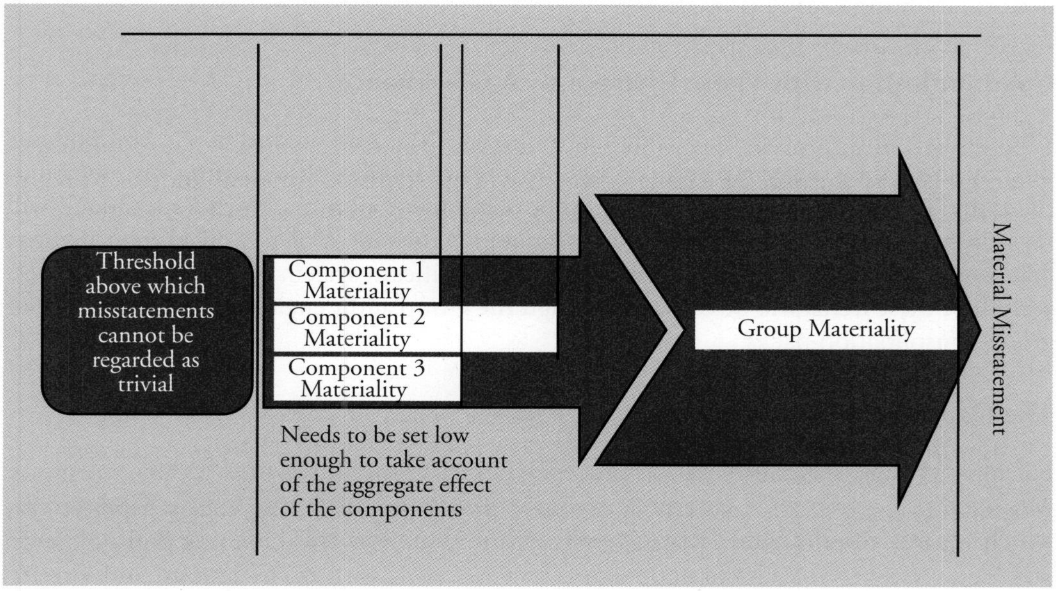

the group financial statements. However, the group auditor needs to consider the aggregate impact of undetected errors and must therefore set materiality for each component lower than that of the overall group materiality, albeit still relevant to the significance of the component.

Once materiality is set at the component level, the component auditor will set performance materiality; however, the group audit team must assess the reasonableness of this.

20.5 GROUP AUDIT CONCLUDING ACTIVITIES

As the group audit process reaches its final stages there are still important audit concluding activities to take place. The group auditor must assess if **sufficient appropriate audit evidence** has been obtained from all components. Any material matters to be brought to the attention of **those charged with governance** must be collated and assessed. While the process of consolidating all of the component financial information will have been completed, technical issues regarding accounting treatment or disclosures could arise and will need to be addressed. Each of these possible concluding activities are now outlined.

Review of Sufficiency and Appropriateness of Component Auditor Work

Throughout the audit, it will have been necessary for the group auditor to maintain a close involvement in the work of the component auditors, which can include a review of their files or a re-performance of some of the audit activities facilitated through an onsite visit (should the review of electronic files be deemed insufficient). This will be particularly necessary should the group auditor determine that significant risks exist relating to the component itself or should he have concerns regarding the component auditor. Should the group auditor determine that the work of the component auditor does not represent **sufficient appropriate audit evidence,** then the group audit engagement team should perform additional audit procedures.

Communication with Those Charged with Governance

The group auditor is required to discuss not only the issues arising in the components directly audited by the group audit engagement team, but also those arising with regard to the individual components audited by other component auditors. Such issues noted will include non-compliance with laws and regulations, instances of perceived management bias, unadjusted errors (shown by components), significant system or control deficiencies, etc. All of these items will be collated through the group audit engagement team review of group consolidation packs.

The Consolidation Process

For most groups, the consolidation process will be a complicated one. Ideally, the group will operate a group-wide enterprise resource planning (ERP) system (see **Chapter 9**), which reports the individual components in the same format. This will greatly reduce the work of the group auditor. However, in the absence of such a system, the group audit engagement team will have an onerous task in checking that:

- all components are included in the consolidated financial statements;
- all necessary consolidation adjustments have been accounted for, as per IFRS 10 *Consolidated Financial Statements*, and consistent accounting policies have been applied;
- all intergroup balances and transactions have been disclosed and eliminated, where appropriate on consolidation.

This will be one of the key areas where the group auditor will use **computer-assisted audit techniques (CAATs)** – see **Chapter 9**.

20.6 IMPORTANCE OF COMMUNICATION IN GROUP AUDITS

Co-ordinating the audit process in any audit can be difficult, even for a straightforward audit, so when it comes to the audit of a complex group, e.g. with different worldwide geographical locations, etc., the importance of coordination is critical. Co-ordination is necessary to ensure that the audit is planned and performed in an effective and efficient manner, and completed:

- within specified timeframes;
- within specified requirements (applicable financial reporting standards, consistent group accounting policies and legal and regulatory requirements); and
- in compliance with ethical requirements and applicable auditing standards.

The timeframe of the group audit commences with identifying with group management the planned date for the issue of the audited financial statements, allowing the group auditor to build a plan that works backwards from this date. Once the timeframe is determined it then needs to be communicated. The group auditor communicates with the component auditors through a combination of group audit instructions, onsite visits to component auditors or conference calls and video-conferencing.

It is essential that the group auditor maintains a control checklist of the issue of the group audit instructions to each component, as well as the return receipt of their responses, and that these are documented on the audit file. Additionally, any other meetings held with the component auditors should be documented and recorded on the audit file.

20.7 CONCLUSION

While for group audits the audit procedures surrounding the actual audit of the financial statements remain unchanged from those for non-group audits, and the ISAs, as discussed throughout previous chapters of this textbook, are applied consistently to group audits as they are to non-group audits, the process of managing a group audit is very different and poses its own set of challenges and risks to the group audit firm.

The overriding point is that the group audit partner holds ultimate responsibility for the audit opinion expressed on the group financial statements and for this reason he must be confident with regard to:

- adequate scoping of components;
- adequate review of component auditor competency and eligibility; and
- adequate review of component auditor work.

SUMMARY OF LEARNING OBJECTIVES

Learning Objective 1 Understand the additional considerations with regard to acceptance and continuance of group audits.

The group auditor must consider whether the audit firm has sufficient resources to manage a group audit, which requires the audit of components as well as component auditor reviews. He must also consider if the firm has adequate policies and procedures to deal with the requirements of ISA 600.

Learning Objective 2 Understand the requirements of ISA 600 with regard to risk-assessment procedures and communication of group audit instructions to component auditors.

A comprehensive assessment of audit risk is necessary. A thorough understanding of the group and its components is vital for this assessment. Key risks identified will be notified to all component auditors.

Learning Objective 3 Be able to identify the considerations of the auditor with regard to group components, component auditors and materiality when performing an audit of group financial statements.

From the outset, it is essential to establish the scope of the group audit (what components are included) and carry out an assessment of the professionalism and competency of the component auditors.

Learning Objective 4 Understand the importance of adequately scoping in and out significant and non-significant components.

The auditor must give consideration to the scoping in and out of significant and insignificant components, ensuring that he has adequate coverage of key balances in the financial statements.

Learning Objective 5 Know the auditor's responsibilities with regard to materiality when auditing group financial statements.

Determining audit materiality for the group and for each of its components is critical to the audit process. This information needs to be clearly communicated to the component auditors.

Learning Objective 6 Understand the concluding activities required by the group auditor prior to the issue of an opinion.

The auditor has a very large task in checking the consolidation of the financial statements of a group and must **check that all components have been consolidated** with **consistent accounting policies** and that **all intercompany items have been eliminated**.

Prior to issuing the audit opinion, the group auditor needs to ensure that he has performed **adequate scoping of components**; an **adequate review of component auditor competency and eligibility** and an **adequate review of component auditor work**. All of this is necessary to ensure that the group auditor issues the appropriate audit opinion on the group financial statements.

Additionally, the group auditor must ensure **adequate documentation** is maintained with regard to component auditor communication.

QUESTIONS

Self-test Questions

20.1   What is a component of a group?

20.2   What is a component auditor?

20.3   Is it correct that the group auditor can rely on the opinion of the component auditor?

20.4   Is the process of a group audit entirely different from that of a non-group audit?

20.5   What additional acceptance and continuance considerations might the auditor have in relation to a group?

20.6   What deems a component 'insignificant'?

20.7   What audit procedures must the group auditor perform on insignificant components?

20.8   Why is setting materiality for a group more difficult?

20.9   Name eight items that might be included in a set of 'group audit instructions'.

20.10   Why might an insignificant component need to be scoped back in for full audit procedures?

20.11   Why does the group auditor need to consider the appropriateness of the component auditor work if the component auditor has told him he carried out all audit procedures and no material errors exist?

20.12   Why is communication so important for group audits?

20.13   What should the auditor take into consideration when at the consolidation process stage of the audit?

Review Questions

(See Suggested Solutions to Review Questions in **Appendix D**.)

Question 20.1

The external, independent audit of group financial statements poses particular challenges for auditors at the audit planning stage. At the commencement of a group audit, the auditor is required to set the audit plan and strategy for the overall group.

Puretrans Plc is a global-reach group of companies with component entities in North and South America, Canada, Mongolia and China. Your firm has been auditors of the group for the past three years.

The audit is for the year ending 31 December 2012. In May 2012, Puretrans plc acquired a wholly owned subsidiary in Mongolia, its first investment in that country. For convenience, in the first year the local firm of auditors is not an affiliate of the parent auditors. This will change for 2013.

Requirement
(a) Describe **six** matters of significance that you would include in the group audit planning document for Puretrans plc.
(b) There have been recent calls for widening the incidence of joint audits from what is currently a voluntary option to a mandatory regime for Plcs. Discuss **two** advantages and **two** disadvantages of joint audits.

CHALLENGING QUESTIONS FOR PART IV

(Suggested Solutions to Challenging Questions are available through your lecturer.)

These challenging questions aim to test your knowledge of **Chapters 18** to **20**, relating to audit work conclusion, audit reports and group audits. They are intended to test your practical application of what you have learned in these chapters and so you are presented with a case study on which you are asked to deliver on a number of requirements.

Question IV.1

You have reached the completion stage of the audit of Large Company Limited and as audit senior, you are carrying out the audit procedures relating to audit work conclusions.

Requirement
(a) Going concern is one of the key principles on which a set of financial statement is based and as such the audit manager wants to be sure you are aware of the respective responsibilities relating to going concern. Outline the responsibilities in the form of a memo, including:
   (i)   the directors and auditors responsibilities with respect to going concern;
   (ii) the basic steps required by the auditor under ISA (UK and Ireland) 570 *Going Concern*; and
   (iii) a list of financial and operational events that may impact on the going concern assumption.
(b) A junior member of the audit team asks if during an audit you note that there is a future event that could result in the company no longer being a going concern, what type of audit opinion you would issue. Advise the audit junior of the possible opinions
   (i)   where there is **full disclosure** of the event and its possible outcome is included in the financial statements; and
   (ii) where there is **no disclosure** of the event and its possible outcome is included in the financial statements.
(c) The completeness assertion is always the most difficult to prove for the auditor, particularly when it comes to provisions and contingent liabilities. Outline how the auditor might search for unrecorded liabilities.

Question IV.2

It is March 2013 and you have performed all audit work conclusion, except for the preparation and review of the error schedule. Appendix 1 below is a summary of all the errors collected throughout the audit.

Requirement
(a) Collate the errors shown in Appendix 1 and provide the audit manager with a summary of the error schedule (which shows the impact on the statement of comprehensive

income and on the statement of financial position). Assume all transactions are VAT-exempt and ignore tax.

(b) Considering the error schedule that you have prepared, are these financial statements materially misstated (performance materiality is €2,731,875 and overall materiality is €3,642,500)?

(c) If management refuse to amend the contents of the financial statements, what type of an audit opinion would you issue?

(d) Draft the 'basis of opinion' and 'opinion' paragraphs to support the opinion you believe is necessary.

APPENDIX 1: SUMMARY OF ERRORS FOUND THROUGHOUT THE AUDIT

Error 1 – The review of management's bad debt provision revealed that it was understated by €315,000. Additional audit procedures performed revealed a further understatement of €450,000.

Error 2 – Analytical procedures performed on accruals revealed an omission of accruals to the value of €670,000. Further procedures revealed a further omission of €800,000 (all expense-related).

Error 3 – Stock was overvalued by €150,000 due to the incorrect application of bill of material (BOM) values – this was assigned to a lack of controls in the area.

Error 4 – Revenue recognition issues considered:

• Goods sold on a sale-or-return basis in December 2012, where the return period did not end until February 2013, were recognised as sales in 2012. The value of the sale was €550,000.

• Goods dispatched on 31 December 2012 but which did not arrive at the customer's premises until 4 January 2013 were included in revenue in 2012. The contract stipulated that ownership passed on arrival of the goods at the customer's premises. The value of the sale was €1,500,000.

• Goods dispatched on 31 December 2012 but which did not arrive at the customer's premises until 4 January 2013 were included in revenue in 2012. The contract stipulated that ownership passed on dispatch of the goods and payment was received on date of dispatch. The value of the sale was €800,000.

• A customer balance showing a credit balance of €300,000 was included within trade receivables.

Appendix A

EXTANT LIST OF ETHICAL AND AUDITING STANDARDS AND OTHER SELECTED MATERIAL (FRC)

The primary chapter in which the standard is addressed is noted alongside; however discussions on the standard may appear in other chapters.

Standard	Standard Name	Primary Chapter Reference
ES 1	Integrity, Objectivity and Independence (Revised) (December 2011)	2
ES 2	Financial, Business, Employment and Personal Relationships (Revised December 2010)	2
ES 3	Long Association with the Audit Engagement (Revised October 2009)	2
ES 4	Fees, Remuneration and Evaluation Policies, Litigation, Gifts and Hospitality (Revised December 2010)	2

ES 5	Non-Audit Services Provided to Audit Clients (Revised) (December 2011) Provisions available for Small Entities (Revised December 2010) Ethical Standard for Reporting Accountants (October 2006)	2
ISQC 1 (UK and Ireland)	International Standard on Quality Control (UK and Ireland) – Quality Control for Firms that Perform Audits and Reviews of Financial Statements, and other Assurance and Related Service Engagements	2
ISA (UK and Ireland) 200	Overall Objectives of the Independent Auditor and the Conduct of an Audit in Accordance with International Standards on Auditing (UK and Ireland)	1
ISA (UK and Ireland) 210	Agreeing the Terms of Audit Engagements	5
ISA (UK and Ireland) 220	Quality Control for an Audit of Financial Statements	5
ISA (UK and Ireland) 230	Audit Documentation	6
ISA (UK and Ireland) 240	The Auditor's Responsibilities Relating to Fraud in an Audit of Financial Statements	3
ISA (UK and Ireland) 250 – Section A	Consideration of Laws and Regulations in an Audit of Financial Statements	3
ISA (UK and Ireland) 250 – Section B	The Auditor's Right and Duty to Report to Regulators in the Financial Sector	N/A
ISA (UK and Ireland) 260	Communication With Those Charge With Governance – Revised October 2012	3 and 18
ISA (UK and Ireland) 265	Communicating Deficiencies in Internal Control to Those Charged with Governance and Management	8 and 18

ISA (UK and Ireland) 300	Planning an Audit of Financial Statements	5
ISA (UK and Ireland) 315	Identifying and Assessing the Risks of Material Misstatement Through Understanding of the Entity and Its Environment – Revised January 2013	7, 8 and 10
ISA (UK and Ireland) 320	Materiality in Planning and Performing an Audit	5
ISA (UK and Ireland) 330	The Auditor's Responses to Assessed Risks	7
ISA (UK and Ireland) 402	Audit Considerations Relating to an Entity Using a Service Organisation	10
ISA (UK and Ireland) 450	Evaluation of Misstatements Identified During the Audit	18
ISA (UK and Ireland) 500	Audit Evidence	6
ISA (UK and Ireland) 501	Audit Evidence – Specific Considerations for Selected Items	6
ISA (UK and Ireland) 505	External Confirmations	6, 13, 14 and 16
ISA (UK and Ireland) 510	Initial Audit Engagements – Opening Balances	6 and 11–17
ISA (UK and Ireland) 520	Analytical Procedures	5, 7 and 11–18
ISA (UK and Ireland) 530	Audit Sampling	6
ISA (UK and Ireland) 540	Auditing Accounting Estimates, Including Fair Value Accounting Estimates, and Related Disclosures	6 and 11–17
ISA (UK and Ireland) 550	Related Parties	18
ISA (UK and Ireland) 560	Subsequent Events	18
ISA (UK and Ireland) 570	Going Concern	18
ISA (UK and Ireland) 580	Written Representations	18
ISA (UK and Ireland) 600	Special Considerations – Audits of Group Financial Statements (Including the Work of Component Auditors)	20
ISA (UK and Ireland) 610	Using the Work of Internal Auditors	10

APB (FRC) Bulletin	Developments in Corporate Governance Affecting the Responsibilities of Auditors of Companies Incorporated in Ireland	2
Practice Note 25 (Revised)	Attendance at Stocktaking	12
Briefing Paper	Professional Scepticism – Establishing a common understanding and reaffirming its central role in delivering audit quality	3

Appendix B

PAST EXAM[1] QUESTIONS REFERENCE LIST

Ethics

CA Proficiency 2 Autumn 2012 Q1d, Q2d
CA Proficiency 2 Summer 2012 Q1e
CA Proficiency 2 Autumn 2011 Q1e, Q2d
CA Proficiency 2 Summer 2011 Q1c
CA Proficiency 2 Summer 2010 Q1f
CA Proficiency 2 Autumn 2010 Q3b
CA Proficiency 2 Autumn 2010 Q1e
CA Proficiency 2 Autumn 2009 Q1e, Q2a
CA Proficiency 2 Summer 2009 Q1
CA Proficiency 2 Sample Paper 1 Q1f
CA Proficiency 2 Sample Paper 2 Q2d
CA Proficiency 2 Summer 2009 Q1
Professional Three Summer 2007 Q1a
Professional Three Summer 2006 Q1e
FAE Autumn 2012 Simulation 1
FAE Autumn 2007 Q1a
FAE Autumn 2003 Q1a, e

Laws and Regulations

CA Proficiency 2 Sample Paper 2 Q2a
Professional Three Autumn 2006 Q1a
Professional Three Summer 2005 Q1c

Non-current Assets

CA Proficiency 2 Autumn 2012 Q2a, b
CA Proficiency 2 Autumn 2011 Q2b

CA Proficiency 2 Summer 2011 Q1b
CA Proficiency 2 Summer 2010 Q3a, b, c
CA Proficiency 2 Autumn 2009 Q1b, Q3a
CA Proficiency 2 Summer 2009 Q2b, Q4
Professional Three Summer 2008 Q3
Professional Three Summer 2006 Q3
Professional Three Summer 2005 Q6
FAE Autumn 2005 Q3
FAE Autumn 2004 Q2

Intangible Non-current Assets/Research and Development

CA Proficiency 2 Autumn 2010 Q3c, d, e
Professional Three Summer 2005 Q6
FAE Autumn 2006 Q5

Investments

CA Proficiency 2 Autumn 2009 Q2d
Professional Three Summer 2007 Q1d
Professional Three Autumn 2006 Q3

Inventories

CA Proficiency 2 Autumn 2012 Q1a, b
CA Proficiency 2 Summer 2010 Q2a, b, c
CA Proficiency 2 Autumn 2009 Q2c
CA Proficiency 2 Sample Paper 1 Q1c, Q1d, Q1e
CA Proficiency 2 Summer 2009 Q1

---

[1] Chartered Accountants Ireland.

Professional Three Summer 2008 Q4
Professional Three Autumn 2008 Q3
Professional Three Autumn 2007 Q3
Professional Three Autumn 2006 Q6
Professional Three Autumn 2005 Q4, Q5
FAE Autumn 2008 Q2
FAE Autumn 2005 Q1d
FAE Autumn 2005 Q4
FAE Autumn 2003 Q4

Revenue and Trade Receivables

CA Proficiency 2 Autumn 2012 Q2c
CA Proficiency 2 Summer 2012 Q1c
CA Proficiency 2 Autumn 2011 Q1c
CA Proficiency 2 Autumn 2010 Q1d
CA Proficiency 2 Autumn 2009 Q3a, b
CA Proficiency 2 Sample Paper 1 Q1a, b
CA Proficiency 2 Sample Paper 2
Q1a, b, e, Q3
CA Proficiency 2 Summer 2009 Q1
Professional Three Autumn 2008 Q4
Professional Three Summer 2007 Q1b,
Q3
Professional Three Autumn 2007 Q1b,
Q4
Professional Three Summer 2006 Q6
Professional Three Autumn 2006 Q1b
Professional Three Summer 2005 Q4
Professional Three Autumn 2005 Q1e
FAE Autumn 2012 Simulation 3
FAE Autumn 2011 Simulation 3
FAE Autumn 2007 Q2, Q4
FAE Autumn 2006 Q1a
FAE Autumn 2004 Q3
FAE Autumn 2003 Q3, Q5

Bank and Cash in Hand/Bank Loan

CA Proficiency 2 Summer 2011 Q2
CA Proficiency 2 Summer 2009 Q1,
Q2e, Q4
Professional Three Summer 2007 Q1e
Professional Three Summer 2006 Q3
Professional Three Summer 2005 Q1b,
Q2

FAE Autumn 2008 Q5
FAE Autumn 2007 Q4

Purchases and Trade Payables

CA Proficiency 2 Summer 2012 Q2b
CA Proficiency 2 Autumn 2011 Q2a, Q3
CA Proficiency 2 Summer 2010 Q1e
CA Proficiency 2 Autumn 2010 Q4b
CA Proficiency 2 Autumn 2009 Q1c, d,
Q4a, b, c
CA Proficiency 2 Sample Paper 1 Q3
CA Proficiency 2 Sample Paper 2 Q4
Professional Three Autumn 2008 Q6
Professional Three Autumn 2007 Q1a,
Q5, Q6
Professional Three Summer 2006 Q4
Professional Three Autumn 2005 Q1c
FAE Autumn 2006 Q5
FAE Autumn 2004 Q5

Payroll

CA Proficiency 2 Autumn 2009 Q3a
CA Proficiency 2 Summer 2009 Q3
Professional Three Summer 2008 Q6
Professional Three Summer 2007 Q2
Professional Three Autumn 2006 Q1c
Professional Three Summer 2005 Q3
Professional Three Autumn 2005 Q6
FAE Autumn 2005 Q5

Provisions

CA Proficiency 2 Autumn 2009 Q2b
Professional Three Summer 2008 Q4
Professional Three Autumn 2007 Q2
Professional Three Summer 2006 Q1c, Q4
Professional Three Autumn 2005 Q5

Dividends

CA Proficiency 2 Summer 2010 Q4c
Professional Three Summer 2006 Q1b, Q3

Related Parties

Professional Three Summer 2008 Q1a
Professional Three Autumn 2008 Q4

Professional Three Summer 2007 Q6
Professional Three Autumn 2006 Q5
FAE Autumn 2006 Q3

Controls and Reporting to Those Charged with Governance

CA Proficiency 2 Autumn 2012 Q1c
CA Proficiency 2 Summer 2010 Q1d
CA Proficiency 2 Autumn 2010 Q1c
CA Proficiency 2 Autumn 2009 Q1a, b
CA Proficiency 2 Sample Paper 2 Q1c
CA Proficiency 2 Summer 2009 Q2a
Professional Three Summer 2008 Q6
Professional Three Summer 2007 Q5
Professional Three Summer 2006 Q1d, Q5
Professional Three Autumn 2005 Q4, Q6
FAE Autumn 2011 Simulation 3
FAE Autumn 2010 Simulation 3
FAE Autumn 2010 Simulation 2
FAE Autumn 2007 Q4

Audit Planning

CA Proficiency 2 Summer 2012 Q2a
CA Proficiency 2 Autumn 2010 Q3a
FAE Autumn 2011 Simulation 2
FAE Autumn 2006 Q3
FAE Autumn 2004 Q4

Engagement Letter

Professional Three Autumn 2008 Q1b
Professional Three Summer 2005 Q1a
FAE Autumn 2012 Simulation 1
FAE Autumn 2005 Q1a

Audit Sampling

CA Proficiency 2 Sample Paper 2 Q1d
Professional Three Autumn 2007 Q1c
Professional Three Summer 2006 Q1a
Professional Three Autumn 2005 Q1a

Materiality

CA Proficiency 2 Summer 2012 Q1b
CA Proficiency 2 Summer 2010 Q1a
Professional Three Summer 2007 Q6

Professional Three Summer 2006 Q5, Q6
FAE Autumn 2011 Simulation 3
FAE Autumn 2007 Q1d
FAE Autumn 2004 Q1a

Audit Estimates

CA Proficiency 2 Summer 2010 Q4

Audit Confirmations

CA Proficiency 2 Autumn 2011 Q4c
CA Proficiency 2 Autumn 2010 Q1a

Audit Acceptance

FAE Autumn 2010 Simulation 1

Audit Risk

CA Proficiency 2 Summer 2012 Q1a
CA Proficiency 2 Summer 2011 Q1a
CA Proficiency 2 Autumn 2011 Q1a, b
CA Proficiency 2 Summer 2010 Q1c
CA Proficiency 2 Autumn 2010 Q1b
CA Proficiency 2 Autumn 2009 Q1a
CA Proficiency 2 Sample Paper 2 Q2b, Q2c
Professional Three Summer 2008 Q5
Professional Three Autumn 2008 Q5, Q6
Professional Three Summer 2007 Q5, Q6
Professional Three Autumn 2006 Q4
Professional Three Summer 2005 Q1d
Professional Three Autumn 2005 Q5
FAE Autumn 2012 Simulation 2
FAE Autumn 2011 Simulation 3
FAE Autumn 2010 Simulation 1
FAE Autumn 2008 Q3

Analytical Review

CA Proficiency 2 Summer 2010 Q1a, b
CA Proficiency 2 Autumn 2009 Q1c, Q3a
FAE Autumn 2012 Simulation 2

Audit Completion

CA Proficiency 2 Autumn 2012 Q4
CA Proficiency 2 Summer 2011 Q3b, c
CA Proficiency 2 Autumn 2010 Q2b

Professional Three Autumn 2008 Q2
Professional Three Summer 2007 Q4
Professional Three Autumn 2007 Q5
Professional Three Autumn 2006 Q1e
FAE Autumn 2011 Simulation 1

Audit Reports

CA Proficiency 2 Autumn 2012 Q3
CA Proficiency 2 Summer 2011 Q3a
CA Proficiency 2 Autumn 2011 Q3b
CA Proficiency 2 Summer 2010 Q4b
CA Proficiency 2 Autumn 2010 Q2b
CA Proficiency 2 Autumn 2009 Q2c, Q3a
CA Proficiency 2 Summer 2009 Q4
CA Proficiency 2 Sample Paper 1 Q2
CA Proficiency 2 Sample Paper 2 Q3
Professional Three Summer 2008 Q2
Professional Three Autumn 2008 Q2
Professional Three Summer 2007 Q2
Professional Three Autumn 2007 Q2
Professional Three Summer 2006 Q2
Professional Three Autumn 2006 Q2
Professional Three Summer 2005 Q2
Professional Three Autumn 2005 Q2
FAE Autumn 2012 Simulation 3
FAE Autumn 2011 Simulation 1
FAE Autumn 2010 Simulation 2
FAE Autumn 2008 Q2
FAE Autumn 2007 Q3
FAE Autumn 2006 Q2
FAE Autumn 2005 Q2
FAE Autumn 2004 Q1c, Q2
FAE Autumn 2003 Q2

Subsequent Events and Going Concern

CA Proficiency 2 Summer 2012 Q3
CA Proficiency 2 Autumn 2011 Q4a
CA Proficiency 2 Summer 2010 Q4a
Professional Three Summer 2008 Q1e
FAE Autumn 2008 Q4
FAE Autumn 2004 Q1b

Management Representations/Letter of Representation

CA Proficiency 2 Autumn 2010 Q2a, c
CA Proficiency 2 Summer 2010 Q4a
Professional Three Summer 2008 Q1b
Professional Three Autumn 2006 Q5
Professional Three Autumn 2005 Q1b
FAE Autumn 2003 Q1b

Fraud

Professional Three Autumn 2007 Q1d
Professional Three Summer 2005 Q4
Professional Three Autumn 2005 Q3
FAE Autumn 2011 Simulation 2
FAE Autumn 2008 Q5

Internal Audit

CA Proficiency 2 Sample Paper 2 Q5
Professional Three Summer 2008 Q1c
FAE Autumn 2008 Q1b

Sufficient Appropriate Audit Evidence

FAE Autumn 2010 Simulation 2

Miscellaneous

CA Proficiency 2 Autumn 2011 Q4
CA Proficiency 2 Autumn 2010 Q4a
CA Proficiency 2 Summer 2009 Q2c, d
CA Proficiency 2 Sample Paper 1 Q4
Professional Three Autumn 2008
Q1a, c, d
Professional Three Autumn 2008 Q1e
Professional Three Summer 2007 Q1c
Professional Three Autumn 2007 Q1e
Professional Three Summer 2005 Q1e, Q5
Professional Three Autumn 2005 Q1d
FAE Autumn 2008 Q1a, Q1c, Q1d
FAE Autumn 2007 Q1b, Q1c
FAE Autumn 2006 Q1b, Q1c, Q1d, Q4
FAE Autumn 2005 Q1b, Q1c
FAE Autumn 2004 Q1d

Appendix C

LARGE COMPANY LIMITED[1]

Directors' Report and Financial Statements
Year Ended 31 December 2012

Registered Number (Specify)

June 2013

NOTE: REQUIREMENT FOR LARGE COMPANY STATUS

To qualify the company must satisfy at least two of the following criteria for two years in a row:

Turnover greater than: €15.24 million
Balance Sheet total greater than: €7.62 million
Employees greater than: 250

(Note: These Financial Statements are for Illustrative Purposes only, and are NOT intended as the Study Source for Financial Reporting. Further note that the cash flow has been excluded and full disclosure requirements with respect to defined pension contribution and financial derivatives are also excluded as they are not relevant to support discussions in this textbook.)

---

[1] Source: based on *Pro Forma Financial Statements 2011 (Republic of Ireland)* (© Charted Accountants Ireland, 2011).

LARGE COMPANY LIMITED

Directors' Report and Financial Statements

CONTENTS

LARGE COMPANY LIMITED: DIRECTORS, ADVISORS AND OTHER INFORMATION

Directors (Executive)	Thomas Hogan (Chairperson)
	Mark Hogan (Managing Director)
	Kevin Byrne
	Linda Connolly
	Deirdre Hogan
	David Stuart (British)
Directors (Non-Executive)	Francis Day
	John Night
	Fred Afternoon (American)
Secretary	Timothy Byrne
Auditors	Opinion & Co
	Chartered Accountants
	Balance Street
	Dublin 2
Bankers	General Bank Limited
	Money Street
	Dublin 9
Solicitors	Legal and Co
	Barrister Street
	Dublin 2
Registered office	123 Principal Street
	Dublin 5

LARGE COMPANY LIMITED: DIRECTORS' REPORT

The directors present their report and audited financial statements for the year ended 31 December 2012.

Principal Activities and Review of the Business

The company's principal activity continued to be the manufacture of furniture.

Revenue has increased by 41% to €280,250,000. The directors believe that this trend will continue for the foreseeable future as a new line of furniture has effectively broken into the luxury market. Demand for this range has also increased in foreign countries with €42,625,000 of the increase being attributable to exports.

All other ranges are selling successfully and are expected to do so for the coming year.

Future Developments

The directors are hopeful that the new line of furniture will expand into the United States. At present all sales are either in Ireland or in the United Kingdom. Market research has indicated that turnover could as much as double in the next three years if the major retail outlets in the United States accept the range. Negotiations are ongoing and should be completed by July.

Results and Dividends

	€000
The profit for the financial year amounted to	60,394
It is recommended that this be dealt with as follows:	
Ordinary dividends	
– dividends paid [*State date*] 2012 of 30.34c per share	(25,500)
	34,894
Statement of comprehensive income at beginning of year	50,360
Reserve movements	200
Statement of comprehensive income at end of year	85,454

Research and Development

The company is involved in the development of two new ranges of furniture for future commercial production. These ranges are the "Authentic Mexican Pine range" and the "Mahogany Cast Iron range". An additional employee has been employed to investigate these designs and to develop accompanying accessories.

Branch Operations

The company has overseas branch operations as follows:

Name of branch	Country of operation
Wood kit	Northern Ireland
Wood fit	England

Directors

The present membership of the Board is set out in the schedule of Directors, Advisors and Other Information. Details of directors' shareholdings, related interests and transactions are provided in note 6 to the financial statements.

Mr Kevin Byrne and Ms Linda Connolly retire from the board by rotation in accordance with the Articles of Association and, being eligible, offer themselves for re-election. Ms Deirdre Hogan was appointed to the board during the year and, in accordance with the Articles of Association, retires and offers herself for election. Mr John Hogan retired from the board during the year and the directors express their sincere appreciation for his contribution to the company over the many years he served as a director.

Political Donations

The company made the following disclosable political donations in the current year:

- Party A   –   €60,000
- Party B   –   €60,000
- Party C   –   €5,500

Principal Risks and Uncertainties

Financial Risk Management Objectives and Policies

The company uses financial instruments throughout its business. It uses derivatives to manage interest rate and currency exposures and to achieve a desired profile of borrowings. All transactions in derivatives are designed to hedge against risks without engaging in speculative transactions. The core risks associated with the company's financial instruments (i.e. its interest-bearing loans and debt, cash and cash equivalents, short-dated liquid investments and finance leases, on the operational level trade receivables and payables) are currency risk, interest rate risk, credit risk and liquidity risk. The board reviews and agrees policies for the prudent management of these risks as follows.

Currency Risk

The company's activities in the UK are conducted primarily in sterling, this results in low levels of currency transaction risk, variances affecting operational activities in this regard are reflected in operating costs or in cost of sales in the statement of comprehensive income in the years in which they arise. The principal foreign exchange risk is translation-related, arising from fluctuations in the Euro value of the company's net investment in sterling. The company manages its borrowings, where practical and cost-effective, to partially hedge the foreign currency assets. Hedging is done using currency borrowings in sterling (same currency as the assets), or by using currency swaps.

Finance and Interest Rate Risk

The company's objective in relation to interest rate management is to minimise the impact of interest rate volatility on interest costs in order to protect recorded profitability. A long-term strategy for the management of the exposure considers the amount of floating rate debt that is anticipated over the period and the sensitivity of the interest charge on this debt to changes in interest rates, and the resultant impact on reported profitability. The company has a mix of fixed and floating rate debt, and uses interest rate swaps to exchange at predetermined intervals the difference between fixed and floating interest rates by reference to a predetermined notional principal. The majority of these swaps are regarded as hedging financial instruments.

Liquidity and Cash Flow Risk

The company's objective is to maintain a balance between the continuity of funding and flexibility through the use of borrowings with a range of maturities. The company's policy is to ensure that sufficient resources are available either from cash balances, cash flows and near-cash liquid investments to ensure all obligations can be met when they fall due. To achieve this the company ensures that its liquid investments are in highly-rated counterparties; when relevant, it limits the maturity of cash balances and borrows the majority of its debt needs under term financing.

Credit Risk

The fair value of the company's financial assets are provided in the following table.

	2012	2011
	€000	€000
Cash and cash equivalents	104,200	105,530
Trade and other receivables	15,200	17,500
Derivative financial instruments	2,290	1,630
Other financial assets	36,400	15,300
	158,090	139,960

Other financial assets includes holdings in listed and unlisted share capital.

The company's credit risk is predominantly attributable to its trade receivables. Provisions for bad debts are made based on historical evidence and any new events which might indicate a reduction in the recoverability of cash flows. The company's receivables are made up of a large number of customers and hence the risk of default is reduced. In addition, the company uses credit insurance when allowing credit to more risky customers, requests letters of credit, parent company guarantees or cash collateral.

The company may be exposed to credit-related loss in the event of non-performance by counterparties in respect of cash and cash equivalents and derivative financial instruments. However, the company considers the risk to be negligible as it only transacts with financial institutions that are rated as investment grade or above. Information on the derivative financial instruments is provided in note 25.

Payment of Payables

The directors acknowledge their responsibility for ensuring compliance with the provisions of the EC (Late Payment) Regulation 2012. Procedures have been implemented to identify the dates upon which all invoices fall due for payment and to ensure that payments are made by such dates. Such procedures provide reasonable assurance against material non-compliance with the regulations.

Books of Account

The measures taken by the directors to ensure compliance with the requirements of Section 202, Companies Act 1990, regarding proper books of account are: the implementation of necessary policies and procedures for recording transactions; the employment of competent accounting personnel with appropriate expertise; and the provision of adequate resources to the financial function. The books of account of the company are maintained at [address/es].

Events After the Reporting Period

Details of important events affecting the company which have taken place since the end of the financial year are given in note 31 to the financial statements.

Auditors

In accordance with Section 160(2) of the Companies Act, 1963, the auditors, Opinion & Co., Chartered Accountants, will continue in office.

On behalf of the board

Thomas Hogan   Mark Hogan   [*state date*] 2012
Director   *Director*

LARGE COMPANY LIMITED: STATEMENT OF DIRECTORS' RESPONSIBILITIES[2]

The directors are responsible for preparing the Directors' Report and the financial statements in accordance with Irish law and regulations. Irish company law requires the directors to prepare financial statements giving a true and fair view of the state of affairs of the company and the profit or loss of the company for each financial year. Under that law, the directors have elected to prepare the financial statements in accordance with Irish Generally Accepted Accounting Practice (accounting standards issued by the Financial Reporting Council and promulgated by the Institute of Chartered Accountants in Ireland and Irish law).

In preparing these financial statements, the directors are required to:
• select suitable accounting policies and then apply them consistently;
• make judgements and accounting estimates that are reasonable and prudent;
• prepare the financial statements on the going concern basis unless it is inappropriate to presume that the company will continue in business.

The directors are responsible for keeping proper books of account that disclose with reasonable accuracy at any time the financial position of the company and enable them to ensure that the financial statements comply with the Companies Acts 1963–2012. They are also responsible for safeguarding the assets of the company and hence for taking reasonable steps for the prevention and detection of fraud and other irregularities.

---

[2] FRC Bulletin 1(I) *Compendium of Illustrative Auditor's Reports on Irish Financial Statements.*

INDEPENDENT AUDITOR'S REPORT TO THE MEMBERS OF LARGE COMPANY LIMITED[3]

We have audited the financial statements of Large Company Limited for the year ended 31 December 2012, which comprise the Statement of Financial Position, the Statement of Comprehensive Income, the Statement of Cash Flows and the Statement of Changes in Equity and the related notes 1–35. The financial reporting framework that has been applied in their preparation is Irish law and International Financial Reporting Standards (IFRS) as adopted by the European Union.

This report is made solely to the company's members, as a body, in accordance with section 193 of the Companies Act 1990. Our audit work has been undertaken so that we might state to the company's members those matters we are required to state to them in an auditor's report and for no other purpose. To the fullest extent permitted by law, we do not accept or assume responsibility to anyone other than the company and company's members as a body, for our work, for this report, or for the opinions we have formed.

Respective responsibilities of directors and auditor As explained more fully in the Statement of Directors' Responsibilities, the directors are responsible for the preparation of the financial statements giving a true and fair view. Our responsibility is to audit and express an opinion on the financial statements in accordance with applicable law and International Standards on Auditing (UK and Ireland). Those standards require us to comply with the Financial Reporting Council's Ethical Standards for Auditors.

Scope of the audit of the financial statements An audit involves obtaining evidence about the amounts and disclosures in the financial statements sufficient to give reasonable assurance that the financial statements are free from material misstatement, whether caused by fraud or error. This includes an assessment of: whether the accounting policies are appropriate to the company's circumstances and have been consistently applied and adequately disclosed; the reasonableness of significant accounting estimates made by the directors; and the overall presentation of the financial statements. In addition, we read all the financial and non-financial information in the Large Company Limited annual report to identify material inconsistencies with the audited financial statements. If we become aware of any apparent material misstatements or inconsistencies, we consider the implications for our report.

Opinion on financial statements In our opinion the financial statements:
• give a true and fair view, in accordance with IFRS as adopted by the European Union, of the state of the company's affairs as at 31 December 2012 and of its profit for the year then ended; and

---

[3] Based on APB Bulletin 1(I): Compendium of Illustrative Auditor's Reports on Irish Financial Statements, Example 5, and adapted to reflect a clean audit opinion for 'Large Company Limited'.

- have been properly prepared in accordance with the requirements of the Companies Acts 1963–2012.

Separate opinion in relation to IFRS as issued by the IASB As explained in the financial statements in the statement of accounting policies under the 'Basis of Preparation' paragraph, the company, in addition to applying IFRS as adopted by the European Union, has also applied IFRS as issued by the International Accounting Standards Board (IASB).

In our opinion the financial statements comply with IFRSs as issued by the IASB.

Opinions on other matters prescribed by the Companies Acts 1963–2012:
- We have obtained all the information and explanations which we consider necessary for the purposes of our audit.
- In our opinion, proper books of account have been kept by the company.
- The financial statements are in agreement with the books of account.
- In our opinion, the information given in the directors' report is consistent with the financial statements.
- The net assets of the company, as stated in the balance sheet, are more than half of the amount of its called-up share capital and, in our opinion, on that basis there did not exist at 31 December 2012 a financial situation which, under section 40(1) of the Companies (Amendment) Act 1983, would require the convening of an extraordinary general meeting of the company.

Matters on which we are required to report by exception We have nothing to report in respect of the provisions in the Companies Acts 1963–2012 which require us to report to you if, in our opinion, the disclosures of directors' remuneration and transactions specified by law are not made.

John Smith   **31/03/2013**   13 The Crescent, Dublin 2.

John Smith
for and on behalf of ABC & Co.

LARGE COMPANY LIMITED: STATEMENT OF ACCOUNTING POLICIES

(for the year ended 31 December 2012)

The following accounting policies have been applied consistently in dealing with items which are considered material in relation to the company's financial statements.

Basis of Preparation

The financial statements have been prepared on the going concern basis and in accordance with IFRS as adopted by European Union (additionally Large Company Limited has applied IFRS, as issued by the International Accounting Standards Board (IASB) and Irish statute comprising the Companies Acts 1963 to 2012). Accounting Standards generally accepted in Ireland in preparing financial statements giving a true and fair view are those published by Chartered Accountants Ireland and issued by the Financial Reporting Council.

Revenue Recognition

Revenue is stated net of trade discounts, VAT and similar taxes and derives from the provision of goods falling within the company's ordinary activities.

Goodwill

Goodwill represents the excess of the cost of an acquisition over the fair value of the identifiable net assets acquired at the date of acquisition. After initial recognition, goodwill is stated at cost less any accumulated impairment losses, with the carrying value being reviewed for impairment at least annually, and more frequently if events or changes indicate that the carrying value may be impaired.

Other Intangible Assets

Intangible assets acquired separately from a business are capitalised at cost. They are amortised using the straight-line basis over their estimated useful lives. For example, the cost of a patent for a new design of furniture is amortised over the term of the patent, which is three years on a straight-line basis.

In all cases intangible assets are reviewed for impairment at the end of the first full financial year following acquisition, and in other periods if events or changes in circumstances indicate that the carrying value may not be recoverable.

Investment Properties

Investment properties are recognised using the fair value model, revalued annually and are not depreciated or amortised. This treatment is a departure from the requirement of company law to provide depreciation on all fixed assets which have a limited useful life. However, these investment properties are not held for consumption but for investment. The directors believe that the policy of not providing depreciation is necessary in order for the financial statements to give a true and fair view, since the current value of investment properties, and changes to that current value, are of prime importance rather than the calculation of annual depreciation.

Changes in fair value are recognised in the comprehensive income statement.

Property, Plant and Equipment

All tangible fixed assets are initially recorded at historic cost. Freehold land and buildings (all non-specialised properties) are revalued on the basis of fair values.

Revaluation gains are recognised in other comprehensive income.

Revaluation losses caused by a clear consumption of economic benefits are recognised in other comprehensive income to the extent that there is a revaluation surplus relating to the asset. Beyond this the loss is recognised as an expense in the comprehensive income statement.

Finance costs directly attributable to the construction of freehold buildings are capitalised as part of the cost of these assets. The capitalisation rate used is the weighted average rate of general borrowing outstanding during the period. Only capital items with a net of VAT cost in excess of €1,000 are capitalised.

Depreciation

Depreciation is provided on all property, plant and equipment other than freehold land and investment properties, at rates calculated to write off the cost or valuation, less estimated residual value, of each asset systematically over its expected useful life, as follows:

Freehold buildings   – straight-line over 22 years
Leasehold land and buildings   – straight-line over the term of the lease
Plant and machinery   – straight-line over 3 years
Motor vehicles   – straight-line over 4 years

The carrying values of tangible fixed assets are reviewed annually for impairment in periods if events or changes in circumstances indicate the carrying value may not be recoverable. A full year's depreciation is charged in the year of addition and in the year of disposal.

Available-for-sale Securities

The company usually holds certain equity securities (listed and unlisted) which are classified as available-for-sale and are measured at fair value, less incremental direct costs, on initial recognition. At the reporting period end the investments are revalued to fair value and any increase in value is credited to equity. Impairments are debited to equity (fair value reserve) to the extent that they were previously credited to equity, with further reductions in value beyond this amount being charged to the comprehensive income statement. When the investment is derecognised (for example, on sale) the cumulative revalued amount to that point is released from the fair value reserve to the comprehensive income statement.

Government Grants

Grants are recognised when there is reasonable assurance that the grant will be received and all attaching conditions have been complied with. Grants towards capital expenditure are credited to deferred income and are released to the comprehensive income statement over the expected useful life of the related assets, by equal annual instalments. Grants towards revenue expenditure are released to the comprehensive income statement as the related expenditure is incurred.

Inventories

Inventory is stated at the lower of cost and net realisable value. In the case of finished goods and work in progress, cost is defined as the aggregate cost of raw material, direct labour and the attributable proportion of direct production overheads based on a normal level of activity. Net realisable value is based on normal selling price, less further costs expected to be incurred to completion and disposal.

Research and Development

Research expenditure is written off to the comprehensive income statement in the year in which it is incurred. Development expenditure is written off in the same way unless the directors are satisfied as to the technical, commercial and financial viability of individual projects. In this situation, the expenditure is deferred and amortised over the period during which the company is expected to benefit.

Leasing and Hire-purchase Commitments

Assets held under finance leases and hire purchase contracts are capitalised in the balance sheet and are depreciated over their useful lives with the corresponding lease or hire purchase obligation being capitalised as a liability. The interest element of the finance lease rentals is charged to the comprehensive income statement over the period of the lease and represents a constant proportion of the balance of capital repayments outstanding.

Operating lease rentals are charged to the comprehensive income statement on a straight-line basis over the lease term.

Provisions for Liabilities

Provisions for the expected legal costs are charged against profits when an action against the company commences. The effect of the time value of money is not material, therefore the provisions are not discounted.

Income Taxes

Current tax assets and liabilities are measured at the amount expected to be recovered or paid to the taxation authorities, based on tax rates and laws that are enacted or substantively enacted by the date of the statement of financial position.

Deferred income tax is recognized using the statement of financial position (SoFP) liability method, providing for temporary differences between the tax bases and the accounting bases of assets and liabilities. Deferred tax is calculated on an undiscounted basis at the tax rates that are expected to apply in the period when the liability is settled or the asset is realised, based on tax rates and laws enacted or substantively enacted at the date of the statement of financial position.

Foreign Currencies

Functional and Presentation Currency

Items included in the financial statements are presented in Euros, the currency of the primary economic environment in which the entity operates (the "functional currency").

The principal exchange rates used for the translation of results, cash flows and balance sheets into Euro were as follows:

	2012	2011
	€1=Stg£	*€1=Stg£*
Average	0.810	0.867
Year end	0.816	0.835

Transactions and Balances

Transactions in foreign currencies are recorded at the rate ruling at the date of the transaction. Monetary assets and liabilities denominated in foreign currencies are retranslated at the rate of exchange ruling at the date of the statement of financial position or the contracted rate. All differences are taken to the statement of comprehensive income. Translation differences are disclosed separately in a "foreign currency reserve", within equity reserves.

Dividends

Dividends to the company's equity shareholders (holders of ordinary shares) are recognised as a liability of the company when approved by the company's shareholders. Preference share dividends are cumulative and cannot be waived, therefore they are treated in the same manner as debt interest and are accrued for, if not paid when due.

Pension Costs

The company operates both defined benefit and defined contribution schemes. The asset recognised in the statement of financial position represents the fair value of the scheme assets offset by the present value of the scheme liabilities.

Defined Contribution Scheme

Pension contributions in respect of defined contribution schemes for employees are charged to the comprehensive income statement as they become payable in accordance with the rules of the scheme. The assets are held separately from those of the company in an independently administered fund. Differences between the amounts charged in the comprehensive income statement and payments made to pension funds are treated as assets or liabilities.

Defined Benefit Scheme

For defined benefit retirement benefit plans, the cost of providing benefits is determined using the Projected Unit Credit Method, with actuarial valuations being carried out at each statement of financial position date. Actuarial gains and losses that exceed 10% of the greater of the present value of the company's defined benefit obligation and the fair value of plan assets as at the end of the prior year are amortised over the expected average remaining working lives of the participating employees. Past service cost is recognised immediately to the extent that the benefits are already vested, and otherwise is amortised on a straight-line basis over the average period until the benefits become vested.

The retirement benefit obligation recognised in the statement of financial position represents the present value of the defined benefit obligation as adjusted for unrecognised actuarial gains and losses and unrecognised past service cost, and as reduced by the fair value of the plan assets. Any asset resulting from this calculation is limited to unrecognised actuarial losses and past service cost, plus the value of available refunds in future contributions to the plan.

Stock Compensation Scheme

Certain employees have been granted stock options with an exercise price less than the quoted market price on the date of grant. This is recorded as deferred compensation within shareholders' equity and recognised in the comprehensive income statement over the vesting period (three years) of the inventory options. To hedge the related exposure the company buys, or transfers from existing portfolios, the number of shares necessary to satisfy all potential outstanding obligations under the plan.

Capital Instruments

Shares are included in shareholders' funds. Other instruments are classified as liabilities if not included in shareholders funds and if they contain an obligation to transfer economic benefits. The finance cost recognised in the comprehensive income statement in respect of capital instruments other than equity shares is allocated to periods over the term of the instrument at a constant rate on the carrying amount.

Issue Costs of Capital Instruments

The cost of issue of preference shares and debentures are charged to the comprehensive income statement on a straight-line basis over the life of the instrument. A corresponding amount is transferred from reserves to the share premium account.

LARGE COMPANY LIMITED

STATEMENT OF COMPREHENSIVE INCOME

For the year ended 31 December 2012

	Notes	2012 €000	2011 €000
Revenue	1	280,250	198,500
Cost of sales		(140,250)	(120,800)
Gross profit		140,000	77,700
Other operating income		750	700
Investment revenue	3	350	330
Distribution costs		(23,000)	(20,000)
Administration costs		(35,000)	(34,000)
Profit/(loss) on sale of tangible fixed assets	2	420	(120)
Loss on disposal of available-for-sale investments	2	(120)	–
Impairment of investment property	2	(10,000)	–
Finance costs	4	(550)	(550)
Profit before tax		72,850	24,060
Income tax expense	10	(12,456)	(8,500)
Profit for the year	29	60,394	15,560

Other comprehensive income

	Notes	2012 €000	2011 €000
Unrealised surplus on revaluation of investment property		–	10,000
Impairment of revalued investment property		(10,000)	–
Unrealised deficit on revaluation of freehold property		(17,200)	–
Actuarial gain on market value of the defined benefit pension scheme's assets and liabilities (note 8)		200	80
Currency translation effects on foreign borrowings		(200)	150

Fair value movement on effective cash flow financial instruments	100	(200)
Income tax on other comprehensive income	–	–
Other comprehensive income net of tax	(27,100)	10,030
Total comprehensive income for the year	33,294	25,590

Thomas Hogan Mark Hogan   [*state date*] 2013
Director   *Director*

LARGE COMPANY LIMITED

STATEMENT OF FINANCIAL POSITION

As at 31 December 2012

	Notes	2012	2011
ASSETS		**€000**	**€000**
Non-current assets			
Property, plant and equipment	13	130,050	140,500
Other intangible assets	12	1,150	1,140
Derivative financial instruments	25	1,900	1,460
Financial assets	14	112,200	110,200
Pension asset		1,200	1,000
		246,500	254,300
Current assets			
Inventories	15	49,774	35,020
Trade and other receivables	16–17	15,200	17,500
Derivative financial instruments	25	390	170
Available-for-sale investments	18	4,200	5,000
Cash and other cash equivalents		104,200	105,530
		173,764	163,220
Total assets		**420,264**	**417,520**

		2012	2011
EQUITY AND LIABILITIES		**€000**	**€000**
Equity attributable to owners			
Capital and Reserves			
Share capital	28	84,050	78,160
Share premium account	29	2,990	570
Retained earnings	29	85,254	50,360
Other components of equity	29	1,600	28,700
Total equity		**173,894**	**157,790**
Non-current liabilities			
Long-term borrowing	20	20,350	27,560
Other liabilities	20	89,590	89,070
Long-term provisions	24	750	500
Total non-current liabilities		**110,690**	**117,130**
Current liabilities			
Trade and other payables	19	109,320	114,650
Short-term borrowing	19	4,250	9,650
Other	19	19,420	15,560
Current tax payable	19	2,690	2,740
Total current liabilities		**135,680**	**142,600**
Total liabilities		**246,370**	**259,730**
Total equity and liabilities		**420,264**	**417,520**

Approved by the directors on (*specify date*) 2013

On behalf of the board

Thomas Hogan   Mark Hogan
Director   Director

LARGE COMPANY LIMITED

STATEMENT OF CHANGES IN EQUITY

For the year ended 31 December 2012

	Share Capital €000	Share Premium €000	Other Components of Equity €000	Retained Earnings €000	Total Equity €000
At 1 January 2012	78,160	570	28,700	50,360	157,790
Comprehensive Income:					
Profit for year				60,394	60,394
Other Comprehensive Income:					
Impairment of investment property			(10,000)		(10,000)
Deficit on revaluation of freehold property			(17,200)		(17,200)
Actuarial gains on defined benefit pension scheme			200		200
Exchange adjustment			(200)		(200)
Fair value gains on cash flow hedge			100		100
Transactions with owners:					
Share issue	5,890				5,890
Share premium		2,420			2,420
Equity dividends paid				(25,500)	(25,500)
At 31 December 2012	**84,050**	**2,990**	**1,600**	**85,254**	**173,894**

(*Note:* that a statement of cash flows is excluded from this proforma set of accounts as it is not relevant to support discussions in this textbook.)

LARGE COMPANY LIMITED

NOTES (*FORMING PART OF THE FINANCIAL STATEMENTS*)

1. Revenue and Segmental Analysis

The company operates in one industry and within two geographical markets, Ireland and the United Kingdom.

Area of activity

	Ireland		United Kingdom		Total	
	2012 €000	2011 €000	2012 €000	2011 €000	2012 €000	2011 €000
Revenue by origin						
Continuing	168,150	129,025	112,100	69,475	280,250	198,500
Revenue by destination						
Continuing	180,000	140,000	100,250	58,500	280,250	198,500
Profit						
Continuing	68,714	24,674	22,476	13,286	91,190	37,960
Common costs					(8,840)	(13,950)
Operating profit					82,350	24,010
Exceptional items					(9,700)	(120)
Investment and other income					200	170
Profit on ordinary activities before taxation					72,850	24,060
Net assets						
Continuing	190,728	186,180	63,042	46,170	253,770	232,350
Unallocated net liabilities					(81,076)	(75,560)
Total net assets					172,694	156,790

Unallocated net liabilities comprise some dividends, taxation and net debt.

2. Exceptional Items

	2012		2011
	€000	€000	€000
Recognised in arriving at operating profit			
Bad debts		(1,000)	–
Recognised below operating profit			
Profit/(loss) on sale of property, plant and equipment	420		(120)
Impairment of investment property	(10,000)		
(Loss) on disposal of fixed asset investments	(120)		–
		(9,700)	
		(10,700)	(120)

Details of the impairment of the investment property is disclosed in note 14 to the financial statements.

The company also disposed of a rare cutting machine. This transaction resulted in the above exceptional gain of €420,000.

Shares costing €1,700,000 were also disposed off, resulting in an exceptional loss of €120,000.

3. Investment Revenue

	2012	2011
	€000	€000
Available-for-sale non-current asset investment income	210	209
Available-for-sale current asset investment income	75	71
Other investment income	10	9
Net return from defined benefit pension scheme (note 8)	20	11
Bank interest receivable	30	23
Other interest receivable and similar income	5	7
	350	330
Of which derived from listed investments	215	205

4. Finance Costs

	2012 €000	2011 €000
On bank loans, overdrafts and other loans wholly repayable within 5 years	95	98
On other loans	15	19
Mark to market of designated fair value hedges and related debt*	5	8
Finance lease interest in respect of finance leases and hire purchase contracts	18	20
Finance costs in respect of completed freehold building	12	15
On overdue tax	5	-
Dividends on preference shares	300	300
Additional finance costs of financial liabilities	100	90
	550	550

* The company uses interest rate swaps to convert fixed rate debt to floating rate debt. Fixed rate debt which has been converted to floating rate debt using interest rate swaps is stated in the statement of financial position at adjusted fair value to reflect movements in the underlying interest rates. The movement in this adjustment, together with the offsetting movement in the fair value of the swaps, is taken to the statement of comprehensive income each year.

5. Statutory and Other Information

Operating profit is stated after charging/(crediting):	2012 €000	2011 €000
Depreciation and amounts written off assets:		
Depreciation of property, plant and equipment owned	48,580	42,200
Depreciation of property, plant and equipment held under finance leases	32,625	31,300
	81,205	73,500
Amortisation of development costs (see below: also included in research and development)	250	225
Amortisation of patents	200	200
Goodwill – impairment	50	50
	500	475

	2012 €000	2011 €000
Exceptional item – Impairment in value of investment property	10,000	–
Total depreciation, amortisation and impairment in value of non-current assets	91,705	73,975
Exchange differences	25	23
Provision for legal costs charged	50	15
Provision for legal costs released	(15)	–
Operating lease rentals	800	800
Government grants amortised	(1,500)	(850)

	2012 €000	2011 €000
Auditor's remuneration:		
Ireland audit services	45	42
United Kingdom audit services	11	10
	56	52
Research and development:		
Amortisation of deferred development expenditure	250	225
Expenditure written off	1,800	1,530
Total research and development	2,050	1,755

6. Directors' Remuneration and Transactions

6a. Directors' Remuneration

Staff costs include the following in respect of directors of the company:

	2012 €000	2011 €000
Fees	250	235
Amounts paid to third parties for the service of directors	25	20
Company pension contributions to money purchase schemes	45	36
Pensions to former directors	15	5
Amounts receivable under long-term incentive schemes	15	25
Compensation for loss of office (note 6h)	10	-
	360	321

	No.	No.
The number of directors for whom benefits accrued under the money purchase scheme during the year were:	6	6
The number of directors for whom retirement benefits are accruing under defined benefit schemes amounted to:	1	1

6b. Loans to Directors

Included in "Other receivables" (note 17) is a loan to a director, Deirdre Hogan, to purchase a house. The loan is permitted by the Companies Act 1990, to enable Deirdre Hogan to carry out her duties as director. It is an unsecured interest-free loan repayable in monthly instalments.

	2012 €	2011 €
At 1 January 2011	58,000	66,000
Monies advanced by company during the year	25,000	30,000
Amount repaid during the year	(23,000)	(38,000)
At 31 December 2011	60,000	58,000

The maximum amount outstanding during the year was €62,000 (2011: €66,000).

An amount of €20,000 is included in receivables in respect of goods supplied at favourable rates by the company to Mr Byrne. The total arm's-length value of the transaction was €22,000. The whole amount has been paid since the statement of financial position date. The maximum amount outstanding from Mr Byrne to the company at any time during the year was €5,000.

6c. Directors and Secretary and their Interests

The directors at 31 December 2012 and their interests in the share capital of the company were as follows:

	At 31 December 2012		At 1 January or on Subsequent Appointment	
	Ordinary Shares	Preference Shares	Ordinary Shares	Preference Shares
Thomas Hogan	26,601,000	100,000	26,600,000	100,000
Mark Hogan	130,500	-	130,000	-
Kevin Byrne	131,000	-	130,000	-
Linda Connolly	750	-	-	-
Deirdre Hogan	200,250	100,000	200,000	100,000
David Stewart	101,000	-	100,000	-
Timothy Byrne	550,500	-	550,000	-

On 20 February 2013 Timothy Byrne acquired another 2,000,000 shares in the company, increasing his total holding to 2,550,500 shares. In all other respects the interests of the directors were unchanged as shown above, except for exercising options to purchase shares.

6d. Interests in the Share Option Scheme

The group operates a directors' share option scheme and in addition to the interests disclosed above certain directors have options to acquire shares in Large Company Ltd. Full details are as follows.

Directors	Number of Options Over Ordinary Shares of €1 Each in Large Company Limited				Exercise price	Market Price at Date of Exercise	Date from Which Exercisable	Expiry Date
	01/01/12	Granted	Exercised	31/12/12				
T. Hogan	5,000	-	1,000	4,000	€1.10	€1.35	Jan 2011	Jan 2014
M. Hogan	5,000	-	500	4,500	€1.20	€1.40	Jan 2011	Jan 2014
K. Byrne	5,000	-	1,000	4,000	€1.20	€1.37	Jan 2012	Jan 2015
L. Connolly	1,000	-	750	250	€1.10	€1.42	Jan 2010	Jan 2015
D. Hogan	5,000	-	250	4,750	€1.05	€1.56	Jan 2011	Jan 2014
D. Stewart		2,000	1,000	1,000	€1.25	€1.58	Jan 2013	Jan 2014
T. Byrne		1,000	500	500	€1.25	€1.49	Jan 2015	Jan 2015
	21,000	3,000	5,000	19,000				

No options lapsed during the year. The market price of the shares at 31 December 2012 was €1.60 and the range during the year was €1.30 to €1.72. See the accounting policy and note 7 for further details of the option scheme.

6e. Controlling Party

Thomas Hogan, the chairman of the company, is considered by the directors to be the company's ultimate controlling party as he holds 32% of the ordinary share capital of the company. Included in this are 5,000,000 shares which are held in trust for his children.

6f. Material Interests of Directors in Contracts with the Company

The following information relates to transactions between the company and companies in which Thomas Hogan is considered to have an interest:

(a) The Pine Timber Company supplied materials to the value of €3,500,000 (2010: €3,000,000) for the pine bedroom range of furniture. The maximum amount outstanding at any time during the year was €300,000. Nothing was outstanding at the year end.
(b) The company has a loan from Wood Timber Company of €200,000 (2010: €250,000). This loan is included in bank and other loans (note 21). €50,000 is repayable within one year, the balance being repayable after more than one year.

(All transactions were made at arm's length.)

Trading Transactions

These are summarised below.

	€000
Aggregate sales to the directors of the company	1,005
Aggregate purchased from the directors of the company (including the €3,500,000 mentioned above)	4,000
Aggregate net amounts due from the directors of the company	60
Aggregate value of all the arrangements with directors at the end of the year expressed as a percentage of the company's relevant assets at the time.	1.1%

All the transactions were made on normal trading terms.

6g. Dividends

Details of the directors' shareholdings in the company are set out in the Report of the Directors.

The rates of dividends on all shares are set out in note 11 of the financial statements.

6h. Other

John Hogan retired as director on 30 April 2012 and was paid compensation for loss of office of €10,000. There were no amounts due to or from John Hogan at the balance sheet date.

During the year security was provided on a bank loan of €4,000 for J. Matthews, a senior officer of the company. The maximum amount owing on the loan in the year was €4,000. The balance on the loan at the year-end was €3,800.

7. Staff Costs

	2012 €000	2011 €000
Wages and salaries	9,256	8,856
Social security costs	1,110	954
Pension costs (see note 8)	1,523	1,230
	11,889	11,040

The average number of persons employed by the company (including executive directors) during the year analysed by category, was as follows:

	2012 No.	2011 No.
Management	39	37
Administration	56	54
Production	208	198
Research and development	7	3
Sales	23	18
	333	310

Directors and senior management staff are entitled to participate each year in a share option plan without payment if the company achieves, on average, a 5% increase in profitability each year, for the next three years. The benefits consist of the right to buy Large Company Limited shares at a predetermined price. This plan started on 1 August 2008 and has a rolling seven-year duration, with the rights being vested after three years.

In order to hedge the related exposure the company buys – or transfers from existing treasury portfolios – the number of shares necessary to satisfy all potential outstanding obligations under the plan when the benefit is awarded and holds them until the maturity of the plan or the exercise of the rights. Movements in the options and the relevant prices are as follows:

Number of Options Over Ordinary Shares of €1 Each in Large Company Limited				Exercise price	Weighted Average Price at Date of Exercise	Date from Which Exercisable	Expiry Date
01/01/12	Granted	Exercised	31/12/12				
25,000	-	15,000	10,000	€1.10	€1.35	Jan 2012	Jan 2014
15,000	-	10,000	5,000	€1.20	€1.40	Jan 2012	Jan 2014
15,000	-	7,500	7,500	€1.20	€1.37	Jan 2012	Jan 2014
10,000	-	5,000	5,000	€1.10	€1.42	Jan 2012	Jan 2013
15,000	-	2,000	13,000	€1.05	€1.56	Jan 2012	Jan 2014
	200,000	-	200,000	€1.25		Jan 2013	Jan 2016
	150,000	-	150,000	€1.25		Jan 2013	Jan 2015
80,000	350,000	39,500	390,500				

The weighted value of the share options granted in the period was 50c. This was measured using a binomial model which incorporated the following assumptions:

	2012
Weighted average share price	€1.58
Exercise price	€1.25
Expected volatility	17%
Option life (average from date granted)	4 years
Expected dividend	10c per year
Risk-free interest rate	5%

Expected volatility is based on an annualised standard deviation of the continuously compounded rates of return on the share price over time. It is assumed that market conditions will not change materially and the probability of the company achieving the target profitability is estimated at 60%.

Amount included in the wages and salaries expense relating to the bonus accrued for the option compensation scheme is as follows:

	2012	2011
	€000	€000
Granted 2012	35	–
Total charge for the period	35	–

8. Pension information

Analysis of the total amount charged to operating profit:

	2012	2011
	€000	€000
Current service cost	1,338	1,075
Past service cost	150	125
Cost of other post-retirement benefits (note 9)	35	30
Total operating charge (note 7)	1,523	1,230

The company operates both defined benefit and defined contribution schemes in Ireland. The majority of the schemes are defined contribution with defined benefit schemes still in existence for those employees who joined before 1985 who did not want to transfer benefits to the contribution scheme.

The total pension cost for the company was €1,338,000 (2011: €1,075,000) of which €1,200,000 (2011: €975,000) relates to the defined contribution schemes and €138,000 (2011: €100,000) to the defined benefit schemes.

Defined Contribution Scheme

The company operates the defined contribution scheme, Pension Scheme Fund, for its employees. The assets of the scheme are held separately from those of the company in an independently administered fund.

Defined Benefit Scheme

The pension cost of the defined benefit scheme is assessed on an annual basis in accordance with the advice of qualified actuaries using the projected unit method. The funding policy for this scheme is to make the maximum annual contributions that are deductible for income tax purposes.

(Note that the full disclosure requirements for Defined Benefit Scheme are not included as they are not relevant for the purpose of this textbook.)

9. Post Retirement Benefits Other than Pension Schemes

The company operates a plan which provides employees with over 30 years' service with benefits, other than pensions. The liabilities in respect of these benefits are assessed by qualified independent actuaries, applying the projected unit method. The charge for the year is €35,000 (2011: €30,000).

	Medical & Golf Fund
Main assumptions	
Discount rate for obligations (% per annum)	8.5%
Inflation rate (% per annum)	5%

10. Income Tax Expense

(a) Analysis of Charge in Period

	2012		2011	
	€000	€000	€000	€000
Current tax:				
ROI corporation tax on profits of the period	12,275		7,628	
Adjustment in respect of previous period	–		–	
	12,275		7,628	
Double taxation relief	(22)		(19)	
Total RoI current tax		12,253		7,609
Foreign tax on income for the period	23		21	
Adjustment in respect of previous period	–		–	
Total foreign current tax		23		21
Total current tax (note 10(b))		12,276		7,630
Deferred tax:				
Origination and reversal of timing differences		150		830
Effect of increased tax rate on opening liability		27		36
Derivative financial instruments		3		4
Total deferred tax (note 24)		180		870
Tax on profit on ordinary activities		12,456		8,500

The tax effect on the profit and loss account relating to the exceptional items recognised below operating profit is a charge of €90,000 (2011: Credit of €36,000).

(b) Factors Affecting the Tax Charge for the Period:

The tax assessed for the period is lower than the standard rate of corporation tax in the RoI (31%). The differences are explained below:

	2012 €000	2011 €000
Profit on ordinary activities before taxation	72,850	24,060
Profit on ordinary activities multiplied by standard rate of corporation tax in the RoI of 31% (2011: 30%)	22,584	7,218
Effects of:		
Expenses not deducted for tax purposes	864	2,352
Capital allowances for period in excess of depreciation	(9,076)	(1,472)
Utilisation of tax losses	(2,100)	(470)
Rollover relief on profit on disposal of property	–	–
Higher tax rates on overseas earnings	4	2
Adjustment to tax charge in respect of previous periods	–	–
Current tax charge for period (note 10(a))	12,276	7,630

(c) Factors that may Affect Future Tax Charges

Based on current capital investment plans, the company expects to continue to be able to claim capital allowances in excess of depreciation in future years but at a slightly lower level than in the current year. The company has now used all brought-forward tax losses, which have significantly reduced tax payments in recent years.

Suggested Disclosure where there has been a Gain on Revaluation The company's overseas tax rates are higher than those in Ireland because the profits earned in the United Kingdom are taxed at a rate of 45%. The company expects a reduction in future tax rates following a recent announcement that the rate of tax in the United Kingdom is to reduce to 40%.

11. Dividends

	2012 €000	2011 €000
Equity Dividends on Ordinary Shares		
Dividend paid of 30.34c (2010: 12.79c) per share	25,500	10,000
	25,500	10,000

A dividend is proposed of €15,500 (18.44c per share); (2011: €25,500 (30.34c per share))

12. Other Intangible Assets

	Patents €000	Goodwill €000	Development Costs €000	Total €000
Cost:				
At 1 January 2012	600	1,000	415	2,015
Additions	–	–	510	510
At 31 December 2012	600	1,000	925	2,525
Amortisation:				
At 1 January 2012	200	600	75	875
Provided during the year	200	50	250	500
At 31 December 2012	400	650	325	1,375
Net book value				
At 31 December 2012	200	350	600	1,150
At 1 January 2012	400	400	340	1,140

13. Property, Plant and Equipment

	Freehold Land and Buildings €000	Plant and Machinery €000	Motor Vehicles €000	Total €000
Cost:				
At 1 January 2012	400,000	113,625	28,800	542,425
Additions	–	82,250	35,000	117,250
Deficit on revaluation	(355,000)	–	–	(355,000)
Disposals	–	(49,000)	(14,655)	(63,655)
At 31 December 2012	45,000	146,875	49,145	241,020
Depreciation				
At 1 January 2012	319,800	61,725	20,400	401,925
Charge for year	18,000	48,705	14,500	81,205
Elimination on revaluation	(337,800)	–	–	(337,800)
Disposals	–	(29,000)	(5,360)	(34,360)
At 31 December 2012	–	81,430	29,540	110,970
Net book value				
At 31 December 2012	45,000	65,445	19,605	130,050
At 1 January 2012	80,200	51,900	8,400	140,500

Freehold Land and Buildings

Freehold land (€15,000,000) which is not depreciated is included in land and buildings. On 31 December the land was valued at its original cost by the external surveyors (details in next paragraph).

The freehold buildings were valued at €30,000,000 being their value in use, in accordance with the Appraisal and Valuation Manual of the Royal Institution of Chartered Surveyors, on 31 December 2012 by external professional surveyors, Big Value Valuers and Co., Chartered Surveyors. The property had been revalued to €385,000,000 but by 31 December 2012 was depreciated to €47,200,000. The sudden decline in value of the freehold buildings was caused by the upsurge of political trouble and the exit of commercial businesses in the local area. The total reduction in the net book value is €17,200,000. The year-end valuation (€30,000,000) is not materially different to the open market value.

Modified Historical Cost

Particulars relating to revalued land and buildings are given below:

	2012	2011
	€000	**€000**
Opening book amount	65,200	95,200
Depreciation	(18,000)	(30,000)
Adjusted book amount	47,200	65,200
Revaluation gain/(loss)		
Recognised in the statement of changes in equity	(17,200)	–
Closing book amount	30,000	65,200

Finance Costs

Where applicable finance costs were capitalised at 10% (2011: 12%). The cost of Freehold buildings includes €5,000,000 of finance costs which were capitalised in 2011. No finance costs were capitalised in 2012.

Historical Cost Information for the Property Included at Valuation

On the historical cost basis, land and buildings would have been included as follows:

	€000
Cost:	
At 1 January 2012 and 31 December 2012	100,000
Cumulative depreciation based on cost	
At 1 January 2012	74,320
Charge for the year	6,500
At 31 December 2012	80,820
Net book values	
At 1 January 2012	25,680
At 31 December 2012	19,180

Other tangible fixed assets are included at cost.

Assets held under Finance Leases or Hire-purchase Agreements

	Plant and Machinery €000	Motor Vehicles €000	Total €000
Net book values			
At 1 January 2012	81,500	6,500	88,000
At 31 December 2012	92,750	17,250	110,000
Depreciation charge for the year			
To 31 December 2012	31,000	1,625	32,625
To 31 December 2011	27,000	4,300	31,300

14. Financial Assets

	Investment Properties €000	Available-for-sale Investments €000	Total €000
Fair value:			
At 1 January 2012	100,000	10,500	110,500
Additions	–	23,700	23,700
Diminution in value	(20,000)	–	(20,000)
Disposals	–	(1,700)	(1,700)
At 31 December 2012	80,000	32,500	112,500
Provision for diminution in value			
At 1 January 2012	–	300	300
Charge for year	–	–	–
Disposals	–	–	–
At 31 December 2012		300	300
Net book value			
At 31 December 2012	80,000	32,200	112,200
At 1 January 2012	100,000	10,200	110,200

Non-current Asset Investments

The statement of financial position value of €112,200,000 reflects the market value of the company's investment properties and available for sale investments as at the year end (2011: €110,200,000). In accordance with the company's accounting policy, these assets are held at fair value. The available-for-sale investments represent an equity stake in an unlisted entity. The stake is classified as available for sale as the company has no power to exercise any influence over the underlying entity.

Investment Properties

The investment properties were valued at €80,000,000, being their fair value for existing use, in accordance with the Appraisal and Valuation Manual of the Royal Institution of Chartered Surveyors, on 31 December 2012 by Big Value Valuers and Co., Chartered Surveyors. This has resulted in an impairment in value to €10,000,000 below the original cost price.

The historical cost and aggregate depreciation based on historical cost calculated at a rate of 5% per annum are as follows:

	€000
Cost	
At 1 January 2012 and 31 December 2012	90,000
Cumulative depreciation based on cost	
At 1 January 2012	18,000
Charge for the year	4,500
At 31 December 2012	22,500
Net book values	
At 1 January 2012	72,000
At 31 December 2012	67,500

True and Fair View Override

Had the investment properties been depreciated in accordance with companies legislation, the reported profit for the year would have been €4,500,000 less and assets and reserves in the statement of financial position €12,500,000 lower.

15. Inventories

	2012 €000	2011 €000
Raw materials and consumables	9,320	7,770
Work in progress	12,530	10,750
Finished goods and goods in transit	27,924	16,500
	49,774	35,020

16. Trade and Other Receivables

Due after One Year

	2012 €000	2011 €000
Loan notes	6,000	8,000
Other receivables:		
Called up share capital not paid	685	875
Prepayments and accrued income:		
Pension prepayment	65	25
Other prepayments	1,950	1,350
	8,700	10,250

17. Trade and Other Receivables

Due within One Year

	2012 €000	2011 €000
Loan notes	1,500	1,500
Trade receivables	3,250	4,100
Other receivables	750	600
Prepayments and accrued income	1,000	1,050
	6,500	7,250

"Other receivables" include amounts advanced to finance the acquisition of shares in the company.

Trade receivables are stated net of a provision of €500,000 (2011: €750,000) for estimated bad debts based on historical experience.

	2012	2011
	€000	€000
Opening balance	750	700
(Decrease)/increase in provision	450	150
Bad debts written off	(700)	(100)
Closing balance	500	750

An aged analysis is utilised to determine the likelihood of payment default.

Aged analysis of trade receivables:

	2012	2011
	€000	€000
Current (within credit terms)	3,100	4,250
30–60 days	420	350
60–90 days	150	140
Greater than 90 days	80	110
	3,750	4,850

The directors consider the net trade receivable value to be representative of fair value.

18. Available-for-sale Investments

	2012	2011
	€000	€000
Other unlisted equity investments	1,200	850
Listed equity investments	3,000	4,150
	4,200	5,000

The unlisted equity investments are recorded at cost. The directors consider that these shares have not diminished in value and that their market value at the date of the statement of financial position is similar to their cost.

The listed equity investments (all of which are listed on the Irish Stock Exchange) are measured at fair value in line with the company's accounting policy.

19. Trade and other Payables: Amounts Falling Due within One Year

	2012	2011
	€000	€000
Bank and other loans (note 21)	4,250	9,650
Obligations under finance leases and hire purchase contracts (note 22)	2,500	4,000
Derivative financial instruments (note 25)	120	80
Trade payables	109,320	114,650
Bills of exchange payable	150	230
Other payables	16,150	10,500
Accruals and deferred income	500	750
	132,990	139,860

Tax payables:

	2012	2011
Corporation tax	2,310	2,280
PAYE	100	120
VAT	80	60
Capital Gains tax	120	80
Other tax	30	110
	2,640	2,650
Social welfare (PRSI)	50	90
	2,690	2,740
	135,680	142,600

Trade payables includes the following:

	2012	2011
Due at the year end to suppliers who claim reservation of title	20,000	21,000

20. Payables: Amounts Falling Due after More than One Year

	2012	2011
	€000	€000
Bank and other loans (note 21)	20,350	27,560
Obligations under finance leases and hire purchase contracts (note 22)	85,000	85,000
Preference shares	3,000	3,000

Derivative financial instruments (note 25)	70	50
	108,420	115,610
Other payables		
Government grants (note 23)	1,308	808
Pension commitments	212	174
Other	–	38
	1,520	1,020
	109,940	116,630

21. Bank Loans

	2012	2011
	€000	**€000**
Current		
Galway bank loan	1,000	1,000
Dublin bank loan	3,250	8,650
	4,250	9,650
Non-current		
Eurobond	3,750	350
Galway bank loan	14,000	15,000
Dublin bank loan	2,600	12,210
	20,350	27,560
Total Bank Loans	24,600	37,210

Analysis of loans

	2012	2011
	€000	**€000**
Not wholly repayable within five years	13,050	17,720
Wholly repayable within five years	11,960	19,990
	25,010	37,710
Issue costs	(410)	(500)
Total	24,600	37,210
Included in current liabilities	(4,250)	(9,650)
Included in long-term liabilities	20,350	27,560

Loan Maturity Analysis

	2012 €000	2011 €000
Bank and other loans comprise amounts repayable:		
In one year or less, or on demand	4,250	9,650
Between one and five years	7,300	9,840
After more than five years	13,050	17,720
	24,600	37,210

The Eurobond is secured by a fixed charge on the land and buil ngs and a ating char on the other assets of the company. It carries a fixed interest ra of 6.9%.

The Dublin bank loan is repayable in instalments over the next six years. It is subject to a variable interest rate based on EURIBOR. The weighted average interest rate during the year was 4.9% (2011: 4.9%).

The Galway bank loan is repayable in instalments over the next eight years. It has a fixed interest rate for 75% of the loan at 5.5%, with the remainder at EURIBOR plus 2%. The weighted average interest for the period was 5.2% (2011: 5.1%).

22. Obligations Under Finance Leases and Hire-purchase Contracts

Analysis and Maturity Schedule

	2012 €000	2011 €000
Repayable within one year	2,500	4,000
Repayable between one and two years	2,500	2,500
Repayable between two and five years	12,000	13,300
Repayable after five years	83,000	82,200
	100,000	102,000
Finance charges and interest allocated to future periods	(12,500)	(13,000)
Total	87,500	89,000
Included in liabilities falling due within one year	2,500	4,000
Included in liabilities falling due after more than one year	85,000	85,000

23. Government Grants Deferred

	Government Grants
	€000
At 1 January 2012	808
Grants received during the year	2,000
Amortisation in the year	(1,500)
At 31 December 2012	1,308

Under agreements between the company and [*state name of agency*] which are dated on various dates between 2010 and 2016, the company has a contingent liability to repay in whole, or in part, grants received amounting to €500,000 (2011: €300,000) if certain circumstances set out in those agreements occur within [10] years of the date of the agreement.

The agreements to which the company was a party were signed between 2010 and 2012 and the amounts received under those agreements amounted to €800,000 (2011: €350,000).

24. Provision for Liabilities

	Deferred Tax	Legal Costs	Post Retirement Benefits	Total
	€000	**€000**	**€000**	**€000**
At 1 January 2012	250	15	235	500
Charged to statement of comprehensive income account	180	50	35	265
Utilised during the year	–	(15)	–	(15)
At 31 December 2012	430	50	270	750

For details on the movements to the legal costs provision see note 34.

Deferred Taxation

	2012 €000	2011 €000
Accelerated capital allowances	430	270
Tax losses carried forward	–	(20)
Undiscounted provision for deferred tax	430	250

25. Derivative Financial Instruments

The company's principal risks and uncertainties and the financial risk management objectives and policies used to manage these, including the use of derivative financial instruments to hedge forecasted transactions and the exposure of the company to credit risk, liquidity risk, interest rate risk and cash flow risk are included in the directors' report.

(Note that the full disclosure requirements for derivative financial instruments are not included as they are not relevant for the purpose of this textbook.)

26. Sensitivity Analysis – Financial Instruments

Interest Rate Risk

At 31 December 2012, if interest rates had been 1% lower with all other variables held constant, post-tax profit for the year would have been €12,000 higher (in 2011 post-tax profits would have been €13,000 higher), arising mainly as a result of lower interest expense on variable borrowings, and other components of equity would have been €11,000 (2011: €11,800) higher, arising mainly as a result of an increase in the fair value of fixed rate financial assets classed as available for sale.

If interest rates had been 1% higher with all other variables held constant, post-tax profits would have been €9,500 lower (in 2011 post-tax profits would have been €11,000 lower), arising mainly as a result of higher interest expense on variable borrowings, and other components of equity would have been €12,950 (2011: €11,500) lower, arising mainly as a result of an increase in the fair value of fixed rate financial assets. Profit is more sensitive to interest rate decreases than increases because of borrowings with capped interest rates. The sensitivity is lower in 2011 than in 2012 because of the increase in outstanding borrowings (see note 21).

Foreign Currency Exchange Rate Risk

At 31 December 2012, if the Euro had weakened 10% against sterling with all other variables held constant, post-tax profits for the year would have been €56,000 lower (in 2011 the post-tax profit would have been €21,000 lower), and other components of equity would have been €18,000 (2011: €17,000) higher.

Conversely, if the Euro had strengthened 10% against sterling with all other variables held constant, post-tax profits for the year would have been €56,000 higher (in 2011 the post-tax profit would have been €25,000 higher), and other components of equity would have been €18,000 (2011: €17,000) lower. The lower foreign currency exchange rate sensitivity in losses/profits in 2012 compared with 2011 is attributable to an increase in foreign denominated debt. Equity is more sensitive in 2012 than in 2011 because of the increased use of hedges of foreign currency purchases, offset by the increase in foreign currency debt.

Commodity Price Rate Risk

At 31 December 2011, if the price of wood had increased in value by 10% with all other variables held constant, post-tax profits for the year would have been €186,000 lower (in 2011 the post-tax profit would have been €121,000 lower).

Conversely, if the price of wood had decreased in value by 10% with all other variables held constant, post-tax profits for the year would have been €186,000 higher (in 2011 the post-tax profit would have been €121,000 higher). The higher commodity price rate sensitivity in losses/profits in 2012 compared with 2011 is attributable to an increase in purchases to meet increased sales demand.

27. Management of Capital

The company's objectives when managing capital are:
(a) to safeguard the entity's ability to continue as a going concern, so that it can continue to provide returns for shareholders and benefits for other stakeholders, and
(b) to provide an adequate return to shareholders by pricing products and services commensurately with the level of risk.

The company sets the amount of capital in proportion to risk. The company manages the capital structure and makes adjustments to it in light of changes in economic conditions and the risk characteristics of the underlying assets. In order to maintain or adjust the capital structure, the company may adjust the amount of dividends paid to shareholders, return capital to shareholders, issue new shares, or sell assets to reduce debt.

Consistently with others in the industry, the company monitors capital on the basis of the debt-to-capital ratio. This ratio is calculated as net debt to capital. Net debt is calculated as total debt (i.e. loans and finance lease liabilities) less cash and cash equivalents. Capital comprises all components of equity (i.e. share capital, share premium, minority interest, retained earnings, other equity reserves and revaluation reserve).

During 2012, the company's strategy, which was unchanged from 2011, was to maintain the debt-to-capital ratio at a level which did not exceed 1:1, in order to secure access to finance at a reasonable cost by maintaining an AAA credit rating. The debt-to-capital ratios at 31 December 2012 were as follows:

| | 2012 | 2011 |
	€000	€000
Total debt	(107,850)	(116,560)
Less: cash and cash equivalents	111,650	110,380
Net cash and cash equivalent/(debt)	3,800	(6,180)
Total equity	173,894	157,790
Debt-to-capital ratio	– 0.02:1	0.04:1

The reduced debt-to-equity ratio during 2012 resulted primarily from a reduction in fixed rate interest bearing debt. As a result of this reduction in net debt, improved profitability and lower levels of managed receivables, the dividend payment was increased to €25.5 million for 2012, from €10 million for 2011.

28. Share Capital

| | 2012 | 2011 |
	€000	€000
Authorised		
100,000,000 A ordinary shares of €1 each	100,000	100,000
5,000,000 10% redeemable preference shares of €1 each	5,000	5,000
Allotted, called up and fully paid		
84,050,000 (2011: 78,160,000) ordinary shares of €1 each	84,050	78,160
3,000,000 10% redeemable preference shares of €1 each	3,000	3,000

Preference Shares

The preference shares, which were issued at par, are redeemable on 31 December 2023 at par. They carry a dividend of 10% per annum, payable half-yearly in arrears on 30 June and 31 December. The dividend rights are cumulative.

Share Issue

On 30 June 2012, 5,890,000 ordinary shares were issued at €1.40 each.

Share Option Scheme

The company has a share option scheme under which options to purchase shares are granted to senior employees (see note 7).

29. Share Premium, Other Components of Equity and Retained Earnings

	Share Premium €000	Other Components of Equity €000	Retained Earnings €000	Total €000
At 1 January 2012	570	28,700	50,360	79,630
Premium on share issue	2,356	–	–	2,356
Finance cost of share issue	(36)	–	–	(36)
Exchange difference on loan	–	(200)	–	(200)
Derivative financial instruments		100		100
Impairment of investment property		(10,000)	–	(10,000)
Revaluation of tangible assets	–	(17,200)	–	(17,200)
Actuarial gain on market value of defined benefit scheme's assets		200	–	200
Additional finance cost of preference shares to share premium account	100		–	100
Profit for the year	–	–	60,394	60,394
Dividends distributed in the year (note 11)	–	–	(25,500)	(25,500)
At 31 December 2012	2,990	1,600	85,254	89,844

Analysis of retained earnings:

	2012 €000	2011 €000
Retained earnings excluding pension asset	84,054	49,360
Pension reserve	1,200	1,000
Retained earnings	85,254	50,360

Other components of equity:

	Currency Reserve €000	Revaluation Reserve €000	Fair Value Reserve €000	Total €000
At 1 January 2012	250	28,300	150	28,700
Exchange difference on loan	(200)	–		(200)
Actuarial gains	–	–	200	200
Impairment of investment property		(10,000)		(10,000)
Revaluation of tangible assets		(17,200)		(17,200)
Derivative financial instruments		–	100	100
At 31 December 2012	50	1,100	450	1,600

30. Reconciliation of Movements in Total Equity

	2012 €000	2011 €000
Recognised gains and losses for the year	33,294	25,590
Dividends paid	(25,500)	(10,000)
New shares subscribed	5,890	–
Premium on new shares	2,356	–
Finance cost of issue	(36)	–
Additional finance cost of non-equity shares	100	90
Net increase in Total Equity	16,104	15,680
Opening Total Equity	157,790	142,110
Closing Total Equity	173,894	157,790

31. Events After the Reporting Period

The company sold a franchise licence in Cork on 28 February 2013 and realised a gain on disposal of €10,000,000.

32. Capital Commitments

At the date of the statement of financial position the company had entered into contracts for future capital expenditure amounting to:

	2012	2011
	€000	€000
Contracted	3,000	–
Authorised but not contracted	750	500
	3,750	500

	2012	2011
Government grants reclaimable in respect of the above future capital expenditure are estimated at:	1,500	–

33. Other Financial Commitments

Finance Leases and Hire Purchase Contracts

In addition to the capital commitments set out above, the company has entered into contracts whose inception occurs after the year-end amounting to:

	2012	2011
	€000	€000
Finance leases and hire purchase contracts	750	1,000

Operating Lease Commitments

Annual commitments exist under non-cancellable operating leases as follows:

	2012 Land and Buildings €000	2012 Other €000	2011 Land and Buildings €000	2011 Other €000
Expiring:				
Within one year	300	500	300	500
Between two and five years	800	2,000	800	2,000
More than five years	400	200	100	700
	1,500	2,700	1,200	3,200

The rentals payable in respect of leases of land and buildings are subject to rent review at three yearly intervals as specified in the lease agreement.

34. Contingent Liability and Subsequent Provision

A customer who purchased furniture in 2011 has commenced an action against the company. He claims that the furniture was defective resulting in injury to one of their customers. The company's solicitors have advised that the action is unlikely to succeed. Therefore no provision for any liability has been made.

A provision of €65,000 for legal costs in connection with the defence has been provided for under other provisions (Note 24). €15,000 of this provision has been utilised in the year leaving a closing balance on the provision account of €50,000.

It has been estimated that the maximum liability should the action be successful is €6,000,000 to the plaintiff with an additional €500,000 in court costs. No provision has been made for these costs based on the solicitor's advice and the directors' judgement on the matter.

35. Approval of Financial Statements

The board of directors approved these financial statements for issue on [*state date*].

Appendix D

SUGGESTED SOLUTIONS TO REVIEW QUESTIONS

(a) **Explaining auditing and the role of auditor**

Auditing is one of the key accounting disciplines and forms the backbone of many accounting practices. In very simple terms an audit involves an independent firm of auditors examining financial information prepared by a client in order to verify its authenticity and accuracy. The process of an audit is to enhance the degree of confidence of intended users in the financial statements. This is achieved by the expression of an opinion by the auditor on whether the financial statements are prepared, in all material respects, in accordance with an applicable financial reporting framework.

The term 'audit' refers to the process undertaken by the auditor to gather and assess a range of audit evidence that will enable such an opinion to be formed and expressed by the auditor. Evidence is gathered in a number of forms and using a wide variety of methods.

When most people think of the discipline of auditing, they most commonly associate it with the annual statutory audit of a company's financial statements (statutory requirements are discussed in more detail below). In this case, the auditor gathers evidence on the items included within the company's financial statements and then expresses an opinion on how these statements were prepared. This is the most common form of auditing in practice, and as such it is the most closely regulated, with guidance and requirements to be found in auditing standards issued by accounting bodies (e.g. international standards on auditing (ISAs)) and within government legislation. This regulation adds a degree of uniformity to procedures applied and reports produced in the financial statement audit.

The independent external auditor provides 'reasonable assurance' that the financial statements are free from material misstatements. The assurance is not a guarantee;

it provides a high degree of assurance but not absolute assurance that the financial statements are correct. For this reason the term 'true and fair' is used when expressing the opinion.

(b) **Eligibility requirements to be an auditor in the Republic of Ireland and the UK**

The independent oversight bodies operating under IAASA ROI and the FRC through the Professional Oversight team in the UK operates stringent entrance requirements, a strict code of ethics and technical updating of members in order to maintain a level of professionalism and competence within the auditing profession. The requirements cover the following areas:

Education and Work Experience An auditor must complete a required level of education supported by examination and must support this by a minimum training period (representing relevant experience).

Eligibility Those acting as auditors must be members of a recognised supervisor body (such as the Institute of Chartered Accountants in Ireland). The 'auditor' can be a body corporate, partnership or sole practitioner. Should you have close connections to a company you may not act as their auditor. Additionally there are ethical requirements which must be adhered to should one wish to operate as an auditor. Should you have ever been convicted of an offence or been bankrupt and not yet cleared those debts then you will not be permitted to act as auditor.

Supervision and Monitoring While acting as an auditor you will be subject to monitoring and review. Firstly you will be required to maintain a certain level of continuing professional development to ensure you maintain technical excellence. Additionally, you will be monitored and reviewed to ensure you are acting within a properly structured audit approach, abiding by quality control procedures, adhering to the fit and proper criteria as well as maintaining strong audit files.

Should you wish to operate as an auditor you will also be required to hold professional indemnity insurance.

(c) **Audit exemption criteria**

In order to be audit exempt a company must satisfy **all** of the following three criteria for **ROI**:

 (i) Turnover: €8.8 million (or less) – this is breached as the company has €9.3 million turnover.
 (ii) Balance sheet total: €4.4 million (or less) – this has not yet been breached but is likely it will be in the near future.
 (iii) Average number of employees: 50 (or less) – this is breached.

In addition the Annual Returns must be fully up to date and filed on time.

A company Limited by Guarantee cannot avail of audit exemption.

Therefore, the family retail business has two of the criteria breached and the company is required to have an audit.

In order to be audit exempt a company must satisfy two of the following criteria for **UK**:

  (i) Turnover: £6.5 million (or less) – this is breached as the company has €9.3 million turnover.

 (ii) Balance sheet total: £3.26 million (or less) – this has not yet been breached but is likely it will be in the near future.

(iii) Average number of employees: 50 (or less) – this is breached.

Therefore, the family retail business has two of the criteria breached and the company is required to have an audit.

QUESTION 1.2

(a) **Regulatory framework – diagram[1] and roles**

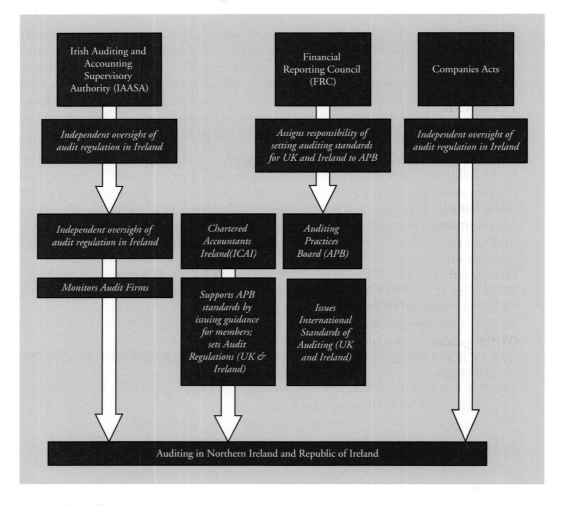

---

[1] Louise Kelly, *Advanced Auditing and Assurance* (Chartered Accountants Ireland, 2013)

The Role of the FRC – the FRC has overall responsibility for the regulation of auditing, accounting and the actuarial professions. The role of the Auditing Practice Board (APB) is overseen by the FRC.

The Role of the APB – the APB is responsible for the development of auditing practice in the UK and Ireland. Their responsibilities include the setting of standards and issuing guidance on the application of standards in particular circumstances and industries.

The Role of IAASA – the IAASA provides an independent oversight of the regulation in the Republic of Ireland. It also provides information relating to the registration and regulation of audit firms.

Essentially, they serve in the public interest by setting high-quality international standards for:
- auditing,
- quality control,
- review,
- other assurance, and
- related services.

The Role of CARB – the Chartered Accountants Regulatory Board (CARB) was established by Chartered Accountants Ireland to provide, among other things, monitoring of the quality of the audit function. CARB assists in regulating members, in accordance with the provisions of the Institute's bye-laws, independently, openly and in the public interest. CARB is responsible for developing standards of professional conduct and supervising the compliance of members, member firms and affiliates and this is done by regular reviews of member firms.

(b) Appointment/removal of auditors in the RoI and UK

Auditors are appointed by shareholders at the Annual General Meeting and may be removed only by shareholders at a general meeting. The directors may fill a casual vacancy either before the convening of the first annual AGM, whereby a vote will be taken as to the continuance, or otherwise, of that appointed auditor. Additionally, should the auditor be removed or resign during office the directors may fill that vacancy until the next shareholder meeting.

(c) **ODCE guidance on auditor resignation**

The ODCE outlines the duties and rights of an auditor should he wish to resign, these include:

Duties:
- To notify the shareholders in a 'statement of circumstances', which outlines the circumstances giving rise to the resignation?
- To notify the respective RSB (should the resignation be during a term of office).
- To notify the Companies Registration Office (CRO).

Rights:
- To request an Extraordinary General Meeting (EGM) – where the auditor can explain the contents of the statement of circumstances.

- To request the company to circulate notice of the holding of the EGM and the circumstances relating to the resignation.

QUESTION 1.3

Auditor's duty of care – case law and judgments

An auditor, generally speaking, owes a duty of care only to the shareholders. An auditor can face claims under contract law, or under the tort of negligence. He must be able to show that he gave the expected duty of care to the plaintiff if a legal action is taken. However, if an auditor can show that he carried out the engagement in compliance with generally accepted auditing standards, this may act in his defence. It is up to the courts to decide if the required standard of skill and care has been given. The *Caparo* case is a landmark case that brought the most important ruling with respect to the duty of care of the auditor. The auditor should be mindful of proximity, which is said to arise where, for example, a company's financial condition is such that it is a likely takeover target, the auditor in such circumstances should be aware that the accounts may be relied upon by potential investors and a duty of care thus arises.

Caparo Industries plc v. Dickman and Others (1990)

Caparo Industries held shares in Fidelity plc. After viewing the audited accounts of March 1984, which showed company profits of £1.3 million, Caparo purchased more shares in Fidelity. Later in the year Caparo successfully took over Fidelity.

After the takeover, Caparo brought an action against Touche Ross, the auditors, claiming that the accounts were inaccurate and should have shown a loss of some £400,000. Caparo claimed that, as auditors, Touche Ross owed a duty of care to the investors and those potential investors in respect to the audited accounts.

Caparo claimed that: (a) the auditors would have known that the company was vulnerable to a takeover as the reported profits had fallen short of those projected of £2.2 million and the share price had fallen by nearly 50% in the month of March 1984; and (b) that the auditors were negligent as they should have known that any potential investor would be likely to rely on the audited accounts before making their investment decision.

The first issue was if a duty of care was owed to Caparo. The High Court held that Touche Ross had no duty of care to Caparo.

A plaintiff wishing to bring a claim under negligence must prove three things:
1. that a duty of care which is enforceable in law existed;
2. that this said duty of care was breached, i.e. that the auditor was negligent;
3. that the breach caused the injured party to suffer a loss which is able to be measured, be it a physical or a financial loss.

Negligence is conduct which is careless or unintentional in nature and entails a breach of any contractual duty or duty of care in tort owed to another person or persons.

If the auditor has been negligent, the client may sue him for breach of an implicit term of contract to exercise reasonable care and skill in order to recover any consequential loss suffered. The judge will seek to establish not only that the auditor's ultimate decision was incorrect but also that the method in arriving at the decision was flawed (i.e. the requirements of the auditing standards and company law were not followed).

Compliance with ISAs to help avoid liability

If the auditor can reliably demonstrate, that they followed the ISAs as laid out by the FRC, in performing their audit then this evidence will strongly support the auditor's contention that they were not negligent.

QUESTION 1.4

Landmark legal cases – outline, judgment and impact

(1) Royal Bank of Scotland v. Bannerman, Johnstone, Maclay and Others (2002)

Royal Bank of Scotland (RBS) provided overdraft facilities to APC Limited who in turn were audited by Bannerman Johnstone Maclay. Included in the bank facility letter was the requirement for the company to provide audited accounts each year to the bank. It subsequently transpired that the auditors had failed to detect fraud which had occurred in the company. RBS claimed that they were therefore owed a duty of care by APC's auditors as they knew they would be relying on the audited accounts. The auditor knowing this should have disclaimed liability to RBS but they did not do so.

The ruling judge held that the in the absence of the disclaimer, the auditors did owe a duty of care to RBS and found in their favour.

Following the ruling in *Royal Bank of Scotland v. Bannerman, Johnstone, Maclay and Others* (2002), Chartered Accountants Ireland issued guidance to its members on the appropriate action for members to take for additional wording in their audit reports to protect against the exposure to third party claims.

The inclusion of this wording is not to be seen to reduce the value of the audit. Audits are still to be carried out to the highest standards and in accordance with Generally Accepted Accounting Principles. Its purpose is to inform third parties that, by relying on the financial statements, the auditor does not accept any responsibility to the third party.

(2) Kingston Cotton Mill Co (1896)

This case involved a manager who had exaggerated stock values for years to fraudulently overstate profits. It eventually came to light when the company could not pay debts.

The auditors had relied on certificates from management to confirm stock value and had not attended stocktakes, nor attempted to validate the opening balance of stocks or to cross-reference to sales and purchases – all of which would have highlighted the issue.

The judge held that "auditor must rely on some skilled person (i.e. the manager) for the materials necessary to enable him to enter the stock in trade at its proper value in the statement of financial position….. he (the auditor) has to perform that skill, care and caution which a reasonably competent, careful and cautious auditor would use – he (the auditor) is a watchdog but not a bloodhound.

Learning – laid down some fundamental auditing principles such as the "watchdog" rule and the notion of reasonable skill and care.

(3) Caparo Industries plc v. Dickman and Others (1990)

Caparo Industries held shares in Fidelity plc. After viewing the audited accounts of March 1984, which showed company profits of £1.3 million, Caparo purchased more shares in Fidelity. Later in the year Caparo successfully took over Fidelity.

After the takeover, Caparo brought an action against Touche Ross, the auditors, claiming that the accounts were inaccurate and should have shown a loss of some £400,000. Caparo claimed that, as auditors, Touche Ross owed a duty of care to the investors and those potential investors in respect to the audited accounts.

Caparo claimed that: (a) the auditors would have known that the company was vulnerable to a takeover as the reported profits had fallen short of those projected of £2.2 million and the share price had fallen by nearly 50% in the month of March 1984 and (b) that the auditors should have known that any potential investor would be likely to rely on the audited accounts before making their investment decision.

The first issue was if a duty of care was owed to Caparo, the High Court held that no duty of care was owed to Caparo.

Auditors can face claims under contract law, or under the tort of negligence. The auditors must be able to show that they gave the expected duty of care to the plaintiff if an action is taken. However, if the auditors can show that they carried out the engagement in compliance with generally accepted auditing standards, this may act as their defence. It is up to the courts to decide if the required standard of skill and care has been given. The *Caparo* case is a landmark decision which brought the most important ruling with respect to duty of care of the auditor.

QUESTION 2.1

There are a number of threats to integrity, objectivity and independence arising in the case of Trafford Ltd:
- **Familiarity Threat** Your firm has been auditor of Trafford Ltd for 10 years, indeed the company has not had any other auditors. In addition, your audit partner appears to have a close relationship with the client's managing director and has been audit partner on the engagement for 10 years. All these factors indicate a familiarity threat which could potentially impact on your firm's ability to adequately challenge the client's

management where required, thus impacting on the firm's ability to arrive at the correct audit opinion.

- **Intimidation Threat** The managing director of the client entity, Arnold Ferguson, appears to be a rather domineering figure and has shown tendencies towards intimidating members of the audit team in the past. This increases the risk that your firm may be pressurised into accepting his judgements even where these may not be appropriate. This may result in your firm issuing an inappropriate audit opinion.
- **Self-interest Threat** The fees generated by the audit of Trafford Ltd are now extremely significant in the context of your firm's total income from audit activity – over 20% of total audit income. As a result, the loss of this audit client could have a serious impact upon your firm's income in the future. This may lead to your firm being reluctant to challenge management on difficult issues for fear of displeasing the client's management resulting in the client changing auditors.
- **Self-review Threat** Arnold Ferguson has recently raised the idea that your firm may wish to perform internal audit services for Trafford Ltd. Should your firm accept this internal audit engagement, it may result in work performed by your firm in its capacity as internal auditor being relied upon by your firm in its capacity as external auditor. This is a clear self-review threat as the adequacy of internal audit work needs to be assessed by the external auditor prior to placing reliance on it.

Action to be Taken Prior to accepting the external audit engagement for the next financial year, your firm should assess whether adequate safeguards have been put in place to guard against each of the threats identified above, and reduce the threat to an acceptable level. This is in accordance with Ethical Standard 1(Revised) *Integrity, Objectivity and Independence* (ES 1). In particular the involvement of the current audit partner should be seriously considered. The long association is a real threat and this could be resolved by appointing a new engagement partner. The domineering role of the managing director could have a pervasive effect on the organization and raises the risk of financial misreporting and fraud. The continuation as auditor needs to be evaluated. The fees dependency issue needs to be tackled. The firm is now in breach of independence guidelines. The firm cannot take on work more work with the client due to the already existing level of fees. There would be a clear conflict of interest if the firm took up the internal audit assignment.

QUESTION 2.2

MEMO

To: Mr Rick Parry, Istanbul Ltd
From: XYZ Chartered Accountants
Subject: Corporate governance practices in listed companies

The standard for best practice in corporate governance is contained in the *UK Corporate Governance Code* which was issued in September 2012.

- If Istanbul Ltd is to become listed, it would be required, under Stock Exchange Listing Rules, to report within their financial statements annually on their compliance with the requirements of this code.
- Some of the key structures/practices that the directors in Istanbul should consider implementing in advance of listing include:
  - undertaking a thorough review of the effectiveness of the systems of internal control. This review should be updated on an annual basis going forward;
  - holding formal board meetings on a regular basis;
  - appointing a number of non-executive directors to the company's board, ensuring that there is a reasonable balance on the board between non-executives and executives;
  - establishing an audit committee to liaise with external and internal auditors and to manage the appointment of auditors. This committee should be chaired by an independent non-executive director;
  - separating the roles of chairman and chief executive of the board;
  - establishing a formal, rigorous and transparent procedure for appointing new directors to the board;
  - ensuring all board members are supplied with information on a timely basis prior to board meetings; and
  - establishing a procedure whereby the Board undertakes an annual review of its own performance.
- By establishing the above procedures and practices, corporate governance procedures will be enhanced and the transition to listed status will be eased.

QUESTION 3.1

Audit Planning Memorandum

Qualitax Ltd. Audit for year ending 31 December 2012

Subject: Key Requirements of ISA 240 (UK and Ireland) *The Auditor's Responsibilities Relating to Fraud in an Audit of Financial Statements* (ISA 240).

First, it should be noted that for the purposes of the ISAs (UK and Ireland) an auditor is concerned with fraud that causes a material misstatement in the financial statements. This can be broken down into fraudulent financial reporting and misappropriation of assets.

As auditor we are responsible for obtaining reasonable assurance that the financial statements taken as a whole are free from material misstatement, whether caused by fraud or error.

We need to adopt an approach of professional scepticism throughout the audit, considering the potential for management override of controls and recognising the fact that audit procedures that are effective for detecting error may not be effective in detecting fraud.

Our objective is to identify and assess the risk of material misstatement of the financial statements due to fraud. We need to respond to those risks through performing appropriate audit procedures.

As an audit team we are required to discuss how and where the entity's financial statements may be susceptible to material misstatement due to fraud, including how fraud might occur.

We need to discuss the risk of fraud with management and those charged with governance.

Our audit procedures are likely to include:
- testing journal entries for validity;
- reviewing accounting estimates for reasonableness and lack of bias;
- scrutinising transactions outside the normal course of business and ascertaining their business rationale; and
- paying particular attention to the recognition of revenue.

At the conclusion of our audit we shall obtain written representations from management and those charged with governance regarding their knowledge of any allegations of fraud, or suspected fraud, affecting the entity's financial statements.

QUESTION 3.2

(a) **The auditor's responsibility for detecting fraud**
ISA 240 (UK and Ireland) *The Auditor's Responsibilities Relating to Fraud in an Audit of Financial Statements* (ISA 240) states that the primary responsibility for the prevention and detection of fraud rests with both those charged with governance of the entity and management.
The auditor is responsible for obtaining reasonable assurance that the financial statements taken as a whole are free from material misstatement, whether caused by fraud or error. Accordingly, the auditor should assess the risk of fraud and plan and perform appropriate audit procedures in order to have a reasonable expectation of detecting material frauds or error.

(b) **Whether fraud by management or employees (not in management positions) is more easily perpetrated**
In general it is easier for management to perpetrate fraud. Management is frequently in a position to directly or indirectly manipulate accounting records and thereby influence financial information drawn there from. Management may be in a position to override controls that otherwise seem to be operating effectively. There is also the likelihood of collusion, either through the direct instruction of employees, or the seeking of their co-operation in carrying out fraud.

QUESTION 5.1

(a) **The procedures an auditor should adopt before accepting an appointment**
The prospective engagement partner should consider the following matters when deciding whether to accept a new client.
1. The integrity of the prospective client's management and the integrity of its principal owners.
2. The legality of the entity's activities, and entity's reputation.

3. The entity's business environment and who will use the financial statements.
4. The entity's financial position and prospects.
5. The likelihood that the scope of the audit will be restricted or subject to an unacceptable time constraint.
6. Any key accounting policy issues.

Before accepting a new engagement, the auditor should determine that a sufficient number of **competent staff** will be available to provide the services that the client has requested.

Before commencing any services on an engagement for a new client, the auditor should determine whether the firm is **independent** with respect to that client. It should also be confirmed that the firm has no potential conflict of interests.

Where a registered auditor is a corporate practice, it should obtain written confirmation from a potential audit client or associated undertaking that it **holds no interests** in the firm, before accepting the audit appointment.

(b) **Matters that should be included in a letter of engagement**

Addressee For clients incorporated under the Companies Act(s), the auditor should address the engagement letter to the directors of the company.

Confirmation of the Terms of the Engagement The auditor should always discuss the scope of the engagement with the client's management, and should then confirm the matters agreed in the engagement letter. In the case of a new engagement, the auditor should normally discuss and agree the contents of the engagement letter with the client's management before accepting the audit appointment.

The auditor should obtain the client's confirmation of the terms of the engagement by sending an additional copy of the engagement letter and asking the client to sign this and return it.

In the case of a company, the auditor should request that the letter be tabled at a board meeting or, where the board delegates this responsibility, at a meeting of a suitable committee of the board, and for the approval of the letter to be minuted.

A copy of the engagement letter should be filed with the audit working papers.

Contents of the Letter Audit firms may wish to send their corporate clients an engagement letter covering additional services, e.g. corporate tax advice and assistance in preparing tax computations.

Corporate Finance Clients If the only incidental investment business the firm is likely to undertake for the client consists of corporate finance type activities, and the client has agreed that it is appropriate for the firm to treat the client as a 'corporate finance' client, the engagement letter should include a specific paragraph highlighting this.

If the client does not agree to be treated as a corporate finance client, or the investment business anticipated would not be a corporate finance activity, the engagement letter should include an appropriate paragraph.

Other matters that may be dealt with in the engagement letter include:
- fees and billing arrangements;
- procedures in the event the client has a complaint about the service;
- where appropriate, arrangements concerning the involvement of:
  - other auditors and experts in some aspect of the audit;
  - internal auditors and other staff of the entity;
  - any restriction of the auditors' liabilities to the client;
  - where appropriate, the country by whose laws the engagement is governed;
  - a reference to any further agreements between the auditors and the client;
  - a proposed timetable for the engagement.

QUESTION 5.2

Engagement Letter – Leoville Ltd
The Board of Directors,
Leoville Ltd

XXXX Date:

Re: PROPOSED PRESENTATION OF BUSINESS PLAN FOR LAS CASES LTD TO YOUR BANKERS

Dear Sirs,

I refer to our recent meeting. It is our understanding that Leoville proposes to raise €4 million to fund its investment in Las Cases Ltd.

We further understand that your shareholding in Las Cases Ltd will be 50% of the share capital; the balance of the share capital will be held by Poyferre Ltd.

The purpose of this letter is to set out the basis on which we are to assist Leoville Ltd in its formal presentation to your bankers of:
- a business plan for the new venture, Las Cases Ltd; and
- the preparation of management accounts of Leoville Ltd, for the six months ended 30 June 2012.

Each of the above issues is dealt with separately below.

Leoville's Management Accounts for the Six Months Ended 30 June 2012

As directors of the company, you are responsible for ensuring that the company maintains proper accounting records and for the preparation of the management accounts based on such accounting records.

Our responsibility is to **review** the accounts as prepared by you and to discuss any issues arising therein with the management of the company. We will not carry out an audit on the management accounts and, accordingly, we will **not** express an audit opinion.

We will review the balance sheet and related statements of comprehensive income and cash flows and will report on this review to the directors of the company. Our report on the management accounts is at present expected to read as follows:

"Our review consisted principally of obtaining an understanding of the process for the preparation of the financial statements, applying analytical procedures to the underlying financial data, assessing whether accounting policies have been consistently applied, and making enquiries of management responsible for financial and accounting matters. Our review excluded audit procedures such as tests of control and verification of assets and liabilities and was, therefore, substantially less in scope than an audit performed in accordance with Auditing Standards. Accordingly, we do not express an audit opinion on the financial information.

On the basis of our review,
• we are not aware of any material modification which should be made to the financial information as presented; and
• in our opinion the financial information has been prepared consistent with the accounting policies set out on pages — to —.

Clearly, the limited nature of our review work will thus be conveyed to your bank who will examine the management accounts of which our report will form a part."

Business Plan for Las Cases Ltd

The drafting of a business plan and preparation of trading projections for this company for the period from 1 January 2013 to 31 December 2013 is a matter for which the directors of Las Cases Ltd are solely responsible. We further understand, from our recent discussions, that you will retain specialist textile industry consultants to advise on particular aspects of this new venture. Our responsibility will be to report to the directors of Leoville Ltd on our management of the plan's preparation. As the nature of the plan and the trading projections relate to a future accounting period, we clearly cannot offer any audit opinion on these matters.

The responsibilities of the directors of Las Cases Ltd are to make the underlying commercial assumptions which will form the basis of the plan. In this respect you will use the input of senior management of Leoville and Poyferre to assist you in the preparation of this plan and the related projections. You are also solely responsible for engaging the input of consultants and for deciding on the scope and nature of their engagement. Furthermore, your responsibility is to select appropriate accounting policies in line with generally accepted accounting principles and which reflect the activities of the proposed business.

Our report on the trading projections for the new venture is at present expected to read as follows:

"We have reviewed the accounting policies and the calculations for the trading projections of Las Cases Ltd for which the directors are solely responsible. In our opinion, the forecasts so far as the accounting policies and the calculations are concerned have been properly compiled on the basis of the assumptions made by the directors of the company. Also the projections are presented, in our opinion, on a basis consistent with the accounting policies normally adopted by the company."

Other Issues

Unless otherwise agreed, it will not be our responsibility to undertake or assist in the formal presentation to your bankers in relation to the application for finance.

Additionally, in order to ensure that the work we have agreed to can be done in sufficient time to enable the presentation to be made four weeks from now, we must have your agreement to the timetable set out in the Appendix to this letter. You should be aware that, without adhering to the numerous deadlines for information identified in this Appendix, it will not be possible to complete the assignment within the given timescale.

Our fees are based on the time required by the individuals assigned to the engagement plus direct out-of-pocket expenses. Individual hourly rates vary according to the degree of responsibility involved and the experience and skill required.

We would be grateful if you would confirm in writing your agreement to these terms by signing and returning the enclosed copy of this letter to indicate that it is in accordance with your understanding of the arrangements in relation to the preparation of the business plan for the new venture and Leoville's management accounts for the six months ended 30 June 2012. Alternatively, you should inform us if your understanding of the proposed arrangement is not in accordance with the terms of the engagement as set out in this letter.

Yours faithfully,

We agree to the terms of this letter.

Signed for and on behalf of Leoville Ltd

QUESTION 5.3

Conway Chartered Accountants

Memorandum

To: Audit Trainees
From: Audit Senior

Re: Planning, Controlling and Recording of an Audit

In order to ensure an effective and efficient audit it is essential that the audit is properly planned, recorded and controlled. Auditors are required by professional standards and guidelines to adequately plan, control and record their work.

(a) **Planning** The nature of the planning required will vary from audit to audit and will be dependent on the complexity of the client's business, the auditor's knowledge of the client and his business and the reporting requirements to which the audit is subject.

Adequate Planning

- establishes the intended means of achieving the audit objectives;
- assists in the direction and control of the work;
- helps to ensure that attention is devoted to the critical areas of the audit; and
- helps to ensure that the work is completed expeditiously.

Business Review

One of the first stages of the audit planning process is to carry out a review of the client's business. This will comprise gaining an understanding of the business, carrying out a preliminary analytical review, reviewing significant accounting policies and making a preliminary assessment on materiality.

Evaluating Audit Risk

Audit risk can be divided into two main categories:
1. **The risk of material misstatement.** This is the risk that items in the financial statements either individually or in aggregate will be materially misstated and that the client's controls will not be effective in detecting those misstatements.
2. **Detection risk.** This is the risk that misstatements will not be detected by the audit work.

It should be possible for the auditor to assess the risk of misstatement – this will be done through his assessment of inherent risk and control effectiveness. The auditor can control detection risk by varying the nature, extent and timing of his audit tests.

Inherent risk is the susceptibility of an account balance or type of transaction to material misstatement through fraud or error, before taking into account the effectiveness of the client's internal controls.

The auditor should carry out a search for inherent risks, evaluate the significance of those risks and relate such risks to account balances, classes of transactions and his audit objectives. The auditor's assessment of these risks will form the basis of his audit testing and will impact on his audit emphasis.

Review of Internal Controls for Audit Strategy Purposes

A business must have some form of internal control systems in order to function. The nature and complexity of these systems will vary from business to business and will depend on the complexity of the business. An internal control structure can be divided into three main categories:
1. the control environment;
2. the accounting system; and
3. the internal controls.

The control environment is the overall attitudes, abilities, awareness and actions of the individuals in the organisation, particularly those of management, concerning the importance of control and the emphasis attached to it.

Accounting systems normally comprise the financially significant computer applications and the computer environment within which these are developed, implemented, maintained and operated. These systems will form the basis for the preparation of periodic financial statements and other information required by management to control the business.

Internal accounting controls are the specific procedures established by management to ensure that transactions are completely and accurately processed, transactions are recorded as authorised by management, assets are safeguarded and that the accounting systems are reliable and the account balances are correct.

The auditor's initial assessment of the control environment is crucial. If he forms the opinion that the control environment is unfavorable he is unlikely to carry out further procedures to assess the controls with a view to placing reliance on them in performing his audit.

Regardless of whether he is going to place reliance on internal controls he will need to understand the accounting systems. This will enable him to design his audit tests to ensure an efficient and effective audit.

If the auditor decides to rely on the internal control system he will need to make a detailed assessment of that system in order to design his tests of controls.

The review of the internal control systems will influence the audit strategy and is therefore a crucial element of the audit planning stage.

Determining the Strategy

The audit strategy sets out the principal features of the planned audit approach. The auditor develops his strategy by considering his knowledge of the client together with more up to date information obtained through the business review and the preliminary assessment of internal control.

Substantive Testing Plan

Having determined his audit strategy the auditor can then set about developing his substantive testing plan. This forms the link between the audit strategy and the detailed tests to be performed during the audit.

In respect of each audit area the substantive testing plan should set out the following information:
- the audit objectives that are relevant to the particular account balance or class of transactions;
- an evaluation of the inherent risks;
- a general assessment as to the extent to which control effectiveness reduces those risks and any specific control risks identified; and
- the nature, extent and timing of the substantive tests.

Administrative Matters

For a new client it is necessary to ensure that all necessary steps regarding the firm's appointment have been carried out. This includes clearance from previous auditors and agreeing the terms of the engagement with the client.

The staff needed to carry out the audit must be assigned, ensuring that they have the experience required to carry out the assignment and that there is no conflict of interest.

Consideration needs to be given as to whether it will be necessary to engage the services of other experts and the timing and nature of their report.

The audit partner and manager will then set timetables, time and fee budgets.

Before the audit work is commenced it is essential that all members of staff are properly briefed.

(b) Controlling The reporting partner needs to ensure that the audit work is being performed to an acceptable standard and that problems are quickly identified and brought to the attention of the partner or manager. The most important elements of control are the direction and supervision of audit staff and the review of the work they have done.

Roles of Partners and Managers

An audit team usually comprises people of different levels of experience and seniority. It is usual for all work to be reviewed by a person more senior than the person who performed the work. In some cases, for larger, high-risk clients it is usual to have a second partner review.

Procedures

The nature of the procedures needed to control an audit and the extent to which they need to be formalised will depend on the organisation of the audit firm and the degree of delegation of the audit work. The procedures established should be designed to ensure:
- work is allocated to audit staff who have the appropriate training, experience and proficiency;
- audit staff of all levels clearly understand their responsibilities and the objectives of the procedures they are carrying out;
- the working papers provide an adequate record of the work done and the conclusion reached; and
- the work performed is reviewed by a more senior member of staff to ensure that the work was adequately performed and to confirm that the results obtained support the audit conclusions reached.

Quality Assurance Inspection

Each registered auditor is required to establish and maintain quality control procedures appropriate to its circumstances. The audit firm's programme of quality assurance inspection has, as its main objective, to ensure that the audits are conducted in accordance with the relevant policies and procedures.

(c) Documenting The quantity, type and content of audit working papers will vary with the circumstances, but they must meet the following overall objectives:
- assist in the efficient conduct of work;
- enable the work carried out to be independently reviewed; and
- demonstrate that the auditor has properly performed all the audit work necessary to enable an opinion to be formed on the financial statements.

For this reason the following procedures are important:
- remove all lists of outstanding work once the work required has been completed;
- record all relevant information received and its source when questions of principles or judgement arise;
- the working papers should be consistent with the financial statements and audit report given;
- each working paper should be dated, record the preparer's initials, give the client's name;
- record the period covered by audit;
- detail the subject matter;
- show evidence of review;
- no unnecessary information should be kept on file;
- appropriate conclusions on the result of work performed should always be recorded; and
- all working papers should be kept confidential.

QUESTION 6.1

(a) **Substantive tests and financial statements**

Test of Detail	Financial Statement Area	Financial Statement Assertions Covered by Test
Recompute depreciation charge	Fixed Assets and comprehensive income statement depreciation charge	Accuracy
Search for unrecorded liabilities	Accruals and accounts payable	Completeness Cut-off
Perform debtors circularisation	Accounts receivable	Existence/Occurrence Rights and Obligations

(b) **Obsolete and unsaleable inventory**
- Review client procedures for identifying and making obsolete inventory provisions.
- Examine any quality control reports available and discuss with management.

- Check the system in place to monitor the ageing of inventory.
- Compare stock quantities held at year end with past and projected sales performance.
- Physically inspect the condition of the inventory at the stock-take and follow up on any points noted.
- Check outcome of previous provisions to consider how accurate management estimates have been in the past.

It is unlikely that any one test will be sufficient to draw a conclusion on the risk of obsolescence or unsaleability of inventory. It is very important for this reason that where inventory is a material balance that the auditor attends the year-end stock take to help in assessing the condition of inventory. Whether inventory will sell or not can be assessed through looking at post year-end sales and sales order books.

QUESTION 6.2

(a) **Further information/audit evidence needed: liability of €/£350, 000 in company statement of financial position**
- Examine documentation, e.g. minutes of meetings of shareholders or board of directors, which support the dividend amount issued to shareholders.
- Ensure that dividends paid during the year were recorded at the appropriate amount, e.g. inspection of the payment of dividends to shareholder by tracing cheque payments to bank statements.
- Ensure that dividends payable at the year end were recorded at the appropriate amount, e.g. inspection of post year-end payment of dividends to shareholders by tracing cheque payments to bank statements.
- Ensure dividends payable at year end were posted to the correct accounts by inspecting, the actual postings made by the client.
- Determine when dividends were declared and authorised by the board in order to ensure dividends paid and payable have been recorded in the proper period from inspection of board minutes. Under IAS 10 *Events After the Reporting Period* (IAS 10), dividends declared to shareholders after the balance sheet date should not be provided for as a liability in the financial statements but should be disclosed in the notes to the financial statements.
- Ensure the transactions were authorised and approved from inspection of board minutes.
- Ensure that any dividend paid was not paid illegally, i.e. review reserves and confirm that there were sufficient reserves available to issue the dividends during the year.
(b) **Further information/audit evidence needed: revalued company land and buildings**
- Gain or update understanding of how management organises and controls the process for determining fixed asset valuations and disclosures for fixed assets.
- Obtain information as to who performed the revaluation, e.g. directors or chartered surveyors.

- Consider how the revaluation has been accounted for and if this is in line with IFRS, if the disclosures are appropriate and if the method of valuation is applied consistently or if changes are appropriate.
- For external valuations, obtain and inspect the valuation report issued by the surveyor, gain an understanding of how the valuation has been performed and assess the reasonableness of the valuation.
- For internal valuations performed by directors, gain an understanding of how the valuation has been performed and assess the reasonableness of the valuation.
- Verify asset recording is appropriate, including the depreciation calculation and valuation reserves.

(c) **Further information/audit evidence needed: customer liquidation and unsold inventory**
- Verify whether any of this inventory has been sold post year end and paid for.
- Confirm whether any of this inventory will be recovered from the customer, review correspondence with the liquidator.
- Confirm whether the client is attempting to secure contracts with new customers for the sale of this inventory.
- Consider if the inventory has been recorded in the financial statements at an appropriate amount.
- If it is probable that the inventory will not be sold, considered if it should be treated as obsolete inventory.

(d) **Further information/audit evidence: legal fees**
- Contact the client's solicitor and confirm details of the pending litigation such as: the nature of the claim, the status of the claim, the probability of an economic outflow arising and the probable amount of any such outflow.
- Consider if a provision is necessary in the financial statements for any possible losses arising from the case.
- If no provision is necessary consider if disclosure of a contingent liability is necessary in the financial statements.

QUESTION 6.3

1. Conduct a numerical sequence check on sales invoices to ensure that all sales are recorded.
2. Review and vouch the debtors control account reconciliation to underlying books and records.
3. Perform detailed cut-off testing.
4. Carry out analytical procedures.

QUESTION 6.4

(a) Supplier statement reconciliations are a useful procedure as they verify each financial statement assertion:
   (i) existence – that the liability exists at the year end;
   (ii) rights and obligations – that the liability pertains to the entity at the year end;

(iii) occurrence – that the purchase pertains to the entity during the relevant period;
(iv) completeness – that there are no unrecorded liabilities;
 (v) valuation – that the liability is recorded at an appropriate carrying value; and
(vi) measurement – that the creditor is recorded at the proper amount and the purchase is allocated to the prior period.

(b) Request the following from the audit junior assistant:

Supplier A – verify the actual reason for not recording the invoice and establish if there is a cut-off error.

Supplier D – ensure the assistant follows up as to the reason for not posting the credit note. If it is an error it should be recorded on the schedule of unadjusted differences.

Supplier R – bring to schedule of unadjusted differences and no further work is necessary.

Supplier W – get the assistant to establish why there is a delay in the posting of the October payment. This could have implications for the reliance the auditor places on the system of internal control. Ensure the assistant enquires as to the present status of the discount claim. If there is no evidence that the discount is to be given then bring it to the schedule of unadjusted differences as an error.

QUESTION 7.1

(a) **Outline approach to address significant risk in relation to inventory**
- Choose a sample of inventory items and test the post-period-end sale price of those items of inventory.
- Inspect the sales invoice raised when these items were sold.
- Consider whether the year-end valuation is appropriate based on inventory valued at cost or net realisable value (NRV), whichever is lower.
- Where the NRV is lower than the carrying value of stock items, year-end inventory has been overstated and a stock provision against these stock items will be necessary.
  - Calculate a reasonable inventory provision which will restate inventory at a value which is not overstated.
  - Adjust inventory for the provision.

(b) **Impact on the audit plan in the absence of the finance director**

For five months in the year, in the absence of supplier statements reconciliations and daily till reconciliations, the controls around the following areas and financial statement assertions have been absent:
- accounts payable: completeness, accuracy and existence/occurrence
- purchases: completeness, accuracy and existence/occurrence
- sales: completeness, accuracy and existence/occurrence.

Accounts Payable

In the absence of adequate controls at the period end, accounts payable balances must be tested substantively through the performance of period-end supplier statement reconciliations. A greater amount of creditor balances may need to be reconciled in order to test the balance down to the materiality level, whereas if the control was operating effectively during the year the level of substantive testing would be reduced.

Sales

As this is predominantly a cash business, in the absence of daily till reconciliations, gaining comfort over the completeness, accuracy and existence/occurrence of total sales figure per the financial statements may not be possible. The auditor may not be able to express an opinion on the financial statements given the inability to validate the assertions noted above in relation to cash sales. As a result a qualified audit opinion may be issued.

(c) **Audit considerations if contract is to be agreed**

This will be a contract with a related party and as a result has inherent risk attached to it. As the company is experiencing a downturn in sales, the related party relationship with Gorgeous Shoes Ltd could be manipulated in order to improve the sales figures for Oh So Chic Ltd through sales invoices being raised at overstated amounts. When performing an audit with such a related party, the auditor will have to inspect and review all sales invoices raised in respect of Oh So Chic Ltd and ensure that sales have been made on an arm's length basis, i.e. that they have neither been inflated – which would be likely in this scenario – or reduced to an unrealistic selling price due to the related party relationship.

The auditor must also ensure that the following are disclosed in the financial statements in relation to related parties:
- the names of all related parties;
- the basis of how the related party relationship has arisen; and
- the nature and amount of transactions with related parties which took place during the period – together with period-end balances with those related parties.

QUESTION 7.2

The key risk to the audit is the ability of the company to continue to trade as a going concern. It has incurred significant losses and its gearing is rapidly increasing. The auditor should discuss with the company's directors their assessment of the going concern status of the company and what this is based on. Detailed budgets for at least two years (2014 and 2015) and related cash flow projections would be necessary. The auditor must consider the cash position of the company and the interest payments which the company must make on loan balances.

When performing the audit the auditor must remain alert for fraudulent accounting which could be used by the company directors in order to present results going forward which do not represent a going concern risk, for example, fictitious sales and debtor balances.

QUESTION 7.3

- Select a sample of weekly time sheets and confirm that they have been reviewed by line managers.

- From the weekly time sheets select a sample of employees and confirm that the correct numbers of hours have been inputted onto the payroll system for processing.
- Select a sample of employees and agree 'hourly wage rate per personnel records' to 'hourly wage rate per payroll system'.
- Select a sample of employees and obtain payslips for each employee; recompute PAYE and PRSI/ NIC charges and compare to deductions from the employees' payslips. Assess for reasonableness.
- Select a sample of BACS payment listings and agree 'total per BACS listing' to 'total per payroll report'.
- Validate that the BACS payments listings selected above have been authorised by the payroll manager.
- Observe the payroll manager and accounts manager processing weekly wages and validate that authorisation codes are required.

QUESTION 7.4

The existence of dominant directors introduces the risk of override of internal controls resulting in misstated financial statements which do not reflect accurately the results and financial position of the company for any given period. The following are some risks that may arise as a result of dominant directors running a company:
- creation of fictitious customer accounts and sales transactions;
- creation of fictitious supplier accounts and purchases;
- overstatement of stock value in order to increase assets of the company;
- risk of hidden bank accounts;
- inaccurate valuation of tangible fixed assets and investments;
- directors may limit the auditor's access to books and records therefore hindering performance of audit work; and
- directors may attempt to manipulate the auditor or provide false representations.

Possible Risks	Auditor Response
Creation of fictitious customer accounts and sales transactions	Performance of debtors circularisation. Unexpected visit to customer premises where significant doubt exists.
Creation of fictitious supplier accounts and purchases	Investigate existence of supplier by phone call or research on the internet. Unexpected visit to supplier premises where significant doubt exists.
Overstatement of inventory value in order to increase assets of the company	Perform period-end stock count. Visit premises unexpectedly and inspect site to ensure similar inventory levels are maintained during the year. Perform NRV testing.

Risk of hidden bank accounts	Contact bank and confirm accounts held and period-end balances.
Inaccurate valuation of tangible fixed assets such as land and buildings	Use professional valuers who are independent of the client.
Directors may limit the auditor's access to books and records therefore hindering performance of audit work	Qualified audit opinion may be issued.
Directors may attempt to manipulate auditors or provide false representations	Qualified audit opinion may be issued.

QUESTION 7.5

(a)
Memo
To: James Brett
From: John Smith
Re: Parallel Ltd
Inherent and Controls Risk identified during initial meeting with client for Year Ended 31 Dec 2012

Date 12 Jan 2013

As requested please find below details of identified inherent and controls risk noted during my discussion with management.

Inherent Risks
- 80% of sales are to Irish supermarkets that are currently under pressure to reduce prices due to cross-border sales and the recessionary environment. This may put pressure on Parallel Ltd to reduce prices to allow the supermarkets to maintain margins and entice consumers to continue purchasing.
- Management are under pressure from the group company to reduce costs which may indicate an incentive to under-record expenses.
- Inexperienced staff may have been carrying out tasks during the strike period.
- Impact on reputation/sales due to strike.
- Marketing costs have been cut by 60% which may further impact the ability to sell.
- Replacement of financial controller will result in loss of knowledge. In addition there was a month where no financial controller was in place.
- Management were reluctant to discuss reason for his departure which in itself is concerning.

Overall the turnover in key staff and the absence of key staff raises concerns with respect to the reliability of the accounting function throughout the year.

In addition a number of factors indicate pressure on ability to sell and pressure on cost reduction may be a motive for management to under-accrue expenses. These may also be indicative of a threat to the going concern.

Control Risks
- Controls around purchasing may be weak as a number of unexpected costs suddenly arose in the last two months of the prior year, further investigation may be required to see if these were unrecorded/un-accrued expenses that came to light late. In addition pressure to keep costs low may motivate management to hide costs and override controls.
- Many of the members of staff on strike were from accounts receivable and payable functions – this may have affected the operation of the controls within these departments during this period.
- Many of the staff on strike were distribution related and some of the signed PODs were not returned and hence sales were finalised without signed PODs – this may have an impact on the validity of sales.
- The payroll provider changed during 2012 which may have changed the control environment.

Overall from a controls perspective it may be wise to substantively test receivables, payables and payroll due to the possibility of control weaknesses in these areas. The assertion with respect to occurrence of revenue may also be a concern and focused substantive procedures should be performed in this area.

(b)
- Despite budgeted sales of just €4.8 million and pressures in the economy, sales came in at €4.9 million. What factors have contributed to these higher than expected sales?
- Why has material B cost 18% more than expected despite only a 2% increase in sales?
- Why is factory electricity 6% higher than budget considering sales are just 2% higher than expected?
- Considering wage reductions (reason for strike) why are labour costs 22% greater than budget?
- Distribution and finance administration salaries are down just 2% despite wage reductions and a period of strike, why is this?
- Office rent is 52% lower than budgeted – it is unusual to be able to reduce a fixed cost by such a substantial amount, how was this achieved?
- During our discussions you indicated an intended 60% reduction in marketing costs which are showing 40% lower than budgeted. How did you manage to maintain sales while cutting marketing?
- Budgeted receivables write off was €/£100,000 but actual is just €25,000, this seems unusual considering the environment. What is the reason for the difference?
- Depreciation of office equipment is 72% higher than budgeted, was there a significant purchase of office equipment during the year?

QUESTION 8.1

Where the controls process surrounding the revenue and receivables cycle is weak this means that a greater level of substantive testing will be necessary in order to gain comfort over management assertions surrounding total sales and the period-end debtors balance.

- The auditor may consider vouching sales down to the materiality level. Sales would be vouched to invoices raised/contracts/rental agreements depending on the nature of the business in order to gain comfort over accuracy of total sales.
- The auditor may perform a debtors circularisation in order to gain comfort over the existence/occurrence of the balances.
- The auditor may perform post year-end cash receipts testing on balances that are not confirmed by the debtors circularisation in order to confirm the existence/occurrence of the balances.
- The auditor may perform cut-off testing to verify that sales invoices around the period end have been included in the correct period in order to gain comfort over the cut-off of the debtors balance and total sales included in the accounts.
- The auditor may perform a substantive analytical review on trade debtors.
- The auditor may consider credit notes issued post-period end by the client and determine if any adjusting journal entries are necessary.

Where the control environment is weak the auditor will perform further substantive testing to compensate for the poor internal controls. For example, when performing debtors circularisation and post-period-end cash receipts, testing down to materiality will be necessary. In contrast, in a strong control environment testing down to materiality would not be necessary and a lower level of substantive testing would be supplemented by strong controls.

QUESTION 8.2

Where the controls process surrounding the revenue and receivables cycle is strong this means that a lower level of substantive testing will be necessary in order to gain comfort over management assertions surrounding total sales and the period-end debtors balance.
- Substantive testing of sales in the form of vouching total sales to invoices raised/contracts/rental agreements depending on the nature of the business in order to gain comfort over accuracy of total sales will not be necessary.
- Performance of substantive analytical procedures over sales will be sufficient combined with a strong controls environment to gain assurance over total sales. The auditor may perform a debtors circularisation in order to gain comfort over the existence/occurrence of the balances.
- The auditor may perform post year-end cash receipts testing on balances which are not confirmed by the debtors circularisation in order to confirm the existence/occurrence of the balances.
- The auditor may perform cut-off testing to verify that sales invoices around the period end have been included in the correct period in order to gain comfort over the cut-off of the debtor balance and total sales included in the accounts.
- The auditor may perform an analytical review on trade debtors instead of a substantive analytical review given the strong control environment.
- The auditor may consider credit notes issued post-period-end by the client and determine if any adjusting journal entries are necessary.

Where the control environment is strong the auditor will perform a lesser extent of substantive testing due to the significant comfort obtained from controls work, for example, when performing debtors circularisation and post-period-end cash receipts, testing down to materiality will not be necessary. In contrast, in a weak control environment testing down to materiality would be necessary and a greater level of substantive testing would be necessary to compensate for a lack of controls.

QUESTION 8.3

(a) **Weaknesses in the revenue and receivables cycle and impact on audit evidence**
- No controls are exercised by head office over cash sales at sites (a) and (b) as tills are not networked.
- Till reconciliations are retained. Therefore, there is no evidence of reconciliations being performed. Lack of control could result in misappropriation of cash.
- Transfer of cash from sites (a) and (b) is not secure.
- Lodgements are not made to bank on a timely basis, increasing the risk of loss due to theft.
- A manual cash received/lodgement book is not maintained by the client and analysis of weekly lodgements to the bank is not possible meaning that a cash audit trail does not exist. No analysis of weekly lodgements in respect of customer accounts/receivables is maintained. The reliability of the receivables balance is questionable.

(b) **Changes that could be implemented to improve controls around the revenue and receivables cycle**
- maintain a manual cash received book;
- retain till reconciliations; and
- network tills between head office and sites (a) and (b), and implement head office review of till reconciliations for sites (a) and (b) on a weekly basis.

QUESTION 8.4

(a) **Outsource of payroll function – further information needed**
At the planning stage the auditor needs to identify audit risks, i.e. the risks that an auditor may give an inappropriate audit opinion on the financial statements. As part of this process the auditor is required to obtain sufficient knowledge of the business to enable him to identify and understand transactions and events that affect the financial statements. The outsourcing of the payroll function is such an event and the following is the information that will need to be obtained:

1. The auditor will need to review the contract between the company and the payroll bureau, documenting an understanding of it and how Barrow Ltd monitors the work carried out by the payroll bureau.
2. The auditor will need access to the payroll records to carry out audit work and should enquire who holds the payroll records and, if it is the payroll bureau, arrange with them to gain access to the records.

3. The degree of authority delegated to the payroll bureau will have to be assessed in the context of evaluating the internal controls of the company. Such issues as: who approves payroll payments, who authorises payroll changes and what controls are in place for authorising overtime etc., will form part of this assessment.

4. The auditor will have to assess the quality of the work of the payroll bureau and this should be planned at the start of the audit. The auditor will assess, at the planning stage, the reputation and expertise the service organisation has in this area.

5. The auditor will have to report, as part of his audit opinion on Barrow Ltd, whether the company has kept proper accounting records. The quality of the payroll bureau's work will need to be assessed in this context and this should be considered at the planning stage.

(b) **Outsource of payroll function – additional audit procedures**

Additional audit procedures may not be necessary as a result of the decision to outsource the payroll function. As part of the systems testing the auditor will have assessed control risks relating to the payroll bureau. Provided that the auditor is satisfied that the bureau has the expertise and a good reputation within the industry, it may be possible to reduce the auditor's detailed testing and rely on evidence produced by the bureau. In order to do this the auditor may need to review information from the payroll bureau concerning the design and operation of its control system.

When considering whether to rely on work undertaken by the payroll bureau, the auditor considers the professional qualifications, experience and resources of the bureau's personnel.

The auditor will need to obtain representations to confirm balances and transactions from the payroll bureau and inspect records and documents held by them. In some cases the auditor may decide that they need to visit the premises of the bureau to obtain audit evidence.

(c) **Reporting of control weaknesses**

The following are the key considerations for the reporting of control weaknesses to the directors of the company:
- There is a need for the auditor to document the weaknesses based on audit findings.
- There is a need for the auditor to report the potential impact of the weaknesses.
- The auditor will need to consider if further audit work is required as a result of control weaknesses.
- The auditor needs to consider the effects of the weaknesses on the financial statements in arriving at their audit opinion.
- The auditor should consider the requirements of ISA (UK and Ireland) 265 *Communicating Deficiencies in internal Control to those Charged with Governance and Management.*

QUESTION 8.5

(a) Weakness
- HR are not involved in the recruitment process.

Risks

1. Employee hire may not have been authorised.
2. Employee salary or rate decided by one person (may be excessive).
3. Bias or poor judgement may exist in the recruitment process without the independence and expertise of HR (i.e. adequately experienced/qualified not hired for the position).

- Employee details are provided to HR by the individual managers.

Risk

1. The employee may not exist and the bank details may be those of the manager or a connected person.

- There is a lack of segregation of duties as Terry, the payroll supervisor, enters the new starters into the payroll system.

Risks

1. Terry could add an employee not included on the list and use his own or a connected person's bank account details.
2. Terry could input the incorrect salary or hourly rate.

- There is a lack of segregation of duties as Terry, the payroll supervisor, enters the terminations into the payroll system.

Risk

1. Terry may avoid terminating an employee for a period of time, change their payroll details and process wages for himself.

- No review is performed to match the entries made by James, the payroll assistant, to the spread sheets sent by the individual managers.

Risks

1. Data entry errors would go undetected meaning employees get paid too much or too little.
2. James may add additional hours for people he knows meaning employees get paid too much.

- No independent review is carried out on the Gross to Net reports or any payroll reports prior to the instruction being given to the bank to pay employees.

Risk

1. Fraud and error in the payroll processing would go unnoticed.

- Only one authorisation is required to pay 1,000 employees

Risk

1. Additional payrolls may be processed
2. Errors may go unnoticed

(b)

- HR should sign off on all new hire requirements to confirm vaUd business need.
- HR should be part of the interview process to ensure the best candidate is hired and no bias exists in the interview process.
- HR should sign off on wage/salary rate.
- HR should obtain bank details directly from the new recruit.
- HR, not Terry, should be responsible for inputting new recruits into the payroll system as Terry has too many other payroll tasks.

- If HR does not input new recruits, they should review the exception report generated by the system and compare it to the authorised list sent to Terry.
- HR, not Terry, should terminate all employees directly in the payroll system as Terry has too many other payroll tasks.
- If HR does not terminate leavers in the system, they should review the exception report generated by the system and compare it to the authorised list sent to Terry.
- Terry should review inputs by James by using batch totals at the end of each manager's spreadsheet ensuring that the total number of basic, overtime and holidays hours entered for each manager on the system equals that on their spreadsheet.
- Alternatively, each manager should be given their exception report showing summary hours, holidays etc. per the payroll system and be requested to sign off. This will also ensure that terminations and new starts are captured.
- A reconcihation of the headcount per the payroll system and the headcount per HR should be performed periodically.
- There should be two authorised individuals required to sign off on the file before it is sent to the bank for payment (similar to cheques).

(c)

#	Cycle	Assertion	Suggested Test
A	Revenue	Occurrence	1. Select a sample of invoices from the General Ledger and trace them back to customer signed purchase order delivery dockets to confirm goods were delivered to support the transaction.
B	Receivables	Valuation	**Any one of below** 1. Review the aging of customer balances and enquire of any balances that are outside of customer agreed terms. 2. Review post year end receipts from customers.
C	Fixed Assets	Existence	**Any one of below** 1. Observe fixed asset count at year end. 2. Compare listing of assets to insurance certs. 3. Compare listing of assets to ownership documents.
D	Purchases	Completeness	**Any one of below** 1. Select a number of suppliers and review supplier reconciliation. 2. Review post year-end invoices. 3. Review post year-end payments. 4. Review debit balances on the supplier listing.

QUESTION 9.1

(a) **Key aims and objectives of an IT audit**

The main aim of an IT audit is similar to a Financial Statement Audit objective, i.e. to determine whether an organisation's financial statements and financial position are presented fairly in accordance with generally accepted accounting principles (GAAP).

The objective of an IT audit is to review and evaluate an organisation's information system's availability, confidentiality, and integrity. Availability refers to the access to the organisation's computer systems to ensure they would be available to the business at all times when required. Confidentiality review is necessary to ensure that information is only disclosed to authorised users. The final aim is to ensure the integrity of the information, i.e. that the information provided by the system is accurate, reliable, and timely.

(b) **Main areas of an IT audit**
- information security,
- change control, and
- IT operations and data interfaces.

Information Security

In the area of information security the key risks include allowing access to the information by more people than is necessary, either by a failure to implement appropriately logical security (including user names and passwords), or, a failure to implement a secure user access management process including a process to approve the set-up of new users and to denying access once a person leaves employment. It is also important to ensure that there is an appropriate segregation of duties.

The key controls include:
- implementing logical security tools, such as passwords, firewalls, and virus protection to govern access;
- taking appropriate physical and environment security measures e.g. no physical access to computer facility without relevant code etc.; and
- introducing a process to govern the granting or denying of access to the systems; and a process to regularly review access to ensure that any segregation of duties issues are identified.

OR

Change Control

The key risks associated with the area of IT change control include:
1. that changes are not properly approved by management; and
2. that changes are not fully tested so that they deliver their objectives.

The key controls to address these risks include:

- the use of formal acquisition and development procedures which ensure that before any changes are implemented they are fully approved by management to ensure that they are in line with the organisation's IT aims and objectives;
- procedures to ensure that all data converted from older systems is fully reviewed to ensure that it has been transferred correctly;
- controls to restrict access to programmes and the ability to make changes so that changes cannot be made without approval by a senior responsible official; and
- procedures to ensure that formal testing is carried out before the changes are implemented. This should include testing by users to ensure that they achieve their aims and by IT to ensure that the changes are correctly developed from a technical point of view.

OR

IT Operations and Data Interfaces

The main risks in the area of IT operations and data interfaces are:
- that all scheduled programme processing e.g. sales update do not run successfully;
- that data does not flow accurately from one application to another;
- that data is not appropriately backed up; and
- that additional or unapproved tasks are run on the systems.

The key controls include:
- a process to monitor all overnight or batch jobs to ensure that these have completed successfully;
- controls to restrict the ability to make changes to scheduled processing jobs; and
- a process to identify and follow up on any jobs that fail to run correctly.

(c) **Benefits of CAATs**
The main advantage of CAATs is the ability to test 100% of the transactions under review rather than the normal sampling approach. The use of CAATs is also more effective and efficient than a manual approach. In addition when using CAATs software it is possible to define scripts or commands which can be re-run multiple times and used when tests are repeated thus bringing greater efficiencies.

QUESTION 9.2

Smith & Smith
Registered Auditors & Chartered Accountants,
Smith House,
10 Main Street,
Dublin 2

1 July 2013

Dear Sirs,

(a) **General application of Computer-Assisted Audit Techniques**

We are very pleased to have been appointed as auditors to Large Company Ltd. As part of this appointment you asked that we provide an outline of Computer Assisted Audit Techniques (CAATs) and how we might utilise these as part of our audit. Set out below is a summary of how we might use CAATs as part of the audit at Large Company.

CAATs are a set of data analysis tools that are used to provide detailed data analysis and review to support the auditor and to understand and integrate large amounts of data in order to identify any risk or unusual transactions which should be investigated.

CAATs are used as part of an audit as they provide the ability to test 100% of the population rather than rely on a sample of transaction which would be used for manual testing. It is also possible to design and develop tests which can be re-run for different periods or files. This increases the efficiency associated with the audit.

(b) **Specific application of CAATs to Large Company**

Specifically, in relation to Large Company, we have noted the information that you have provided in relation to your inventories. In particular we note the large value of raw materials and consumables. We propose to validate the value of this category of inventory by re-aging the inventory to ensure that the valuation is correct and remains current. We also propose to validate the calculation of the inventory value by recalculating the value of inventories using CAATs. We will also review inventory movements and identify slow moving inventory items which might indicate obsolete products which may not be correctly valued.

We look forward to working with you as part of the audit this year and to delivering a robust and fair assessment of your annual financial statements.

Yours faithfully,

_____

Smith & Smith

QUESTION 9.3

(a) **Definition of terms**

Input Controls

Input controls are exceptionally important as many errors can occur at the input stage. Input controls are those controls designed to ensure that the input data has been correctly authorised, is complete, and accurate. If input errors are detected, these need to be reviewed, corrected and resubmitted for inputting into the system again. Examples of input controls are input validation checks, for example restricting date fields to a particular date format.

Processing Controls

Processing controls are those designed to provide reasonable assurance that the computer processes have performed as intended. They ensure that the transactions are not duplicated, lost or improperly changed in any way and errors are identified and corrected on a timely basis. An example of a processing control is a 'before and after report' showing the value of transactions before and after processing.

Data Reporting Controls

Data reporting controls are those designed to ensure that the processing has been correctly carried out, and that the output reports are distributed to authorised personnel only. An example of a data reporting control is a 'reconciliation of reports to source data'.

(b) **General IT security controls – key considerations**

Information Security

In the area of information security the key risks include:

- allowing access to the information by more people than is necessary
- failure to implement appropriately logical security including user names and passwords
- failure to implement a secure user access management process including a process to approve the setting up of new users and to remove access once a person leaves employment
- failure to ensure that there is an appropriate level of segregation of duties

The key controls include:

- implementing logical security tools, such as passwords, firewalls virus protection to govern access;
- taking appropriate physical and environment security measures;
- introducing a process to govern the granting and removing of access to the systems; and
- implementing a process to review access from time to time to ensure that any segregation of duties issues are identified.

QUESTION 9.4

(a) **Physical and logical security controls**
Physical security controls refer to measures that are in place to restrict physical access to the organisations computer and information assets. Examples include the use of swipe cards, logging and monitoring of people entering and leaving key areas of the building and the use of other technology including CCTV.

Logical security controls refer to the use of tools, such as passwords, firewalls and virus protection to govern access to information assets even for those who may have physical access to the premises.

(b) **Change controls**

Change controls around key IT systems are important for the IT auditor as the failure to adequately control changes made to IT systems can impact on the integrity of the data stored in those systems. As this data is relied upon to generate the financial statements, if its integrity is not maintained then there is a risk that the financial statements will not reflect the accurate financial position of the company.

Given that data integrity is of primary importance to the production of the financial statements, some of the key risks that should be tested include:
- that unauthorised changes might be made to the IT systems,
- that changes are not fully tested before implementation; and
- that there is no formal process in place to move changes from the test environment to the live environment.

In addition, it is also important that there is an appropriate segregation of duties between those who can makes changes to the computer systems and those with access to the live data. System developers should not be able to access live data.

(c) **Unauthorised access controls**

Controls that may be used to detect unauthorised access include:
- logging and monitoring of access;
- alerts for access out of hours or at unusual times; and
- alerts to record attempts to use invalid user names and passwords.

QUESTION 9.5

(a) **Sales and trade receivables**
- Extract a sample to be circularised and print out the confirmation.
- Select a sample using an appropriate statistical approach such as monetary unit sampling (MUS).
- Search for usual items such as large and unusual balances or credit balances in receivables balances.
- Totalling the accounts receivable ledger and comparing it to the general ledger total.
- Age the receivables listing in order to help identify possible bad debts

(b) **Inventories**
- Testing overhead allocations.
- Checking the mathematical accuracy of the inventory records by multiplying the cost by the quantity.
- Adding the total values of inventory items to arrive at a total value of inventory included in the financial statements.
- Identifying slow-moving items by comparing to sales records.

(c) **Purchases and trade payables**
- Comparison of goods received with purchases orders as part of cut-off testing.
- Identify any large or unusual purchases.
- Identify any employees who are also suppliers.
- Stratify purchases by month to detect unusual patterns.

(d) **Wages and salaries**
- Recalculate the payroll cost for the year which could be agreed to the General Ledger.
- Identify employees that might have worked excessive hours for further follow-up by the auditor.
- Confirm that all employees on the payroll file are valid employees.

(e) **Fixed assets (PPE)**
- Analysis of assets by different classes.
- Re-performing depreciation calculations to ensure that they have been correctly calculated.
- Verifying the mathematical accuracy of different asset classes and agreeing them to the financial statements.
- Selecting a sample of additions during the year for further testing.
- Selecting a sample from the repairs and maintenance account for further testing to ensure that those items should not have been capitalised.

QUESTION 9.6

(a) **Benefits of computerised system**
The key risks associated with the use of IT systems for bedroom and bar revenue include:
- that the system's availability, confidentiality, and integrity are compromised. This means that access to the organisation's computer systems is interrupted and that it is not available for the business at all times when required (Availability). Provision of bills to customers may be delayed.
- that the confidentiality of its information is not maintained and that information is disclosed to unauthorised users.
- that integrity of the information is compromised, which means that the information provided by the system is inaccurate, unreliable, or not provided in a timely manner.

Key benefits include:
- faster transaction times
- more accurate and reliable information
- standard pricing and the ability to monitor and track business operations more accurately.

(b) **Application and benefits of CAATs**
1. To avoid the risk that revenue is overstated, the auditor may use CAATs to validate the revenue numbers, recalculating the numbers reported by multiplying the

number of nights sold by the rate per room. This could be done on a 100% basis using CAATs rather than a sample basis where a manual process might be used.

2. For bar revenue a comparison of sales form the IT system could be made to purchases of stock in order to validate revenue figures reported.

3. A comparison of revenue and sales can be made to the previous year's performance in order to identify any anomalies or unusual trends that might point to a mistake in the revenue reported.

QUESTION 9.7

(a) **Controls for maintenance of computer systems**

   (i) Key areas for consideration in relation to the maintenance and development of IT systems include the risks that changes are not properly approved by management, and that changes are not fully tested to ensure they achieve their objectives. Controls need to be designed, tested and implemented to deal with proposed changes to the IT system. For changes to implemented there should be an appropriate sign off by appropriate responsible officials.

   (ii) In order to assess the controls in place over the development process the auditor would review a number of changes that have been made to the IT systems and confirm that the appropriate approval for the change was received; that changes were appropriately planned and tested; and that changes were accurately implemented.

(b) **Review of operational controls**

In order to assess these controls any review should consider the following headings:

1. The use of Formal Acquisition and Development Procedures which ensure that before any changes are implemented they are fully approved by management to ensure that they are in line with the organisation's IT aims and objectives.

2. Procedures to ensure that all data which is migrated from an older system is fully reviewed to ensure that it has been migrated completely and correctly.

3. Controls to restrict access and the ability to make system changes, requiring approval before changes can be implemented.

4. Procedures to ensure that formal testing is carried out before the changes are implemented. This should include user-testing to ensure that the changes achieve their stated aims; and testing by IT professionals to ensure that the changes are correctly developed from a technical point of view.

QUESTION 9.8

(a) **E-commerce audit**

When conducting an audit of an e-commerce organisation, the steps outlined below should be completed:

1. **Map flow of transactions and data** – e-commerce can increase the complexity of processes. In order to identify key risks and controls, auditors should consider using process or data flow diagrams to map the flow of transactions.

2. **IT general controls** – testing of ITGCs should be completed for applications and infrastructures. Interfaces from externally facing websites and internal systems should be tested to obtain assurance that all data transferred is complete and accurate.

3. **Key application controls** – data input controls are typical of the application controls that should be tested as part of an e-commerce audit.

4. **Network controls** – as key elements of the IT environment are externally facing, the auditor should consider engaging the services of Information Security Technical specialists to perform a penetration test of websites and mobile applications. A penetration test is where the actions of a computer hacker are emulated in order to identify security vulnerabilities or weaknesses. Firewalls are used by organisations to separate external internet traffic from internal network traffic. The firewalls in place between externally facing technology and other internal systems are key controls. The processes in place for managing firewall rules should be tested as part of an e-commerce audit.

(b) **Key controls in e-commerce environments**

The key control considerations for the finance director centre on completeness, accuracy and reliability of the processing of transactions. Each element of the provision of services online needs to examined in detail and measured against the objectives of completeness, accuracy and reliability.

In relation to security in an online environment the need for appropriate security is vitally important. The e-commerce enabled website is equivalent to a shop and should be secured appropriately. Businesses will typically be responsible for collecting sensitive information such as credit card numbers and personal details and will need to ensure that these are not lost or accessed by intruders.

QUESTION 10.1

- There is a need to evaluate and perform audit procedures to confirm their adequacy for the external auditor.
- Establish if the internal auditor has adequate technical training/proficiency and determine if the work of assistants is supervised/reviewed/documented.
- Ensure sufficient appropriate audit evidence has been obtained to be able to draw reasonable conclusions there from.
- Determine the conclusions reached are appropriate in the circumstances and any reports prepared are consistent with the results of the work performed.
- Ensure any exceptional/unusual matters disclosed by the internal auditor are properly resolved.

It is difficult to determine until the above is complete whether the internal audit work carried out will reduce the work of the external auditor as the external auditor cannot simply take the work at face value. The auditor must remember he holds sole responsibility for the audit opinion expressed and while he might find the need to obtain expert advice, he does so knowing he must obtain sufficient appropriate audit evidence with respect not only to the subject matter but also to the calibre of the appointed expert.

QUESTION 10.2

Dear John,

I felt I had to write to you and express my concerns about your plans to reduce the time on your upcoming audit of XYZ Limited. I think it is admirable that you are taking the training so seriously and trying to increase the margins for our firm, but some of your intentions are of concern to me.

Before I discuss these with you there is one resounding issue with your plans and that relates to the responsibility with respect to the opinion given on the financial statements. While the auditor may call on various sources to assist him in concluding his opinion, he holds sole responsibility for that opinion. For that reason he makes no reference to the use of the service organisation auditor, the internal auditor or the auditor's expert in his audit report, as doing so would be perceived as an attempt to diminish his own responsibility with respect to the conclusion drawn.

For this reason, when using the work of others, the auditor must satisfy himself as to the adequacy of the qualifications, expertise and competence of individuals involved as well as satisfying himself as to the reasonableness, accuracy, relevance and completeness of the conclusions drawn by others.

Internal audit Before you proceed with the work of the internal auditor you will need to satisfy yourself with regard to the competence, experience and quality of the internal audit team work.

ISA 610 *Using the Work of Internal Auditors* (ISA 610) will help you when deciding on whether to use the work of the internal auditor – it outlines the following audit procedures that may be carried out by the external auditor prior to relying on the work of the internal audit team. These include:
• examination of items already examined by the internal auditors;
• examination of other similar items; and
• observation of procedures performed by the internal auditors.

Service organisation Type 1 report A Type 1 report is the use of a service auditor to report on the description and design of the service provider's controls with respect to the entity. This report does not make any reference to the operation and effectiveness of the controls. To gain assurance around the operation and effectiveness of the controls you will need to obtain a Type 2 report. The principle auditor remains responsible for the opinion provided on the financial statements and for this reason he must satisfy himself that the Type 2 report constitutes sufficient appropriate audit evidence with respect to the competence and professionalism of its preparer and its form and content. ISA 402 *Audit Considerations Relating to an Entity Using a Service Organisation* (ISA 402) will offer further guidance to you on your responsibility when the entity uses a service organisation.

Using the work of an auditor's expert Before engaging the work of the expert, the auditor is responsible for evaluating the necessary qualifications, competence, capabilities and objectivity of the expert. The auditor cannot simply accept a second opinion on a valuation and perform no further work. The auditor is not the expert and therefore he cannot judge the assumptions and methods used but should seek to obtain an understanding of them to consider their reasonableness. This will involve discussions with the expert as well as with the client.

QUESTION 10.3

The code of ethics of the IIA are principles relevant to the profession and practice of internal auditing , and Rules of Conduct that describe behaviour expected of internal auditors. The Code of Ethics applies to both parties and entities that provide internal audit services. The purpose of the Code of Ethics is to promote an ethical culture in the global profession of internal auditing.

Being independent, however, is somewhat more difficult for the internal auditor due to his direct employment by the entity. The threats to external auditor independence are similar to those of the independence issues facing the internal auditor although they present themselves in different ways for example:

1. **Self-interest threat** The internal auditor has his remuneration package agreed within the organisation. Quite often the individual to whom the internal auditor reports will influence, if not dominate, the performance reviews of the internal auditor. For this reason it is essential that the head internal auditor report directly to the audit committee. Consider a situation where the internal auditor reports directly to for example, the CFO, identifying a control failing or even a fraud with respect to the CFO or his department. A self-interest threat arises due to the internal auditor's concern for his remuneration, or possibly his employment, should he report these failings with respect to his superior.
2. **Intimidation threat** The head of internal audit will often sit on the line below senior management and may be intimidated by his superiors into not reporting certain instances of fraud or error. The audit committee should ensure the company enforces a whistleblowing hotline to permit the anonymous reporting of concerns over fraud or error.

It is impossible to show an exhaustive list of independence threats which an internal auditor may face but the above demonstrates examples of such independence threats.

QUESTION 11.1

Select a sample of additions from the fixed asset registers and ensure they have adequate supporting documentation.

QUESTION 11.2

It is more economical to audit fixed assets using substantive testing because of the relatively few associated transactions compared with other balances.

QUESTION 11.3

To: Audit Assistant
From: Audit Senior
Date: 1 May 2013
Re: Builder Limited
        Audit of Tangible Fixed Assets
        Year ended 31 March 2013

The following is the audit programme to be followed when auditing Builder's tangible fixed assets:

- Prepare or obtain a fixed asset register showing the date of purchase of assets and the make up of the opening balance.
- Agree the client's fixed asset schedule to the closing nominal ledger. Check the totals on the schedule.
- Agree opening balances to prior-year signed financial statements.
- Physically verify assets. Ensure assets brought forward have been inspected.
- Vouch additions to supporting documentation.
- Vouch disposals to supporting documentation.
- Examine title documents (if not held as security by a lender). Ensure title is in the name of the company.
- Examine vehicle registration documents. Note details of model and user.
- Review hire purchase and lease agreements and ensure the assets and related obligations have been properly accounted for in accordance with IAS 17 *Leases*.

QUESTION 11.4

The following audit tests should be completed on each of the reconciling items:

1. Plant held on operating lease – as per IAS 17 *Leases* (IAS 17), paragraph 33: "Lease payments under an operating lease shall be recognised as an expense on a straight-line basis over the lease term". The operating lease agreement should be reviewed and the transaction should be traced through the statement of comprehensive income.
   As per IAS 17, assets held under operating leases should not be capitalised, therefore Handitel is correct in omitting this from its final tangible fixed asset listing.
2. Repairs posted in error to fixed asset register – these items should be vouched to purchase invoices to verify that they are in fact repairs and not of a capital nature. An analytical review should also be completed on the repairs and maintenance expenses, and fluctuations should be discussed with the client.
3. Assets purchased on 5 January 2012 – vouch receipt of goods to 'goods despatch notes' and invoice and vouch payment for goods to the bank. Inquire of management when the asset was brought into use.
   From inquiries and tracing to backup documentation determine if it is correct to capitalise 20% or 100% of the cost of the asset.

4. Assets excluded from register – vouch receipt of goods to 'goods despatch notes' and invoices. Vouch payment to the bank. If receipted before year end then it is correct to capitalise them at year end. Review the depreciation on these assets to ensure it is accurate and complete.

5. Adjustment for capitalisation of interest – as per IAS 23 *Borrowing Costs* (IAS 23), interest can be capitalised if it is directly attributable to the construction of fixed assets. Capitalisation should cease when the asset is ready to be brought into use. The interest capitalised should be recomputed by the auditor.

   Ensure there is consistency in treatment across all fixed asset classes.

   Ensure the new accounting policy is reflected in the notes to the financial statements.

6. Assets constructed internally – inspect the supporting documentation for labour costs, materials and overheads, ensure they are directly attributable and cease being charged to the asset account when the asset is ready to be brought into use.

   Verify that only expenditure relating to design, construction or installation of the asset is capitalised and that no abnormal costs are included. Review the depreciation policy and review if depreciation has been charged since October.

QUESTION 12.1

(a) **Castlelyons inventory schedule testing**
   - Check arithmetical accuracy of totals, costs and calculations of the schedule.
   - Verify that the cost of each Product No. is correct to their supporting purchase invoices.
   - Ensure that inventory is valued at lower of cost and net realisable value in accordance with IAS 2 *Inventories* (IAS 2).
   - The net realisable value of the inventory should be tested by agreeing sales to recent sales invoices.
   - Review stocktake reports for evidence of obsolescence.
   - Agree inventory figures to the nominal ledger.
   - For products where the components can be sold separately, the component value should be tested.
   - Discuss with management the saleability of all products and substantively test the responses, e.g. look at orders placed and post year-end sales.
   - Review the level of sales of the products in the last few months to determine if any provision may be required.

(b) **Stocktake error**
   - Contact person who attended the stocktake and inquire if they remember anything unusual.
   - Inquire from management how the error was detected.
   - Re-count the inventory of the products relating to the errors as soon as possible.
   - Reconcile the movement of the inventory from the year end to the subsequent re-count – the movements should be agreed to the sales and purchases ledgers.
   - Review stocktake error and consider whether it has any material impact for the audit report.

(c) **Explicit and implicit assertions**

Explicit assertions:
- inventory exists (existence);
- the correct amount of inventory is €808,264 (valuation).

Implicit assertions:
- all inventory that should be reported has been included (completeness);
- all reported inventory is owned by the entity (ownership) – there are no restrictions on the use of the inventory (presentation and disclosure).

QUESTION 12.2

(a) **Stocktake procedures**
- Ensure adequate stocktaking instructions are given to all counters.
- Check that there is no physical movement of inventory during the count.
- Review for possible evidence of slow-moving inventory.
- Check that all inventory is counted.
- Perform test counts from the stock sheets to the floor to test existence of stock; and counts from the floor to the sheet to test the completeness of the count sheets.
- Obtain cut-off information i.e. last goods received notes and despatch dockets.

(b) **Cut-off checks**
1. Test cut-off at the date of stocktake:
   - Purchases cut-off:
     - select the last goods received notes for goods delivered pre stocktake and check that they have been recorded in the inventory records before the stocktake began; and
     - select a sample of goods received notes for stock received after the stocktake and ensure they were not recorded in the stock system until after the stocktake was finished.
   - Sales cut-off:
     - select the last despatch dockets for goods despatched before the stocktake and ensure the sale has been recorded before the stocktake; and
     - select the first despatch dockets for goods despatched after the stocktake and ensure the sale has been recorded after the stocktake.
2. Test cut-off at year end:
   - Purchases cut-off:
     - select the last goods received notes for goods delivered pre year end and check that they have been recorded in the inventory records before the year end;
     - check that the purchase invoice relating to the goods received note has been recorded in the purchases ledger or accruals at year end;
     - select a sample of goods received notes for stock received after the year end and check thatthey were not recorded in the stock system until after year end; and
     - check that the purchase invoice relating to the goods received note has not been recorded in the purchases ledger or accruals at year end.

- Sales cut-off:
  - select the last despatch dockets for goods despatched pre year end and check that the sale has been recorded before the year end.
  - select the first despatch dockets for goods despatched after year end and check that the sale has been recorded after the year end; and
  - trace the despatch documentation through to the relating sales invoice and check that the sales invoice was posted to debtors and sales in the correct period.

(c) **Inventory value verification**
  1. Review the number and value of adjustments posted to the inventory records at the end of each stocktake. If there are only minor adjustments posted this will give the auditor comfort that the inventory system at any one time is fairly accurate.
  2. Obtain a summary report from the inventory manager which details how often all inventory was counted and ensure that all inventory was counted at least three times a year.
  3. Check the level of adjustments posted just before and after the year end;
  4. Review the inventory listing for negative items, obtain an explanation and ensure that the error is corrected.
  5. Test completeness of raw material receipts between the stocktake and the year end. This may be tested by checking the sequence of goods received notes (GRNs) and tracing a sample of the GRNs to the raw material sub-ledger.
  6. Test the completeness of the transfer to work in progress (WIP) from raw materials and the transfer out of WIP to finished goods. This may be completed by testing a sample of journal entries for transfers of raw materials to WIP and WIP to FG.
  7. Check completeness of despatches of finished goods (FG). This should be tested by checking the sequence of despatch notes and tracing a sample of items in sales/cost of sales reports to the FG sub ledger.

QUESTION 13.1

(a) **Total sales revenue expectation (2012)**

	€	
Total sales to 31/12/2011	462,000	
Increase in revenue due to new DVDs brought to market	130,280	See a) below
Decline in revenue due to DVDs discontinued	(21,930)	See b) below
Increase in revenue due to introduction of children's sweatshirt range	17,550	See c) below
Decline in revenue due to reduction in directory prices	(15,800)	See d) below
Total expectation for sales to 31/12/12	**572,100**	

Expected Sales FY 2012
€

	€
DVDs	335,350
Sweatshirts	54,550
Magazines	182,200
Total	572,100

(i) **New DVDs**

DVD	Number of Months on the Market	Expected Revenue (No. of months on market × selling price × budgeted monthly sales)
1	11	11 × €10 × 250 = €27,500
2	9	9 × €17 × 300 = €45,900
3	6	6 × €12 × 485 = €34,920
4	4	4 × €15 × 245 = €14,700
5	2	2 × €22 × 165 = €7,260
Expected increase in revenue		**€130,280**

(ii) **Discontinued DVDs**
DVD 1

Lost revenue = €22 × 565

= €12,430

DVD 2

Lost revenue = €19 × 500

= €9,500

Expected decline in revenue = €21,930

(iii) **Children's Sweatshirts**
Number of months on the market = 2
Average selling price = €13.50
Expected monthly sales = 650
Expected increase in revenue = 2 × €13.50 × 650
= €17,550

(iv) **Magazines**

Price Cut	No. of Months During Which Price Cut was in Operation	Prior-Year Annual Sales Volume	Lost Revenue
€0.2	12	20,000	€0.2 × 20,000 = €4,000
€0.2	12	13,500	€0.2 × 13,500 = €2,700
€0.3	10	10,000	€0.3 × 10/12 × 10,000 = €2,250
€0.4	12	11,000	€0.4 × 11,000 = €4,400
€0.15	7	28,000	€0.15 × 7/12 × 28,000 = €2,450

Decline in revenue   €15,800

(b) **Additional information to determine reliability**

New DVDs

- Determine the basis of budgeted figures, understand the budget and assess its robustness.
- Consider who prepares the budget.
- Consider who authorises the budget.
- Determine if actual results are traced to budget on a timely basis and if remedial action is taken.
- Understand why budgeted figures have not been achieved and validate the reasons for this.
- Confirm the month of introduction of new DVDs to the market, for example, by inspection of sales catalogue or sales records.
- Validate selling prices of DVDs, for example, by inspection of sales catalogues or sales invoices.

Discontinued DVDs

- Confirm that selling prices for DVDs 1 and 2 were €22 and €19 respectively for all of the prior year.
- Confirm the month of discontinuation of DVDs to the market, for example, by inspection of sales catalogues or sales records.

Sweatshirts

- Confirm month of introduction of children's sweatshirts to market, for example, by inspection of sales catalogue or sales records.
- Validate selling prices of children's sweatshirts, for example, by inspection of sales catalogue or sales invoices.
- Inspect market research and assess reliability of data to confirm expected monthly sales figure.
- Consider if average selling price is a reliable basis for use when determining expectation.

Magazines

- Assess reliability of using prior-year sales volume when determining expectation.
- View sales records to confirm selling price cut for amount of price cut and date of price cut, e.g. inspect invoice 'before' and 'after' date and confirm that price cut has taken place.

(c) **Completion of the four-step approach**

- Develop the threshold for further investigation based on the planning materiality of €10,000, for example, 75% of €10,000, i.e. €7,500.
- Compute the difference between expectation and the actual result:

	€
Expected sales	572,100
Actual sales	568,000
Difference	4,100

- Where the difference is greater than the threshold, perform additional testing. In this case this is not deemed necessary as the difference is below the threshold for further investigation.

QUESTION 13.2

(a) **Bad debt provision audit procedures**
1. Obtain an analysis of the bad debt provision showing which customer balances have been provided for by the client.
2. Obtain an analysis of the invoice numbers, invoice dates and invoice amounts which have been provided for.
3. Discuss with management/directors how provision amounts have been determined and assess reasonableness and basis of provision amounts.
4. Attention should be given to the following when considering the amount provided for by the client and if it is necessary or adequate:
   - Has the customer gone bankrupt? If so the total customer balance on the ledger should be provided for in full.
   - Is there a dispute over a balance which has been provided for?
   - Is the customer experiencing financial difficulties?
   - How long has the balance which has been provided for been outstanding?
   - How recent was the last payment received from the customer? The greater the length of time the greater the risk that future payments will not be received.
   - Is the customer's account on hold or is the client still trading with the customer?
   - Is the client actively chasing the debt?
5. It will be important for the auditor to confirm any of the circumstances above in order to validate the need for the provision amount:
   - as bankruptcy must be publicly disclosed, it can be validated with reasonable ease;

- where balances are disputed, inspect correspondence with the customer (letters/e-mails/faxes) pertaining to the dispute;
- a review of the customer's payment patterns may indicate cash flow problems; for example, if the customer is making round sum payments on a timely basis such as €1,000 each month, this could suggest that the customer is experiencing difficulties and may cast doubt over the recoverability of the balance and confirm the need for a provision;
- inspect invoices making up the unpaid balance which have been provided for and confirm how long they have been outstanding;
- by inspection of customer accounts and cash receipts book, verify the date of the final payment made by the customer;
- inspect the client's accounting system to confirm if the customer account is on hold or if it remains active; and
- inspect correspondence with the customer (letters/e-mails/faxes) requesting payment for aged balances.

In view of the information obtained from testing, the auditor must consider if the provision is adequate, i.e. whether an over- or under-provision has been made. If necessary the auditor will propose an adjustment to the amount of the provision.

(b) **Other accounting estimates and their audit approach**

1. Accruals
   - discuss with management the method of determining the balance and understand the basis of the accrued amount;
   - evaluate whether the assumptions used are consistent with each other, the prior year, supporting data, relevant historical data, and industry data;
   - consider whether accounting estimates are in compliance with generally accepted accounting policies;
   - re-compute accrued amounts;
   - apply analytical procedures;
   - assess reasonableness of the period-end balance;
   - confirm that significant estimates are disclosed appropriately in the financial statements; and
   - verify post year-end payment of accrued amounts.

2. Depreciation
   - consider reasonableness of depreciable life;
   - consider appropriateness of depreciation policy;
   - re-compute depreciation for significant fixed asset classes and assess reasonableness; and
   - where significant differences arise, investigate reasons for these differences.

3. Inventory provision
   - discuss with management the method of determining the balance and understand the basis of the inventory provision;
   - evaluate whether the assumptions used are consistent with each other, the prior year, supporting data, relevant historical data, and industry data;
   - apply analytical procedures;

- assess the reasonableness of the period-end balance;
- confirm that significant estimates are disclosed appropriately in the financial statements; and
- investigate post-period-end sales of inventory items and confirm that the selling price is greater than the carrying value in the accounts, i.e. confirm that inventory balance is not overstated.

QUESTION 13.3

(a)
To: All members of audit engagement team
From: Audit Senior
Re: Audit approach to testing of receivables balances aged greater than 90 days
Date: June 2013

On review of the aged receivables listing for Ballycane Metals Ltd it is clear that half of the year-end balance is aged 90 days plus. The total balance is material to the financial statements; therefore, it is important that we perform suitable audit procedures around the aged balances in order to gain sufficient comfort over the valuation of the receivables balance and the recoverability of the aged debts. In order to obtain sufficient appropriate audit evidence I suggest the following approach:

- Obtain an analysis of all debts aged 90 days plus by customer name which provides a breakdown of all invoices making up the aged balance.
- Obtain an analysis of the bad debt provision (if a provision has been made) and consider how much has been provided for in relation to debts aged 90 days plus.
- Confirm ageing of invoices on the receivables ledger is accurate by re-performing the aging of a sample of customer invoices.
- Discuss with the credit controller/financial controller/directors the circumstances surrounding each aged debt as each balance will likely have unique circumstances. The following should be given consideration:
  - Has the customer been declared bankrupt suggesting that the balance is not recoverable?
  - Is the customer experiencing cash flow problems? This could be noted on review of the customer's payment pattern, e.g. if the customer is making round sum payments on a timely basis such as €1,000 each month, this could suggest that the customer is experiencing difficulties and may cast doubt over the recoverability of the balance.
  - How recently was the last payment received from the customer? The greater the length of time the greater the risk that future payments will not be received.
  - Confirm if the customer's account remains active. Has the account been put on stop or is the client still supplying the customer? Where the account has been put on stop this suggests that a dispute is ongoing between the customer and the client.
  - Is there an ongoing dispute between the customer and the client over particular invoices, for example, due to faulty inventory being supplied or the customer being invoiced for goods which it did not receive? Have credit notes been issued post period-end to correct the account balance? Are adjustments still necessary to the year-end accounts?

- Has a payment been received from the customer post period end? If so, the payment should be vouched to the cash receipts book.
- Is the client actively chasing the aged debt? Confirm via inspection of letters which the client has sent to the customer seeking payment or memos detailing phone calls which the client has made for the same reason.
- Based on experience with the client, are any of the customers historically slow payers?
- Are all customer balances legitimate? Is there any issue of existence? If you have concerns include such customer balances within the receivables to be circularised.
- Include customers with overdue balances within the receivables to be circularised.

It is essential that at all times you keep in mind the valuation of the receivables balance included in the period-end accounts and the recoverability of the balances, asking the questions:
- Have all balances which are unlikely to be recovered in view of investigations performed by the audit team been adequately provided for? Should the provision be increased? Are adjustments needed?
- Has the receivables balance been overstated?
- If significant debts are written off what are the implications for the results of the client?

(b) **Prompt payment discount**

In determining an expectation for prompt payment discount the auditor should consider the following:
- Is the discount available to all customers or only to key customers?
- If only available to key customers, details of activity on the customers' accounts during the period under review should be obtained, i.e. total value of goods invoiced to the customer, determine expectation by calculating 3% of total sales value (assuming that all key customers always took advantage of prompt payment discount – this can be confirmed by reviewing a sample of invoice dates and when they were paid by the customer throughout the period under review to determine whether, generally, payment was made promptly).
- Where discount is available to all customers, it should be ascertained from the sales manager which customers generally, during the period under review, have taken advantage of the discount available. It is unlikely that all customers will have availed of the facility, but for those who have it should be validated that they have paid promptly during the period by performing the same review of invoices and payments as noted above. Customer activity should be reviewed to ascertain the total sales value to those customers using the prompt payment facility, calculating the expected discount in the same way as above.

QUESTION 13.4

The auditor should scan the period-end receivables listing and review it for any credit balances. Where credit balances are noted the auditor should:
- Determine why the balances have arisen, i.e. are they deposits received from customers, payments on account, overpayments or amounts posted in error to the receivables ledger?

- When the reason for the credit balances appearing on the ledger are ascertained, the auditor should consider if any correcting adjustments are necessary.
- Where credit balances are deposits received from the customer, the auditor should vouch the receipt of the deposits to the cash receipts book/bank statement and inspect any supporting documentation such as a signed agreement with the customer for the deposit. Where deposits are refundable, the balances should be disclosed within other creditors and not netted off against the total receivables balance.
- Where credit balances are payments on account the auditor should vouch the receipt of the deposits to the cash receipts book/bank statement. Where payments on account are refundable the balances should be disclosed within other creditors and not netted off against the total debtors balance.
- Where credit balances are overpayments by the customer, the auditor must determine whether the client has informed the customer of the overpayment. Where the customer has not been informed, the possibility of money laundering should be considered. Where the customer has been informed, the auditor must verify this by inspection of any correspondence with the customer notifying them of the overpayment. Overpayments should be disclosed within other creditors and not netted off against the total debtors balance.
- Where credit balances have arisen due to amounts being posted in error to the receivables ledger the auditor must obtain details of how the error arose and understand the impact of the error on the financial statements, i.e. should a correcting adjustment be made to correct the accounts?

QUESTION 13.5

(a) **Debtors circularisation on trade receivables balance**
  1. Obtain an aged list of trade receivables balances.
  2. Stratify the list into value ranges.
  3. Analyse the list to identify credit balances.
  4. Select balances for circularisation.
  5. Prepare a control schedule of balances selected.
  6. Send circularisation letters.
  7. Follow up on replies and, where necessary, carry out alternative procedures.
(b) A receiavables circularisation may not need to be performed where any of the following are identified:
  - debtors balance is immaterial to the financial statements;
  - the use of confirmations is deemed to be ineffective, e.g. based on past audit experience the auditor is unlikely to get an adequate response rate to the confirmations or that responses are known or expected to be unreliable and, in such cases, the auditor may conclude that the use of confirmations would be ineffective; or
  - based on the auditor's assessment of risk and assurance from controls testing, the risk in relation to the receivables balance has been reduced to an acceptably low level to allow alternative forms of substantive testing.
(c) Where a debtor does not respond to the debtors circularisation the auditor should perform alternative procedures which include the following:

- agree period-end receivable balance to sales invoice/goods delivered note;
- vouch post-period end payment of the receivable balance by agreeing payment to the client cash receipts book and bank statement and verify that post-period-end payment is in respect of invoices included on the receivables ledger at the period end; and
- consider whether it is necessary to confirm the existence of the customer, for example, by a telephone call or visiting the customer's business premises.

SOLUTION 13.6

Risk	Financial Statement Assertion	Testing Performed to Mitigate Risks
1. Recoverability of the trade receivables balance, i.e. will the client recover the trade debtors balance in full?	Valuation	(a) Testing of post-period-end receipts from customers in respect of period-end balances. (b) Review of aged receivables balances, e.g. all balances aged greater than 90 days and discussion with relevant personnel of the reasons why the balances have not been settled at the period end. (c) Consideration of the bad debt provision and its adequacy in view of findings from (b) above.
2. Are all customer balances legitimate, i.e. do the balances represent real sales made to real customers?	Existence/ Occurrence	(a) Performance of a debtors' circularisation to confirm the existence of the customers and to verify the period-end balance per the client records.
3. Have all sales invoices raised during the period under review been posted to the receivables ledger?	Completeness	(a) Select a sample of invoices raised during the period and confirm that they have been posted to the receivables ledger. (b) Perform period-end cut-off procedures and confirm that invoices raised around the period end – where the greatest risk exists – have been posted to the ledger in the correct period, i.e. vouch that only pre-period-end invoices have been posted to the ledger and that post-period-end invoices have only been posted to the ledger post-period-end.

(c) Review credit notes issued to customers post-period-end by the client in respect of pre-period-end invoices and consider if adjusting journal entries are necessary to correct the sales figure and receivables balance included in the financial statements.

QUESTION 13.7

(a) **Advertising revenue – substantive analytical procedure**

Type of Advert	% Use by advert type	No of Pages	No of Ads	Price Per ad €	Revenue €
2 Page	30%	225	113	4,500	506,250
1 Page	30%	225	225	2,500	562,500
1/2 Page	25%	188	375	1,500	562,500
1/4 Page	15%	113	450	1,000	450,000
	100%	750	1,163		2,081,250

Less 2 Pages Spread discount	16%		–
			81,000
Net Monthly Revenue			2,000,250
Annualised (net monthly revenue x 12)			24,003,000

Subscriptions Revenue Analytical Procedure

Listing Fees	€200
No. of Subscribers	1,800
Total Subscriptions	**€360,000**
	€
Annual Subscription Revenue	4,320,000
Advertising Revenue	24,003,000
Subs revenue	4,320,000
Expected Revenue	**28,323,000**

Actual Revenue   28,525,000
Difference   202,000
Threshold   300,000

Within Threshold no further investigation

(b) **Valuation of receivables test**
   1. First approach, adopted for verifying the general provision, is to obtain management's procedures for determining the estimate and considering the adequacy of the provision; checking that the procedures have been followed and have been appropriately approved; considering the reasonableness of assumptions used in the calculation; checking calculations and considering reliability of prior year provisions.
   2. Review the aged debtor listing for debts aged 60–90 days and older. The auditor should also, at this point, review a sample of sales invoices included on the period-end ledger to assess the reasonableness of the aging of the invoices by the system on the period-end ledger.
   3. Confirm and verify if such balances have been received post year end.
   4. Where balances have not been settled post year end, the auditor should enquire from management if there are any circumstances surrounding the non-payment of the balance; such as a dispute between the customer and the client, the customer being declared bankrupt or the customer experiencing cash flow difficulties.
   5. Where, after the above testing is performed, receipt of the balance outstanding on the aged listing at the year end is deemed unlikely, the auditor should consider if the client has provided for the relevant balances.
   6. Where the client has not provided for the relevant balances and the auditor deems that a provision is necessary then an adjusting journal entry should be proposed.
   7. The bad debt provision created by the client is known as an accounting estimate, as the final payment amount which will be received from the customer for the provision is made is not known with any certainty. It is the role of the auditor to assess the facts surrounding the aged balances and to determine if the provision appears reasonable based on what is known.

(c) **Audit tests for occurrence**
   1. for a sample of sales transactions that appears on the sales listing agree that the related customer is included in the company's list of subscriber businesses.
   2. count the number of advertisements in each monthly directory and ensure the count matches the number of invoices on the subscription sales listings.
   3. confirm debtor balances/sales transactions with customer by sending out debtors circularisation letters.

QUESTION 14.1

The auditor should first obtain the year-end bank statement for the loan account. If there is a difference between the figure in the accounts and the figure on the bank statements (e.g. due to a repayment in transit etc.), he should then review the year-end bank reconciliation performed by the client to verify the figure disclosed in the financial statements. Additionally, a bank confirmation letter should be obtained directly from the bank, and the auditor should check that interest accrued on the loan has been properly accounted for.

QUESTION 14.2

To determine whether the amount of detailed testing carried out by the external auditor on bank and cash could be reduced, the internal auditors would be expected to conduct the following:
1. branch visits, involving:
   - checking compliance with standard procedures;
   - cash counts to confirm amounts agree with point of sale record; and
   - all branches being covered on a rotational basis;
2. a review of bank reconciliations to check that:
   - reconciliations have been performed;
   - amounts banked agree with point of sale records; and
   - any delays in banking are investigated.

The internal auditors should also investigate the use and review of exception reports for identifying and investigating the differences between the recorded cash amount and the actual amount of cash on hand.

Ideally, the retail outlet should undertake weekly inventory counts and reconcile inventory movements to sales. The internal auditors should attend these counts and review the reconciliations.

QUESTION 14.3

The audit confirmation of all bank accounts is a very important part of the audit of bank and cash as it provides the auditor with reliable, independent, third-party audit evidence. The confirmation request should be sent on the auditor's letterhead and clearly identify all information required. The auditor must maintain complete control over the process.

The bank confirmation request letter will disclose bank balances, loans and details of all accounts in the name of the audit client as at the balance sheet date.

QUESTION 14.4

In order to ensure that all bank accounts are confirmed at the year end the auditor should obtain details of accounts held by and on behalf of the entity by:
- inquiring of management details of bank accounts held by the entity;
- reviewing details of any new accounts opened; and
- seeking details from the banks where accounts are kept of any changes to banking arrangements.

QUESTION 14.5

A full audit provides management with assurance that it is complying with statutory duties and that information filed with the registrar of companies meets legal requirements. It also provides other stakeholders, such as the tax authorities, with assurance on the credibility of the figures.

Audited financial statements are more reliable and will result in better informed decisions by management. The company will also benefit from the by-products of an audit such as the identification of weaknesses and recommendations for reducing risk and improving performance.

An audit imposes discipline which is useful for control purposes in a growing company.

Audited financial statements will assist a future sale of an entity by providing a basis for the determination of the purchase consideration.

QUESTION 15.1

(a) **Investment audit work**
  - Vouch each of the investments to its supporting documentation.
  - Verify that each of the investments is in the name of Meridian.
  - Obtain copies of the investments' reports to confirm the net market values of each of the investments.
  - Investigate where cost of investment is greater than market value, i.e. Golden and Yellow.
  - Where the cost of the investment is greater than its market value, inquire from management if the investment has been impaired and assess the need for an impairment review.
  - For any new investments, agree the purchase to its supporting documentation in the year of purchase; consideration paid should be agreed to bank statements.
  - The Yellow investment should not have been included in the client schedule, as it had been sold before year end – the schedule should only include investments still held.
  - The sale of the Yellow investment should be vouched and the loss reviewed to ensure that it is appropriately calculated and correctly accounted for and disclosed.

(b) **Potential audit issues**
- The market value of the investment in Golden equals €1,320,000 which is €334,000 lower than the cost of the investment, therefore an impairment of €334,000 exists.
- The impairment on investments may need to be adjusted for as the investment in Yellow is still appearing on the client's year-end schedule despite the fact that it was sold before the year end.
- The circumstances surrounding why Yellow is still appearing on the year-end schedule needs to investigated and understood.

(c) **Proposed adjustments**
Please find outlined below the adjustments to the investment balance that I would recommend:

	€000	€000
DR Statement of comprehensive income – loss on sale	811	
CR Investment Yellow – Balance Sheet		811
(Being the sale of the investment not recorded)		
DR Statement of Comprehensive Income – impairment provision	334	
CR Investment Golden – Balance Sheet		334
(Being the recording of the investment at the lower of cost or market value)		

QUESTION 15.2

The procedures that should be adopted in order to obtain the required assurance concerning the standard audit objectives for the current asset balances detailed are as follows:

Trade Investments (Listed and Unlisted)

Completeness

The auditor will normally obtain sufficient assurance on the completeness objective for investments from work in conjunction with other objectives, particularly that relating to existence and to rights and obligations.

Re-computation in total is an efficient method of auditing income from fixed interest investments such as loans, debentures, fixed rate preference shares, and government securities. The auditor should re-compute the total income by using the principal amount and a known interest rate.

A substantive analytical review may, for example, be based on a comparison of the average recorded yield and the investment portfolio (or outstanding loans) with prior years and with budget. Alternatively, the audit may develop an estimate by applying an average yield to the average market value of investments.

Accuracy

The auditor will obtain part of the required assurance concerning the accuracy objective from work on the other objectives. For example, the work carried out to verify the existence and ownership of investments should provide secondary assurance that those investments have been accurately recorded. However, it is still necessary to check the following:

- the control account reconciliation;
- the carrying values of investments;
- the classification of investments in subsidiaries and associates; and
- that the amounts in the financial statements agree with the accounting records.

Where there is an investment control account in the general ledger, the auditor should check the reconciliation of the control account with the total of the individual investment balances by:

- tracing the totals to the general ledger;
- testing individual balances with the investment ledger (or equivalent records); and
- checking the additions of the reconciliation.

As part of the business review, the auditor should review the client's accounting policies for determining the carrying value of investments. This should include checking that such policies conform with relevant legislation and accounting standards, that they are appropriate to the circumstances, and have been consistently applied.

The auditor should examine supporting documents for additions (e. g. broker's contract notes), ascertain that the transaction was properly authorised and approved and trace the acquisition to the investment ledger or equivalent detailed record.

The auditor should examine supporting documents such as broker's contract notes ensuring that disposals have been authorised and approved. The disposals should be checked to the investment ledger or equivalent detailed records. The correct calculation and recording of any gain or loss on disposals should also be checked. If only part of the investment has been sold, the auditor should check that the unsold balance is recorded correctly.

It is not normally necessary to investigate the selling price if it is possible to rely on the independence of the broker who has originated the contract note. However, if there is any doubt about the independence of the broker, or if the investment is not listed, it is important to consider whether the sale price appears reasonable. If necessary, the auditor should make reference to a stock exchange official list (if the investment is listed), or to audited financial statements or PE ratios of similar companies (if the investment is not listed).

If there are any investments carried at a valuation the auditor should check the market value to the stock exchange daily list or the *Financial Times* (for listed investments). For unlisted investments, the valuation by the directors is often based on the underlying net assets or a PE ratio of similar companies using reports or valuations made by experts. The auditor should discuss the basis of the valuation with the client, review the available financial statements, and inspect any reports of the experts on whom the directors have relied.

Existence: Rights and Obligations

The principal substantive test for the existence and ownership of investments is the inspection of documents of title, or confirmation from third parties (normally independent, reliable authorised custodians) that they are holding such documents on behalf of the client. The auditor should also obtain direct confirmation of loans.

To ascertain whether investments have been pledged as collateral or as security for liabilities (of either the client or a third party), the auditor should make enquires of the client's management, and review board minutes, loan agreements and other appropriate documentation.

Cut-off

The auditor will normally obtain sufficient assurance relating to the cut-off objective from work carried out on the completeness, accuracy, existence and rights and obligations objectives. For example, work on additions and disposals will also provide evidence that purchases and sales of investments and income from investments have been recorded in the appropriate period.

Valuation

Clients may classify investments as either fixed or current assets and the treatment of any diminution in value will vary accordingly. In the case of fixed asset investments, provision is required for any permanent diminution in value whereas, for current asset investments carried at cost, provision is also required for any temporary diminution in value (i.e. so that the current asset is carried at the lower of cost and net realisable value).

There are two complementary procedures that the auditor may use with regard to assessing any diminutions in value. These are:
• checking individual investments and making specific enquiries into their current status and prospects; and
• reviewing the investment portfolio in the light of background knowledge of the client acquired during the business review, and discussing the portfolio with members of management who possess an adequate level of knowledge and seniority.

For listed investments carried at cost, a significant decrease in the market value may suggest a permanent diminution in value. However, market value might not be an appropriate indicator if the market in the shares is small or infrequent, or if the dealings have been suspended. In these cases the auditor may need to follow the procedures relating to unlisted investments.

Unlisted investments should be examined by reference to all the available information, such as recent audited financial statements, reports by independent accountants or investment advisers, and operating forecasts and budgets produced by the investee. The auditor should consider the marketability of the investment and, in the case of overseas investments, any restriction on the remittances of funds.

Management is frequently reluctant to recognise that an apparent reduction in the value of an investment is permanent, particularly if the client is committed to some form of continued support to the investee. Whilst it is important to recognise that decisions concerning the permanent impairment of value involve judgement, the auditor should not accept unrealistic optimism on the part of management.

Presentation and Disclosure

To help achieve the objective the auditor should, at the end of the audit, review the financial statements and consider whether full and proper disclosure has been achieved.

Prepayments

The auditor should be aware that the prepayments balance in total only equals the audit materiality balance and, as such, only limited work should be carried out.

The auditor should carry out a substantive analytical review of prepayments based on prior period amounts adjusted for any relevant changes in the business. The auditor should be aware of the client's major items of income and expenditure from which prepayments, accrued income and other debtors might arise.

Examination and checking of supporting documents should only be carried out where prepayments appear to be out of line with the expected amount and where the difference is material (say one-third of the audit materiality level).

Bank and Cash Balances

Completeness

The auditor should derive the required assurance that all bank balances have been identified and accounted for principally from the understanding of the business which has been acquired through the business analytical review.

In particular, the auditor should consider whether the number of bank accounts appears adequate for the level of business.

Additionally, the following procedures may be appropriate:
- reviewing the list of balances at the previous balance sheet date and enquiring into any changes; and
- scrutinising bank confirmations, cash books, bank statements and board minutes for evidence of accounts opened during the period.

Accuracy

Detailed checking of the bank reconciliations should normally provide sufficient assurance that bank and cash transactions have been accurately processed. The auditor should normally check the bank reconciliation at the same date that confirmation of balances are obtained from the bank.

The auditor should carry out the following work:
- checking the balances on the reconciliations to the general ledger, the bank confirmations and the bank statements.
- testing the additions of the reconciliations, and of the lists of unpresented cheques and outstanding lodgements.
- tracing entries in the cash records before the substantive testing date to the bank statements or reconciliations.
- checking unpresented cheques and outstanding lodgements recorded in the bank reconciliation to the cash records and the bank statement; and
- investigating and verifying any other reconciled items.

The auditor should select from the receipts and payments recorded in the cash records for the period before the substantive testing date, and should ensure that the items selected are either:
- recorded on bank statements prior to the substantive testing date; or
- included in the bank reconciliation as unpresented cheques or outstanding lodgements.

The auditor should check that any material payments to creditors, identified in work on creditors' reconciliations and not recorded on the creditors' statement at the reconciliation date, are traced to the unpresented cheque listing.

The auditor should review the detailed list of represented cheques for all large amounts (especially any large round sum amounts) that have not been cleared by the bank since the substantive testing date, and should trace these cheques to original documentation and discuss with the client why they have not been cleared.

With regard to unpresented cheques not cleared by the time the work is carried out, the auditor should:
- obtain explanations for any large or unusual items; and
- investigate any cheques which have been outstanding for more than six months and consider whether they should be added back to the bank balance.

Existence

The auditor would normally acquire sufficient evidence that recorded bank and cash balances exist by obtaining direct confirmation from the client's bankers. Confirmation should cover all banks with which the client held an account during any part of the period under audit, including payroll and dividend accounts, even though the account might have been closed before the balance sheet date. This should be done to identify possible unrecorded bank borrowings and contingent liabilities.

Many clients' cash balances are immaterial and, depending on the assessment of the risk of misstatement, the auditor may decide not to carry out any substantive testing on them.

In the current circumstances, however, the cash balances are very material and the auditor will need to specifically address them.

The auditor should attend the year-end cash count – unannounced. To avoid any possibility that a shortfall could be blamed on the audit staff, it is essential to count cash in the custodian's presence, insist that he or she stays until the count is completed, and ask the custodian to sign the record of the amount counted to confirm acceptance of the findings. The auditor should check the amount counted to the general ledger and to the petty cash records.

Cash funds often include cheques that have been cashed for directors or employees. However, shortages of cash are often concealed by the inclusion of fictitious, forged, or worthless cheques and IOUs in the funds. The auditor should therefore:
- examine cheques carefully and ensure that they bear a recent date and are not post-dated;
- check that they are subsequently banked and cleared; and
- check that there is authority for the issue of IOUs and test that they are subsequently repaid.

Cut-off

The auditor should normally obtain much of the required assurance concerning the cut-off of bank and cash balances from the work on bank reconciliations.

The auditor should identify any significant transfers of funds between two or more of the company's bank accounts in the period prior to the balance sheet date. In respect of such transfers, the auditor should check that receipts and payments are recorded in the accounting records in the same accounting period and that any such items not reflected by the bank in the same accounting period appear in the appropriate bank reconciliation.

The auditor should review the accounting records for evidence of the inclusion of lodgements which were physically received after the balance sheet date.

The auditor should review the lapse of time between the date of issue of unrepresented cheques as recorded in the accounting records and the date of their subsequent presentation at the bank and consider whether any of these cheques might not have been released by the client until after the balance sheet date.

Valuation

If balances are held with reputable banks the auditor should not need to question recoverability.

If there are substantial balances in other countries or currencies, the auditor should determine whether there are any restrictions on the transferability of funds which could affect the value of the asset or which, for any other reason, should be disclosed in the financial statements.

Rights and Obligations

As a rule this objective should be accomplished through the normal bank confirmation procedures.

Presentation and Disclosure

The auditor will normally achieve this objective at the end of the audit by reviewing the financial statements and considering whether full and proper disclosure has been achieved.

QUESTION 16.1

The audit test being performed by the audit junior is a typical audit procedure used to search for unrecorded liabilities to gain assurance over the completeness of creditors/payables within the financial statements.

Issue 1. This relates to goods delivered post year end. There is, therefore, no liability in existence at the year end. The current treatment of this transaction by the company is therefore appropriate, and no audit adjustment.

Issue 2. Although the invoice for these goods has not been received until post year end, the goods themselves have been delivered pre year end, and should therefore be accounted for within the December 2012 financial statements. As the value of the goods involved (€9,000) is greater than materiality (€5,000), an audit adjustment is required to account for this transaction:

DR	Purchases	€9,000	
CR	Accruals		€9,000
DR	Inventory (Balance Sheet)	€9,000	
CR	Inventory (Statement of Comprehensive Income)		€9,000

Issue 3. This invoice relates to goods received post year end and therefore should not be accounted for in the December 2012 accounts. However, the goods are currently included within year-end accruals. This is incorrect, and assuming the goods have also been included within year-end inventory, represents an overstatement of accruals and inventory in the balance sheet. As the amount involved is material, an adjustment is required:

DR	Accruals	€5,000	
CR	Purchases		€5,000
DR	Inventory (statement of comprehensive income)	€5,000	
CR	Inventory (Balance Sheet)		€5,000

Issue 4. Although this invoice relates to goods received pre year end which have not been accounted for in the correct period, the amount involved is immaterial and, indeed, is clearly trifling. As a result no audit adjustment is required.

QUESTION 16.2

- In the accounts payable reconciliation agree the balance per the accounts payable ledger to the actual creditors listing as at 31 May 2013.
- In the accounts payable reconciliation agree the balance per supplier's statement to actual statement received from supplier.
- Check arithmetical accuracy of the accounts payable reconciliation.
- The payment made of €720,000 should be agreed to supporting documentation.
- Invoices on statements but not on ledger accounts: need to verify that the goods were not received by Lactic before the year end or, if received, have been appropriately accrued.

- The auditor should inquire about the statement dated 28 May, as it does not coincide with the year end.
- Inquire as to why invoice No. 14255 has not been posted to the ledger.
- Investigate the reasons for the remaining unreconciled difference of €100,000.

QUESTION 16.3

(a) **Substantive analytical procedures**

Substantive analytical procedures means the analysis of relationships between items of data (financial or non-financial) deriving from the same period, or comparable information from different periods or entities, in order to identify consistencies, predicted patterns, significant fluctuations or unexpected relationships, and to investigate the results thereof.

Analytical procedures can be used to obtain audit evidence, at the substantive testing stage, in order to detect material misstatements in the financial statements.

(b)

Memorandum

To: Audit Partner
From: Audit Senior
Re: Bistro Ltd
       Analytical review of operating expenses year ended 31 March 13
Date: 08/06/2013

Expense	Work Required
Insurance	Vouch the balance to insurance invoices to corroborate the explanation given for the increase in insurance costs.
Administration Salaries	Vouch temp's salary and payments made for correct period of maternity leave to payroll records.
Depreciation	Cross-reference and agree to work on fixed assets.
Distribution Costs	Policy adopted in current year is not consistent with that of prior year. This seems to be a change in accounting policy and if material would require a prior-year adjustment. This requires further investigation.
	Sales have increased by 10%. I would expect a direct correlation with distribution costs, but overall distribution costs have decreased. This requires further investigation.
Repairs and Maintenance	Vouch to supporting invoices.
	Investigate whether any amounts expensed should have been capitalised and cross-reference to the tangible fixed-asset section of file.
Rent and Rates	Vouch to supporting documentation from local authority and to cheque payments.

(c) Computer-assisted Audit Techniques could be used in the audit of each significant account balance. Generally they could be used to:
- perform additions and calculations;
- select a sample of items for testing, e.g. select a sample of trade receivables for confirmation or inventory items to test the accuracy of the pricing of items;
- re-perform calculation of extraction of items, e.g. aged listings, from inventory, receivables and payables lists;
- perform analytical procedures and comparisons; and
- compare data elements, e.g. names of suppliers, in different files for agreement.

QUESTION 17.1

The following are the audit procedures which would be undertaken in the audit of the increase in share capital.
1. Obtain a copy of a company search report from the CRO for XYZ Limited.
2. Review the documents filed during the period under review.
3. Request/obtain a copy of the share issue certificates.
4. Agree the increase in share capital to the share issue certificates.
5. If shares issued were to a director or secretary ensure this is appropriately disclosed in the financial statements.
6. Ensure the share issue was within the authorised limits set out in the Memorandum and Articles of Association of ZYZ Ltd.
7. Vouch the transaction and trace the cash receipt to the bank statement.

QUESTION 17.2

As the new shares have been issued at a premium, the following should be completed.
1. Ensure the issue of share capital at a premium is in line with the provisions of Printer Limited's Memorandum and Articles of Association.
2. Determine the correct disclosure for the financial statements.
3. An audit adjustment is necessary to reflect the issue of the new shares.
4. Ensure the issue of shares at a premium is correctly disclosed in the financial statements.
5. Vouch the transaction and trace the cash receipt to the bank statement.
6. Inquire as to why the transaction was not included in the draft accounts.

QUESTION 18.1

The auditor should conduct the following in order to ensure that they have obtained sufficient evidence about the entity's subsequent events.
1. Review management procedures to ensure that subsequent events are identified.
2. Read minutes of meetings held by management, shareholders and those charged with governance.

3. Inquire of the client's legal counsel.
4. Inquire of management.
5. Review latest management accounts for unusual trends.

QUESTION 18.2

The most important period for the auditor after the balance sheet date is the time between the year end and up to and including the date of signing of the audit report.

QUESTION 18.3

An important consideration is the true and fair view given by financial statements taken as a whole. Individual figures may be accurate, but they may be presented in a biased manner or important notes that help clarify the figures may be missing.

Also the concept of 'substance over form' is a very important concept as it requires transactions to be recorded based on their substance and not just their legal form.

QUESTION 18.4

The review of audit papers ensures the following:
- The work completed by the audit staff was accurate, thorough and in accordance with the audit programme.
- Judgements exercised by the audit staff during the course of the audit were reasonable and appropriate and have been properly documented to support the audit opinion.
- All audit work was completed in accordance with the conditions and terms specified in the engagement letter.
- The audit staff resolved any significant accounting, auditing and reporting questions raised during the audit.
- The review will ensure that the audit working papers reflect the requirements of the International Standards on Auditing (UK and Ireland) and that the audit firm's quality control policies and procedures have been met.

QUESTION 18.5

The following are the benefits that arise from performing final analytical procedures:
- Final analytical procedures help reduce the detection risk of failing to discover material misstatements in the financial statements.
- Final analytical procedures provide support for the audit conclusions.
- The auditor can conclude on the reasonableness of the financial statements with added assurance.

QUESTION 18.6

Memo to Monitor Limited File
From: A. Senior
Re: Subsequent events procedures
Date: 01/07/2013

Following my meeting with the financial controller on 11 June 2013 the following post-balance sheet events require attention:

Customer gone into liquidation

Further verification work required:
1. Confirm that the debt was fully provided for and no further provision is required.
2. Inspect any liquidator's report to determine if the company will recover any of its debt.
3. Consider if any further doubtful debt provisions are necessary in light of this customer going into liquidation.

Another procedure that may need to be carried out would be to evaluate the effect the loss of this customer will have on future trading and on the going concern assumption.

Change of banking arrangements, review of contracts and proposed sale and leaseback

Further verification work required:
1. Inspect latest post year-end management accounts.
2. In light of this new information, extend going concern audit procedures.
3. Inquire of management what is their exact intention regarding contracts and what stage they are at regarding the proposed sale and leaseback of premises.

Other procedures that may need to be carried out:
- Consider if there are any further going concern disclosures required in the accounts.
- Consider if there is any impact on the audit opinion based on the revised going concern review.
- Consider if there are any post-balance sheet disclosures required in the financial statements in accordance with IAS 10 *Events after the Reporting Period* (IAS 10).
- Consider the accounting impact the proposed sale and leaseback will have on next year's financial statements.

QUESTION 18.7

(a) **Further audit work required**
  1. No further audit work is required – bring the error straight to the schedule of 'unadjusted differences'.

2. Verify that the bonus payments should have been accrued in full at the year end and if this is the case inquire as to why it was not.
3. Confirm that your calculation is correct, e.g. you may have included fully written down assets in your calculation in error. If there is an error bring it to the schedule of 'unadjusted differences'.
4. Verify adjustments to prior-year working papers, ensuring that closing reserves are correct and can be agreed to the closing trial balance.

(b)
Client: Santa Limited
Period End:

Schedule of Unadjusted Differences

		Statement of Financial Position		Statement of Comprehensive Income	
		DR	**CR**	**DR**	**CR**
		€	€	€	€
DR	Prepayments	50,000			
CR	Trade payables		50,000		
	Being correction of mis-posting				
DR	Staff bonus costs			150,000	
CR	Accruals		150,000		
	Being correction of understatement of Bonus Costs				
DR	Depreciation			44,000	
CR	Fixed Assets		44,000		
	Being correction of depreciation charge				

(c) **Review of schedule of unadjusted differences**
  The audit partner will need to take the following into account when reviewing the schedule of unadjusted differences:
  • Materiality of each error – if an individual item on its own is material the financial statements should be adjusted. Where a number of errors add up to a material amount then consideration will be required as to which item(s) to adjust for.
  • The reason for the error in payroll – if there is evidence of fraud then this should be reported to the directors and the auditor may have an obligation to report to a third-party regulator.
  • The need for further investigation of any of the matters.

- Whether any of the errors found impact on other aspects of the audit, e.g. the reliance the auditor places on internal controls, the auditor's assessment of the integrity of management etc.
- The year-on-year impact, i.e. the auditor may have to review the prior-year schedule of differences.
- The result of any discussion with the client and explanations received.

QUESTION 18.8

(a) Schedule of unadjusted errors

	Statement of Financial Position		Statement of Comprehensive Income	
	DR	**CR**	**DR**	**CR**
	€	**€**	**€**	**€**
DR Bad Debt provision			30,000	
CR Bad Debt provision		30,000		
Being Correction of Bad Debt provision understatement				
DR Depreciation charge			100,000	
CR Depreciation		100,000		
Being Correction of Depreciation understatement				
DR Claims Provision			75,000	
CR Provision for Legal Claims		75,000		
Being Correction of Legal Claim understatement				
DR Bank	150,000			
CR Payables		150,000		
Being Correction Classification error on Bank and Payables				

Summary	150,000	355,000	205,000	–
Net Impact on the SOCI		205,000	205,000	

Note: the cut-off error was adjusted by the client and is not brought to the error schedule.

			€
Workings			
1	Beds Express		
	Owed at year end		75,000
	Paid		15,000
	Still outstanding at time of liquidation		60,000

Required bad debt provision	60,000
Actual bad debt provision	30,000
Understatement of bad debt provision	30,000

(b)

(i) Yes, these accounts are materially misstated. While the statement of comprehensive income remains under the €270,000 materiality threshold, the liabilities on the balance sheet in aggregate are €355,000 understated. Errors must be considered both individually and in aggregate. While no one error is material when all are considered together a material error exists.

(ii) The classification error of €150,000 is the most significant and if it were adjusted the liabilities would no longer be an aggregated material error. In addition, this adjustment would not change the statement of comprehensive income of the client.

(c) **Adjusting post balance sheet events**
   • The settlement of a court case that confirms the entity has a present obligation at the balance sheet date.
   • The receipt of information after the balance sheet date which indicates an asset was impaired at the balance sheet date.
   • The determination after the balance sheet date of the cost of assets purchased or proceeds of assets sold before the balance sheet date.
   • Details of fraud or errors which show the financial statements are incorrect.

(d) **Property valuer**
   1. Check he is professionally qualified to undertake the valuation.
   2. Check he has the expertise and experience to undertake the valuation.

QUESTION 18.9

(a) (i) Directors'/auditors' responsibilities for the management assertion of going concern
   • The primary responsibility for assessing the appropriateness of the going concern assumption rests with directors and management.
   • If financial statements are prepared on a going concern basis, the auditors must consider and assess whether applying this basis is appropriate in the valuation and measurement of items appearing in the financial statements.
   • ISA 570 (UK and Ireland) *Going Concern* (ISA 570) requires the auditor, when planning an audit, to identify risks whereby the entity's ability to continue trading as a going concern may be uncertain and, as such, to include appropriate audit procedures in the audit programme.
   • The auditor will evaluate the management's assessment of the entity's ability to continue as a going concern and be alert for evidence of events or conditions that may cast doubt on that assumption.

(a) (ii) Financial and operational events affecting going concern

Financial

- The entity has not met the necessary borrowing agreements.
- There is an indication of the withdrawal of financial support by debtors and other creditors of the entity.
- The entity has negative operating cash flows, indicated by historical or prospective financial statements.
- The entity is unable to pay creditors on the appropriate due dates.
- The entity sells substantial fixed assets when it has no intention of replacing the assets.
- The entity has not complied with capital or other statutory requirements e.g. banks.
- Legislative changes that may adversely impact the entity.
- An inability to finance new products and/or product development.

Operational

- Loss of key management or staff.
- Labour difficulties
- Shortage of key suppliers.
- Loss of a major market.
- Fundamental changes in the marketplace, e.g. new technology to which the company cannot respond.
- Excessive dependence on a few products where the market is depressed.

(a) (iii)

Where full disclosure is possible – an unqualified opinion to include an explanatory 'emphasis of matter' paragraph in the 'basis of opinion' section.

Where the client entity refuses to make the necessary disclosure – a qualified opinion of an 'except for' type, due to disagreement over adequacy of disclosures.

(b) **Unrecorded liabilities**

- Review subsequent and post balance sheet events up to date of approval of the financial statements.
- Inquire of management.
- Inquire of legal counsel and banks (by confirmations) of possible unrecorded liabilities.
- Review original signed minutes of board and management meetings.
- Review contracts and loan agreements.
- Review current and prior year tax returns.
- Request written confirmation from the entity's lawyers, solicitors etc. of any existing, pending or expected contingent liabilities.
- Review open purchase orders (POs).
- Inspect books of prime entry such as Cheque Payments Book and Purchases Book for the period subsequent to the balance sheet date for evidence of transactions that perhaps should be dealt with in the period under audit.

QUESTION 19.1

(a) **Implications for audit report**

(i)

1. Repairs Provision
   - *Individual impact* At the year end, Merlin Ltd is not committed to the repairs, there is no contract and no work has yet been carried out, accordingly the provision is not justified in accordance with IAS 37 *Provisions, Contingent Liabilities and Contingent Assets* (IAS 37).
   - *Overall impact* This will result in a qualified opinion (Except For or Adverse) due to disagreement in accounting treatment if the provision is not reversed prior to the approval of the financial statements.

2. Information Technology General Controls Review
   - *Individual impact* No audit report implications arise as a result of the weaknesses identified with regard to infrastructure security. The auditor would have assessed the likely effect of such weaknesses on the financial statements during the planning and execution of the audit.
   - *Overall impact* Whilst an issue exists, this issue does not have any significant impact on the financial statements.

3. Consultancy Payment
   - *Individual impact* No impact on the audit report. Amount is immaterial and does not impair the true and fair view of the financial statements.
   - *Overall impact* Possible 'related party' transaction in accordance with IAS 24 *Related Party Disclosures* (IAS 24) as it may be material to the brother. Further audit investigation is required. It is possible that the audit report would need to be qualified (Except For) if the auditor considers that appropriate disclosure was not made.

4. Fixed Assets
   - *Individual impact* This item has not been correctly treated in accordance with IAS 16 *Property, Plant and Equipment* (IAS 16). However, the amount is immaterial and does not impair the true and fair view of the financial statements.
   - *Overall impact* As a result, there is no impact on the audit report.

5. Management Bonus
   - *Individual impact* There is no impact on the audit report. (Assuming no further information can be obtained to verify the increase on the prior-year's figure, the amount is immaterial and does not impair the true and fair view of the financial statements.)
   - *Overall impact* As a result, there is no impact on the audit report.

(ii)

   - *Overall audit opinion* Any decision regarding the overall opinion is a matter of professional judgement. The most likely outcome is a qualified opinion (Adverse) arising as a result of disagreement in accounting treatment regarding the repairs provision of €500,000, excess capitalisation of employee costs of €50,000 and possible overprovision of the management bonus.

(b) **Capitalised salary costs**

Salary costs included in fixed assets:
- Verify that the individuals are employees of the company.
- Agree the salary costs to supporting documentation.
- Verify that the estimate of percentage involvement of the employee in the capital project is reasonable by looking at supporting documentation evidencing involvement in the project, e.g. attendance at meetings, compilation of reports, timesheets etc.
- Obtain a copy of the calculation and check its arithmetical accuracy.

(c) **Accounting adjustments**

MERLIN LTD

UNCORRECTED MISSTATEMENTS – YEAR ENDED 30 MARCH 2013

Uncorrected Misstatement	Statement of Financial Position		Statement of Comprehensive Income	
	DR	**CR**	**DR**	**CR**
	€	€	€	€
1.				
Repairs Provision				
Provisions	500,000			
Operating expenses – Repairs and Maintenance				500,000
Being provisions not relating to financial year				
2.				
Capital Project				
Fixed assets		50,000		
Operating expenses – Wages and Salaries			50,000	
Being expense items incorrectly capitalised				
Total	**500,000**	**50,000**	**50,000**	**500,000**

QUESTION 19.2

(a) **Implications for audit report**
1. Audit Issue 1:
   - This could potentially result in a limitation of the scope of the auditor's work if the crash resulted in a loss of evidence that could not be corroborated by alternative audit means.

- However, the creditor information was only lost for one day and this information has been reposted.
- On the basis that there is no issue with the reposted information and it is supportable by source documentation, there is no limitation on scope.
- Therefore on this basis there is no impact on the audit report arising from the crash in the creditor system.

2. Audit Issue 2:
   - IAS 10 *Events After the reporting Period* (IAS 10) states that the bankruptcy of a customer that occurs after the balance sheet date usually confirms that a loss existed at the balance sheet date on a trade receivable, and that the entity needs to adjust the carrying amount of the trade receivable.
   - Consequently, the amount of €250,000 should be provided for at the year end.
   - In addition, the €100,000 of additional business would be disclosed as a non-adjusting post-balance sheet event (IAS 10), as the sale took place in the post-balance sheet period.
   - The effect of the incorrect treatment has resulted in profit before tax being overstated by €250,000 and net assets being overstated by the same amount. The level of misstatement is material from an audit reporting point of view as it represents 75% of profit before tax.
   - If unadjusted this would cause the financial statements to be misleading – therefore an adverse opinion will be issued on the basis of a disagreement with management.

3. Audit Issue 3:
   - The amounts are quantitatively immaterial.
   - However, bonuses are required to be disclosed as part of Directors' Emoluments by the Companies Act(s) and consequently will result in a disagreement with management over the adequacy of disclosure.
   - This will likely result in a qualified audit opinion ('Except for') and the information omitted from the financial statements will be disclosed in the audit report.

(b) **Adverse opinion**

Basis for Adverse Opinion

As more fully explained in Note X to the financial statements, no provision has been made in the financial statements for a significant receivable balance relating to a customer that went bankrupt in January 2013. This is not in accordance with International Accounting Standards IAS 10 *Events after the Reporting Period.* The bankruptcy of a debtor in the post-balance sheet period confirms that a loss existed at the balance sheet date and consequently a provision should have been made for the amount of the irrecoverable debt. Accordingly, the profit for the year should be reduced by €250,000 and trade receivables, current assets and net assets should each be reduced by that amount.

Qualified Opinion

In our opinion, because of the significance of the matter discussed in the Basis for Adverse Opinion paragraph, the financial statements do not give a true and fair view of the financial position of Denark Ltd as at 31 December 2012, and of its financial performance and cash flows for the year then ended in accordance with International Financial Reporting standards.

In all other respects, in our opinion, the financial statements have been properly prepared in accordance with the Companies Act(s) etc.

QUESTION 19.3

(a)

Memo to:	Audit partner
From:	A. Senior
Re:	Worldglobal Ltd
	Year ended 31/12/12
Date:	08/06/13

The following is the audit evidence I require and the implication that I see for the audit opinion in respect of the matters raised regarding the above company:

Breach of Covenants Management has indicated that they have received assurances from their bank that none of the financing facilities would be withdrawn. With the client's permission, I propose communicating with the bank directly and requesting them to confirm this to us in writing. Should we receive such confirmation, this would form part of the basis for our conclusion as to whether the entity is a going concern. The net assets of the company are €5.5 million. Whether the entity can continue as a going concern in the foreseeable future will depend on the working capital of the entity, which I will investigate further. Provided that this investigation proves positive, then the matter will have no implications for our audit report.

If no confirmation is received from the bank and they state that they have not given assurances that the financing facilities would not be withdrawn, then a going concern issue exists and requires further consideration.

If we conclude, post our analysis of all the pertinent facts, that it is appropriate to prepare the financial statements on a going concern basis and the relevant disclosures in the financial statements are adequate, then an explanatory paragraph should be given in the audit report referring to the relevant disclosures.

If we consider the disclosures to be inadequate but that the entity is a going concern, we should qualify the audit report on the basis of an 'Except for' disagreement type qualification as well as giving an explanatory paragraph outlining the going concern uncertainty.

If the financial statements are prepared on a going concern basis and we disagree with that basis, and the effect of using that basis is so material or pervasive that the financial statements are seriously misleading, an adverse audit opinion should be given.

Carrying Value of Investment The company cannot provide us with the evidence we require to support the carrying value of the investment in Horizon Ltd. We need to establish if there is any alternative evidence we can use to support the carrying value. I will try to obtain the last financial statements issued by Horizon and review the net asset position of the company. If there is no alternative evidence available then there is a potential limitation of scope issue. The maximum impairment is €100,000 which would reduce the net assets of the company and increase the loss by that amount. Given the loss-making nature of the entity, it could be argued that the amount is material and if we conclude this to be the case then this would lead to an 'Except for' limitation in scope qualification.

(b) **Draft qualification paragraphs**

Basis for Qualified Opinion

Worldglobal Ltd's investment in Horizon Ltd, a trade investment, is carried at cost of €100,000. We were unable to obtain sufficient appropriate audit evidence about the carrying amount of Worldglobal Ltd's investment in Horizon Ltd as at 31 December, 2012. Consequently, we were unable to determine whether any adjustment to the amount was necessary.

Qualified Opinion Arising from Limitation in Audit Scope

In our opinion, except for the possible effects of the matter described in the Basis for Qualified Opinion paragraph, the financial statements give a true and fair view of the financial position of Worldglobal Limited as at 31 December, 2012, and of its financial performance and its cash flows for the year then ended in accordance with International Financial Reporting Standards.

(c) **Audit report checks**
The following are the checks that should be performed on audit reports prior to signing:
- ensure legal references are correct;
- ensure the page references refer to the actual pages of the financial statements being audited;
- the correct result is reflected in the opinion paragraph, i.e. a profit or loss;
- ensure consistency with relevant financial reporting framework;
- check name of company being audited and year end are correct;
- ensure final audit opinion is correct, i.e. unqualified or qualified;
- ensure consistency with the audit firm's standard audit report wording whereby

two members of staff should 'call over' the report i.e. one member should read the final draft to the other staff member who checks it against the firm's standard audit report format to ensure the wording is correct.

QUESTION 20.1

(a) **Group audit planning**

Six matters of significance to include in the group audit planning document for Puretrans plc are as follows:

1. **Risk identification, assessment and response to such audit risks**
   - Group auditor to outline material risks identified and the assessment of these risks at group level that could impact on the group and local component entity accounts.
   - Group auditor to suggest audit procedures in response to the identified risks.

2. **Materiality**
   - Group auditor to set out overall audit planning materiality based on projected group results for 2012.
   - Performance materiality for the group financial statements to be applied to specific transactions or balances.
   - Group component materiality to be set at a lower level than group materiality (approximately 60%) and communicated to component auditors.
   - Component auditors if reporting separately for local statutory purposes will set materiality for that purpose.

3. **Response to audit risks**
   Group auditor to determine the audit procedures in response to the identified risks and communicate same to component auditors.

4. **Use by the auditor of external experts**
   Group auditor to outline any planned use of external experts, e.g. actuaries.

5. **Acquisition of subsidiary in Mongolia and component auditor**
   Group auditor to provide brief summary of financial position of new subsidiary to highlight any risks regarding local GAAP and any implications for consolidation. May be need for audit visit as component auditor not affiliates of parent audit firm.

6. **Audit timetable**
   Key Milestone Dates e.g. commencement date of interim audit visits, date for issuance of interim management letter, date that first draft management accounts will be available for audit etc. and audit fees billing dates.

(b) **Joint audits**

A joint audit is when two audit firms are appointed as auditors to a company. The two firms will provide one audit opinion which is signed by both firms. The occurrence of joint audits is infrequent in the UK and republic of Ireland. However, joint audits are more frequent in some European countries such as Denmark and France.

The joint auditors will work together to plan and execute the audit on an agreed basis. The usual workload of an audit be shared by both firms and care will be taken to ensure that all necessary audit procedures are performed. The following documents will be issued on a joint basis: Letter of Engagement, Letter of Management to Those Charged with Governance and the Letter of Representation.

There are a number of perceived advantages to a joint audit as follows:

1. There will be greater audit assurance as there are two firms carrying out the audit and they will doing their best to compete against each other in providing the best service possible.
2. For large companies with activities across many countries there is likely to be a greater range of services available from two multinational audit firms.

There are also possible disadvantages of joint audits as follows:

1. A joint audit could be more costly due the involvement of two firms and possible duplication of work.
2. There is a risk of overlooking some important audit work due to lack of coordination.

Index